Ghana

the Bradt Travel Guide

Philip Briggs

Updated by
Sean Connolly

edition
7

www.bradtguides.com

Bradt Travel Guides Ltd, UK
The Globe Pequot Press Inc, USA

KEY
■ Capital city
● Other city
○ Town
✈ Airport
⛴ Ferry
Surfaced road
Unsurfaced road
Railway
International boundary
National park/reserve

Bradt

N

0   80km
0   50 miles

BENIN

TOGO

BURKINA FASO

IVORY COAST

Paga: famed for its sacred crocodiles, Paga also offers access to traditional Sahelian Paga Pia's Palace
pages 467–70

Eastern Highlands: the lush highlands of eastern Ghana offer a plethora of accessible waterfalls and out-of-the-way gems
pages 305–36

Mole National Park: guided walks and superb birdwatching are highlights of Ghana's largest national park
pages 439–51

Bawku
Zebilla
Bolgatanga
Bongo
Paga
Navrongo
Sandema
Tumu
Hamile
Lawra
Jiripa
Nadawli
Wa
Wechiau Hippo Sanctuary
Black Volta
Gbele Resource Reserve
Kulpawn

Nakpanduri
Gambaga
Nalerigu
Walewale
Gushiega
Cherepeni
Yendi
Bimbilla
N2
N2
Tamale
N10
N10
Salaga
Daboya
Tolon
Yapei
N10
Larabanga
Damongo
Sawla
Bole
N12
N12
Bui National Park
N12
White Volta
Mole National Park
Mole
Nasia
Daka
Oti

TOGO

GOLD COAST

LOMÉ

Ho
ACCRA
Koforidua
Kumasi
Sunyani
Cape Coast
Sekondi
Takoradi

Accra: from trendy Oxford Street to historic Jamestown, Ghana's capital is one of Africa's most invigorating cities
pages 103–50

Cape Coast and Elmina: these historic ports, set only 15km apart, are watched over by the best preserved European-built castles in West Africa
pages 195–207 and 213–23

encounters with cheeky Lowe's monas at this popular monkey sanctuary
pages 413–15

Kumasi: the chaotic capital of Ashanti contains a wealth of cultural and architectural landmarks
pages 356–76

Kakum National Park: teeming with rare birds, this national park is home to Africa's oldest canopy walkway
pages 207–13

Nzulezo: this unique stilted village in the Amansuri Wetlands can be visited by canoe from Beyin
page 265

Busua: this scenic stretch of coast near Takoradi is the ultimate Ghanaian beach relaxation spot
pages 240–8

Digya National Park

Bomfabiri Wildlife Sanctuary

Baabeng-Fiema Monkey Sanctuary

Owabi Wildlife Sanctuary

Kalakpa Resource Reserve

Shai Hills Resource Reserve

Kakum National Park

Ankassa Protected Area

Lake Volta

Lake Bosomtwe

Keta Lagoon
Songor Lagoon

Mt Afadjato 885m

Cape Three Points

Kadjebi
Jasikan
Kete-Krachi
Hohoe
Kpandu
Kpeve
Kpetoe
Af017
Aflao
Keta
Ada Foah
Sogakope
Teshie
Tema
Akosombo
Begoro
Abudi
Nsawam
Winneba
Saltpond
Agona Swedru
Assin Foso
Nkawkaw
Bunso Junction
Kade
Akim Oda
Asamankese
Odumasi
Agogo
Mampong
Ejisu
Ejura
Atebubu
Mampong
Nkoranza
Techiman
Wenchi
Berekum
New Drobo
Domea-Ahenkro
Tepa
Goaso
Bibiani
Wiawso
Obuasi
Dunkwa
Bogoso
Prestia
Tarkwa
Agona
Busua
Axim
Enchi
Nzulezo
Elubo
Twifo Praso
Elmina
Agordeke
Sogonkope
Begoro
Kpeve

N1
N2
N6
N8
N10
N12

Ghana
Don't
miss...

National parks
Ghana's largest wildlife
sanctuary, Mole National Park
is the best place in West Africa
for general game viewing and
superb savannah birdwatching
(AVZ) pages 439–52

History
The former Gold Coast is dotted
with historic castles such as
Elmina's St George's, founded
in 1482, which is the oldest
surviving European building in
sub-Saharan Africa
(AVZ) page 221

Villages

Situated along the Volta River, villages such as this one in Ada Foah illustrate a slice of rural Ghanaian life
(AVZ) pages 275–88

Culture

hana is well known for its innovative musical style, often mixing traditional drum-based beats (such as those played by this band in okrobite) with myriad foreign influences
(AVZ) pages 30–1

Wildlife

National parks and sanctuaries throughout the country provide ample opportunities for wildlife spotting — head to Boabeng-Fiema Monkey Sanctuary for a close view of the cute mona monkeys
(AVZ) pages 413–15

Ghana in colour

above left Vivid murals decorate the walls of the Brazil House Museum in Accra, built by Portuguese-speaking freed slaves (AVZ) page 143

above right A traditional medicine seller displays her wares in the Centre for National Culture (AVZ) pages 144–5

below The Central Post Office is an impressive example of the historic colonial architecture dotted around the capital (AVZ) page 143

above Located on Independence Square, the Soviet-inspired Black Star Arch celebrates Ghana's pioneering position as the first independent former African colony (AVZ) page 145

right The Presbyterian Church in Osu, Accra's most easterly neighbourhood (AVZ)

far right Nkrumah Mausoleum in Kwame Nkrumah Memorial Park – the 5ha site is located in the grounds of a former colonial polo club (AVZ) page 144

below Jamestown's old fishing harbour is a riot of colourful pirogues in the morning (AVZ) page 142

above Local taboo prevents anything but customised *padua* tree trunks from being used on Lake Bosomtwe, held sacred by the Ashanti — fishermen must also use their hands to paddle (AVZ) pages 384–9

left Africa's oldest canopy walkway can be found in Kakum National Park, an ideal spot for spectacular birdwatching (AVZ) page 211

below Plunging about 70m in three separate stages, Kintampo Falls is at its most impressive after the rains (AVZ) page 417

AUTHOR

Philip Briggs (e *philip.briggs@bradtguides.com*) has been exploring the highways, byways and backwaters of Africa since 1986, when he spent several months backpacking on a shoestring from Nairobi to Cape Town. In 1991, he wrote *South Africa: the Bradt Travel Guide*, the first such guidebook to be published internationally after the release of Nelson Mandela. Over the rest of the 1990s, Philip wrote a series of pioneering Bradt travel guides to destinations that were then – and  in some cases still are – otherwise practically uncharted by the travel publishing industry. These included the first dedicated guidebooks to Tanzania, Uganda, Ethiopia, Malawi, Mozambique, Ghana and Rwanda (co-authored with Janice Booth), all now in their sixth to eighth editions. More recently, he authored the first English-language guidebooks to Somaliland and Suriname, as well as a new guide to The Gambia, all published by Bradt. He spends at least four months on the road every year, usually accompanied by his wife, the travel photographer Ariadne Van Zandbergen, and spends the rest of his time battering away at a keyboard in the sleepy village of Wilderness in South Africa.

UPDATER

Sean Connolly has been an English teacher in Somaliland, a student in Ghana, a writer in Malawi, and a backpacker across much of the African continent. When he's not discussing verb tenses, diplomatic recognition or the merits of camel meat, you may find him riding in the back of a grain truck, sampling questionable local delicacies or seeking out a country's funkiest records. Raised in Chicago and educated in New York, Sean is a full-time culture fiend (read: anthropology graduate), has updated or  contributed to the Bradt guides to Somaliland, Rwanda, Malawi, and Mozambique, and is the author of the first Bradt guide to Senegal. He stays on the move whenever possible, though lately you'll most often find him in Berlin.

PUBLISHER'S FOREWORD   *Hilary Bradt*

We've become used to praise from readers for Philip's books. They seek us out at travel fairs to tell us, and he receives more 'fan' mail than any of our other authors. But the real test of a guidebook is if it's as useful to local residents as to visitors. Here's an extract from a reader in Accra:

> I have the impression that I started discovering fantastic new and unknown places only last year when I got a copy of your guide in one of the local bookshops. I am extremely grateful to you for introducing me to so many beautiful new places outside of Accra. While some guides on Ghana are far too positive and enthusiastic and thereby evoke possible disappointment on the traveller's side, other guides are too negative and almost scare any prospective traveller off. You have found the right mixture and reading your guide is a real pleasure. Even for my life here in general I found your guide useful: the big and small struggles of everyday life sometimes make me forget all the beautiful things this country has to offer. You reminded me that sometimes it is important just to take a step back and look at the greater picture and you are so right. Once again: thanks a million!

Seventh edition published January 2017
First published in 1998

Bradt Travel Guides Ltd
IDC House, The Vale, Chalfont St Peter, Bucks SL9 9RZ, England
www.bradtguides.com
Print edition published in the USA by The Globe Pequot Press Inc,
PO Box 480, Guilford, Connecticut 06437-0480

Text copyright © 2017 Philip Briggs
Maps copyright © 2017 Bradt Travel Guides Ltd; includes map data © OpenStreetMap contributors
Photographs copyright © 2017 Individual photographers (see below)
Project Manager: Laura Pidgley
Cover research: Pepi Bluck, Perfect Picture

ISBN: 978 1 78477 034 1 (print)
e-ISBN: 978 1 78477 199 7 (e-pub)
e-ISBN: 978 1 78477 400 4 (mobi)

British Library Cataloguing in Publication Data
A catalogue record for this book is available from the British Library

Photographs
Ariadne Van Zandbergen (AVZ); Dave Coles (DC); FLPA (FLPA); Shutterstock: Eunika Sopotnicka (ES/S), Felix Lupov (FL/S); SuperStock (SS)

Front cover Mud house, Sirigu (AVZ)
Back cover Mona monkey (AVZ); Wa Na's Palace, Wa (AVZ)
Title page Atia Kusia Kwame Shrine (AVZ); Traditional dancer, Kokrobite (AVZ); Pirogue, Busua (AVZ)
Part openers Page 101: Independence Arch, Accra (FL/S); Page 175: Cape Coast Castle (ES/S); Page 175: Kakum National Park (DC); Page 271: Wli Falls (DC); Page 353: Seller at Kejetia Market (AVZ); Page 419: Nakore Mosque (AVZ)

Illustrations Annabel Milne, Carole Vincer
Maps David McCutcheon FBCart.S; relief map base by Nick Rowland FRGS

Typeset by Ian Spick, Bradt Travel Guides and www.dataworks.co.in
Production managed by Jellyfish Print Solutions; printed in India
Digital conversion by the www.dataworks.co.in

Acknowledgements

PHILIP BRIGGS Thanks are due to my wife, Ariadne Van Zandbergen, for her company on the research trips for four editions of this guide, and to one-off updaters Katherine Rushton and Kim Wildman for their comprehensive work on the other two editions. I'm also grateful to the many readers of previous editions who have written in with useful updates, as reproduced on the Bradt updates website (*www. bradtupdates.com/ghana*) and in many cases incorporated into this seventh edition.

I doubt that any edition of any of my guides has benefited from the input of quite so many previous readers, travellers, locals and folk in the travel industry. More specifically, for this edition, I am indebted to the following (listed in first-name alphabetical order) for their help, input and/or company: Adam Riley, Adrian Landry, Alexander Kwame Nketia, Andrew Murphy, Andrews Agyekumhene, Anita Low, Annie Terminet Schuppon, Aubrey Malcolm-Green, Bernhard and Gabrielle Hagspiel, Bob Baldry, Bob and Jacqueline (Rootsyard), Brett Davies, Callan Cohen, Cara Schildtknecht, Chloe Grant, Chris and Charity Scott, Chris den Engelsman, Christiane Milev, Claudia Kleinbudde, Daniel Rössler, Danielle and Olivier Funfschilling, Edith de Vos, Edwin Owusu-Mensah, Eef Bijlsma, Elodie (Green Ranch), Emmanuel Chance, Esperanza Delores Adjei, Festus Kayang, Frederic Beroud, Gordon Rattray, Graham Douglas, Heidi Bancroft, James Fraser, Jeanne Donkoh, Jeanne Marie Pittman, Johan Verhagen, John Collins, John Mason, John Tsrakasu, Julia Overas, Justine Spencer, Kojo Bentum-Williams, Kwame (Aylos Bay), Kwame Sarpong, Laura Doak, Lianne van Rijssel, Liz Gentilcore, Manchán Magan, Marian Thompson, Margriet Langeveld, Noëlle and Hervé Jacob, Patricia Zoer, Patrick Adjewodah, Patrick Badiako Mantey, Patrick Kpikpi, Patrick Sarpong, Paul Ramlot, Peter Nardini, Peter Nizette, Phil Allman, Princess Akosua Love Kpedekpo, Rod McLaren, Thomas Adjei, Tom and Jo Miles, Sietske Gramsma, Stephanie Versteeg, Steven Cole, Steven Wilson, Sylvester Kubi, Walisu Alhassan, Wendy Lubin and Yaba Badoe.

SEAN CONNOLLY Thanks are first and foremost due to Philip Briggs for entrusting me with another of his extraordinary guides. My thanks also go out to Imke Rueben for her unending support and companionship; to Jeff Martin for accompanying me for part of the journey; to Julian Prieto, Jana Schröder and Jack Grady for their patience as this book was written.

And in Ghana itself, a coterie of welcoming hosts and gracious companions made my long-awaited return to this friendliest of countries a delight. In no particular order, my thanks are due to Max Gross, Geoffrey Zanu, Dim Attipoe and Atsu Devine (Somewhere Nice); Paul Ramlot (Lou Moon); Danielle Funfschilling (Busua Inn); Trevor Stephens (Akwidaa Inn); Bob (Africa Beach); Akwasi McLaren (Escape3points); Annelies and Nol (Ko-Sa); Elodie (Green Ranch); Brother Basilio Zaa-Liebe (Kristo Buase); Andy, Arvind, PK, Udit and Araba (Zaina); Eef Bijlsma (Asempa); Joel (Magaya); Muhammad (Upland); Robyn Emory; Patricia Zoer

(Moon and Star); Steve (Stumble Inn); Victoria Obiakor and Gabriella Glymin (Kempinski); Eric Tenkorang (Jays Lodge); Frank Scott (Four Villages); Claudia (Biriwa Beach); Wendy Lubin (Big Milly's); Leonard Miller (Ezime Guesthouse); Antonella and Yaw (Wild Camp Ghana); Stephen Asare and Frederick Adams (Rocklyne); Emma and Vinny (Bajevo); Bernhard Hagspiel and Sabine Weitze (Waterfall Lodge); Jacqueline and Bob (Rootsyard); Aubrey Malcolm-Green and Nana Preston (West African Safaris); Marian Thompson (M&J Travel); and Anthony Arthur for his amiable company and skills behind the wheel.

To all the friends I met along the way – Marije Maliepaard; Abhimanyu Jadhav; George; Ezra Davis; James Caunt; Joyce Fas; Kay Rainford; Blake Frederick; Chichi; Brandon Payne; Luis Beirao; Edson Barros; Cleiton Santos; and Hugo – *medaase paa* for the Clubs, Stars, *nacionais*, laughs, bowling and/or mini-golf, and the occasional shove in the right direction.

And finally, to everyone at Bradt – Laura Pidgley, Rachel Fielding, Hugh Brune, Hugh Collins, Deborah Gerrard and Julie May – it's a pleasure to work with such an expert team.

AUTHOR'S STORY

Incredibly, almost 20 years have passed since I researched the original Bradt guide to Ghana. Much has changed over the course of that time. In the mid 1990s, Ghana – still widely associated with the series of economic and political disasters that marred its first few decades of independence – was generally thought of as a country best avoided by travellers. Today, by contrast, it is routinely cited as a nascent African success story: a genuine democracy whose relative economic health is reflected in the ease of travel conditions compared with most of West Africa.

When we first travelled around Ghana, reliable travel information was scarce, and we relied mainly on the hit-and-miss combination of instinct, serendipity, the advice of locals and a chat with the occasional other traveller. Mostly, it was hits, but the misses were spectacular. On one misinformed occasion, I recall spending 12 hours waiting for a non-existent trotro before retiring to the room where we'd spent the previous night. Elsewhere, we were forbidden from seeing the only room in the only guesthouse in the village until we paid upfront, whereupon the caretaker opened the door to reveal a squealing mass of bats flapping and crapping through the trashed ceiling – fortunately, it was early enough in the day to move on.

Of course, facilities have improved greatly since then; indeed, barely a month goes by without us receiving news of a new tourist hotel, backpacker resort or ecotourism project. And I'd like to think that this book has contributed to that process. But, cheeringly, one thing that hasn't altered is that Ghana remains a singularly unpackaged destination – you'll find no snap-happy coachloads here, little in the way of prescribed tourist circuits or wallet-emptying 'must-do' excursions, and plenty of opportunity for whimsical exploration. Ghana today, as it was in 1997, is the ideal destination for the genuinely independent-minded travellers at whom Bradt guides are aimed.

Contents

LIST OF MAPS

GHANA UPDATES WEBSITE AND FEEDBACK REQUEST

Administered by author Philip Briggs, Bradt's Ghana update website (*www. bradtupdates.com/ghana*) is an online forum where travellers can post and read the latest travel news, trip reports and factual updates from Ghana. The website is a free service to readers, or to anybody else who cares to drop by, and travellers to Ghana and people in the tourist industry are encouraged to use it to share their comments, grumbles, insights, news or other feedback. These can be posted directly on the website, or emailed to Philip (e *philip. briggs@bradtguides.com*).

It's easy to keep up to date with the latest posts by following Philip on Twitter (*@philipbriggs*) and/or liking his Facebook page (*fb.me/pb.travel.updates*). You can also add a review of the book to www.bradtguides.com or Amazon.

Introduction

Ghana is often referred to as Africa for Beginners. It might as easily be described as Africa in Microcosm. Not only does this amiable and largely hassle-free country form an obvious entry-level destination for nervous newbie independent travellers, but it also boasts a remarkably varied set of attractions within an unusually compact travel circuit.

The southern part of Ghana is much as you'd expect of West Africa, all lush jungle, heavily hung banana plantations and picture-postcard beaches, albeit with a unique dimension in the form of the string of 500-year-old European forts and castles that line the former Gold Coast. But the real surprises begin as you travel further north, to the game-rich savannah of Mole National Park, a setting that evokes East Africa more than West, or to the Burkina Faso border region, whose deeply Islamic mood and striking adobe architecture lean towards the Sahel and North Africa. What's more, practically wherever you go in Ghana, English is spoken to an unusually high standard, making it easy for English-speaking travellers to get around, and to interact with locals.

What Ghana does lack is that one drop-dead, big-name attraction, the sort of place that friends who've visited will say you simply have to see once in your lifetime. Zimbabwe has Victoria Falls, Tanzania has Kilimanjaro, South Africa has Cape Town, Ethiopia its rock-hewn churches. The closest thing Ghana has to offer in the not-to-be-missed stakes is the above-mentioned castles. Not quite the pyramids in terms of impact, I grant you, but nevertheless a unique and chilling memorial to an episode as sickening as any in the recorded history of Africa: the cruel trade in human life that resulted in several million Africans being displaced to a life of bondage in the plantations of the Americas and the Caribbean.

If Ghana lacks one truly great tourist attraction, then it is equally true that busy travellers will find that barely a day goes by without at least one memorable experience, be it swimming below one of the gorgeous waterfalls of the eastern highlands, the thrill of walking to within a few metres of a wild elephant, climbing to the roof of one of the surreal mosques that dot the northwest, taking a dugout canoe through papyrus swamps to the stilted village of Nzulezo, watching colourful mona monkeys play between the houses of Boabeng village, watching the sun set over the Atlantic, or just making new friends in a down-to-earth local 'spot' (bar) or 'chop shop' (restaurant).

Ghana is also largely free of the trappings associated with mass tourism. Seldom are you made to feel part of some tourist treadmill, and the country remains endowed with some remarkably exciting off-the-beaten-track possibilities. There are, for instance, several national parks and reserves ideally suited for equipped independent travellers, yet which currently go weeks on end without seeing a visitor.

In recent decades, there has been much talk about an African renaissance. And regardless of what one thinks of such generalisations, Ghana is frequently cited as being at the forefront of this movement. Not only is post-millennial Ghana one of the few African countries to have truly embraced the democratic process (and the regular changeovers of elected government, and the freedom of speech and free press that go with it), but it has also boasted one of the world's fastest-growing and diversifying economies. Trailblazing of this sort is not a new role – the former Gold Coast was the first country in Africa to have extended contact with Europeans, one of the first to be formally colonised and, in 1957, it became the first to be granted independence in the post-war era. Less prestigiously, it also became one of the first African countries to slide into post-independence chaos and, while it never plummeted to the depths reached by many of its neighbours, the modern visitor will find it difficult to reconcile accounts of Ghana in the 1980s with the vibrant country they see today.

Tangibly steeped in history and tradition, yet paradoxically also building towards a brighter future, Ghana is simply one of Africa's most rewarding and exciting travel destinations

Part One

GENERAL INFORMATION

GHANA AT A GLANCE

Location Western Africa, on the Gulf of Guinea
Neighbouring countries Bordered to the west by Ivory Coast (Côte d'Ivoire), to the north by Burkina Faso, to the east by Togo and to the south by the Atlantic Ocean
Size/area 239,460km^2 – roughly equal to Great Britain or the state of Oregon, USA
Climate Tropical. Hot and humid in the south; hot and dry in the north.
Status Republic; member of the Commonwealth; independent since 1957.
Population 28 million (2016 estimate)
Life expectancy 66 years
Capital Accra (population 2.3 million)
Other main towns Kumasi, Tamale, Sekondi-Takoradi, Cape Coast, Obuasi, Tema
Economy Major industries include agriculture – most notably cocoa farming – bauxite and gold mining, oil production, aluminium smelting, and tourism
GDP US$113.3 billion, with a per capita GDP of US$4,300
Languages Official language is English. At least 46 African languages are spoken, with the major ones including Twi, Fante, Ewe, Ga, Dagomba and Halisa.
Religion Predominantly Christian, but largely Muslim in the north
Currency Cedi (GHC) (1 cedi = 100 pesewa)
Exchange rate The exchange rate in September 2016 was roughly GHC3.97 to US$1, GHC4.44 to €1 and GHC5.18 to £1
Main airport Kotoka International Airport, Accra (ACC)
International telephone code +233
Time GMT
Electrical voltage 200/220V
Flag Horizontal stripes in red, yellow and green (top to bottom), with a black star in the centre
National anthem 'God Bless our Homeland, Ghana'
Public holidays 1 January, 6 March, 1 May, 25 May, 1 July, 21 September, first Friday in December, 25 December, 26 December (see also page 82)

1

Background Information

GEOGRAPHY AND LOCATION

Ghana is a West African country between latitudes of 4°N and 12°N, and longitudes of 4°W and 2°E. Its 540km southern coastline is part of the Gulf of Guinea, the name given to the tropical region of the Atlantic Ocean bounded by Cape Palmas (Liberia) in the far west and Cape Lopez (Gabon) in the far south. Ghana is bisected by the Prime Meridian (also known as the Greenwich Meridian, or 0° longitude), which runs through the port city of Tema, 25km east of the capital Accra. Cape Three Points, the most southerly peninsula in Ghana, is distinguished by being the closest land to the oceanic intersection of the Prime Meridian and the Equator. Ghana is neighboured by Ivory Coast (Côte d'Ivoire) to the west, by Togo to the east, and by Burkina Faso to the north and northwest.

Most of Ghana could be classified as flat and low-lying. Almost half the country lies below an altitude of 150m, and nowhere does it cross the 1,000m contour, with the highest point being the 885m Mount Afadjato near the Togolese border. The far south of Ghana is dominated by flattish plains that typically run for 100–150km inland of the Atlantic coastline, except near Accra, where the Akwapim Mountains around Aburi rise from the coastal plain only 20km inland. Other mountainous areas topping the 500m contour include the Atewa Range west of Koforidua, the extensive Kwahu Plateau running east of Koforidua and Kumasi, the Togo-Atakora ranges (which stretch from the southeastern highlands of Ghana through Togo to Benin, and include Mount Afadjato). These highlands are characterised by numerous waterfalls, most famously Wli Falls, which is reputedly the highest feature of its type in West Africa. The north of Ghana is mostly flat, and lies at low to medium altitudes, but it is much dryer than the forested south. The most notable highland in northern Ghana is the Gambaga Escarpment east of Bolgatanga.

Hydrographically, Ghana is practically synonymous with the Volta Basin, a 407,093km^2 drainage basin that also extends northwards into Burkina Faso and is centred upon the 1,600km-long Volta River (a Portuguese name that refers to its meandering course). The 1,350km Black Volta, also known as the Mouhoun, rises in the southwest of Burkina Faso, flows along the Ghana–Ivory Coast border then enters Ghana near Bui National Park, where it has been dammed since 2013, forming a nearly 444km^2 reservoir, and subsequently continuing its circuitous route through northwest Ghana before converging with the other tributaries. These are the White Volta, or Nakambe, which originates in eastern Burkina Faso and flows into Ghana close to Bawku, and the Red Volta, whose source is near the Burkinese capital Ouagadougou. Much of the Volta River is now submerged by Lake Volta, which has the largest surface area of any artificial lake in the world, extending over some 8,500km^2 along several forks formed by drowned tributaries. Lake Volta is contained by the Akosombo Dam, which was built in the 1960s about 60km inland of the river mouth at Ada Foah.

The main urban conglomeration in Ghana is focused on the capital city Accra, which lies on the Atlantic coastline 25km west of the Prime Meridian. Population estimates for Accra vary greatly, but most sources place the figure at around 2.3–2.5 million. However, considering that eight other cities listed in the national top 20 population-wise are part of Greater Accra (a compact administration region whose 3,245km² accounts for less than 1.5% of Ghana's surface area but supports more than 15% of the population), this feels like a gross underestimate. Include these other significant population hubs, ie: Ashaiman, Teshie, Tema, Madina, Nungua, Tema New Town, Dome and Lashabi, several of which are all but contiguous with Accra, and the city's real population is probably closer to four million.

Kumasi, the former capital of the Ashanti Empire and modern capital of the synonymous administrative region, is Ghana's second-largest city, with a population of around two million. Since different sources quote wildly divergent population figures for other large towns in Ghana, it is difficult to rank them by size with any great conviction. However, based on the available sources and our own impressions, we would regard the following to be the largest towns outside of Greater Accra and Kumasi, in approximate descending order of population: Tamale, Sekondi-Takoradi, Cape Coast, Obuasi, Koforidua, Wa, Techiman, Ho and Sunyani.

ADMINISTRATIVE REGIONS

Ghana is divided into ten administrative regions, all of which, to some degree, have borders dating from the earliest days of colonialism. Several of the regions also have names that date from the earliest colonial times in a manner that can create some confusion to new arrivals to the country. The Western, Central and Eastern regions, as delineated by the British administration before the annexation of Ashanti in 1902, still go by those names, even though Eastern Region today lies to the west of Volta Region, and Central Region lies nowhere near the centre of modern Ghana, but on its southern coast. Likewise, the original Northern Region as delineated by the colonial authorities has since been split in such a manner that Northern Region lies to the south of Upper East and Upper West regions. It is worth being aware of this, because the regions have a high profile in Ghana today, and when most Ghanaians speak of 'eastern', 'central', or 'northern', they mean the administrative region rather than the most easterly, central, or northerly part of the country.

The ten modern administrative regions of Ghana are as follows:

Region	Km²	Pop*	Capital	Other large towns
Ashanti	24,390	4,780,380	Kumasi	Obuasi, Tafo, Mampong
Brong-Ahafo	39,557	2,310,983	Sunyani	Techiman, Wenchi, Kintampo
Central	9,826	2,201,863	Cape Coast	Elmina, Winneba, Dunkwa
Eastern	19,223	2,633,154	Koforidua	Nkawkaw, Akosombo
Greater Accra	3,245	4,010,054	Accra	Tema, Ada, Dodowa, Ashaiman
Northern	70,384	2,479,461	Tamale	Yendi, Bimbilla, Nalerigu
Upper East	8,842	1,046,545	Bolgatanga	Navrongo, Bawku, Zebilla
Upper West	18,476	702,110	Wa	Jiripa, Tumu, Lawra
Volta	20,334	2,118,252	Ho	Hohoe, Aflao, Kpandu, Keta
Western	23,921	2,376,021	Sekondi-Takoradi	Tarkwa, Elubo

*As recorded in the 2010 census

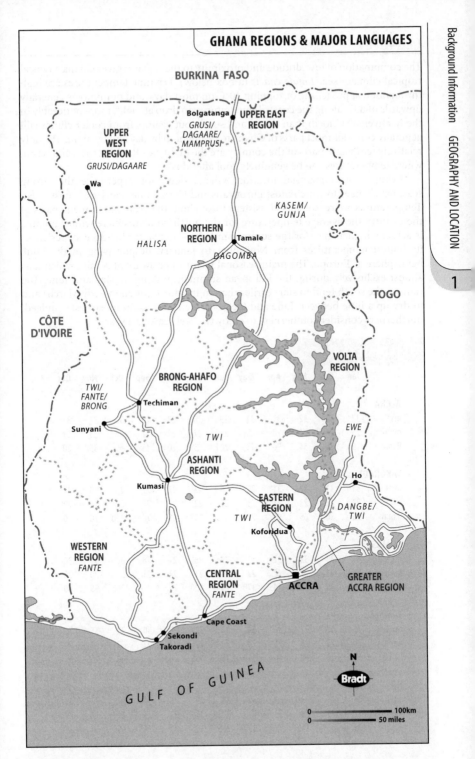

GHANA REGIONS & MAJOR LANGUAGES

BURKINA FASO

UPPER WEST REGION
GRUSI/DAGAARE

Wa

Bolgatanga
GRUSI/ DAGAARE/ MAMPRUSI

UPPER EAST REGION

KASEM/ GUNJA

NORTHERN REGION
Tamale

HALISA

DAGOMBA

TOGO

VOLTA REGION

CÔTE D'IVOIRE

BRONG-AHAFO REGION

TWI/ FANTE/ BRONG
Techiman

Sunyani

TWI

EWE

ASHANTI REGION

Kumasi

Ho

EASTERN REGION

DANGBE/ TWI

TWI
Koforidua

WESTERN REGION
FANTE

CENTRAL REGION
FANTE

ACCRA

GREATER ACCRA REGION

Cape Coast

Sekondi
Takoradi

GULF OF GUINEA

N

Bradt

0 ——————— 100km
0 ——————— 50 miles

CLIMATE

The combination of low altitude and proximity to the Equator gives Ghana a typical tropical climate (see *climate charts* in box below). Daytime temperatures are high throughout, approaching or topping 30°C on most days, and humidity is generally upwards of 80% along the coast. Temperatures do drop at night, more noticeably in the relatively dry north than the humid south, but visitors from cooler climes will generally consider most parts of Ghana to be hot both by day and by night. The only relatively temperate parts of the country are the highlands flanking the Volta Basin, where temperatures can be genuinely cool after dusk.

Owing to its equatorial location, Ghana does not experience the strong seasonal changes to which most Europeans and North Americans are accustomed. Temperatures are reasonably consistent throughout the year, and in many parts of the country the average temperature for the northern hemisphere winter months is actually higher than for the summer months – Accra, for instance, experiences its hottest temperatures from November to January, despite lying in the same hemisphere as Europe. The main seasonal factor to be aware of is rain, which falls almost exclusively during the European summer, peaking in May and June. The rains in the south tend to start earlier than in the north (often in early March) and to dry up a little between June and October, then start again in earnest – indeed, northerners consider southerners to enjoy two wet seasons a year.

CLIMATE CHARTS

	Jan	Feb	Mar	Apr	May	Jun	Jul	Aug	Sep	Oct	Nov	Dec
ACCRA												
mx°C	32	32	32	31	31	29	28	28	29	30	31	31
mn°C	23	24	24	24	23	23	22	22	22	23	23	23
R mm	15	30	55	90	135	201	53	20	45	65	35	20
TAKORADI												
mx°C	31	31	32	31	30	28	27	27	27	29	30	31
mn°C	22	23	23	23	23	23	22	21	22	22	22	22
R mm	25	30	65	95	210	315	135	65	70	100	70	30
KUMASI												
mx°C	31	33	32	32	31	29	28	27	28	30	31	30
mn°C	20	21	22	22	22	21	21	21	21	21	20	20
R mm	20	45	140	145	170	230	120	75	170	200	95	60
TAMALE												
mx°C	35	37	37	36	34	31	30	29	30	32	35	35
mn°C	20	23	25	25	24	23	22	22	22	22	21	20
R mm	5	10	40	85	110	150	155	200	230	80	15	5
HO												
mx°C	34	35	34	33	32	31	29	29	30	31	32	33
mn°C	22	23	23	23	23	22	21	21	21	21	22	22
R mm	25	65	115	130	190	205	135	95	145	165	50	35

Rainfall figures are highest in the forested southwest, where some areas regularly experience in excess of 2,000mm per annum, and are lowest in the north and the plains immediately around Accra, where it is unusual for more than 800mm of rain to fall in a calendar year. The reason why the eastern coastal belt of Ghana is drier than the western coast is because its slopes tend to have a southwestern orientation that causes rain-bearing westerly winds associated with the monsoon to flow past without yielding much moisture. Indeed, Accra and eastern Ghana, together with Togo and Benin, form a geographic region often known as the Dahomey Gap, a tract of relatively dry savannah that divides the Upper Guinean forests (running from central Ghana through to Liberia) from the Lower Guinean forests (running from southern Nigeria southwards to the Congo).

Another noteworthy climatic phenomenon in this part of the world is the harmattan winds, which blow from the northeast during the dry season, bringing dust from the Sahara and reducing visibility to as little as 1km. Generally, the winds come in late November or early December and continue until sometime in March. The harmattan will have little effect on most tourists (except perhaps those flying to or from Tamale), but it is a nightmare for photographers and will cause disappointment to those who've come to admire the scenery in mountainous areas.

HISTORY

Ghana, like the other modern states of West Africa, is fundamentally a European creation of the late nineteenth century. For this reason, it would be thoroughly misleading to write about Ghana as a meaningful entity prior to the colonial era. True, as long ago as 1700, the coast of modern-day Ghana stood firmly at the epicentre of the European maritime trade out of West Africa, while the Ashanti Empire gave political and social cohesion to much of the area between the coastal belt and the Black Volta. But even as recently as 1873, when Britain established its Gold Coast Colony, few would have foreseen the eventual existence of a political state with borders approximating present-day Ghana. Indeed, it was only in 1902 that the central and northern parts of Ghana were annexed to the colony, while the interior east of what is now Lake Volta, which formed part of German Togoland before World War I, was mandated to Britain by the League of Nations in 1919.

Bearing the above in mind, we have started this history with a section offering a broad overview of West African history prior to 1500. In the sections that follow, which focus more specifically on modern-day Ghana, we refer to the coastal belt of what is now Ghana prior to colonisation as the Gold Coast; to the interior south of the Black Volta as Ashanti; and to the interior north of the Black Volta as the northern regions (in colonial times, this area was in fact called Northern Region, though it has since been divided into three administrative regions: Northern, Upper East and Upper West). Following this logic, we refer to Ghana in colonial times as the Gold Coast Colony, and reserve use of the name Ghana to describe the country after it gained independence in 1957. To preclude confusion between the modern state of Ghana and the ancient state from which its name is taken, the latter is referred to as Ancient Ghana. For the sake of consistency, the term 'Ancient Mali' has been used to refer to another vanished West African empire that was to bequeath its name to a modern state.

WEST AFRICA BEFORE 1500 The northwestern 'bulge' of Africa can be divided into four economic units prior to 1500. The most northerly of these is the Mediterranean coastal belt of North Africa, an area that has had direct links with the other Mediterranean civilisations since ancient times, and that assimilated the influence of Islamic invaders as early as the 8th century AD, barely a century after the religion was founded. To the south of this lies the Sahara, almost as large as Europe, yet devoid of permanent human settlement since time immemorial. South of the Sahara is the Sahel, an ever-expanding belt of dry savannah, thinly populated except where it's crossed by large rivers, such as the Niger, Senegal and Volta. And further south still, there is the belt of moister savannah and forest that terminates at the Atlantic coast, the area we normally think of when we refer to West as opposed to North Africa, and the area to which the modern state of Ghana belongs.

Prior to the arrival of the Portuguese on the Gold Coast in the late 15th century, there had existed for centuries a trade relationship between these four regions. Merchant caravans would cross the Sahara from north to south, bringing with them salt, fine cloth and other luxury items that they would trade for goods such as gold, ivory and kola nuts. It is difficult to ascertain exactly when this epoch of trade started, but the available physical evidence would appear to show that a trade route across the Sahara similar to the modern one has existed since before 500BC. It can probably be assumed, too, that the spread of Iron Age know-how into the Sahel and areas further south before 600BC was influenced by trade routes that, for all we know, may have existed in some form or other for several millennia.

The specifics of this trade and of the societies south of the Sahel are difficult to determine prior to the 8th century AD. Some scholars suggest that there was a substantial increase in trade at around this time, based on the rather unconvincing argument that the first written record of the area south of the Sahel dates to AD773. It is just as likely that the reason no earlier records exist is linked to the rapid increase in written documentation in northwest Africa following the introduction of the Islamic faith in the 8th century AD. What is clear from this first written reference to the Sahel is, firstly, that its Arabic writer regarded it to be the 'Land of Gold', and, secondly, that it had long supported a powerful centralised trading empire that effectively acted as the 'middleman' between areas south of the Sahel and north of the Sahara.

This empire was the ancient state of Ghana, which – somewhat confusingly – lay completely to the north of its modern namesake. (Kwame Nkrumah's choice of the name 'Ghana' in 1957 was largely symbolic, as the former Gold Coast was the first African colony to gain independence from a European power; contemporary claims by some local historians that many of modern Ghana's main groupings descend from Ancient Ghana have subsequently been discredited.) Ancient Ghana was founded by Mande-speakers at sometime between AD300 and AD700; at its peak, it spread for roughly 300km from north to south and 500km east to west between the rivers Niger and Senegal. The capital of Ancient Ghana at Kumbi Saleh (now a ruined city in southern Mauritania less than 100km from the Malian border) supported a population of roughly 15,000, and its emperor was able to muster an army numbering 200,000.

In AD992, Ancient Ghana was at the height of its powers and its leadership decided to cement its hold on the trade routes out of the southern Sahara by capturing the important terminus of Awdaghast, 300km northwest of Kumbi Saleh. In the long term, this proved to be the downfall of the state, as the displaced Berbers of Awdaghast consolidated under a somewhat fanatical religious movement known as the Almoravids (meaning 'the people of the hermitage') and waged a jihad culminating in the capture of Kumbi Saleh in 1076. The Almoravids held the Ancient Ghanaian capital for little more than a decade, but their brief tenure appears to have been the catalyst that caused the vast empire to fissure into several smaller and less powerful states, a situation that evidently persisted throughout the 12th century.

The beginning of the 13th century saw the emergence of a clear successor to Ancient Ghana in the omnipotence stakes, and this was the Ancient Mali Empire founded by the Mandinka people of Kangaba. Accounts of the early days of this empire tend to be somewhat vague, but, so far as anybody can ascertain, the Mandinka had by 1205 taken over large parts of what had formerly been Ancient Ghana. In 1230, the leadership of Mali was assumed by Munsa Sundiata, an inspirational expansionist who had doubled the area of Mali by the time of his death in 1255. In 1240, Sundiata captured Kumbi Saleh, and relocated the capital to the fringe of the Sahara: the exact location selected is a matter of some debate amongst historians, but it evidently proved unsatisfactory, as all later accounts place the capital of Mali at Niani in the vicinity of the Guinean and Ivorian border.

You might reasonably wonder what bearing all the above has on modern Ghana. The best answer, in the broadest sense, is simply that it puts paid to the common misconception that this part of Africa was some sort of stagnant backwater prior to the arrival of Europeans. More specifically, the area that lies within the modern state of Ghana played a palpable role in the trade patterns of this era – it was, indeed, the empires of the Sahel that controlled the southern end of the Saharan caravan routes, but it was through a more localised trade system involving the people of the moist savannah and rainforest region that they obtained most of their trade goods. Centuries ago, Ghana was the major supplier of kola nuts to the empires of the Sahel, as well as an important source of ivory. Of more lasting significance, the rainforest belt of modern Ghana was in medieval times – as it would be in the era of coastal trade, and remains today – one of the region's richest sources of gold; the gold that not only lay at the heart of the trade route across the Sahara to Morocco, but also would later be one of the factors that caused the Portuguese to set sail in search of a trade route to sub-Saharan Africa.

Another lasting effect of the cross-Sahara trade was the spread of Islam into West Africa. It is not certain when or how deeply Islam first took hold in the region, but the writings of the Arab Al-Bakri in 1067 testify to the presence of a permanent Islamic community situated roughly 10km from Kumbi Saleh. While it is clear from this that the rulers of Ancient Ghana were not converts, the fact that this community boasted 12 mosques suggests it was reasonably significant.

The rulers of Ancient Mali almost certainly were Muslim converts right from the empire's earliest days. As early as 1200, Mansa Uli of Ancient Mali undertook a pilgrimage to Mecca. More famous was the pilgrimage of Mansa Musa in 1324–26, when the empire would have been at its economic prime. Contemporary records state that Musa gave away so many gifts of gold that the market for the metal was seriously undermined for some time after. His visit also put Ancient Mali on the world map in the most literal sense; the West African empire first appeared by name on an Arabic map drawn up in 1339. And it is well documented that Musa returned home with several Islamic scholars who did much to entrench the exotic religion among the common people of Ancient Mali, and were responsible for designing the mud-and-stick style of mosque construction that visitors to modern Ghana will see in places such as Larabanga and Wa.

Islam was the state religion of the Songhai Empire, centred to the north of what is now Burkina Faso. One of several small empires that were ruled by the Mansa of Ancient Mali following the collapse of Ancient Ghana, Songhai was revived in the mid 15th century by a leader called Sunni Ali, from his capital at the Niger River port of Gao, and it replaced Ancient Mali as the dominant Sahelian state from roughly 1464. One of the most powerful of Songhai rulers, Askia Mohammed, made the pilgrimage to Mecca in the 1490s, after which Islam was forced on the commoners of the empire. The Songhai Empire collapsed in 1591, following an attack on Gao by an army from Morocco. This event is generally seen as signalling the beginning of what many historians refer to as the West African interior's

THE AKAN

The most numerically significant of Ghana's four ethno-linguistic groupings, the Akan of the southern and central part of the country embrace several dozen culturally similar and historically allied peoples, the best known of whom are probably the Ashanti of the Kumasi area and the Fante of the central coast. Most travellers to Ghana will come into regular contact with several Akan cultural institutions, as the country's two main travel circuits pass almost exclusively through Akan territories. Even those who travel further afield – into the Ewe heartland of Volta Region, for instance – will soon recognise the Akan influence over the cultural and political organisation of many of their neighbours.

Every Akan village has its chief, whose position is not purely hereditary. Most, although generally of matrilineal aristocratic birth, are selected by a Council of Elders for their perceived capabilities and may be stripped of their powers if they do not perform satisfactorily or they indulge in tyrannical behaviour. Practically throughout Ghana the power of the chief is denoted by his possession of the royal stool, which is typically made of wood and blackened after the death of the monarch (notable exceptions being the famous golden stool of Ashanti and the silver stool of Mampong). Akan chiefs are referred to as having been 'enstooled' when they ascend to power and 'destooled' should they lose that position. In many Akan territories, a traditional hierarchy of chiefs is maintained – the King of Ashanti, for instance, is considered paramount to the chiefs of such vassal states as Mampong and Jauben, who in turn preside over several small local chieftaincies. It is customary in Akan societies as well as in other parts of Ghana for visitors to a village to pay their respects to the chief, a custom that is still enforced in villages receiving few foreign visitors.

Most Akan societies show remarkably similar political structures. Every chief is served by a Council of Elders, a body to which he must refer all important matters and which has the power to destool him. Another very important figure is the Queen Mother, a misleading title since she will not necessarily be the mother of a queen, but serves as spiritual mother to the chief. She will work closely with the Council of Elders in selecting a new chief, will sit in on all council meetings, and preside over all births and menstruation rites. Other key figures include the Akyeame, the chief's official spokesman and carrier of a royal staff, and the Adontenhene, the leader of the main military body. Some Akan societies are divided into several *asafo*, military companies that play an important role in defence as well as in the arts (see box, pages 182–3), and one of the few Akan institutions to follow purely patrilineal lines of inheritance.

The basic unit of traditional Akan society is the extended family, an institution that is maintained along matrilineal lines, evidently on the basis that one can always be certain of the identity of a child's mother. In modern Ghana, patrilineal inheritance lines are now assuming greater importance, and (in urban areas particularly) the nuclear family is valued more highly by many than the extended one. Traditionally, the Akan regard every person to be composed of three parts: blood, semen and soul. Blood, the most significant, is inherited from the mother as a signifier of family. Semen is the father's contribution, and determines personality and other individual attributes. The soul is believed to be the part of God that

'Dark Age', a 300-year period of economic stagnation attributable less to any one single attack than to the reorientation of trade patterns that followed the arrival of Portugal at the Gold Coast in 1471.

enters each child at birth. Interestingly, the Akan regard a person's soul to be linked to the day of the week on which they were born.

For this reason, most Ghanaians' first name is not a given name, but one determined by their day of birth. It is the child's second name that is chosen by the parents eight days after birth, and is normally that of a respected family member, in the belief that the child will have some of the attributes of the person after whom he/she has been named. Names associated with the day of birth are as follows:

Day	Male	Female
Sunday	Kwasi	Akosua, Asi, Ese
Monday	Kwadwo, Kojo	Adwoa, Ajao
Tuesday	Kwabena, Kobina	Abena, Araba
Wednesday	Kwaku	Akua
Thursday	Yao, Ekow	Yaa
Friday	Kofi	Afua, Afia, Efua
Saturday	Kwame, Kwamena	Ama

The religious beliefs of the Akan are too complex to do justice to here. Briefly, all Akan societies believe in one omnipotent God, but also pay homage to any number of minor local deities (some villages in Ghana have more than 70 local shrines, which may take the form of trees or rocks or any other natural feature) and like most African societies place high emphasis on the veneration of ancestors. Many Akan villages have a totem, often a particular type of animal that may not be killed or eaten by members of that village. Selection of the totem is often bound up in the oral history of that village. The people of Boabeng-Fiema, for instance, believe the sacred monkeys descend from villagers transformed into monkeys by the magical powers of a king who died before he could return them to human form.

At some point visitors are likely to encounter one of the most remarkable aspects of Akan society: its colourful and vibrant funerals. Unusually, Ghanaian societies tend to separate the burial ceremony from the actual funeral – generally by at least three months, but sometimes by as long as two years! At the risk of great oversimplification, burial is generally a quiet and dignified moment, though often preceded by wailing and singing, and is followed by at least nine days of quiet mourning and fasting by close relatives. The funeral itself was traditionally held on a Monday or Thursday several months after the person died, but is now most often held on a Saturday for pragmatic reasons. The general tone is one of celebration rather than mourning, marked by exuberant drumming and dancing, not to say heavy drinking – on attending a Ghanaian funeral, you can't help but feel that it displays an altogether more convincing belief in some sort of afterlife than its sombre Christian equivalent.

For a good overview of Akan culture, we recommend Peter Sarong's book *Ghana in Retrospect* (Ghana Publishing Company, 1974), which is readily available and inexpensive in most Accra bookshops.

GHANA BEFORE 1500 On the basis of archaeological evidence, it has been established that modern-day Ghana was inhabited by humans 300,000 years ago, though current knowledge of human movements prior to this would suggest that the country has been occupied for millions of years. The earliest people to inhabit the region were hunter-gatherers, of whom little concrete can be said. It has yet to be determined when agriculture and pastoralism were adopted in the area, but this could have been as early as around 5000BC. Certainly, by 2000BC, both exotic creatures, such as cattle, and indigenous ones, such as guinea fowl, were being raised in domesticity, while archaeological findings near Kintampo demonstrate that substantial villages had been established at this time – a sure indication that hunting-gathering was no longer the predominant lifestyle in what are now Ashanti and Brong-Ahafo regions. From around AD1000, it appears that an increased trend towards urbanisation was under way, with population centres of more than 2,000 people forming in the central and northern parts of what is now Ghana, presumably as a result of an economy that depended increasingly on trade with the great empires of the Sahel.

Oral tradition suggests that most modern Ghanaian population groups migrated to their present homeland from elsewhere in West Africa. The traditions widely agree that these migrants moved into territory occupied by the Guan, who are still regarded by other Ghanaians to be the true aboriginals of the country, though they are now assimilated into more recently arrived groups, with the exception of a few isolated Guan pockets at places such as Adokrom, Winneba and Efutu. It is difficult to tell whether these migration traditions reflect the influx of an entire group of people who would presumably have gained territory through conquest, or whether they relate to a small group of migrants who formed a ruling class over the existing occupants of an area. What does seem reasonably certain is that the modern country's broad pattern of population had taken a recognisable shape by the late 15th century, when the Portuguese arrived at the coast.

The people of modern Ghana are generally divided into four main regional groupings, each of which shares a similar language and culture. The **Mole-Dagbani** of the Northern Region were possibly the first to establish their approximate modern territory; tradition has it that they migrated from the Lake Chad region in the 13th century, settling briefly at Pusiga (on the modern border with Togo) before establishing the Mamprusi Kingdom at Gambaga. Other northern chieftaincies, such as Dagomba, Nanumba and Mossi, are traditionally regarded to be offshoots of the Mamprusi, and even today secession disputes in most parts of the region are referred to the Chief of Gambaga (known as the 'Nayiri'), quite possibly the oldest extant chieftaincy in modern Ghana. The only significant exception to the above generalisations regarding the people of the Northern Region is the Gonja Kingdom, which is traditionally said to have been founded by Mande migrants from Ancient Mali in the early 16th century.

As a result of its proximity to the ancient empires of the Sahel, the Northern Region has enjoyed a strong Islamic influence for centuries, though exactly when and how this exotic religion reached the area is a matter of conjecture – some sources place its arrival as early as the 13th century, while others date it to the 17th. This discrepancy in dates might be accounted for by a long delay between the establishment of the first Islamic settlements in the northern regions and a more widespread acceptance of the religion. It has been suggested that the large-scale influx of Islamic ideas into present-day Ghana was blocked for centuries by a powerful anti-Islamic kingdom in what is now Burkina Faso, but this would not have prevented Islamic traders from establishing their own settlements along the main trade routes through the region. The mud-and-stick mosques found in several villages in the northwest of modern Ghana almost certainly pinpoint some of the country's earliest Islamic settlements but, since the antiquity of these mosques is open to debate, it is difficult to draw any firm conclusions about when Islam first reached these villages.

The area to the east of Lake Volta is inhabited by the **Ewe**, 15th-century migrants from eastern Nigeria. Ewe society is the least centralised of any in modern Ghana; each of the roughly 130 small Ewe chieftaincies is entirely autonomous (in other words, there is no paramount chief), though the larger Anlo Kingdom based around the port of Keta is something of an exception. The other important grouping of the east is the **Ga-Adangbe**, which consists of the Ga people of the Accra coastal plain and the Adangbe of Ada and Somanya. The Ga and Adangbe have practically identical languages, and they share several customs, such as ritual circumcision and a defined order of child-naming, though over the centuries they have adopted a great many customs from the neighbouring Akan. Like the Ewe, the Ga-Adangbe are originally from eastern Nigeria, and it is more than probable that the Ga had settled the Accra area and gelled into a cohesive state by the time the Portuguese arrived.

The most significant population group in modern Ghana, territorially and numerically, is the **Akan** (see box *The Akan*, pages 10–11). The Akan comprise more than half the country's population and inhabit five of its ten administrative regions: Western, Central, Eastern, Ashanti and Brong-Ahafo. Although every Akan village has its own chief, political centralisation into larger kingdoms has been a recurrent feature of Akan history, from the 14th-century Bono Kingdom of Techiman to more recent entities such as Denkyira, Ashanti and Fante. Superficially, oral traditions relating to the origin of the Akan vary greatly from one society to another, but in essence they tend to run along one of two basic themes: a migration from somewhere further north, or a sudden emergence from the sky or a hole in the ground or somewhere equally improbable. There does, however, appear to be a reasonable degree of consensus among historians that the Akan migrated to modern-day Ghana from the Sahel. Since most traditions claim Bono as the cradle of the Akan, and Bono was firmly established as a gold-mining and trading empire under King Akumfi Ameyaw I (1328–63), any migration must have occurred before the end of the 13th century. On this evidence, it seems reasonable to assume that the Akan migrated to their modern territory as a result of the dissolution of Ancient Ghana. It strikes me that those Akan societies lacking a migration tradition could be older groupings that adopted Akan culture either through long periods of association with, or colonisation by, one of the larger Akan empires.

THE GOLD COAST 1471–1665 In 1415, Portugal captured the Moroccan port of Ceuta, one first small step in an era of naval exploration that would result in the circumnavigation of Africa before the end of the 15th century. The motives that lay behind the Portuguese crown backing such a venture were manifold. Portugal believed that by sailing south around Africa it would be able to wrest control of the lucrative eastern spice trade and, although the Portuguese had no idea just how large an obstacle Africa would prove to be, they were ultimately correct in this. Religion, too, was an important factor, in that the Portuguese crown was eager to forge links with the Christian kingdom of Prester John (a legend referred to in many medieval writings, probably based on rumours emanating from Christian Ethiopia) and to spread Christianity to areas lying beyond the Islamic lands north of the Sahara. Finally, through having a foothold in Morocco, Portugal was keenly aware of the quantity of gold being transported across the Sahara, and recognised that finding a sea route to the source of the gold would be a more realistic goal than trying to take direct control of the Arabic caravan routes through the Sahara.

In 1471, the Portuguese arrived at the village that was subsequently named Elmina, after the Portuguese 'De Costa da el Mina de Ouro' – 'the Coast of Gold Mines' (a phrase that would also give rise to the moniker 'Gold Coast') – and entered into trade with a powerful chief whose name is recorded as Caramansa. Eleven years later, with a written lease from Caramansa, the Portuguese built the castle of St George on a rocky outcrop next to Elmina. Architecturally reminiscent of the castles built by the Crusaders, St George was separated from the village by a dry moat and its strongest bastion faced inland, suggesting that the Portuguese perceived their greatest threat of attack to come not from the sea, but from the interior. St George was the first of several forts and lodges established by the Portuguese – in 1515 and 1523, respectively, they built forts at Axim and Shama, close to the mouths of the rivers Ankobra and Pra (both of which flowed from parts of the interior rich in gold), and later in the 16th century they constructed a short-lived trading lodge in what is now downtown Accra.

Elmina, however, was to remain the centre of the Portuguese gold trade throughout their 150-year tenure on the Gold Coast. The fact that Portugal found such bountiful gold at Elmina was no mere coincidence. On the contrary, Elmina's importance as a salt-production centre gave Portugal effortless access to a trade route established at least a century before its arrival, connecting Elmina to the Akan gold mines near what are now Tarkwa and Obuasi via the empire of Eguafo. Gold was far and away the most important export from the West African coast at this time – £100,000 worth annually throughout the 16th century, or roughly 10% of the world supply – but surviving Portuguese ledgers show that there was also a thriving trade in ivory, cotton and animal hides, while major imports included metal pots and bowls, beads, leatherware, alcoholic spirits and guns. Odd as it may seem with hindsight, the Portuguese also imported to Elmina a quantity of slaves, captured or bought in Benin during the period 1486 to 1506, and at São Tomé after 1506.

Some readers may wonder why Ghana (as opposed to, say, Senegal or Liberia) became the centre of European activities in West Africa. First and foremost, this is because Ghana is the only West African country with a coast that lies close to significant gold deposits. But this alone doesn't really explain why all but two of the roughly 60 forts and trading lodges built on the Gulf of Guinea were sited in what is now Ghana – especially as many of these forts were built to service the slave trade rather than the gold trade. Just as important as the presence of gold inland was the physical nature of the Gold Coast. Studded with large rocky outcrops rather than mangrove swamps and sprawling shallow lagoons, Ghana boasts a great many good natural harbours, easily approached by ship, but also easily guarded and protected, with ample local material for constructing fortified buildings.

It is also interesting to note that Portugal's tenure on the Gold Coast was in no respect colonialism as we think of it today. The Portuguese had no jurisdiction beyond their forts, which were built with the permission of the local chiefs on land that was formally leased for the purpose. The Portuguese did make a concerted effort to spread Christianity, but even this was restricted to the immediate vicinity of the forts. They made no serious attempt to venture inland, or to capture the Akan gold mines, but instead traded with the local chiefs and merchants on an even footing. And, it should be noted, what is true of Portugal is largely true of the European powers that followed. The arrival of the Portuguese ushered in an era of trade that lasted more than three centuries. Only when describing events from the mid 19th century onwards is it valid to talk in terms of colonists.

The level of Portuguese trade out of the Gold Coast had probably peaked as early as 1530, its decline thereafter a result largely of the increasingly widespread Portuguese global 'empire' that spread from Goa, Malindi and Mozambique in the Indian Ocean to South America and the Caribbean. Nevertheless, Portuguese dominance of the Gold Coast was not substantially threatened in the 16th century, although it did not go entirely unchallenged. The first English ships reached the west coast of Africa in roughly 1530, and in 1542 a French ship landed at Dixcove, where it purchased 28kg of gold. From the 1550s, non-Portuguese ships were an increasingly common sight off the coast – in 1553, Captain Thomas Wyndham returned with a stash of gold that he sold for £10,000, and a few years later the coast was visited by Francis Drake as part of his successful attempt to circumnavigate the globe. The Dutch, by comparison, were latecomers, and when their first ship did arrive on the Gold Coast, blown off course *en route* to Brazil in 1593, its captain was imprisoned – though he still managed to return home with a healthy amount of gold.

That the Dutch were the first seriously to challenge Portugal's monopoly on the Gold Coast is often attributed to the tension that already existed between these two countries in Europe. In reality, economics was probably the greater factor. The first Dutch attack on Elmina was an unsuccessful naval bombardment in 1596. From that time on, between ten and 20 privately owned Dutch ships visited the Gold Coast annually. The Portuguese responded to this influx of new traders first by attacking Dutch ships whenever possible, and second by punishing brutally any African caught dealing with a rival European power. The offender's ears would be cut off for a first infringement; a second offence was rewarded with execution. Possibly as a result of this cruel policy, the chief of the Asubu sent two ambassadors to Holland requesting that a fort be erected at his capital 20km east of Elmina, at Moree. In 1612, the Dutch did just this, shipping skilled artisans and the requisite materials direct from Holland so that the fort would be built too quickly for the Portuguese to mount an attack during its construction.

With a secure foothold at Moree, the Dutch were positioned to mount a concerted attack on Portugal's Gold Coast possessions, especially after 1621, when the powerfully backed West India Company (WIC) was formed in Amsterdam. By 1622, some 40 Dutch ships were assigned to the Gold Coast trade. Then, in 1630, what was in effect a Dutch navy took to the Atlantic, capturing several Portuguese possessions in the West Indies and Brazil before turning its attention on the West African coast. After an aborted naval attack, Elmina fell in 1637, bombarded from the nearest hill. Shama followed in the same year, and Axim was captured by Dutch boats in 1642, effectively ending Portugal's influence in this part of the world (though Portugal would remain a major player for centuries to come in the Indian Ocean and on the coast of what is now Angola).

The Dutch capture of Portugal's Gold Coast possessions signalled the beginning of a period of intense rivalry for dominance between several European powers, some of which had little lasting impact on what is now Ghana. The Swedes, for instance, occupied Fort Carolusbourg, which they built at Cape Coast in 1653, for a mere 11 years. The Brandenburgers built Fort Gross Friedrichsburg at Pokesu (Prince's Town) in 1683, only to vacate it in 1717. Even the French, later to become so powerful in West Africa, had little influence on the Gold Coast, never occupying any one place for longer than a decade.

A more important rival to Dutch dominance was Denmark, though, on the whole, the Dutch tolerated the Danish presence in a tacit alliance against stronger powers. Aside from their rather obscure outpost at Keta, the Danes restricted their activities on the Gold Coast to Osu in modern-day Accra. The Danish castle at Osu

1

grew to be one of the most impressive on the Gold Coast, and the Danes occupied it almost continuously from 1642 to 1850, when it was sold to Britain. The most significant interruption in the Danish occupation of Osu occurred in 1681–83, when the castle was captured and occupied by Portugal; part of a rather desperate last bid at recapturing some of the Gold Coast trade.

The first British 'West Africa Company', formed in 1618, met with little success – its efforts at occupying the Gold Coast climaxed in 1640 with the construction at Cormantin of a small trading lodge that burnt down shortly after it was built, possibly with the assistance of a Dutch saboteur. More successful was the snappily titled 'Company of Royal Adventurers of English Trading to Africa', established in 1660 with a royal charter and the hearty backing of the Duke of York (later King James II, and – take note, trivia lovers – rewarded for his efforts in backing the 'Adventurers' by being not only the James of Accra's James Town, but the York of the USA's New York, known as New Amsterdam until it was captured from the Dutch by his charges).

In 1665, the British company launched a concerted attack on Holland's West African possessions, capturing the forts at Takoradi, Shama, Moree and Anomabu, as well as Fort Carolusbourg at Cape Coast, which the Dutch had occupied since 1664. The British company was unable to hold on to all of its newly captured forts, so it concentrated its efforts on ensuring that Fort Carolusbourg was impregnable, converting the modest fort into a castle covering roughly three-quarters of the area it does today. The British company had its foothold on the Gold Coast, one that was strengthened with its transformation to the wealthily backed Royal Africa Company in 1672, and by the end of the century Britain had become, if anything, more economically powerful than its more established rival. The reason for this is perfectly simple: instead of trading in gold, Britain decided to enter an altogether more lucrative arena of trade. The British capture of Cape Coast in 1665 can be seen as the critical point in the process that would, by 1700, cause a Dutch official to bemoan that 'the Gold Coast had changed into a virtual Slave Coast'.

THE SLAVE COAST 1665–1807 However convenient it might be to see the trade in slaves as an abomination introduced to Africa by Europeans, there is no escaping the reality that a slave trade was in existence from the very earliest days of the trans-Sahara caravans, when people captured in the sub-Sahelian region were transported across the desert to be sold into domestic bondage in North Africa and parts of Europe. Neither can it be denied that a slave class has formed a part of practically every centralised African society on record, at least until modern times. And, while it is true that, in many past African societies, slaves have had the opportunity to climb the social ladder, it is also true that in many such societies slaves were treated as subhuman, and cruelly sacrificed to mark special occasions or entreat deities.

None of which makes Africa in any way unusual, since slavery in name or in kind has been a feature of most ancient societies until this century. It is merely worth noting that the slave trade out of the Gold Coast emerged in an environment where not only slavery, but also trading in slaves were established practices, just as it should be noted that the Europeans who conducted this trade came from societies where it was customary to hold public executions for crimes as paltry as stock theft, and to burn alive witches and other perceived heretics on a stake. Viewed from the lofty moral heights of the early 21st century, there is a certain uncomfortable irony in the realisation that the very earliest form of slave trade entered into by Europeans on the Gold Coast, as mentioned above, involved not the export of slaves, but their import, as captives bought by Portuguese merchants from African sellers in Benin were sold to African buyers in Elmina.

Nevertheless, the transatlantic slave trade is a singular event in human history, not simply because it operated on an unprecedented scale, but also because it was so ruthlessly well organised, and so shattering and wide-ranging in its effects. Before the arrival of Europeans, slaves were generally incidental captives of inter-tribal war, relatively few in number, and in most cases able to integrate themselves into the society that enslaved them. By the time the transatlantic slave trade hit its peak, it would be an understatement to say that the capture of slaves had been transformed into the *raison d'être* for war; closer to the mark, perhaps, to say that the entire West African interior had deteriorated into a hunting ground wherein slave raiders with firearms attacked village after comparatively defenceless village, trading their booty at the coastal forts for yet more firepower. It is estimated that between 12 million and 20 million Africans were transported across the Atlantic between the late 17th century and the early 19th, a five-week trip in conditions so cramped and unhygienic that it was not unusual for a boat to lose half its human cargo in passage. It is impossible to tell how many more people – those who were too young or too old or too weak to be saleable – died in the course of the raids.

Most of us are familiar with the fate of the victims of these raids. Rather less well documented is the devastating effect that the slave trade had on African society. It has been noted, for instance, that many traditional industries were lost to the Gold Coast interior – iron-smelting and gold-mining are good examples – as the product of these industries became increasingly worthless by comparison with slaves, and their practitioners were taken into bondage. Worse still was the arms race that built up between neighbouring groups, as, in the 17th century, Britain alone supplied around 100,000 guns annually to West Africa – and it is not difficult to see how this situation forced even the most unwilling of chiefs into finding slaves to trade for the firearms they needed to protect themselves. For two centuries, Africa lost a high proportion of its most able-bodied men and women to the slave trade. In return, it received items that were, at best, of no lasting value – alcoholic spirits and tobacco – and at worst entirely destructive.

In the 16th and 17th centuries, the Gold Coast was spared the worst of this. Both Portugal and, later, Holland made it policy not to buy slaves at the Gold Coast – not for any moral reason, but because they believed (correctly, as it turned out) that the slave trade would interfere with the gold trade. Instead, they concentrated their slaving efforts further south, along the stretch of coast between modern-day Nigeria and Angola. This was to change towards the end of the 17th century; firstly, because the recently arrived British had difficulty breaking into the Dutch-controlled gold trade, and, secondly, as a result of the rise of the Akwamu Empire, which, at its peak, controlled a 350km stretch of coast east of Accra crossing into what is now Togo, but at no point had access to the gold mines at Akan. The British and, to a lesser extent, the Danes started trading in slaves from around 1665, a situation that was rapidly exploited by the Akwamu, and the floodgates were opened in 1698, when the Royal African Company (RAC) forsook its monopoly on British trade, allowing any British boat to trade freely, provided that a 10% custom was paid to the company. This policy was a failure in so far as few of the so-called 'ten-percenters' actually paid the required levy, but it did ensure that the market for slaves expanded exponentially from 1698 onwards, with Anomabu in particular becoming a major centre for 'free trade'.

In the late 17th century, two empires dominated the interior immediately north of the coast. These were Akwamu, already mentioned above, and a much older Akan empire called Denkyira, the region's main repository of gold-working skills and the centre of the gold trade to the coast. In 1701, Denkyira was conquered by the recently established Ashanti Empire of Kumasi, creating what was perhaps the most radical power shift in the Ghanaian interior since Portugal had first arrived at the coast. One result of Denkyira's defeat was that the lease papers for Elmina Castle passed into the hands of the Ashanti, who were far more interested in empire-building and trading slaves for guns than they were in such pastoral pursuits as scratching around for gold. Another was that the flow of gold to the coast, already stemmed by the emergent slave trade, dried up to such an extent that, in 1703, the governor of Elmina formally requested that Amsterdam allow him to abandon the gold trade in favour of slaves.

The threat posed by the rampant Ashanti, whose king was courted by both the major European powers almost as soon as he conquered Denkyira, appears to have been pivotal in the expansion of the Fante state in the early 18th century. Based in the area around Mankessim and Anomabu, the Fante were, in 1700, the most powerful and wealthy of perhaps 20 small Akan kingdoms running along the coast west of Accra, all of which were linked by a common culture and used to having a degree of control over trade with the Dutch and English, both of whose headquarters lay in this part of the country. Between 1707 and 1720, the Fante gradually exerted control over all these groups, including the Oguaa of Cape Coast and Edina of Elmina, using a combination of force and coercion as it became obvious to all that unity was their best weapon against an Ashanti attack. Ashanti, meanwhile, grew in power with almost every passing year, capturing Akwamu in 1730, Brong-Ahafo in 1744–45, and much of what are now Burkina Faso and the northern regions of Ghana in 1745–50. By the end of this period of expansion, Ashanti was probably bigger than Ghana is today, and, along with Fante, it was by far the most dominant power in what is now Ghana. Unexpectedly, perhaps, the two empires maintained a relatively peaceful coexistence, motivated partly by the recognition that a tacit alliance was the best way to exclude other kingdoms from the lucrative coastal trade, but also enforced to a degree by the British and Dutch, on whom they relied for weapons.

The slave trade out of the Gold Coast continued unabated throughout the 18th century. Roughly 5,000 slaves passed annually through each of the main British trading posts, Cape Coast and Anomabu, and were stored in cold, dark dungeons that are chilling to visit today. The Dutch tried in vain to revive the flagging gold trade in 1702 by building a new fort they named 'Good Hope' at Senya Beraku; ten years later, the fort was extended to include slave dungeons. Ashanti prospered, as Kumasi lay at the heart of all three major trade routes to the coast west of Accra; and, although it was forbidden for an Ashanti to enslave another Ashanti, their frequent military expeditions and slave raids ensured the flow of human cargo to the coast never abated.

As the 18th century drew to a close, the anti-slavery lobby became an increasingly powerful voice in Europe, a result not only of the strengthening liberal attitudes that emerged following the Industrial Revolution, but also of a greater public awareness as to how the slave trade actually operated, following several publications on the subject. In 1804, Denmark abolished the slave trade, followed by Britain in 1807, the USA in 1808, and Holland, France, Portugal and Spain between 1814 and 1817. Also in 1817, several of the above nations signed a Reciprocal Search Treaty, which in effect allowed Britain to search boats captained by people of other nationalities. The slave trade was subdued by this, but it was by no means halted – it became common practice among slavers to throw all their human cargo overboard at the approach of a British naval patrol. Britain soon recognised that it would take nothing less than the abolition of slavery to end the trade, and it banned slavery throughout its colonies in 1833, followed by France in 1848, the USA in 1865 (after a bloody civil war dominated by the issue) and, finally, Brazil in 1888.

THE BUILD-UP TO COLONIALISM 1806–1902 By 1800, Britain was the major European trading power on the Gold Coast and, although the Danes were to retain a presence there until 1850, and the Dutch until 1872, developments in the 19th century, in hindsight though perhaps not at the time, show a clear trend towards British colonisation. So far as the interior was concerned, a clear pattern had emerged by 1800 wherein various Fante chieftaincies acted as middlemen between the Ashanti and British traders. This arrangement suited the British, who believed that if Ashanti were to take full control of the interior it would be able to dictate terms of trade to Britain. It suited the Fante, too, since without the tacit backing of Britain they would never have had the military prowess to resist an Ashanti invasion. The arrangement was, however, less agreeable to the Ashanti, who lost out substantially by having to deal through the Fante. Nevertheless, a few minor skirmishes aside, Fante and Ashanti had a reasonably healthy relationship in the second half of the 18th century, several times combining forces against upstart states to ensure they retained their joint trade monopoly.

The relationship between the European occupants of the forts and the surrounding chieftaincies changed little in essence between the construction of St George in 1482 and 1820. Theirs was a commercial not a colonial relationship: European control barely extended beyond the forts, and even those chieftaincies closest to the forts remained autonomous political units, though inevitably they were offered a degree of protection by their well-armed European neighbours. This long-standing balance was to waver in the first decade of the 19th century, partly as a result of Britain's wish to curb the slave trade at its Ashanti roots from 1807 onwards, no less because of escalating tension between Fante and Ashanti following a military skirmish between these states in 1806.

There are two main reasons why the Ashanti attacked Fante in 1806. The first is that Fante, always more a federation of disparate states than a cohesive empire, had been weakened by internal disputes, such as the wars between Oguaa and Komenda in 1788, Anomabu and Mankessim in 1789, Oguaa and Anomabu in 1802, and Komenda and Shama in 1805. The second was the escalation of a long-standing dispute over trade with Elmina Castle. Ashanti had held the lease to the castle since 1701, for which reason they believed they had the right to trade with its Dutch occupants directly, but the Fante regularly blocked Ashanti access to Elmina in the late 18th century, and even attacked the town on a number of occasions. The above points noted, it was inevitable that sooner or later the vast Ashanti Empire would decide to take direct control of the coast, and the remarkable thing is that they waited so long to try.

Between 1806 and 1874, there were nine military clashes between Ashanti and Fante, and three more were averted at the last moment. Up until 1820, these clashes were wholly internal affairs, resulting in one or other of the two dozen or so Fante states being conquered by Ashanti. The Fante, however, refused to recognise Ashanti's traditional rights of conquest, and tension between the two states meant that trade of all forms ground to a virtual halt. In this, the Fante were supported by the British, not only because Britain favoured dealing with several small competitive states over an Ashanti monolith, but also because it was eager to end the slave raids in which the Ashanti still indulged. To this end, the British parliament placed all the Gold Coast forts formerly run by its companies under crown government in 1821. Three years later, Britain for the first time gave military support to the Fante, in a battle at the Adaamso River that ended in an Ashanti victory – one contemporary account claims that the wounded British governor was beheaded by his Ashanti counterpart, and that his head was taken to Kumasi as a trophy. In 1826, Britain and Ashanti clashed again at Akatamanso, to the north of Accra: a battle that ended in a resounding British victory. It would be three decades before another major clash took place between these powers.

By 1828, the British government was prepared to withdraw entirely from the Gold Coast, due to the high cost of maintaining the forts and the massive drop in trade following a decade of instability. In the end, however, it bowed to pressure from British merchants and the beleaguered Fante, selling the forts to a company called the London Committee of Merchants. In 1830, a new governor was installed, George MacLean, who more than any other person would lay the foundation of future British rule. In 1831, MacLean pressed the humbled Ashanti into signing a tripartite treaty that required them to refrain from any further attacks on their southern neighbours. As a sign of good faith, the Ashanti left a large sum of gold with MacLean, to be returned after six years, as well as two Ashanti princes to be educated in Europe. Six years after the treaty was signed, MacLean returned the gold, and, in 1841, the princes went back to Kumasi in order to help establish a Methodist mission there, creating a new atmosphere of trust between Ashanti and the British. In addition to his role as peacemaker, MacLean made great efforts to end the slave trade; and he turned around the Gold Coast economy, ushering in a new era of 'legitimate trade' as the value of exports leapt by 275% during the first decade of his governorship, and imports by more than 300%. This remarkably successful administration ended in 1843, when the British government decided to claim back the Gold Coast forts and to install its own governor. Many of MacLean's achievements were formalised with the so-called Bond of 1844, a sort of proto-protectorateship over several Fante states, in exchange for which the chiefs had to pledge allegiance to the Queen of England and give up practices regarded to be barbaric, such as human sacrifices and *panyarring* (the seizure of a debtor's relatives, to be sold into slavery if the debt wasn't met within a specified period). MacLean himself died in 1847, and was buried in the courtyard of Cape Coast Castle. It is said that the chiefs of southern states mourned his passing for months afterwards.

The two decades that followed the MacLean administration were relatively uneventful. In 1850, the year in which the governances of Sierra Leone and the Gold Coast were finally separated, Britain bought the forts at Keta and Osu from Denmark. It is doubtful that the British saw much use for these forts at the time of their purchase, but didn't want them falling into French or Dutch hands, and perhaps hoped to have more success than Denmark in curbing the clandestine slave trade running out of Keta. (As it turned out, Osu Castle would become the seat of government in 1876, a position it retained until the controversial relocation to Flagstaff House in 2013.) In 1852, the British authorities introduced a poll tax system, which sparked a series of riots and battles (most famously, the violent Anglo–Krobo confrontation that took place on Krobo Mountain) without ever raising a great deal of revenue – it was abandoned in 1861.

The year 1863 saw renewed tension between the British and Ashanti, caused by the former's refusal to hand over refugees from Ashanti justice. In 1864, the two armies clashed once again. The battle went the way of the Ashanti, largely because so many British troops died in an outbreak of fever or dysentery brought on by unusually heavy rain. It also signalled the beginning of a rush of events that would conspire to make the period 1867–74 of unparalleled decisiveness in the history of the Gold Coast.

The rush started in 1867, when Britain and Holland arrived at the mutual conclusion that every aspect of their increasingly unprofitable administrations would be improved were Britain to control a continuous strip of coast east of Cape Coast, and the Dutch a strip of coast to the west of Elmina. The two countries signed the so-called Fort Exchange Treaty, much to the consternation of several Fante states, long allied to a nearby British fort and now suddenly forced to live alongside the Dutch, whom they regarded as foes due to their involvement with the Ashanti who still held the lease to Elmina fort. King Aggrey of Cape Coast led a protest against the treaty, and was arrested by the British and exiled to Sierra Leone. The arrest of Aggrey, along with widespread dissatisfaction with the new status quo, triggered the formation of the Fante Confederation. Founded at Mankessim in 1868, this was the first formal alliance incorporating all the Fante states from Axim to just east of Accra, and, although it was to prove short-lived, the movement had some success in preventing the Dutch from occupying forts they had traded with Britain. In 1871, Britain arrested the confederation leaders and imprisoned them for a month. In the following year, Holland finally limped away from the Gold Coast, selling its remaining possessions to Britain. In 1873, the Fante Confederation disbanded, having lost direction after the Dutch evacuation of the coast – and in any case riddled with leadership squabbles. By this stage, the British parliament was of the opinion that it would have to take one of two approaches to the governing of the increasingly fractious Gold Coast: in its own words, a 'very evil choice' between following the Dutch and withdrawing completely, or pursuing an active policy of territorial expansion and colonisation. On 24 July 1874, Britain formally declared the Gold Coast a crown colony.

The withdrawal of Holland from Elmina proved to be the trigger of the notorious Anglo–Ashanti war of 1873–74. Fearing that Britain wouldn't honour the ancient lease, the Ashanti occupied Elmina in 1873. Britain responded with a naval bombardment that flattened the old town to the west of the castle, leaving around 20,000 people without a home. In 1874, British troops entered Ashanti for the first time, defeating its army at Bekwai and – after the Ashanti king refused to accept their initial terms of treaty – burning Kumasi to the ground. The Treaty of Fomena, signed in Adanse towards the end of 1874, forced the Ashanti to renounce all claims on territories lying to the south of their core state, most of all Elmina. At the same time, several vassal states to the north (for instance Gonja, Bono and Dagomba) took advantage of the defeat to assert their independence from Ashanti, and so an empire that had once been larger than modern Ghana was reduced to an area similar in size to present-day Ashanti Region.

In its earliest incarnation, the Gold Coast Colony was a fraction of the size of modern Ghana, with an identical coastline, but barely extending more than 50km inland. So it might have remained were it not for the so-called 'Scramble for Africa', initiated in the late 1870s when Belgium and France entered into a race for control of the Congo. By 1888, most of the modern states of Africa had more or less taken shape, though not Ghana, presumably because its most interesting asset, the Gold Coast, had been British long before the scramble started. By the 1890s, however, both France and Germany were eyeing the interior of what is now Ghana. As a result of this, Britain extended its borders to cover the whole of the modern Western and Central provinces in 1893, while the northern border was settled with France in 1898, and the eastern border with Germany agreed in 1899 (though the latter was to move further east exactly 20 years later, when the League of Nations divided German Togoland between Britain and France).

In the 1890s, Britain's attention turned once again to Ashanti, which it was desperate not to let fall into German or French hands. In 1891, British protectorateship was offered to Ashanti, and soundly rejected by the recently installed King Prempeh I. Britain decided it would have to install a British resident in Kumasi to prevent the French from doing the same, and so it was that, in 1896, a British military expedition (whose numbers, incidentally, included the future Lord Baden-Powell, just in case you ever wonder why the Scout movement regularly comes up as a topic of small talk with students in this part of the country!) entered Kumasi without firing a shot. Prempeh, along with many other members of the royal family, was arrested and imprisoned in Elmina Castle before being exiled to Sierra Leone, and, later, the Seychelles. Britain then demanded that the remaining Ashanti elders in Kumasi hand over the Golden Stool (not so much the symbol of the king as its embodiment, handed down from generation to generation), a request that had been anticipated to the extent that they had a fake stool ready to hand to Britain (the fake is now on display in the Prempeh II Museum in Kumasi).

In 1900, the Ashanti rose one last time against British colonisation in the war named after its main instigator, Yaa Asantewaa, the Queen Mother of Ejisu. After heavy loss of life on both sides, Ashanti was defeated again in 1901, and yet another contingent of dignitaries, Yaa Asantewaa among them, was imprisoned and exiled to the Seychelles. On 1 January 1902, Ashanti was formally annexed to the British Gold Coast Colony, along with the territories that today make up Ghana's three northern regions.

GOLD COAST COLONY 1902–57 The Gold Coast, like most other British colonies in Africa, was run along the system of indirect rule, a sharp contrast to the French and Portuguese systems whereby African colonies were – in theory, if not in practice – run as an extension of the so-called mother country. The basic principle underlying indirect rule, as patented by Lord Lugard, first in Uganda and later in Nigeria, was that traditional chiefs would continue to rule locally as before, but under the supervision of the colonial administration. The motivations for adopting this system were twofold. Firstly, Britain believed that the Gold Coast would be better served in the long run if it developed a system of government rooted in its own traditions rather than one imposed entirely from outside. More to the point, perhaps, the lack of funding and shortage of European manpower created by Britain's insistence that all colonies should be economically self-sufficient would have made it impossible for most colonial governors to rule in any other manner. Indirect rule was, in the words of eminent Ghanaian historian Albert Adu Boahen (1932–2006), 'in reality, the most indirect way of ruling directly'. It was also, doubtless, the cheapest.

The core problem with indirect rule as it was administered in the Gold Coast is that it undermined the very institution it was nominally designed to protect. A traditional chief in pre-colonial Ghana was not, as might be supposed, a hereditarily determined autocrat, but an appointee of the council of elders. And the elders who appointed a chief had not only a right to veto any ruling he made, but also the customary right to remove him from the stool. Prior to the colonial era, then, the authority of the chief was rooted in the council of elders over whom he presided. Under Britain, the authority of the chief came from the colonial administration, a situation that was bound to become a problem the moment that the administration tried to enforce an unpopular ruling through the chief.

The first steps towards indirect rule took place in 1883, when all chiefs in the Gold Coast (then only a fraction of what is now Ghana) were required to apply for recognition by the colonial administration. The policy took a more formal shape with the formation of so-called Native Authorities, comprising a paramount chief and his main sub-chiefs; an institution that, to its credit, paved the way for the modern regional and district councils of Ghana. In reality, Britain often tried to appoint a chief who was wholly unacceptable to his subjects. The clearest example of this occurred in Ashanti, where King Prempeh I and many other important chiefs were held in exile from 1896 until 1924, while the British authorities attempted to gain recognition for a dummy king of their choosing. Even when Prempeh I was returned to the stool in 1926, it was as King of Kumasi rather than King of Ashanti. Only in 1935 did Britain come full circle and restore the Ashanti Confederacy Council that it had abolished following the Yaa Asantewaa war in 1901, at the same time allowing the recently enstooled King Prempeh II to assume his full traditional role.

Resistance to colonial rule emerged as early as 1897, when the Aboriginal Rights Protection Society successfully blocked a bill that would have made all physically unoccupied territory in the colony the property of the colonial administration. It appeared in a more orchestrated form in the wake of World War I with the formation of the National Congress of British West Africa (NCBWA) by the Gold Coast barrister, Casely Hayford. The formation of the NCBWA is widely seen as the beginning of a formal split between educated nationalists, who were excluded from government under the system of indirect rule, and the uneducated and generally conservative traditional chiefs who gained from it. The inaugural meeting of the NCBWA took place in Accra in 1920, bringing together a total of 20 nationalist delegates from Gambia, Nigeria, Sierra Leone and, of course, the Gold Coast. The delegates drew up a list of demands, notably that the government should provide equal job opportunities for Africans and Europeans with equivalent qualifications, that at least half of the legislative council in all countries should be freely elected, and that the colonial administration should cease interfering in the selection and removal of traditional chiefs. An NCBWA delegation was sent to London to present these demands to the Colonial Secretary, but was refused an appointment. Nevertheless, a great many changes along the lines suggested by the organisation had been set in place by the time of Casely Hayford's death in 1930, by which time the organisation was close to disintegration.

It was World War II, however, that proved decisive in ending the colonial era in the Gold Coast, as elsewhere in Africa. In the Gold Coast specifically, at least 65,000 African volunteers were shipped to fight in the European war (mostly in East Africa and Burma), where they were exposed on a daily basis to the democratic and anti-imperialistic ideals of the Allied Forces. The Atlantic Charter signed by Roosevelt and Churchill stated categorically that the signatories would 'respect the right of all peoples to choose the form of government under which they will live'. Churchill would later retract the statement in so far as colonies were concerned, but the American government affirmed that by 'all people', they meant all people. When these African servicemen returned home after the war, they had high hopes of benefiting from the democratic ideals for which they had been obliged to fight. Instead, in at least 50,000 cases in the Gold Coast alone, the ex-servicemen returned home to unemployment, not to say a capital city whose population had increased threefold as a result of short-lived employment opportunities created by the European war.

In the Gold Coast more than any other British colony, the immediate post-war period saw events move with remarkable speed and purpose. In 1946, Governor Burns responded to the mood of the time with a new constitution that allowed 18 of the 30 seats in the colony's Legislative Council to be elected, 13 by the Provincial Council of Chiefs of the southern regions and Ashanti, and five by the small number of registered African voters in Accra, Cape Coast and Sekondi. In 1947, the United Gold Coast Convention (UGCC), formed by Dr J B Danquah, demanded 'self-government within the shortest possible time' and objected to the new constitution on the valid grounds that the Provisional Council of Chiefs was seen as a stooge organisation by most commoners, that the electoral roll in the above-mentioned cities was laughably unrepresentative, and that the Northern Region had no vote at all. November 1947 saw the return from 12 years in the USA and UK of the nationalist and pan-Africanist Dr Kwame Nkrumah, invited home by Danquah to act as Secretary General to the UGCC.

On 28 February 1948, colonial officers opened fire on a peaceful march organised by ex-servicemen to deliver a petition to the governor. Three marchers were killed, including the leader of the ex-servicemen, and another 12 died in the rioting that followed. This event proved decisive in the history of modern Africa. The Gold Coast was Britain's 'model colony', the most prosperous, educated and organised of them all, and the administration reasoned that if this could happen in the Gold Coast, then colonialism in Africa was surely doomed. Even before 28 February 1948, Britain had generally seen self-government as the end goal for its colonies, but it had been thinking ahead to a time decades, perhaps even centuries away. After 28 February 1948, that time span changed to one of years.

In the short term, however, the colonial administration put the UGCC leadership in jail, hoping that would help quieten things down. On his release in July 1949, Nkrumah formed the new and more radical Convention People's Party (CPP) – motto, 'self government now!' – and set about organising a series of strikes and boycotts that peaked in January 1950, with the aim of making the colony ungovernable. Nkrumah was once again thrown in jail, but the colonial administration backed down by installing a new constitution that allowed 36 seats in the government to be elected by the African population. In the 1951 election, the CPP won 33 of the seats, and Nkrumah was released to enter government. In March 1952, Nkrumah became the Gold Coast's first African prime minister. He then set about writing a new constitution that gave the Gold Coast virtual self-government after the 1954 election, in which the CPP won 79 out of 104 seats. Nkrumah then lobbied for full independence from Britain, but this was held up while the UN resolved the so-called Ewe Question (a legacy of the split of the Ewe homeland when the former German Togoland was divided between Britain and France by the League of Nations in 1919) with a referendum that went in favour of the British section becoming part of independent Ghana. In the election of July 1956, the CPP won 74 out of 104 seats on a pro-independence ticket. Britain had no choice but to acquiesce to popular demand, and so, on 6 March 1957, the former Gold Coast Colony became independent Ghana. It was the first African colony to be granted independence in the post-war era, and its name was adopted from the most ancient of West African empires; in the words of Nkrumah, 'as an inspiration for the future'.

GHANA 1957–81 Ghana's pioneering status as the first independent former colony in Africa is pivotal to understanding much of what occurred in the country under Nkrumah, who evidently perceived himself as a spokesman not merely for his country, but also for the far broader goal of liberating Africa from colonial rule. It is for this reason that the grass-roots development of agriculture and the mining era were often ignored in favour of frittering away the country's financial reserves on a variety of grand schemes and empty gestures. Nkrumah's role as an African statesman cannot be denied – he was, for instance, the prime mover behind the formation of the Organisation of African Unity (OAU) in 1963, and he frequently gave generous financial support to other newly independent countries. But neither can one ignore a level of economic mismanagement and wastefulness that resulted in Ghana having accumulated a foreign debt of US$1 billion by 1966, despite having had foreign reserves ten times greater than its foreign debt at the time of independence. Characteristic of the Nkrumah era was the construction of an enormously expensive OAU headquarters in Accra, one that was never to be used after the OAU decided to base itself in Ethiopia instead.

The Nkrumah government did have several far-reaching successes, eg: the vast improvement in the country's transport network between 1957 and 1966 – notably the laying of the 'new' Kumasi–Tamale road and surfacing of several other major trunk routes, and the construction of Akosombo Dam and a deepwater harbour at Tema. Another success was the expansion of an education system that already ranked among the best in Africa, resulting in a fivefold to twentyfold increase in enrolment at every level from primary school to university. And if Nkrumah's biggest failings were in the development of the crucial agricultural sector, then the 60% drop in the externally determined cocoa price during his rule must be cited as an important mitigating factor. It is also the case that post-independence Ghana was something of a victim of the Cold War mentality – Nkrumah's espoused policy of African socialism, not to say his strong diplomatic ties with the Eastern bloc, made him an increasingly unpopular figure in the West, so that many Western governments were unwilling to provide Ghana with the support they might otherwise have given.

On the political front, the Nkrumah regime followed a path that, in hindsight, feels naggingly familiar. In July 1958, the Preventative Detention Act was passed in response to the formation of the opposition United Party under the leadership of Dr Kofi Busia, allowing for the detention without trial of perceived political opponents for a period of up to five years. In July 1960, following a national referendum, Ghana was decreed a republic with Nkrumah elected as executive president. Shortly after the presidential election, Nkrumah's main opponent for the presidency, J B Danquah, was placed in detention, where he would eventually die, as would another former ally of Nkrumah, Obetsebi Lamptey. It is estimated that, by this time, the jails of Ghana held some 3,000 political detainees, a number that would increase dramatically following the attempted assassination of the president in 1962. It was this harsh repression of criticism, combined with the elevated status given to the Presidential Guard of the normal military, which would result in Nkrumah's downfall. On 24 February 1966, while the president was away in Hanoi, control of the country was assumed by the military. Nkrumah never returned home, and he died of cancer in exile in 1972.

Between 1966 and 1969, Ghana was ruled by the military National Liberation Council under the leadership first of Lieutenant General Joseph Ankra, and later (and more briefly) Brigadier Akwasi Afrifa. This regime did much to restore democracy by releasing all political detainees and allowing a reasonable degree of free speech and a free press. It also restored Ghana's credibility in the West by breaking ties with the Eastern bloc and initiating a widespread policy of privatisation. In May 1969, in line with a freshly drawn-up Bill of Rights, political parties were legalised. The election held a few months later was won by the Progress Party (PP) under Dr Kofi Busia, recently returned to the country after having fled to exile in 1959.

Busia's most notable contribution to the country was a remarkable drive towards rural improvement, eg: by building several new clinics and hospitals, drilling boreholes, and installing electricity in many places. By and large, the Busia regime maintained a policy of free speech and a free press, but these democratic ideals were undermined somewhat by their inconsistent application – at one point, for instance, Busia made it a criminal offence to mention Nkrumah by name, a response to the increasing lionisation of the former president. Busia's biggest failings were on the economic front and, although much of this can be blamed on a legacy of mismanagement left by former regimes, it would be an economic decision – the devaluation of the cedi by 44% – that triggered the coup that removed him from power on 13 January 1972.

The six-year presidency of General Ignatius Acheampong started out well enough, but all the initial grand talk of economic self-reliance and democracy soon deteriorated into a more familiar scenario. Acheampong's gross economic mismanagement and stubborn refusal to take advice regarding the freeing of the exchange rate resulted in an annual inflation rate of 130%, prompting an economic collapse that was exacerbated by two severe droughts during the early years of the regime. The repression of political activity continued with the mass detention of perceived political opponents. Meanwhile, the national coffers were drained by the regime, nepotism was rampant, and the level of corruption soared so high it caused one prominent Ghanaian to coin the term 'kleptocracy' – rule by thieves. Amid an increasing level of civil unrest and widespread cries for a return to civilian rule, the military sacked Acheampong in 1978, and installed in his place Lieutenant General Akuffo. The ensuing months saw the unveiling of a new constitution, as well as a lift on the six-year-old ban on political parties, and an election date was set for 1979.

On 4 June 1979, exactly two weeks before the scheduled election date, power was seized in a coup led by Flight Lieutenant Jerry Rawlings, a 32-year-old Ghanaian of mixed Scottish descent. Rawlings vowed that the election would go ahead, but that before power was transferred to the victor it was essential to purge corruption from the military and civil service. In the bout of bloodletting that followed, a great many civil servants were removed from office, tax offenders were forced to pay their debts, and several high-ranking members of the military were executed publicly by firing squad, among them three former heads of state: Afrifa, Acheampong and Akuffo. Remarkably, on 24 September, a week ahead of schedule, civilian rule was restored when Rawlings handed power to the newly elected People's National Party under President Hilla Limann. The initial popularity of this government, however, was soon offset by the country's continued economic slide, and within a year the new government had become as corrupt as any before it.

GHANA 1982–2000: THE RAWLINGS YEARS AND BEYOND On 31 December 1981, Ghana suffered its fourth coup in 15 years, as power was seized once again by the popular figure of Jerry Rawlings. The constitution was abolished, parliament was dissolved, political parties were banned, and a number of prominent figures were jailed, President Limann among them. Rawlings installed a Provisional National Defence Council comprising three civilians and four military men, and at a local level he replaced councils with People's Defence Committees (later called Committees for the Defence of the Revolution). The next few years were marked by two clear trends. The first was unprecedented economic growth (a result of Rawlings's massive devaluation of the cedi), large-scale paring down of the civil service, privatisation of several state assets, and improved payments at the grass roots of the crucial cocoa industry. The second trend was one of repeated political instability, including several attempted coups and the unravelling of alleged assassination conspiracies against Rawlings, as well as a great many strikes and protests.

Things came to a head in 1989, when universities nationwide were closed for four months after protests and rioting, and Rawlings had introduced severe press restrictions. An attempted coup against the government was foiled in September, and, a few months later, one of its instigators was found hanged in his cell, prompting an international outcry led by Amnesty International, as well as providing a rallying point for the many Ghanaians who wanted a return to civilian rule. In December 1990, Rawlings announced that a new constitution would be put in place within a year – it would, in fact, be enacted in April 1991, following a 92% approval among the 44% of the population who turned out for the national referendum. In May 1991, Rawlings endorsed the implementation of a multi-party system; the next month, he passed amnesty on all political detainees, and six opposition groups were granted legal status. The most important of these were Dr Limann's People's National Convention (PNC) and Dr Boahen's New Patriotic Party (NPP), while Rawlings announced that he would retire from the military as per the new constitution and stood as president for the National Democratic Congress (NDC). The election was held in two phases. The presidential elections in November 1992 saw Rawlings poll a clear majority of 58%, almost twice as many votes as his closest rival Boahen, who polled 30%. The election was declared substantially free and fair, but this was contested by the NPP and PNC who decided to boycott the constituent elections held on 29 December 1992 in protest. As a result, the NDC took 189 out of a possible 200 seats, with only a 29% poll recorded.

Rawlings's years as an elected president saw many positive developments on the economic front, as well as an increased level of political freedom with the release of political detainees and the re-emergence of a free press. The government managed to weather two major storms during Rawlings's first term. The first of the crises to beset Ghana in recent years was an outbreak of ethnic violence in the northern regions, which originated from a land dispute between the Konkomba and Nunumba of the Bimbilla district in February 1994. Within months, the violence had spread to many parts of the north, leaving as many as 6,000 people dead and a further 100,000 displaced as 200 villages were razed. The second was an attempt to replace the existing sales tax with a new VAT system in February 1995, an unpopular decision that resulted in widespread rioting, the death of five people in Accra, and – eventually – the reinstatement of the familiar sales tax system. The above events notwithstanding, Rawlings was voted back into power in December 1996, defeating John Kufuor's New Patriotic Party (NPP) with a diminished, but still comfortable, majority of 133 seats.

GHANA TODAY That the days of coup and countercoup were long gone was confirmed when the momentous election of December 2000 ushered in the first transfer of power from one elected leader to another in Ghanaian history. The 2000 election also marked the end of the Rawlings era, as the former president stepped down after 18 years in power, having served his maximum of two terms as stipulated in the 1991 constitution. In the first round of Ghana's 2000 election, neither of the two main parties seized enough seats to assume outright power, but in run-off elections that followed a few days later, John Kufuor, the leader of the former opposition NPP, defeated Rawlings's handpicked successor, Vice President John Atta Mills, by a substantial margin. Despite some fears to the contrary, the election took place in a peaceful atmosphere; both the result and the process by which it was obtained drew widespread international praise. Kufuor and Rawlings appeared together on television shortly after the election, to demonstrate their mutual commitment to smooth transition. 'We need to co-operate to find solutions to the economic problems that are going to beset this country for the next years to come,' Rawlings said generously. Kufuor's response was: 'We welcome very much your constructive criticism, because that is the essence of multi-party democracy.'

Kufuor was re-elected as leader of the NPP in 2004, and the party won 128 out of 230 seats in the election in the same year. The NDC won 94.

But with Ghana facing severe economic problems, Kufuor had a difficult task ahead of him. Despite boasting one of the highest growth rates in Africa throughout the 1990s, by the beginning of the new millennium the country was in the midst of a currency crisis that saw the sudden but rapid devaluation of the cedi to the order of 200% against the US dollar during 2000. Although experts tied the crisis to a drop in international gold and cocoa prices, as well as the rise in international fuel prices, the reasons for the scale of devaluation were difficult to identify. According to government estimates, inflation in Ghana at the time was around 10%, but local expatriates pinned it at up to 27%. The truth was probably somewhere between the two, but the re-denomination of the currency in July 2007 – which involved dropping four zeros and reintroducing the pesewa (100th of a cedi) – did manage to bring inflation under short-term control.

Despite significant achievements, such as compulsory universal basic schooling, Kufuor's presidency faced some major criticisms, most notably for its programme of privatisation. In 2007 and 2008, the government came under heavy attack for its decision to sell 70% of the state-owned Ghana Telecom to Vodafone and was accused of failing to subject the sale to a competitive tendering process, as required by law, and for then agreeing a low price. Kufuor was also accused of wasting money on the 2008 African Cup of Nations football tournament. This was then coupled by dramatic rises in fuel and food prices in 2008. All in all this spelled disaster for the government in an election year.

With parliamentary and presidential elections set for 7 December 2008, Kufuor stepped down having served the maximum two terms under the constitution, and the NPP selected Nana Akufo-Addo as its presidential candidate. In a controversial move, the NDC once again selected John Atta Mills, who had been defeated twice previously as its candidate. But in a case of third time lucky, John Atta Mills secured the presidency on 3 January 2009 by a margin of less than 1% after a second round of voting. Mills suffered a fatal stroke on 24 July 2012, aged only 68, and his vice-president John Dramani Mahama was sworn in as his successor the same day. Less than five months later, Mahama led the National Democratic Congress to another tight electoral victory, obtaining 50.7% of the vote, while his nearest rival Nana Akufo-Addo got 47.74%.

The government has said it intends Ghana to be a 'first-world' country by 2020. Such expectations are more than a touch optimistic, but nevertheless the country has recently experienced a level of economic development and diversification almost unprecedented in Africa, one fostered by high levels of social and political stability (it was placed 54th among 162 countries surveyed in the 2015 Global Peace Index). As a result, Ghana was ranked as the world's fastest-growing economy in 2011, thanks to an astonishing 20% increase in its annual GDP (the next best was Qatar with 14%), and its per capita GDP almost doubled between 2007 and 2012. Partly this was due to the discovery of offshore oil and gas in 2007, but Ghana's economic boom has also been fostered by a sustained atmosphere of political freedom and stability in recent years. At the same time, however, growth has slowed from 2011's frenzied heights, and averaged at around 8% for the past six years, with a significant dip to around 4% over 2014–15 thanks to ongoing inflation, energy shortages caused by insufficient water levels at Akosombo and Bui dams, and a significant drop in global oil prices. A 2013 cut in fuel subsidies that saw prices jump by more than 20% contributed to the inflationary trends at work, but this seems to have largely stabilised and economists predict continued steady growth through the second half of the decade, meaning the outlook for Ghana probably remains as bright as it has been at any time since independence.

The campaign season for the November 2016 presidential and parliamentary elections was just ramping up as this book went to print, and it's set to be another matchup between incumbent president John Dramani Mahama representing the NDC and seeking his second full term, versus the NPP's Nana Akufo-Addo, who is making his third attempt at winning the presidency.

ECONOMY

Ghana is a country of great mineral and natural wealth, for which reason it has been an important centre of trade since prehistoric times. Skipping briefly through subjects covered more fully in the history section above, Ghana is thought to have been the main West African producer of kola nuts (sharp tasting and mildly narcotic, favoured by Muslims who are forbidden from drinking alcohol, and available in any Ghanaian market today) prior to the 15th century, at which time it also supplied amounts of gold and salt to Islamic traders in the Sahelian region to its north. From 1471 until the late 17th century, the Gold Coast supplied roughly 10% of the world's gold, as the empires of the south entered into a maritime trade with Portuguese and, later, Dutch traders. From the late 17th until the early 19th century, this trade in gold and other natural assets was swamped by the nefarious transatlantic slave trade, operated by British and Dutch traders out of the Gold Coast and by several other European powers elsewhere off the west coast of Africa.

The roots of the modern Ghanaian economy can be traced to Britain's attempts to re-establish what they termed 'legitimate trade' after the slave trade was legally abolished in 1807. The main problem facing Britain in this regard was that many traditional trade-related skills, such as gold mining, were lost during the era when slaves were the main item in demand by European merchants. In any case, the powerful Ashanti Empire of the interior had been built largely on the slave trade, so that it was in both of their interests and those of many European merchants to continue operating a clandestine trade in slaves, one that continued out of the Gold Coast at least until Britain's first defeat of Ashanti in 1826.

The first important item of legitimate trade to emerge in the 19th century was palm oil, used for cooking and in the manufacture of detergents, and exported from the Gold Coast as of 1820. This was of necessity a small-scale trade harvested from wild palms (the oil palm still cannot be properly cultivated), but plantations were slowly established in many areas, notably in what is now the interior of Eastern Region, and the emergent industry had the important effect of restoring respectability to agriculture after a century in which cultivation had been seen by many Africans as work fit only for slaves. By 1850, palm oil was the principal export from the Gold Coast, and by the 1880s it accounted for almost 75% of export revenue raised by the recently established Gold Coast Colony. At the peak of the palm-oil era in 1884, some 20,000 tonnes of pure oil and twice that of palm kernels were exported, mostly to Germany.

Two other relatively important crops that took hold in the 19th century were cotton and rubber. The former never became an export crop due to infestations of insects and disease, but the crop was generally adequate to supply local needs, sometimes with a bit to spare for export. Rubber trees, by contrast, had been grown and tapped in the forest zone since the 17th century, but it was only in the 1870s that rubber was cultivated on a large scale, when its global importance

West Africa is well known for its vibrant and largely self-contained music scene, and for many years Ghana was perhaps the leading innovator when it came to styles that combined traditional African sounds with foreign influences. More recently, Ghana has, by and large, relinquished its status as innovator to its francophone neighbours; nevertheless, a practically incessant backdrop of music remains a notable feature of travelling in urban parts of the country, and visitors will find themselves exposed to a rich variety of novel sounds (alongside more familiar genres such as reggae, with the late South African singer Lucky Dube being particularly well known).

The most popular music to have emerged out of Ghana is 'highlife', a term that covers a broad spectrum of home-grown styles fusing traditional percussive beats with various European, American and even Caribbean influences. Highlife, developed in the 1920s along the ports of what was then the Gold Coast, was first recorded in the late 1930s, reaching a popular peak in the period 1950–70. Its leading practitioners included E T Mensah, the African Brothers International Band and, more recently, Alex Konadu and Koo Mino's Adadam Band.

Less easy to hear are the myriad traditional musical styles that hark from all around the country, generally drum-based in the south, more reliant on fiddles and other string instruments in the far north. It is in the north, though, that you are most likely to hear the peculiar 'talking drum', an instrument associated with the Sahel, as well as colourfully robed ensembles of Dagomba drummers (one of which we encountered by chance at a funeral in Bolgatanga).

Within Ghana, locally recorded music is largely drowned out by a plethora of exotica, not only the familiar contemporary Western hits, but also vibrant guitar music from the Congo and other parts of francophone Africa, as well as reggae. Traditional Ghanaian music is most likely to be encountered by chance, at a street funeral or similar public festival, though in the north you could ask whether there is a specific day when music will be performed for the chief.

Cassettes, CDs and mp3s of popular Ghanaian recording artists – admittedly not always of the highest quality sound-wise – can be bought for next to nothing in lorry parks and markets in most substantial towns. The selection can be daunting; perhaps the simplest way to go about choosing a few cassettes as mementos of your trip is to make a habit, when you hear something you like in a bar or on a trotro, of asking somebody what's playing.

The most useful practical handbook to exploring Ghanaian and other contemporary and traditional African music forms is Rough Guide's comprehensive *World Music*. Split across two volumes, the first of which deals with Africa and the Middle East, this now seems to be out of print, but the most recent edition, published in 2006, is available secondhand through the usual online sellers. Sterns Music (*www.sternsmusic.com*) boasts an extensive catalogue of African recordings, as do online sellers such as Amazon. A commendable source of traditional and more contemporary Ghanaian music is www.emusic. com, a treasure trove of affordable legitimate downloads that's especially strong on so-called 'world music' and other obscure genres; streaming service Spotify (*www.spotify.com*) has a massive selection as well.

We are aware of two private organisations within Ghana dedicated to preserving and archiving its recorded musical heritage. The better known of these is probably Kwame Sarpong's Gramophone Records Museum and

Research Centre (GRMRC), which is based in Cape Coast and covered under that section (pages 206–7), though Mr Sarpong's death in 2015 has called the future of the centre into question. The other, based in Accra, is the Bokoor African Popular Music Archives Foundation (BAPMAF) (\ *03024 21964;* m *0243 239488;* e *newbapmaf@yahoo.com; www.bapmaf.com*), founded in 1990 by Professor John Collins of the University of Ghana (a collector of old shellac and vinyl since the 1960s) to research and preserve 'classical' highlife styles. The archive, which has since expanded into other areas of popular and traditional African music, was housed at Bokoor House on the Accra-Nsawam prior to a devastating flood that left it 2m under water in October 2011. The restored display collection thankfully reopened to the public in late 2013, and BAPMAF also operates as a resource for students. Their website is well worth checking out, and some other websites dealing more specifically with Ghanaian music include www.ghanamusic.com and www.ghanabase.com.

Also worth investigating is the aptly named and dangerously addictive website Awesome Tapes From Africa (*www.awesometapes.com*). Established in 2006 by Brian Shimkovitz after a stint as a student in Ghana, this site showcases literally hundreds of obscure and out-of-print cassettes' worth of music from Ghana and elsewhere in Africa, most of which was never released on any other format and remained practically unheard outside its country of origin. Most of the music featured on the website can be downloaded, and Awesome Tapes has now branched out to become a specialist reissue label whose releases can be bought through the likes of eMusic and iTunes. Another site worth checking out is the wonderful Electric Jive (*http://electricjive.blogspot.com*), which focuses mainly on vintage and otherwise unavailable South African music, but also has some worthwhile material from Ghana free to download.

As for individual releases, a good starting point is E T Mensah's *All for You*, a stalwart 'greatest hits' package re-released in 2003, and available on eMusic. Recent years have seen a spate of exciting reissues, including classic and long-unheard albums from legends such as Ebo Taylor and Gyedu-Blay Ambolley, along with numerous 'various artist' compilations of Ghanaian music, most of them focusing on the 1960s and 1970s heyday. Top picks include *Ghana Special: Modern Highlife, Afro-Sounds and Ghanaian Blues 1968–1981* (Soundway, 2009); *Ghana Soundz Vol 1: Afrobeat, Funk and Fusion in 70s Ghana* (Soundway, 2007); *Ghana Soundz Vol 2* (Soundway, 2007); *Black Stars: Ghana's Hiplife Generation* (Out Here, 2008) and the *Rough Guide to Highlife* (Rough Guides, 2007).

If you want to get deeper into traditional Ghanaian chants, Smithsonian Folkways has no less than a dozen albums of Ghanaian field recordings, ranging from ethnographic records like *Traditional Women's Music from Ghana: Ewe, Fanti, Ashanti and Dagomba* to the La Drivers Union's *Por Por: Honk Horn Music of Ghana*, played by a collection of trotro mates on nothing but squeeze-bulb horns, bells, and car parts. At the other end of the modernity scale, Ghana has also produced its fair share of hiplife (a fusion of hip-hop and highlife) artists, among them Shatta Wale, Samini, VVIP, Sarkodie, Castro, Reggie Rockstone, Kae Sun, Buk Bak, Lil Shaker, and Yaa Pono. It's easier to get hold of their music in Ghana than outside the country, though once again eMusic has a pretty decent selection for downloading, and YouTube and Spotify have even more available for streaming.

soared as a result of the invention of the pneumatic tyre. In 1880, the Gold Coast exported a mere 0.05 tonnes of rubber. By 1886, that figure had increased to 692 tonnes, and by the early 1890s rubber was a bigger earner than palm oil, and the Gold Coast had become the world's third-largest supplier. In the early 1900s, however, the bottom fell out of the rubber market; prices slid, and the industry in the Gold Coast collapsed, never to recover. (You can still, however, take a (presumably short) gander at the first-ever Firestone tyre manufactured in Ghana in 1969 at Accra's Museum of Science and Technology – see pages 145–6.)

Perhaps the pivotal moment in Ghana's future economic development came in 1879, when Tetteh Quarshie returned home to the Gold Coast from Fernando Po with a few cocoa seedlings that he planted in his garden in Mampong. The climate and soil of the Gold Coast proved ideal for growing cocoa, and the crop was exported from 1891. By the turn of the 20th century, cocoa had replaced rubber as the colony's biggest earner of foreign revenue, and by 1935 the Gold Coast was supplying half the world's cocoa. Cocoa remains to this day Ghana's most important agricultural earner (though it lies second on the production table after neighbouring Ivory Coast), and the failure of the annual crop due to disease has, along with the rise and fall of the internationally determined cocoa price, often had a major influence on the country's politics. This is largely because the cocoa industry still favoured the small-scale farmer – it has been estimated that in 1951 roughly 500,000 people were employed by the cocoa industry, or earned their primary income from cocoa production.

Much of Ghana's modern transport infrastructure dates to the colonial era, and there is little doubt that in this regard, if no other, Ghana was reasonably well served by its colonists, particularly by Gordon Guggisberg, the governor from 1919 to 1927. By the end of World War II, the Gold Coast had some 10,000km of roads (about one-third of the present road network), and all its present rail systems had been constructed – the Tarkwa–Sekondi line was completed as early as 1901 and extended to Kumasi in 1903, while the Accra–Kumasi line was finished in 1927. Under Guggisberg, the colonial administration provided a solution to the country's lack of a natural deep-water harbour with the construction of an artificial one at Takoradi in 1928. It was extended in 1956 as the colonial era drew to a close, and is still the most important harbour in the country.

Two major engineering projects that were first mooted in the colonial era, but only brought to fruition later, largely at the instigation of Nkrumah, were the development of Tema as a deep-water harbour close to Accra, and the linked construction of a dam on the Volta at Akosombo, the latter not only important to the transport network of the north and east, but also capable of producing enough electricity for the whole country, as well as for export to neighbouring countries.

Just as important to economic development as a healthy transport infrastructure is good education, and here again the colonial administration was unusually forward-looking, with primary school attendance reaching 300,000 by 1951, and secondary school attendance 7,700. By the time of independence, the Gold Coast had 29 teacher-training colleges as well as a highly regarded university and a number of trade colleges. The adult literacy rate at this time stood at roughly 25% – nothing to shout about by Western standards, perhaps, but remarkable by comparison with many other African countries at the end of the colonial era.

It is difficult to be so positive about the colonial administration's development of the mining industry – not because the colony's great mineral wealth was left unexploited, but because the industry was structured in such a manner that very little of the significant profit it raised would stay in the colony. Formal gold mining in the Gold Coast started at Tarkwa in 1877 and at Obuasi two years later, and it was also soon discovered that the colony had significant deposits of several other minerals, notably diamonds and manganese. By 1951, the year in which Nkrumah's CPP entered government, annual gold exports exceeded £8 million annually, with manganese and diamonds close behind at around £7 million and £6 million, respectively. For the sake of comparison, the value of cocoa exports in this year was a massive £60 million, and timber, the second most important agricultural export, stood at £5 million.

At the time of independence in 1957, Ghana had one of the strongest economies in Africa, with foreign revenue reserves ten times greater than the foreign debt. By 1966, the situation had practically reversed, with foreign debt in the region of US$1 billion. The reasons for Ghana's economic decline in the decades immediately following independence, and particularly between 1966 and 1981, are clearly linked to the political instability of that era, though exacerbated by external factors such as the 60% drop in the cocoa price during the Nkrumah era.

More important here and now is that Ghana has experienced more than three decades of substantial economic growth since productivity reached a post-independence nadir in the early 1980s. Many people – not just Ghanaians – regard the country to be the most promising economic prospect in Africa at the moment. Real gross domestic product (GDP) growth since 1984 has typically hovered at above 5%, culminating in the 20% leap made in 2011, when Ghana was officially named the world's fastest-growing economy. It's slowed considerably since then, but continues to tick along at or around 5%.

Despite a marked increase in industrialisation in recent times, industry (mining, manufacturing, and construction) contributes less than 30% of GDP, while services account for roughly half. Agriculture's role in the economy has been shrinking, and today it contributes just over 20% of GDP, down 12% from 2009 alone, but still employing more than 45% of the Ghanaian workforce. Cocoa remains the most important crop in export terms and, although output dropped from over 500,000 tonnes annually in the early 1960s to 158,000 tonnes in 1983, production has increased by an average of around 10% annually since 2000. Other important crops include cassava, plantains, coco yams, yams, maize, groundnuts, millet, rice, sorghum and sugarcane.

In recent years, mining has become the most important source of foreign revenue: renewed development in the goldfields of the south means Ghana is now Africa's largest gold exporter after South Africa, and the tenth-largest in the world, with production having risen from a mid-1980s nadir of around 300,000 ounces to one million ounces in 1992 and 3.5 million ounces in 2014. Diamond exports have declined by nearly 75% since their 2005 peak of more than 1,000,000 carats, but this still places Ghana in the top 20 diamond-producing countries globally. Ghana is also a major producer of bauxite and manganese. In 2007, Ghana received another economic boost when oil reserves estimated at three billion barrels were discovered offshore. Oil production began in 2010, and stood at around 100,000 barrels daily in mid-2015, accounting for nearly 7% of GDP. Since the initial discovery, 23 further wells have been discovered, and output is scheduled to double by 2020. While tourism remains an important earner of foreign revenue, its contribution sits behind gold, oil and cocoa, and tourism receipts generated US$1.3 billion, or just under 3% of GDP, in 2013, as compared with US$233 million in 1995 and US$19 million ten years earlier.

LANGUAGE

English is the official national language, and it is widely spoken as a result of the country's long links with Britain and an unusually high standard of education from colonial times to the present day. A total of at least 46 African languages and 76 dialects are spoken in Ghana, generally divided into the Akan, Mole-Dagbani, Ewe and Ga language groups. Twi is the main Akan tongue, first language to roughly half the population, including both the Ashanti and Fante, and widely spoken elsewhere in central and southern parts of the country. See also pages 486–8.

GETTING STARTED IN TWI

See also *Appendix 1, Language,* pages 486–8

Hello	*Mima ache*
	(response is *yemu*)
Goodbye	*Nanti ye*
Thank you	*Meda ase*
Please	*Me pawocheo*
Yes	*Aane/Nyew*
No	*Dabe*

RELIGION

According to a 2012 poll conducted by the *Christian Science Monitor*, Ghana is the world's most religious country, with 96% of respondents stating that they are religious (next were Nigeria and Armenia, with 93% and 92% respectively). It is the only country in West Africa where Christians outnumber followers of Islam, but there is no official state religion, and freedom of religion is a constitutional right. No official figures seem to be available, but at least 60% of Ghanaians are Christian (though Christian slogans and music are so prevalent that you might easily think that should be 150%) and around 30% Muslim. Minority religions include Hinduism, Buddhism, Baha'i and various traditional faiths. Islam is the predominant faith in the north of Ghana, having reached West Africa via the trans-Sahara trade routes as early as the 8th century AD. It has been practised in what is now northern Ghana for at least 500 years, probably longer.

Christianity dominates in the southern and central parts of the country. Catholicism was first introduced at the coast by the Portuguese in the late 15th century (the first public Mass was said at Elmina in January 1482), but its influence dwindled after the Portuguese withdrew in 1637. Christianity in modern Ghana dates mostly to the latter half of the 19th century. Catholicism, now the most widespread and popular denomination, was reintroduced to the south with the establishment of a French mission at Elmina in 1880, and it arrived in the north in 1906, when the White Fathers opened a mission in Navrongo. The Presbyterian Church reached Ghana in 1828, with the foundation of a Swiss mission at Danish Osu Castle. After initial setbacks as several missionaries were claimed by malaria, Presbyterianism spread into much of what is now Eastern Region in the 1840s. The separate Evangelical Presbyterian Church, established by German missionaries in the 1850s, has had its stronghold in what is now Volta Region for almost 150 years. The Methodist Church, formerly the Wesleyan Mission, is almost as widespread as Catholicism – it was established around British castles in the 1830s and spread largely through the pioneering work of the Reverend Thomas Birch Freeman, who served in the Gold Coast and Ashanti from 1838 to 1890. In addition to denominations familiar to most Europeans, a large number of American churches have been established in Ghana, most significantly the AME Zion Church, which spread out of Keta from 1896, as well as more recent ones.

RELIGIOUS SLOGANS

One of the more idiosyncratic ways in which Ghanaians like to demonstrate their faith is by naming their businesses after religious sayings. Cumulatively, it can start feeling like you are trapped in a world designed by an evangelical Hallmark copywriter, but their unintentional humour can also make for some light relief on long journeys. Here are some of the best:

* Innocent Blood Restaurant
* Talk To Jesus Phone Shop
* Fear God Electricity Services
* He Is Able To Deliver Store
* Jesus Loves Fashion
* Joy Fumigation Services
* Consuming Fire Fast Food
* Blood of Jesus Hair Care

And a few non-religious ones for good measure:

* No Rush in Life Taxi Services
* Observers are Worried Chop Bar
* Fred's Tact Shop
* Virgin Lips Bar
* No Condition is Permanent Vulcanising Service (for *Star Trek* cultists?)
* Snob Against Cornmill (eh?)
* Mary Immaculator Rewinding Service (double eh?!)
* You Are Welcome To Happy Yourself Spot Mind Your Own Business And Happy Yourself

Despite Ghana being the most flagrantly Christian country that we've visited – exasperatingly so at times for non-subscribers – various traditional beliefs and customs have also retained an unusually high profile in the country. It's difficult to establish whether this is essentially a case of Christians and traditionalists existing alongside each other, or whether it's simply that a significant number of Ghanaians somehow manage to adhere to what appear to be two contradictory systems of belief. Either way, it makes for an interesting, if occasionally bemusing, cocktail of faiths to the outsider. 'To more religious visitors,' reader Bruce Billedeaux recommends that 'visiting a local church service will be very rewarding, as the services have a great African feel'.

SEND US YOUR SNAPS!

We'd love to follow your adventures using our *Ghana* guide – why not send us your photos and stories via Twitter (@BradtGuides) and Instagram (@bradtguides) using the hashtag #ghana. Alternatively, you can upload your photos directly to the gallery on the Ghana destination page via our website (*www.bradtguides.com/ghana*).

2

Natural History

Most of southern Ghana – that is, for about 250km inland of the Atlantic – supports a natural cover of rainforest or moist semi-deciduous forest. Unfortunately, while southern Ghana remains very lushly vegetated, the clearing of forest for cultivation together with logging activities mean there are now few areas of true rainforest left intact outside designated reserves. For most visitors, exposure to this habitat is limited to a day trip to Kakum National Park, which is noted for its unique and spectacular canopy walkway, but there are countless other opportunities for more adventurous travellers to explore Ghana's forests. These include the readily accessible Owabi Forest Reserve and Bobiri Butterfly Sanctuary close to Kumasi, the Ankassa Resource Reserve in the far southwest, and a handful of more obscure national parks and reserves suited to self-sufficient hikers.

The central and northern parts of the country support a habitat of savannah, as does the far southeast. Typically comprising a combination of grassland and open canopy woodland, the savannah of Ghana tends to become drier and more sparsely vegetated as you head further north. In conservation terms, Ghana's most important savannah reserve is Mole National Park, which can be visited as an overnight trip from Tamale. Other protected savannah habitats include Shai Hills close to Accra and the Gbele Resource Reserve in the far northwest.

WILDLIFE

Ghana lacks the vast conservation areas and huge herds of wildlife associated with eastern and southern Africa. Indeed, several large mammals typically associated with Africa do not occur in Ghana at all, for instance rhino, zebra, wildebeest and gorilla, while many other large mammal species have been driven to extinction in Ghana, notably giraffe, cheetah and African wild dog. The status of several other large mammal species, including lion, is highly vulnerable.

For all that, Ghana still offers some great opportunities for game viewing, with a wide variety of large mammals present, and monkeys, in particular, well represented and easily observed. The following overview of the more interesting mammals to be found in Ghana is designed to help readers who are not carrying a field guide of any sort, but it should also be useful to those carrying a continental guide and seeking more specific information about the distribution and status of various mammal species within Ghana.

Ghana boasts 16 integrated protected areas, which are managed by the Wildlife Division, and cover a total area of 13,489km² (5.66% of the total land area). These are Nini Suhien National Park and Ankasa Resource Reserve, Bia National Park and Resource Reserve, Kakum National Park, Bui National Park, Digya National Park, Kyabobo National Park, Mole National Park, Gbele Resource Reserve, Kalapka

Resource Reserve, Shai Hills Resource Reserve, Kogyae Strict Nature Reserve, Agumatsa Wildlife Sanctuary, Boabeng-Fiema Monkey Sanctuary, Bomfobiri Wildlife Sanctuary, Owabi Wildlife Sanctuary, and Keta Lagoon Complex. The Wildlife Division is also responsible for five coastal wetland areas designated under the Ramsar Convention, as well as the zoological gardens in Kumasi.

CARNIVORES Africa's largest predator, the **lion** (*Panthera leo*) is a sociable creature, typically living in prides of five to ten animals, which hunt collaboratively at night, their favoured prey being large or medium-sized antelope. Lions naturally occur in any habitat but desert and rainforest, and they once ranged across much of the Old World, but these days they are all but restricted to a few large conservation areas in sub-Saharan Africa. In Ghana, a small population of lions theoretically remains in Mole National Park, though few tourists see them.

The powerful **leopard** (*Panthera pardus*), the most solitary and secretive of Africa's large cats, is also the most habitat tolerant, though it typically favours areas with plenty of cover, such as riverine woodland and rocky slopes. It is the most common large felid in Ghana, but secretive and seldom seen.

Leopard

Of the smaller cats, the **serval** (*Felis serval*), built rather like a miniature cheetah, with black-on-gold spots giving way to streaking near the head, is seldom seen, but widespread and quite common in moist grassland, reed beds and riverine habitats. The **caracal** (*Felis caracal*) closely resembles the European lynx with its uniform tan coat and tufted ears, and it favours relatively arid savannah habitats. The not-dissimilar **golden cat** (*Felis aurata*) lives in forested areas, lacks ear tufts, and has a spotted underbelly. The

Caracal

markedly smaller **African wild cat** (*Felis sylvestris*) ranges from the Mediterranean to the Cape of Good Hope and is similar in appearance to the domestic tabby cat.

The **spotted hyena** (*Crocuta crocuta*), probably the most common large predator in Ghana, has a bulky build, sloping back, brown-spotted coat, powerful jaws and dog-like expression. Contrary to popular myth, it is not exclusively a scavenger, nor is it hermaphroditic (an ancient belief that stems from the false scrotum and penis covering the female's vagina). Sociable animals, and fascinating to observe, hyenas live in loosely structured clans of about ten animals, led by females who are stronger and larger than males.

Spotted hyena

The North African **striped hyena** (*Hyaena hyaena*), pale brown with several dark vertical streaks and a blackish mane, may occur in the very far north of Ghana.

A great many small nocturnal predators occur in Ghana. The **side-striped jackal** (*Canis adustus*) occurs sparsely in the north and is listed for Mole National Park. The **African civet** (*Civettictus civetta*) is a bulky, long-haired creature with a rather feline appearance, primarily carnivorous, but also partial to fruit, and widespread and common in many habitats but very rarely seen. The smaller, more

African civet

slender **tree** or (**two-spotted**) **palm civet** (*Nandinia binotata*) is an arboreal forest animal with a dark-brown coat marked with black spots. The **small-spotted genet** (*Genetta genetta*), **Hausa genet** (*Genetta thierryi*), **panther genet** (*Genetta pardina*) and **Johnston's genet** (*Genetta johnstoni*) are Ghanaian representatives of a taxonomically confusing genus comprising perhaps ten species, all very slender and rather feline in appearance, with a grey to gold-brown coat marked with black spots and a long ringed tail.

The **ratel** or **honey badger** (*Mellivora capensis*), black with a puppyish face and grey-white back, is an opportunistic feeder best known for its symbiotic relationship with a bird called the honeyguide, which leads it to a beehive, waits for it to tear open the hive, then feeds on the scraps. The **Cape clawless otter** (*Aonyx capensis*) is a brown freshwater mustelid with a white collar.

Honey badger

Six **mongoose** species occur in Ghana, most of them diurnal, terrestrial and reasonably common – all six have, for instance, been recorded in Mole National Park. The **marsh mongoose** (*Atilax paludinosus*) is large, normally solitary, with a very scruffy brown coat, often seen in the vicinity of water. The **Egyptian** or **large grey mongoose** (*Herpestes ichneumon*) is also large and often associated with water, but its grey coat is grizzled in appearance, and it is most often seen in pairs or family groups. Restricted to rainforest habitats, where it is often quite common, the **cusimanse** (*Crossarchus obscuras*) is a small, sociable mongoose with a shaggy brown coat, almost always seen in family groups. The **white-tailed mongoose** (*Ichneumia albicauda*) is a large, solitary, brown mongoose, generally found in savannah country and easily identified by its bushy, white tail. The **slender** or **pygmy mongoose** (*Galerella sanguinea*) is another solitary inhabitant of the savannah, but very much smaller and with a uniform brown coat and blackish tail tip. The **Gambian mongoose** (*Mungos gambianus*), dark brown with the distinctive combination of pale throat and black cheek stripe, is the most sociable mongoose found in savannah country, occurring in groups of up to 30 animals.

Gambian mongose

PRIMATES The **common chimpanzee** (*Pan troglodytes*) is one of two species (the other being the extralimital bonobo or pygmy chimpanzee) placed a genus more closely related to humans than to any other living creature. It is naturally a widespread and common resident of the African forest, but numbers are in rapid decline throughout its range, with a wild population estimated at several million in the early 20th century now thought to be around 150,000. No reliable figures are available for Ghana, where it has been accorded full legal protection since the 1970s. In 1997, based on limited data, the Ghanaian population was estimated at 1,500–2,200, but recent reports suggest it is now much scarcer, possibly even on the verge of local extinction. The main population centre is in the southwestern rainforest, where a small but viable population is known to occur in Ankassa, but its status in other reserves is uncertain. There are no habituated chimps in Ghana, and they are most unlikely to be seen by tourists.

Chimpanzee

The **anubis** or **olive baboon** (*Papio anubis*), a powerful terrestrial primate distinguished from any monkey by its much larger size, inverted U-shaped tail, and distinctive dog-like head, is fascinating to watch from a behavioural perspective. It lives in large troops that boast a complex, rigid social structure characterised by matriarchal lineages and plenty of intra-troop movement by males seeking social dominance. Omnivorous and at home in almost any habitat, the baboon is the most widespread primate in Africa. It is quite frequently seen in Ghana, especially in Mole National Park and Shai Hills.

The **green monkey** (*Chlorocebus sabaeus*) is a type of vervet monkey, probably the world's most common primate superspecies. It is an atypical monkey in that it inhabits savannah and woodland rather than true forest, spending a high proportion of its time on the ground. Even more terrestrial is the **patas monkey** (*Erythrocebus patas*), which is larger and more spindly than the vervet, with an orange-tinged coat and black forehead stripe. Essentially a monkey of dry savannah, the patas occurs in northern Ghana, and is quite easily observed in Mole National Park.

Patas monkey

Probably the easiest to see of Ghana's true forest monkeys is the **mona monkey** (*Cercopithecus mona*), of which six long-recognised races are now regarded by some authorities to be distinct species on the basis of recent chromosome studies. The most widespread mona in Ghana is **Lowe's monkey** (*Cercopithecus mona lowei*), a pretty and cryptically coloured grey, white and black guenon distinguished by the pale stripe over its eye. Lowe's mona is the common monkey at Boabeng-Fiema Monkey Sanctuary, and it occurs in most Ghanaian forests, where it is offered some protection against hunting. It is replaced in Tafi Atome in the east by the **true mona** (*Cercopithecus mona mona*), which is similar in overall appearance, but can be distinguished by the prominent white discs on its hips, easily seen when it moves away from the observer.

Mona monkey

Two other distinctive species of forest guenon occur in Ghana. The **lesser spot-nosed monkey** (*Cercopithecus petaurista*) is a small guenon easily distinguished by its prominent white nose. Though widespread in Ghana's forests, the lesser spot-nosed monkey is most likely to be seen on Monkey Hill in Takoradi, where a small and relatively habituated troop survives within a few hundred metres of the city centre. Much rarer, the beautiful white-bearded orange-rumped **Roloway monkey** (*Cercopithecus roloway*), sometimes considered to be a race of Diana monkey (*Cercopithecus diana*), was thought to be extinct in Ghana prior to the discovery of a small population in the community-owned Kwabre Forest in the Western Region in 2013. Though not seen elsewhere in Ghana since 2001, it might also survive in the Ankassa or Bia forests near the Ivorian border.

The **western** or **Geoffrey's black-and-white colobus** (*Colobus vellerosus*) is a beautiful jet-black monkey with bold white facial markings and a long white tail, widespread where it hasn't been hunted to extinction, and easily seen at Boabeng-Fiema Monkey Sanctuary. Almost exclusively arboreal, it is capable of leaping distances of up to 30m, a spectacular sight with its white tail streaming behind. The Miss Waldron's race of **western red colobus** (*Procolobus badius waldroni*) is a distinctly red, long-limbed forest monkey formerly

Black-and-white colobus

restricted to a few forests in southwestern Ghana. It is now officially regarded to be extinct in Ghana, though recent reports suggest a relic population survives in the remote Krokosua Hills Forest Reserve near Bia National Park. The smaller and duller **olive colobus** (*Procolobus verus*), an olive-grey monkey distinguished by two light-grey patches on its forehead, occurs in several forests in southern Ghana, including Kakum National Park, but is most likely to be seen on Monkey Hill in Takoradi.

The one other forest monkey to occur in Ghana, the **sooty mangabey** (*Cercocebus atys*), is the only West African representative of a genus associated with the central African rainforest. It is the only uniform dark-grey monkey to occur Ghana, where it is confined to western forests such as Bia and Ankasa. The race found in Ghana, *Cercocebus atys lunulatus*, has a small white collar, and is sometimes referred to as the white-naped or white-cheeked mangabey.

Also present in Ghana are a few species of nocturnal **bushbaby**, often quite easy to locate if you know where to find them and have a good spotlight. The **Demidoff's bushbaby** or **dwarf galago** (*Galagoides demidoff*) is found in the southerly rainforests of Kakum and Ankasa, while the **northern lesser bushbaby** (*Galagoides senegalensis*) is found in the savannah regions to the north, and is very common in Mole. In 2005, **Thomas's bushbaby** (*Galagoides thomasi*) was discovered in the forested hills east of the Volta. The **potto** (*Perodicticus potto*) is a sloth-like nocturnal primate of rainforest interiors, also most easily located with the aid of a spotlight.

Roan antelope

ANTELOPE The **roan antelope** (*Hippotragus equinus*) is the largest plains antelope found in Ghana, with a shoulder height of 120–150cm. It is a handsome horse-like creature, uniform fawn-grey with a pale belly, short decurved horns and a light mane. It occurs in several savannah reserves and is the common antelope of Gbele Resource Reserve near Tumu in the north. The roan is quite likely to be seen by visitors spending a few days in Mole National Park.

The **Defassa waterbuck** (*Kobus ellipsiprymnus defassa*) is another very large antelope, easily recognised by its shaggy brown coat, white rump and the male's large, lyre-shaped horns. It is normally seen in small family groups grazing near water, and is almost certain to be seen in the vicinity of the hotels at Mole National Park. The closely related **kob** (*Kobus kob*) is a beautiful, red-gold antelope with a white throat, but otherwise few distinguishing features. It is probably the most common large antelope in Ghana and family herds are almost certain to be seen by visitors to Mole National Park and Shai Hills.

Defassa waterbuck

Kob

Hartebeest

The **western hartebeest** (*Alcelaphus buselaphus*) is a large, ungainly antelope readily identified by the combination of large shoulders, sloping back, red-brown or yellow-brown coat, and smallish horns in both sexes. It is resident in several savannah reserves in Ghana, but quite rare everywhere.

Bushbuck

Secretive and scarce, the **bongo** (*Tragelaphus euryceros*) is a very large, stocky and clearly striped rainforest species, isolated populations of which occur in several Ghanaian reserves, including Kakum National Park. It is highly unlikely to be seen by a casual visitor. A far more common and widespread resident of forest and thick woodland, though also quite secretive, the **bushbuck** (*Tragelaphus scriptus*) is an attractive, medium-sized antelope. The male is dark brown or chestnut, while the much smaller female is generally a pale reddish brown. The male has relatively small, straight horns. It can be seen in just about any Ghanaian forest or game reserve, and is quite frequently observed in Shai Hills and Mole National Park.

Less common, the **Bohor reedbuck** (*Redunca redunca*) is a plain, light-fawn, medium-sized antelope generally seen in pairs in open country near water. The **oribi** (*Ourebia ourebi*) is rather like a miniature reedbuck, uncommon in grassland habitats. Even smaller, the **common** or **grey duiker** (*Sylvicapra grimmia*) is an anomalous member of the duiker family in that it occurs in savannah and woodland rather than true forest. Distinguished by the black tuft of hair between its small horns, it is the only small, grey antelope likely to be seen in non-forested habitats in Ghana.

Reedbuck

The **forest duikers** are a taxonomically confusing group of 12 to 20 species restricted to the rainforests of Africa. Six species occur in Ghana, all of them widespread (all but the red-flanked, for instance, occur in Kakum National Park), but secretive and rather unlikely to be seen in the wild by tourists. The largest of these is the nocturnal **yellow-backed duiker** (*Cephalophus leucogaster*), a bushbuck-sized antelope with a blackish coat and yellow patch on its back, which occurs sparsely in most true rainforests, including Kakum National Park.

Three of Ghana's remaining duiker species are also rather large by the standards of the family, with a shoulder height of up to 55cm. The most distinctive of these, the **black duiker** (*Cephalophus niger*), with a thick off-black coat and red forehead and throat, is realistically likely to be seen clearly only at Owabi Wildlife Sanctuary outside Kumasi. More widespread, the **bay duiker** (*Cephalophus dorcas*), red-brown with a wide, black, dorsal stripe, would be difficult to tell apart at a glance from **Ogilby's duiker** (*Cephalophus ogilbyi*), which is similar, but has a narrower dorsal stripe.

Common duiker

The most common forest antelope in Ghana, **Maxwell's duiker** (*Cephalophus maxwelli*), is a small, grey duiker with a distinctive, pale eye-stripe, likely to be seen in any forest in southern Ghana. Similar in size to Maxwell's, but with colouring closer to the bay duiker, the **red-flanked duiker** (*Cephalophus rufilatus*) is best distinguished from members of its genus by habitat and distribution, since it is essentially a species of forest fringe and woodland that differs from all other forest duikers in that it occurs only in the northern half of Ghana.

Also occurring in the Ghanaian rainforest, the **royal antelope** (*Neotragus pygmaeus*) is a common, but infrequently observed, brown antelope with a red throat collar, which, with a shoulder height of up to 28cm, is regarded as the world's smallest horned ungulate. More closely related to European deer than any antelope, the **water chevrotain** (*Hyemoschus aquaticus*) is an odd, hare-sized nocturnal creature with a brown coat and white stripes and spots, generally associated with wet habitats within rainforests.

Since 1999, there have also been sightings in the Avu Lagoon of the **sitatunga** (*Tragelaphus spekei*) – the world's only aquatic antelope, which is adapted to swimming with widely splayed hoofs and a thick oily coat that repels water. This rare mammal was previously thought to have been extinct from Ghana for over 20 years.

OTHER MAMMALS The **African elephant** (*Loxodonta africana*) is the world's largest land animal, and both the savannah and smaller forest species occur in Ghana. It is an intelligent, social animal, and often very entertaining to watch. Elephants are widespread and common in habitats ranging from desert to rainforest and, despite heavy poaching, they are still present

African elephant

in several national parks and reserves. Mole National Park, with a population of several hundred, is the best place to see them.

Characteristic of Africa's large rivers and lakes, the **hippopotamus** (*Hippopotamus amphibius*) is a large, lumbering animal that spends most of the day submerged, but emerges at night to graze. Strongly territorial, herds of ten or more animals are presided over by a dominant male who will readily defend his patriarchy to the death. Hippos are present in Mole National Park, and they were once very common in the part of the Volta River protected by Bui National Park, but have generally moved to more remote stretches of the river since the Bui Dam came online in 2013, flooding much of their original habitat.

The **West African manatee** (*Trichechus senegalensis*) is an unmistakable large, grey, hairless mammal, related to the marine dugong, but entirely restricted to freshwater habitats. Increasingly very rare, manatees are still seen from time to time on Lake Volta and the Volta estuary area near Ada.

The **African buffalo** (*Syncerus caffer*) is a distinctive ox-like animal that lives in large herds on the savannah and occurs in smaller herds in forested areas. It is common and widespread in sub-Saharan Africa, and historically both the black savannah race and the smaller, redder, forest race occur in Ghana, though the latter is now very rare and possibly extinct. The country's largest buffalo population,

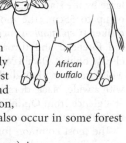
African buffalo

of roughly 1,000 animals, is found in Mole, but buffalo also occur in some forest reserves and in Kalapka Resource Reserve near Ho.

The rather endearing **warthog** (*Phacochoreus africanus*) is grey in colour with a thin covering of hairs, wart-like bumps on its face, and rather large upward-curving tusks. Africa's only diurnal swine, the warthog is often seen in family groups, trotting off briskly with its tail raised stiffly (a diagnostic trait) with a determinedly nonchalant air. In Ghana, it occurs in most savannah reserves, though is only likely to be seen in Mole National Park, where it is common. The **red river hog** (*Potamoccoerus porcus*) is a larger forest swine, common but primarily nocturnal, and regarded by some authorities to be a race of the East African bushpig,

Warthog

from which it is readily distinguished by a decidedly red coat and clear white stripe along its back. Larger still, the **giant forest hog** (*Hylochoerus meinertzhageni*), a very hairy, dark-brown swine that weighs up to 250kg, is a fairly common but difficult-to-observe nocturnal resident of most rainforests in Ghana.

Pangolin

The **aardvark** (*Orycteropus afer*) is a singularly bizarre insectivore, quite common in dry savannah country and unmistakable with its long snout and huge ears, but rarely seen due to its nocturnal habits. Equally distinctive, **pangolins** are rare nocturnal insectivores with armour plating and a tendency to roll up in a ball when disturbed. Spiky rather than armoured, several **hedgehog** and **porcupine** species occur in the region, the former generally no larger than a guinea pig, the latter generally 60–100cm long.

One small mammal species that you're quite likely to encounter in the right habitat is the **rock hyrax** (*Procavia capensis*), a rodent-like creature more closely related to elephants and often seen sunning itself in rocky habitats. Probably more numerous in Ghana, but less easily seen, the similar-looking **tree hyrax** (*Dendrohyrax dorsalis*) is a nocturnal forest creature that announces its presence with an unforgettable shrieking call.

Rock hyrax

Ground squirrel

Of the great many **squirrel** species present in Ghana, all but one are essentially restricted to forest and woodland. The exception, a widespread inhabitant of the northern savannah, is the **unstriped ground squirrel** (*Xerus inauris*), a terrestrial animal with a white eye-ring, silver-black tail and the characteristic squirrel mannerism of holding food in its forepaws while standing on its hind legs. Occasionally seen at Kakum and in other forests, the **anomalures** (also known as flying squirrels) are large rodents with a flap of skin stretched between their front and hind legs, enabling them to glide for quite significant distances through the canopy.

Also common in Ghana, the **savannah cane-rat** (*Thryonomys gregorianus*) is a large grizzled-brown rodent that can be as heavy as 8kg and is associated with marshes and elephant grass. Known locally as the 'grass-cutter', it is prized as bushmeat by Ghanaians of all religious groups, and is reputedly very low in cholesterol, though many Westerners find it an acquired taste (like gamey mutton or goat meat). Commercial grass-cutter farming is rapidly catching on in Ghana, and makes for a more ecologically sound option than farming non-indigenous stock.

REPTILES

Nile crocodile The order Crocodilia dates back at least 150 million years, and fossil forms that lived contemporaneously with dinosaurs are remarkably unchanged from their modern descendants, of which the Nile crocodile (*Crocodylus niloticus*) is the largest living reptile, regularly growing to lengths of up to 6m. Widespread throughout Africa, the Nile crocodile was once common in most large rivers and lakes, but it has been exterminated in many areas in the past century – hunted professionally for its skin as well as by vengeful local villagers. Contrary to popular legend, Nile crocodiles generally feed mostly on fish, at least where densities are sufficient. They will also prey on drinking or swimming mammals where the opportunity presents itself, dragging their victim underwater until it drowns, then storing it under a submerged log or tree until it has decomposed sufficiently for them to eat. A large crocodile is capable of killing a lion or wildebeest, or an adult human for that matter, and in certain areas, such as the Mara or Grumeti rivers in Tanzania, large mammals do form their main prey. Today, large crocodiles are mostly confined to protected areas throughout Africa. In Ghana, they are most easily observed at Paga or any of several other ponds countrywide where they are held sacred by locals.

Snakes A wide variety of snakes is found in Ghana, though – fortunately, most would agree perhaps – they are typically very shy and unlikely to be seen unless actively sought. One of the snakes most likely to be seen on safari is Africa's largest, the **rock python** (*Python sebae*), which has a gold-on-black mottled skin and regularly grows to lengths exceeding 5m. Non-venomous, pythons kill their prey by strangulation, wrapping their muscular bodies around it until it cannot breathe, then swallowing it whole and dozing off for a couple of months while it is digested. Pythons feed mainly on small antelopes, large rodents and similar animals. They are harmless to adult humans, but could conceivably kill a small child. A slumbering python might be encountered almost anywhere in Ghana.

Of the venomous snakes, one of the most commonly encountered is the **puff adder** (*Bitis arietans*), a large, thick resident of savannah and rocky habitats. Although it feeds mainly on rodents, the puff adder will strike when threatened and it is rightly considered the most dangerous of African snakes, not because it is especially venomous or aggressive, but because its notoriously sluggish disposition means it is more often disturbed than other snakes. The related **Gabon viper** (*Bitis gabonica*) is possibly the largest African viper, growing up to 2m long, very heavily built, and with a beautiful cryptic geometric gold, black and brown skin pattern that blends perfectly into the rainforest litter it inhabits. Although highly venomous, it is more placid and less likely to be encountered than the puff adder.

Several cobra species, including various **spitting cobras** (*Naja* spp), are present in Ghana, most with characteristic hoods that they raise when about to strike, though they are all very seldom seen. Another widespread family is the mambas, of which the **black mamba** (*Dendroaspis polylepis*) – which will attack only when cornered, despite an unfounded reputation for unprovoked aggression – is the largest venomous snake in Africa, measuring up to 3.5m long. Theoretically, the most toxic of Africa's snakes is said to be the **boomslang** (*Dispholidus typus*), a variably coloured and, as its name – literally 'tree snake' – suggests, largely arboreal snake that is reputed not to have accounted for one known human fatality, as it is back-fanged and non-aggressive.

Most snakes are in fact non-venomous and not even potentially harmful to any other living creature much bigger than a rat. The **mole snake** (*Pseudaspis cana*) is a common and widespread grey-brown savannah resident that grows up to 2m long and feeds on moles and rodents. The remarkable **egg-eating snakes** (*Dasypeltis* spp) live exclusively on birds' eggs, dislocating their jaws to swallow the egg whole, then eventually regurgitating the crushed shell in a neat little package. Many snakes will take eggs opportunistically, for which reason large-scale agitation among birds in a tree is often a good indication that a snake (or small bird of prey) is around.

Lizards All African lizards are harmless to humans, with the arguable exception of the giant monitor lizards that could, in theory, inflict a nasty bite if cornered. Two species of monitor occur in West Africa, the **water** and the **savannah** (*Varanus niloticus* and *Varanus exanthematicus*), the latter growing up to 2.2m long and

CHAMELEONS

Common and widespread, but not easily seen unless they are actively searched for, chameleons are arguably the most intriguing of African reptiles. True chameleons of the family Chamaeleontidae are confined to the Old World, with the most important centre of speciation being the island of Madagascar, to which about half of the world's 120 recognised species are endemic. Aside from two species of chameleon apiece in Asia and Europe, the remainder is distributed across mainland Africa. In Ghana, you're most likely to come across a chameleon by chance when it is crossing a road, in which case it should be easy to take a closer look at it, since most chameleons move painfully slowly and deliberately.

Chameleons are best known for their capacity to change colour, a trait that has often been exaggerated in popular literature and that is generally influenced by mood more than the colour of the background. Some chameleons are more adept at changing colour than others, with the most variable being the common chameleon (*Chamaeleo chamaeleon*) of the Mediterranean region, with more than 100 colour and pattern variations recorded. Many African chameleons are typically green in colour, but will gradually take on a browner hue when they descend from the foliage in more exposed terrain, eg: while crossing a road. Several change colour and pattern far more dramatically when they feel threatened or are confronted by a rival of the same species. Different chameleon species also vary greatly in size, with the largest being Oustalet's chameleon of Madagascar, known to reach a length of almost 80cm.

A remarkable physiological feature common to all true chameleons is their protuberant round eyes, which offer a potential 180° vision on both sides and are able to swivel around independently of each other. Only when one of them isolates a suitably juicy-looking insect will the two eyes focus in the same direction as the chameleon stalks slowly forward until it is close enough to use the other unique weapon in its armoury. This is its sticky-tipped tongue, which is typically about the same length as its body and remains coiled up within its mouth most of the time, to be unleashed in a sudden, blink-and-you'll-miss-it lunge to zap a selected item of prey. In addition to their unique eyes and tongues, many chameleons are adorned with an array of facial casques, flaps, horns and crests that enhance their already somewhat fearsome prehistoric appearance. Another oddity is the spectrally pale nocturnal colouring, which shows up clearly under a spotlight and explains why these creatures are regarded with both fear and awe in many local African cultures.

occasionally seen in the vicinity of termite mounds, the former slightly smaller, but far more regularly observed by tourists in moist habitats. Their size alone might make it possible fleetingly to mistake a monitor for a small crocodile, but their more colourful yellow-dappled skin precludes sustained confusion. Both species are predatory, feeding on anything from birds' eggs to smaller reptiles and mammals, but will also eat carrion opportunistically.

Visitors to Ghana will soon become familiar with the **common house gecko** (*Hemidactylus mabouia*), an endearing, bug-eyed, translucent white lizard, which, as its name suggests, reliably inhabits most houses as well as hotel rooms, scampering up walls and upside down on the ceiling in pursuit of pesky insects attracted to the lights. Also very common in some hotel grounds are various *Agama* species, distinguished from other common lizards by their relatively large size of around 20–25cm, basking habits and almost plastic-looking scaling – depending on the species, a combination of blue, purple, orange or red, with the flattened head generally a different colour from the torso. Another common family is the skinks: small, long-tailed lizards, most of which are quite dark and have a few thin black stripes running from head to tail.

Tortoises, terrapins and turtles *with help from Tricia Hayne*

These peculiar reptiles are unique in being protected by a prototypal suit of armour formed by their heavy exoskeleton. The most common of the terrestrial tortoises

WEAVERS

The weavers of the family Ploceidae, which also incorporates the closely related sparrows, are a quintessential part of Africa's natural landscape, common and highly visible in virtually every habitat from rainforest to desert. The name of the family derives from the intricate and elaborate nests – typically, but not always, a roughly oval ball of dried grass, reeds and twigs – that are built by the dextrous males of most species.

It can be fascinating to watch a male weaver at work. First, a nest site is chosen, usually at the end of a thin hanging branch or frond, which is immediately stripped of leaves to protect against snakes. The weaver then flies back and forth to the site, carrying the building material blade by blade in its heavy beak, first using a few thick strands to hang a skeletal nest from the end of a branch, then gradually completing the structure by interweaving numerous thinner blades of grass into the main frame. Once completed, the nest is subjected to the attention of his chosen partner, who will tear it apart if the result is less than satisfactory, and so the process starts all over again.

All but 12 of the 113 described weaver species are resident on the African mainland or associated islands, with roughly 30 represented within Ghana alone. Most of these species are placed in the genus *Ploceus* (true weavers), which is surely the most characteristic of all African bird genera. *Ploceus* weavers are typically slightly larger than a sparrow, and display a strong sexual dimorphism. Males are generally very colourful, but females, with a few exceptions, tend to be drab buff- or olive-brown birds, with some streaking on the back, and perhaps a hint of yellow on the belly.

Most male *Ploceus* weavers conform to the basic colour pattern of the 'masked weaver' – predominantly yellow, with streaky back and wings, and a distinct black facial mask, often bordered orange. Several Ghanaian weaver species fit this masked weaver prototype more or less absolutely, and a similar number approximate it rather less exactly, eg: by having a chestnut-brown mask, or a full black head, or a black back, or by being more chestnut than yellow on the belly. Identification of the masked weavers can be tricky without experience – useful clues are the exact shape of the mask, the presence and extent of the fringing orange, and the colour of the eye and the back.

The various species of golden weaver are also brilliant yellow and/or light orange with some light streaking on the back, but they lack a mask or any other strong distinguishing features. The handful of forest-associated *Ploceus* weavers,

in the region is the **leopard tortoise** (*Testudo pardalis*), which is named after its gold-and-black mottled shell, can weigh up to 30kg, and has been known to live for more than 50 years in captivity. Several species of terrapin – essentially the freshwater variant – are resident in West Africa, all somewhat flatter in shape than the tortoises, and generally with a plainer brown shell. They might be seen sunning on rocks close to water or peering out from roadside puddles, and in rare instances might reach a length of almost 1m.

Turtles – the saltwater equivalent of terrapins – live largely in the water, coming ashore only to nest, and, unlike their landlubber cousins, they are unable to retract either their heads or their flippers into their shell for protection. The world's eight species of marine turtle are all protected under the Convention on International Trade in Endangered Species (CITES), and four are known to nest on the beaches

by contrast, tend to have quite different and very striking colour patterns, and although sexually dimorphic, the female is often as boldly marked as the male. The most aberrant among these is the common Vieillot's black weaver (*Ploceus nigerrimus*), the male of which is totally black except for its eyes, while the black-billed weaver (*Ploceus melanogaster*) reverses the prototype by being all black with a yellow face mask.

Many *Ploceus* species are gregarious breeders, forming single or mixed species colonies of hundreds, sometimes thousands, of pairs, often in reed beds or other waterside vegetation (Hans Cottage Botel is a good site; see pages 210–11). Most weavers don't have a distinctive song, but they compensate with a rowdy jumble of harsh swizzles, rattles and nasal notes that can reach deafening proportions near large colonies. One more cohesive song you will often hear seasonally around weaver colonies is a cyclic 'dee-dee-dee-Diederik', often accelerating to a hysterical crescendo when several birds call at once. This is the call of the Diederik cuckoo (*Chrysococcyx caprius*), a handsome green-and-white cuckoo that lays its eggs in weaver nests.

Most of the colonial weavers, perhaps relying on safety in numbers, build relatively plain nests with a roughly oval shape and an unadorned entrance hole. The nests of certain more solitary weavers, by contrast, are far more elaborate. Several weavers, for instance, protect their nests from egg-eating invaders by attaching tubular entrance tunnels to the base – in the case of the spectacled weaver, sometimes twice as long as the nest itself. The Grosbeak weaver (a peculiar, larger-than-average brown-and-white weaver of reed beds, distinguished by its outsized bill and placed in the monospecific genus *Amblyospiza*) constructs a large and distinctive domed nest, which is supported by a pair of reeds and woven as precisely as the finest basketwork, with a neat, raised entrance hole at the front. By contrast, the scruffiest nests are built by the various species of sparrow- and buffalo-weaver, relatively drab but highly gregarious dry-country birds likely to be seen in Mole National Park and elsewhere in the north.

and lagoons of the Ghanaian coast. The most common of these are the **green turtle** (*Chelonia mydas*), so called because its fat is a greenish colour, the **olive ridley turtle** (*Lepidochelys olivacea*), and the **leatherback** (*Dermchelys coriacea*), which can reach a length of greater than 2m. Also indigenous to these waters is the very rare **hawksbill turtle** (*Eretmochelys imbricata*), whose exquisite shell is the source of traditional 'tortoiseshell', long coveted for ornamental purposes and an important trade item since Ancient Egyptian times.

Turtles do not nest until they are at least 25 years old, when they lay their eggs deep in the sand. The eggs take around 60 days to hatch, at which time the hatchlings make their way towards the sea, attracted by the play of moonlight on the waves. The green turtle, the most likely of the four species to be seen by visitors, lays between 300 and 540 eggs per season in the wild, nesting every three or four years, with the eggs hatching from May to September. In captivity, these figures increase, with up to 1,700 eggs in total laid over several batches in a season. In their first year, the hatchlings grow up to 2.7kg, and they can be expected to weigh up to 24kg by the time they are three or four. Green turtles may live to be centuries old, and can weigh in excess of 200kg. Turtles are cold-blooded animals, requiring warm water to survive. In fact, water temperature

BUTTERFLIES

Ghana's immense wealth of invertebrate life is largely overlooked by visitors, but is perhaps most easily appreciated in the form of butterflies and moths of the order **Lepidoptera**. An estimated 1,000 butterfly species, including several endemics, have been recorded in Ghana, as compared with roughly 650 in the whole of North America, and a mere 56 in the British Isles. Several forests in Ghana harbour 400 or more butterfly species, and one might easily see a greater selection in the course of a day than one could in a lifetime of exploring the English countryside. Indeed, I've often sat at one roadside pool and watched ten to 20 clearly different species converge there in the space of 20 minutes.

The Lepidoptera are placed in the class Insecta, which includes ants, beetles and locusts, among others. All insects are distinguished from other invertebrates, such as arachnids (spiders) and crustaceans, by their combination of six legs, a pair of frontal antennae, and a body divided into a distinct head, thorax and abdomen. Insects are the only winged invertebrates, though some primitive orders have never evolved wings, and other more recently evolved orders have discarded them. Most flying insects have two pairs of wings, one of which, as in the case of flies, might have been modified beyond immediate recognition. The butterflies and moths of the order Lepidoptera have two sets of wings and are distinguished from all other insect orders by the tiny, ridged wing scales that create their characteristic bright colours.

The most spectacular of all butterflies are the swallowtails of the family **Papilionidae**, of which roughly 100 species have been identified in Africa. Named for the streamers that trail from the base of their wings, swallowtails are typically large and colourful, and relatively easy to observe when they feed on mammal dung deposited on forest trails and roads. The West African giant swallowtail (*Papilio antimachus*), a black, orange and green gem with a wingspan of up to 20cm, is probably the largest butterfly in the world, but it's seldom seen as it tends to stick to the forest canopy.

The **Pieridae** is a family of medium-sized butterflies, generally smaller than the swallowtails and with wider wings, of which almost 100 species are present in

affects the sex of the hatchlings: at 28°C, a balance between male and female is to be expected; cooler than that, and males will dominate; hotter, and there will be a predominance of females.

Sadly, female turtles – which go into a trance for several hours while they lay eggs – are routinely captured as food by local villagers, and the egg sites are also often disturbed. This problem is being countered in some areas by public-awareness campaigns, in which tourist interest can play a major role. Among the best sites for turtle spotting in Ghana are Ada Foah and Winneba, but they might be seen on any sandy and reasonably deserted beach – November to March is the best season.

BIRDS *by Adam Riley, whose company, Rockjumper Birding Tours (www.rockjumper/birding.com), specialises in guided birding tours to Ghana and elsewhere in Africa*
Although Ghana has, of recent times, been seldom visited and explored by birders, it is a country with great birding potential. Its obvious advantages as a politically stable, English-speaking nation with friendly people are complemented by a decent network of national and regional parks and ecotourism facilities, with the cherry on the top being the fabulous Kakum canopy walkway (see page 211). These factors, combined with the wide variety of habitats within this small country, make Ghana a very worthwhile

Ghana, several as seasonal intra-African migrants. Most species are predominantly white in colour, with some yellow, orange, black, or even red and blue markings on the wings.

The most diverse family of butterflies in Africa is the **Lycaenidae**, which accounts for almost 500 of the 1,500 species recorded continent-wide. Known also as 'gossamer wings', this varied family consists mostly of small to medium-sized butterflies, with a wingspan of 1–5cm, dull underwings, and brilliant violet-blue, copper or rufous-orange upper wings. The larvae of many Lycaenidae species have a symbiotic relationship with ants – they secrete a fluid that is milked by the ants and are thus permitted to shelter in their nests.

Another well-represented family is the **Nymphalidae**, a diversely coloured group of small to large butterflies, generally associated with forest edges or interiors. The Nymphalidae are also known as brush-footed butterflies because their forelegs have evolved into non-functional brush-like structures. One of the more common and distinctive species is the African blue tiger (*Tirumala petiverana*), a large black butterfly with about two dozen blue-white wing spots, often observed in forest paths near puddles or feeding from animal droppings.

The family **Charaxidae**, regarded by some authorities to be a subfamily of the Nymphalidae, is represented in Africa by roughly 200 species. Typically large, robust, strong fliers with one or two short tails on each wing, the butterflies in this family vary greatly in coloration, and several species appear to be scarce and localised since they inhabit forest canopies and are seldom observed.

Rather less spectacular are the grass-skipper species of the family **Hersperiidae**, most of which are small and rather drably coloured, though some are more attractively marked in black, white and/or yellow. The grass-skippers are regarded as forming the evolutionary link between butterflies and the generally more nocturnal moths, represented in Ghana by several families of which the most impressive are the boldly patterned giant silk moths of the family **Saturniidae**.

birding destination, with more than 750 species recorded. The two main climatic zones (dry north and wet south) spawn several distinct habitat biomes, including the southwestern Guinea–Congo forest zone, the southeastern coastal savannah, the central and northern Guinea savannah, and the far northeastern dry Sudan savannah.

Ghana's premier birding region is its lowland forests, which fall within the Upper Guinea forest block. This stretches from Guinea to Ghana and harbours 15 endemic species, of which 14 are globally threatened. Ghana is currently the only safe country in which this internationally recognised Endemic Bird Area can be visited. Kakum National Park provides a superb opportunity for sampling the avian delights of this threatened lowland forest biome. Other reserves that protect lowland forests and are recognised as Important Bird Areas by BirdLife International are Atewa Range FR (Forest Reserve), Bia NP, Boin River FR, Boin Tano FR, Bosomtwe Range FR, Bura River FR, Cape Three Points FR, Dadieso FR, Draw River FR, Ebi River Shelterbelt FR, Fure River FR, Jema-Asemkrom FR, Mamiri FR, Mount Afadjato-Agumatsa Range Forest, Nini Suhien NP and Ankasa Resource Reserve, Nsuensa FR, Pra-Suhien FR, Subri River FR, Tano-Anwia FR, Tano-Ehuro FR, Tano-Nimiri FR, Tano-Offin FR and Yoyo River FR. Sadly, only 11% of Ghana's forests remain intact, and even within reserves, logging, illegal hunting and forest destruction continue.

Within Ghana, a remarkable 180 species, many of them beautiful and highly sought-after avian gems, are restricted to these forests. Some of the key birds that occur here are white-crested tiger-heron, Congo serpent eagle, the dashing long-tailed hawk, white-breasted guineafowl (an Upper Guinea Forest Endemic (UGFE) and very rare), white-spotted flufftail, the strange Nkulengu rail, yellow-billed turaco, black-throated coucal, rufous fishing owl (UGFE and very rare), brown nightjar, brown-cheeked hornbill (UGFE), the huge yellow-casqued and black-casqued wattled hornbills, Bates's swift, chocolate-backed kingfisher, western wattled cuckoo-shrike (UGFE and very rare), green-tailed bristlebill (UGFE), yellow-bearded greenbul (UGFE), rufous-winged illadopsis (UGFE), white-necked rockfowl or picathartes (UGFE and very rare), Sharpe's apalis (UGFE), black-headed rufous warbler (UGFE and very rare) and copper-tailed glossy starling (UGFE).

Kakum National Park (see pages 207–13) is arguably the best site for these rarities and for other forest birds. Another excellent forest birding site is the Atewa Range, which is situated on the South Volta Scarp and is one of the only higher-lying forests in Ghana (see pages 345–6). The best base for birding in the extensive belt of pristine broadleaved Guinea woodlands running across the centre of Ghana is the vast Mole National Park (see box, page 444).

The welcome publication of the dedicated *Helm Field Guide to the Birds of Ghana* by Nik Borrow and Ron Demey (A&C Black Publishers, 2010) has greatly enhanced Ghana's allure as a birding destination. This 352-page guide illustrates all 758 confirmed resident, migrant and vagrant species across 145 plates, and also has useful short descriptions and distribution maps.

3

Practical Information

WHEN TO VISIT

In most respects, the best time to visit Ghana is during the northern hemisphere winter. The months of October through to April are not significantly hotter or cooler than other times of the year, but they are a great deal more comfortable since humidity levels are lower.

More importantly, these months form the dry season, which means fewer mosquitoes (and a correspondingly decreased risk of contracting malaria), dirt roads are in better condition, and there is less likelihood of you or your luggage being drenched in an unexpected storm. The dry season is particularly suitable for those with a strong interest in natural history, since game viewing is best when the grass is low and resident bird populations are supplemented by all sorts of Palaearctic migrants.

The main disadvantage of the dry season, particularly from December through to February, is that visibility is seriously impeded by sands blown from the Sahara by the harmattan winds. This won't greatly affect most travellers, but the beaches lose much of their beauty, people who plan on doing a lot of hiking will miss the best of the mountain scenery, and serious photographers will find the dull ambient light and grey skies not at all conducive to getting decent pictures.

TOURIST INFORMATION

The **Ghana Tourism Authority** (03022 22153/44794; e *ghanatourismgar@gmail. com; www.ghana.travel*) has a head office in Accra and regional offices in each of the other regional capitals, ie: Bolgatanga, Cape Coast, Ho, Koforidua, Kumasi, Sunyani, Takoradi, Tamale and Wa. These offices are worth visiting if you want to check up on new developments in the region, though do be warned that staff are sometimes surprisingly ignorant about even the most important local attractions, and often have a tendency to invent a plausible but inaccurate answer to a query rather than admit that they don't know. Details of the individual office are included in the relevant chapter.

The **Nature Conservation Research Centre (NCRC)** (*www.ncrc-ghana.org*) is a useful source of information about wildlife reserves and ecotourism in Ghana, though their website hasn't been updated in years.

Also worth a look is the informative site of the **Ghana Museums and Monuments Board** (*www.ghanamuseums.org*), the authority responsible for the upkeep of all the country's museums, UNESCO World Heritage Sites and other national monuments.

ITINERARIES AND HIGHLIGHTS

Itineraries are personal things, dependent on such factors as your specific interests, preferred style of travel, budget and available time. As such, an itinerary that might be thoroughly suitable to an active traveller with a keen interest in natural history might be anathema to somebody looking to chill out on a beach for a few days, and vice versa. Bearing this in mind, we prefer not to list a bunch of prescribed itineraries, but rather to make a few general points.

This book is divided into five main regional parts – Accra and surrounds, the Coast West of Accra, Eastern Ghana, Kumasi and Central Ghana, and Northern Ghana – each of which contains more than enough of interest to keep you busy for a week (see the list of ten regional highlights in the 'Best of …' overview box at the start of each part). Active travellers who are happy to move at a fast pace and want a good look at the best of what Ghana has to offer could see most of the country in a month, though five to six weeks might be more relaxed. At the other extreme, it is not unusual to come across travellers who spend a week or more at one beach resort – the cluster along the west coast between Busua and Cape Three Points are particularly recommended – bookended perhaps by a few days in Accra and Cape Coast or Elmina.

In a typical two-week holiday, we would recommend you focus on no more than two regions (discounting Accra, assuming you just spend a night or two there in transit). The most popular region with travellers is probably the west coast, which contains an excellent choice of beach resorts, historical sites and interesting urban centres, as well as offering access to some fine forest reserves, notably Kakum. For a combination of traditional cultural sites, Sahelian architecture and good general wildlife viewing, Northern and Central Ghana stand out, while Eastern Ghana is great for budget-conscious outdoors types seeking a mix of scenic hikes and beach retreats. A one-week holiday is feasible but limited, and you'd have to pick just one or two of the highlights below.

Our top 12 highlights for all of Ghana are as follows:

ACCRA From historic Jamestown to vivacious 'Oxford Street' in the trendy suburb of Osu, the Ghanaian capital is one of Africa's most invigorating cities, whether you are into craft shopping, museums, nightlife, eating out or just hanging out at La Beach. See pages 103–49.

CAPE COAST AND ELMINA Situated just 15km apart along the coast between Accra and Takoradi, these historic towns are home to a pair of hulking castles that formed the nerve centre of the transatlantic slave trade during the 18th century. See pages 195–207 and 213–223.

KAKUM NATIONAL PARK Teeming with rare birds and other rainforest wildlife, this popular national park a short drive north of Cape Coast is home to Africa's oldest canopy walkway. See pages 207–13.

BUSUA, AKWIDAA AND CAPE THREE POINTS This short and scenic stretch of coast west of Takoradi is the ultimate Ghanaian beach chill-out venue and the centre of a nascent surfing scene. See pages 240–8 and 250–5.

ADA FOAH Set at the mouth of the Volta River, this small riverside town is known for its relaxed beach resorts, and a bordering marine turtle-viewing site. See pages 275–81.

WLI FALLS The scenic showpiece of Volta Region is West Africa's tallest and most spectacular waterfall, set in the forested Agumatsa Wildlife Sanctuary on the Togolese border east of Hohoe. See pages 329–30.

KUMASI The likeably chaotic capital of Ashanti boasts a wealth of cultural and architectural landmarks, as well as the labyrinthine Kejetia Market, and access to several ancient kente-weaving villages and UNESCO-protected fetish shrines. See pages 356–76.

LAKE BOSOMTWE Hiking, birdwatching and horseriding are all on offer at this lovely crater lake nestled south of Kumasi, though many people just opt to relax at a lakeshore resort. See pages 384–8.

BOABENG-FIEMA MONKEY SANCTUARY Close-up encounters with the cheeky Lowe's mona and more serene black-and-white colobus monkey, both held sacred by the local villagers, are the main attractions of this popular community reserve between Kumasi and Tamale. See pages 413–15.

MOLE NATIONAL PARK Thrilling guided walks in search of elephant and antelope are the highlight of Ghana's largest national park, which also offers superb savannah birdwatching, serene canoe trips and two scenically located hotels. See pages 439–51.

PAGA Set on the Burkinese border north of Tamale, Paga is famed for its tame sacred crocodiles, but also offers access to the Paga Pia's Palace, an impressive example of traditional Sahelian architecture, and the chilling Pikworo Slave Camp. See pages 467–70.

LARABANGA, BOLE AND NAKORE MOSQUES Larabanga, near the entrance to Mole National Park, is the oldest of northern Ghana's surreal West Sudanese-style mud-and-stick mosques, but its less publicised counterparts at Bole and Nakore offer a more satisfying experience to visitors. See pages 445–8.

HEADING OFF THE BEATEN TRACK Ghana is dotted with little-visited and poorly publicised ecotourism projects and small reserves that don't quite seem sure themselves whether they are properly operational or not. Often, you'll find that these sort-of-not-quite scenarios – which are most prevalent north of Kumasi – have evolved from a situation where a volunteer or NGO helped to set up an ecotourism project, often building a visitor centre and training a few guides, but failed to see it through properly, leaving the community to its own devices (which, in Ghana, often means 'to the whims of local politics'). These things tend to come and go, so we have removed projects that are clearly no longer functional from this edition, and have also tried to make it obvious when a project is running well. However, the situation is sometimes not so clear-cut, particularly where less regularly visited sites are concerned, and we can only advise travellers to visit such off-the-beaten-track spots in a spirit of adventure.

TOUR OPERATORS

The following international companies offer tours to Ghana. See also the list of Accra-based operators on pages 118–20. Three overland truck companies also offer trips that include Ghana in the itinerary.

UK
Ashanti African Tours `07841 577276 (UK), 03321 31679; m 0245 289736; e info@ashantiafricantours.com; www. ashantiafricantours.com; see ad, 3rd colour section

Explore Worldwide Adventure Holidays `01252 888 768; e res@explore.co.uk; www. explore.co.uk
Native Eye `020 3286 5995; e info@ nativeeyetravel.com; www.nativeeyetravel.com

com. This Suffolk-based operator specialises in personalised tours to off-the-beaten-track destinations worldwide, & offers small group trips to Ghana & more than 2 dozen other African countries.
Responsible Travel ⟍01273 823700; e rosy@ responsibletravel.com; www.responsibletravel.com

Fulani Travel ⟍(+1) 646 290 5028 (US); e info@ fulanitravel.com; www.fulanitravel.com

OVERLANDING
Dragoman Overland ⟍(+1) 855 273 0866; e info@dragoman.co.uk; www.dragoman.com

TOP PRACTICAL TIPS

As guidebooks become bigger, denser and more detailed, it becomes easier for key advice to get lost in the verbiage. Here are a few important summary points (mostly elaborated upon elsewhere) worth highlighting for first-time visitors:

ASK BEFORE YOU SWIM IN THE OCEAN All beaches in Ghana, even those generally regarded to be safe, can be dangerous in certain conditions due to rip tides, strong undertows, etc. See pages 61–2.

APPLY FOR A GHANAIAN VISA AS EARLY AS YOU CAN Visas must be obtained in advance, a laborious procedure best initiated as early as possible, especially for visitors from the USA. See pages 56–7.

BRING A VISA CARD The most viable way to access cash is to use a credit or debit card to draw local currency at ATMs, which can be found in all larger towns. Visa is widely accepted in Ghana, MasterCard to a lesser extent, and other cards are virtually worthless. See page 137.

GET USED TO CONVERTING US DOLLAR PRICES IN THIS BOOK TO LOCAL CURRENCY Most things are best paid for in local currency, but due to the nearly 400% devaluation of the cedi over 2007 to 2016, we have opted to quote prices as a US dollar equivalent, which should prove more reliable in the medium term. See page 137.

COUPLES SHOULDN'T ASSUME THEY NEED A DOUBLE ROOM Ghanaian hotels often advertise a double room as a single, and a twin as a double, so make a habit of checking out a 'single' room before assuming you need to pay more for a double or twin. (And do note that in this guidebook, we reflect what a room actually is, rather than what the hotel calls it, so if it has a double bed, we call it a double, and if it has two beds, we call it a twin). See pages 77–9.

BE AWARE OF OLD CEDI PRICES In 2007, the cedi (the local currency) was redenominated by a factor of 10,000. Confusingly, many Ghanaians have yet to adjust to this dramatic change, and will, for instance, say '50,000 cedi' or just '50' when they mean 5 cedi. See page 67.

BE PREPARED TO TRAVEL WITHOUT TIMETABLES In this book we have made every reasonable effort to give the best transport options and departure points for all routes, but road transport tends to be rather chaotic by Western standards, so it is

RED TAPE

Check well in advance that your **passport** hasn't expired and will not do so for a while, since you may be refused entry on a passport that's due to expire within six months of your intended departure date.

not an exact science. Main routes are covered by a wide variety of vehicles, most of which simply leave when full, rather than operating to a fixed schedule, and departure points in larger towns are often not centralised. See pages 72–7.

THEY'RE CALLED MOBILE PHONES FOR A REASON The ubiquity and efficiency of mobile phones has had many positive effects on business in Ghana. But when it comes to hotels, restaurants and tourist centres, contact numbers – often those of an individual manager, guides or receptionists – tend to change more regularly than fixed lines. There is nothing we can do about this, but readers are welcome to alert us to any such changes by posting on our updates website.

MAPS OF GHANA ARE NOTORIOUSLY INACCURATE No reliable road map of the country exists, and neither is there anything much available for most towns. For this seventh edition, the author has made every reasonable effort to make town plans and regional maps as accurate as possible, but still, in many circumstances, travellers will feel the lack of a reliable foldout colour map of the sort that are ten a penny in most countries. See pages 71–2.

DOUBLE CHECK DISTANCES Many Ghanaians treat miles and kilometres as interchangeable measures. Worse still, at least a dozen times in the course of researching this seventh edition, we were given estimates so wildly out as to be inexplicable – a drive we were told would take 2 hours was actually only 3km, a hotel 200m down the road was actually 10km away, etc. See pages 88–90.

AVOID GETTING 'CAUGHT SHORT' Public toilets are thin on the ground, and where they do exist, they tend to be quite dirty, and may not have running water or toilet paper. Try to get in the habit of going to the toilet before you go out, and carrying toilet paper with you. Hotels, banks and filling stations are the best places to head for if you need a toilet urgently. See page 90.

ADJUST YOUR HOTEL EXPECTATIONS Accommodation standards in Ghana are generally quite low, and facilities tend to be very poorly maintained. Hotels in this book are generally reviewed in this context, and use of words like 'clean', 'smart' or 'stylish' is relative. See pages 77–9.

CHECK FOR ONLINE UPDATES Our updates website (*www.bradtupdates.com/ghana*) is there to publicise important update information sent to us between editions by travellers and people within the industry.

Visitors of practically all nationalities require a **visa**, which must be applied for in advance at the Ghanaian diplomatic mission (embassy or high commission) in your country of residence, where one exists. This is often a complicated and costly process, not least because many such missions are notoriously unhelpful and unresponsive (the Ghanaian embassy in the USA has a particularly bad reputation for mislaying passports, not answering phone calls, etc), so it is advisable to set things in motion as far in advance as possible. People travelling overland to Ghana should be aware that it is no longer possible to get a Ghanaian visa in neighbouring countries unless you are a resident of that country (for instance, the embassy in Ouagadougou, Burkina Faso, will only process visas for Burkinese residents).

Most Ghanaian embassies require applicants to fill in the application form in quadruplicate and send/hand it in accompanied by their passport, a copy of a paid-up air ticket, a letter of invitation from somebody in Ghana together with a copy of their passport, four identical passport-sized photos, and a fee of around US$50–100, depending on whether you want a single-entry visa (valid for one stay of up to 60 days from the date of entry) or a multiple-entry visa. A handful of Ghanaian embassies have begun using an online application form in lieu of the quadruplicate forms mentioned above – we were required to apply online in Berlin for our latest trip, and it's presumable this will eventually be rolled out to other embassies as well. If all goes well, visas typically take three days to issue if you hand in and collect the application personally, or around ten days by post, but we have heard of people waiting longer than a month. As with many developing countries, journalists are likely to face a considerably longer wait.

Should you want to stay in Ghana for longer than 60 days, you will have to apply for a visa extension once you are in the country (normally a straightforward process) and to pay an additional fee for every extra 30 days, regardless of whether you have paid for a single- or multiple-entry visa. It's worth knowing that a visa extension in Accra might take two weeks to process, whereas it shouldn't take more than 48 hours at any other regional capital – although a considerably more attractive option might be to buy a multiple-entry visa and then to cross into one of the neighbouring countries and get an extra 60 days on your return.

The recent initiative of several other African countries in allowing tourists to purchase a short-term **visa upon arrival (VOA)** at airports and land borders has yet to be reciprocated in Ghana, but it's now possible to get a visa on arrival in very limited circumstances if you're travelling at short notice from a country where there's no Ghanaian representation. Applications for this 'emergency entry visa' must be made to the director of immigration (✆ 03022 21667/24445/58250; e director@ myzipnet.com or info@ghanaimmigration.org) and you'll need a letter of invitation, round-trip itinerary, hotel reservation or other proof of lodging, and copy of your passport to start with. Should you be approved, you'll be sent a letter of confirmation to bring to the port of entry. The emergency visa is good for 14 days (it's unclear whether extensions to this type of visa are possible), costs US$150, and can only be issued at Kotoka International Airport, Paga, Aflao, or Elubo. Since July 2016, all AU citizens are eligible for 30-day visas on arrival at the same cost. As this book went to print, the VOA for AU citizens was only available at Kotoka International Airport, but it will likely be rolled out to major land borders during the lifespan of this edition. More info is available at www.ghanaimmigration.org/Em_entryvisa_arrival.html.

Within Ghana, the main objections to scrapping the current visa system are either to do with security (in particular a frequently voiced fear that VOA will make it easier for homosexuals and other 'perverts' to enter the country) or with reciprocity (many Western countries require Ghanaians to jump hoops in order to get a visa). We strongly support the scrapping of visas or conversion to VOA, and will post any news on the updates website (*www.bradtupdates.com/ghana*) as we are made aware of it.

We've had reports of travellers having visas issued in January stamped a year behind – eg: a visa issued on 3 January 2014, but accidentally dated 3 January 2013 – which effectively means it will have expired on the date of issue! It's an easy mistake, and most (not all) border officials will be reasonable about it, but best to check your visa is dated correctly when you collect it.

In theory, it's compulsory to have a valid **yellow fever vaccination certificate** to enter Ghana, but in practice it seems quite random whether or not it's checked. Over the course of researching the seventh edition of this guide in 2016, it was requested of us perhaps 50% of the time.

In case you might want to drive or hire a vehicle in Ghana, do organise an **international driving licence** (any AA office will do this for a nominal fee).

For security reasons, it's advisable to write up all your important information in a document and email copies to yourself and a few trusted friends or relatives, together with a scan of your passport (which will facilitate getting a quick replacement if it is lost or stolen). Other information you might want to include on the document are your flight details, travel insurance policy details and 24-hour emergency contact number, passport number, details of relatives or friends to be contacted in an emergency, bank and credit card details, camera and lens serial numbers, etc.

The Ghanaian Ministry of Foreign Affairs keeps a well-updated list of **embassies and consulates** around the world at www.mfa.gov.gh (see also pages 138–9).

GETTING THERE AND AWAY

BY AIR Among the better-connected cities in West Africa, Accra is served by direct flights from numerous European and North American hubs. It's about 6½ hours non-stop from London, and airlines with scheduled flights to Accra include:

✈ **British Airways** ✆03022 14996; www.britishairways.com

✈ **Brussels Airlines** ✆03022 43893; www.brusselsairlines.com

✈ **Delta Airlines** ✆03022 13111; www.delta.com

✈ **Emirates** ✆03022 13131; www.emirates.com

✈ **Egypt Air** ✆03022 43537/8; www.egyptair.com

✈ **Ethiopia Airways** ✆03026 64856–8; www.ethiopianairlines.com

✈ **Iberia** ✆03022 14970; www.iberia.com

✈ **KLM** ✆03022 14700; www.klm.com

✈ **Kenya Airways** ✆03070 01333; www.kenya-airways.com

✈ **Lufthansa** ✆03022 43894; www.lufthansa.com

✈ **Royal Air Maroc** ✆03027 87182; www.royalairmaroc.com

✈ **RwandAir** ✆03027 97486; www.rwandair.com

✈ **South African Airways** ✆03027 83558; www.flysaa.com

✈ **TAP Portugal** ✆03029 84524; www.flytap.com

✈ **Turkish Airlines** ✆03027 34560/1; www.turkishairlines.com

Flights from the US and Canada tend to be expensive, so North Americans with more time than money may find it cheaper to fly to London, or elsewhere in Europe, and organise a ticket to Africa from there.

As with most destinations, round-trip tickets to Ghana are typically a much better deal, so we recommend going this way if possible, rather than buying a one-way ticket and organising your return once you are there. Additionally, you may hit serious problems with airport immigration officials if you can't show them a return ticket on arrival.

There are dozens upon dozens of travel agents in London offering cheap flights to Africa, and it's worth checking out the ads in magazines like *Time Out* and *TNT* and phoning around before you book anything. The following list includes Ghana specialists:

Africa Travel Centre ✎ 020 7843 3587; e info@ africatravel.co.uk; www.africatravel.co.uk
STA Travel ✎ 0333 321 0099; www.statravel. co.uk. There are 50 STA branches in the UK

specialising in cheap round-the-world-type tickets.
Trailfinders ✎ 020 7938 3939; www.trailfinders. com

OVERLAND FROM EUROPE There are two overland routes between Europe and Ghana. Both start in Morocco and involve crossing the Sahara, one via Algeria and the other via Mauritania, then continue through Mali and Burkina Faso. The Algeria option has been impassable for some years now, and more recent events in Mali mean that that country, too, is impossible to enter from the north, making the Mauritania route the only viable Sahara crossing in West Africa at the time of writing. Still, the situation with either route is highly changeable and you should seek current advice. For readers based in the UK, the best way to gauge the situation would be to get in touch with the many overland truck companies that advertise in magazines such as *TNT* and *Time Out*. Frankly, unless you have a reliable 4x4, joining an overland truck trip is almost certainly the best way of doing this difficult route, especially if you have thoughts of continuing through the Democratic Republic of Congo to East Africa.

Travellers visiting Ghana overland from Europe will presumably want to carry a regional or continental guide. If you are taking your own vehicle, get hold of *Sahara Overland* by Chris Scott (Trailblazer, 2004) (*www.sahara-overland.com*), the essential companion, while *Africa Overland* by Siân Pritchard-Jones and Bob Gibbons (Bradt Travel Guides, sixth edition, 2014) is very useful when it comes to general planning. It might also be worth investing in a regional guide to West Africa, or even a more general guide to Africa; but bear in mind that the wider the scope of the guide, the skimpier it will be on individual country detail.

Overland borders Ghana borders three other countries: Togo to the east, Burkina Faso to the north, and Ivory Coast to the west. If you are coming from any of these countries, it is worth knowing that, as things stand, the Ghanaian embassies in their capitals will not issue visas except to residents of that country, so you will need to have arranged your visa in advance in your normal country of residence.

Togo The main border, and the most accessible, is at Aflao (pages 287–8), where you can cross by foot to the Togolese capital Lomé. A more northerly crossing point is between Ho (capital of Volta Region) and Kpalimé (a quite substantial town in Togo about 30km east of the border) via Kpedze, Honuta (the actual border crossing) and Kpadapé. Plenty of shared taxis run between Ho and Honuta, from where you may need to get a motorbike taxi to the Ghanaian and Togolese border posts, which are about 5km apart. Another border crossing lies further north, connecting Hohoe to Kpalime via Golokwati and the crossing point at Leklebi-Kame.

A big advantage of crossing at Aflao/Lomé is that a seven-day visa can be issued at the Togolese immigration office for around US$30 (15,000CFA). This can be extended and/or converted to multiple-entry for US$1 at the passport centre less than 30 minutes' taxi ride from the border, an overnight procedure that requires two passport photos. So far as we are aware, there are two other border crossings at which you can also get a visa on arrival: Kpoglo, which is some 15km northwest of Aflao itself on the road to Ho, and Kpadapé, between Ho and Kpalimé. Note that when taking the Kpadapé route, there are three possible border crossings – Honuta, as mentioned above, and the nearby towns of Shia and Nyive. Regardless of which crossing you take, the roads converge after some 7–10km at Kpadapé, where the Togolese visas are issued. For all other borders, visas must be obtained in advance from the Togolese Embassy in Accra, at around twice the price charged for visas on arrival.

Burkina Faso The main border crossing is at Paga (see pages 467–70), which lies on the main road connecting Bolgatanga (and indeed Tamale, Kumasi and Accra) to the Burkinese capital Ouagadougou. Plenty of shared taxis run between Bolgatanga and Paga, where the immigration office, which closes at 18.00, is clearly signposted to your left opposite the 'border' station. It is a five-minute walk from here to the Burkina Faso immigration post at Dakola. Here you can buy a three-month tourist visa or three-day transit visa for Burkina Faso, but be warned that these currently cost around US$165/45 (94,000/24,000CFA) respectively, so it's much cheaper to arrange this in Accra if you can. From Dakola, it is about 160km to Ouagadougou, and there are plenty of buses, but allow at least 3 hours for the trip. Heading west, there's a little-used crossing north of Tumu from where you can also connect to Ouagadougou, and travellers headed to Bobo-Dioulasso may want to cross the border at Hamile in the Upper West. In the far east, the thoroughly remote crossing north of Bawku at Kulungugu is set to gain in importance as the northern terminus of the Eastern Corridor Road to Tema, due to be completely surfaced during the lifespan of this edition.

Ivory Coast The main crossing point is Elubo, on the main trunk road between Accra and the Ivorian capital Abidjan. You must first go through the Ghanaian immigration office, which is right in town, then walk or take a taxi (which costs around US$2) along the 2–3km road uphill to the Ivory Coast customs, quarantine and immigration offices, from where you can walk directly into Noe, the border town on the Ivorian side. There is a bank about 500m after the border where you can change money, and Ivorian SIM cards can be bought at the border without any fuss, at least for the time being. A shared taxi from Noe to Abidjan will take up to 3 hours minimum, costs around US$13, and might entail stopping at up to a dozen military roadblocks. We would recommend crossing early enough to be in Abidjan comfortably before dark, but if you are delayed, there is accommodation in Noe as well as in Aboisso, about an hour towards Abidjan.

At the time of writing, a biometric visa must be obtained in advance and costs €50 for up to three months. Details of how to do this are posted at www.snedai.com/en. The application form and payment are done online and you'll be emailed a receipt and an approval letter (separately), which must be brought with you to collect the visa at either an Ivorian embassy or at Félix-Houphouët-Boigny International Airport in Abidjan (where the visa costs €70). In either case you'll need to show a return ticket and hotel booking or letter of invitation. Officially (aside from at the airport), visas are only issued in your country of citizenship or residence, though we've had several recent reports of non-resident travellers successfully getting visas at the Ivorian Embassy in Accra (*18th St, Osu, opposite the Royal Blue Hotel*), but it's hard to say if this can be relied upon. There are no visa facilities at overland crossings.

There are several more northerly crossing points, but the only ones with confirmed international facilities are between Dormaa Ahenkro (west of Sunyani) for Agnibilekrou, and Sampa (west of Wenchi) for Bondoukrou. In the past, these have tended to close during periods of political instability in Ivory Coast.

Wherever you cross, ensure that you have a yellow-fever certificate, as men in white coats might be waiting with needle poised on the other side. They may also try to persuade you that a valid certificate is out of date or illegal in Ivory Coast, which is so much nonsense, and can safely be ignored.

SAFETY AND HASSLES

Ghana is, overall, a very safe travel destination, certainly where crime and associated issues are concerned. Indeed, the biggest concerns for most travellers should be malaria (for details, see information on pages 94–5) and road accidents associated with public transport (see page 93). Levels of hassle are low, too, and tolerance for the quirks of outsiders is high, though it should be pointed out that, as is the case almost anywhere in the world, breaking the law – in particular the usage of illegal drugs – could land you in big trouble.

THEFT The level of crime against tourists is generally very low, and almost entirely restricted to a few very specific places along the coast. The main centre of crime, not unexpectedly, is Accra, where muggings and drive-by theft from tourists are reported from time to time, though certainly not with the frequency of many other African capitals. Other spots that have experienced spates of tourist attacks are Kokrobite Beach, the beaches and paths between Cape Three Points, Akwidaa, Dixcove, Busua and Butre, central Cape Coast (particularly around the castle), Tamale after dark, and the beach between Axim and Ankobra.

That said, even in a relatively safe African country, tourists tend to stand out from the crowd, making them easy game for whatever criminal element exists. As things stand, it would be wholly inappropriate to be anything but relaxed and open in your dealings with Ghanaians; you certainly shouldn't be ruled by fear. Nevertheless, the risk of being pickpocketed or mugged does exist, and the basic common-sense precautions appropriate to travelling in any African country are worth repeating here:

* Most casual thieves operate in busy markets and bus stations. Keep a close watch on your possessions in such places, and avoid having valuables or large amounts of money loose in your daypack or pockets.
* Keep all your valuables and the bulk of your money in a hidden money-belt. Never show this money-belt in public. Keep any spare cash you need elsewhere on your person.
* We feel that a button-up pocket on the front of the shirt is the most secure place for money, as it cannot be snatched without the thief coming into your view. It is also advisable to keep a small amount of hard currency (ideally, cash) hidden away in your luggage, just in case you lose your money-belt.
* Where the choice exists between carrying valuables on your person or leaving them in a locked room, we would tend to favour the latter option, particularly after dark, but obviously you should use your judgement and be sure the room is absolutely secure. If you do decide to carry large sums of money or other valuables with you after dark, then use taxis; don't walk around.
* Leave any jewellery of financial or sentimental value at home.

- Avoid quiet or deserted places, such as unlit alleys by night, or deserted beaches by daylight, particularly if they lie close to or within a major urban area. When in doubt, take a guide, though preferably one who has been recommended to you by your hotel or by other travellers.
- Particularly in large cities, Westerners carrying a daypack, handbag or external money-belt are often targeted by bag-snatchers and other thieves. Ideally, carry as little baggage as possible when you're out and about.

BUREAUCRACY Although bribery and corruption are a fact of life in Ghanaian business circles, these issues seldom affect tourists directly, so you probably don't need to worry about them! The tendency to portray African bureaucrats as difficult and inefficient in their dealings with tourists is also often overstated. Sure, you come across the odd unhelpful official, but then such is the nature of the beast everywhere in the world. It is worth noting that the treatment you receive from officialdom will be determined partly by your own attitude. Walk into an official encounter with an aggressive, paranoid approach, and you are quite likely to kindle the feeling held by many Africans that Europeans are arrogant and offhand in their dealings with other races. Instead, try to be friendly and patient, and accept that the person to whom you are talking may not speak English as fluently as you, or may struggle to follow your accent.

MARINE DANGERS An element of risk is associated with swimming from any Ghanaian beach – even those generally regarded as relatively safe – in the wrong conditions. The currents off the Ghanaian coast can be very dangerous, and swimmers risk being dragged away from shore by rip tides, strong undertows and whirlpools, particularly in stormy or windy weather. It is common for those swimmers who underestimate the dangers associated with these currents to drown. Our understanding is that swimming conditions are most likely to be dangerous during the rainy season, between July and October, and are safest from December until the beginning of the rains. However, in both cases, this is dependent on weather conditions on the day, and the presence of a strong undertow may not always be apparent until you are actually in the water.

There are a few rules of thumb, bearing in mind that most beaches in Ghana lack for dedicated lifeguards, and very few display flags indicating whether swimming conditions are safe. If conditions look rough, at any time of year, don't swim. If they look calm, you should still not swim without first asking local advice, perhaps not at all if you are a weak swimmer. And even the strongest of swimmers on relatively safe beaches should not be in water deeper than their waist without some sort of flotation device. Once in the water, if you sense the presence of a strong undertow, get out immediately. If you are caught in a rip tide or whirlpool, it is generally advisable not to fight the current by trying to swim directly to shore, but rather to save your strength by floating on your back or swimming parallel to shore until the tide weakens, and only then to try to get back to land.

The coastal residents of Ghana evidently view beaches in a less aesthetic way than we do. It is customary in most seaside towns and villages for the beach to serve as a communal toilet. While this may not constitute a health threat in most circumstances, dodging around freshly deposited faeces does tend to take the edge off a pleasant stroll on the sand, and imagining what the last tide washed away might also deter swimmers. Fortunately, most beaches that are regularly visited by tourists are no longer put to the traditional use.

Don't swim or walk barefoot on the beach, or you risk getting coral, urchin or venomous fish spines in your feet. If you tread on a venomous fish, soak the foot in hot (but not scalding) water until sometime after the pain subsides; this may be for 20–30 minutes in all. Take your foot out of the water to top up, otherwise you may scald it. If the pain returns, re-immerse the foot. Once the venom has been heat-inactivated, get a doctor to check and remove any bits of fish spine in the wound.

WOMEN TRAVELLERS Women travelling alone have little to fear on a gender-specific level, and will often find themselves the subject of great kindness from strangers who want to see that they are safe.

The most hassle you are likely to face is heightened levels of flirtatiousness from many Ghanaian men, with the odd direct proposition and a million marriage proposals thrown in. They can be persistent, but barring the marriage part, it's nothing that you wouldn't expect in any Western country, or – probably with a far greater degree of persistence – from many male travellers.

It may sometimes help to pretend you have a husband at home or waiting for you in the next town – in which case, a wedding ring is accepted as 'proof' – but be aware whilst you are fabricating that he is almost worthless without having given you some 'issue', or children. Being married without offspring attracts the twin reactions of vigorous proposals from 'better' men, and sorrowful looks based on the assumption that your husband is impotent or, to call it by that most mystifying of Ghanaian euphemisms,

PERSPECTIVES FROM WOMEN TRAVELLERS

Helen Beecher Bryant

I spent several months teaching English and French in a preparatory school in Ghana, then travelling around during the school holidays. I was 19 at the time, though always claimed to be at least 24 when questioned, as 19 sounds very young. I loved travelling alone – people always want to talk with the 'white lady' and there wasn't a single journey where I didn't make several friends. Obviously, you have to be sensible about giving personal information, and I very rarely gave personal contact details.

I found Ghanaians immensely protective of the lone *obruni*. They would walk me to hotels and places to eat, tell me where the transport was (though never when it would depart!), and they even bargained with taxi drivers for me at times. *En route* to Akosombo in a minibus, there was a near-fatal crash and we all had to pile out of the vehicle. I had no idea where I was, and a friendly man called Mr Happy paid for a taxi to take me to Akosombo!

The number of marriage proposals was ridiculous; I was single at the time, but always claimed to have a boyfriend waiting for me in whichever town or village I was heading for. Even then, they wanted to know what colour he was. I never had to produce my fake wedding photo and didn't bother with a fake ring. People tend to believe what you say.

Although I had many hair-raising experiences on public transport, I was never threatened in any way whilst travelling alone. It is important to be sensible and to look confident, however scared you feel. The people are fascinated by your wish to see their country, particularly in the smaller towns and certainly in rural places; they all want to know why you are there and how they can keep in touch with you. They will often go out of their way to help you, and often don't expect anything back as they do in the tourist areas of Mali, like Mopti and Timbuktu.

'without portfolio'. If anyone does overstep the mark – by touching you, for instance – do make a fuss and slap the offending hand away to underscore that it is not acceptable.

It would also be prudent to pay some attention to how you dress in Ghana, particularly in the more conservative Muslim north, where covered shoulders and skirts or trousers that come below the knee are advisable. It's not that Ghanaians would be deeply offended by women travellers wearing shorts or other outfits that might be seen to be provocative, but it pays to allow for local sensibilities, and under certain circumstances revealing clothes may be perceived to make a statement that you don't intend. Even in the south, where heart-stoppingly tight clothes are the order of the day, try to keep your midriff and the area just below covered, as this is where Ghanaian women often wear their beads and is seen as highly sexual.

More mundanely, tampons are not readily available in smaller towns, though you can easily locate them in Accra and Kumasi. If you're travelling in out-of-the-way places, it's advisable to carry enough to see you through to the next time you'll be in a large city, although, in an emergency, sanitary pads are available in most towns of any size. It is also worth bearing in mind that travelling in the tropics can sometimes cause women to have heavier or more regular periods than they would at home – often alarmingly so. This is quite normal, but any pharmacist will be able to recommend something to stem the flow if necessary.

For the experiences of two readers of previous editions of this book, see their stories in the box below.

However, I was usually genuinely grateful and happily bought whoever had helped me a drink or a few oranges.

Alexandra Fox
I think it may be helpful, for the benefit of single female travellers, to mention something about the amount of hassle they should be prepared to expect from men in Ghana. Nearly everywhere I went (even around the village where I was staying), I was approached by men wanting to talk to me. Usually within 20 seconds, they would be telling me that they were in love with me! I managed to clock up around 32 marriage proposals in three months, and although at times you just had to laugh, at other times I found it incredibly tedious. I never got to the bottom of why they were so keen to declare their love to any white girl they met; however, one Ghanaian told me that it could be because in order to get Ghanaian women to go out with you, you have to tell them you love them so they take you seriously. The way I found to deal with it, though, was to start counting them so I would say, for example, 'You are number 22; when I've been through the first 21 husbands then I'll move on to you.' This seemed to work as it made them laugh, and gave me an easy exit. Although the unwanted attention was annoying at times, I didn't, however, feel overly threatened by any of it, and not all Ghanaian men are the same.

Something else for the girls: if you've ever wanted to have your hair braided, get it done while you're in Ghana. I have fairly long hair and found having it braided much cooler in the hot weather as, although there is a lot of artificial hair braided into your own natural hair, it enables more air to get to your scalp so feels less hot. I had it done just before coming home – a hairdresser in my village came to my house to do it; it took her 5 hours, and she only charged me the equivalent of a few US dollars.

GAY TRAVELLERS Any act of male homosexuality (defined as being 'deemed complete upon proof of the least degree of penetration') is criminal in Ghana. Offenders risk a prison term of up to three years if the act is found to be consensual, and between five and 25 years if it isn't. The law is ambiguous when it comes to sexual activity between females.

Legalities aside, the vast majority of Ghanaians would regard any homosexual act or relationship, whether between male or female, or local or foreigner, to be profoundly unnatural and sinful. Over the past ten years or so, ugly anti-gay rhetoric spouted by religious leaders, much of which links homosexuality to satanic influences and a broader Western decadence, has been reported prominently by the sensationalist local press, affording the issue a far higher profile than was the case ten years ago.

None of which means that homosexuality doesn't exist in Ghana, only that, of necessity, it is somewhat clandestine. Also that, setting aside the rights and wrongs of the matter, and at risk of stating the blindingly obvious, Ghana clearly isn't a destination suited to single travellers in search of anything approximating a gay scene, while same-sex couples who do visit the country should exercise maximum discretion. One other practical consequence of this widespread homophobia is that many hotels in Ghana now forbid two males (and occasionally two females), irrespective of their orientation, to share a double room.

Founded in 2012, the Solace Brothers Foundation (e *solacebfoundation@gmail. com*; */solacefoundadtion*) may be Ghana's first and only LGBT advocacy group, and offers paralegal and human-rights training to members of the community to fight for their rights under the law (such as they are), and resist the arbitrary accusations, attacks and arrests LGBT Ghanaians are often subject to.

WHAT TO TAKE

The key to packing for a country such as Ghana is finding the right balance between bringing everything you might possibly need and carrying as little luggage as possible, something that depends on your own priorities and experience as much as anything. Worth stressing, however, is that almost all genuine necessities are surprisingly easy to get hold of in Ghana, especially in Accra, and that most of the ingenious gadgets sold in camping shops will be deadweight on the road. Indeed, if it came to it, you could easily travel in Ghana with little more than a change of clothes, a few basic toiletries and a medical kit.

CARRYING LUGGAGE Assuming that you'll be using public transport, you'll want to carry your luggage on your back, either in a backpack or in a suitcase that converts into one, since you'll tend to spend a lot of time walking between bus stations and hotels. Which of these you choose depends mainly on your style of travel. If you intend doing a lot of hiking, you definitely want a proper backpack. On the other hand, if you'll be doing things where it might be a good idea to shake off the sometimes negative image attached to backpackers, then there would be obvious advantages in being able to convert your backpack into a conventional suitcase.

If you don't plan on carrying camping gear, there is much to be said for trying to compress your needs into a robust 35-litre daypack. The advantages of this are manifold. For starters, you can rest it on your lap on bus trips, avoiding extra charges for luggage, arguments about where your bag should be stored, and the slight but real risk of theft. A compact bag also makes for greater mobility, whether you're hiking or looking for a hotel in town. If your luggage won't squeeze into a daypack, a sensible compromise is to carry a large daypack in your rucksack, so you can leave much of it in storage when it suits. Either way, make sure your backpack or case is designed in such a way that it can easily be padlocked. This won't prevent a determined thief from slashing it open, but in Ghana you are still unlikely to encounter theft of the sort to which a lock would not be a real deterrent.

CLOTHES Bearing in mind that you can easily and cheaply replace worn items in Ghana, or, even better, get them made to measure, take the minimum. That might be one pair of long trousers and two shorts for men, or two skirts or shorts for women, plus three shirts or T-shirts, one light sweater, maybe a light waterproof windbreaker during the rainy season, enough socks and underwear to last five to seven days, one solid pair of shoes or boots for walking, and one pair of sandals, thongs or other light shoes.

When you select your clothes, remember that jeans are heavy to carry, hot to wear and slow to dry. Far better to bring light cotton trousers, or skirts made of a light natural fabric such as cotton. For reasons of protocol, women may prefer to keep their shoulders covered and wear a skirt that goes below the knees in the Muslim north – true, Ghanaians are relatively relaxed about dress codes, but still, single women in particular might find that a dress draws much less attention than skimpier attire.

T-shirts are lighter and less bulky than proper shirts, though the top pocket of a shirt (particularly if it buttons up) is a good place to carry spending money in markets and bus stations, since it's easier to keep an eye on than trouser pockets. One sweater or sweatshirt will be adequate, since no part of Ghana lies at an altitude above 1,000m, which means night-time temperatures are almost invariably comfortable to sweaty.

Socks and underwear must be made from natural fabrics. Bear in mind that re-using sweaty undergarments will encourage fungal infections, such as athlete's foot, as well as prickly heat in the groin region. Socks and underpants are light and compact enough that it's worth bringing a week's supply. As for footwear, genuine hiking boots are worth considering only if you're a serious off-road hiker, since they are very heavy whether on your feet or in your pack. A good pair of walking shoes, preferably with solid ankle support, is a good compromise. It's also useful to carry sandals, thongs or other light shoes.

There is a massive used-clothing industry in Ghana (known in Twi as *obroni wawu*, or 'dead white man's clothes'), and at most markets you'll find stalls selling jumpers of variable aesthetic but impeccable functional value for next to nothing – you might consider buying such clothing on the spot and giving it away afterwards. Having new clothes made from local fabrics is also quick and relatively inexpensive. The markets sell all sorts of cotton-based cloth by the yard (slightly shorter than a metre) and the vendors will be able to take you to reliable local seamstresses.

CAMPING GEAR The case for bringing camping equipment to Ghana is compelling only if you intend hiking or visiting some of the more obscure reserves where there is no other accommodation. The main argument against carrying camping equipment is that it will increase the weight and bulk of your luggage by up to 5kg, all of which is deadweight except for when you camp. If you decide to carry camping equipment, look for the lightest available gear. It is now possible to buy a lightweight tent weighing little more than 2kg (but you must make sure it is mosquito-proof). Other camping essentials include a sleeping bag and a roll-mat, which will serve as both insulation and padding. There is no need to bring a portable stove, but you might think about carrying a pot, plate, cup and cutlery.

ELECTRICAL DEVICES Electricity is 220V AC at 50 cycles. Stabilisers are required for sensitive devices and adaptors for appliances using 110V. Batteries are useful during power cuts.

OTHER USEFUL ITEMS Many backpackers, even those with no intention of camping, carry a **sleeping bag** – but a much better plan in this climate would be to carry a **cotton sheet** or **sheet sleeping bag** (also known as a sleeping-bag liner), something you can easily make yourself or have run-up cheaply when you arrive in Accra. For the most part, the bedding in local lodgings will be far cleaner than any sweaty rag you haul around with you, but it can be a relief if faced with super-synthetic sheets on a humid night, or something less than sanitary.

If you're interested in natural history, it's difficult to imagine anything that will give you such value-for-weight entertainment as a pair of light, compact **binoculars**, which these days needn't be much heavier or bulkier than a pack of cards. Binoculars are essential if you want to get a good look at birds (Africa boasts a remarkably colourful avifauna, even if you've no desire to put a name to everything that flaps) or to watch distant mammals in game reserves. For most purposes, 7x21 compact binoculars will be fine, though some might prefer 7x35 traditional binoculars for their larger field of vision. Serious birdwatchers will find a 10x magnification more useful.

All the **toilet bag** basics (soap, shampoo, conditioner, toothpaste, toothbrush, deodorant, basic razors) are very easy to replace as you go along – so there's no need to bring family-sized packs – but women planning on longer stays might want to stock up on some **heavy-duty, leave-in conditioner** to minimise sun damage to their hair. Those staying outside Accra and Kumasi should also carry enough **tampons** and/or **sanitary pads** to see them through, since these items may not always be easy to find. If you wear **contact lenses**, be aware that the various cleansing and storing fluids are not readily available in Ghana and, since many people find the intense sun and dry climate irritates their eyes, you might consider reverting to glasses. Some readers have recommended daily disposable contact lenses to save the hassle and risk of re-using. Most budget hotels provide **toilet paper** and many also provide **towels**, but it is worth taking your own with you to make sure you don't get caught short. Also keep an eye out for street vendors selling short lengths of neon-coloured netting; these are **bath scrubs** and we couldn't recommend them more highly. They're more abrasive than your average loofah, but perfectly suited to the climate and just the thing for scrubbing off a long day of trotro sweat.

You should carry a small **medical kit**, the contents of which are discussed on page 94, as are **mosquito nets**. Two items of tropical toiletry that can be difficult to get hold of outside Accra are **mosquito repellent** of a type suitable for skin application, and **high-factor sunscreen**. In both cases, you are advised to bring all you need with you. A pack of **wet or facial cleansing-wipes** can help maintain a semblance of cleanliness on long, dusty journeys, and **antibacterial gel** is a good way of making sure you don't make yourself sick with your own grime if you're eating on the move.

Other useful items include a **padlock** for your bag (preferably a combination lock, since potential thieves are more likely to have experience of picking locks with keys), a **torch**, a **penknife** and (if you don't have one on your phone) a compact **alarm clock**. A **universal sink plug** will get around the fact that many baths in Ghana don't come with a plug – useful for doing the laundry, if not for bathing in, and a twisted **no-peg washing line** is great for hanging clothes out. Some people wouldn't travel without a good pair of **earplugs** to help them sleep at night (or through morning mosque calls in the north) and a **travel pillow** to make long bus journeys that bit easier to endure. Some travellers carry **games** – most commonly a pack of cards, less often chess or draughts or Travel Scrabble.

MONEY

The unit of currency is the Ghanaian cedi (GHC) (pronounced 'seedy'), which is named after the Akan word for cowry shell, once widely used as a medium of exchange, and divided into 100 pesewa, after the Akan *pesewabo*, a dark-blue seed formerly used as the smallest gold weight. The cedi has experienced consistent devaluation since it replaced the Ghanian pound in 1965, pegged at an exchange rate of GHC2.4 to the British pound. By 2007, it had plummeted to around GHC10,000 to the US dollar, leading the Bank of Ghana to re-denominate it by a factor of 10,000 (in other words, removing the last four zeros, so that, for instance, the GHC20,500 in the old denomination became the GHC2.05). This meant that the 'new' Ghanaian cedi was on rough parity with the US dollar when it was introduced. Since then, however, it has continued to devalue, and in April 2016 it stood at around GHC3.83 to the US dollar, GHC4.33 to the euro and GHC5.49 to the British pound. Since re-denomination, banks notes have been available in denominations of GHC1, 2, 5, 10, 20 and 50, supplemented by coins of 1, 5, 10, 20 and 50 pesewa, as well as GHC1.

Although the new cedi had been in use for nearly a decade when this seventh edition was researched, a surprising number of Ghanaians had still not adjusted to it, particularly in smaller towns and rural areas, and would still quote prices in the old cedi equivalent. This can lead to some confusion, not least because it is conventional for Ghanaians to abbreviate old cedi prices so that the 'thousand' is unspoken, which makes something sound ten times more expensive than it actually is. For instance, you might be told a meal at a chop bar costs an outrageous-sounding '50', meaning GCH50,000 in the old denomination, or GHC5 in the new denomination, or that a hotel room costs '300 cedi', ie: 300,000 old cedi, which is actually only GHC30. Occasionally, this discrepancy can lead to serious misunderstandings, so bear in mind that any price that feels out by a factor of ten is probably being quoted in the old denomination.

ORGANISING YOUR FINANCES There are three ways of carrying money: hard currency cash, travellers' cheques or a debit/credit card. These days, however, travellers' cheques are of extremely limited use in Ghana, which means you ideally need to carry a combination of hard-currency cash, to exchange into local currency as you go, and a widely recognised credit, debit or ATM card to draw local currency at ATMs. Visa is by far the most useful brand, since it is accepted at all international ATMs in regional capitals and large towns (which basically means any ATM outside a branch of Ghana Commercial, Barclays, Standard Chartered, Stanbic and most other banks; see www.visa.com/atms). A poor but improving second best is MasterCard or Visa Electron, which will be accepted at most Ghana Commercial, Access, UniBank, and EcoBank ATMs, but is far less useful overall (see www.mastercard.us/cardholder-services/atm-locator.html for details of individual ATMs). Cards belonging to other brands (including American Express) are borderline useless in Ghana.

It is important to note that, with the exception of a few upmarket hotels, mainly in Accra, very few tourist facilities accept direct payments by credit or debit card. This means that you usually need to settle hotel and almost all other bills in Ghana with cash. So if your card is your main source of funds, it is vital to plan ahead when it comes to ATM withdrawals. Typically, ATMs are easily located anywhere in Accra, and you can draw the equivalent of around US$400 daily, usually over two transactions. There are also usually several ATMs in most larger towns, but smaller towns will often only have one or two – which may not be available during a power cut or when out of service – and rural areas such as isolated beach resorts and forest reserves will have none.

A few precautions if you will rely primarily on your Visa card for funds. The first is to let your bank know you will be travelling to Ghana, and the dates, so they don't become suspicious and put a hold on your account. The second is that an individual or group relying on only one card could hit real complications if that card is stolen, swallowed by an ATM, or otherwise rendered useless, so best carry a second card as a backup, and keep it apart from the rest of your funds. Finally, though credit/debit card scams are not commonplace, several incidents have been reported by readers, sometimes involving the direct theft of a card, but more frequently hotel staff copying a card number and using it to make a fraudulent payment. This sort of thing can largely be avoided by not letting the card out of your sight at any time, and it presents another argument in favour of using your card to withdraw money from ATMs rather than to pay hotel bills directly.

As already noted, travellers' cheques are now close to useless in Ghana. About the only places where you can exchange them, with daily limitations, are the Barclays Bank head offices in Accra and Takoradi, and it seems likely this facility will eventually close, too. So the best backup for a Visa card is hard-currency cash, perhaps to a total value of around US$500, ideally carrying a healthy mix of denominations of up to US$100, which can be changed into the local currency at most banks and at any private bureau de change. In the worst instance, should your card let you down and your cash run out, Western Union is widely represented in Ghana and can be used for quick cash transfers from anywhere in the world.

Carry your hard currency and cards (plus passport and other important documentation) in a money-belt, ideally one that can be hidden beneath your clothing. The money-belt should be made of cotton or another natural fabric, and everything inside it should be wrapped in plastic to protect it against sweat.

In theory, any excess local currency can be changed back into dollars when you leave Ghana. However, you are best doing this at one of the foreign-exchange bureaux in town rather than waiting until you get to the airport.

FOREIGN EXCHANGE The most widely recognised and exchangeable foreign currency is the US dollar, although the euro is fast catching up, and the pound sterling is often just as exchangeable but tends to fetch a slightly poorer rate. US dollar, euro and pound sterling banknotes can be exchanged for local currency in practically any town or border post, often at a bank or a private bureau de change (forex bureau), though smaller bills often fetch a poor rate compared with US$50/US$100 bills. In Accra, Kumasi and, to a lesser degree, the other regional capitals, there's generally a choice of places to exchange hard-currency cash and the rate may vary by a few per cent, so it's worth shopping around. In smaller towns, your options will probably be limited to one bank or forex bureau, so you'll have to take whatever rate you're offered.

In towns where there are no banks, or if you want to exchange money outside the normal banking hours of 08.30 to 16.00 weekdays, you'll rarely have a problem finding a private individual to exchange your US dollars. There is always a danger of being conned in such a situation, however – particularly when you deal with 'professional' money-changers at borders who occasionally deal in counterfeits – so we would advise against changing significantly more money than you need to get to the next town with banking facilities.

PRICES IN THIS BOOK With a few exceptions (basically, a handful of upmarket hotels and car rental companies, which charge in US dollars), pretty much every price in Ghana is quoted in the local currency – in fact it's required by law – and can be paid for that way. Indeed, in many situations, attempting to pay for something in any currency other than the cedi would create complete confusion. In an ideal world, we would follow suit in this book, by quoting all prices in cedis (as we did in some previous editions). Sadly, however, the recent weakness of the local currency, which devalued by approaching 400% against the US dollar between 2007 and 2016, has fuelled high rates of local inflation that tend to make any price quoted in Ghanaian cedis look obsolete a year later. The exchange rate was reasonably stable at roughly 4GHC to US$1 from autumn 2015–spring 2016, but there's no guarantee this will last. Thus, for this edition, we feel we have no sensible option but to quote cedi prices as a US dollar equivalent, which will almost certainly prove to be a more reliable medium-term guideline than any price given in the inflation- and devaluation-prone local currency.

TAXES AND LEVIES VAT of 17.5% is charged on most goods and services in Ghana, including accommodation and restaurant meals. In addition, as of October 2012, all private tourism-sector operators, including hotels, are compelled to pay a Tourism Development Levy of 1%. In both cases, these taxes are usually built into the prices quoted on the ground and in this book, but several restaurants in particular charge both taxes over and above the price quoted on the menu.

BARGAINING AND OVERCHARGING Tourists to Ghana do sometimes need to bargain over prices, particularly in Accra, but generally only in reasonably predictable circumstances, such as when chartering private taxis, organising guides or buying curios and other market produce. Prices in hotels, restaurants, shops and public transport are generally fixed, and overcharging in such places is too unusual for it to be worth challenging a price unless it is blatantly ridiculous (though many hotels will be open to negotiating a discounted rate, particularly for longer stays).

You're bound to be overcharged at some point in Ghana, but it is important to keep this in perspective. Some travellers, after a couple of bad experiences, start to haggle with everyone from hotel owners to old women selling fruit by the side of the road, often accompanying their negotiations with aggressive accusations of dishonesty. Unfortunately, it is sometimes necessary to fall back on aggressive posturing in order to determine a fair price, but such behaviour is also very unfair on those people who are forthright and honest in their dealings with tourists. It's a question of finding the right balance, or, better still, looking for other ways of dealing with the problem.

The main instance where bargaining is essential is when buying curios. What should be understood, however, is that the fact a curio seller is open to negotiation does not mean that you were initially being overcharged or ripped off. Curio sellers will generally quote a price knowing full well that you are going to bargain it down (they'd probably be startled if you didn't), and it is not necessary to respond aggressively or in an accusatory manner. It is impossible to say by how much you should bargain the initial price down. Some people say that you should offer half the asking price and be prepared to settle at around two-thirds, but my experience is that curio sellers are far more whimsical than such advice allows for. The sensible approach, if you want to get a feel for prices, is to ask the price of similar items at a few different stalls before you actually contemplate buying anything.

In fruit and vegetable markets and stalls, bargaining is often the norm, even between locals, and the most healthy approach to this sort of haggling is to view it as an enjoyable part of the African experience. There will normally be an accepted price band for any particular commodity. To find out what it is, listen to what other people pay and try a few stalls. A ludicrously inflated price will always drop the moment you walk away. When buying fruit and vegetables, a good way to get a feel for the situation is to ask for a bulk discount or a few extra items thrown in. And bear in mind that when somebody is reluctant to bargain, it may be because they asked a fair price in the first place.

Above all, don't lose your sense of proportion. No matter how poor you may feel, it is your choice to travel on a tight budget. Most Ghanaians are much poorer than you will ever be, and they do not have the luxury of choosing to travel. If you find yourself quibbling with an old lady selling a few piles of fruit by the roadside, stand back and look at the bigger picture. There is nothing wrong with occasionally erring on the side of generosity.

COSTS AND BUDGETING Ghana used to be a relatively inexpensive travel destination by Western standards, but prices have jumped in recent years, and it is now rather expensive by any standards, and very costly by comparison with many parts of Asia.

So far as travel basics go, **accommodation** for one or two people will probably average out at around US$15 per day if you always go for the cheapest option, though it will be cheaper for single travellers where dorm beds are available, which is mainly along the coast. You're looking at more like US$20/25 per day for a budget self-contained double with fan/air conditioning, and from US$40–100 upwards for mid-range comfort.

For **food**, expect to spend around US$5–10 per head per day if you stick to street food and very cheap restaurants, US$10–15 if you eat once daily in a restaurant, and maybe US$25–30 per day to eat pretty much what you like (excluding really upmarket places).

Depending on how often and how far you travel, **public transport** shouldn't come to more than US$5 per day per person, while a charter taxi ride in most towns costs no more than US$3.

The main thing you need to add to the above on a daily basis is **liquid**. Unless you restrict yourself to tap water (not advisable) or the slightly chemical-tasting but perfectly acceptable water in sachets, you'll spend a fair bit of money just keeping your thirst quenched in Ghana's hot climate – say US$4 per head daily if you stick to sachet water and soft drinks, perhaps US$10 daily if you add on a couple of beers.

Put this together, and you're looking at a rock-bottom budget of US$30/40 daily for one/two people using dorms or camping where possible, and avoiding bottled drinks and restaurants. To travel thriftily but with a bit more freedom and comfort, a budget of around US$55/75 for one/two people would be feasible. If you want air-conditioned rooms, two solid meals, and the rest, budget on upwards of US$80/100 for one/two people.

The above reckoning excludes one-off expenses such as entrance fees to museums or guiding fees in parks, factors that tend to create the occasional expensive day, markedly so for those on a tight budget.

GETTING AROUND

MAPS Good general road maps of Ghana are difficult to come by. The only internationally published option is the 1:500,000 *Ghana* International Travel Map produced by the Canadian company ITMB (*www.itmb.com*). This can be bought on the likes of amazon.com for around US$12, and is just about worth the expense if you want a proper map, since it is compact and folds out easily. Be warned, however, that it falls far short of Ordnance Survey (OS) standards. Indeed, it is truly difficult to believe anybody involved in the production of this map has ever set foot in Ghana, or knows the first thing about the country. In particular, watch out for the omission of several minor roads and towns, misspelt town names, and unnecessarily inventive naming and delineation of national parks and other reserves. It also lacks important features such as road distances and altitudes of peaks. The best online resources are OpenStreetMap (*www.openstreetmap.org*) and Google maps *(http:// maps.google.com)*, but they can both be patchy, being quite accurate for some areas and completely out for others. Taken together and compared, though, you can usually get a pretty good idea of where things stand.

Within Ghana, a large number of wall maps are available, most more or less accurate when it comes to major routes, but often wildly out for minor towns and routes, fairly useless when it comes to geographic landmarks, and not really designed for travel. A better option than any of these is the 1:500,000 *Road Map of Ghana* sold by the map sales office in the Survey Department of the Land Commission in Accra. Despite being shockingly out of date (the eighth and current edition is copyrighted to 1994), this does seem to have been very accurate when it was originally produced, though it omits newer roads and often shows recently surfaced roads as dirt. It is also useful when it comes to road distances (given in miles) and topographic features such as mountains and rivers, but no national parks or other reserves are shown, and some spellings are also unusual or archaic. For hikers and walkers, the map sales office also stocks more detailed 1:50,000 sheets covering most parts of the country. These have proved to be reasonably reliable in our experience, though they are clearly far older than the copyright date would have you think, so there are often curious omissions, inclusions and displacements, as well as unusual spellings for some towns and villages.

As for town and city plans, numerous foldout maps (as well as an A–Z map book) cover Accra (see page 118), but little in the way of printed maps is available for most other towns. Google maps can be quite useful for some larger towns, though one suspects map details have been added remotely from satellite images, which makes it wildly unreliable for many places – again, best to double-check things with OpenStreetMap as well. The map sales office in Accra also stocks plans of a few larger towns but these are mostly very old – in fact, some seem not to have been updated since the colonial era – and not much use except for general orientation.

Which brings me, rather defensively, to the maps in this book. For the sixth edition of this guide, most town plans were completely redrawn, based on original maps compiled by the author, who walked and drove around most large towns tracking every road and marking every major landmark with GPS. The same procedure was undertaken in updating the maps for this seventh edition. We are confident not only that these town plans are far more accurate than their counterparts in previous editions, but also represent the most accurate maps in existence for the towns they cover. The situation with regional road and locator maps is more problematic, since no wholly reliable source exists, and it goes beyond the resources of a guidebook writer to map a country to OS standards. Nevertheless, a great deal of effort has gone into making these maps as accurate and useful as possible, and where errors do exist, we hope readers will not be too critical, but rather let the author know so they can be corrected in future editions.

CAR RENTAL AND DRIVING Formal car rental options in Ghana are more or less restricted to Avis, Europcar, and a number of private tour operators in Accra (see pages 118–20). In most cases, they will only rent a car with a local driver, whose expenses should be covered in the asking rate. An affordable alternative to renting a vehicle formally is to charter a taxi driver for one or more days – which, if you choose the right driver, means you also have a guide, interpreter and evening companion for the bar. The rate for this sort of service is highly negotiable, and it will depend on the distance you want to travel, the number of days, and whether fuel and the driver's meals and room are included, but at worst you should be looking at around US$30 daily, exclusive of extras such as fuel – and a lot less in rural areas or the north of the country. If you want to rent a taxi as a private charter on a one-off basis, bank on a fee of around US$7–10 per hour inclusive of fuel and unlimited kilometres.

So far as driving practicalities go, filling stations are plentiful, fuel is reasonably cheap by international standards, and shortages are uncommon, though certainly not unknown. There are tolls on most major routes, often at bridges, charging nominal fees. Official road signs exist, usually at junctions, and have white text on a green background. Otherwise, there is little indication of distances or route confirmation on the roads.

Unusually for a former British colony, Ghana drives on the right-hand side of the road (except on dual carriageways, where two-way traffic has been known to flow down *both* sides!). Twenty years ago, the state of Ghana's roads was appalling. In recent times, however, there has been large-scale upgrading of the main routes, all of which are now surfaced (except where roadworks are under way). You could easily drive the entire coastal road from Aflao to Elubo in a saloon car, as you could the main north–south road from Accra to Paga via Kumasi and Tamale. In fact, there are now very few parts of the country that aren't accessible to practically any carefully driven vehicle – as attested by the ancient taxis that cover the most unlikely of routes throughout Ghana. All the same, it would be prudent to seek local advice repeatedly as you move around the country, particularly if you visit more remote areas during the rainy season.

If you've never driven in Africa before, be aware that the general approach to driving is quite different from that in more developed countries. Ghanaians tend to be complete maniacs on the road, and visitors should be very cautious, particularly if they are also adapting to driving on the right-hand side of the road. In addition to a heart-stopping approach to overtaking, you will have to contend with pot-holes, pedestrians and domestic animals on the road, as well as insane levels of traffic in Accra and Kumasi during rush hour. And be acutely aware that it's customary not to slow down on a blind curve, but to race around it hooting wildly – if you don't hoot back, it will be assumed that no vehicle is coming! Driving at night is inadvisable, not so much for security reasons, but because the general chaos on the road is exacerbated by a lack of street lights and many vehicles without headlights.

Foreigners may drive for up to 12 months in Ghana on an international driving licence. Other foreign licences might be accepted in theory, but not in practice.

BY PUBLIC TRANSPORT
Rail The passenger service on the triangle of railway lines connecting Accra, Kumasi and Takoradi has been non-operational since 2006 due to high fuel prices. The

government reputedly secured a substantial Chinese loan to rehabilitate the line in 2011, and works were visibly under way between Takoradi and Kumasi during 2016.

Road Major roads through Ghana are covered by a variety of public transport, divisible into five broad categories, in descending order of comfort: air-conditioned coaches, air-conditioned vans (known variously as Fords, Stanbics or Yutons), Metro Mass buses, trotros (also sometimes called lorries) and shared taxis. In small towns and villages, all public transport generally arrives at and departs from one central terminus (usually referred to as the 'station', or 'lorry station'). Most larger towns have several different stations, sometimes serving different types of transport or individual operators, other times a set of destinations in one direction. Most road transport doesn't operate to a fixed schedule. Instead, vehicles simply wait at their designated station, and leave as soon as they are full. This can all seem rather chaotic to first-time Africa visitors used to more formal train and bus timetables, especially where departure points are decentralised, but once you adapt, you'll find that getting around Ghana's roads is very cheap and straightforward, though the standard of driving leaves a great deal to be desired on the safety front.

Throughout this book, we have indicated the most important stations in most large towns, but it can all become quite confusing. If in doubt, an easy solution is to catch a charter taxi, and ask the driver to take you to the right place. The convention is to ask for the 'station' for the destination you want – in other words, should you be looking for transport to Kumasi, then ask to be taken to Kumasi Station. The exception is where you want a specific bus company, such as Metro Mass, VIP or STC, in which case ask for the station by the company's name.

Fares are generally very cheap. The priciest air-conditioned coaches from Accra to Kumasi, for instance, cost US$13 one-way, while those from Accra to Tamale (almost the full length of the country) cost around US$20, and Metro Mass buses, trotros and other light vehicles are significantly cheaper. Most buses and trotros charge an additional (and often negotiable) fee for large luggage, such as a backpack. In most cases, the fee is legitimate, but travellers are sometimes overcharged, and may occasionally be asked to pay a luggage fee where a local wouldn't. We are more inclined to accept the legitimacy of a fee we are asked for upfront than one first mentioned at the end of the trip.

Details of individual routes are scattered under relevant headings throughout this book, but an overview of the transport types follows:

Air-conditioned coaches As a rule, the safest and most efficient way of travelling long distances (for instance from Accra to Kumasi or Tamale) is by air-conditioned coach, which typically cover at least 80km per hour, with scheduled 15-minute meal breaks every few hours, and blaring Nigerian films to keep you entertained (or aggravated) through the trip. The coach market used to be dominated by the STC, which still operates a small handful of routes, but this institution has become increasingly unreliable (and seemingly moribund) in recent years, and most Ghanaians now favour newer operators such as VIP or VVIP (which dominates the Accra–Kumasi route and also runs north to Tamale, Bolgatanga and Wa) and OA, which usually have their own stations away from the main one. Some coach operators have fixed departure times for some routes, and can be booked in advance. On other routes, it's generally possible to pitch up at the appropriate station and buy a ticket for the next bus leaving, but this can't be relied on completely, and buses may well be booked solid over long weekends and holiday periods, such as the week before Christmas or Easter weekend.

3

Air-conditioned vans Known by various nicknames, such as Ford, Yuton or Stanbic (the last after the bank that provided the financing for several individual owners a few years back), these spacious air-conditioned vans offer an excellent compromise between comfort, cost and efficiency. Stanbics provide the optimum light transport option between Accra and Kumasi, while Fords are available along most other routes, for instance Accra to Wa, Bolgatanga, Cape Coast or Takoradi. They invariably operate on a fill-up-and-go basis, and most often leave from the same station as trotros to the same destination.

Metro Mass buses This ubiquitous parastatal operates cheap (and distinctive bright orange) buses along every major route in the country, and most minor ones. These buses are just as safe as the private air-conditioned coaches (perhaps more so, as the drivers tend to be less gung-ho), but they are generally older, slower, more crowded, less comfortable and not air conditioned. Every town usually has its own Metro Mass station, often quite far from the centre and from other stations. On major routes, such as Accra to Kumasi, dozens of Metro Mass buses might depart daily on a fill-up-and-go basis. On quieter routes, it is usually just two or three buses daily, and these do operate to fixed departure times.

Trotros A sort of catch-all term covering any licensed passenger vehicle that doesn't slot into any of the above categories, the word trotro is usually applied to any van or minibus that isn't air conditioned, but it is also applied (more or less interchangeably with 'lorry') to a type of customised covered truck with densely packed seating, a pervasive aura of sweat, and little chance of finding an escape route should you be involved in an accident. Trotros cover the length and breadth of Ghana's roads and you will have little choice but to depend on them when you travel between smaller towns. Nonetheless, we would strongly advise you to use other transport wherever possible, not so much because trotros are slower or less comfortable than buses (though generally they are both), but because the risk of being involved in a fatal accident is so much greater. Most trotros work on a fill-up-and-go basis, and you will rarely wait more than 30 minutes for a vehicle heading in your direction on main roads. Only on routes where there is very little transport do you need to think in terms of set departure times, and in such circumstances you should definitely check the situation the day before – it may, for instance, be the case that all the transport leaves before 06.00. It is also worth being aware that fewer trotros run on Sundays, particularly in Christian parts of the country, which means you'll generally wait longer for something to leave along main roads and may be delayed for hours or find that nothing is going at all along minor routes.

Many of the touts whose task it is to fill up trotros have a quite neurotic need physically to 'see' bums on seats. It can take all your powers of persuasion to convince them that if they could only use their imagination and pretend you are sitting in your seat, then you could stand outside while you wait for the vehicle to fill up rather than having to practise being uncomfortable in a sweaty, cramped, motionless vehicle for half an hour. And even when you think that you've had an incandescent moment of cross-cultural communication, as the tout appears to light up with recognition of the good sense of your position, he'll be edging up to you two minutes later hissing, 'You sit, white man, you sit!'. One blessing is that the Ghanaian government is starting to crack down on overcrowded vehicles, although they are still common on rural routes where there are fewer police checks.

In many places, you have to buy a ticket at the booth of the **Private Transport Union** (or the GRPTU of TUC, to give its full set of initials) for a specific route, and even when you just pay the conductor (known as the 'mate') on the road, fares are fixed and overcharging is not a significant concern. As with buses, some trotros charge the full fare to passengers alighting along the way. If you're going to be picking up trotros on the roadside (which most travellers will), it is useful to know a few of the many hand signals used to indicate where you want to go. Universal signs include jabbing the air with your index finger to indicate that you want to go 'far', making the same gesture downwards to demonstrate a short trip, or using your thumb sideways to point in the direction you will eventually want to turn or 'branch'.

Taxis Ghanaian taxis can be split into dropping and shared (or 'passenger') taxis. The dropping system is essentially the one we are familiar with, where you charter a taxi privately, with the major difference being that Ghanaian taxis are not metered, so a price must be agreed in advance. The shared taxi system is like a mini trotro, where a taxi plies a specific route at a fixed fare, either picking up passengers along the way, or else filling the vehicle at a recognised terminal, and is often the most convenient way to get around quickly and cheaply. Whichever system you use, taxis in Ghana are quite inexpensive, and it is well worth making use of them.

Shared taxis are often the main form of transport between two nearby towns. They also often cover short roads between a junction and a nearby town, especially along the coast, where many towns and villages lie a few kilometres south of the main road. Officially, these taxis should take four passengers, but on routes where the drivers think they can get away with it, the convention is still six: two in the front and four in the back. It will often be assumed by taxi drivers that any foreigner prefers a private taxi, so always specify when you want a 'passenger', not a 'dropping' vehicle. In most towns, you can normally assume that any empty taxi that stops for you will be offering you a 'dropping' service to wherever you like at a negotiable fare, whereas a vehicle that already has passengers will be offering you a lift in a specific direction at a fixed fare.

There may often be circumstances where you do want to use a private taxi. In Accra, for instance, it's barely worth figuring out the passenger taxi routes if you're only spending a night or two there. When you arrive in a town with luggage, it is often pleasant to catch a taxi to a hotel. Likewise, you may consider it a waste of time to wait an hour for a passenger taxi to fill up when, for instance, it is covering a 6km road at a cost of US$0.50 per person, and you could charter the whole thing for US$3. And note that in such circumstances it would be perfectly acceptable to pay the difference where the taxi is partially full – using the example above, if two passengers each paying US$0.50 were already sitting in the taxi when you arrived, you could offer to pay US$2 to make up the full fare.

Shared taxi fares, like those for other public transport, are fixed by the government for specific routes, often at rates that make it difficult for the taxi driver or owner to make any significant profit. Dropping fares, by contrast, are not fixed and are thus perceived to be negotiable. You might ask a cab driver how much a passenger fare is and he'll tell you it's US$0.50, then when you ask how much to charter the same taxi on the same route he'll ask ten times as much. It's very difficult to come up with a rule of thumb for determining the right dropping fare – you might ask two different taxi drivers for the same route and one will ask half what the other does – but you'll quickly get a feel for what seems reasonable, and should bear in mind that the dropping fare between two spots should work out at between four and six times the passenger fare.

Motos A cheap and popular alternative to charter taxis, especially in small towns and rural areas, or when heading to out-of-town reserves and other sites, is a moto – the local name for a motorbike fitted out to carry one passenger. The fares are usually a fraction of the taxi equivalent, but be warned that moto drivers are often

Practically speaking, cycling is probably easiest in the far north and in the far south, for rather different reasons. A dry climate, flat landscape and plenty of tarmac characterises the north, and we found 125km a day was not unreasonable. As we pedalled south, the landscape became more spectacular and we were glad of the shade as we toiled up hills set in incredibly lush and jungly surroundings. After leaving Mole National Park, we encountered some very rough roads – corrugations and deep gravel made the going pretty tough (though the road to Mole has since been surfaced). Once south of Kumasi, however, the roads were good again and the fairly flat coastal strip made for some very scenic cycling.

The east is perhaps a mixture of the two – hilly, but well-surfaced roads and spectacular scenery mean it is definitely an area to explore on two wheels. We found the northern and eastern regions to be less hard going in human terms – friendlier reactions from locals and less of the hassle typical of coastal tourist resorts. Areas we would particularly recommend against are Kumasi and Accra, where traffic volumes are high and driver patience low. Like the locals, you may feel that pulling off on to the verge is the safest option on narrow roads when a vehicle approaches.

Ghana is a fantastic place to indulge in a spot of birdwatching, and perhaps cycling is the ideal way to appreciate the birdlife without having to set off on specific twitching expeditions. On the quiet forest roads, we found birds to be abundant and unperturbed by a passing cyclist. But be warned that craning to watch birds means you can't hole-in-the-road watch so closely, which can be rather dangerous! Cycling in Ghana, you'd be wise not to let your eyes stray from the road at all, in fact – judging by the abundance of tangled trotros and rusting wrecks on the verges, it was miraculous that we didn't witness a single crash in almost two months of cycling.

It pays to double-check your information for less-used routes – maps can be wrong, and even relying on a single source of local information is risky. Ghanaians have, in general, no sense of distance – so as not to disappoint, they will tell you

even more reckless than car and trotro drivers, and the risk of serious injury or fatal accidents on a bike is far higher. So do at least try to go with a driver who can provide you with a helmet.

By plane Several domestic carriers run reasonably affordable flights from Accra to Kumasi, Tamale, Takoradi and other locations. These cost around US$80 one-way to Kumasi and US$90–100 to Tamale. Carriers include **Starbow** (m 0245 000000; *www.flystarbow.com; online booking at www.ghanaticketservice.com*), and **Africa World Airlines** (m 0242 438888; *www.flyawa.com.gh*).

It's worth noting that there is now an online ticketing service (www. ghanaticketservice.com) that allows you to compare prices and book tickets for domestic flights with Starbow and Africa World. If you wish to use this service, payments can be made either with PayPal, credit card or bank transfer. Tickets are then sent to the passenger by email.

By boat A number of ferry services operate on Lake Volta, of which the most extensive is the weekly ferry service between Akosombo and Yeji, details of which are on page 292. There are also local 'short-hop' ferries between Yeji

how many kilometres it is to a certain place, but it rarely bears any relation to the real distance! Where settlements are close together, or the road a fast one, it doesn't matter too much, but, at the end of a long day on the piste, it can be demoralising to find yourself 10km from your destination ... then still 10km from your destination ...

As well as a willingness to give directions, the Ghanaians we encountered displayed a keen curiosity and surprise at our decision to explore their country by bike. It was assumed that we were too poor to afford other forms of transport and we were treated with great kindness on several occasions. Following a hold-up and robbery near Larabanga in the north, we were badly shaken but unhurt. Pedalling madly back to the village and safety, we were surrounded by a crowd of about 50 shocked and outraged villagers within minutes. Despite the sorry circumstances, this episode led to a display of real concern and kindness on the part of the villagers, who went out of their way to help us retrieve our possessions and apprehend the culprits. Shouts from the roadside – 'Who are you?' or 'Where are you going?' – can seem rude and abrupt, but it's only a first impression. Typically, the Ghanaians we got to know were exceedingly helpful and welcoming.

It's easy to burn 4,000 calories in a long day in the saddle, so finding and eating food took on great importance for us on our journey. We were happy to find that good cycling grub – especially for veggies – was easy to come by in Ghana. Some of the culinary colonial relics – British-style white bread, shandy, baked beans, Horlicks – provoked a bout of homesickness as well as a heightened appreciation of tasty indigenous cuisine! The fruit was perhaps the best thing – we found ourselves screeching to a halt by a roadside stall to fill our bar bags with pineapple, or papaya or bananas several times a day. By eating fresh produce, and staying in cheap hotels or camping, we found cycle-touring to be a really cheap way to explore Ghana. With our own transport, we had none of the hassles associated with trotro travel, and the added flexibility and slow pace meant we felt we got a real insight into the life of this very beautiful country.

and Makongo, Kpandu and Agordeke, and Ekye-Amanfrom and Adowso. Downriver of the lake, there are also ferry services from Ada Foah to Akuse and Anyanui.

ACCOMMODATION

By international standards, accommodation in Ghana tends to be of poor quality and rather overpriced. True, there are a handful of Ghanaian hotels – in Accra, Kumasi, Takoradi and a few of the major coastal resorts – that genuinely conform to international four- or five-star standards, but these tend to be exceptionally expensive, since their main clientele comprises government, NGO, business and other travellers who are not footing their own bills. The country also boasts a scattering of genuinely characterful and attractive budget to mid-range beach resorts and urban bed and breakfasts, many of them owner managed, and highlighted in the book as an 'Author's Favourite' (marked with the symbol ✳). But the overwhelming majority of accommodation options in Ghana consist of unremarkable town or beach hotels geared primarily to the local market, and characterised by some or all of the following flaws: indifferent staff, aesthetically challenged décor, ugly furniture, low standards of cleanliness, an erratic power or water supply, and slack maintenance (often manifested by broken fittings, leaky plumbing, noisy air conditioning, or advertised facilities that don't work). Having stated this upfront, it should be noted that we review hotels in this book in a Ghanaian context, so that use of words like 'clean', 'smart' or 'stylish'

HOTEL PRICE CODES	
$$$$$	US$180+
$$$$	US$100–180
$$$	US$40–100
$$	US$15–40
$	under US$15

might often seem unduly kind to new arrivals not yet used to local standards.

Unless they rent a car, most travellers will find that accommodation is proportionally the biggest drain on the budget. For the most budget-conscious, rooms typically start at around US$10-15, and come with fans, electricity and shared washing facilities, though cheaper dorms are available in some places. In most towns, US$20 will get you a self-contained room with a fan, while for upwards of US$30 you can expect to find a room with air conditioning, television, running hot water and a fridge. Note that in Ghana, rooms with en-suite toilet and bath are ubiquitously referred to as self-contained.

One quirk to watch out for in Ghana, particularly if you are travelling as a couple, is that a room advertised as a single will often have a double bed, while one advertised as a double might actually be a twin (ie: with two beds). Occasionally, and more bizarrely, you'll also find that by single room the hotel actually means a double room sharing toilet and shower facilities, while a double room has exactly the same bed but is self-contained. Generally, a couple will first be shown a room with two beds, presumably because it's the most expensive option, so if your preference is to share a bed, then ask to look at a single room first. If you're having trouble making your meaning clear, Ghanaians often talk about big and small beds – you're less likely to be misunderstood if you ask for a room with one big bed as opposed to asking for a double room. Note, too, that room prices quoted in this book's listings refer to what a room actually is rather than what the hotel bills it as: for instance, if the 'single' at any given hotel in in fact a double, then we refer to it as a double, not a single.

It is customary for cheaper hotels to supply guests with an under-sheet only. Many hotels will supply you with a sheet to sleep under upon request, but many won't. Most of the time in Ghana you don't really need a top-sheet to keep you warm, but it can be pleasant to have something to break the direct effect of a fan and to help keep off mosquitoes.

There are relatively few opportunities for camping in Ghana and, accommodation being as cheap as it is, for most people the hassle of carrying a tent and other camping equipment will outweigh the advantages. The major exception is if you expect to spend a lot of time visiting remote wildlife reserves and national parks, many of which are only realistically accessible to people with camping equipment. In addition, many backpacker-orientated resorts along the coast also allow camping.

Accommodation entries for this edition of this guide have been categorised under five main headings: **exclusive/luxury**, **upmarket**, **moderate**, **budget** and **shoestring**. This categorisation is not rigid, but should nevertheless help travellers to isolate the range of hotels in any given town that best suits their budget and taste. Broadly, exclusive or luxury hotels are truly world-class institutions that meet the highest standards, while upmarket hotels are three-star-plus affairs that meet international standards. Moderate hotels are typically one- or two-star lodgings that approach, but don't quite meet, international standards, and are still comfortable enough for most tourists, offering a range of good facilities such as air conditioning, DSTV (see page 86), en-suite hot showers and toilet. Budget accommodation mostly consists of ungraded hotels aimed largely at the local market, which definitely don't approach international standards, but are still reasonably comfortable and in many cases have air conditioning and en-suite facilities. Shoestring accommodation consists of the cheapest rooms around, usually unpretentious local guesthouses or church-affiliated hostels. The categorisation has been decided on the feel of the hotel as much as the price; it is often relative to the other options in that town, and there are many borderline cases.

EATING AND DRINKING

FOOD Local dishes generally comprise a starchy staple and some sort of soup or stew, often liberally flavoured with a hot, red powdered-pepper seasoning. Among the great many staples you're likely to encounter, the most popular are *fufu*, *kenkey, banku, akple, tuo zafi* (TZ), *omo tuo* (rice balls), boiled rice, and fried yam or plantain. Particularly popular in the south, fufu is made of cassava, plantain or yam, mashed until the starch breaks down and it becomes a gooey ball, then cooked with no water to form an even gooier one. It is served submerged in a soup, typically palm nut, groundnut (peanut), or a chicken-and-tomato-based 'light soup', and is not supposed to be chewed, but rather mashed against the palate with your tongue and swallowed that way, as otherwise you could chew on it for ages! Similar to each other in taste and sticky texture are banku and akple, both made of fermented maize and cassava, and often eaten with *okro* stew for double helpings of that gelatinous feel! Akple is particular to the Volta Region, while banku is found throughout Ghana. Kenkey is especially common among the Fante and Ga (indeed, they make two separate varieties of it) and also made of fermented maize, but is much firmer than banku or akple, as it's boiled in a removable wrapping of plantain leaves or corn husks before being served with a spicy tomato sauce or similar. Largely restricted to the north, tuo zafi is a millet- or maize-based porridge. Fried yam, often sold at markets, is not dissimilar in taste and texture to potato chips – though, when bought on the street, it often has a lingering, petroleum-like taste, presumably a result of using the same oil for too long – and is great eaten with spicy tomato relish, or soft green *palava sauce* made from spinach-like cocoyam leaves.

Other dishes worth trying include *red-red*, a delicious stew of black-eyed peas commonly eaten along the coast that's typically cooked with red palm oil and served over fried plantains. Red-red is potentially a good vegetarian option as well, as it's often served with an accompanying piece of chicken or fish, but neither are integral parts of the dish. Other plantain-based favourites include kalawole (pronounced 'keliweli'), which consists of soft, deep-fried cubes of plantain liberally seasoned with ginger, pepper and salt; and *titale*, which is very similar to *kalawole*, but mashed with flour and deep fried as fritters. Most travellers find Ghanaian staples to be an acquired taste, but stick around long enough and you might just find yourself looking up your local Ghanaian restaurant every now and then when you get back home. If you want to try and cook some up yourself, there's no better place to start than Fran Osseo-Asare and Barbara Baëta's vibrant and comprehensive *The Ghana Cookbook* (Hippocrene Books, 2015).

Local food can be eaten in small restaurants known as '**chop bars**', where you will generally be served a plate of fufu or kenkey or plain rice along with a portion of meat or vegetable stew, but perhaps the most characteristic of all chop-bar dishes is *jollof* rice – a savoury rice dish that shares a common origin with Senegal's *thiéboudiène*, where the rice is cooked in a tomato and vegetable stew rather than water, and often paired with some kind of meat or fish. Another easily found and perennially satisfying dish is *waakye*, which is basically the Ghanaian take on rice and beans, usually made with black-eyed peas. The beans and rice are cooked together and served with a complex (and always spicy) sauce known as *shito*, and usually a bit of fried tilapia on the side. A more interesting way of eating local food, and dirt cheap, is on the street. Most towns have at least one place where vendors sell a huge variety of dishes from informal stalls, often near the lorry station or the market. One advantage of eating on the street is you can try a bit of this or that, rather than be confronted with one specific dish. In addition to the usual staples, street vendors often sell grilled poultry (chicken or, in the north, guineafowl), spicy beef or goat kebabs, delicious sweet fried plantain with pepper seasoning, smoked fish, hard-boiled eggs stuffed with chilli and tomato relish, and deep-fried doughnut-like balls called *bofrot*. Sugar kenkey is sold in smaller bundles than savoury kenkey, and is sort of like semolina/tapioca, but more solid and eaten with super-hot pepper sauce. If you're craving dairy products, *wagashi* is a farmer's cheese made by the Fulani that can be eaten raw, but is most often available fried on the roadside.

Fresh fruit and vegetables are widely available, with a degree of regional and seasonal variety. The most characteristic fruits are probably pineapples, coconuts and oranges, the last skinned in a way that makes it easy to suck the liquid out without getting sticky fingers. Another unexpected pleasure for the sweet of tooth is the locally manufactured chocolate – not a complete surprise when you consider that Ghana is one of the world's major cocoa producers, but unexpectedly good all the same. As for 'vegetables', tomatoes, onions and yams are available practically everywhere, but most others are mainly restricted to the south and the larger towns of the north.

When it comes to **breakfast**, you'll pay a small fortune for an egg, bread and tea in your hotel, so head rather for one of the tea stalls that are to be found in most markets and lorry stations. These places serve fresh, tasty tomato and onion omelettes, as well as bread and hot drinks. Note, however, that in Ghana, 'tea' seems to be a blanket term covering all hot drinks, so instead of asking for tea or coffee, you should ask by brand name for Lipton (tea), Nescafé (coffee) or Milo (a chocolate malt drink). Bread, meanwhile, comes in three forms. The ordinary loaves, squarish but often with a pattern baked in, are known as sugar bread, and – appropriately enough – can be quite sweet. Better to eat with eggs or other savoury food is tea bread, a slightly crustier loaf that's often not much bigger than a large roll. You'll normally be able to find fresh tea bread somewhere around the market or lorry station, though you may want to resist any offer to have it smothered in margarine, since this is often rancid. Butter bread is light and soft, and frequently easier to find than tea bread.

Finally, most towns of substance have at least one restaurant serving exotic dishes, most often straight Western chicken or steak with chips or rice. Quite why, we don't know, but there are a large number of Chinese restaurants in Ghana, and many of the more Westernised places and superior chop houses serve Chinese-style fried rice and spring rolls. Outside Accra, a meal in a proper restaurant generally costs around US$5–10 per head excluding drinks, so it is a lot more expensive than eating on the street or in chop bars, which will generally work out at anywhere in the US$2–5 range, depending on what you order and which part of the country you're in. If you are not carrying a lot of cash on you, remember to check the small print of the menu before

RESTAURANT PRICE CODES

All prices below are quoted for a main course.

$$$	US$10+
$$	US$5–10
$	US$5 and below

you order, since many restaurants quote prices exclusive of VAT and service charge – so that you actually pay around 20% more than the stated price.

Vegetarians used to have a hard time of it in Ghana, and vegans might still struggle to establish whether any given restaurant dish is totally untainted by animal products, but these days most restaurants that regularly cater to travellers offer a few vegetarian options, and you are also pretty safe with staples like red-red or jollof rice. One vegetarian reader notes: 'My biggest piece of advice for vegetarians is come prepared with protein bars and nutritious spreads like Marmite, so you get plenty of iron and B vitamins, and multivitamins. Vegetarians should always think ahead when a Sunday or a public holiday is approaching, as many places are shut – we spent a few Sundays with some stale bread and whatever else we could get our hands on, which wasn't much.'

DRINKS Most visitors to Ghana drink a lot more than they would at home, thanks to the hot sticky climate, and since tap water is not recommended, you will probably find yourself going through several bought litres of water daily. This can be purchased in several forms. Conservative travellers will probably prefer to stick with 1.5-litre bottled mineral water, which is known locally as *Voltic* (after a well-known brand), and is widely available, inexpensive by international standards, and can usually be bought chilled on request. A far cheaper option, which most travellers drink without any problem, are the factory-sealed 500ml sachets known as 'pure water'. These labelled sachets contain genuine purified water (often with a strong chemical taste to prove it), are usually chilled, and cost the equivalent of US$0.05 (or if you are based somewhere for a while, you can buy a pack of 30, containing a total of 15 litres, for US$1). Elsewhere, mainly in small villages, 'ice water' is sold in unmarked plastic bags and comes from an undetermined source, so is perhaps best avoided. For a change of flavour, you can spice up the water with a sachet of Tang, a powdered orange or mango drink with added vitamins.

The usual brand-name sodas are widely available in Ghana's fridges, and are very cheap by any standards (though as a tourist you may sometimes be urged to buy an imported can of the same drink for twice the price. In addition to the international brands, there are a few uniquely Ghanaian minerals available. At most bus stations, for instance, you'll also see men trundling around with a selection of Fan Ice products, which include great strawberry frozen yoghurts in sachets, frozen chocolate milk, ice cream and a refreshing citrus-based drink called Tampico. Bottled pure orange and pineapple juice from Accra is also widely available at bars and restaurants catering to tourists. Also worth trying are the surprisingly good, sweetened Kalyppo fruit juices that come in 250ml packs. A cheap, refreshing and highly nutritious drink is fresh coconut juice. You'll often see street vendors selling piles of coconuts, particularly along the coast – just ask them to chop one open and you can slurp down the liquid.

The most widespread alcoholic drink is lager, which is brewed locally, generally pretty good (though occasionally flat) and drunk most cheaply at local bars, usually called 'spots'. A standard 750ml bottle costs anything from US$1 to US$3, depending on where you drink, but be aware that the smaller 375ml bottles are often relatively overpriced, especially at tourist hotels that don't stock large beers. Several brands are available, most commonly Club and Star, both with an alcohol level of around 5%. Also widely available are litre boxes of very cheap Don Garcia red and white wines, but imported bottled wine is also increasingly easy to locate, starting at around US$5 per bottle in garages and supermarkets. Draught beer (sometimes referred to as 'bubra') is typically only available at upmarket bars or hotels.

If you're interested in trying local tipples, several are available, all very cheap and generally rather potent. *Pito* is a type of millet beer, similar to the local beer brewed in villages in many parts of Africa, and most easily located in the pito bars that can be found in most towns, especially in the north. Palm wine, easily located on the coast, is called *ntunkum* in its mildest form and *doka* when it is older and stronger. *Akpeteshie* is a fiery spirit distilled from palm wine. It's frequently offered to visitors when they visit a village chief – the correct protocol is to spill a few drops on the ground in honour of the ancestors before you swig it down. Akpeteshie is also commonly infused with a variety of roots and bark to create a powerful herbal liquor known as bitters, which is commonly believed to do wonders for your virility. In addition to the home-brew variety, it's widely available from commercial producers such as Alomo and Kasapreko. Another popular drink is schnapps, which is the customary liquor used when it comes to visiting chiefs and making libations, a preference that dates back several centuries to the Dutch presence on the Gold Coast.

PUBLIC HOLIDAYS

Although several public holidays are recognised in Ghana, the only major impact they will have on tourists is that banks and government offices are closed and the volume of public transport decreases to a level you'd expect on a Sunday. There are four variable-date public holidays: the Christian Good Friday and Easter Monday, and the Muslim Eid al-Fitr and Eid al-Adha.

In addition, the following fixed-date public holidays are recognised:

1 January	New Year's Day
6 March	Independence Day
1 May	May Day
25 May	Africa Unity Day
1 July	Republic Day
21 September	Founder's Day (Kwame Nkrumah's birthday)
1st Friday in December	Farmers' Day
25 December	Christmas Day
26 December	Boxing Day

If the holiday falls at the weekend, the 'free day' shifts to the following Monday. One reader adds that: 'On two occasions during our six months in Ghana, public holidays were announced at short notice – both on Mondays! If you're travelling when this happens, public transport will be minimal and banks are closed, so keep your ear to the ground.'

MEDIA AND COMMUNICATIONS

NEWSPAPERS Several English-language newspapers are printed in Ghana, of which the well-established *Daily Graphic* (*www.graphic.com.gh*) is probably the best and gives you a good grounding in what are the hot debates during your visit. Other titles include the well-respected *Ghanaian Times* (*www.ghanaiantimes.com.gh*) and *Ghanaian Chronicle* (*www.thechronicle.com.gh*). In Accra, you can buy imported newspapers at a highly inflated price.

TELEPHONE Ghana Telecom was privatised in 2008, with Vodafone Ghana (*www. vodafone.com.gh*) now the country's main service provider for landlines. If you're

FARMERS' DAY   *Ama Branford-Arthur*

Farmers' Day was instituted in 1984, after a particularly bad period of drought and hunger the previous year, when it hardly rained, there was a very bad harvest, widespread bush fires, and many Ghanaians starved. To compound the problem, Nigeria deported a great number of Ghanaians who were working in that country, who arrived to swell the population.

I remember that at that time, kenkey, a staple food of many Ghanaians, was not allowed to be cooked at the kenkey seller's house, so great was the demand. The trick was to arrive early, buy as many uncooked balls as you were allowed, and then to take them home and cook them yourself. These were the early days of Jerry Rawlings's revolution, which started on 31 December 1981, and the economy was in serious trouble – it's amazing that the drought didn't cause it to collapse entirely.

In 1984, the IMF and the World Bank stepped in to help, but, more fortunately, it rained. The harvest was much better, and so Farmers' Day was instituted to thank the hard-working and often unrewarded farmers for their efforts. It was not initially a holiday, though. Indeed, we believe it was not until 1988 that it was declared a national holiday.

Farmers from all over the country are assessed by visits to their farms from extension officers of the Ministry of Agriculture, who evaluate their farming methods, acreage, diversity of products and their yield. Winners are chosen in each category by a central committee. There are two sets of best farmers – those that are entered at national level, and those that win at regional level.

A couple of weeks before Farmers' Day proper, all the national-level farmers are invited to Accra. Accompanied by 'chaperones' from the ministry, they tour the sights, go on the Akosombo Lake, visit the president, and are royally wined and dined. Note that none of them knows, at this stage, who will be chosen National Best Farmer.

On the actual day, all the winning farmers are taken to the durbar grounds, which have been different each year. The event is broadcast on national television. Starting in reverse order, and with appropriate prizes, each of them is honoured. The crowning moment is the unveiling of the National Best Farmer (NBF), with an impressive reeling off of his/her achievements by the MC. When he/she is called to the podium, he/she receives from last year's NBF a traditional sword, symbolising a passing on of the responsibility for feeding Ghana's very hungry population.

When the awards first started, the NBF received a pair of farming wellington boots, a set of cutlasses, a power tiller and 12yds of wax cloth. Prizes have expanded to include a visit to the Royal Agricultural Festival in Kew, UK, and even houses and trucks. Ibrahim Musa, the 2015 NBF was awarded a car, laptop and 3,000GHC cash prize. Though he was away in South Africa this year, typically when the farmer has received a car, the president has been his driver, chauffeuring him around the durbar grounds to the cheers of the crowd. Throughout the year, whoever won will take part in programmes and discussions, and past NBFs have set up training for young people.

going to be in Ghana for any length of time, rather than roaming on your home number, which can be very costly, it is worth buying a local SIM card and inserting it in your phone. This is a simple and inexpensive procedure that also allows you to

TRADITIONAL FESTIVALS

A notable feature of Ghanaian society, and one that is of great interest to travellers, is the enormous number of local festivals that take place in various parts of the country throughout the year. Few travellers are likely deliberately to select the dates of their trip to Ghana to coincide with any one particular festival, but it's certainly worth taking note of any festivals that will take place while you are in Ghana and making the effort to be in the right place at the right time, bearing in mind that accommodation may be in relatively short supply in some areas during the most important festivals.

If you are visiting Ghana in early May, do try to get to Winneba for the first weekend of the month, in time for the renowned **Aboakyir deer-hunting festival**, one of the most ancient in the country, described in detail in the section on Winneba (see page 179).

Most other festivals in coastal parts of Ghana take place during the European autumn. The most important annual festival in Greater Accra Region, celebrated in the capital as well as in other Ga towns such as Prampram, is **Homowo**, which literally means 'mocking hunger'. It takes place in August and September, the months that normally yield the largest harvest of fish and grain. A similar festival, called **Damba**, takes place in Northern Region, centred on Tamale, during the same months.

The most important festival in the Fante calendar is the colourful **Oguaa Fetu Afahye** (the last word literally means 'adorning of new clothes'), on the first Saturday of September, when local chiefs and *asafo* companies dressed in full traditional regalia lead processions through the streets of Cape Coast.

The main festival in Anomabu is the five-day-long **Bontungu** in August, in which a variety of drumming and dancing rituals are held to bring God's blessing for the forthcoming year.

In Elmina, the **Bakatue Festival** takes place a bit earlier in the year, on the first Tuesday of July, the beginning of a new fishing season. Characterised by a variety of processions and competitions, this festival is said to pre-date the arrival of the Portuguese at Elmina 500 years ago, making it one of the most ancient in Ghana.

link other facilities on your phone (internet access, emails, etc) to a local provider. The major networks are MTN (*www.mtn.com.gh*), Tigo (*www.tigo.com.gh*) and Vodafone (*www.vodafone.com.gh*), all of which offer good network coverage, even in quite out-of-the-way places. Mobile phone numbers all start with '02' or '05'. In this book, the ten digits are transcribed with a space between the fourth and fifth digit to distinguish them from landlines, which are now also ten digits but are transcribed with a space between the fifth and sixth digit.

Ghana's fixed-line telephone system is reasonably efficient. From overseas, it's one of the easiest African countries to get through to first time. The ringing tone is a single short tone followed by a longer pause, and the engaged tone is equal lengths on and off. International calls out of Ghana can be made at official telecommunication centres, and a bit more expensively (but with less queuing) at many upmarket hotels and at private telecommunication centres offering IDD (International Direct Dialling) – the latter is usually available even in small towns. Dialling overseas, the country code should be preceded by 00. Dialling into Ghana, the international code is +233.

The ubiquity and relative efficiency of mobile phones in Ghana mean that many hotels and other organisations have discontinued their landlines. Unfortunately,

In Volta Region, the whole of September is given over to the **Yam Festival**, and two other important festivals take place during November. In Anloga, near Keta, on the first Saturday of the month, **Hogbetsotso** (pronounced 'Hobejojo') or the 'Exodus' Festival, commemorates the escape of the Ewe people from a tyrannical ruler in what is now Togo. It is marked by processions of traditionally dressed chiefs as well as lively drumming and dancing (note that a similar festival called the Godigbeza takes place in nearby Aflao every April). Later in November, the **Agumatsa Waterfall Festival** in Wli traditional area is also characterised by dancing, drumming and colourful costumes.

There is a small festival in Kumasi and other parts of Ashanti twice during each of the nine 42-day cycles, or *adae*, into which their annual calendar is divided. It is difficult to give dates for these, since they change from year to year (as astute mathematicians will realise, 9 x 42 does not equal 365), but basically the festival days fall on every sixth Sunday, and then the 17th day after that, always a Wednesday.

The most important annual festival in Ashanti is **Odwira**, a week-long affair that climaxes on Friday with a procession through town to the palace. The Odwira generally takes place during the ninth adae of the calendar, which falls in September. Among the most lively celebrations are those in Kumasi, Akwapim, Akrapong, Akuapem and Akwamu.

Visitors to northern Ghana may want to note the following festival dates:

22 January	Kpini Kyiu Festival	Wa
7 March	Kyiu Sung Festival	Upper East and West regions
14 May	Don Festival	Wa, Bawku, Bolgatanga
11 June	Dzimbi Festival	Upper East and West regions
1–12 November	Daa Festival	Tongo
9 November	Sabre Dance Festival	Lawra
15 November	Kobina Festival	Lawra
28 November	Boarim Festival	Tongo
1 December	Fao Festival	Navrongo

when it comes to hotels, this means that contact numbers tend to change more regularly than is the case with fixed lines – indeed, the number for many hotels is simply that of the receptionist or the manager's personal mobile phone. Unfortunately, there is nothing we can do about this, but we have included both numbers where they exist, on the basis that the mobile will usually be easier to get through to, but there's a far greater chance a landline will still be in place in two or three years' time. Readers are welcome to alert us to any such changes by posting on our website (*www.bradtupdates.com/ghana*).

POST Ghana's international postal service is cheap and reasonably reliable, but often very slow. One reader who worked in Ghana for a while reckons that sending mail from Ghana to Europe (Holland, England and Belgium) was generally about six times faster than the other way around (about one week to Europe, but up to eight weeks from Europe).

RADIO AND TELEVISION The Ghana Broadcasting Corporation (*www.gbcghana. com*) produces a reasonable television service by African standards, though it's nothing to shout about by any other. The state-owned radio service, by contrast, is quite exceptional, with some good news and issue coverage and an eclectic mix of music – except on Sundays when it's hijacked by God, or rather his earthly representatives. You can pick it up on 95.7 FM. The last few years have seen a boom in commercial radio stations, most of which seem to combine chat shows with local and international music (dominated by reggae and contemporary R&B).

Most hotels in Ghana now subscribe to a South African satellite multi-channel pay service called DSTV, or to a more limited local package called Multi. The DSTV package varies from one hotel to the next, but it generally includes M-Net, which shows reasonably current movies and serials, as well as Movie Magic (mostly one- to two-year-old movies), BBC World, CNN and Supersport, the last showing a good selection of current sporting events, with an inevitable bias to sports popular in South Africa (football, cricket, rugby) and events involving South African teams.

INTERNET AND EMAIL Internet is widely available throughout the country. Travellers carrying smartphones, tablets, laptops or other such devices can easily obtain 24-hour internet access by buying a local SIM card or a portable modem with a USB port from a local provider such as MTN or Vodafone. Most mid-range to upmarket hotels (and even some cheaper ones) now offer a free Wi-Fi service, and for those without, dozens of internet cafés can be found in Accra, concentrated in Osu and, to a lesser extent, Adabraka, and there are private internet cafés in most other substantial towns. Rates are very reasonable, and while servers are generally quite slow by comparison with Europe or North America, this is improving all the time. The cafés operated by Vodafone are particularly recommended.

BUSINESS

The first port of call for anybody thinking of establishing a business in Ghana should be the **Ghana Promotion Investment Centre** (✆ 03026 65125–9; m 0244 318252/4; e info@gipcghana.com; www.gipcghana.com).

CULTURAL ETIQUETTE

Ghana, like any country, has its rules of etiquette, and while allowances will normally be made for tourists, there is some value in ensuring that they don't have to be made too frequently!

Visitors to the north of Ghana should bear in mind that it is considered highly insulting to use your left hand to pass or receive something, or (a common custom in Muslim countries) when shaking hands. If you eat with your fingers, it is customary throughout Ghana to use only the right hand.

Greeting procedures tend to be more formalised in Ghana than in modern Western societies, especially in small towns and villages, and elderly people in particular should be treated with special respect. If you need to ask somebody directions, or anything else for that matter, it is considered very rude to blunder straight into interrogative mode without first exchanging greetings – even when shopping. At village level, it is polite for strangers to say hello to anybody they pass along the way.

It is customary to visit the chief of any village where you intend to stay overnight or to do any local sightseeing. In practice, this is no longer necessary in many villages, and where the custom has been continued in places that regularly receive tourists it tends to feel a bit showy. Only when you travel in really out-of-the-way

TAKING IT EASY   *Conal Ho*

Having lived in Ghana for some time, I would advise Westerners to take things as light-heartedly as they can. Laugh at ridiculous situations and act in a humorous way when you find yourself in a situation that seems ridiculous, or you are being asked absurd questions. For instance, there are times when the traveller can find the calls of, '*Obruni! Obruni!*', tiring. Of course it is silly, but if you lightly call back, '*Bebeni! Bebeni!*' (which means 'black person'), people will generally like the fact that you can speak a few Twi phrases and enjoy you being funny with them, too.

I think the most important single point of etiquette is *always* to greet someone first and ask them how things are going. I typically begin with the salutation 'Sister', 'My friend', 'Auntie', 'Uncle' or 'Brother', as applicable. Then, after they answer and return the greeting, you can start asking them for a favour, begin bargaining, or enquire about the price of something. Greetings are the first and foremost single point of etiquette to learn in Ghana, especially for many Westerners, who may not find it intuitive to greet their waiters or hotel clerk before asking something.

areas is a visit to the chief likely to feel like a matter of etiquette over commerce, and here you should be especially careful to observe protocol. You will be expected to pay tribute in the form of kola nuts, a bottle of schnapps or money (the equivalent of about US$2 is normally fine). In return, you may receive a glass of *akpeteshie* (local gin), and it would be rude to refuse unless you use the excuse that you don't touch alcohol. Before drinking the gin, pour a few drops on the ground as a tribute to the forefathers. You should always take off your hat or cap in the presence of a chief (or any old person), and should never sit with your legs crossed in his presence.

INTERACTING WITH GHANAIANS   Ghana has a reputation as one of the friendliest countries in West Africa, a title that is patently absurd, but probably quite justified. Taken as a whole, Ghanaians do seem to be remarkably affable and friendly both among themselves and in their dealings with tourists, and we find it difficult to think of any other African country where we felt so safe or unhassled. First-time visitors to Africa, or at least those with a white skin, may be surprised at the amount of attention they draw by virtue of their conspicuous foreignness – symptoms of which range from having every passing taxi in Accra blare its horn at you, to being greeted by mobs of exuberant children chanting '*Obruni*' as you walk past. At times, this can be exhausting, but we cannot recall an incident of this type that was underscored by anything approaching malice. Put simply, Ghana is an amazingly welcoming country, and although you'll sometimes encounter people who treat all Westerners like a walking ATM, they are the exception, not the rule. You'd have to be extraordinarily unlucky to experience anything that could be described as seriously threatening or unpleasant. If you do feel mobbed by Ghanaians asking you 'one thing', or who want to 'take you as a friend', a good way of moving on is enthusiastically to wave goodbye or just say, 'Later'. Generally, Ghanaians will happily accept your promise without any real expectation that you will stick to it, and you will be able to make an exit without their facing the social humiliation of having you shake your head or say no. If hassle starts to become more intrusive and less good-humoured – and certainly if a Ghanaian touches you without permission – it is perfectly acceptable and nearly always more effective to make a big fuss of saying no.

Guides and tipping Based on our 2016 research trip, it seems that the constant stream of aspirant guides who used to attach themselves to travellers in Ghana, contributing little to their experience other than chit-chat and arbitrary requests for money, is largely a thing of the past. However, there are still many situations where tourists are required or expected to take a guide. Often, this is an unambiguously worthwhile investment, eg: when visiting game reserves (where it is not permitted to walk without an armed guide), or at many historical sites (where knowledgeable guides are generally provided by request only), or at community ecotourism sites such as Tafi Atome or Paga. In such clear-cut circumstances – basically, where you are allocated a guide by an institution – you *will* normally pay a fee, but since this will not go directly to the guide (who in all probability is poorly paid), it is proper and customary to tip. It's difficult to give an exact guideline for tipping, since this depends on group size and the quality of service, but at current exchange rates, a figure of around US$1 per group member per hour feels about right. Another approach would be to tip the equivalent of half of the guide fee, bearing in mind that these are generally very reasonable.

The guide situation becomes more ambiguous when it isn't institutionalised. Even here, though, there are some reasonably straightforward scenarios. At places such as Bonwire, for instance, visitors are normally approached by a cluster of prospective guides on arrival. There is no reason why you should take one on in such circumstances but, once you've selected somebody who seems a good bet and you've agreed a fee, you'll be left in peace by the other guides, and the one you've chosen will generally be able to add a great deal of insight to what you see. One cautionary note in this sort of situation is that guides will often agree to a fee, but then when you pay them this amount they go on a major sulk because you haven't tipped them. We don't see any valid reason why an additional tip should be given to a private individual with whom you've already agreed a fee, and nine times out of ten, when people sulk, they are simply chancing it.

The right approach to this sort of situation – particularly when the guide comes up with the old 'you pay whatever you like' line – is to talk through costs at the negotiation stage. Stress to the guide that whatever fee is agreed is final and inclusive of a tip. Check, too, what other fees must be paid – it's not unusual to agree to a guide fee thinking that it covers the full excursion, only to find that the village chief also wants his fee, the caretaker his fee, the guy who thrusts himself unbidden into the middle of your photo his modelling fee, etc. This may feel like nit-picking to our Western mentalities, but Africans are accustomed to negotiation and will not be offended if it is conducted in good humour. The reality is that most of us in most situations are more comfortable when we get a full quote than when there are hidden extras. The overwhelming argument in favour of clarifying things at the outset is that it will decrease the likelihood of bad feeling later.

It is not customary to tip for service in local bars and chop bars, though you may sometimes want to leave a small something (in fact, given the difficulty of finding change in Ghana, you are often practically forced to). Many restaurants catering to Western palates automatically add a service charge to the bill. In theory, the tip goes to the waiter, but we are not convinced about how often this happens in practice, so you may still want to give a cash tip. Restaurant tipping standards are more in line with Europe (around 10% of the bill) than with the USA.

Asking directions There is no polite way of saying it: most Ghanaians are utterly clueless when it comes to estimating distance (or time) in any measure more objective than 'far' and 'not far'. Travellers, particularly those needing directions off the beaten track, will have to allow for this.

VOLUNTEERING IN GHANA   *Dominic Durose*

Volunteer projects in Ghana offer an amazing opportunity for individuals to live, work and have fun in a new and exciting country; having lived in Accra for six months myself, working in an advertising firm with i-to-i Volunteer & Work Abroad (*www.i-to-i.com*), I can thoroughly recommend the experience. However, there are a few things that are worth considering before you leave.

To begin with, it can often feel restrictive and unsettling living in a new and unfamiliar environment, so much so that there can be the temptation to neglect your placement. It is important to think carefully before you depart about the things that you wish to achieve as a volunteer, as this can go a long way to ensuring that your time in Ghana is as beneficial to both yourself and your placement as possible.

This is not to say that volunteer projects are all work and no play; the laid-back lifestyle in Ghana lends itself to flexibility. If I wanted an afternoon off to do a little relaxing at the beach, or even a couple of weeks to explore the wilds of Ghana, my placement was more than happy to accommodate me.

The working style in Ghana is very different from that in the West, with a much more relaxed approach to working hours and productivity. It can be frustrating when things appear to be at a standstill, but be patient; once you get used to the rhythm and pace of life, you'll tend to find that things have a way of running smoothly of their own accord.

During the first few weeks, you are certain to feel the effects of culture shock to one degree or another. Nevertheless, as you begin to settle into your placement you will learn to accept the differences in your new environment, and who knows, you may even prefer them.

The fact that I was living with other volunteers served as an ideal parachute to settle me into Ghanaian life. Many of them had been in the country for a few months already and had acquired local knowledge that was invaluable in helping me through those first few disorientating weeks. I found that socialising with the Ghanaian people I was working with was hugely beneficial, too; after all, they were the people guaranteed to be with me for the entirety of my placement.

Overall, volunteering in Ghana was a fantastic experience, one that I will cherish for the rest of my life. For me, it was the little things that mattered most: the greeting of a bread seller as I walked to work and the friendly shouts of the local schoolchildren as I joined in their game of football. Becoming part of my community is something that, although it wasn't easy, brought me the most enormous amount of satisfaction during my stay.

One regular and reasonably straightforward area of confusion is the difference between miles and kilometres, measurements that many Ghanaians seem to treat as interchangeable. It's always better to ask for a distance in miles, the measure still used by most people, even though signposts generally show distances in kilometres. If you're not familiar with one or other system of measurement, you can convert distances using the equation that five miles is roughly equivalent to eight kilometres, while three feet (or a yard) is basically the same as one metre – imprecise equations, we grant you, but more than adequate for practical travel purposes. Another way of verifying distances is to ask both the distance and the time – in reasonably flat conditions, a reasonably fit walker will not cover significantly more than 6km (3½ miles) in an hour.

That said, it's difficult to figure out how a bar worker who not only speaks good English, but also has the capacity to make drawing a pint of draught look as exhausting as running a marathon, can say that a hotel 2km distant is three minutes' walk away. Or how people living at Larabanga and Mole, not to say various books, can come up with estimates as divergent as 3km and 10km for the road between Larabanga and Mole Motel. Or how a signpost at Vane reads 'Amedzofe 5km' when the two towns are less than 3km apart by road. We hit this sort of problem on a daily basis, and found it difficult to escape the conclusion that a lot of Ghanaians simply say whatever figure first comes into their head – not with the deliberate intent of misleading visitors, but either to oblige you with the information they think you want to hear, or because the measurements that are so important to us mean very little to somebody who has lived in a small town all their life and 'knows' how far one place is from another without ever having had reason to translate that knowledge into hours or kilometres.

It goes without saying that a great deal more interrogation about distances is required when you're researching a travel guide than when you are using one. Still, two points ought to be passed on to readers. The first, particularly if you are hiking, is to ask at least three or four people how far away somewhere is, to use some judgement in interpreting the answers, and to accept that you'll probably never know for sure until you walk there yourself. The second is that we've had to 'guestimate' a great many walking distances in this guide, but they are informed and generally based on first-hand experience, and – unlike many of the short distances that are quoted so emphatically by other books, by people you meet, and even on some maps – they will not be wildly out.

PUBLIC TOILETS For those unused to travel in the developing world, it should be noted that public toilets in Ghana, as in most other parts of Africa, leave much to be desired by Western standards. Often, few such facilities are available – in many rural areas, specific stretches of beach or patches of wasteland serve as communal dumping grounds – and where they do exist, they tend to be dirty and may not have running water. Restaurants, hotels and bars are your best bet if you are caught short, though smaller chop shops and drinking spots won't normally have a toilet. Many bus stations have public toilets that are kept reasonably clean by virtue of charging a small fee for use and toilet paper. It's still a good idea always to carry some toilet paper around with you however, as not all toilets will have it. One reader suggests: 'When you need to use the loo urgently, a bank is a great place – maybe the staff take pity on a wandering obruni, but not once have I been turned down!'

Among Ghanaians, it seems to be perfectly acceptable to urinate publicly – men pretty much anywhere, women more generally in rural areas than in towns – a solution more likely, perhaps, to appeal to male travellers than to female ones. To be sure of not offending anybody, it's a good idea to ask a local person of the same gender where you can urinate. Nobody will find this strange – in my experience, Ghanaians are not at all coy about this sort of thing (I've often asked for a toilet in a bar and been asked bluntly – sometimes with graphic miming gestures – whether I need to urinate or the other thing). What will create total confusion is if you resort to euphemisms or more informal, slangy terms!

SMOKING *based on information by Carole Allsop and Tony Kaleda*
Smoking is pretty uncommon in Ghana, and often associated with fast or immoral living by the Ghanaian middle classes – although it is better understood

by foreigners. As such, it's not easy to find cigarettes in small towns, and you will usually have to ask for an ashtray in bars. Some cigarettes are readily available in cities and larger towns, with the most popular brands being Rothmans and 555s, which are very cheap by international standards (about 10% of the UK price). You can also try Tusker, which are even cheaper, but also very rough. Marlboro cigarettes are rarely available, but, when you can find them, they are still pretty inexpensive by international standards. Loose tobacco is very hard to find, so roll-up fans should bring their own tobacco with them.

UPDATES WEBSITE

Go to www.bradtupdates.com/ghana for the latest on-the-ground travel news, trip reports and factual updates. Keep up to date with the latest posts by following Philip on Twitter (🐦 @philipbriggs) and via Facebook: 📘 fb.me/pb.travel.updates. And, if you have any comments, queries, grumbles, insights, news or other feedback, you're invited to post them directly on the website, or to email them to Philip (e philip.briggs@ bradtguides.com) for inclusion.

M&J TRAVEL AND TOURS

Ghana • Togo • Benin • Burkina Faso • Ivory Coast

Location: Opposite U.N.D.P Head Offices Ring Road East
Office: 0302 773498
Mobile: 0244 156309
　　　　0244 514824

Your full service DMC founded in 1991 by locals

- Extensive Local Knowledge, Expertise & Resources
- Planning Professional & Hassle Free Land Arrangements
- 24/7 Service

Themed Events & Meeting Organizers

Transportation:
Experienced Driver Guides
Vehicle Rentals of Mini Buses, Coaches, Sedan and 4 by 4

Transfers:
Airport/Harbour Drop Off or Pick Up for Individuals & Groups
Tamale to Mole National Park
Meet & Greet
VIP lounge
Visa Upon Arrival

Flight Bookings:
Domestic & International

Tours:
Professional & Experienced Bilingual Guides
Tailor Made for Individuals & Groups
Packaged Half Day & Multi Days

Accommodation Bookings:
Budget, Mid-Range and Luxury

Medical Services & Treatment

Relocation & Domiciliation Services

Visa Assistance & Work Permits

info@mandjtravelghana.com | www.mandjtravelghana.com

4

Health

with Dr Felicity Nicholson

This is the chapter that always gives us the creeps when we read a travel guide, and we're quite sure that some readers will question the sanity of travelling to Ghana by the time they finish this one. Don't let it get to you – with the right vaccinations and a sensible attitude to malaria prevention, the chances of serious mishap are small. It may help to put things into perspective to point out that, after malaria, your greatest concern in Ghana should not be the combined exotica of venomous snakes, stampeding elephants, gun-happy soldiers or the Ebola virus, but something altogether more mundane: a road accident.

Road accidents are very common in many parts of Ghana so be aware and do what you can to reduce risks: try to travel during daylight hours, always wear a seatbelt, and refuse to be driven by anyone who has been drinking. Listen to local advice about areas where violent crime is rife, too.

There are private clinics, hospitals and pharmacies in most large towns, and doctors generally speak fluent English. Consultation fees and laboratory tests are remarkably inexpensive when compared with most Western countries, so if you do fall sick it would be absurd to let financial considerations dissuade you from seeking medical help. Commonly required medicines, such as broad-spectrum antibiotics and Flagyl (though tinidazole is easier to take, it is not generally available in Ghana), are widely available and cheap throughout the region, as are malaria cures and prophylactics. It is advisable to carry all malaria-related tablets (whether for prophylaxis or treatment) with you, and only rely on their availability locally if you need to restock your supplies.

If you are on any medication prior to departure, or you have specific needs relating to a known medical condition (eg: if you are allergic to bee stings, or you are prone to attacks of asthma, which may be exacerbated by the high dust levels), then you are strongly advised to bring any related drugs and devices with you.

PREPARATIONS

Sensible preparation will go a long way to ensuring your trip goes smoothly. Particularly for first-time visitors to Africa, this includes a visit to a travel clinic to discuss matters such as vaccinations and malaria prevention. A list of recommended travel clinic websites worldwide is available at www.itsm.org, and other useful websites for prospective travellers include www.travelhealthpro.org.uk and www.netdoctor. co.uk/travel. The Bradt website now carries a health section online (*www.bradtguides. com/africahealth*) to help travellers prepare for their African trip, elaborating on most points raised below, but the following summary points are worth emphasising:

- Don't travel without comprehensive medical **travel insurance** that will fly you home in an emergency.

- Make sure all your **immunisations** are up to date. Proof of vaccination against **yellow fever** is needed for entry into Ghana for all travellers aged nine months and over. If the vaccine is not suitable for you, then obtain an exemption certificate from your GP or a travel clinic. However, you need to consider the risks involved in travelling to Ghana without protection for a potentially fatal disease. It is also wise to be up to date on **tetanus, polio** and **diphtheria** (now given as an all-in-one vaccine, Revaxis, which lasts for ten years), **typhoid** and **hepatitis A**. Immunisations against meningococcus, hepatitis B, cholera and rabies may also be recommended.

- The biggest health threat is **malaria**. There is no vaccine against this mosquito-borne disease, but a variety of preventative drugs is available, including mefloquine (Lariam), atovaquone/proguanil (Malarone) and the antibiotic doxycycline. The most suitable choice of drug varies depending on the individual and the country they are visiting, so consult your GP or a travel clinic for medical advice. If you will be spending a long time in Africa, and expect to visit remote areas, be aware that no preventative drug is 100% effective, so carry a cure, too. It is also worth noting that no homeopathic prophylactic for malaria exists, nor can any traveller acquire effective resistance to malaria. Those who don't make use of preventative drugs risk their life in a manner that is both foolish and unnecessary.

- Though advised for everyone, a **pre-exposure rabies vaccination**, involving three doses taken over a minimum of 21 days, is particularly important if you intend to have contact with animals, or are likely to be 24 hours away from medical help.

- Anybody travelling away from major centres should carry a **personal first-aid kit**. Contents might include a good drying antiseptic (eg: iodine or potassium permanganate), Band-Aids, suncream, insect repellent, aspirin or paracetamol, antifungal cream (eg: Canesten), ciprofloxacin or norfloxacin (for severe diarrhoea), antibiotic eye drops, tweezers, condoms or femidoms, a digital thermometer and a needle-and-syringe kit with accompanying letter from a health-care professional.

- Bring any **drugs or devices relating to known medical conditions** with you. That applies both to those who are on medication prior to departure, and those who are, for instance, allergic to bee stings, or are prone to attacks of asthma.

- Prolonged immobility on long-haul flights can result in **deep vein thrombosis** (DVT), which can be dangerous if the clot travels to the lungs to cause pulmonary embolus. The risk increases with age, and is higher in obese or pregnant travellers, heavy smokers, those taller than 6ft/1.8m or shorter than 5ft/1.5m, and anybody with a history of clots, recent major operation or varicose veins surgery, cancer, a stroke or heart disease. If any of these criteria apply, consult a doctor before you travel.

COMMON MEDICAL PROBLEMS

MALARIA Along with road accidents, malaria poses the single biggest serious threat to the health of travellers in most parts of tropical Africa, Ghana included. It is unwise to travel in malarial parts of Africa whilst pregnant or with children unless there is a compelling reason: the risk of malaria in many parts is considerable and these travellers are likely to succumb rapidly to the disease. The *Anopheles* mosquito that transmits the parasite should be assumed to be present at all altitudes below 1,800m, a category that includes all of Ghana.

LONG-HAUL FLIGHTS, CLOTS AND DVT

Any prolonged immobility, including travel by land or air, can result in deep vein thrombosis (DVT) with the risk of embolus to the lungs. Certain factors can increase the risk and these include:

- Previous clot or having a close relative with a history
- Being over 40, but there is a greater risk of clots in those over 80 years old
- Recent major operation or varicose veins surgery
- Cancer
- Stroke
- Heart disease
- Obesity
- Pregnancy
- Hormone therapy
- Heavy smoking
- Severe varicose veins
- Being very tall (over 6ft/1.8m) or short (under 5ft/1.5m)

A deep vein thrombosis (DVT) causes painful swelling and redness of the calf or sometimes the thigh. It is only dangerous if a clot travels to the lungs (pulmonary embolus). Symptoms of a pulmonary embolus (PE) include chest pain, shortness of breath and sometimes coughing up small amounts of blood, and commonly start three to ten days after a long flight. Anyone who thinks that they might have a DVT needs to see a doctor immediately.

PREVENTION OF DVT
- Keep mobile before and during the flight; move around every couple of hours
- Drink plenty of fluids during the flight
- Avoid taking sleeping pills and excessive tea, coffee and alcohol
- Consider wearing flight socks or support stockings

If you think you are at increased risk of a clot, ask your doctor if it is safe to travel.

Since no malaria prophylactic is 100% effective, it makes sense to take all reasonable precautions against being bitten by the nocturnal *Anopheles* mosquitoes that transmit the disease (see box, page 98). Malaria usually manifests within two weeks of transmission (though it can be as short as seven days), but it can take months, which means that short-stay visitors are most likely to experience symptoms after they return home. These typically include a rapid rise in temperature (over 38°C), and any combination of a headache, flu-like aches and pains, a general sense of disorientation, and possibly even nausea and diarrhoea. The earlier malaria is detected, the better it usually responds to treatment. So if you display possible symptoms, *get to a doctor or clinic immediately*. A simple test, available at even the most rural clinic in Africa, is usually adequate to determine whether you have malaria, though if the test is negative it is important to repeat it, so stay close to the facility. And while experts differ on the question of self-diagnosis and self-treatment, the reality is that if you think you have malaria and are not within easy reach of a doctor, it would be wisest to start treatment.

TRAVELLERS' DIARRHOEA Travelling in Ghana carries a fairly high risk of getting a dose of travellers' diarrhoea; perhaps half of all visitors will suffer, and the newer you are to exotic travel, the more likely you will be to suffer.

Rule one in avoiding diarrhoea and other sanitation-related diseases is arguably to wash your hands regularly, particularly before snacks and meals, and after handling money (1 cedi notes in particular are often quite dirty). As for what food you can safely eat, a useful maxim is: PEEL IT, BOIL IT, COOK IT OR FORGET IT. This means that fruit you have washed and peeled yourself should be safe, as should hot cooked foods. However, raw foods, cold cooked foods, salads, fruit salads prepared by others, ice cream and ice are all risky. It is rarer to get sick from drinking contaminated water but it happens, so stick to bottled water, which is widely available.

If you suffer a bout of diarrhoea, it is dehydration that makes you feel awful, so drink lots of water and other clear fluids. These can be infused with sachets of oral rehydration salts, though any dilute mixture of sugar and salt in water will do you good, for instance a bottled soda with a pinch of salt. If diarrhoea persists beyond a couple of days, it is possible that it is a symptom of a more serious sanitation-related illness (typhoid, cholera, hepatitis, dysentery, worms, etc), so get to a doctor. If the diarrhoea is greasy and bulky, and is accompanied by sulphurous (eggy) burps, one likely cause is giardia, which is best treated with tinidazole (four x 500mg in one dose, repeated seven days later if symptoms persist).

BILHARZIA Also known as schistosomiasis, bilharzia is an unpleasant parasitic disease transmitted by freshwater snails most often associated with reedy shores where there is lots of water weed. It cannot be caught in hotel swimming pools, but should be assumed to be present in any freshwater river, pond, lake or similar habitat, probably even those advertised as 'bilharzia free'. The riskiest shores will be within 200m of villages or other places where infected people use water, wash clothes, etc. Ideally, however, you should avoid swimming in any fresh water other than an artificial pool. If you do swim, you'll reduce the risk by applying DEET insect repellent first, staying in the water for under ten minutes, and drying off vigorously with a towel. Bilharzia is often asymptomatic in its early stages, but some people experience an intense immune reaction, including fever, cough, abdominal pain and an itching rash, around four to six weeks after infection. Later symptoms vary but often include a general feeling of tiredness and lethargy. Bilharzia is difficult to diagnose, but it can be tested for at specialist travel clinics, ideally at least six weeks after likely exposure. Fortunately, it is easy to treat at present.

HIV/AIDS The risks of sexually transmitted infection are extremely high in Ghana, whether you sleep with fellow travellers or locals. About 80% of HIV infections in British heterosexuals are acquired abroad. If you must indulge, use condoms or femidoms, which help reduce the risk of transmission. Condoms are widely available in Ghana; however, it is always best to bring your own reputable brand, eg: with the British Kitemark. If you notice any genital ulcers or discharge, get treatment promptly since these increase the risk of acquiring HIV. If you do have unprotected sex, visit a clinic as soon as possible; this should be within 24 hours, or no later than 72 hours, for post-exposure prophylaxis.

MENINGITIS This nasty disease can kill within hours of the appearance of initial symptoms, typically a combination of a blinding headache (light sensitivity), blotchy rash, and high fever. Outbreaks tend to be localised and are usually reported in newspapers. Fortunately, immunisation with the conjugate ACWY vaccine (eg Menveo, Nimenrix) protects against the most serious bacterial form of meningitis. Nevertheless, other less serious forms exist, and a severe headache and fever – possibly also symptomatic of typhoid or malaria – should be sufficient cause to visit a doctor immediately.

RABIES This deadly disease can be carried by any mammal and is usually transmitted to humans via a bite or deep scratch. Beware village dogs and habituated monkeys, but assume that *any* mammal that bites or scratches you (or even licks your skin) might carry rabies, even if they look perfectly healthy. First, scrub the wound with soap under a running tap, or while pouring water from a jug, then pour on a strong iodine or alcohol solution, which will guard against infections and might reduce the risk of the rabies virus entering the body. Whether or not you underwent pre-exposure vaccination, it is vital to obtain post-exposure prophylaxis as soon as possible after the incident. However, if you have had the vaccine before exposure treatment is very much easier. It removes the need for a human blood product (Rabies Immunoglobulin (RIG)) which is not pleasant to have, expensive and often hard to find. Death from rabies is probably one of the worst ways to go, and once you show symptoms it is too late to do anything – the mortality rate is 100%.

TETANUS Tetanus is caught through deep, dirty wounds, including animal bites, so ensure that such wounds are thoroughly cleaned. Immunisation gives good protection for ten years, provided you do not have an overwhelming number of tetanus bacteria on board. If you haven't had a tetanus shot in ten years, or you are unsure, get a tetanus booster as quickly as possible. Keep immunised and be sensible about first aid.

TICK BITES Ticks in Africa are not the rampant disease transmitters that they are in the Americas, but they may spread tick-bite fever along with a few dangerous rarities. They should ideally be removed complete as soon as possible to reduce the chance of infection. The best way to do this is to grasp the tick with your fingernails as close to your body as possible, and pull it away steadily and firmly at right angles to your skin (do not jerk or twist it). If possible, douse the wound with alcohol (any spirit will do) or iodine. If you are travelling with small children, remember to check their heads, and particularly behind the ears, for ticks. Spreading redness around the bite and/or fever and/or aching joints after a tick bite imply that you have an infection that requires antibiotic treatment, so seek advice.

SKIN INFECTIONS Any mosquito bite or small nick is an opportunity for a skin infection in warm, humid climates, so clean and cover the slightest wound in a good drying antiseptic such as dilute iodine, potassium permanganate or crystal (or gentian) violet. Prickly heat, most likely to be contracted at the humid coast, is a fine pimply rash that can be alleviated by cool showers, dabbing (not rubbing) dry and talc, and sleeping naked under a fan or in an air-conditioned room. Fungal infections also get a hold easily in hot, moist climates, so wear 100% cotton socks and underwear and shower frequently.

EYE PROBLEMS Bacterial conjunctivitis (pink eye) is a common infection in Africa, particularly for contact-lens wearers. Symptoms are sore, gritty eyelids that often stick closed in the morning. They will need treatment with antibiotic drops or ointment. Lesser eye irritation should settle with bathing in salt water and keeping

The *Anopheles* mosquitoes that spread malaria are active at dusk and after dark. Most bites can thus be avoided by covering up at night. This means donning a long-sleeved shirt, trousers and socks from around 30 minutes before dusk until you retire to bed, and applying a DEET-based insect repellent (around 50% DEET) to any exposed flesh. It is best to sleep under a net, or in an air-conditioned room, though burning a mosquito coil and/or sleeping under a fan will also reduce (though not entirely eliminate) bites. Travel clinics usually sell a good range of nets and repellents, as well as Permethrin treatment kits, which will render even the tattiest net a lot more protective, and helps prevent mosquitoes from biting through a net when you roll against it. These measures will also do much to reduce exposure to other nocturnal biters. Bear in mind, too, that most flying insects are attracted to light: leaving a lamp standing near a tent opening or a light on in a poorly screened hotel room will greatly increase the insect presence in your sleeping quarters.

It is also advisable to think about avoiding bites when walking in the countryside by day, especially in wetland habitats, which often teem with diurnal mosquitoes which can carry diseases like dengue fever. Wear a long loose shirt and trousers, preferably 100% cotton, as well as proper walking or hiking shoes with heavy socks (the ankle is particularly vulnerable to bites), and apply a DEET-based insect repellent to any exposed skin.

the eyes shaded. If an insect flies into your eye, extract it with great care, ensuring you do not crush or damage it, otherwise you may get a nastily inflamed eye from toxins secreted by the creature.

SUNSTROKE AND DEHYDRATION Overexposure to the sun can lead to short-term sunburn or sunstroke, and increases the long-term risk of skin cancer. Wear a T-shirt and waterproof sunscreen when swimming. When visiting outdoor historical sites or walking in the direct sun, cover up with long, loose clothes, wear a hat, and use sunscreen. The glare and the dust can be hard on the eyes, so bring UV-protecting sunglasses. A less direct effect of the tropical heat is dehydration, so drink more fluids than you would at home.

UNUSUAL MEDICAL PROBLEMS

SNAKE AND OTHER BITES Snakes are very secretive and bites are a genuine rarity, but certain spiders and scorpions can also deliver nasty bites. In all cases, the risk is minimised by wearing closed shoes and trousers when walking in the bush, and watching where you put your hands and feet, especially in rocky areas or when gathering firewood. Only a small fraction of snakebites deliver enough venom to be life-threatening, but it is important to keep the victim calm and inactive, and to seek urgent medical attention.

OTHER INSECT-BORNE DISEASES Although malaria is the insect-borne disease that attracts the most attention in Africa, and rightly so, there are others, most too uncommon to be a significant concern to short-stay travellers. These include dengue fever and other arboviruses (spread by diurnal mosquitoes), sleeping sickness (tsetse flies), and river blindness (blackflies). Bearing this in mind, however, it is clearly sensible, and makes for a more pleasant trip, to avoid insect bites as far as possible (see box on page 98). Two nasty (though ultimately relatively harmless) flesh-eating insects associated with tropical Africa are *tumbu* or *putsi* flies, which lay eggs, often on drying laundry, which hatch and bury themselves under the skin when they come into contact with humans, and jiggers, which latch on to bare feet and set up home, usually at the side of a toenail, where they cause a painful boil-like swelling. Drying laundry indoors and wearing shoes are the best way to deter this pair of flesh-eaters. Symptoms and treatment of all these afflictions are described in greater detail on Bradt's website (*www.bradtguides.com/africahealth*).

OTHER SAFETY CONCERNS

CAR ACCIDENTS Dangerous driving is probably the biggest threat to life and limb in most parts of Africa. On a self-drive visit, drive defensively, being especially wary of stray livestock, gaping pot-holes, and imbecilic or bullying overtaking manoeuvres. Many vehicles lack headlights and most local drivers are reluctant headlight-users, so avoid driving at night and pull over in heavy storms. On a chauffeured tour, don't be afraid to tell the driver to slow or calm down if you think he is too fast or reckless.

Part Two

ACCRA AND SURROUNDS

OLD ACCRA Readily explored by foot over a day, the historic old quarter of Accra is studded with interesting landmarks, ranging from the venerable fort and lighthouse overlooking Jamestown beach to the moving Kwame Nkrumah Memorial Park and wonderfully chaotic Makola Market.

OXFORD STREET The main thoroughfare through trendy Osu, referred to as Oxford Street for all the obvious reasons, is flanked by boutique shops, craft stalls and the country's biggest concentration of eateries, bars and nightspots.

ACCRA NATIONAL MUSEUM Under renovation since 2015, this primarily ethnographic museum is set in a sculpture garden on Barnes Road and while it wouldn't have won any awards in its previous incarnation, it was a great introduction to various Ghanaian cultures nonetheless, and should be even more so after its reopening.

TRASHY BAGS No better souvenir or gift than one of the funky bags made by this eco-friendly social enterprise from recycled plastic sachets and other similar trash.

LA BEACH Accra's best swimming beach is a great chill-out spot at any time of day, but Thursday night is party time.

NIMA DAY TOURS Explore the densely populated and impoverished suburb of Nima, which was established in the 1950s by rural migrants, with an articulate Nima resident who will ensure your safety.

ABURI BOTANICAL GARDEN Established as a sanatorium in the early colonial era, this historic botanical garden inland and uphill of the capital still makes for a refreshingly breezy day or overnight break from the sweltering coast.

SHAI HILLS RESOURCE RESERVE The closest wildlife viewing to Accra – baboons, antelope and an abundance of birds – is offered at this small low-key reserve along the road to Akosombo.

KOKROBITE Dominated by the legendarily relaxed Big Milly's Backyard, a favourite weekend party retreat for volunteers and backpackers, this beachfront village west of Accra is a sociable place to hang out at any time of the week.

FETE AND SENYA BERAKU Site of the spectacular clifftop Fort of Good Hope, which has rough and ready accommodation, these twin towns also boast several smarter beach resorts within easy weekender distance of the capital.

5

Accra

It is tempting to introduce Accra as Ghana's historical capital, or something similarly portentous. This, after all, is a city whose oldest Ga inhabitants (page 13) settled there 500 years ago, whose coastline is guarded by a trio of 17th-century European-built forts, and which became a colonial capital back in 1877, when many other African metropolises – for instance Nairobi, Johannesburg and Addis Ababa – were still tracts of empty bush. Knowing this, Accra is perhaps something of a disappointment. Historic landmarks are sparse on the ground, and for the most part either closed to the public or surprisingly underwhelming – one notable exception is the colonial-era Jamestown Lighthouse, which offers an informal welcome to the curious visitor, and a superb gull's-eye view over the old town.

In feel, Accra is a modern city. Emphatically so. Since the dawn of the colonial era, its population has grown from a few thousand to several million, so that it now ranks 11th on the list of Africa's largest metropolitan areas. And while bespoke tourist attractions are few and far between, the old Ga quarters of Jamestown and Usshertown do possess a certain faded charm, while the more vibrant and modern districts of Adabraka and Osu are serviced by an alluringly cosmopolitan selection of bars, restaurants and other social venues.

Not the least of Accra's assets is its amiability. Hectic it may be, chaotic in places, but few 'developing world' cities of comparable size feel as comparably safe and relaxed. As such, the Ghanaian capital tends to reward casual exploration. Scruffy lanes lined with open sewers and colonial-era homesteads might lead to grandiose independence monuments, to dazzling modern skyscrapers, to unkempt open spaces, or to rundown concrete blocks harking from the headiest days of Soviet town planning. Indeed, the more you try to pin any one adjective to this sprawling city of incongruities, the more you're likely to find yourself floundering. Famed Polish journalist Ryszard Kapuściński described Accra's seeming incoherence as 'like an overgrown small town that has reproduced itself many times over', and indeed the city often feels more like an amalgamation of historically distinct villages – not unlike the sprawling neighbourhoods of Berlin, for example – than it does a city unto itself. And it is in this respect – the way in which the former Danish outpost of Osu, say, still feels like a separate entity to Usshertown or Jamestown – that Accra is, if not a historical city, then certainly one whose multiple personalities reflect its organic growth over centuries of habitation.

HISTORY

EARLY DAYS The coast around Accra has presumably supported human habitation for many millennia. The earliest known residents were probably the La and Kpeshie, who settled there during or before the 13th century, and for whom La Beach and the nearby Kpeshie Lagoon are named. In the late 15th century, according to oral tradition, a group of **Ga** settlers founded a small village immediately east of

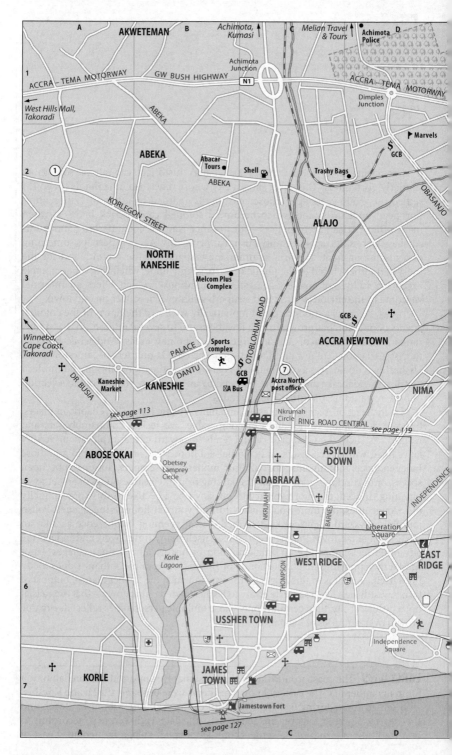

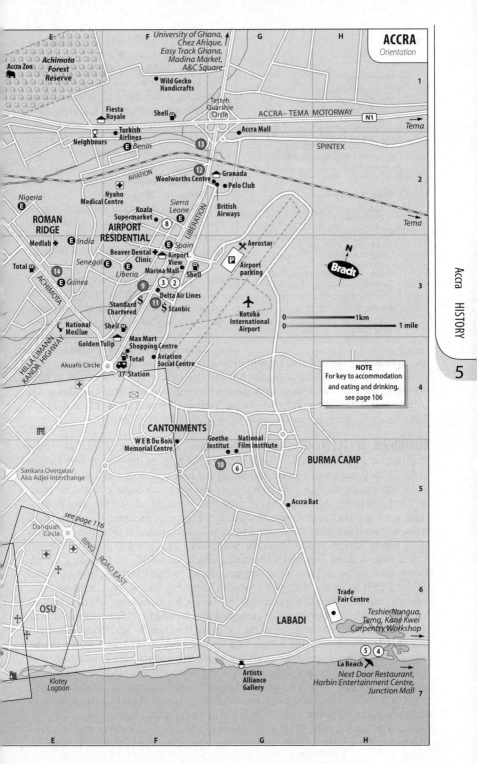

ACCRA
Orientation

University of Ghana,
Chez Afrique,
Easy Track Ghana,
Madina Market,
A&C Square

Accra Zoo

Achimota Forest Reserve

Wild Gecko Handicrafts

Tetteh Quarshie Circle

ACCRA–TEMA MOTORWAY N1

Tema

Fiesta Royale

Shell

Accra Mall

SPINTEX

Turkish Airlines

Neighbours

Benin

13

AVIATION

Woolworths Centre

12

Granada

Polo Club

Tema

Nigeria

Nyaho Medical Centre

Koala Supermarket

Sierra Leone

British Airways

ROMAN RIDGE

8

Medlab

India

AIRPORT RESIDENTIAL

Spain

Aerostar

Beaver Dental Clinic

Airport View

P

Airport parking

N

Total

Senegal

Liberia

Marina Mall

Shell

Bradt

14

Guinea

9

3 2

Delta Air Lines

Kotoka International Airport

3

Standard Chartered

11

Stanbic

0   1km

0   1 mile

National Mosque

Shell

Golden Tulip

Max Mart Shopping Centre

Aviation Social Centre

Akuafo Circle

Total

37 Station

NOTE
For key to accommodation
and eating and drinking,
see page 106

4

CANTONMENTS

W E B Du Bois Memorial Centre

Goethe Institut

National Film Institute

BURMA CAMP

10

6

Sankara Overpass/
Ako Adjei Interchange

Accra Bat

5

Danquah Circle

see page 116

RING ROAD EAST

Trade Fair Centre

6

OSU

LABADI

Teshie-Nungua,
Tema, Kane Kwei
Carpentry Workshop

5 4

Klotey Lagoon

Artists Alliance Gallery

La Beach

Next Door Restaurant,
Harbin Entertainment Centre,
Junction Mall

7

Korle Lagoon (the site of present-day Jamestown), from where they started trading with passing Portuguese ships. The Ga had relocated to this site from Ayawaso, which lies only 15km inland, and is now part of Greater Accra, but most likely they originated from somewhere further east, possibly present-day Benin (though one improbable tradition states their original homeland was Israel and that they travelled to the Ghanian coast via Egypt and Nigeria).

In the first decade of the 16th century, the Ga settlers at Korle founded a state called Nkran, which literally means 'ants' (and was later bastardised by European settlers to become Accra). Some say this name alludes to a supposed profusion of ants (or anthills) in the vicinity. A less arbitrary and more credible explanation, however, is that it was coined by an enemy who was faced by hundreds of canoes carrying Ga soldiers across the lagoon, and likened the apparition to a formation of black driver ants. The paramount chief of Nkran is the Ga Mantse, the earliest of whom is said to have been enstooled in 1510, though only the most recent 20 or so – from Ga Mantse Ayi (ruled 1680–1700) through to Nii Tackie Tawiah III (ruled 2006–12) and Tackie Teiko Tsuru II (2015–present) – seem to be remembered by name.

EUROPEAN SETTLEMENT The first Europeans to settle at Accra were the Portuguese, who built a small lodge close to the present-day site of Fort Ussher in 1557. They started to expand and fortify the lodge in 1576, but it was attacked and destroyed by locals a year later, before the work was complete, and no trace of it remains today. Although Nkran presumably continued to trade with passing ships after the Portuguese were ejected, any European presence there remained transitory until the mid 17th century, when the construction of three different forts along barely 3km of coastline transformed it into a focal point of foreign rivalries. The first of these was Fort Crèvecœur, which started life in 1642 as a simple Dutch-built lodge, but was vastly expanded and fortified in 1649, and occupied by the Dutch for more than two centuries thereafter. The second, built in 1652, was the earthen Swedish precursor of Fort Christiansborg, which changed hands several times before being expanded and fortified in 1661 to serve almost uninterrupted for two centuries as the capital of the Danish Gold Coast. The third was Fort James, built by the British as a trading post in 1673, and joined by the original Jamestown Lighthouse in 1871. Despite this unparalleled concentration of European fortifications, pre-colonial Accra was never as politically or commercially important as Cape Coast or Elmina. However, it did become an important focal point of British military interests following their purchase of Fort Christiansborg in 1850 and Fort Crèvecœur in 1868. Fort Christiansborg later become known as Osu Castle, after the Ga village that surrounded it, while Fort Crèvecœur was renamed in honour of H T Ussher, the British administrator of the Gold Coast from 1867–72.

THE COLONIAL ERA The Gold Coast officially became a British colony in 1873. Four years later, the capital was relocated from Cape Coast to Accra. The reasoning behind this was largely climatic. Accra, due to its location in the Dahomey Gap, is significantly drier than Cape Coast, which made it less prone to outbreaks of malaria, and relatively free of the tsetse-borne diseases that routinely felled horses (then an important form of transport) elsewhere along the coast. It also helped that Osu Castle, recently evacuated by the Danish, made an ideal seat for the colonial government, while the relatively mountainous hinterland around Aburi (rather like the 'hill stations' of India) formed a perfect sanatorium site for ailing administrators. In addition, Accra was somewhat better suited to modern steamers than Cape Coast, even though it lacked an obvious site for a proper harbour, so that ocean-going ships had to anchor about 1.5km offshore of Jamestown Lighthouse, and goods and passengers were landed in surf boats.

Prior to becoming the capital, Accra had supported only a few thousand people, split between a trio of villages centred on the three forts. From west to east, these were British Accra or Jamestown, Dutch Accra or Crèvecœur (now Usshertown) and Danish Accra or Christiansborg (now the southern end of Osu). The main centre of urbanisation, a warren of mostly mud houses bounded by Korle Lagoon to the west and Fort Ussher to the east, was also known as Ga Mashie, the traditional capital of the Ga Mantse. At the time of colonisation, Ga Mashie was still being rebuilt in the wake of the 1862 earthquake that had flattened a great many buildings. The old town suffered further losses in 1894, when it was swept through by a fire – attributed by some sources to the British authorities, acting in response to an outbreak of plague – that razed many of its more temporary structures, and led to the construction of more substantial replacements.

In 1896, Accra became the first town in the Gold Coast to be granted municipal status and to be governed by a dedicated town council. By this time, the colonial authorities were actively expanding the town limits. The exclusively European residential suburb of Victoriaborg was laid out along Otoo Street (now John Atta Mills High Street), the 3km-long thoroughfare that ran eastwards from Fort Ussher and what is now the Central Business District (CBD) towards Osu Castle. Contemporaneously described by George MacDonald as 'a piece of England grafted into the townscape of Accra', Victoriaborg was graced by several fine examples of colonial architecture, of which the old Post Office Building and Anglican Holy Trinity Cathedral are among the best-known survivors. It also boasted a whites-only golf course, cricket pitch, race course and polo field, all now buried below the many spacious Africanist and independence-related memorials characteristic of this part of town.

Accra grew exponentially in the early 20th century, which is when most of the suburbs that now lie within the ring road were established. However, a strict policy of racial segregation was applied to residential areas at this time, one rationalised by the fear of diseases spreading beyond poorly sanitised 'native' areas such as Jamestown and Adabraka (the latter established as a Muslim enclave in the aftermath of a bubonic plague outbreak that claimed more than 100 lives in 1908). By 1911, the city supported a population of 18,500, including 150 European settlers and administrators, and its sea frontage extended for about 5km east of Korle Lagoon. An important impetus for Accra's early growth was the completion of the railway connecting it to Kumasi and the main inland cocoa production regions in 1923. The same year also witnessed the construction of a bridge across the Korle Lagoon, which opened up new areas for settlement and prompted a fresh influx of rural migrants in search of work. By 1921, the population had risen to 38,000, ten years later it stood at 61,000, and by the end of World War II it had increased to approximately 130,000.

MODERN ACCRA Accra was the fulcrum of the struggle for independence. On 28 February 1948, three demonstrators were killed and another 237 injured when police opened fire on an anti-colonial demonstration outside Osu Castle, a landmark event in the tidal change that led to almost all of Britain's African colonies being granted independence within 15 years. The Palladium Theatre in Ga Mashie is where Dr Kwame Nkrumah made many of his most influential anti-colonial speeches, and also where he launched the Convention People's Party (CPP) in 1949. Nkrumah and many of his CPP supporters were imprisoned in Fort Ussher in 1950, and it was as the constituent for Old Accra (Ga Mashie) that Nkrumah was elected to parliament (whilst still in jail) and released to form a government in February 1951. And it was in Victoriaborg, on the former whites-only polo ground – now, fittingly, the site of the Nkrumah Mausoleum – that Nkrumah made a formal declaration of Ghanaian independence on 6 March 1957.

Nkrumah also had an important influence on the development of Accra. It was he who prevented the enactment of the so-called Fry/Treavallion Plan – devised by city planner Maxwell Fry in 1944 and revisited by his successor B D W Treavallion in the 1950s – to reorganise and gentrify the CBD, Usshertown and Jamestown to become an elite administrative extension of upmarket Victoriaborg. Instead, Nkrumah decided to leave Usshertown and Jamestown as they were, and to replace the old playing fields of Victoriaborg with more populist landmarks such as the Independence Arch, Black Star Square and Liberation Monument. Economically, Nkrumah's biggest contribution to the future growth and industrialisation of Greater Accra was the commissioning of the country's second deep harbour (after Takoradi) at Tema, only 25km east of the capital. Meanwhile, a series of newer residential suburbs – including Asylum Down, Nima and Odorkor – were created outside the present-day Ring Road to accommodate a population that increased threefold, to more than 400,000, between the late 1940s and the coup that deposed Nkrumah in 1966.

Accra's recent economic fortunes have mirrored those of the country it governs. But throughout the past 50 years, a steady influx of job-seeking migrants to the city

---

HOTEL 'HIJACKING' BY DRIVERS   *Chris Scott*

You have done your homework preparing for your trip to Ghana using the Bradt Travel Guide and the internet. You have made your hotel bookings over the net and you have arrived in Ghana. To get to your hotel, you charter a more expensive, less hassle, airport taxi found to the left of the exit to 'Arrivals', or a public taxi found across the road from 'Arrivals' in the public parking area. You give the driver the name of your hotel only to receive a comment to the effect that the hotel is closed temporarily for some reason or another and such and such hotel is a better choice. This is a scam. Many drivers have made prior arrangements with certain hotels to get hefty commissions when they bring tourists. Insist on your hotel – whatever.

Or … you have chartered a car hire company to take you around to major centres outside Accra. You are approaching a certain city and the driver says he will call on his mobile, or yours, the hotel you have booked over the internet to ask for directions. Often the driver will feign the call and then give you some excuse why you can't go there – 'they are fully booked', 'they are overbooked' – and then take you to the hotel where, again, he would collect a big commission. Insist on talking to the hotel yourself or, better still, call the night before to confirm your reservation.

has spurred an average annual population growth of around 5%, roughly double the national average. Indeed, the Greater Accra Metropolitan Area, supporting a population of more than four million, is now the 11th-largest such agglomeration on the continent. As a result of its rapid growth, fewer than half of the city's 50 recognised neighbourhoods are a product of proper town planning. Mostly, these are the older suburbs that lie within the inner Ring Road, or the smarter residential and administrative districts that run northeast in the direction of Kotoka International Airport and University of Ghana. The remainder – supporting the overwhelming majority of the city's inhabitants – are unplanned slum-like suburbs suffering from poor drainage and sewerage, limited road access, and an insufficient supply of water and electricity. Despite this, Accra is clearly riding high on the (admittedly uneven) economic boom that has characterised post-millennial Ghana, and the city's infrastructure and facilities have grown enormously since the first edition of this guidebook was published. It is a measure of Accra's burgeoning stature that in 2010, the influential Globalisation and World Cities Research Network ranked it along with Lagos and Nairobi as the only three 'world cities' in Africa south of the Sahara and north of the Limpopo.

GETTING THERE AND AWAY

BY AIR All international flights arrive at the unusually central **Kotoka International Airport** [105 G3] (✆ 03027 76171; e info@gacl.com.gh; www.gacl.com.gh; IATA code ACC), which lies only 4km north of Sankara Overpass and 500m east of Liberation Avenue. The airport is named after Lieutenant General Emmanuel Kotoka, who served on the National Liberation Council following the coup that ousted Kwame Nkrumah in 1966, but was shot dead during a failed coup a year later (his statue now stands at the location where he was killed). The airport consists of two passenger terminals connected by an internal walkway. Most international airlines land at (and depart from) Terminal 2, whereas Terminal 1 mainly serves domestic flights.

Assuming that your passport and visa are in order, immigration and customs procedures are usually quite speedy and straightforward. A few years back, the maximum period immigration would stamp in any visitor's passport (regardless of what visa they had or how long they intended to stay) was 30 days. This has been extended to up to 60 days, usually by request only, so do specify any intent to spend longer than 30 days in Ghana *before* your passport is stamped. Theoretically, it is possible to buy a visa on arrival at the airport, but only by prior arrangement, and at a hugely inflated fee, so travellers who chance it risk being deported on the spot at vast expense (see pages 56–7 for details).

There is a cash-only foreign exchange desk at the airport, as well as an ATM where you can draw local currency against a Visa card. It makes sense to ensure you leave the airport with at least enough local currency to get a taxi to your hotel. If you've got some time to kill, the Aerostar Bar & Restaurant [105 G3] (✆ 03027 72664; ⊕ 09.00–22.00 daily) serves grills, Ghanaian dishes, and draft beer in a garden setting just 100m opposite the terminal to the right of the parking lot.

Should your flight be scheduled to arrive after dark, it might be wise to make an advance booking at a mid- to upper-range hotel that has a shuttle service to and from the airport. Otherwise, you can expect to be mobbed by taxi drivers as soon as you leave the terminal building. A passenger taxi from the airport to anywhere in central Accra should cost around US$5–10, but you may be asked a lot more and, while you ought to negotiate the fare, this probably isn't the moment to get overtly confrontational. Arriving in daylight, there is nothing to prevent you from pushing past the taxis and hopping into a shared taxi or trotro, but it's probably fair to say that most freshly landed visitors laden down with luggage prefer to save first acquaintance with Accra's bemusing public-transport routes for another time.

Airlines All international flights land in Accra. For further connections within Ghana, there are now two domestic carriers that run affordable flights to Kumasi, Tamale, Takoradi and other locations. These are **Starbow** (m *0245 000000; www. flystarbow.com; online booking at www.ghanaticketservice.com*) and **Africa World Airlines** (m *0242 438888; www.flyawa.com.gh*).

For a full list of daily flight schedules, click the 'Flight Status' tab at www.gacl. com.gh, though we don't recommend relying on this to find out if a flight is delayed or cancelled. For a list of airlines flying to Accra, see page 57.

BY ROAD There are numerous different coach and trotro stations in Accra, some serving specific lines, and others a specific group of destinations. If in doubt, cab drivers usually know the departure points for the most obscure of destinations, so the simplest way to find the terminal you need is often just to hail down a taxi, tell the driver that you want, for instance, a VIP Coach to Kumasi, or a Ford to Cape Coast, and let them deposit you there. Likewise, when you arrive in Accra, it really is worth the small price of a taxi to get to your hotel swiftly and simply.

The most central stations are **Tudu Station** (also known as Aflao Station) [127 C2] on Kinbu Road north of Makola Circle, the **Tema Station** [127 D2] a block to its east, and **Agbogbloshie Station** [127 A1] to the west of the old railway station. An equally important group of long-haul coach and trotro terminals, including all the VIP/VVIP stations, the OA Tours station, the STC station, and the bustling trotro station known as Neoplan (after a type of bus that used to be assembled locally in Kumasi), are clustered within a few hundred metres of Nkrumah Circle [119 B1]. A little further out of town, **Kaneshie Station** [113 A1] is situated on Dr Busia (Winneba) Road about 1km northwest of Lamptey Circle, almost adjacent to the sprawling Kaneshie Market. Less central still is **Madina Station** [105 G1], which lies along the Aburi–Koforidua road near Madina Market, a few kilometres north of Legon and the University of Ghana.

In addition, several terminals are run exclusively by **Metro Mass** (\ *0302 237539; e info@metromass.com; www.metromass.com*), which is by far the largest coach operator in Ghana, though rather more downmarket and cramped than the likes of VIP/VVIP and OA Tours, and not generally recommended for getting out of Accra. These include two central stations, one on Independence Avenue between Tema and Tudu stations [127 D2] and the other on Kwame Nkrumah Avenue near the old railway station [127 C2]. There is also the more out-of-town main Metro Mass Terminal [113 A1], which lies on Nii Teiko Din Street, about 200m northeast of the Winneba Road between Lamptey Circle and Kaneshie Station.

From the mid 1990s until several years back, coach transport was dominated by the **STC**, whose station lies on the south side of the ring road about 500m west of Nkrumah Circle [113 B1]. Sadly, this once ubiquitous operator has gone precipitously downhill in recent years, with a dramatic decrease noted both in the number of services and their reliability. Destinations still served by the STC include Kumasi, Tamale, Bolgatanga, Wa, Cape Coast, Takoradi and Ho.

To Kumasi The best operator is VIP/VVIP, which operates around 20 air-conditioned coaches a day from its **main station** [119 A1], on the south side of the ring road, just past the drainage canal a few hundred metres west of Nkrumah Circle.

(There were also some Kumasi-bound VIP coaches departing from the northeast side of Nkrumah Circle in 2016, but these may relocate when roadworks on Nkrumah Circle are complete.) These coaches leave throughout the day on a fill-up-and-go basis, and the fare is in the US$9–13 range depending on the type of bus. Other reliable operators to Kumasi in this part of town include **OA Tours** [104 C4] (m *03022 36917*; m *0244 284713*; *www.oatravels.com*), but they only run a handful of buses daily and advance booking is usually required. Alternatively, a regular stream of air-conditioned Stanbic and Ford vans to Kumasi, as well as more basic trotros, leaves from Neoplan Station. Metro Mass also operates several buses daily to Kumasi.

To Tamale, Bolgatanga and Paga Once again, the best coach operator is VIP/VVIP, which runs two to four fixed-departure air-conditioned services to Tamale daily, one or two of which continue on to Bolgatanga. Coaches leave daily at 15.00 and 16.00, taking 14 hours to Tamale and another 4 hours to Bolgatanga, and the fare is around US$15–20 for either destination. There is also one VVIP coach to Tamale only, leaving at 15.00 and costing around US$20. These leave from a small station a few hundred metres north of the main VIP station to Kumasi, on the east side of the back road to the OA station. Advance bookings can be made at m 0243 543337/0245 414456, but if you do this we recommend you get there an hour early to confirm your seat.

Also recommended for Tamale and Bolgatanga, and slightly cheaper, is OA Tours whose office is about 200m further north. OA runs two buses daily, leaving at noon and 16.00, and continuing on from Bolgatanga to Paga, the main border crossing for Burkina Faso. The STC also runs one bus daily to Tamale and Bolgatanga. Air-conditioned Fords to Tamale and Bolgatanga leave from Agbogbloshie Station.

To Wa The best service to Wa (and Nandom) is an air-conditioned overnight coach run by OA Tours. This leaves from the same station as their coaches to Tamale and Bolgatanga at 19.00 daily, and costs US$16–23 depending on the type of bus. There's also a once-daily VIP coach from the main VIP station (m *0560 027233*) at Nkrumah Circle, departing at 18.30 for US$22, or you could conceivably pick up the once-daily VIP bus that goes to Hamile (m *0248 576608*) from Madina Station and drop at Wa as well. If you can't get a seat on any of these coaches, we recommend taking a VIP or VVIP coach as far as Kumasi then picking up transport to Wa from there. In addition a few air-conditioned Fords to Wa leave from Agbogbloshie Station daily. Another (significantly inferior) option is the slower non-air-conditioned Metro Mass service.

To the west coast The most useful terminal for coastal destinations west of Accra is Kaneshie Station. Comfortable air-conditioned Yuton, Stanbic or Ford minibuses to Cape Coast (*US$4–6*) and Takoradi (*US$8–10*) steam out of here on a fill-up-and-go basis throughout the day. Kaneshie is also the best place to pick up transport for Kokrobite, Winneba and other destinations between Accra and Cape Coast. Cape Coast and Takoradi are also serviced by cheaper trotros from Neoplan Station, but these are generally a lot more crowded and uncomfortable, and feel like a false economy unless you are seriously strapped for cash. Heading to Elmina, it is best to travel as normal to Cape Coast and then pick up a shared taxi from there. Heading to Busua or destinations further west, catch a Yuton, Stanbic or Ford as far as Takoradi, where you can downgrade to local transport. STC coaches between Accra, Cape Coast and Takoradi have stopped running almost entirely.

To Aburi and Koforidua Comfortable air-conditioned Stanbic or Ford minibuses run from Madina Station to Koforidua (*US$4*), which is also the best place to pick up transport directly to Aburi. There are also trotros to Koforidua from Neoplan and Tudu stations, but these are not air-conditioned.

To Volta and the east coast Formerly the best option running eastwards from Accra was the air-conditioned VVIP coach service to Ho via Atimpoku (Akosombo) departing from Nkrumah Circle, but these have been discontinued.

Today, most transport to destinations east of Accra leaves from the central Tema or Aflao/Tudu stations. This includes regular trotros to Tema from Tema Station, and to the likes of Aflao, Akosombo, Ho and Hohoe, and Keta from Aflao Station. Air-conditioned trotros to Ho depart fairly regularly for US$6. If there is no direct transport to where you are headed (for instance Shai Hills and Prampram), you may have to pick up a trotro from Tema Station to the junction town of Ashaiman, and change vehicles there.

International services Heading for Lomé (Togo), most people catch a trotro or bus from Tudu Station as far as the Ghanaian border town of Aflao, then cross on foot. Reliable operators to Cotonou (Benin) and Lagos (Nigeria) via Lomé include **Chisco** (m *0242 372433/0277 806272; www.chiscotransportng.com*), which has a terminal between Nkrumah Circle and the VIP station for Kumasi, and **Efex Executive** (m *0245 522510; www.efex-executive.com.ng*), which lies on the ring road east of Nkrumah Circle, more or less opposite the Paloma Hotel. For direct buses to Abidjan (Ivory Coast) or Ouagadougou (Burkina Faso), the **STC** (\ *03022 21414*) is still recommended, and operates one bus daily in either direction.

ORIENTATION

Central Accra is bounded by the Atlantic Ocean to the south and by Korle Lagoon to the west. In other directions, it is hemmed in by the Ring Road, which starts at the old Winneba Road on the seafront immediately west of Korle Lagoon, before running northeast via Lamptey Circle to Nkrumah Circle, then east to Sankara Overpass, then southeast via Danquah Circle to the junction with Labadi Road near the seafront.

Tourists who spend some time in Accra will probably come to regard Nkrumah Circle – often just referred to as 'Circle' – as its most significant landmark. Not only is this the city's most important local transport hub, but it also marks the intersection between the Ring Road and Nkrumah Road, the latter the main north–south thoroughfare through the busy suburbs of Adabraka (in the north), Usshertown and Jamestown (on the seafront). Running parallel to and east of Nkrumah Avenue are Kojo Thompson and Barnes, arguably the city's second- and third-most important north–south thoroughfares, the former well supplied with budget accommodation, the latter effectively the eastern border of the most built-up part of the city centre,

ACCRA *Inner Ring Road*
For listings, see pages 121–32

🛏 **Where to stay**
1 Access Inn..................................F4
2 Avenida....................................C2
3 Calvary Methodist
   Guesthouse........................ C2
4 Chez Delphy..........................G4
5 Lake Bosumtwi.....................F4
6 Mariset Plaza........................F4
7 Somewhere Nice...................D1

✖ **Where to eat and drink**
8 +233 Jazz Club.......................E2
9 Afrikiko Complex.................. E2
10 Auntie Gracie Special...............C2
11 Bamboo Chinese Fusion..........F1
12 Café dez Amis.........................E2
13 Eat By Fine Things...................E2
14 Khana Khazana........................C2
15 Jokers Pub & Grill......................G4
16 Le Magellan............................F3
17 Maquis Tante Marie..................G2
18 Melting Moments...................F2
19 Zanzibar...................................G2

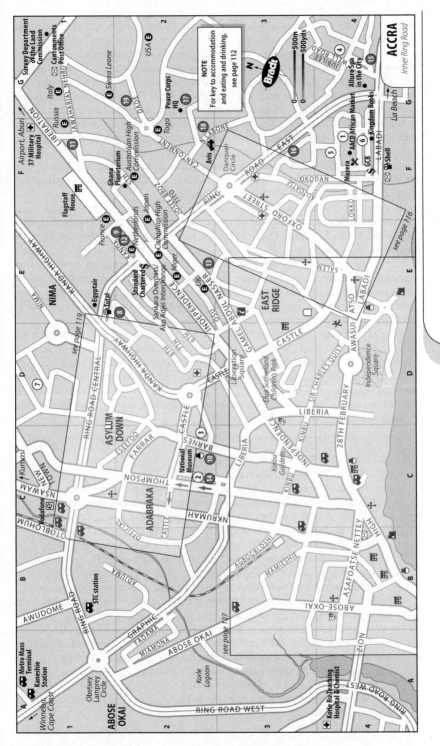

ACCRA
Inner Ring Road

NOTE
For key to accommodation
and eating and drinking,
see page 112

Survey Department
of the Land
Commission
Cantonments
Post Office

Italy

Russia

Sierra Leone

USA

Togo

Peace Corps
HQ

Airport, Aburi
37 Military
Hospital

Australian High
Commission

Ghana
Planetarium

Flagstaff
House

France

Netherlands

Japan

Canadian High
Commission

Niger

UK

Standard
Chartered

Egyptair

Total

Avis

Danquah
Circle

Mazera

GCB

AKO African Market
Allure Spa
in the City
Kingdom Books
Shell

La Beach

EAST
RIDGE

NIMA

ASYLUM
DOWN

ADABRAKA

National
Museum

Efua Sutherland
Children's Park

Liberation
Square

Independence
Square

Metro Mass
Terminal
Kaneshie
Station

STC station

Vodafone

Korle Bu Teaching
Hospital & Chemist

Obetsey
Lamprey
Circle

ABOSE
OKAI

Korle
Lagoon

RING ROAD WEST

and notable for two important landmarks: the National Museum [113 C2] and Novotel Hotel [127 D1].

The suburbs that lie within the Ring Road can be divided into three broad clusters. In the west, Adabraka, Usshertown and Jamestown essentially form the old commercial city centre. Of these, Adabraka is a popular haunt of budget travellers since it is dotted with cheap accommodation, bars and restaurants, while Usshertown and Jamestown together form Old Accra, an area of some historical interest. To the east of this, bounded roughly by Barnes Road to the west and an imaginary north–south line running between Sankara Overpass and Independence Square, lies a cluster of more spacious, green suburbs comprising, from north to south: Asylum Down, North Ridge, East Ridge, West Ridge and Victoriaborg. The main thoroughfare through this part of Accra is Independence Avenue, which connects Sankara Overpass on the Ring Road to the seafront at the south end of Barnes Road.

Last but by no means least, the most easterly central suburb is Osu (aka Christiansborg), another old part of town that runs south from Danquah Circle on the Ring Road towards Osu Castle. The main thoroughfare through Osu, an extension of Cantonments Road known as Oxford Street, vies with Nkrumah Circle as the city's best-known hub of activity. Accra's greatest concentration of restaurants, bars and nightlife venues are clustered along Oxford Street and the 18 short numbered 'lanes' that flank it (all of which have recently been given new, non-numeric, names), and the area is also studded with craft stalls, mid-range hotels, boutiques and other places of interest to travellers.

Several important trunk roads fan outwards from the Ring Road. The main road to Winneba and the west coast leaves the Ring Road at Lamptey Circle; the main road to Nsawam, Kumasi and the north leaves from Nkrumah Circle; while Liberation Road, which leaves from Sankara Overpass, heads past Kotoka International Airport to Tetteh Quarshie Circle and the Kwame Nkrumah Highway for Tema and other destinations east of Accra. At the very southeast of the Ring Road, Labadi Road heads to La Beach, Coco Beach and Tema via the coast.

A NOTE ON STREET NAMES

In early 2013, President Mahama issued a directive to municipal assemblies across Ghana to begin cataloguing and naming the roads under their jurisdiction as part of a nationwide street-naming initiative that remained ongoing in early 2016 as we conducted research for this seventh edition of the guide. Blue-and-white street signs have gone up all across the country, and though people still tend to navigate by landmarks and almost no-one (including taxi drivers) knows the location of these newly named streets, they can still be a help when it comes to demystifying Accra navigation for a visitor.

The naming process has been a consultative affair, and communities retain the right to propose names or petition changes in their neighbourhoods. Unfortunately, however, the fact that some road names may still change was given as the reason to deny us access to the newly produced maps when we visited the Accra Municipal Assembly's Town and Country Planning Department to request information on the new names. Thus, we've done our best to collect the most current information from street signs across the city, but there are bound to be at least a few changes, omissions and errors in the final product, so don't be shocked if you find yourself on the same old street with an unfamiliar new name.

SAFETY

Accra ranks among the safest capital cities in Africa. Violent crime against tourists is reassuringly unusual, certainly by comparison with the likes of Nairobi, Lagos or Johannesburg, and there is very little risk attached to walking around by day. That said, no city is entirely free of crime, and tourists, being relatively wealthy and conspicuous, are inevitably seen as an easy target for whatever casual criminal element might exist.

Based on reader feedback, the most common form of crime against tourists is bag snatching, often from a passing vehicle and generally after dark. La Beach, to the east of the city centre, is a hotspot for this sort of thing, as is Oxford Street and surrounds in central Osu. Far more unusual, but not unheard of, nocturnal hold-ups at knifepoint or gunpoint are most likely to happen along quiet roads abutting popular nightspots such as Adabraka or Osu, or around the Tudu lorry station. Should you be unfortunate enough to be held up like this, the risk of being injured is very slight, provided that you comply with your assailants' demands.

The most effective measure against crime is to avoid attracting the attention of criminals in the first place. If possible, never carry a daypack or other bag, especially after dark, and if you must do so then wear it on the opposite side of your body from the street, with the entrance facing your body. Wearing expensive (or for that matter cheap) jewellery might also attract the interest of robbers, as would flashing around any other valuables. In Accra, as elsewhere in Africa, we would strongly advocate that travellers carry on their person only as much cash as they will need for any given excursion, especially at night. All travellers (but especially women) are advised against walking around alone after dark, particularly in known trouble spots or along quiet unlit roads, as this will increase their appearance of vulnerability.

The above warnings notwithstanding, there really is very little about Accra to strike serious fear into the heart of any traveller who adheres to the common-sense rules of urban survival that one might follow in any unfamiliar modern city.

GETTING AROUND

Accra is serviced by a cheap and efficient system of trotros, passenger (shared) taxis and dropping (charter) taxis, though getting to grips with the main routes used by passenger vehicles takes time and a certain degree of trial and error. In our opinion, travellers who are spending only a couple of days in Accra may as well stick to dropping taxis, which can be picked up practically anywhere and at any time. You're unlikely to have to pay more than US$5 for a daytime trip within the bounds of the Ring Road, though you may sometimes have to negotiate to get a fair price, and fares are understandably higher on days when traffic is particularly heavy. Dropping taxis to places outside Ring Road will cost more, but are still very cheap by international standards. Women travellers may also be interested in taking advantage of the new **Miss Taxi** (✆ *02332 55074*; m *0555 050950*; e *misstaxigh@ gmail.com*; ◼ *fb.me/misstaxighana*) service, which offers female-driven taxis for short trips, airport pickups and hourly or daily hiring/tours.

Passenger taxi and trotro fares are even cheaper – seldom more than US$0.50, depending on the exact route – and we've neither heard nor experienced anything to suggest there is any serious need to worry about pickpockets and other petty thieves on public transport. In fact, the presence of a whole minibus of Ghanaians (who will get noisy if something happens that they don't like) actually seems to work as insurance against getting ripped off. Once you are reasonably well orientated to Accra, the system is quite easy to assimilate.

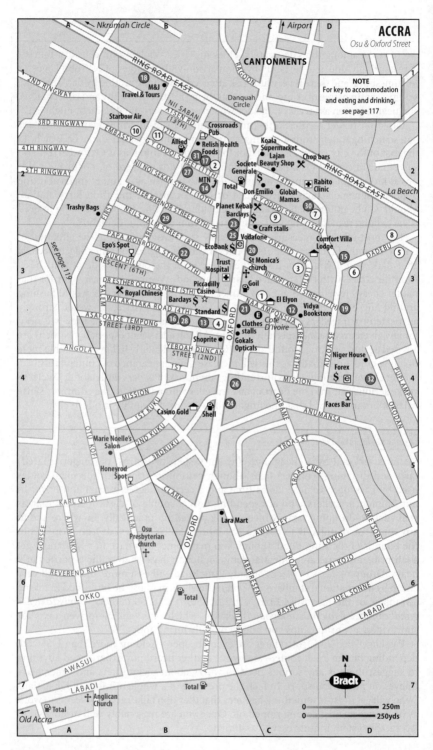

ACCRA
Osu & Oxford Street

NOTE
For key to accommodation and eating and drinking, see page 117

CANTONMENTS

Nkrumah Circle
Airport
RING ROAD EAST
2ND RINGWAY
3RD RINGWAY
4TH RINGWAY
5TH RINGWAY
EMBASSY
RAGOON
Danquah Circle
La Beach
RING ROAD EAST

18 M&J Travel & Tours
Starbow Air
10 11 Allied
NII SABAN ATSEN RD (13TH)
G Y ODDOI STREET (11TH)
NII NOI SEKAN STREET (10TH)
Crossroads Pub
Relish Health Foods
31 17 2
27
14 MTN
Total
Koala Supermarket
Lajan Beauty Shop
Chop bars
Societe Generale
Don Emilio
Global Mamas
Rabito Clinic
30
Trashy Bags
MASTER BARNOR STREET
NEIL'S PALM STREET (8TH)
PAPA MONROVIA STREET (8TH)
Epo's Spot
KUKU HILL CRESCENT (6TH)
29
22
Planet Kebab
Barclays
23
25
Vodafone
20
EcoBank
Craft stalls
9
OXFORD LINK
Comfort Villa Lodge
15
8
5
6
DADEBU
St Monica's church
Trust Hospital
Piccadilly Casino
DR ESTHER OCLOO STREET (5TH)
Royal Chinese
Barclays
WALAKATAKA ROAD (4TH)
Standard
ASAFOATSE-TEMPONG STREET (3RD)
Goil
1 El Elyon
3
NII KOFI ANIEFI STREET (17TH)
El Elyon
12 Vidya Bookstore
19
16 28
13 4
21
Cote D'Ivoire
Clothes stalls
Shoprite
Gokals Opticals
YEBOAH DUNCAN STREET (2ND)
1ST
ANGOLA
MISSION
26
24
Casino Gold
Shell
Niger House
Forex
32
ADFOATSE
Faces Bar
ANUMANSA
MISSION
OGBAME
1ST KUKU
2ND KUKU
3RD KUKU
CLARK
Marie Noelle's Salon
Honeyrod Spot
KARL QUIST
AUMANKO
GORSEE
OXFORD
SALEM
OTU KOFI
Osu Presbyterian church
Lara Mart
AWULETEY
TROAS ST
TROAS CRES
LOKKO
SAI KOJO
NII ETSOBU
PUPTAMPO
OKODAN
REVEREND RICHTER
LOKKO
Total
AWASUI
LABADI
Total
Anglican Church
Old Accra
AWULA KPAKPA
WENTUM
ABEBRESEM
TROAS
BASEL
JOEL SONNE
LABADI
Total

N
Bradt
0   250m
0   250yds

The most important local transport hub is **Nkrumah Circle** [119 B1], known locally as 'Circle', and the adjacent stations under the Nsawam Overpass. You can safely assume you'll find a shared taxi or trotro from 'Circle' to anywhere in central or Greater Accra, at the worst involving one change of vehicle. Shared taxis to Osu and the vicinity of the National Theatre (via Farrar Avenue and Barnes Road) leave from the south side of 'Circle', while those to Sankara Overpass, '37' Station, the airport, La Beach and Nungua leave from the station next to Nsawam Overpass. Trotros from Circle to Osu (Danquah Circle), La Beach, Teshie-Nungua and Tema follow the Ring Road and (coastal) Labadi Road back and forth and can be easily picked up anywhere along this route. Minibuses heading down Nkrumah Road to Usshertown and Jamestown can generally be picked up by waiting on the west side of Nkrumah Road immediately south of the Circle. Trotros to destinations slightly further out of town, for instance the University of Ghana at Legon, generally leave from the northwest side of the Circle.

The most important station in the city centre for local trotros is **Tema Station** [127 D2] on Independence Avenue, below the Novotel Hotel. Here you can pick up transport to coastal destinations in the direction of Tema as well as northeast along Independence Avenue to Sankara Overpass, and along Liberation Avenue past the airport and on to Aburi.

Outside Ring Road, a landmark worth knowing is **'37' Station** [105 F4] at Akuafo Circle on the junction of Liberation Avenue and Gifford Road. From '37' you can pick up shared taxis to most destinations, including Nkrumah Circle (via Sankara Overpass), Osu (via Cantonments Road and Danquah Circle), and Nungua (via Burma Camp Bypass and La Beach).

It's worth getting to know some of the signals and calls most frequently used by trotro 'mates' within Accra. When they shout 'Accra!', it means they are heading to the central Tema Station. When they shout 'Circle', they will be heading to Nkrumah Circle – there is also a hand sign to show you're going to the Circle, which involves rotating your hand in small circles with your index finger pointed downwards. The trendy part of Osu south of Danquah Circle is usually referred to as 'Oxford Street' by taxi drivers and trotro mates. Other signs – used in Accra and throughout Ghana – are briefly explained on pages 74–5.

If you use 'dropping' taxis, be aware that their drivers seldom know the names of streets or of places of touristic interest. This includes the likes of the National Culture Centre, National Museum, Asylum Down, and important traffic connections like Kanda Overdrive, Liberation Circle and Independence Avenue! When this happens, the driver may show some uncertainty, but that doesn't prevent him from taking you just anywhere, so be prepared and have your maps at hand.

MAPS The most complete map resource for Accra is the *Kingdom A–Z of Accra & Tema*, an 80-odd page book that divides Accra across 18 grid pages and Tema across 16, and has a good street index. The pick of several foldout maps is probably the *Drexmap Modern Map of Accra*, which also includes a moderately useful map of Ghana on one side. You should be able to pick up either of these, as well as several other maps, at any of the bookshops listed on pages 136–7, though note that at the time of writing, neither map offered an edition including the new post-2013 street names. For other requirements, head to the map sales office in the Survey Department of the Land Commission [113 G1] (⏱ *09.00–16.00 Mon–Fri*) on the junction of Airport and Gifford roads, about 500m from '37' Station.

TOURIST INFORMATION AND TOUR OPERATORS

The headquarters and Greater Accra regional office of the **Ghana Tourism Authority** (GTA) [127 F1] (✆ *03022 31817/44612*; e *ghanatourismgar@gmail.com or info@ ghana.travel*; *www.ghana.travel*; ⏱ *08.00–12.30 & 13.30–17.00 Mon–Fri*) are centrally located in a new high-rise building on Second Avenue, behind State House. The people who work here are very friendly, and the office stocks a fair selection of maps and brochures. The best source of current information about Accra, in particular things such as restaurants and nightlife, is the magazine-style guide *Time Out Accra* (*www.timeout.com/accra*), which is easily found at upmarket restaurants and shops around Accra for around US$8. Also very useful are the websites www. enjoyaccra.com and www.noworriesghana.com.

Most tour operators in Accra specialise in visits to the Eastern, Western and Central regions taking in the beaches and castles of the Cape Coast, cruises of Lake Volta and the kente weavers of the Ashanti Kingdom as well as safaris to Mole National Park. For more flexibility, they can also usually arrange car or 4x4 rental inclusive of a driver and his expenses.

Abacar Tours [104 B2] Bobo St #39, Tesano; m 0265 744449/0243 482403; e info@abacar-tours.com; www.abacar-tours.com; see ad, page 172. Running since 2007, this well-thought-of small operator, with its dynamic French-Ghanaian owner-manager team, specialises in tailor-made 4x4 & hiking tours for small groups who want to get a little off the beaten track. All programmes are worked out individually in collaboration with the client.

Easy Track Ghana [105 G1] Kisseman; m 0276 657036; e contact@easytrackghana.com; www. easytrackghana.com. Based out of a family-like compound in the unplanned neighbourhood of Kisseman in northern Accra, this socially committed boutique operator, with its close-knit team of articulate guides & drivers, can arrange everything from tours of the whole country to contemporary or traditional cultural experiences in Kisseman & elsewhere around Accra, using

ACCRA *Adabraka, Asylum Down & Nkrumah Circle*
For listings, see pages 121–32

🛏 **Where to stay**
1	Agoo Hostel	F1
2	Ampaqx Grand	E2
3	Eclipse	C3
4	Greenfield Lodge	F2
5	Gye Nyame	F2
6	Hotel Crown Prince	B4
7	Hotel de California	D3
8	Hotel Kyekyewere	C4
9	Hotel Paloma	E1
10	Hotel President	C3
11	Ingot	C3
12	Niagara	C2
13	Pink Hostel	E2
14	YMCA	E4

✖ **Where to eat and drink**
15	Champs Sports Bar & Grill	E1
16	The Orangery	C3
17	Sky Bar	E3
19	Vienna City	B2
20	White Bell	B3
21	Yoko's Indian	E2

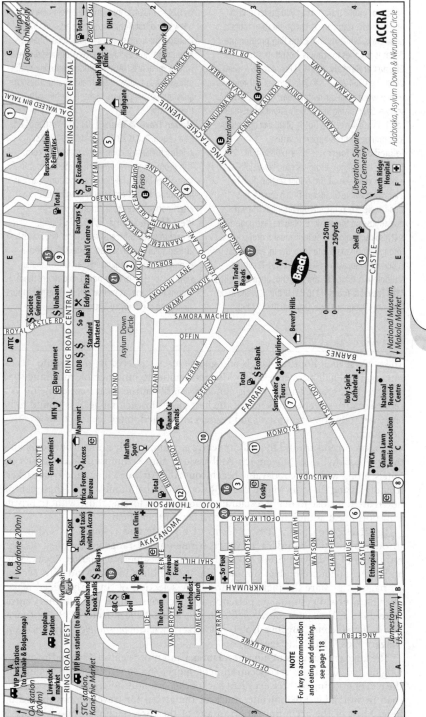

ACCRA
Adabraka, Asylum Down & Nkrumah Circle

private or public transport as you prefer. It also offers airport transfers, Accra orientation tours & homestays, while its 'One Extra Bag' programme donates supplies to schools, hospitals, etc.

Ghana Car Rentals [119 C2] Paradise St, Asylum Down; m 0264 264246; e info@ghana-car-rentals. com; www.ghana-car-rentals.com; see ad, 3rd colour section. Specialising in relatively affordable rentals of car/4x4 with driver, this Dutch-Ghanaian operation also arranges tours & airport transfers.

Jolinaiko Eco Tours m 0208 120856/0247 522173; e info@joli-ecotours.com; www.joli-ecotours.com; see ad, 3rd colour section. Run by a knowledgeable Ghanaian-Dutch couple, this small-scale eco-conscious operator has its own guesthouse on the outskirts of Accra (see page 165), & it also runs tailor-made individual & group tours throughout Ghana & into Togo, Benin, Ivory Coast & Burkina Faso, with a focus on nature & culture. Multiple-day hiking & camping trips are a speciality.

M&J Travel & Tours [116 B1] UNDP HQ, Ring Road East, near Danquah Circle, Osu; ✆03027 73498;

m 0244 514824; e info@mandjtravelghana.com; www.mandjtravelghana.com; see ad, page 92. Probably the longest-serving operator in Ghana, & among the most highly respected, this responsive & vastly experienced IATA-accredited company, with offices in Accra, Kumasi & Tamale, arranges bespoke individual & group tours, flights & car hire all around the country.

Melian Travel & Tours [104 D1] Westlands Bd, East Legon; ✆03029 62411; m 0204 750896; e info@meliantnt.com; www.meliantnt.com. This promising new owner-managed operator specialises in flight & hotel reservations, car/bus hire, airport transfers & tours ranging from an afternoon to 2 weeks in duration.

West African Safaris m 0247 919469; e explore@westafricansafaris.com; www.west.african.safaris.com; see ad, page 225. Based in Elmina, this well-organised joint UK-Ghanaian venture specialises in bringing volunteer school groups to Ghana, as well as offering bespoke tours all around the country & further afield.

⌂ WHERE TO STAY

There are several hundred hotels and guesthouses scattered in and around Accra, ranging from half a dozen with world-class facilities to innumerable mid-range bed and breakfasts, and budget hotels aimed primarily at the local market. Below is a representative selection of some of the best places in each range; it is bound to be less than fully comprehensive, and readers are invited to tell us about any exciting new finds.

Options in and around the **old city centre** are numerically limited, but do include the peerless five-star Mövenpick Ambassador and Kempinski Gold Coast City hotels, along with the good-value beachfront Afia African Village and backpacker-friendly Rising Phoenix Magic Beach Resort. Note that in most cases these central hotels are not close to many restaurants, more or less forcing those without private transport to eat at their hotel or to catch a taxi further afield.

The liveliest part of Accra in terms of nightlife and restaurants is **Osu**, run through by hectic Oxford Street. Osu is strong on mid-range hotels, most of them rather bland and overpriced, but it also hosts the superb upmarket Roots Hotel and a few adequate budget options. The three hotels in the 'Moderate' section on pages 122–3 are the pick of a fairly large selection of similarly priced places offering a broadly similar experience and facilities. These include the **Central Hotel** [116 C3] (*www.centralhotels.com.gh*), **Mariset Plaza Hotel** [113 F4] (*www. marisethotels.com*), **Byblos Hotel** [113 B2] (*www.bybloshotelghana.com*) and **Niagara Plus** [116 C2] (page 124).

The adjacent suburbs of vibrant **Adabraka** and more genteel **Asylum Down** have long hosted Accra's main concentration of budget and shoestring options, but with the recent opening of three excellent backpacker-friendly hotels just across the ring road in workaday **Kokomlemle**, much of the action for travellers has moved up here. Most of the accommodation in any of the three neighbourhoods above is within walking distance of Nkrumah Circle, which is surely the single largest public transport hub in Ghana.

Unsurprisingly, **suburban Accra** hosts an ever-increasing number of upmarket and luxury hotels catering mainly to business travellers. In terms of location, the two large luxury hotels at La Beach are hard to beat, while Villa Monticello and Mahogany Lodge, both close to the airport, have lesser settings but the more intimate atmosphere one would expect of the city's top boutique hotels. The more affordable Marcus Garvey Lodge and Crystalline Hostel are both citywide standouts in their price range.

CITY CENTRE
Luxury

⌂ **Mövenpick Ambassador Hotel** [127 D1] (260 rooms) Independence Av; ☎03026 11000; e hotel.accra@moevenpick.com; www.moevenpick.com. Opened in 2011 on the site of the original 1950s Ambassador Hotel, centrally located opposite the National Theatre, this completely rebuilt 5-star member of the Swiss Mövenpick chain is without doubt one of the 2 most stylish & prestigious hotels in Ghana. The high-ceilinged reception & other public areas are adorned with superb contemporary African artworks, creating a genuine sense of place, yet the super-efficient staff & blasting AC ensure that it also has a truly international feel (indeed, coming here directly from elsewhere in Ghana has been known to induce low-key culture shock). Facilities include a superb restaurant, a bar serving relatively affordable snacks, a great little deli, a superb buffet b/fast (included in the room rate), a wonderful free-form swimming pool & pool bar, a small but well-equipped shopping mall, lobby lounge, meeting facilities, forex desk & on-site Stanbic Bank & ATM, health club, spa & tennis court. The spacious rooms, tastefully decorated with modern African art, come with king-sized bed, large-screen satellite TV, Wi-Fi, minibar, safe & en-suite combined bath/tub. Unlike any other hotel in Ghana, this would probably earn a 5-star ranking anywhere in the world, though the hefty prices, however justified, mean it is mainly frequented by business travellers on account. *US$355/395 B&B standard sgl/dbl, US$455/495 executive sgl/dbl; suites from US$750 upwards.* **$$$$$**

⌂ **Kempinski Gold Coast City Hotel** [127 E1] (269 rooms) Gamel Abdul Nasser Av; ☎0242 436000; e reservations.accra@kempinski.com; www.kempinski.com/accra. The newest African property in the prestigious Kempinski chain, the Kempinski Gold Coast City Hotel sits in a rapidly developing new neighbourhood atop what was once the colonial-era Accra racecourse. Its late-2015 opening marks the 2nd international 5-star hotel to take root in Accra, & is a good barometer for the capital's fortunes as a whole – the yet-to-be-completed developments surrounding the hotel will include high-end condos, shopping, restaurants & more. The hotel itself is the height of style, with a fountain-lined drive opening on to a wide & artistic reception area, adorned with wood & reed accent pieces, glass & wire chandeliers, adinkra-inspired art throughout, & plush seating at the hotel's several top-notch bars. One sumptuous buffet restaurant was open at the time of writing, but there are eventually set to be 3 (not including the brilliantly located 3rd-floor rooftop pool bar), including fine dining inside & a Lebanese-inspired terrace restaurant in the designer courtyard. Rooms come with either city or pool & garden views, along with king-sized beds, flatscreen satellite TV, safe, Wi-Fi, minibar, hardwood floors, writing desk & rainfall showers. The sauna & yoga studio were still under construction in 2016, but the handsomely equipped gym, pool & business centre were already up & running when we stopped in. Even if staying here is well beyond your budget, the attached Gallery 1957 (*www.gallery1957.com*) hosts rotating exhibitions by contemporary Ghanaian artists & is absolutely worth stopping in for. *US$395–525 B&B dbl depending on facilities* **$$$$$**

Upmarket

☀ ⌂ **Afia African Village** [127 E3] (30 chalets) Beachfront south of High St; ☎03026 81462/4; m 0247 758685; e info@afiavillage.com; www.afiavillage.com. One of the best-value lodges in Accra, with the added bonus of having a central location right on a rocky beach, earthy Afia Village offers the winning combination of comfortable accommodation, delicious home-cooked food in the open-sided Tribes Restaurant designed to catch a sea breeze, & plenty of African character. The spacious chalets have terracotta-tile floors, fan, fridge, kettle, AC, satellite TV, 2 sgl or 1 dbl bed, & en-suite hot shower. Other facilities include Wi-Fi

& a brilliantly stocked antiques shop, which sells artefacts the owners have collected from all over West Africa. Negatives are the lack of a swimming beach or pool, & a few recent complaints about tardy service. Still, great value for pricey Accra. *US$123/143 B&B standard sgl/dbl, US$153/173 sgl/ dbl with oceanfront balcony.* **$$$$**

Budget

✳ ⌂ **Rising Phoenix Magic Beach Resort** [127 C3] (12 rooms) Beachfront south of High St; m 0244 315416 or 0204 332051; e myopenspace@ yahoo.co.uk; www.magicbeachresort.com. Set on a low cliff above a small beach behind the Anglican Cathedral in Usshertown, this quirky central lodge won't be to everybody's taste & as such it gets mixed reviews from readers. We rate it as the best-value option in Accra for music-loving backpackers who enjoy a sociable party atmosphere, but it can't be recommended to more fastidious travellers or those seeking a tranquil beach escape. The variably sized rooms, though a little rundown, all have fans & nets, & most have ocean-facing balconies. The large outdoor dance floor hosts live music on the last Sat of the month, dance parties on other Sats, & acrobatics/martial arts on most other afternoons. The restaurant/bar has an excellent vegetarian-only menu. Ask about sea conditions before swimming. Though only about 200m from the main road, it is rather well hidden: coming from the old city centre, turn right (towards the beach) into a dirt road immediately after the Vodafone office, then left when you hit a row of old green wooden buildings after about 100m, then right, walking through the market, then left again. Usefully, you can book online & pay with PayPal. *US$12–28 dbl with shared facilities, US$22–31 self-contained dbl.* **$$–$**

⌂ **Calvary Methodist Guesthouse** [113 C2] (6 rooms) Barnes Rd; m 0242 562910. One of the best-value central budget options in Accra, this hostel is opposite the National Museum. There's a communal lounge with TV. Inexpensive meals are served, & plenty of other eateries lie within walking distance. *US$18/24 self-contained sgl/dbl with AC, fan, balcony & hot shower.* **$$**

⌂ **YMCA** [119 E4] (7 rooms) 03022 24700. Situated in a quiet compound on Castle Rd, about 500m east of Kojo Thompson, this central but peaceful set-up has agreeable self-contained rooms with king-sized bed, fan & AC. *Good value at US$8–13 old block dbl, US$13–18 new block dbl.* **$$–$**

Shoestring

⌂ **JayNii Beach Resort** [127 A4] (2 rooms) Jamestown Beach; m 0277 117286/0264 117286; e jaynii@jaynii.com; www.jaynii.com. This hospitable foundation for street children (see box, page 144) has 2 very basic dorms – 1 for males & 1 for females – where travellers are welcomed. Ignore the touts near the lighthouse who say they're closed. *A donation of around US$10pp per night is expected, FB at US$20pp.* **$**

OSU
Upmarket

⌂ **Roots Hotel** [116 C2] (43 rooms/apts) 15th Ln; 03070 13276; m 0243 310310; e info@roots-hotel.com; www.roots-hotel.com. This smart & newish high-rise in the heart of lively Osu offers exceptional value in self-catering apts with attractively earthy décor, well-equipped kitchenette, sitting area, large-screen satellite TV, modern furnishings & AC. There's also a good 7th-floor restaurant with fab views over the city. *US$190 self-contained dbl, exec suites from US$420.* **$$$$$**

⌂ **Olma Colonial Suites** [116 D3] (8 units) Dadebu Rd; m 0502 579952/0246 830741; e bookings@olmacolonialsuites.com; www. olmacolonialsuites.com. A few blocks off the main drag in Osu, this new hotel might as well be miles away. Set in a prim whitewashed compound, the suites here, surrounded by gardens & done up in dark woods & calm colours, are likely the most characterful accommodation in Osu. All are handsomely equipped with full kitchen, AC, Wi-Fi, flatscreen TV, private terrace & living area. There's a small but especially scenic swimming pool, & it pays to reserve ahead as they're often booked out. *US$200 B&B bungalow, US$300 B&B 2br apt.* **$$$$$**

Moderate

⌂ **Frankie's Hotel** [116 B3] (22 rooms) Oxford St; 03027 73567; m 0249 680000; e reserve@ frankieshotel.com; www.frankieshotel.com. This high-rise in the heart of fashionable Osu, though ideally placed for nightlife & eating out, has clean & modern but rather small rooms that though recently remodelled, no longer stand out for their value after a recent price hike. *US$100/130 dbl/twin.* **$$$$**

⌂ **Blue Royal Hotel** [116 C3] (32 rooms) 18th Ln; 03027 83075; m 0545 518899; e blueroyalghana@yahoo.com. Intensely blue, not quite so obviously royal, this well-established hotel ranks among the better of several similarly characterless but serviceable high-rises in central Osu. The spacious, clean semi-suites are a little on the floral side, but all have hot water, sitting area, Wi-Fi, AC & satellite TV. *US$69/89/99 self-contained sgl/dbl/twin.* **$$$**

🏠 **Lake Bosumtwi Hotel** [113 F4] (12 rooms) Klannaa St; 📞 03027 87298; m 0264 018810; e bonsukojo@yahoo.co.uk. Major renovations in 2016 mean this is no longer the budget option it once was, but the rooms on offer today come in several configurations, all of which are pleasant & modern with AC & flatscreen TVs. It's within easy walking distance of Osu's restaurants & nightlife & seems good value. *US$60 dbl, US$100–150 suite with kitchenette & living area.* **$$$$–$$$**

Budget

🏠 **World Link Hotel** [116 B2] (11 rooms) 9th Ln; 📞 03027 74602; e worldlinkhotel@yahoo. com. Formerly known as the Kohinoor & still next to the good Indian restaurant of the same name, this budget hotel is a little tatty at the edges, but still one of the few budget options in the heart of Osu. The en-suite rooms with fan, AC, TV & fridge seem quite good value, all things considered. *US$25/29 self-contained dbl/twin.* **$$**

🏠 **Joska Lodge** [116 D3] Dadebu Rd; 📞 03027 74808/03039 62821. A pretty good deal by Osu standards, though pricey perhaps by any other, this adequate hotel has small but clean rooms with AC, fridge & Wi-Fi. *US$26–37/31–37 self-contained sgl/dbl.* **$$**

🏠 **Access Inn** [113 F4] (8 rooms) Otswe St; m 0241 285949/0207 582529. Warmly recommended by readers, this clean & friendly hotel stands out among a dwindling number of budget options in Osu as particularly good value for the neighbourhood. Rooms use spotless shared bathrooms, & all come with AC, Wi-Fi, & b/fast to be taken on the communal terrace. *US$50 B&B dbl.* **$$$**

🏠 **Hotel Christianborg** [116 D3] (12 rooms) 📞 03027 76074. This vintage multi-storey block looks like it's been around almost as long as its namesake fort, but the dated 1st-floor rooms are clean & well kept for the price, & all come with AC, TV, & fan. *Good value at US$17/20 self-contained dbl/king.* **$$**

Shoestring

🏠 **Salvation Army Hostel** [116 B2] (45 rooms) First St; m 0243 829112/453025. The cheapest acceptable option for single travellers, this has the bonus of a brilliant location for nightlife & eating out at the end of Embassy Rd in Osu (though be warned that there is an official but laxly enforced curfew of 22.30). *US$5 per bed in a 5- or 6-bed dorm, US$8–16 self-contained dbl.* **$$–$**

ADABRAKA, ASYLUM DOWN & KOKOMLEMLE
Upmarket

🏠 **Hotel Paloma** [119 E1] (65 rooms) Ring Rd; 📞 03022 28700; m 0244 336070; e reservations. rrc@palomahotel.com; www.palomahotel.com. Conveniently located on the north side of Ring Rd, between Nkrumah Circle & Sankara Overpass, the Paloma is a reliable though perhaps slightly overpriced multi-storey with a Mediterranean feel & large, comfortably furnished rooms with satellite TV, AC & hot water. There are also suites with kitchenettes. The complex hosts a good selection of popular restaurants, & often has live music at w/ ends (salsa dancing on Sat). Prices have increased, but it's still good value. *US$125/145/170 B&B self-contained sgl/dbl/suite.* **$$$$**

Moderate

🏠 **Greenfield Lodge** [119 F2] (8 rooms) 4th Crescent Link; 📞 03022 64360; m 0202 886590; e info@greenfieldghana.com; www. greenfieldghana.com. Tucked away in Asylum Down, this relatively stylish lodge has spacious clean rooms with Wi-Fi, satellite TV, AC, writing desk & hot showers, & a bright little restaurant serving a varied selection of Ghanaian & international dishes. *US$65/78/105 self-contained dbl/exec/suite.* **$$$**

🏠 **Gye Nyame Hotel** [119 F2] (22 rooms) Kaanyemi Crescent; 📞 03022 23321; m 0245 186834; e gyenyamehotel@hotmail.com. Set in Asylum Down, just off Ring Rd, this modest & sparklingly clean hotel is a pleasant enough escape, but the small rooms with AC, satellite TV & hot water feel ever so slightly overpriced. *US$52/63/73 B&B self-contained sgl/dbl/suite.* **$$$**

🏠 **Niagara Hotel** [119 C2] (19 rooms) Kojo Thompson Rd; 📞 03022 30118; m 0245 933639; e niagara@ighmail.com. This long-serving hotel can be a useful 1st base in Accra, thanks to the responsive owner-manager, though it can be noisy at the w/ends. The large rooms are starting to look their age but come with hot water, AC, satellite TV & Wi-Fi. It arranges reasonably priced car hire, & there's a Lebanese restaurant with AC. The affiliated **Niagara Plus** [116 C2] in Osu is similar in standard & price. *From a negotiable US$66/88 self-contained sgl/dbl.* **$$$**

Budget

✳ 🏠 **Somewhere Nice** [113 D1] (12 rooms) Manye Nanobeng Av; m 0543 743505; e info@ hostelaccra.com; www.hostelaccra.com; see ad, page 150. With an effortlessly sociable vibe that most hostels aim for but few actually manage to achieve, this new place, part of the Czech Bohemian Hostels group, stands out as an excellent choice for those looking to kick back & connect with other travellers. Opened in 2015, it's set in a newly restored colonial-era building surrounded by recently planted gardens & a swimming pool that's pure backpacker catnip. The en-suite rooms are minimalist but quite comfortable & simply furnished with an intriguing collection of recycled/upcycled materials (like old soda crates & chairs made from tyres). All rooms come with AC & ceiling fans (dorms too!), plus shared balcony access on the upper floor. There's Wi-Fi in the popular common area, & though there was no food served at the time of writing (this may soon change), cold drinks are available, several chop stalls line the street out front, & guests can also use the kitchen. *US$50/55/60 B&B sgl/dbl/trpl, US$13 B&B dorm.* **$$$–$**

🏠 **Agoo Hostel** [119 F1] (7 rooms) Keta Close; ☎ 03022 22726; m 0554 598461; e info@ agoohostel.com; www.agoohostel.com. Set about 300m north of the Ring Rd headed towards Nima Roundabout, this pretty new hostel opened in 2013 & feels like a welcoming place to while away the days in Accra. The breezy, wax-print decorated rooms are set in a large converted home & come with AC & clean shared facilities, while the comfortable gender-segregated dorms are equally well kept but have ceiling fans only. There's a daily Ghanaian dinner available at US$4.50, or the large kitchen is also open to guests should you feel like cooking. Outside, there are a couple of shady verandas overlooking the neat gardens. The private rooms seem good value, the dorms somewhat less so. *US$33/44 B&B sgl/dbl, US$17.50 B&B dorm bed.* **$$$–$$**

🏠 **Sleepy Hippo Hotel** [104 C4] (12 rooms) Duade Av; m 0261 113740/1; e info@

sleepyhippohotel.com; www.sleepyhippohotel. com. Opened at the end of 2014, this welcoming Australian-run backpacker hangout has well-priced rooms & dorms set in a newly renovated 3-storey building about 1km north of Nkrumah Circle. All rooms come with AC, hot water & flatscreen TVs, & the dorms happily have AC as well. Outside, there's a rooftop terrace, plunge pool made from a converted water tank, open-air film screenings, BBQ nights out back, a large (indoor) English-language library, & a restaurant-bar serving pizzas, pastas, curries, & snacks for US$5–10 daily. *US$41/50 B&B std/dlx dbl, US$11 B&B dorm bed.* **$$$–$**

🏠 **Pink Hostel** [119 E2] (19 rooms) Anyemi Kpakpa Rd; ☎ 03022 56710; m 0205 438325; e bookings@pinkhostel.com.gh; www. pinkhostel.com.gh. Though it's come in for a fair bit of reader criticism & remains a little overpriced, this Asylum Down stalwart is comfortable & convenient enough, & makes for a fine place to touch down in Accra & meet other travellers. Online booking is available, & the small but neat & clean rooms come with safe, writing desk, AC, satellite TV, Wi-Fi & shower, and there is also a dorm with AC. There is a good inexpensive bar/restaurant on site & great Indian food around the corner at Yoko's. *US$42/50 self-contained sgl/dbl, US$16 dorm bed.* **$$$–$$**

🏠 **Ampaqx Grand Hotel** [119 E2] (15 rooms) Anyemi Kpakpa Rd; ☎ 03022 34157; m 0247 114850. Situated in Asylum Down, a few doors down from the well-known Pink Hostel, this clean & well-kept hotel has spacious & sensibly priced self-contained rooms with TV & hot water. *US$18/27 dbl with fan/AC; US$32 twin with AC.* **$$**

🏠 **Hotel President** [119 C3] (18 rooms) Farrar Av; ☎ 03022 23343; m 0246 286773; e hotelpresident23@yahoo.com. This time-warped (they even had *Shaft* on TV when we visited) multi-storey hotel near the junction with Kojo Thompson has decent rooms with comfortable beds, fan, AC, TV & hot shower. There's a good patio bar & affordable restaurant attached. *US$22/30/43 self-contained sgl/dbl/suite.* **$$$–$$**

🏠 **Avenida Hotel** [113 C2] (30 rooms) Kojo Thompson Rd; ☎ 03022 21354. When it opened way back in 1948, this substantial hotel in Adabraka was one of the fanciest in town. Now it isn't. But it does remain a good budget bet, with friendly staff, large & clean but rather tired rooms with TV, & a spotless kitchen serving decent food in a cavernous canteen-style dining room. *US$18/21 dbl or twin with fan/AC, US$26 dlx dbl with fridge & TV.* **$$**

Shoestring

🏠 **Hotel de California** [119 D3] (16 rooms) Watson Rd; ☏03022 26199. Although it lost much of its former charm when it relocated a few years back, this evocatively named dive remains good value, though rooms are quite dingy & it is often fully booked. *US$7/8 sgl/dbl with shared bath, US$10 self-contained dbl.* **$**

🏠 **Ingot Hotel** [119 C3] (20 rooms) Off Kojo Thompson Rd; ☏03029 57650. Boasting a convenient location on a quiet side road in Adabraka, this good-value hotel has bright, clean rooms with funky tiled floors & fan. *US$8/9/11 self-contained sgl/dbl/queen* **$**

🏠 **Eclipse Hotel** [119 C3] (12 rooms) Off Kojo Thompson Rd; ☏03022 57263. Situated in Adabraka 100m or so uphill of Kojo Thompson Rd, this good-value hotel has small but neat & clean rooms with hardwood furniture & shared bath. It has no restaurant but lies next to the affiliated Eclipse Bar & close to several good eateries. *US$12/16 dbl with fan/AC.* **$$–$**

🏠 **Hotel Kyekyewere** [119 C4] (5 rooms) Amusudai Rd; ☏03022 24179; **m** 0242 883574. This quiet family-run place just opposite the Ghana Lawn Tennis Association on the backroads west of Kojo Thompson looks fair value. *US$11 dbl with fan & shared bath.* **$**

🏠 **Hotel Crown Prince** [119 B4] (16 rooms) Cnr Castle & Kojo Thompson Rd; ☏03022 25381; **e** hotelcrownprince@live.com. Situated at the junction of 2 roads, this rather rundown Adabraka stalwart has a loud courtyard bar, & shabby but convincingly clean & inexpensive rooms with shared showers that are often flooded. *US$11/13 sgl/dbl with shared bath; US$18 self-contained dbl.* **$$–$**

OUTSIDE THE RING ROAD
Luxury

✳ 🏠 **Villa Monticello** [105 F2] (16 rooms) Mankata Av; ☏03027 73477; **m** 0266 307398; **e** reservations@villamonticello.com; www.villamonticello.com. This super-stylish boutique hotel close to the airport consists of contemporary luxury suites, each individually decorated with a different theme, & furnished with Wi-Fi, iPod

docking station, AC, satellite TV, coffee-/tea-making station, large safe, en-suite hot tub & shower, minibar, & cotton bathrobes & slippers. A classy fusion restaurant with a great wine list serves Ghanaian & continental dishes, with a slight emphasis on seafood, & there is a lovely courtyard & swimming-pool area. Service is exceptional. Facilities include a gym, free shuttle service, & in-room massages. *US$385/435 B&B sgl/dbl standard suite, US$445/495 executive suite, US$800/850 presidential suite, rates drop just over 30% on weekends.* **$$$$$**

✳ 🏠 **Labadi Beach Hotel** [105 H7] (164 rooms) La Rd; ☏03027 72501/6; **m** 0547 141662; **e** labadi@legacyhotels.co.za; www.legacyhotels.com. Having hosted both Tony Blair & Queen Elizabeth II in relatively recent years, the 5-star Labadi Beach was comfortably the top hotel in Accra prior to the opening of the Mövenpick & Kempinski, & recent remodelling has seen it regain some of its shine. It still has the edge when it comes to its oceanfront location on one of the country's most attractive & lively public beaches, but it feels a touch faded compared with the super-stylish upstart competition, & though service standards are very high, everything runs a bit less smoothly. Facilities include tennis courts, sauna & health club, an excellent business centre, a poorly stocked curio & book shop, 2 highly regarded restaurants, a free hourly airport shuttle, lush landscaped gardens complete with large reed-fringed dam & adult & children's swimming pools, & a top-notch hairdressing/beauty salon. The comfortable rooms come with king-size bed, 15-channel satellite TV, Wi-Fi & unusually spacious bathrooms with shower & tub. It is also reasonably convenient for business, situated practically opposite the Trade Fair grounds, yet only 10mins by taxi (traffic permitting) from the city centre & not much further from the airport. *US$375/430 B&B sgl/dbl low season, US$430/505 sgl/dbl high season.* **$$$$$**

🏠 **La Palm Royal Beach Hotel** [105 H7] (159 rooms) La Rd; ☏03022 15100/215111; **e** lapalmres@gbhghana.net; www.gbhghana.net. Situated 200m from Labadi Beach Hotel, this flagship hotel for the Golden Beach chain also overlooks La Beach, though it lacks direct access to the shore. The hotel grounds are centred on a massive free-form swimming pool area shaded by palms. Communal areas & rooms are decorated with African art, but starting to look a bit dated & fuddy-duddy compared with its neighbours. Facilities include 3 excellent restaurants, a bar with a snack menu, & a good shop selling curios, books & newspapers. Spacious tiled rooms have flatscreen satellite TV, fan, AC, wooden writing desk, & en-suite hot tub/shower. *US$376/416 standard sgl/dbl, suites from US$450/490 sgl/dbl, check their website for half-price w/end & other specials.* **$$$$$**

⌂ Holiday Inn Accra Airport [105 F3] (168 rooms) ✆ 03027 40930; e accra@ holidayinnaccraairport.com; www.holidayinn. com/accraairport. The main selling point of this smart but characterless chain hotel is its convenient location a mere 1km from the airport, which makes it very popular with fly-in-fly-out business travellers. The modern rooms have AC, satellite TV, safe, coffee/tea maker, minibar & Wi-Fi. Other services include a business centre, laundry, gym, swimming pool, car rental desk & currency exchange. Attached are 2 excellent but pricey restaurants, & it stands right next to the well-equipped Marina Mall. *US$350/650 B&B dbl/suite.* **$$$$$**

Upmarket

✳ ⌂ Mahogany Lodge [105 G5] (14 rooms) ✆ 03027 61163; m 0244 314795; e mahoganylodge@yahoo.com; www. mahoganylodge.com. One of the few genuine boutique hotels in Accra, this highly praised lodge, close to the airport in leafy East Cantonments, is centred around a courtyard with a bar & a small free-form swimming pool. The rooms & apts are comfortable & attractively decorated, with parquet floors, simple but stylish furnishing, AC, satellite TV, safe, writing desk & Wi-Fi. The ground-floor Mango Tree Restaurant has a cosmopolitan menu serving imaginative mains plus snacks, sandwiches & cocktails. The lodge's most outstanding feature is the excellent personalised service, which ensures plenty of repeat custom. *US$185–200 B&B self-contained dbl, US$280 apt.* **$$$$$**

⌂ Ibis Styles Accra Airport [105 F3] (192 rooms) ✆ 03027 42747/46600; e reservation@ ibisstylesaccra.com; www.accorhotels.com. Much cheaper than the neighbouring Holiday Inn but just as close to the airport & still quite trim, bright & modern, this business-orientated hotel's primary appeal is the location. Rooms come with fridge, telephone, tea/coffee facilities, flatscreen TV & safe,

OLD ACCRA
For listings, see pages 121–32

⊖ **Where to stay**
1 Afia African Village......................E3
2 JayNii Beach Resort...................A4
3 Kempinski Gold Coast City.......E1
4 Mövenpick Ambassador...........D1
5 Noble House & Heritage...........G2
6 Rising Phoenix Magic
    Beach Resort...........................C3

✕ **Where to eat and drink**
7 Asaase Pa.................................D3
   The Deli...............................(see 4)
   Rising Phoenix Magic
     Beach Resort.....................(see 6)
   Tribes Bar & Restaurant.......(see 1)

& there's an on-site pool & restaurant. *US$195/215 B&B sgl/dbl, US$450/470 sgl/dbl suite.* **$$$$$**

Moderate

✳ ⌂ Marcus Garvey Guesthouse [105 F5] (5 rooms) 1st Circular Rd, Cantonments; ✆ 03027 76502. Set in the leafy birdsong-filled compound of the W E B Du Bois Memorial Centre, this out-of-the-way but otherwise very agreeable guesthouse has large, comfortable rooms with old-fashioned décor, AC, satellite TV, hot water, Wi-Fi & fridge. You can eat indoors or out in the shady garden of the attached Roots Flavour Restaurant. *US$50 B&B self-contained dbl or twin.* **$$$**

⌂ Chez Delphy [113 G4] (8 rooms) Jubilee Well St; m 0262 989722/0508 979778; e contact@chezdelphy.com; www.chezdelphy.com. In a low-rise garden compound near the junction of Ring Rd East & the Labadi Rd, this Franco-Ghanaian family B&B feels tranquil & tucked away, though it's only a short hop to the action of Osu or Labone. The tiled rooms are done up in pastels & African décor, & all come with AC, satellite TV, hot water & Wi-Fi. Good Ghanaian & continental meals are available at request. *US$70 sgl, US$105/125 street-/garden-facing dbl, US$130 dbl with king-sized bed; all rates B&B.* **$$$$–$$$**

Shoestring

⌂ Crystalline Hostel [104 A2] (15 rooms) ✆ 03023 04634; m 0277 439745; e crystalhostel@ yahoo.com or crystalhostel@outlook.com; www. crystalhostel.com. Situated in Darkuman, about 10mins by trotro from Kaneshie Market, this amiable family-run hostel, centred on a grassy compound, has comfortable rooms & dorms with fan, TV &

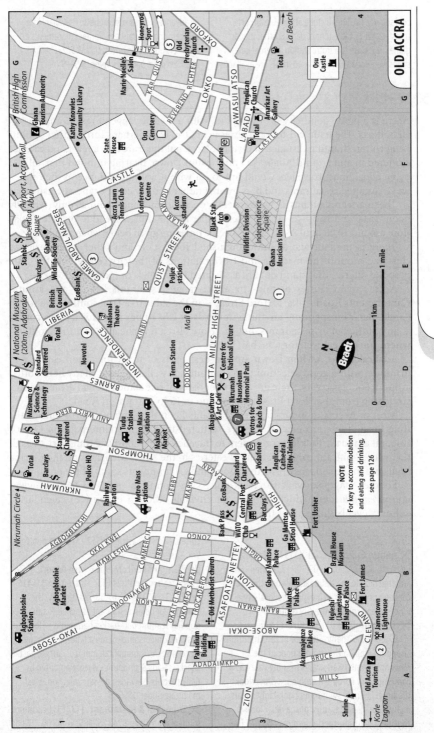

OLD ACCRA

NOTE
For key to accommodation
and eating and drinking,
see page 126

cold shower. Facilities include affordable airport transfers, Wi-Fi, table tennis, darts & other indoor games. It is close to a trotro station, internet cafés & shops. Vegetarian & meat-based meals are available by advance order, & a kitchenette is available for self-catering. It arranges volunteer placements at relatively affordable prices. *US$18.50/25 sgl/dbl, US$10pp dorm bed or camping.* **$$–$**

✖ WHERE TO EAT AND DRINK

Accra is a pretty good city for eating out, with a diverse range of restaurants to suit all budgets. The main cluster of eateries is in Osu, with perhaps three dozen options lying within shouting distance of Oxford Street, but there are also a few good eateries clustered in and around Adabraka and Asylum Down. Bearing in mind that, all else being equal, most travellers would opt to eat within walking distance of their hotel, we've clumped restaurants and bars by area rather than by cost or type of cuisine.

The smarter restaurants in Accra generally open for lunch and/or dinner only (typically noon–15.00 and 16.30–23.00), but the cheaper fast-food places tend to operate all day from around 10.00 until 23.00. More specific times are given below where available.

There is no shortage of undistinguished food stalls and other cheap eateries clustered around the markets and trotro stations of the **city centre**, but the only bespoke eateries that stand out are associated with hotels or lodges.

Accra's main cluster of mid- to upper-range restaurants lies on and around Cantonments Road – aka 'Oxford Street' – in the suburb of **Osu**, south of Danquah Circle. Bank on spending anything upwards of US$10 per head for a main course at any of the better restaurants, but there are also a few cheaper 'fast food' outlets, where you can eat well for less than US$5.

Adabraka and **Asylum Down** are the best parts of town for cheap eating and drinking, with a good selection of restaurants, as well as a great many bars dotted around. For cheap eats, there are a number of jollof rice stands along Farrar Avenue, stretching from the Hotel President back up to Kojo Thompson Road.

Most of Accra's more upmarket restaurants lie in the garden suburbs **outside the Ring Road**. These are inevitably more scattered than their counterparts in Osu or Adabraka, and are thus less convenient to travellers without private transport, though there are significant concentrations of eateries in the Accra Mall, around the Marina Mall, and in the suburbs of North Labone and Cantonments south of the airport.

Foodies may also want to check out Accra Premium (m *0233 668892; www. accrapremium.com*), which puts on an enviable (though expensive) calendar of culinary events throughout the year.

CITY CENTRE

✖ **Auntie Gracie Special** [113 C2] Barnes Rd; m 0262 977250; ⊕ 09.30–17.00 Mon–Fri. Situated next to the National Museum, this is a convenient place for an inexpensive local-style lunch when exploring the city centre. **$**

✖ **The Deli** [127 D1] ✆ 03026 11400; ⊕ 07.00–23.00 daily. Situated in the Emporium Shopping Mall on the ground floor of the Mövenpick Ambassador, this friendly café has a contemporary European ambience & overlooks the hotel lawns & swimming pool. Light meals include sushi, pasta, subs, plus a daily local & continental-fusion special (*around US$10*). The

coffee, cakes & pastries (*US$2–5*) stand out. Good wine list, too. **$$–$**

✖ **Rising Phoenix Magic Beach Resort** [127 C3] Beachfront south of High St; m 0244 315416 or 0204 332051/2; ⊕ 07.30–23.00 daily. The strictly vegetarian restaurant attached to this popular seafront backpacker hangout is within easy walking distance of most landmarks in the city centre. A cosmopolitan menu of curries, pastas, snacks, salads & smoothies is supplemented by daily specials & a varied dessert selection. Most mains are under US$5. **$**

✖ **Tribes Bar & Restaurant** [127 E3] Beachfront south of High St; m 0247 758685; ⊕ 07.00–22.00

Mon–Thu; 07.00–23.00 Fri–Sun. The open-sided seafood-slanted restaurant at Afia African Village serves up hearty Ghanaian & continental mains in the US$8–15 range & chilled drinks – including wine by the glass – to a background of jazz music & overlooking the rocky coast. $$$–$$

✖ **Asaase Pa** [127 D3] Atta Mills High St; m 0277 816017/0241 017842; ⨍ fb.me/asaasepa; ⏲ 08.00–21.00 Sun–Fri. Another good choice for vegetarians, this shady garden restaurant near the Nkrumah Mausoleum does vegetarian & vegan versions of Ghanaian favourites like waakye, jollof rice, & fufu for US$2–3, along with smaller pastries & snacks. $

OSU
EXPENSIVE

❋ ✖ **Bella Roma** [116 B3] 4th Lane; ☎0247 474007; ⨍ fb.me/bellaroma.accra; ⏲ 18.00–late Wed, Fri–Sat. This slick new restaurant-cum-nightspot has a contemporary European feel off-set by African touches to the décor. The predominantly Italian menu using imported meats & cheeses includes pizzas, pasta, grilled seafood, meat & salads, with most mains in the US$15–20 range. There is also a large-screen TV for sporting events, & a dance floor featuring DJs & occasional live music (check the website for upcoming events). $$$

✖ **Burger & Relish** [116 D3] 14th Ln; m 0540 121356; www.burgerandrelish.com; ⏲ noon–23.00 Sun–Wed, noon–02.00 Thu–Sat. In a cool & comfortable industrial-chic building off the main drag in Osu, this new burger joint & cocktail bar is a homesickness cure par excellence, with juicy, generously sized burgers that would easily pass muster in the American heartland or European capitals. The cocktail list is almost as long as the food menu, & there's a stylish front terrace if you're not keen on the air-conditioned interior. Burgers start at around US$9. $$$–$$

✖ **Le Magellan Restaurant** [119 F3] Ring Rd East; ☎03027 77629; m 0244 585858; ⨍ fb.me/LeMagellanGhana; ⏲ noon–15.00 Mon–Sat & 06.30–23.00 Mon–Fri. One of Accra's finest restaurants, this serves French cuisine accompanied by a mostly French wine list. The food is superlative & the service impeccable, though the arctic AC can prove a little overpowering. Mains US$12–20. $$$

❋ ✖ **Monsoon** [116 C3] Oxford St; ☎03027 82307; ⏲ 18.00–22.30 Mon–Thu, 18.00–23.30

Fri–Sat. Located somewhat incongruously on the roof above the Osu Food Court, this owner-managed 3-in-1 restaurant serves fantastic but pricey game meat, as well as Japanese-made sashimi & sushi, hand-rolled to order. Indoor & outdoor seating are available, & a bar is attached. Mains US$10–18. $$$

Moderate

❋ ✖ **Buka Restaurant** [116 B2] 10th Lane; ☎0302 782953; m 0244 842464; ⨍ fb.me/thebukarestaurant; ⏲ noon–21.00 Mon–Sat. Located next to the old American embassy, this well-signposted open-sided restaurant specialising in West African food is the perfect place for new arrivals to sample top-notch Ghanaian cuisine, or for more jaded palates to sample dishes from Nigeria, Togo, Senegal or Ivory Coast, mostly in the US$5–7 range. $$–$

✖ **Eat By Fine Things** [113 E2] Gamel Abdul Rd; ☎03070 20930; m 0204 968130; e vicki@eatfinethings.com; ⏲ 06.00–18.30 Mon–Fri, 08.00–16.00 Sat–Sun. Situated a short walk west of Oxford St, a few doors up from the British High Commission, this deli-like set-up has indoor & outdoor seating, cake & pastries, & a varied selection of Ghanaian, Continental & Asian dishes, with different specials daily. It's a great spot for a snack or a relaxed lunch. Most mains are in the US5–9 range. $$

♀**Honeysuckle Bar & Restaurant** [116 B1] Ring Rd East; m 0275 556006; ⏲11.00–late daily. This sports bar, with pool table & large-screen TVs for major sporting events, feels like a little bit of England in the heart of Accra. There's pub grub (pies, burgers, bangers & mash) for US$10–20. $$

✖ **18th Lane Indian Restaurant** [116 C3] 18th Lane; m 0266 777000/0263 384440; ⨍ fb.me/18thlaneindianrestaurant; ⏲ 08.00–midnight daily. It may not be as posh as the Heritage, but this appealing little restaurant near the Vidya Bookstore is a great spot for authentic Indian food. Vegetarians are well catered for & there's indoor/outdoor seating. Mains US$7–11. $$

❋ ✖ **Mamma Mia** [116 B3] 8th Lane; m 0244 264151; ⨍ fb.me/MammaMiaGhana; ⏲ 17.00–22.30 Tue–Fri, noon–22.30 Fri/Sat. Long regarded as the top Italian eatery in Accra, this earthy owner-managed restaurant is well known for its thin-crust pizzas (made in a wood-fired oven), but the seafood & pasta is also recommended. Most dishes are in the US$10–15 range. Reservations advised. $$$–$$

✳ ✖ **Noble House & Heritage** [127 G2] Salem Rd; ☎03027 85151/85252; www. noblehouseghana.com; ⏰ noon–15.00 & 18.30–23.00 daily. Sharing a large building at the south end of Salem Rd next to the old Presbyterian church, the Noble House & Heritage restaurants might be a bit remote from the action in central Osu, but they are widely regarded as among the very best Chinese & Indian restaurants in the country. The food is well priced & the flavours authentic. Mains US$7–12. $$

✳ ✖ **Pinocchio & La Piazza** [116 B2] 11th Lane; ☎03027 97566; m 0244 432188; ☑ fb.me/ piazzaghana; ⏰ 08.00–23.30 Sun–Thu, 08.00–04.00 Fri–Sat. With a brightly painted gelateria & patisserie out front & a more upmarket restaurant & roof terrace in back, this new go-to spot for pizzas, pastas, paninis & pastries for US$8–12 fits the bill nicely for either a quick lunchtime bite or a classy dinner out. The pizzas are some of the best in town & they keep late hours at w/ends. $$–$$

✖ **Kona Cafe & Grill** [116 C3] Oxford St; m 0264 464712; ➤ @konacafegh; ⏰ 17.00–23.00 Sun–Thu, 17.00–03.00 Fri–Sat. Opened in 2016 in a prime location on Oxford St, this festive & faux-rustic new restaurant & bar is street market-inspired, with furniture made from old pallets on their large ground-floor terrace & a drinks cart serving up traditional brews like the millet-based *pito* & palm wine. The food menu is grill-centric, with kebabs, chips & a late night w/end b/fast that'll keep punters happy, though the focus here seems to be more on the nightlife. There's also a rooftop deck with views over the neighbourhood & big-screen TVs, plus shisha pipes, open mic Thu, & guest DJs at the w/ends. $$$–$$

✳ ✖ **Sunshine Salad Bar** [116 B2] 11th Lane; m 0244 383064/315703; ☑ fb.me/ sunshinesaladbarghana; ⏰ 09.00–17.00 Mon–Sat. This cheery place is repeatedly raved about by readers for its imaginative range of fresh salads (try the chicken, bacon & avocado, oriental or falafel salads), as well as sandwiches, curries, burgers & wraps. Large portions, notably without creamy dressing, are in the US$8–12 range. $$$–$$

✳ ✖ **Zion Thai** [116 D4] Cnr Mission & Okodan Rd; m 0243 610108/0549 967644; ⏰ noon–23.00 Tue–Sat, 17.00–23.00 Sun.

Owned & managed by a friendly Thai-Ghanaian couple, this small & inauspicious restaurant, though a little remote from Oxford St, serves absolutely superb Thai food at very good prices. Be warned that the food here is genuinely hot & spicy, & not suited to those with a blander palate. $$

✖ **Restaurant Chez Clarisse Mama Africa** [116 B2] 8th Lane; m 0242 984828; ⏰ 10.00–21.00 Mon–Sat, noon–21.00 Sun. Universally praised by readers & eaters alike, at first glance this unassuming Ivorian restaurant looks like any of the myriad other chop shops hidden away in the backstreets of Osu, & while the ambiance might be somewhat similar, the food is anything but. The couscous-like *attieke* & tilapia with tomatoes & onions is especially recommended, & checks in at around US$6–8. $$

Snacks and cheap eats
☕ **Frankie's** [116 B3] Oxford St; ☎03027 71877; m 0244 188444; ⏰ 07.00–midnight Sun–Thu, 07.00–01.00 Fri–Sat. Long known for its high-quality pastries, cakes & ice cream, Frankie's now extends over 2 floors (& was being expanded again in 2016), with a patisserie, coffee shop & Lebanese-style take-away at street level, & a more formal restaurant serving an excellent variety of salads & grills (& superb burgers) on the 1st floor. $$–$

✖ **KFC** [116 C3] Oxford St; ☎03029 63086; ⏰ 10.00–23.00 Mon–Thu, 10.00–01.00 Fri–Sat. The Ghanaian branch of this well-known fast-food franchise serves 1-person meals in the US$4–8 range. $$–$

✳ ☕ **Nourish Lab Smoothies** [116 C4] Oxford St; m 0243 939855/0289 333999; ☑ fb.me/smoothysghana; ⏰ 08.00–23.00 daily. Situated opposite the Shell filling station on the south end of Oxford St, this wonderful little café boasts a lengthy list of inexpensive natural fruit smoothies, salads, sandwiches, wraps & paninis, with the added bonus of free Wi-Fi for customers. $

✖ **Osu Food Court** [116 C3] 41 Oxford St; ☎0302 783444; ⏰ 08.00–20.00 daily. An inexpensive fast-food favourite, this southern African implant hosts branches of Galito's (flame-grilled chicken), Pizza Inn & Creamy Inn (ice creams). $

✖ **Papaye Fast Food** [116 C4] Oxford St; ☎03027 73754; ⏰ 10.00–23.00 daily. It may be a little generic, but this small fast-food restaurant still delivers some of Osu's best spicy grilled chicken & fish. Take-away orders can take up to an hour, but the grills are delicious & there's a fun streetside drinking spot opposite where you can have a beer while you wait. $

ADABRAKA AND ASYLUM DOWN

✴ ✘ **Khana Khazana** [113 C2] Off Kojo Thompson Rd; m 0275 834282/0271 591111; ⏲ 10.00–22.00 daily. Accra's only south Indian restaurant, tucked away on a backroad behind the Engen Garage on Kojo Thompson, is well worth seeking out. Comprising a large thatched open-sided dining area set in pleasant gardens, it has a subcontinent-spanning menu with plenty of vegetarian choices, but the speciality is pancake-like savoury filled dosas. Most dishes are in the US$5–8 range. $$

✘ **Champs Sports Bar & Grill** [119 E1] 40 Ring Rd Central; m 0240 959406; www. champsafrica.com; ⏲ 16.00–22.00 Mon–Thu, 16.00–midnight Fri–Sun. Located in the Paloma Centre, this cool & comfortable pub, decorated with international flags, is a popular place to watch major international sporting events on satellite TV. It also serves the usual range of drinks & decent pub grub. $$

✘ **The Orangery** [119 C3] Farrar Av; m 0243 265207; ⏲ 10.30–22.00 Mon–Sat. This attractively decorated tapas bar & fusion restaurant is the most upmarket place to eat in this part of town, with an extensive menu of Ghanaian, Italian & other continental dishes in the US$8–14 range. The prawns & grilled tilapia in pepper sauce are particularly recommended. $$$–$$

✴ ✘ **White Bell** [119 B3] Cnr Farrar Av & Nsawan Rd; m 0244 622389; ⏲ 08.00–23.30 daily. This open-sided 1st-floor restaurant/bar usually catches a good breeze, & has a reasonably eclectic music selection (though it can get a bit loud). The menu (ranging from spicy vegetable or chicken curry to burgers & sandwiches) is a lot more varied than what is actually available on any given day, but it's inexpensive, with nothing much over US$5, & almost invariably good. $

✴ ✘ **Yoko's Indian Restaurant** [119 E2] 5th Av; ☎ 03029 14748; m 0267 225254; ⏲ 11.30–22.30 Tue–Sun. This unpretentious Asylum Down garden eatery on the same road as the Ampaqx Hotel & Pink Hostel serves a varied selection of Indian meat &

vegetarian dishes in the US$6–8 range. Very good & reasonably priced. It was closed for renovations in 2016 but scheduled to reopen. $$

OUTSIDE THE RING ROAD
Expensive
✘ **Bamboo Chinese Fusion Restaurant** [113 F1] Switchback Cresc; ☎ 03029 71272; m 0247 777876; **f** fb.me/BambooAccra; ⏲ noon–15.00 & 18.00–22.00 daily. This excellent & relatively new restaurant, tucked away to east of Liberation Rd, serves an interesting selection of straight & fusion Chinese, continental & local dishes. Mains US$8–15. $$$–$$

✘ **Captain Hook's** [105 G5] Kakramandu St, Cantonments; ☎ 03027 62228; ⏲ noon–16.00 Mon–Sat & 18.00–22.30 daily. The Accra branch of this ever-popular but notoriously pricey Takoradi-based restaurant serves some of the city's best seafood & steaks. The sumptuous seafood platters are enormous, so share one with a friend if you can so you can leave some room for their famously decadent desserts. Mains are mostly around US$25. It has a good wine list. $$$

✴ ✘ **La Chaumiere** [105 F2] Liberation Av; ☎ 03027 72408; m 0244 802013; ⏲ noon–14.30 Mon-Fri & 19.00–23.00 Mon–Sat. Situated opposite the Woolworths Mall, this well-established family-run French restaurant is widely regarded to rank among the finest in Ghana, serving a selection of North African dishes alongside typical French fare. Mains are mostly in the US$15–25 range. $$$

✘ **Simret Restaurant** [105 E3] Roman Rd; m 0507 408938; www.simret-restaurant.com; ⏲ 06.30–22.00 Tue–Sat. Though at roughly US$20pp it's not exactly cheap, this small restaurant feels like a family home, & remains the place to go for authentic Ethiopian flavours in Accra. Meals are served buffet-style, vegetarians are well catered for, & Ethiopian coffee after your meal is included in the price. Reservations strongly recommended. $$$

✘ **Santoku** [105 F2] Azure, Villagio Vista, Tetteh Quarshie Circle; m 0544 311511; www.santoku-restaurant.com; ⏲ noon–14.30 Mon–Fri, 18.30-21.45 Mon–Wed, 18.30-22.45 Thu–Sat. A strong contender for Accra's most stylish restaurant, the *très soigné* Santoku serves sushi, Japanese & fusion cuisine in a luxury designer environment with a sake bar, humidor & long menu of expertly prepared sushi & sashimi. Rolls start around US$7, mains around US$15 & both head upwards from there. No shorts or flip-flops allowed. $$$

Moderate

☀ ✖ **Afrikiko Complex** [113 E2] Liberation Rd; ☎ 03022 29997; m 0244 613677/0543 399100; ⊕ 11.00–23.30 daily. Situated a short distance north of the Sankara Overpass, this long-serving garden bar has evolved into 3 very good & affordable restaurants serving mains in the US$8–10 range. These are the self-explanatory Thai Island & Toras Tapas Bar, & the more intriguing Tamtan, whose pan-African cuisine includes Senegalese chicken yassa, Moroccan-style couscous, Nigerian pepper soup, Ivorian grilled snails, as well as that always welcome north Ghanaian special, spicy grilled guineafowl. The outdoor bar is still there, too, shaded by tall trees & with a dance floor that rocks to salsa on Wed, kizomba on Thu & live music on w/ends. $$

☀ ✖ **Maquis Tante Marie** [113 G2] 5th Norla St, Cantonments; also branches in the Accra Mall & Marina Mall; ☎ 03027 78914; m 0260 726401/0244 612832; ☐ fb.me/MaquisTante; ⊕ 11.00–23.00 daily. Done in the style of an Ivorian *maquis*, the main branch of this popular garden restaurant serves excellent Ghanaian & other West African dishes – including grilled guineafowl, Senegalese rice with red-red & oddities like snail kebab – in the US$6–12 range. Drinks are available. The 2 mall branches are inevitably less outdoorsy, but the food is as good & they are more accessible on public transport. $$$–$$

✖ **Roots Flavour** [105 F5] W E B Du Bois Memorial Centre; ☎ 03027 72122; m 0200 813513; ⊕ 07.00–20.30 Mon–Sat. This pleasant garden restaurant combines a lazy outdoor ambience with a varied selection of Ghanaian & international dishes, including pizzas & sandwiches, in the US$7–10 range. $$

✖ **Zanzibar** [113 G2] 42 Dade St, Labone; m 0240 890990; www.zanzi-bargh.com; ⊕ 11.00–15.00 & 17.00–23.30 daily. This cosy restaurant located on the ground floor of a private home in the residential area of Labone stays true to its name, specialising in authentic spicy Zanzibari cuisine. Low lighting & rich décor add to its intimate appeal. Main courses US$8–12. $$$–$$

Snacks and cheap eats

🍴 **Café dez Amis** [113 E2] Liberation Av; m 0504 990399; ☐ fb.me/cafedezamis; ⊕ 07.30–22.00 Mon–Sat, 08.30–21.00 Sun. Situated alongside the well-known Afrikiko complex, this is a pleasant outdoor spot for b/fast or a snack, serving fresh coffee, delicious smoothies & an inexpensive selection of cakes, biscuits, omelettes & sandwiches. $$–$

✖ **Chez Afrique** [105 G1] Near Yemoh Plaza, East Legon; ☎ 03029 11591; m 0202 112887; ⊕ 11.00–23.30 daily. It's a little out of the way, but this lively outdoor restaurant is a great place to taste-test local dishes like red-red, yams with palava sauce, & banku & fish, with all dishes in US$4–6 range. It's especially known for the live music at w/ends & entrance is free. $$–$

🍴 **Deli France** [105 F3] Marina Mall; ☎ 03027 70223; ⊕ 08.00–20.00 daily. This modern continental-style deli on the top floor of the Marina Mall serves sandwiches, salads, pizza, pasta, pastries & cakes, as well as freshly brewed coffee & a decent selection of wines. $$–$

🍴 **Melting Moments** [113 F2] 1st Norla St, Cantonments; ☎ 03027 70834; ⊕ 07.00–18.00 Mon–Sat. A local expat favourite, this is the perfect place for a mid-morning brunch or a late lunch with a delicious range of homemade cakes & pastries as well as sandwiches, salads & burgers on offer. Current issues of imported magazines are a bonus! $$–$

NIGHTLIFE

Accra is an excellent place to go partying, particularly at weekends, but the most popular venues vary depending on the night of the week.

✖ **Afrikiko Complex** [113 E2] See above.
☆ **Alliance Française** [105 F3] m 0501 287814/12; www.afaccra.org. North of the city centre off Liberation Rd, this popular venue invites renowned

musicians from all over West Africa for occasional performances. It's also home to the excellent Nicolino Pizzeria, offering wood-fired oven pizzas on an open terrace. See the website for upcoming events.

✗ **Bella Roma** [116 B3] See page 129.

☆ **Carbon** [105 F3] Liberation Av; m 0202 261001; 🄵 fb.me/CarbonGhana. With a club designer & mixologist flown straight in from London, this new nightspot is looking to set the bar for luxury when it opens here in 2016. Set on the rooftop of Icon House (where the perfectly styled & co-managed Urban Grill & Coco Lounge can also be found), expect a playground for Accra's elite with first-class style & first-class prices.

✗ **Chez Afrique** [105 G1] See page 132.

🍷 **Duncan's Bar** [116 B3] 3rd Lane; 🄯 17.00–late daily. This inexpensive & popular street bar, next to the Republic Bar & Grill, serves cheap draught beer as well as the usual selection of bottled drinks.

✳ 🍷 **Firefly Lounge Bar** [116 B2] 11th Lane; ✆03027 77818; m 0549 689050; 🄯 17.30–late Mon–Sat. All clean white lines & dim lighting, this industrial venue feels like it belongs more in a wintry European city than tropical Accra, but it is undoubtedly one of the capital's top nightspots. Primarily a lounge bar & restaurant in the early evening, it has an interesting but far from cheap Mediterranean tapas menu, with most dishes in the US$12–20 range, & switches over into nightclub mode at around 23.00 on Thu–Sat nights. No flip-flops!

☆ **Hot Gossip** [116 D3] Osu; m 0240 449666; 🄯 17.00–late daily. The new & unmissably orange Hot Gossip attracts a hip young crowd of partygoers with its heady mix of afro & international club hits, but there are also TVs with sports & videos, snooker tables, & shishas on the 1st-floor terrace. It won the Ghana Tourism Award for best nightclub in 2015. Cover around US$5 for men.

🍷 **Jokers Pub & Grill** [113 G4] m 0244 259911; 🄯 20.00–04.00 daily. A lively but rather seedy pub in Labadi, with pool tables & casino. We've had reports of muggings outside here late at night.

🍷 **Next Door** [105 H7] m 0244 318697; www. next-door.com; 🄯 10.00–late daily. This sprawling restaurant-cum-nightclub, which lies on the coastal road towards Nungua/Tema around 5km past the Labadi Beach Hotel & next door to Harbin Bowling, serves a wide selection of international dishes – though the Ghanaian specialities are the best bet – accompanied by the sound of crashing waves & a varied selection of 'world' music, including live music in the evening at w/ends.

✳ 🍷 **Republic Bar & Grill** [116 B3] 3rd Lane; m 0246 314044; 🄵 fb.me/RepublicBarGH; 🄯 11.00–02.00 Mon–Sat, 16.00–02.00 Sun. Decorated with music-related photos from the mid 20th century & old highlife LP sleeves, this funky & wildly popular retro bar plays an interesting mix of vintage West African & other music, & also hosts occasional live bands, drumming, & karaoke (check their Facebook page for details). There's also plenty of chilled beer, good cocktails, & great-value meals in the US$5–8 range, with seating spilling out on to the street in the evenings.

☆ **Shisha Lounge** [116 C2] Osu; m 0233 551515/0249 059501; 🄯 18.00–late daily. This classy indoor-outdoor restaurant & nightspot has well-priced seafood grills & a wood-fired pizza oven, along with plenty of flavours of shisha tobacco for after dinner, best enjoyed on the upper-level terrace built around a tree. Inside, things are cool, clubby, & open late.

☆ **Sky Bar** [119 E3] Mango Tree Av; m 0248 639802; 🄯 22.00–late Fri–Sun & Wed. In an unmissable building on Mango Tree Av in Asylum Down, this gaudy, glittering nightspot is the successor to the now-closed Citizen Kofi complex in Osu & retains all the overwrought charm & inflated prices of its predecessor. The multi-coloured interior boasts a ground-floor bar, a nightclub with a VVIP section, an upmarket restaurant, pool tables, & a shisha lounge. Admission around US$5.

☆ **Vienna City** [119 B2] ✆03027 75577; www. consulgames.com; 🄯 noon–04.00 daily. More Vegas than Vienna, this entertainment complex on Nkrumah Rd is reputedly (& believably) the biggest in Ghana. It is an acceptable place to eat, drink & play pool by day, but nightfall transforms it into a den of prostitutes – mostly clustered around the attached nightclub or the sizeable casino.

🍷 **Venus Lounge, Bar & Grill** [116 B2] 11th Lane Osu; ✆03027 82250; www. bybloshotelghana.com; 🄯 09.00–01.00 Mon–Thu, 09.00–03.00 Fri–Sat, 16.00–01.00 Sun. This long-serving AC bar & restaurant on the ground floor of the Byblos Hotel has free Wi-Fi, a flatscreen TV & a perennially popular street terrace. It's known locally for great cocktails, but also serves very good Lebanese food & has hookah pipes.

✳ ☆ **+233 Jazz Club** [113 E2] 75 North Ridge Rd; m 0233 233233; www.facebook. com🄵 fb.me/233jazzbarandgrill; 🄯 17.00–late Mon–Fri, 14.30–late Sat–Sun. Situated close to the KLM office near Sankara Overpass, this jazz club, formerly called Bassline, is more a place for listening to music than for dancing, but it hosts good live jazz or highlife most nights except Sun, generally starting at around 20.00 – check their Facebook to see what's on. Cover charge US$8–15pp.

SHOPPING

In common with many other African cities, Accra has experienced a boom in mall construction in the past few years. The biggest and best of these is the newly opened **West Hills Mall** [104 A1] (\ 30708 50817; www.westhillsmallgh.com; ⊕ 10.00–20.00 daily), which upstaged the (also quite large and barely a decade old) **Accra Mall** [105 G2] (\ 03028 23040; www.accramall.com; ⊕ 10.00–21.00 Mon–Sat, noon–18.00 Sun), when it opened in 2015. Accra Mall lies on Spintex Road on the east side of Tetteh Quarshie Circle, while the West Hills Mall unsurprisingly lies to the west along the Winneba Road, 1.5km after Aplaku Junction, the turnoff for Kokrobite. Both are anchored by the large South African chain Shoprite and are home to several big-name stores (the likes of Adidas, Puma and Swatch) and South African chain stores including Game (at Accra Mall) and Truworths (at both). They both also host many of the major banks, half a dozen ATMs, a fast-food court and several restaurants, a decent bookshop, the city's only Apple shop (at Accra Mall), and two Silverbird cinema complexes (fb.me/silverbirdghana).

The **Woolworths Centre** [105 G2], on Liberation Road, south of Accra Mall, is home to the South African clothing chain after which it is named, as well as the offices of British Airways and Iberia. Adjacent to the Holiday Inn Accra Airport, the growing **Marina Mall** [105 F3] (\ 03070 20858/9; www.marinamallghana.com; ⊕ 10.00–21.00 Mon–Sat, noon–20.00 Sun) has plenty of clothing stores as well as a few eateries, ATMs, a supermarket and a bookshop. More centrally, the **Oxford Street Mall** [116 C4] in the heart of Osu is yet to be fully completed, but it's already home to a Shoprite and almost universally known by that name.

Further out of town, East Legon's **A&C Square** [105 G1] (\ 0302 517518; e info@ ancsquare.com; www.ancsquare.com; ⊕ 09.00–17.00 Mon–Fri, 09.00–14.00 Sat) has a fitness centre with a swimming pool, plus a good supermarket and a selection of clothes and other boutiques. Towards Tema, the **Junction Mall** [105 H7] (m 03027 47330; ⊕ 09.00–21.00 Mon–Sat) lies along the coastal road in Nungua and has a Shoprite, Levi's, Puma, MTN Centre, and several ATMs.

SUPERMARKETS AND GROCERIES There are several good supermarkets in Accra, selling a variety of imported goods ranging from breakfast cereals to South African wine. The best is probably **Shoprite** [116 C4] (Accra Mall, West Hills Mall, Junction Mall, Oxford Street Mall; m 0244 779577; www.shoprite.co.za; ⊕ 09.00–22.00 daily), which also incorporates a butchery, bakery, deli and good fresh fruit and vegetable section. Another good option, with a branch on Liberation Road opposite the Golden Tulip Hotel, is the multi-floor **Max Mart** [105 F4] (\ 03027 83750; www. maxmartghana.com; ⊕ 08.30–19.00 Mon–Sat, 11.00–16.00 Sun), which not only sells a superb range of imported foodstuffs, but also has a good appliance section and attached coffee bar and bakery. There are also branches in the A&C Square in East Legon and the University Centre opposite the campus of the University of Ghana.

Also excellent is the main three-storey **Melcom Plus Complex** [104 B3] (\ 0302 221784; www.melcomgroup.com; ⊕ 08.00–17.00 Mon–Fri, 08.30–15.30 Sat), which is basically a very large supermarket that also contains small branches of various book, electronics and other shops. Other smaller (but still substantial) branches of

Melcom can be found on Kwame Nkrumah Road in Adabraka, and on Otublohum Street near Kaneshie Market.

In Osu, the **Koala Supermarket** [116 C2] (◈ *03027 73455; www.koala.com.gh; ⊕ 07.30–21.00 Mon–Sat, 11.00–20.00 Sun*) on Oxford Street, close to Danquah Circle, is one of the best supermarkets in the city centre, with a good ground-floor bakery and probably the best selection of imported goods, though sometimes at inflated prices. They've recently opened a second location on Patrice Lumumba Road in Airport Residential Area offering a similar selection. Opposite Koala Supermarket in Osu, **Don Emilio** [116 C2] (◈ *03027 73366; ⊕ 08.30–21.00 Mon–Sat, noon–20.00 Sun*) stocks what is probably the city's most comprehensive range of wines and other imported drinks.

The excellent (and well-hidden) **Relish Health Foods** [116 B2] (*Akai Hse, 3rd St, Osu Ringway;* ◈ *03027 73590;* e *info@relishhealthfoods.com; www.relishhealthfoods.com;* ⊕ *08.00–21.00 Mon–Fri, 08.00–16.00 Sat*) is the country's largest vegetarian and health food retailer. It also stocks homeopathic products, supplements, natural health-care products and herbal teas.

The small shops attached to many filling stations are often good places to buy luxury goods, from canned food and drinks to chocolates and biscuits. Osu, Adabraka and most other suburbs are dotted with small grocery shops selling everyday goods, as well as bottle stores selling inexpensive local beers and pricier imported wines and spirits. The central Makola Market and suburban Kaneshie Market are also good places for general shopping, albeit in an atmosphere newcomers may find rather chaotic.

ARTS, CRAFT AND CURIOS A number of well-known craft outlets are listed below, but unless you're tremendously pressed for time, you may prefer to do your curio shopping in a more haphazard way. For all but the most esoteric requirements (face masks, for instance), you'll find that there are numerous stalls selling interesting items all over the city – a couple of dozen can be found along and around Osu's Oxford Street, and there are others at '37' and the Golden Tulip Hotel [105 F4], on the Ring Road next to Danquah Circle [116 C2] and on La Beach [105 H7]. Alternatively, the main markets – Makola [127 C2] in the city centre and Kaneshie [113 A1] on Winneba Road – also stock a wide range of textiles, and since the stall owners here are not as dependent on the tourist dollar, the atmosphere is less pushy than at more dedicated tourist outlets. Finally, there is the Centre for National Culture (pages 144–5), where dozens of stalls stock an extraordinary selection of crafts, though the atmosphere can get very pushy and you'll need to bargain pretty hard to get a fair price.

AACD African Market [113 F4] Koi Rd, Osu; m 0262 472057; e aacdafricanmarket@gmail.com; ⊕ 09.00–18.00 Mon–Sat. Started by a Peace Corps volunteer several years ago, this well-stocked shop is not overly inexpensive & items are typically not up for bargain (all have sticker prices). It's a nice place to browse to get an idea of what you can get as souvenirs in Ghana. Some of the profits go to support local artists.

Artists Alliance Gallery [105 G7] Omanye Hse, Beach Rd, La; ◈ 03029 63650; m 0245 251404; ⊕ 09.00–18.00 Mon–Sat, noon–18.00 Sun.

Established under the name Glo Art Gallery by the widely respected Ghanaian artist Ablade Glover in 1968, & renamed in 1993, this gallery showcases work by more than 30 of the country's finest artists under one roof, & allows you to buy directly from the artist. A good fair-trade craft shop, Aid to Artisans operates under the same roof.

Global Mamas [116 C2] 14th Lane, Osu; m 0244 530467; www.globalmamas.org; ⊕ 09.00–20.00 Mon–Sat, 13.00–20.00 Sun. Off the north end of Oxford St near the Koala Supermarket, the ever popular Global Mamas was developed by a former

Peace Corps volunteer as a fair-trade outlet where local women can market their handicrafts for export & local sale. It sells an array of quality batik-printed clothing, purses made from recycled bags, & an assortment of beaded products that blend traditional African design with contemporary European styles.

Kane Kwei Carpentry Workshop [105 H6] Tema Rd, Teshie; ☎0244 114719; www.ghanacoffin. com. If your budget is up to shipping it home, the ultimate in Ghanaian souvenirs must be your very own fantasy coffin, carved *posuban*-style in whatever shape you like (elephant, boat, minibus, whale, uterus!). Get measured up or just go window shopping at Accra's original fantasy coffin workshop, or one of the many other celebrated coffin makers in Teshie on the Tema road.

The Loom [119 B2] Nkrumah Rd, Adabraka; ☎03022 24746; ⊕ 10.00–17.00 Mon–Sat. Established in the 1960s by owner-manager Frances Ademola, this is the oldest & probably the best art gallery in Ghana, with more than 100 artists represented. Some paintings can be bought for less than US$50, but it is also suitable for people willing to spend more for quality work. It also sells souvenirs, craftwork & postcards, has very helpful & reliable staff, & absolutely no bargaining is involved.

Joe's Perspective Art Boutique [127 D1] Mövenpick Ambassador Hotel; ☎03026 11125; ⊕ 09.00–19.00 Mon–Sat, 13.00–19.00 Sun. Perhaps the most interesting gallery-cum-craft outlet in Ghana, this unique conceptual art shop reworks traditional West African pieces to create one-off originals.

Sun Trade Beads [119 E3] Mango Tree Av; ☎03022 35982; m 0244 285056; www.

suntradebeads.com; ⊕ 09.00–18.00 Mon–Fri, 09.00–17.00 Sat. Probably the best place to go bead shopping anywhere in Accra, this stylish boutique designs, manufactures & sells all types of beads (everything from tiny waist beads to ones the size of your fist!), as well as earrings, bracelets & other styles of jewellery. It's also the meeting place for the Ghana Bead Society on the first Tue of every month.

Trashy Bags [104 D2] Shiakle Link, Abelenkpe & Sunkwa Rd, Osu; ☎03027 76060 (Abelenkpe); m 0544 349857 (Osu); e enquiries@trashybags. org; www.trashybags.org; ⊕ 09.00–17.00 Mon–Fri (Abelenkpe); ⊕ 09.30–18.00 Mon–Sat (Osu). This eco-friendly social enterprise recycles plastic waste (a big problem across Africa because of the lack of recycling & waste management infrastructure) into funky & useful bags & other products. It employs over 60 Ghanaians to collect, clean & stitch around 200,000 used plastic sachets monthly, as well as other plastic trash such as old billboards. The bags are easily available at their new shop in Osu & make great souvenirs & gifts, or you can visit the workshop in Abelenkpe on w/ days. The workshop is about 1.5km from the well-known Dimples Junction, & 1km from the junction of Olesegun Obasanjo Way & Abelenkpe Rd.

Wild Gecko Handicrafts [105 F1] Adamafio Cresc, East Legon; ☎03025 08500; m 0244 341117; e info@wild-gecko.com; www.wild-gecko.com; ⊕ 10.00–17.30 Tue–Sat. This wonderful craft centre, dedicated to developing local artisanal skills, makes & sells wood, ceramic, metal & cowhorn artefacts – ranging from large items of furniture to jewellery & other trinkets – that make imaginative use of adinkra symbols.

BOOKS The best bookshop in central Accra is the **Vidya Bookstore** [116 C3] (*18th Lane, Osu;* ☎ *0244 262098;* e *vidyabookstore@gmail.com;* *www.vidyabookstore.com;* ⊕ *08.30–18.00 Mon–Sat*) in Osu, which stocks a decent range of novels, travel guides, children's books and magazines, including a good selection of African authors. The newer and larger **SyTris Bookshop** (*opposite A&C Mall, East Legon;* m *0507 444204/6; www.sytris.net;* ⊕ *08.00–20.00 Mon–Sat, noon–18.00 Sun*) is further away in East Legon, but stocks the best selection of contemporary novels in Ghana, as well as a wide selection of non-fiction.

Less centrally, the sleek **Silverbird Lifestyle Store** [105 G2] (☎ *03028 23040*) in the Accra Mall stocks a good range of contemporary adult and children's fiction at Western prices, as well as non-fiction (including maps and travel guides for Ghana and West Africa), magazines, greetings cards, gift stationery, CDs and DVDs. On the campus of the University of Ghana, the **University Bookshop** [105 G1] (☎ *03025 00398;* ⊕ *w/days, Sat mornings*), stocks all sorts of oddities, with probably the best range of historical books in Accra, as well as a fair selection of cheap secondhand novels.

Also good for secondhand novels are the numerous stalls dotted around Nkrumah Circle, and the anonymous bookshop in Usshertown at the very south end of Nkrumah Road.

OTHER PRACTICALITIES

BANKING AND FOREIGN EXCHANGE Visa cards can be used to draw cash from ATMs outside most branches of Barclays, Ghana Commercial, Standard Chartered, Stanbic and several other smaller banks. There are also stand-alone ATMs that accept Visa cards in Kotoka International Airport, in most shopping malls, on the University of Ghana campus, at several filling stations, and at a few upmarket hotels including the Mövenpick Ambassador and La Palm. In essence, provided you have a valid Visa card, you will seldom be far from a reliable source of cash. While it's still much better to have Visa, a growing number of ATMs now accept MasterCard, including most outlets of Ghana Commercial Bank (GCB), EcoBank, and GT Bank (for a full list for either service, use the ATM locator at www.visa.com or www.mastercard.com). Other credit cards, including American Express, are next to useless in most circumstances.

Visa cards can be used to settle bills at the most upmarket hotels and restaurants, though in practice you might find that many mid-range hotels displaying the facility to accept Visa and/or MasterCard will do so only when 'the machine is working' (for which, read 'as good as never'), and you will need to keep a close eye on your account as it is not uncommon for card details to be stolen and used at even reasonably upmarket hotels.

The best banks for changing foreign currency are the head offices of Barclays and Standard Chartered, both of which are 100m from the Central Post Office in Usshertown [127 C3], with the latter generally offering the best rates. As best we know, their other branches have stopped providing forex services. Generally, however, you'll get a better exchange rate for hard currency cash (and far quicker service) at any of the dozens of forex bureaux dotted throughout the city (there are several in Osu and Adabraka, the suburbs most frequented by travellers). Most of the upmarket hotels also have their own forex bureau, but rates tend to be very poor and many will only serve hotel residents (an exception, worth knowing about in an emergency, is the forex desk at the Mövenpick Ambassador). Another place where you can exchange money at almost any time is Kotoka International Airport.

If you made the mistake of bringing travellers' cheques to Ghana, the only place you can change them, so far as we are aware, is at the main office of Barclays Bank [127 C3] in the old city centre. In theory, this is limited to around £150 per day, but we did hear quite recently from one person who 'cashed around US$1,000, but it took the good part of a morning, and I would certainly not take travellers' cheques to Ghana again.'

BEAUTY AND HAIR SALONS An excellent place for waxing and manicures etc is **Allure Spa in the City** [113 G4] (m *0540 115500/0244 344347; www.allurespainthecity. com;* ⏲ *09.00–19.00 Mon–Fri, 08.00–20.00 Sat*) on Ring Road East near East Labone Junction, which offers Western standards at very reasonable rates. In Osu, the **Lajen Beauty Shop** [116 C2] (*behind Koala Supermarket, 14th Lane;* 03027 77837; ⏲ *08.30–18.00*) and **Marie Noelle's Salon** [116 E5] (*Kuku Hill;* 0302 764154; m *0244 211311; www.marienoellespa.com*) both have a good reputation. Most of the luxury hotels also have salons attached.

BOWLING There's a creaky but surprisingly modern bowling alley in the **Harbin Entertainment Centre** [105 H7] (✎ *03027 13885;* m *0208 381974/0244 320354;* ⏱ *15.00–23.00 Tue–Fri, noon–midnight Sat–Sun*) on the Teshie–Nungua road right next door to Next Door restaurant/nightclub.

MINI-GOLF Another entertainment surprise, the 18-hole mini-golf course at Marvels [104 D2] (✎ *03029 15400/03027 71337;* e *info@marvelsghana.com; www.marvelsghana. com;* ⏱ *10.00–22.00 daily*) near Dimples Junction in Dzorwulu is impressively green and well kept, and it's less than US$5 for a round. There's also an air-conditioned clubhouse restaurant and bar (with Wi-Fi!) selling burgers, snacks and ice cream.

CAR HIRE The better-known international agencies such as Hertz and Budget are not generally represented in Ghana, the two major exceptions being **Europcar** (✎ *03022 44071; www.europcar.com*), based at the airport, and **Avis** [113 F2] (✎ *03027 61752; www.avisghana.com*), which is based at 199 Soula Loop, North Labone and is also represented in Labadi Beach Hotel [105 H7] (✎ *03027 72501*) and La Palm Beach Hotel [105 H7] (✎ *03070 10562*). Both normally offer the car with driver (you pay his expenses), or you can ask for what they call 'self drive', where you pay quite heavy full-cover insurance charges.

Overall, a better bet on any sort of budget would be to contact a few of the tour operators listed on pages 118–20, since they effectively double as car hire agencies, renting out vehicles inclusive of a local driver and his expenses, starting at around US$75 per day for a sedan and US$90 per day for a 4x4. A cheaper option is to make a private deal with a taxi driver to ferry you around for a specified number of days. The agreed rates will normally include the driver's expenses but exclude fuel.

CINEMA The multiplex **Silverbird Cinemas** (m *0275 877474;* f *fb.me/silverbirdghana*) at the Accra Mall [105 G2] and West Hills Mall [104 A1] are Ghana's first dedicated cinemas showing the latest Hollywood blockbusters as well as the latest films from Bollywood and Nollywood. Tickets cost US$5–8. The **Alliance Française** [105 F3] (✎ *03027 60278; www.afaccra.org*) in Airport Residential screens French films and documentaries, while the **Goethe Institut** [105 G5] (✎ *03027 767640; www.goethe.de/accra*) in Cantonments has weekly screenings of films by German directors. Both the Alliance Française and Goethe Institut also have good restaurant-bars attached, should you need some nosh before the credits roll.

EMBASSIES AND DIPLOMATIC REPRESENTATION It might be worth noting that if you intend travelling more extensively around West Africa, you'll technically save money (and passport-page wastage) by obtaining a Visa Touristique d'Entente (VTE), a single visa that costs around US$50 and allows entry to four or possibly five different countries (Ivory Coast, Burkina Faso, Togo, Benin and Niger, though reports suggest the last irregularly honours the VTE). The catch is that the VTE's existence is not actively publicised by several of the embassies concerned, presumably because it's more profitable to sell a one-country visa, and travellers are often told that no such visa exists or that there are no forms available. Historically, your best option is the Togo Embassy, but this is far from certain and it's definitely worth phoning around the relevant embassies in Accra to check.

🄴 **Algeria** 22 Josif Broz Tito Av; ✎ 03027 76719; e embdzacc@africaonline.com.gh

🄴 **Australia** [113 F2] 2 Rangoon Cl, Cantonments; ✎ 03022 16400; www.ghana.embassy.gov.au

🄴 **Belgium** See Netherlands.

ⓔ **Benin** [105 F2] Augustus Akiwumi Rd; \03027 74860; e ambab_accra@yahoo.fr

ⓔ **Burkina Faso** [119 F2] Nyadji Crescent, Asylum Down; \03022 21988; e secretariat@ambafaso-gh.org; www.ambafaso-gh.org.

ⓔ **Canada** [113 E2] 42 Independence Av; \03022 11521; e accra@international.gc.ca; www.canadainternational.gc.ca

ⓔ **China** 6 Agostino Neto Rd; \0302 797437; e chinaemb_gh@mfa.gov.cn; http://gh.china-embassy.org

ⓔ **Ivory Coast (Côte d'Ivoire)** [116 C3] 9 18th Lane, Osu; \03027 74611/2; e acigh@ambaci-ghana.org; www.ambaci-ghana.org

ⓔ **Denmark** [119 G2] 67 Dr Isert Rd; \03022 08730; e accamb@um.dk; www.ghana.um.dk

ⓔ **France** [113 F1] 12th Rd, off Liberation Av; \03022 14550; e info@ambafrance-gh.org; www.ambafrance-gh.org

ⓔ **Germany** [119 G3] 6 Kenneth Kaunda Rd, North Ridge; \03022 11000; e info@accra.diplo.de; www.accra.diplo.de

ⓔ **Guinea** [105 E3] opposite Accra Girls Senior High School, Roman Ridge; \03027 77921; e embagui@ghana.com

ⓔ **India** [105 E3] 9 Ridge Road, Roman Ridge; \03070 20903–5; e hoc.accra@mea.gov.in; www.indiahc-ghana.com

ⓔ **Italy** [113 G1] Jawaharlal Nehru Rd; \03027 75621–2; www.ambaccra.esteri.it

ⓔ **Japan** [113 F2] 5th Av, West Cantonments; \03027 65060; www.gh.emb-japan.go.jp

ⓔ **Liberia** [105 F3] 8 Odoi Kwao St; Airport Residential; \03027 75641

ⓔ **Mali** [127 E2] 1st Bungalow, Liberia Rd, Airport Residential Area; \03026 63276; e ambamaliaccra@yahoo.fr

ⓔ **Mauritania** c/o Embassy of France.

ⓔ **Netherlands** [113 E2] 89 Liberation Rd; \03022 14350; www.ghana.nlembassy.org

ⓔ **Niger** [113 E2] 104–3 Independence Av; \03022 29011/24962

ⓔ **Nigeria** [105 E2] 20/21 Onyasia Crescent, Roman Ridge; \03027 76158/9; e nighicomgh@yahoo.com; www.nigerian-embassy.com/accra.html

ⓔ **Russia** [113 F1] Jawaharlal Nehru Rd, Switchback Lane; \03027 75611; www.ghana.mid.ru

ⓔ **Senegal** [105 F3] Odoi Kwao St, opp Banking College, Airport Residential; \03217 70286.

ⓔ **Sierra Leone** [113 G1] 8 Senchi St, Airport Residential; \03027 69190; e slhcaccra@yahoo.com

ⓔ **Spain** [105 F3] Drake Av Extension, Airport Residential; \03027 74004/5; e emb.accra@maec.es

ⓔ **Switzerland** [119 F3] Kanda Highway/Ridge Street, North Ridge; \03022 28125; www.eda.admin.ch/accra

ⓔ **Togo** [113 F2] Togo Hse, Cantonments Circle; \03027 77950/774521

ⓔ **UK** [113 E2] 1 Gamel Abdul Nasser Av; \03022 13250; e high.commission.accra@fco.gov.uk; www.gov.uk/government/world/organisations/british-high-commission-accra

ⓔ **USA** [113 G2] 24 4th Circular Rd, Cantonments; \03027 41000; http://ghana.usembassy.gov

GYM The **Aviation Social Centre** [105 F4] (\ *03027 80215*; e *enquiries@aviationsocialcentre.com.gh; www.aviationsocialcentre.com.gh*), on the road between the airport and Cantonments post office, is a great place to work out for anyone in Accra for a while. Monthly membership is available. Also recommended is the **Total Fitness Health Club** (\ *03025 43756*; m *0244 275463; www.ancsquare. com/totalfitness.aspx*) in East Legon's A&C Square.

INTERNET Dozens of internet cafés are scattered around Accra, with more opening the whole time. The best are the five **Vodafone** internet cafés. These are situated in Old Accra/Usshertown [127 C3] (*opposite Standard Chartered Bank, High St;* \ *03026 74005/68175;* ⊕ *07.00–23.00 daily*), Osu [116 C3] (*Oxford St, near Trust Hospital;* \ *03027 70000/70481;* ⊕ *24hrs daily*), Adabraka [113 C1] (*Ghana Telecom HQ, Nkrumah Circle;* \ *03022 22213/38000;* ⊕ *07.00–23.00 daily*), Cantonments [113 G1] (*Cantonments Post Office, opposite Lands Department;* \ *03027 64600);* ⊕ *07.00–23.00 daily*) and in the Accra Mall [105 G2] (*near Game Store;* \ *03028 23330/2;* ⊕ *07.00–23.00 daily*).

Also recommended is **Busy Internet** [119 D1] (\ *03022 58800/1; www. busyinternet.com;* ☺ *24hrs),* which lies on Ring Road Central between the Nsawam Overpass and Paloma Hotel, and offers fully serviced offices, a restaurant and bar, a copy centre, teleconferencing, DVD movies and all sorts of other goodies.

MEDICAL FACILITIES

✚ **37 Military Hospital** [113 F1] Liberation Rd near Akuafo Circle & '37' Station; \03027 76111–3. The trauma facility here is the best in Accra; it also has good after-hours facilities, including a 24hr X-ray laboratory & pharmacy.

✚ **Beaver Dental Clinic** [105 F3] 11 Agostino Neto Rd; \03027 71785; m 0244 324639; e beaverdentist@yahoo.co.uk; www. beaverdentist.com. Reliable, modern dental clinic run by UK-trained dentist.

✚ **Ernst Chemist** [119 C1] Ring Rd, near Sankara Overpass; \03022 57140–2; e info@ ernestchemists.com; www.ernestchemists.com. Well-stocked chemist in Adabraka.

✚ **Gokals Opticals** [116 C4] Oxford St, opposite Frankie's Hotel; m 0277 801152; ◼ fb.me/ gokalsopticals. Reliable for replacement glasses or contact lenses.

✚ **Korle Bu Teaching Hospital & Chemist** [113 A4] \03026 65401/70545;

www.kbth.gov.gh. Good hospital with 24hr pharmacy service.

✚ **Medlab** [105 E3] SGS Hse, 14 Ridge Rd; \03027 69680; www.medlab.com.gh; ☺ 08.00– 21.00 Mon–Fri. This is the best laboratory in Accra, & also has branches in Osu's Akai House Clinic (\03027 64676/65335).

✚ **North Ridge Clinic** [119 G1] Off Ring Rd near KLM office & next to Sedco Hse; \03022 27328. Doctor available at all hours.

✚ **Nyaho Medical Centre** [105 F2] 35 Aviation Rd, Airport Residential Area; \03027 75341/75291; e info@nyahomedical.com; www. nyahomedical.com

✚ **Trust Hospital (SSNIT)** [116 C3] Oxford St, 500m south of Danquah Circle; \03027 61974–7; e info@thetrusthospital.com; www. thetrusthospital.com. Reputable clinic for consultations & minor ailments, with 24hr malaria-testing facilities & a convenient location in Osu.

POST The historic **Central Post Office** [127 C3] is on High Street, near the seafront in Usshertown. International mail posted in Accra will arrive at its destination more quickly than mail posted from other towns in the country, but it will still most likely take up to two weeks. Mail posted from the post office in the airport is reputedly a bit quicker. For express and courier services, contact **DHL** [119 G2] on North Ridge Crescent (\ *03022 27035).*

SWIMMING A nominal entrance fee of US$1 is charged to swim on weekdays at the public beach at La, which is popular with locals and lined with bars and restaurants. On weekends, though, prices increase to around US$2–3. Non-guests use the pool facilities and sun loungers on the beach at Labadi Beach Resort for US$13/day. Most of the upmarket hotels have swimming pools available to non-residents for a daily fee of around US$5.

TELEPHONE Dozens of communication centres offer local and international telephone and fax facilities in Osu, Adabraka and elsewhere. Local SIM cards can be bought anywhere, but to be certain of good connectivity, we recommend you take your mobile or tablet with you to one of the providers' customer service centres. Vodafone has centres in the Accra Mall, on Nkrumah Circle and in Usshertown (opposite the Standard Chartered Bank), while MTN has centres in Osu (Oxford Street, near Osu Food Court), on Liberation Road (near the Golden Tulip Hotel) and in the Accra Mall.

TENNIS There are two tennis associations active in Accra that welcome visitors at a small fee. The **Accra Lawn Tennis Club** [127 F1] (\ *03026 66517;* m *0275 121336;*

International telephone code	+233
Tourist information	☏ 03022 31817
Police	☏ 191
Fire	☏ 192
Ambulance	☏ 193
Police Intelligence and Professional Standards (PIPS)	☏ 03027 76435

www.altcgh.com) has nine courts and has been playing at its present location since 1957, while the smaller **Ghana Lawn Tennis Association** [119 C4] (m *0246 997584/0261 485115*) has four courts hidden away on a backstreet in Adabraka. Both have small canteen-bars attached.

WHAT TO SEE AND DO

Accra is not especially rich in sightseeing, but you could easily dedicate a morning to a walking tour through Old Accra and the characterful quarters of Jamestown and Usshertown. With a full day to spare, and sufficient energy, you could head inland from Old Accra to the National Museum, or follow the coast east via the Kwame Nkrumah Memorial Park to Independence Square and (if it ever opens for tourism) Osu Castle, perhaps making use of taxis for longer hops. Many travellers also spend plenty of time in Osu, which is better known for the many shops and restaurants along Oxford Street than for any specific tourist sites. Less centrally, La Beach is perhaps the most obvious excursion for sun-worshippers, while the excellent W E B Du Bois Centre is of some historic interest. In addition to the places listed below, quite a number of more remote sites make for realistic day or overnight trips out of the capital, as covered in the next chapter, *Around Accra*.

INSIDE THE RING ROAD

Jamestown and Usshertown The oldest and most characterful part of Accra, the contiguous suburbs of Jamestown and Usshertown, also sometimes referred to as Old Accra or by the traditional name of Ga Mashie, are the site of the original Ga Mantse Stool House, as well as the palaces of the subsidiary Mantses (Chiefs) of the old quarters of Ngleshie (Jamestown), Asere, Gbese and Sempe. It is an intriguing area to explore on foot, with a strong sense of community, and the roads are dotted with colourful small markets, colonial-era shops and other time-warped buildings, off-set by open sewers, public shitting grounds and accompanying smells. Several of the area's better-known landmarks can be visited independently, but it's worth thinking about exploring the area with a guide, who will help you get into many places where casual visitors might otherwise be unwelcome.

An excellent introduction to Jamestown is the newly launched fixed-departure guided tours offered by **Jamestown Walking Tours** (m *0243 561807 or 0548 850681;* e *jamestownwalkingtours@gmail.com; www.jamestownwalkingtours.wordpress. com*). Guided by locally born guides, these tours leave from outside Jamestown Lighthouse at 14.00 every Saturday, last for 2½ hours, and incorporate the fishing harbour and most major historical streets and sites, as well as cultural visits. No bookings are necessary, but it would be wise to call in advance and make sure the tour is running. Tickets cost US$7 per person.

On other days, visit (or, better, make advance arrangements with) the **Ga Mashie/ Old Accra Development Project** [127 A4] (✆ *03026 70956*; m *0204 300101/0242 850406*), which has an office on the Jamestown waterfront about 100m west of the lighthouse, to arrange a guide. Another recommended contact is the historian and guide Sam Baddoo (m *0243 216187;* e *toursathome@yahoo.com*). Expect to pay around US$10 for one or two people.

The obvious place to start any tour of Old Accra is the prominent red-and-white candy-striped **Jamestown Lighthouse** [127 A4], which stands in front of a station for shared taxis to/from Nkrumah Circle. The lighthouse was originally built by the British in 1871, to be replaced by the 28m-high modern building in the 1930s. Though it isn't formally open to tourists, the caretaker – or any of several aspirant guides who loiter around the area – will most likely allow you to climb the 82-step spiral staircase for a negotiable fee (around US$1–3 per person). The view from the top is fantastic, but if you prefer not to fork out, a climb to the seventh floor of the City Car Park will give you a partial view for free.

Jamestown is named after **Fort James** [127 B4], which stands next to the lighthouse. Built by the British in 1673, possibly on the site of an older Portuguese lodge, Fort James served as a prison during the colonial era right through until 2008. Despite long being listed as open to visitors on the Ghana Museums website (*www.ghanamuseums.org*), the fort has been very much closed over the last several editions of this guide.

Directly below the lighthouse you'll find **JayNii Beach Resort** [127 A4] (see box, page 122), a friendly beach bar whose proceeds go towards a non-profit organisation that helps educate Jamestown's disadvantaged children. The wannabe guides near the lighthouse often tell visitors that JayNii has closed – this is a lie told in order to lead you somewhere else where they'll get a cut of whatever donation they're imagining you'll fork out – ignore them and head down the steps directly to the right of the lighthouse. Facing the lighthouse and fort on the north side of John Atta Mills High Street is the **Ngleshie (Jamestown) Mantse's Palace** [127 A4], whose exterior is decorated with drummers and cannons, and which gives its location as 'British Accra'. Also opposite the lighthouse, the Sea View Hotel, built in 1903 and supposed to be Ghana's oldest, was torn down in 2015 after years of dereliction.

Also worth visiting, the **old fishing harbour** [127 B4] on the beach below Fort James was the second-largest in Ghana prior to the construction of Tema. A riot of colourful traditional pirogues in the early to mid morning after the fishermen come in, the harbour also doubles as a vibrant fish market, and you can see traditional smoking ovens at work on the beach. At one point, tourists were required to report to the office at the harbour entrance and to pay a small fee before they strolled around, but this no longer seems to be the case. Note, however, that the people here can be very funny about photography – it is difficult to say whether this is because it is forbidden to take pictures of Fort James, or just plain contrariness.

Following the High Street west from Jamestown Lighthouse you'll find two sites of interest. The first, tucked away behind the Old Accra Development Project office, is the **Attoh Quarshie Gym**, also known as the House of Pain, and the other is the adjacent **Will Power Gym**. These are two of the leading current proponents of a Ga Mashie street-fighting tradition that has produced five world champion boxers, among them Azumah Nelson, who won three world titles in the course of a 20-year career starting in the late 1970s, and is widely rated to be the greatest boxer to have emerged from Africa. Visitors are welcome to watch the boxers training at both gyms. About 100m further west, an intriguing **posuban-like shrine** [127 A4], evidently associated with the Asere Mantse, stands on a traffic island in the main road leading to Korle Lagoon.

Following High Street east from Jamestown Lighthouse, take the first turn to your right then wander through the alleys for about 100m to reach the now-disused **Brazil House Museum** [127 B4]. Restored with the support of UNESCO in 2007, this attractive two-storey building was the first house built and used by the Tabom (or Tabon), a group of around 70-odd Portuguese-speaking freed slaves who sailed from Brazil to Jamestown on the SS *Salisbury* in 1836. Led by Nii Azumah Nelson (an ancestor of his modern pugilistic namesake), the migrants were christened the Tabom by their Ga hosts, a derivation of the Portuguese '*Ta bom*', literally 'fine', their customary response to the greeting '*Como esta?*' Today, there's nothing much to be seen in the 'museum', save a few neglected art pieces (and it seems to be locked up most of the time anyway), but the exterior is painted in colourful modern murals that are nonetheless worth a peek.

Back on High Street, a short walk northeast leads to **Fort Ussher** [127 B3], which is the oldest of Accra's fortified buildings, founded by the Dutch in 1642 and known as Fort Crèvecœur prior to being sold to the British more than two centuries later. Until the mid 1990s, Fort Ussher, like nearby Fort James, served as a prison, but it is now semi-ruinous, though the western bastion houses a small museum (*entrance US$2.50/1.50 foreign adults/students*) dedicated to the history of the slave trade. The museum has very few displays and it lacks the impact of its counterparts at Cape Coast Castle, and while it used to be possible to visit the cell where Kwame Nkrumah was detained in 1950 prior to his becoming prime minister, this derelict part of the fort is now reputedly too dangerous to go inside.

Past Fort Ussher, follow John Atta Mills High Street to the intersection with Bank Lane, where the **Holy Trinity Cathedral** [127 C3], built in 1895–96 to a design by Sir Aston Webb, architect of London's Victoria and Albert Museum, stands tall to your right. From here, you could either continue along the seafront High Street towards the **Kwame Nkrumah Memorial Park** [127 D3] (page 144) or turn left into Bank Street, which is lined by several old buildings, notably the impressive **Central Post Office** [127 C3] built in the early colonial era. Here, you might want to turn left into Asafoatse Nettey Road and follow it for a block to enjoy a drink or local meal at the **WATO Club** [127 B3] (m *0242 647727;* ☉ *08.30–midnight daily;*), a distinctive curved and balconied three-storey building that started life as a bazaar in the 1920s but has served as a live-music venue since the colonial era (legend has it that Louis Armstrong and the local guitar hero E T Mensah jammed here during the former's first visit to the then Gold Coast in 1955).

From here, head north up Nkrumah Road for two blocks to Makola Square, from where you can join the throngs that mass around the incredibly vibrant **Makola Market** [127 C2], the largest open-air market in Accra. It is a good place to buy fabrics, with a warehouse-like building stacked to the ceiling with the batik for which Ghana is famous. Close by, Agbogbloshie Market is also not for the faint of heart, but it is the best place to buy traditional beads in Accra, and one of the best anywhere in the country. If you prefer to explore these markets with a guide who knows them well, Dela Fumador (✆ *03446 67092*) has been recommended.

Those who like colonial architecture should walk another couple of blocks north to the intersection with Station Road. Here, on the north side of Ushertown, the disused **railway station** [127 C1/2] is possibly the best-preserved 19th-century building in Accra. It looks closed, but if you can slip through the gate you will find the railway station on the left and the railway offices on the right.

Other buildings of interest in Old Accra include the **old Methodist church** [127 B2] and adjacent Methodist school. This is reputedly the oldest school in Accra, having been founded close to Fort James in the 1830s, and relocated to its present spot on the junction of Asafoatse Nettey and Hansen roads after the church was built in the late 19th century. Also on Asafoatse Nettey Road, opposite the church, is the **Palladium Building** [127 A3], a former music hall and cinema where Nkrumah launched the CPP in 1950. In addition, the central block of alleys running through the quarters of Asere, Abola and Gbese, immediately inland of Fort Ussher, are dotted with **ancient Ga shrines and palaces** best visited with a guide.

Kwame Nkrumah Memorial Park [127 D3] (⏲ *10.00–17.00 daily; entrance US$3; camera fees for commercial use only*) This attractively landscaped 5ha park lies on the seafront side of John Atta Mills High Street, between the junction of Thorpe and Barnes roads, on the former site of a colonial polo club. It was here that Louis Armstrong performed to a crowd of around 100,000 at the invitation of Kwame Nkrumah in 1956, the year before independence. The park's centrepiece is the Nkrumah Mausoleum, the third and final resting place of the former president's body, after it was first buried in Conakry (Guinea) then relocated to a small mausoleum at his home town of Nkroful on the west coast. The monument is altogether colder and more ostentatious than its quaintly low-key precursor in Nkroful, but the site is still emphatically worth visiting to explore an adjoining museum, which contains a collection of photos and other artefacts relating to the Nkrumah era. Before heading on from here, you might think about walking the few hundred metres south to the superbly located Rising Phoenix Magic Beach Resort for a clifftop drink or meal overlooking the Atlantic Ocean.

Centre for National Culture [127 D3] (⏲ *08.30–17.00 Mon–Fri, 09.00–15.00 Sat*) Standing on the seaward side of the intersection of John Atta Mills High Street and Barnes Road, this somewhat misleadingly named centre is basically Ghana's biggest craft market. There are many dozens of stalls where you can buy just about anything from traditional medicines and genuine kente and other local cloths, to carvings, masks and statues from all over Ghana and elsewhere in West Africa. It's also a good place to pick up colourful dyed shirts and cheaper trinkets such as imitation kente

wallets and bead necklaces. Be warned, however, that reader feedback splits down the middle as to whether the level of hassle and pushiness is acceptable or not. Even if you're not looking for crafts, the new **Abajo Culture & Art Café** (\03039 61168; m *0201 111138;* ⊕ *10.00–22.00 Mon–Sat, noon–21.00 Sun*) is a most welcome addition to the centre. Set in a sculpture garden just to the right of the centre's western entrance, this warm and welcoming café puts on live performances or a jam session every Friday night, and serves Ghanaian and continental dishes for US$5–10.

Black Star Arch and Independence Square [127 F3] This conglomeration of monuments to pan-Africanism and Ghanaian independence stands about halfway between Usshertown and Osu Castle in an area dominated by 'whites only' sporting and other facilities in the early colonial era. Constructed under Nkrumah, these Soviet-inspired monuments come across as starkly anachronistic, not least because of the absolute lack of African influences apparent in their angular design. (More ironic still, as one one reader points out, is that 'viewed from the right angle, the set of curving arches at the back of the stadium look an awful lot like the McDonald's logo!'). The parade ground between the square and the sea is a barren concrete eyesore, at least when void of the 30,000 people it is intended to accommodate, though it would take a hard heart to be wholly unmoved by the enclosed Flame of African Liberation, lit by Nkrumah himself in 1961.

National Theatre [127 E1] \ *03026 63449;* ☑ *fb.me/alfred4danso;* ⊕ *daily; entrance US$0.50*) Built by China and opened in 1992, this impressive building is adorned with some interesting modern sculptures and there is a small ethnographic display of traditional instruments and carvings, including the huge ceremonial male and female drums in the lobby, each decorated with features specific to individual Ghanaian tribes. It is home to the National Theatre Players, National Symphony Orchestra and National Dance Company, and it also hosts occasional movie screenings, plays and dance performances. These performances are quite irregular, but it's still worth checking whether anything is on while you are in town.

National Museum [113 C2] (\03022 21635; m *0203 221633; www.ghanamuseums. org;* ⊕ *09.00–16.30 daily; entrance US$10/8/1 foreign adult/student/child*) This was closed in December 2015 for renovations of indeterminate length, and it's not entirely clear whether the changes will be cosmetic or curatorial, or when the museum can be expected to reopen, but it seems likely that things will be up and running again by the time you read this. The description below applies to the museum pre-renovation.

Designed by Sir Denys Lasdun (who also designed the National Theatre in London) and opened by the Duchess of Kent on 5 March 1957, the eve of independence, the National Museum is predominantly ethnographic, with displays ranging from an elaborately carved *oware* board and several *akyeamepoma* (the decorated staffs used by royal spokesmen) to the chair used at the presidential inauguration of Kwame Nkrumah, and various Ashanti ancestral stools. There are also interesting displays about Larabanga Mosque and Cape Coast Castle, and ethnic artefacts from neighbouring countries as well as from South Africa. The outdoor sculpture garden displays life-size statues of musicians and of historical figures such as Kwame Nkrumah. Facilities include a gift shop and optional guided tours. Next door, Auntie Grace Special serves inexpensive local lunches.

Museum of Science and Technology [127 D1] \ *03022 23963;* www. ghanamuseums.org; ☑ *fb.me/mstghana;* ⊕ *09.00–16.30 Mon–Fri; entrance*

US$2.50/1.50/1 foreign adult/student/child) Opened in 1965 at the University of Ghana, this museum relocated to its present site on Barnes Road, a few hundred metres south of the national museum, in 2010. It is currently housed in a temporary building but a permanent one is supposed to be under construction. At the time of writing, there's not much happening here unless you fancy seeing an old TV, gramophone, water pump, hippo skull, and a few small animals in formaldehyde. The exhibit on oil and other natural resources in Ghana includes a block of raw rubber and the first ever tyre produced in Ghana (1969). Although it's unclear when this might be, hopefully the museum will offer a fuller range of displays once it takes on a more permanent form.

Osu Castle [127 G4] One of the three main castles along the Ghanaian coast (the other two being sited at Cape Coast and Elmina), this has a more chequered history of occupation than the others. It started life in 1652, when the Ga Mantse permitted Henrik Caerloff of the short-lived Swedish Africa Company to build a fortified earthen lodge at the clifftop site. Five years later, Caerloff, by then working for the Danish Guinea Company, recaptured the lodge for his new employers. In 1659, Caerloff, clearly not noted for his loyalty, defected to the Dutch, whereupon he tricked the Danish commander to sell the lodge to his new employees. However, the Ga Mantse, unimpressed by Caerloff's chicanery, asked the Dutch to leave Nkran, and sold the site back to the Danish for 3,200 gold florins in 1661.

During the 1660s, the Danish built a proper stone edifice to replace the old lodge at Osu, and named it Fort Christiansborg, after King Cristian V, the reigning monarch of Denmark. In 1680, after the Danish commander was killed in a mutiny, the fort was briefly occupied by the Portuguese, who built a new chapel, raised the bastions by 1m, and renamed it Fort São Francisco Xavier. After being returned to Denmark four years later, the fort was captured by Chief Assameni of Akwama in 1693 and sold back to Denmark barely a year later (though the keys were never returned to the Danes and remain the hereditary property of the Akwama chief to this day). The castle would remain the capital of the Danish Gold Coast for the next 150 years, before being sold to Britain in 1850.

The seat of government from 1876 onwards, Osu Castle etched its name indelibly into the modern Africa history books on 28 February 1948. This was the day when, right outside the castle walls, a demonstration initiated by recently returned veterans of World War II was fired upon by colonial police, who killed three demonstrators and injured another 237 – a landmark event not only in the history of Ghana, but also pivotal to that ushering in the end of British colonialism in Africa. In early 2013, Osu Castle was replaced by Flagstaff House as the seat of government, and while it still cannot be visited without special permission, and photography from any angle is strictly forbidden, there is talk that it will be handed over to the Ghana Museums and Monuments Board in the not too distant future.

OUTSIDE THE RING ROAD
La Beach [105 H7] This is Accra's best swimming beach, situated in front of the Labadi Beach Hotel, and easily reached by using a shared taxi or trotro from Nkrumah Circle or Tema Station to Nungua. In addition to the beach itself, which is reasonably safe for swimming depending on the strength of the undertow, there are several shady outdoor bars here, a couple of cheap restaurants, and at least two pool tables, warped ingeniously by the constant exposure to the sun. Thursday night is the best time to come partying here. Entrance costs US$1–3 depending on the day you visit, and you should keep an eye on your belongings as it's a favourite spot for casual theft.

Kaneshie Market [104 A4] Built in the 1970s, this vast and rather chaotic market lies along the Winneba road next to the synonymous trotro station about 1km past Obetsebi Lamptey Circle. In terms of what you can buy, it differs little from Makola Market in the city centre, but it is generally quieter and less frequented by tourists, so the pressure to buy is minimal.

Ghana Planetarium [113 F2] (📞 03027 69204; www.ghanascienceproject.net) Opened on Osu Avenue Extension behind the Police Headquarters in 2009, this is reputedly the first digital planetarium in sub-Saharan Africa and offers a unique interactive experience for children and adults of all ages. It aims not only to enthuse and inspire Ghanaians about astronomy and the world around them, but also to encourage scientific thinking, and to make science education more creative, innovative and practical. Interactive science exhibits are currently being constructed in the grounds of the planetarium compound, while future projects include fun days, teacher training and build-your-own-telescope sessions. At the

KATHY KNOWLES COMMUNITY LIBRARY *Kim Wildman*

One of the most special places I discovered while updating a previous edition of this guide was the Kathy Knowles Community Library [127 F1] (m *0277 452380/0246 838171;* e *jmansah3@gmail.com; www.osuchildrenslibraryfund. ca;* ⏲ *13.30–17.00 Mon–Fri, 09.00–noon Sat*), which lies on Second Avenue in Ridge, behind State House, only 50m from the Kofi Annan IT Centre and a short walk from the Ghana Tourism Authority office.

Founded by a Canadian volunteer, the story of the library reads like an African fable. It all started in 1990 after Kathy was posted to Accra with her husband John, who worked for a gold-mining company. A doting mother who enjoyed reading stories to her four children, she soon realised that Ghanaian children didn't have the same opportunities. Inspired into action, she decided to offer story times, taking a basket of books into her garden each Thursday afternoon and reading stories to six neighbourhood children under the shade of a tree.

Word soon spread and more and more children began lining up to hear Kathy's stories. To meet the demand, Kathy then converted her garage into a mini library, filling it with shelves, stools and books donated by family and friends in Canada. Before long, the makeshift little library was attracting more than 150 children each week who eagerly turned up to discover Kathy's magical world of books. When it came time for Kathy and her family to return home to Canada in 1992, faced with the prospect of closing her much-loved library she instead transformed a bright-blue 40ft cargo container into the first permanent library.

Since then her foundation, the Osu Children's Library Fund (OCLF), has built seven large community libraries in Accra and more than 170 smaller libraries around the country. The OCLF today also supports similar projects in Tanzania, Zimbabwe and the Philippines, and has begun running free adult literacy classes. If you want to meet the children and perhaps read them a story yourself, plan your visit between 14.30 and 15.30 on weekdays when school is out. Anyone looking for a unique gift can buy copies of Kathy's beautiful children's books (also available at Global Mamas), each of which is illustrated with colourful, captivating photographs and simple text that depict everyday life in Africa.

time of writing, only group bookings are accepted (maximum group size 60 adults or 80 children). Occasional public events include planetarium shows, astronomy film shows and telescope viewing.

Nima Day Tours (m *0246 270095/0235 270095;* e *ghananimatours@gmail.com; http://ghana-nima-tours.yolasite.com;* ◼ *fb.me/gntours; US$75/hour, discounts for larger groups*) Abutting the north side of the Ring Road opposite Adabraka and Asylum Down, the suburb of Nima is among the most densely populated and impoverished parts of Accra, routinely suffering from inadequate provisions of basic facilities such as housing, water, electricity and drainage systems. It was established post-World War II by rural migrants, mainly from northern Ghana, and still hosts a large Islamic population, as well as many settlers of other West African nationalities, creating a rich cultural diversity. Guided tours with Charles Sablah, a Nima resident who will ensure your safety whilst you learn about the district, last for about 2 hours and have been recommended by several readers, both for the quality of guidance and the opportunity to see a part of the city that is decidedly untouristic in feel. Sites visited include St Kizito Catholic Church (the earliest church in Nima), Kardor Mosque, the Islamic School, and Nima Market, and you can also meet local dance and drum groups, kids at a special bilingual school, and ordinary families in their courtyards.

W E B Du Bois Memorial Centre for Pan-African Culture [105 F5] (✆ *03027 76502;* m *0243 535572;* e *web.duboiscentre@gmail.com;* ⊕ *09.00–16.30 Mon–Fri, 10.30–15.30 Sat; entrance US$2 inc a 45min guided tour*). Situated on Du Bois Link between First and Second Circular roads in Cantonments, close to the US Embassy, this is the former home and now burial place of Dr William Edward Burghardt Du Bois, a prominent American anti-segregationist, pan-Africanist and communist who served as leader of all the pan-African congresses between 1919 and 1927. A prolific writer and speaker, Du Bois relocated to Accra at the invitation of Kwame Nkrumah to start work on a project called the Encyclopaedia Africana in 1961, and he became a Ghanaian citizen a few months before his death two years later, at the age of 95. Du Bois's former home in Accra now serves as a research institute and library for students of pan-Africanism, but also doubles as a museum dedicated to his memory. The Du Bois Centre is most easily reached by taking a shared taxi east from '37' Station along Gifford Road, and hopping off after about 1km.

Accra Zoo [105 E1] (⊕ *09.30–17.30 daily; entrance US$5/2.50 non-Ghanaians/ students*) Situated in the 500ha Achimota Forest Reserve, which abuts the southwestern boundary of the University of Ghana campus, about 10km north of the city centre, this small zoo is of interest mainly for the Endangered Primate Breeding Centre (EPBC) operated by the Wildlife Division of the Ghana Forestry Commission in collaboration with an international NGO called West African Primate Conservation Action (WAPCA) (*www.wapca.org*). Something of a work in progress, the EPBC is home to the world's largest captive breeding population of white-naped mangabey (*Cercocebus atys lunulatus*) (15 individuals), as well as the only mixed pair of Roloway monkey (*Cercopithecus roloway*) in Africa following the arrival of a male from a French zoo in early 2013. Both these taxa are officially listed as Endangered, and are endemic to rainforest habitats in western Ghana and Ivory Coast. The scarcer of the two is the Roloway monkey, which features on a 2012 list of the World's 25 Most Endangered Primates (compiled by several conservation agencies including the International Union for Conservation of

Nature and Natural Resources (IUCN)'s Specialist Primate Group) and was not observed in the wild in Ghana between 2001 and 2013, when WAPCA located a population in a community forest in the Western Region.

Aside from providing a unique opportunity to see these rare primates (and the Roloway monkey is a particularly striking creature), the zoo is quite a depressing affair, consisting of a few indigenous Ghanaian animals (among them warthog, striped hyena, Maxwell's duiker, grasscutter, civet and spot-nosed monkey and Lowe's monkey) and some that aren't (camel, ostrich and emu) confined to cramped cages. However, plans exist to upgrade and expand the facility as part of a proposal to convert the encroached forest reserve into the Accra Eco-Park. Ground was first broken on the project in August 2016, and phase one is scheduled to be complete within two years. Final completion, which includes the planting of over one million trees, will take a further three to five years. If all goes to plan, it will reputedly become the largest urban ecological park in West Africa, and include facilities for wildlife safaris, conferencing, eco-lodging, botanical gardens, and an amusement park.

The entrance to the forest reserve lies about halfway along the east side of Achimota Forest Road, which runs for about 1km between Dimples Junction on the Accra–Tema (George Walker Bush) Highway to Achimota Police Station. Shared taxis and trotros from the city centre to Achimota run close by the entrance (just ask for a trotro to Dimples or CP junction), but from there it is another 1.6km walk or drive to the zoo itself, so you might prefer to charter a taxi.

University of Ghana [105 G1] (✆ 03025 00381; e pad@ug.edu.gh; www.ug.edu. gh; ⏲ to the public 08.00–16.00 Mon–Sat) Situated in Legon, 14km north of the city centre along the Aburi road, this is the oldest university in Ghana, set in attractive grounds that include several striking colonial-style buildings. The mellow **Botanical Garden** (behind the Department of Zoology) is of special interest to birdwatchers. In addition to boasting a good bookshop, the university is home to the superb **Balme Library**, whose unparalleled hoard of colonial-era books and documents is of great interest to Ghanaphiles. Even more worthwhile perhaps is the renovated **Museum of Archaeology**, which has a remarkable collection of ancient beads as well as displays about bead making, human prehistory, the first known sub-Saharan agricultural settlement at Kintampo, the early trading town of Begho, the Akan kingdoms, Koma statues and finds from excavations in Elmina.

If you are spending time at the university, a good though rather pricey place to eat is the Tayiba Restaurant (m 0275 900072), which resembles a large thatched-roof hut and is located outside the front gates to the Botanical Garden. It serves well-prepared and tasty Ghanaian fare including grilled tilapia, chicken kebabs and fresh fruit juice, and it sometimes has a live jazz band. Also on campus, Taco Bell, across the street from the Soil Science Department, is a good option for red-red and similar fare, while an anonymous snack joint next door is very popular with exchange students from the USA for its breakfast foods (pancakes, oatmeal) and simple sandwiches.

To get there, catch a trotro from the station located on the northwest side of Nkrumah Circle. After entering the main gate, keep going straight to reach the library or bookshop, but turn right at the roundabout for the Department of Archaeology and the museum.

WE WELCOME YOU

SOMEWHERE NICE

Our major goal is to connect locals and travelers in an environmentally friendly home on a level where they both can learn and grow on each other - a community where we are all the same and learn from our individual personalities.

Double rooms from 25 EUR / twin en-suite from 25 EUR / dorms from 10 EUR *
*Prices (per person per night) for all room types may vary depending on season and day

swimming pool / guest kitchen / all rooms with air-conditioning and ceiling-fans / rainhead showers / homemade breakfast / drinking water

WE ARE LOOKING FORWARD TO MEETING YOU

Cotton Avenue 9, Kokomlemle, Accra
+233 543 743 505 I info@hostelaccra.com I www.hostelaccra.com
facebook.comsomewherenice.gh somewherenicegh

SOMEWHERE NICE
HOSTEL ACCRA

Around Accra

This rather unstructured chapter covers most places of interest within a 30km radius of Accra, generally focusing on spots that could easily be visited as day or overnight trips from the capital. It starts on the east coast with the important seaport of Tema and more resort-like towns of Teshie-Nungua and Prampram, then heads inland to the highland town of Aburi (famed for its botanical garden) and Shai Hills Resource Reserve (the closest wildlife destination to Accra), before continuing to the west coast and the very popular resort of Kokrobite and rather more obscure small towns of Gomoah Fetteh and Senya Beraku. Although most of these sites make for good breaks from the capital, in many cases – particularly Aburi and Kokrobite – they are also useful first stops out of the capital and springboards for travel further afield.

TESHIE-NUNGUA

Situated about halfway along the coastal road connecting Accra to Tema, the coastal town of Teshie-Nungua is one of the 20 largest in Ghana, supporting a population of almost 90,000. It is also the closest bona fide beach resort to Accra, only about 10km east of La, supporting a string of seafront hotels that provide an agreeable alternative to staying in the capital. It's also worth visiting Teshie-Nungua to see some of the fantastic coffin workshops that line the main road, producing wooden coffins sculpted in various bizarre shapes, from beer bottles to whales, and snails to polished uteruses. Note that the Nungua area has acquired something of a reputation for bag snatching and other robberies aimed at Westerners.

GETTING THERE AND AWAY To get to Teshie-Nungua, simply follow the main coastal road east out of the city centre past the Labadi Beach Hotel, a drive that can take anything from 10 minutes to over an hour, depending on traffic. Plenty of trotros cover this route: you can either pick one up at the central Tema Station in Accra, or else just wave something down near the junction of Ring Road East and La Road. Most of the resorts lie about 1km south of the main road towards Tema, so travellers with luggage will probably prefer to charter a private taxi.

🏠 **WHERE TO STAY AND EAT** *Map, page 152*
Upmarket
🏠 **Ramada Resort Coco Beach** (75 rooms)
📞 03027 17235; m 0572 233183; e info@
ramadaresortaccra.com; www.ramadaresortaccra.
com. This once quite smart hotel is definitely
starting to show its age, but still has a superb
beachfront location roughly 500m along a
signposted junction off the coastal road to Tema.
Facilities include a large free-form swimming pool

right above the beach, a children's playground, a
well-equipped business centre, a gym, massage
parlour & hair salon, & live music at w/ends. A
decent restaurant serves Western & Ghanaian
dishes on the beach. The rather dated rooms
are tastefully decorated with muted colours &
hardwood furniture, & come with satellite TV, Wi-
Fi, AC & hot water. *B&B US$140/185 sgl/dbl chalet;
US$150/170 standard sgl/dbl.* **$$$$$–$$$$**

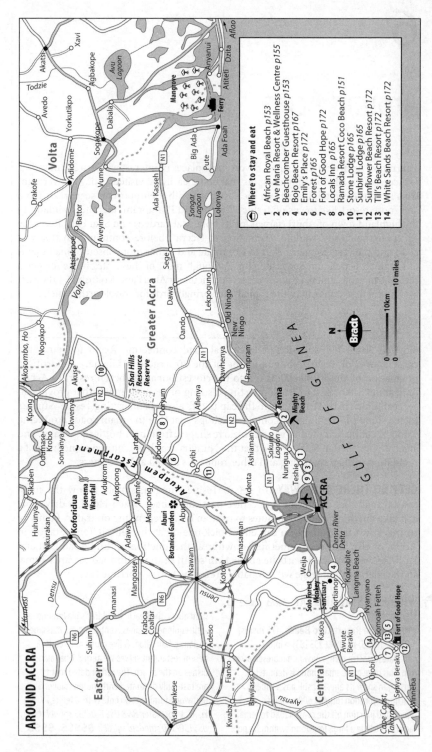

AROUND ACCRA

Eastern

Volta

Akatsi
Xavi
Todzie
Agbakope
Avedo
Avu Lagoon
Yorkutikpo
Dabala
Sogakope
Adidome
Drakofe
Vume
Battor
Atsiekpoe
Aveyime
Volta

Anyanui
Dzita
Atiteti
Aflao
Mangrove
Ferry
Big Ada
Pute
Ada Foah
Ada Kasseh
Songar Lagoon
Lolonya

Huhunya
Nkurakan
Sikaben
Koforidua
Asenema Waterfall
Adukrom
Akropong
Mampong
Mamfe
Aburi Botanical Garden
Aburi

Greater Accra

Akosombo, Ho
Nogokpo
Akuse
Shai Hills Resource Reserve
Kpong
Odumase-Krobo
Somanya
Okwenya
Larteh
Dodowa
Owibi
Afienya
Dawa
Sege
Lekpoguno
Oando
Old Ningo
New Ningo
Prampram

Akuapem Escarpment

Mangoase
Amanasi
Kraboa Coaltar
Suhum
Adeiso
Adawso
Nsawam
Amasaman
Kotoku
Weija
Solo Forest Monkey Sanctuary
Bortianor
Kokrobite
Langma Beach

Fianko
Bawjiase
Ojobi
Awute Beraku
Kasoa
Senya Beraku
Somooah Fetteh
Nyanyano
Fort of Good Hope

Ashiaman
Adenta
Amasaman
Adenta
Nungua
Teshie
ACCRA
Densu River Delta

Tema
Mighty Beach

GULF OF GUINEA

Cape Coast, Takoradi
Winneba

Central

Densu
Densu
Ayensu

N6
N6
N2
N2
N1
N1
N1
N1

Bradt

N

0   10km
0   10 miles

Where to stay and eat

1. African Royal Beach *p153*
2. Ave Maria Resort & Wellness Centre *p155*
3. Beachcomber Guesthouse *p153*
4. Bojo Beach Resort *p167*
5. Emily's Place *p172*
6. Forest *p165*
7. Fort of Good Hope *p172*
8. Locals Inn *p165*
9. Ramada Resort Coco Beach *p151*
10. Stone Lodge *p165*
11. Sunbird Lodge *p165*
12. Sunflower Beach Resort *p172*
13. Till's Beach Resort *p172*
14. White Sands Beach Resort *p172*

African Royal Beach Hotel (50 rooms)
03027 11111–9; e info@africanroyalbeachhotel.
com; www.africanroyalbeachhotel.com. This
sharp & agreeable multi-storey hotel lies on an
attractive-looking (but smelly) rocky stretch of
coast about 1km east of the Ramada Resort &
1.5km from the coastal road to Tema. Facilities
include a neat swimming pool area, live music
at w/ends, a children's playground & a good
restaurant serving continental dishes. The bright &
attractively decorated modern rooms all come with
queen-size bed, satellite TV, AC, private balcony
with sea view, & renovations were ongoing
in 2016. *US$130/145 self-contained sgl/dbl;
US$150/165 sgl/dbl seaside suite.* **$$$$**

Budget

Beachcomber Guesthouse (7 rooms) m
0246 259921. This beachfront guesthouse, located
a few hundred metres from the Ramada Resort,
looks a bit higgledy-piggledy on first glance, but
was for some time among the more pleasant
budget options near Accra. The small grassy
grounds run down to a rocky stretch of beach
where swimming is not recommended, but you
can swim in the pool at the Ramada for a small
fee. The thatched chalets with queen-sized or twin
beds, fan, AC, TV, hot shower & fridge are very
reasonably priced, though one reader's report in
late 2016 warned that there was no food available
on site, & lots of construction going on. *US$15–22
self-contained dbl.* **$$**

TEMA

Bisected by the Greenwich Meridian only 25km east of Accra, Tema is the fourth-largest city in Ghana, supporting a population of around 400,000. Often referred to as Harbour Town, it outranks Takoradi as the country's largest shipping port, with 1.7km² of water-enclosed area, 5km of breakwaters, 12 deepwater berths, a huge tanker berth and a vast container yard. It handles 80% of Ghana's import and export cargo, and deals with goods in transit to landlocked Burkina Faso, Mali and Niger. Tema is widely overlooked by tourists and, unless working harbours are your thing, it is a rather dull and nondescript place, one whose bureaucratic roots – it was custom built to serve the harbour in the 1960s – are reflected in its division into a series of numbered 'communities', none of which offers much in the way of worthwhile sightseeing.

HISTORY An obscure fishing village, founded a few hundred years earlier by Kpeshie fishermen who migrated to the area from present-day Nigeria, Tema was originally known as Torman ('Town of Gourds') after a calabash-producing tree that once grew prolifically in the area. In the early 1950s, the village was first earmarked for future development as a deep-water harbour and industrial centre, a project realised under President Nkrumah, who commissioned the construction of a large harbour and bordering township in 1959, not least because of the site's proximity to the planned hydro-electric plant at Akosombo Dam. The harbour started operation in 1962, and Tema soon evolved into a bustling modern harbour city and centre of manufacture, site of Ghana's only crude oil refinery, of the Volta Aluminium Company, and of most of the country's major industries.

GETTING THERE AND AWAY Regular trotros to Tema leave central Accra from Tema Station [127 D2], taking about an hour each way (sometimes a lot longer in traffic). Travellers staying in the Adabraka or Osu area of Accra may find it easier to catch a shared taxi to Nungua and pick up transport to Tema from there.

WHERE TO STAY AND EAT Tema can easily be visited as a day trip from Accra, but it has a profusion of mostly business-orientated hotels, all with their own restaurant. Standalone eateries worthy of note include the excellent **Delhi Palace** [154 B2] (03033 00741; m 026 4460358) for Indian food, as well as **Basilissa Fast Food** [154 B4] for pizza and shawarmas and **Nominom Café** [154 B4] (m 0543 771777)

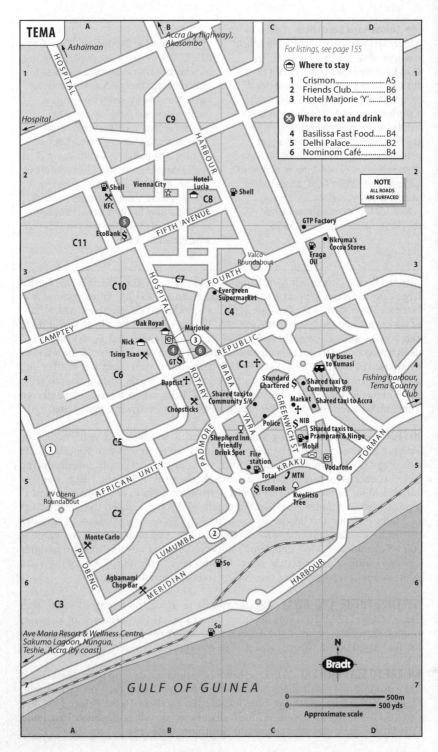

TEMA

Ashaiman

Accra (by highway),
Akosombo

For listings, see page 155

Where to stay
1 Crismon.........................A5
2 Friends Club...................B6
3 Hotel Marjorie 'Y'..........B4

Where to eat and drink
4 Basilissa Fast Food......B4
5 Delhi Palace..................B2
6 Nominom Café..............B4

NOTE
ALL ROADS
ARE SURFACED

Hospital

HOSPITAL

C9

HARBOUR

Shell
KFC
Vienna City
Hotel
Lucia
C8
Shell

FIFTH AVENUE

EcoBank

C11

GTP Factory

Nkruma's
Cocoa Stores
Fraga
Oil

Valco
Roundabout

C10

FOURTH

C7

HOSPITAL

Evergreen
Supermarket

C4

LAMPTEY

Oak Royal
Marjorie
Nick
3
4   6
Tsing Tsao
GT

REPUBLIC

C1

VIP buses
to Kumasi

Fishing harbour,
Tema Country
Club

C6

Baptist

Chopsticks

C5

ROTARY

BABA

Shared taxi to
Community 5/6

Standard
Chartered

Shared taxi to
Community 8/9

Market

Shared taxi to Accra

GREENWICH ST

NIB

Shared taxis to
Prampram & Ningo

Mobil

Vodafone

TORMAN

1

PADMORE

Shepherd Inn
Friendly
Drink Spot

Police

Fire
station

KRAKU

Total

MTN

Kwelitso
Tree

EcoBank

AFRICAN UNITY

C2

PV Obeng
Roundabout

Monte Carlo

PV OBENG

Agbamami
Chop Bar

MERIDIAN

LUMUMBA

2

So

HARBOUR

C3

Ave Maria Resort & Wellness Centre,
Sakumo Lagoon, Nungua,
Teshie, Accra (by coast)

So

N

Bradt

GULF OF GUINEA

0   500m
0   500 yds
Approximate scale

for ice cream, smoothies, coffee, and pastries. There's also now a branch of the ever-expanding **KFC** chain in Tema.

Upmarket

🏠 **Hotel Marjorie 'Y'** [154 B4] (60 rooms) 📞 03032 12566/1; e marjoriehotel@yahoo.com; www.marjorie-y.com.gh. This central 2-star hotel caters mainly to business travellers, but it also makes for an agreeable base for tourists, with its attractive pool area (with its own waterfall) & live music on Sun. For a meal out, Basilissa Fast Food & Nominom Café are both right next door. A range of comfortable rooms all come with fan, AC, hot water & satellite TV. *US$111/116/155 B&B self-contained sgl/dbl/suite.* **$$$$**

🏠 **Crismon Hotel** [154 A5] (47 rooms) 📞 03032 05547; m 0547 366622; e info@crismonhotel.com; www.crismonhotel.com. This smart, friendly hotel in the residential suburb of Community Five offers low-key business travellers a good alternative to the proliferation of multi-storey monoliths in town. The staff at the Crismon are refreshingly professional & very attentive. The large rooms, all with hot bath, hairdryer, AC & satellite TV & free Wi-Fi, are built around a spacious courtyard with a pool & terrace bar. *US$100/129/170 B&B self-contained sgl/dbl/suite.* **$$$$**

🏠 **Ave Maria Resort and Wellness Centre** [map, page 152] (15 rooms) 📞 03270 31074; m 0244 531295; e avemariaresorttema@gmail.com; www.avemariawellness.com. Scoring highly when it comes to curiosity value, this beachfront property, situated off the Accra road a few metres from the Greenwich Meridian Rock, started life in the early 1950s as the Halcrow Beach Club (after its architect Sir William Halcrow, the consultant assigned to the construction of the Tema Harbour). In 1962, it hosted Queen Elizabeth II during her visit in Ghana, after President Nkrumah ordered a new chalet & swimming pool to be built in her honour. In 2002, it reopened in its present guise as a health & wellness centre, with decent facilities including a spa, beauty centre, gym, swimming pool, tennis/squash court, restaurant, & comfortable rooms with AC & satellite TV. It can feel rather moribund when there are no guests, but it does seem quite popular at w/ends. *US$105/125 B&B self-contained sgl/dbl; US$180 Kwame Nkrumah/ Queen Elizabeth Suite.* **$$$$**

Moderate

🏠 **Friends Club Hotel** [154 B6] (16 rooms) 📞 03032 06575; m 0244 718554/0208 111686. This small purple hotel & restaurant in Community Two, close to the town centre, is reasonable value, but it's also come in for some reader complaints. There are clean self-contained rooms with AC, satellite TV, & Wi-Fi. Right around the corner & of a slightly higher standard, the Harbor Terrace Hotel (📞 03032 05437) is under the same management. *US$26–37 self-contained dbl, depending on size.* **$$**

WHAT TO SEE AND DO Should you end up in Tema for whatever reason, it's worth spending some time around the central market area in **Community Seven** [154 B3] and the **fishing harbour** [154 D4], both of which are lively throughout the day. An important landmark is the **Kwelitso Tree** in the grounds of the disused Hotel Meridian – according to local legend, all attempts to uproot this massive baobab during the construction of the hotel failed, and today it is held sacred by Kpeshie traditionalists. Lovers of geographical trivia might be interested to know that the **Presbyterian church** [154 C4] in the market lies right on the Greenwich Meridian. One reader eulogises the vast cylindrical cocoa warehouses constructed under Nkrumah in 1964 but never used, as having a 'monolithic beauty', while another suggests that a tour through the industrial district might be of interest to those with an interest in Ghanaian economics or its manufacturing industry! Golfers can hit the links at the **Tema Country Club** (m *0244 717508;* 📘 *fb.me/temagolfclub*) 3km from the main roundabout towards Aflao.

About 2km west of the city centre, the coastal road to Accra crosses the **Sakumo Lagoon**, a Ramsar Wetland Site separated from the ocean by a narrow sand dune. In addition to marine turtles, more than 70 waterbird species have been recorded in the lagoon, with seasonal mixed flocks of tens of thousands not unusual. Among the more common species are sandwich, common, little and black tern, spotted redshank, and various egrets and plovers. The Sakumo Lagoon is held sacred by Kpeshie traditionalists, and the striking black heron – also known as the umbrella bird for its habit of opening its wings to form an umbrella-like canopy when it fishes – is protected by local taboo. In the first week of April, the annual Kpledjoo Festival marks the end of a traditional three-month ban on fishing and crab-trapping in the lagoon. The chief priest or priestess performs a series of rites on the lagoon's shore, including casting a symbolic net over the water, and this is followed by a celebratory durbar of local chiefs.

The best beach in the vicinity of Tema is the **Regional Maritime Academy Beach** – also known as Mighty Beach – which lies along the coastal road to Accra almost immediately past the bridge over the lagoon. The beach here is also dotted with numerous breezy beach-shack restaurants and bars, which are especially popular with Accra and Tema residents at weekends. Closer to the town centre, a reasonably pleasant place to chill out in views of crashing waves is the Ave Maria Resort and Wellness Centre (page 155).

PRAMPRAM AND NINGO

Situated on the coast about 20km east of Tema, the small towns of Prampram and Ningo, separated by a long sandy beach, are two of the oldest European settlements in this part of Ghana. Prampram was the site of a small British trading post and fort built in 1742, while Ningo was the site of a Danish fort from 1735 until it was handed to Britain in 1850. Neither fort has survived to the modern day: some traces of Prampram's Fort Vernon remain in the walls of a derelict resthouse near the fishing harbour, and even less remains to be seen of Fort Fredenshborg in Ningo. The main attraction of the area today is the beach, which is generally regarded as safe for swimming (though it's always best to ask locally before you take the leap) and dotted with holiday homes. The estuary that separates 'Old' Ningo from 'New' Ningo is also very pretty, its natural beauty enhanced by the colourful fishing boats moored on the beach.

GETTING THERE AND AWAY Both towns lie about 6km south of the main Accra–Aflao road, along a 20km road that loops southwards to the coast between the junction villages of Dawhenya (also known as Prampram Junction) and Oando. Prampram is the main transport hub in the area, but there is no direct trotro transport there from Accra – you will almost certainly have to change vehicles at Ashaiman, a busy junction town to the north of Tema. From Tema itself, shared taxis run from a rank just by the market [154 C5] and take about 45 minutes. If you are coming from the direction of Ada, ask to be dropped at Dawhenya and wait there for a lift. Regular shared taxis connect Prampram to New Ningo and Old Ningo.

⌂ **WHERE TO STAY AND EAT** *Map, page 157*

Moderate

⌂ **Legacy Tribe Beach Resort** (10 rooms) ☏03029 75471; m 0264 430260/0501 315825; e info@legacytribebeachresort.com; www. legacytribebeachresort.com. The smartest option around Prampram is this pleasant resort, which boasts very helpful staff, along with an open-sided restaurant/bar on a private beach, & relatively stylish semi-detached chalets with queen-sized

bed, satellite TV, AC, fridge, kettle & private balcony. *US$92/100 self-contained sgl/dbl; US$106 exec dbl.* **$$$$–$$$**

⌂ **Sealane Hotel** (40 rooms) ☏03039 37960; m 0540 849350/0208 123393; e info@ sealanehotel.com; www.sealanehotel.com. Clearly signposted 500m from the lorry station, this friendly set-up lacks a beachfront location, but facilities include a swimming pool, nightclub &

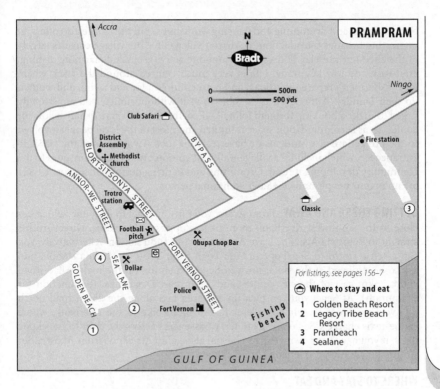

For listings, see pages 156–7

Where to stay and eat

1 Golden Beach Resort
2 Legacy Tribe Beach Resort
3 Prambeach
4 Sealane

Map labels: Accra, N, PRAMPRAM, Ningo, 0 — 500m, 0 — 500 yds, Club Safari, District Assembly, Methodist church, BLORTSITSONYA STREET, BYPASS, Fire station, ANNOR-WE STREET, Trotro station, Classic, Football pitch, FORT VERNON STREET, Obupa Chop Bar, GOLDEN BEACH, SEA LANE, Dollar, Police, Fort Vernon, Fishing beach, GULF OF GUINEA

restaurant serving Western-style food. The large tiled rooms come with king-sized bed, flatscreen satellite TV, W-Fi, & AC, but are starting to look quite rundown. *Middling value at US$26/40 self-contained sgl/dbl.* **$$**

Budget

🏠 **Golden Beach Resort** (30 rooms) ☎03039 10354; m 0248 787362/0244 903952. Set in palm-shaded & well-developed gardens right on the beach on the outskirts of town, this good-value resort offers the choice of older & more basic rooms with dbl bed, cold shower & fan, or smarter new rooms with queen-sized bed, AC & hot shower. It also has a restaurant serving simple local dishes for US$5–7 per plate. *US$9/24 self-contained dbl with fan/AC.* **$$–$**

🏠 **Prambeach** (4 rooms, 6 more under construction) m 0276 1114 29; e info@prambeach. com; www.prambeach.com. Something of a perpetual work in progress, this promising resort has looked rather unfinished for the past 2 editions of this guide. It lies about 1.5km from Prampram in the direction of Ningo. The large seafront gardens could do with having a few trees planted, & they overlook rocky tidal flats (so it isn't much good for swimming) but there is a pleasant enough restaurant serving mains in the US$6–8 range, & the clean tiled rooms with fan seem like good value. *US$21 self-contained dbl with ceiling fan & cold water.* **$$**

ATSIEKPOE

Situated on the northeastern banks of the Volta about 80km distant from Accra as the crow flies, this rustic village – whose name means 'Home of the Cashew Tree' – is the site of a worthwhile ecotourism project initiated by Jolinaiko Eco Tours and centred on the riverside Cashew Village Lodge. It lies in an area adversely affected by the construction of Akosombo Dam, which put an end to the annual flooding that formerly made the riverside farmland so fertile. Formal attractions include a small museum and activities such as a village walk, a longer savannah walk, birdwatching, and drumming and dancing workshops. But the village also offers an interesting broader introduction to African village life. The village consists largely of thatched termite-clay houses, and economic activities include farming, fishing, craftwork and low-key trade. Life is very much centred around the river, where local fishermen prepare their boats and nets, children play and swim, and women do their laundry. Although it is possible to visit without notice, you are strongly urged to make a booking through Jolinaiko Eco Tours (see *Where to Stay* below for contacts), as accommodation space is limited and most of the local people involved in the project are also students or have teaching jobs. Two-thirds of the US$2.50 entrance fee, which includes a village walk and entrance to the museum, goes to the community development fund. Drumming and dancing performances cost US$21 for up to four people and US$5 per additional person.

GETTING THERE AND AWAY From Accra, you must first get to Aveyime, which lies close to the southwest riverbank more-or-less opposite Atsiekpoe. Direct trotros straight to Bator via Aveyime leave Accra from the Tudu station. Alternatively, you can catch a trotro to Sogakope or Ada Foah from Tudu or Madina station, and ask to be dropped at the small town of Sege, which lies on the main Aflao Road about 75km east of the city centre (and 35km past Dawhenya, the junction for Prampram). At Sege, you can pick up a shared taxi along the 25km road north to Aveyime. From Aveyime, walk or take a motorbike to the riverbank, where canoe-taxis charge US$4 one-way to ferry passengers across the river to Atsiekpoe itself. If you have your own vehicle, you can also get to Atsiekpoe from Akosombo/Atimpoko via Akuse, Asetuare and Aveyime.

WHERE TO STAY AND EAT

Cashew Village Lodge (5 rooms) m 0208 120856/0264 432634/0247 230178; e info@joli-ecotours.com; www.joli-ecotours.com. This rustic riverside guesthouse in a mango tree-studded compound offers a good view & a welcoming breeze. It consists of 5 basic guestrooms spread across 2 mud-brick & termite-clay buildings. Facilities include a simple bathhouse (bucket shower), self-composting toilet, local-style kitchen & waterfront summer huts. Tents are also available for hire. *US$11pp per night inc dinner & b/fast.* **$$–$**

ABURI

Situated less than an hour's drive inland of the Ghanaian capital, the small town of Aburi (population 18,000) stands at an altitude of around 450m in the green Akwapim (aka Akuapem) Hills. Thanks to its relatively cool and breezy climate, Aburi has long been favoured as a retreat from Accra, going back to colonial times, when it was the site of an early Basel Mission and later a British sanatorium set in the Aburi Botanical Garden, which is still its main attraction today. Aburi remains a pleasant weekend retreat from the capital, and it is also an excellent first stop for travellers heading deeper into the Ghanaian interior, situated along a road that continues northwards to Koforidua and Kumasi. In addition to the botanical garden, Aburi boasts a selection of decent accommodation catering to most budgets, and it is a good base for hiking and mountain biking.

HISTORY The Akwapim Hills are named after the eponymous kingdom, which was founded in 1733 in rebellion against the oppressive Akwamu Kingdom of the eastern plains, and today consists of 17 townships ruled over by a paramount chief whose throne lies in Akropong.

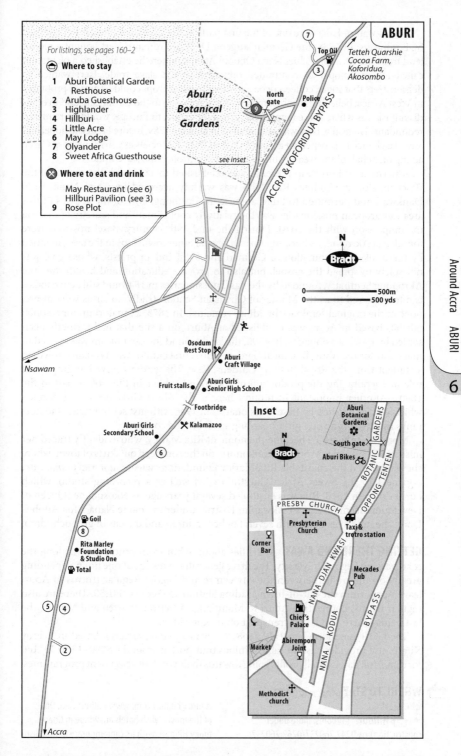

ABURI

For listings, see pages 160–2

🏠 **Where to stay**

1 Aburi Botanical Garden Resthouse
2 Aruba Guesthouse
3 Highlander
4 Hillburi
5 Little Acre
6 May Lodge
7 Olyander
8 Sweet Africa Guesthouse

❌ **Where to eat and drink**

May Restaurant (see 6)
Hillburi Pavilion (see 3)
9 Rose Plot

Top Oil

Tetteh Quarshie
Cocoa Farm,
Koforidua,
Akosombo

Aburi
Botanical
Gardens

North gate

Police

ACCRA & KOFORIDUA BYPASS

see inset

N

Bradt

0 — 500m
0 — 500 yds

Nsawam

Osodum Rest Stop
Aburi Craft Village

Fruit stalls
Aburi Girls Senior High School

Footbridge

Aburi Girls Secondary School
Kalamazoo

6

May Lodge (6)

Goil
8

Rita Marley Foundation & Studio One
Total

5 4

2

Accra

Inset

Aburi Botanical Gardens

South gate

Aburi Bikes

N

Bradt

PRESBY CHURCH

Presbyterian Church

Corner Bar

Taxi & trotro station

Mecades Pub

Chief's Palace

Market

Abirempom Joint

Methodist church

BOTANIC GARDENS
OPPONG TENTEN
NANA DJAN KWASI
NANA A KODUA
BYPASS

The Akwapim Hills were one of the first parts of the Ghanaian interior to be settled by Europeans. In 1788, the German surgeon Dr Paul Erdmann Isert bought a plot of land from the Akwapim chief Nana Obuobi Atiemo, where he established a plantation called Frederiksnopel. A committed opponent of the slave trade, Isert wanted to demonstrate that sugar, coffee, cocoa and other tropical crops could be grown profitably in West Africa, believing that by doing so, the slave trade to the Caribbean, and to other distant islands where these items were grown for export to Europe, would be rendered redundant. Tragically, Isert was assassinated in January 1789, before Frederiksnopel had any real chance to prosper, an act attributed to Danish officials at Christiansborg Castle acting on behalf of the wealthy financiers who controlled the slave trade.

A permanent European presence was established in 1835 with the arrival of the Basel missionary Andreas Riis, who was warmly accepted by Chief Nana Addo Dankwa I and permitted to build a house in Akropong. One of the appeals of this area to European missionaries was the relatively cool climate and scarcity of malaria in comparison with the coast. During the mid 19th century, Basel missions were founded at Akropong, Aburi, Abetifi and several other townships in the area, manned by the unlikely combination of German and West Indian priests, whose goal was not solely to spread the gospel, but also to provide education and healthcare. The Akropong Seminary, founded by the Basel missionaries in 1848 and still active today, is often referred to as the Mother of Ghanaian Schools (sadly, so far as we're aware, none of the original seminary buildings remains). In 1875, a sanatorium for colonial officials based in Accra was established at Aburi, on a site that had formerly been settled by Basel missionaries. In 1890, the land around the sanatorium was cleared to make way for the Aburi Botanical Garden, whose first curator was William Crowther, a student from the Royal Botanic Gardens, Kew. The gardens played an important role in encouraging the production of cocoa and rubber in the Gold Coast in the 1890s. Another important institution here is the Aburi Girls' Secondary School, which was established by Basel missionaries in 1946 with just seven pupils, and now ranks as perhaps the best girls' boarding school in the country.

More recently, Aburi became the home of Rita Marley, who evidently traced her husband Bob Marley's roots to Konkonoru, on the southern outskirts of town, where she established the charitable Rita Marley Foundation (*www.ritamarleyfoundation. org*) next to the Sweet Africa Guesthouse, as well as a recording studio, which burnt down in 2010. Rita was enstooled several years ago as Nkosohene (Queen of Development) of Southeast Akwapim District under the name Nana Afua Adobea I, and she now lives there with several of her children and dozens of grandchildren.

GETTING THERE AND AWAY Aburi lies about 35km from central Accra along the road passing Legon University. The drive generally takes about one hour, depending greatly on the traffic between the city centre and Legon. Regular trotros to Aburi leave Accra from the out-of-town Madina Station, and cost US$1.50. There are also regular trotros connecting Aburi to Mampong, Adokrom, Larteh and Mamfe, the last being where you'll find transport on to Koforidua.

The CO Foundation (m *0540 366848*; *www.co-foundation.org*), based in nearby Kitase, also provides customisable minibus transport at around US$90–120/130–160 for a half/full day, with all profits going towards their youth development programmes.

▲ WHERE TO STAY *Map, page 159*
Exclusive
✳ ▲ Hillburi (3 rooms, more under construction) m 0242 260237/0262 260237;

e info@hillburi.com; www.hillburi.com. One of the most stylish hotels anywhere in Ghana, funky Hillburi, with its contemporary minimalism off-set by warm earthy colours, curvaceous arches & ethnic flourishes, invites comparisons to some of the chicest boutique lodges in eastern & southern Africa. Situated on the east side of the Accra road some 3km south of the town centre, the attractively laid-out grounds, sloping down towards a large free-form swimming pool, also offer lovely views stretching towards Accra. The excellent Pavilion Restaurant has an unusually imaginative menu, & the large uncluttered rooms come with terracotta tiled floor, hardwood furniture, king-size bed, flatscreen satellite TV, tea/coffee station, minibar & luxurious bathroom. The restaurant closes on Mon & Tue nights unless by special arrangement. *US$170 B&B self-contained dbl.* **$$$$**

Moderate

🏠 **Aruba Guesthouse** (12 rooms, more under construction) ➧03470 011011; m 0240 144797; e arubaguesthouse@yahoo.com; www. arubaguesthouse.com.gh. Situated on the Accra road about 200m past Hillburi, this agreeable dbl-storey hotel (with a big new block under construction) has large modern rooms with queen-sized bed, satellite TV, fan, AC, private balcony overlooking the hills, en-suite hot tub/shower & modern African art on the walls. The breezy 1st-floor restaurant has great views & an interesting menu of Asian, continental & local dishes in the US$10–13 range. *US$61/66 self-contained dbl on lower/upper floors.* **$$$**

🏠 **Little Acre Hotel** (35 rooms) ➧03070 91977; e info@littleacrehotelgh.com or littleacrehotell@gmail.com. This smart little hotel is situated in neat green grounds along the Accra road opposite Hillburi. It has comfortable rooms with fridge, hot shower & satellite TV. A restaurant & bar are attached. *US$53/61–66 dbl with fan/AC; US$100–106 large suite.* **$$$$–$$$**

Budget

🏠 **Highlander Hotel** (8 rooms) m 0247 771923/0206 076131; e annakwansa@gmail. com. Situated a few mins' walk from the northern entrance gate to the botanical garden, this very reasonably priced hotel has been warmly recommended by readers. It has nice gardens & comfortable dbl rooms, mostly with AC & TV, but no bar or restaurant (though cold drinks are available at reception). *US$19 self-contained dbl with fan; US$23–37 self-contained dbl with AC, depending on size & facilities.* **$$**

🏠 **Olyander Hotel** (5 rooms) m 0277 580221/0243 582602. Situated about 500m from the northern entrance gate to the botanical garden, this friendly set-up feels like a family home & has comfortable self-contained dbls with sturdy beds, hot water, TV, fridge & fan. Good Ghanaian food can be served in the neatly tended garden. There have been some reports of plumbing problems & a miserly attitude to providing water. *US$13 self-contained sgl; US$17–26 self-contained dbl, depending on size.* **$$**

🏠 **Sweet Africa Guesthouse** (11 rooms) ➧03421 97820; m 0209 041364. Situated along the Accra road about 500m before Hillburi, this agreeable budget lodge has comfortable & spacious AC rooms, & offers good views over the hills, but no food is available. *US$16–24 self-contained dbl.* **$$**

Shoestring

🏠 **Aburi Botanical Garden Resthouse** (20 rooms) m 0244 693068/0248 772027. It's quite rundown & the receptionist clearly never attended charm school, but this characterful former sanatorium, built in 1875, has a wonderful location overlooking the main lawns of the botanical garden about 200m inside the northern entrance gate. The rooms all come with a dbl bed, fan, & en-suite cold bucket shower (no running water). It's advisable to make an advance booking over w/ends & public holidays. *Good value at US$11 self-contained dbl.* **$**

🏠 **May Restaurant & Lodge** (4 rooms) m 0540 503649. This pleasant hotel about 1km south of the town centre has fabulous views over a wooded valley, a restaurant serving generous portions of chicken & rice for around US$4 a plate, & clean, spacious & affordable twin rooms with fans. *US$12 self-contained twin.* **$**

✖ **WHERE TO EAT AND DRINK** *Map, page 159*

✳ ✖ **Hillburi Pavilion** ⏰ noon–18.00 Wed–Fri, 07.30–19.00 Sat–Sun, 11.00–19.00 public holidays. If you can work around the opening hours, this is Aburi's classiest restaurant, serving everything from perfectly seared steaks & grills to an imaginative selection of wraps & sandwiches, some

161

truly decadent desserts & a choice of South African wines. Mains US$10–15. Day visitors must pay to use the swimming pool. $$$
✕ **Rose Plot Restaurant** m 0509 387796/0243 525501; ☺ 07.30–21.00 daily. Situated in the botanical garden next to the

guesthouse, this offers the option of sitting indoors or on the balcony, & serves simple local & Western meals for around US$4–5, as well as chilled beers, soft drinks, spicy barbecued kebabs & pots of delicious local honey. $

SHOPPING Aburi is an excellent place to buy curios: the row of stalls on the junction with the Accra road have been consolidated into the new **Aburi Craft Village** (e *aburicraft2015@gmail.com*) in the same location, where you'll find drums, fertility dolls, stools, etc, sold in a far friendlier atmosphere than in the capital, and at better prices.

WHAT TO SEE AND DO

Aburi Botanical Garden A popular weekend retreat with Accra residents, this 19th-century botanical garden, which extends over 65ha and has an altitudinal span of 370–460m, is planted with a mixture of indigenous and exotic trees, notably the avenue of tall palms that leads to the guesthouse, and an immense 150-year-old kapok tree on the main lawn. It is riddled with footpaths from where visitors can see a large variety of labelled trees as well as many birds. In clear weather, the views back to Accra can be amazing. Entrance to the botanical garden costs US$1.50 for non-Ghanaian adults, with a 50% discount available to students and no additional charge for still photography.

Aburi Bikes (m *0244 209587/0277 666018*; e *ghanabike2@yahoo.com; www. ghanabike2.com*; ☺ *09.00–18.00 daily*) Aburi's attractiveness to adventure tourists is greatly enhanced by the presence of this excellent small operator immediately outside the southern gate of the botanical garden. The fantastically helpful owner used to work with the company's Swiss founders, who marked out three self-guided mountain-bike trails of 2–3 hours' duration in the vicinity of Aburi, as well as a 450km network of guided trails of up to five days in duration. All the mountain bikes have aluminium frames, front suspension forks and V brakes, and are available for hire with helmets, repair kits and maps at US$5 per hour. A variety of fixed one- or two-day tours are also available at US$15–25 per person (minimum 2 people) inclusive of guides, bikes and other transport.

Tetteh Quarshie Cocoa Farm This small farm lies in the small town of Mampong (which, ironically, means 'large town', and should not be confused with its more substantial namesake in Ashanti Region), a short trotro ride north of Aburi. It has an important place in Ghana's economic history as the site of the country's first cocoa farm. This was founded by Tetteh Quarshie, an illiterate but well-travelled Ghanaian who was born in what is now Accra in 1842, and lived on Fernando Po from 1870 to 1876, bringing back with him a bag of cocoa seeds that first bore fruit at Mampong in 1879 and went on to revolutionise the national economy. The Gold Coast first exported cocoa in 1891, just 12 years after this, and by 1911 it had become the world's largest cocoa producer. Even today, Ghana is the world's second-largest producer of cocoa, which was also the country's leading earner of foreign revenue for decades prior to being overtaken by gold and oil. Visitors to Tetteh Quarshie's original farm and homestead can see Ghana's first cocoa plant, still in good health, and they will be shown how cocoa is planted and picked.

SHAI HILLS RESOURCE RESERVE

This 50km² reserve is the closest wildlife sanctuary to Accra, and one of the most accessible in the country, bordered as it is by the main road towards Akosombo. The main vegetation type is coastal savannah, broken by a series of scenic granite inselbergs that rise from patches of dry evergreen forest rich in endemic plant species, some threatened by a recent invasion of the exotic neem tree, *Azadirachta indica*. Originally demarcated as a forest reserve, Shai Hills was listed as a game reserve in 1962 and, uniquely in Ghana, it has since been fenced off to protect the remaining wildlife, which includes several types of antelope and monkey, and at least 175 bird species. The area now protected within the reserve was home to the Shai people for several centuries until 1892, when they were ejected by the British. There are still a great many traces of Shai occupation in the reserve, including pottery dating to about 1600. Several active Shai shrines lie within the reserve, but the most important are closed to casual visitors.

GETTING THERE AND AWAY The main entrance gate and reception centre (℡ *03029 34926–7;* m *0209 010963;* e *shaihillswd@yahoo.com*) is conspicuously signposted on the main Akosombo road opposite Doryumu Junction. A second entrance gate, more difficult to pick up, lies about 10km closer to Akosombo at Sayu Camp. On public transport, the best way to get to the main entrance gate is first to take a trotro from Accra to Ashaiman, from where any trotro heading to Doryumu will drop you outside the main entrance gate. If you want to hire a taxi to explore the reserve, bearing in mind that the internal roads are currently suitable for a 4x4 only (though the rangers claim a saloon car could make it through a few areas), the closest towns from which you could do so are Dodowa, Somanya, Akuse or even Akosombo.

ENTRANCE FEES The rather steep and Byzantine fee structure for Shai Hills is full of ambiguities and was clearly dreamed up by some office bod with nothing better to do and no feel whatsoever for how these things tend to play out in the real world. So far as we can ascertain, there is no entrance fee to the reserve as such, but it cannot be explored without a guide, for which non-Ghanaian adults pay a stiff US$12.50 per person for the first hour plus US$2.50 per additional hour, while students and volunteers pay US$8 per person for the first hour plus US$2.50 per additional hour. Alternatively, birdwatchers and rock climbers pay US$17 per person for the first hour plus US$7 per additional hour, while students and volunteers pay US$12 per person for the first hour plus US$7 per additional hour. In all cases, you will be expected to tip the guide on top of this. The car fee is US$1.50–2.50 per entry (depending on the vehicle type) and campers must pay a US$13 entry fee per person, US$4 camping fee per person, and US$7 guide fee per party.

🏠 **WHERE TO STAY AND EAT**   *Map, page 152, unless otherwise stated*
Note that there is no accommodation within the resource reserve, though **camping** is permitted at the main entrance gate for a fee of US$4 pp per night, exclusive of the US$13 entry fee per person per night and guide fee of US$7 per party per night. You can also camp at **Sayu Camp** in the north of the park, but you must first report to the headquarters at the main entrance gate. Campers will need to be self-sufficient in terms of food and water. Outside the reserve, there is a down-at-heel resort hotel 500m north of the main entrance gate. Other possible bases from which to explore Shai Hills are listed below.

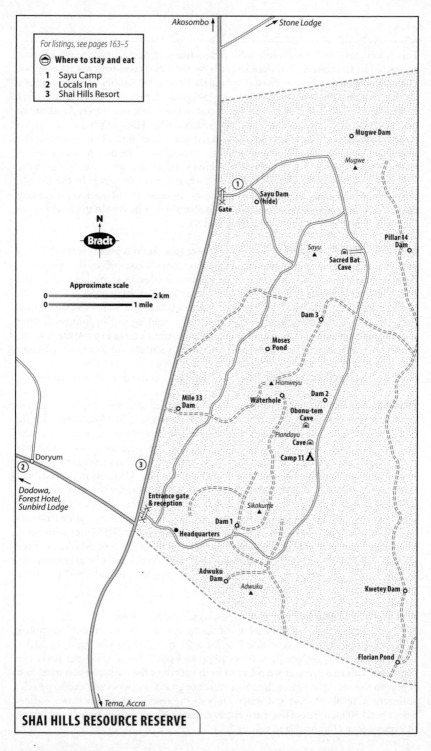

Moderate

🏠 **Stone Lodge** (40 rooms) m 0204 500427/0246 149057; e info@stonelodgeghana. com; www.stonelodgeghana.com. Probably more suited to a family w/end break from Accra than to overseas tourists, this low-key lodge lies on the Kitoma Stock Farm, 5km from the main Accra– Akosombo road along the side road to Asutsuare. Accommodation is provided in a range of chalets, each of which has 2 self-contained dbl rooms & a kitchen (without fan or AC). The Volta River & Shai Hills are both within 15mins' drive of the lodge, while other activities include a private 9-hole golf course, squash, hiking, croquet, volleyball & farm tours. The restaurant serves excellent meals & chilled drinks. *Rates on application.* **$$$**

🏠 **Forest Hotel** (70 rooms) ☎0202 016044; e info@foresthotelgh.com; www.foresthotelgh. com. This rather ambitious 3-star hotel is set in large but crowded grounds just south of the small town of Dodowa on the Accra–Somanya road, about 19km from the main entrance gate to Shai Hills. It has gaudy rooms with AC, fan, satellite TV, Wi-Fi, along with an attached restaurant & swimming pool. To get to the reserve from Dodowa, follow the Somanya road northwards for 8km to Akiyumu Junction, where a right turn will bring you to Doryumu after 6km & the entrance gate at the junction with the Akosombo road after another 2km. Overpriced at *US$75 self-contained dbl.* **$$$**

🏠 **Sunbird Lodge** (2 rooms) m 0208 120856/0264 432634; e info@joli-ecotours.com;

www.joli-ecotours.com/sunbirdlodge.htm. Though you're already about 30km from the reserve at this point (& 20km from Tetteh Quarshie Circle in Accra), this delightful little guesthouse run by Jolinaiko Ecotours (page 120) in the small town of Oyibi is far & away more pleasant & better value than any other hotel on this list. Set in a green & familial compound, the bright & cheerful 1st-floor rooms come with fans, nets, appealing artwork, & a bougainvillea-covered terrace. Meals are available on request. There's Wi-Fi, & reservations must be made in advance. *US$40/46 self-contained sgl/dbl.* **$$**

Budget

🏠 **Shai Hills Resort Hotel** [map, page 164] (90 rooms) m 0244 836883. Set in large but abandoned-feeling wooded grounds 500m north of the reserve's main entrance gate, this rather cheerless & threadbare resort doesn't even begin to live up to its delusional motto ('A Touch of Class'), but it is the most convenient overnight base for a visit, & the carpeted dbls with queen-sized bed, AC, fan & TV aren't bad value at the asking price. A restaurant is attached. *US$19 self-contained dbl.* **$$**

Shoestring

🏠 **Locals Inn** (6 rooms) m 0244 360007. Situated in Doryumu, only 3km from the entrance gate, this basic hotel has self-contained rooms & an attached restaurant. *US$11/13 dbl with fan/AC.* **$**

WHAT TO SEE AND DO All activities must be arranged through the reception centre (☎ 03029 34926/7; m 0209 010963; e *shaihillsswd@yahoo.com*) at the main entrance gate. The reserve is open to day visits between 07.00 and 17.00. Game viewing is most productive in the early morning, and visits can start earlier than 07.00 with advance arrangement.

Game drives Motored visitors can explore the reserve from a circular 17km road network that used to be adequate for a saloon car, except after heavy rain, but now often requires a 4x4. The road loop usually takes 3–4 hours, depending on how often you stop. Wildlife viewing scarcely compares to Africa's major savannah reserves, or even somewhere like Mole National Park, but still there is a fair amount of game around. The most common large mammal is the olive baboon, which most visitors will see (one troop often hangs around the entrance gate). Around 200 kob antelope are resident, and lucky visitors might also encounter the shier bushbuck, green monkey and spot-nosed monkey. At the latest count, 175 bird species were recorded, of which some of the more visible and attractive are the black-bellied bustard, Abyssinian ground hornbill, grey hornbill, Senegal parrot and double-spurred francolin.

Walking and rock climbing The reserve can be explored on foot with an armed guide, using a combination of roads and footpaths, though this does tend to limit you to the area around the main entrance gate. There are more than ten dams in the reserve, with the one closest to Sayu Camp bordered by a (arguably rather optimistically located) game-viewing hide. Also of interest is the bat cave about 4km east of Sayu Camp, which can be visited from the main road through the park following an 800m trail. In addition to the impressive bat colony – several thousand chirruping individuals, with at least three species represented – this cave once served as the chief's palace, and signs of low protective walls can still be seen. Rock climbing is permitted on Elephant Rock and Hieowenya Rock.

KOKROBITE, BOJO AND LANGMA BEACHES

Only 20km west of Accra as the crow flies (though the heavy traffic on the outskirts of the capital can make it feel a lot more distant), the beachfront village of Kokrobite has long been a popular weekend destination for volunteers, while for travellers it is a pleasant alternative base to Accra itself, and a useful springboard for travel further along the west coast. For decades, the action was centred 1km west of the village, at the Academy of African Music and Arts (AAMA), which closed some years ago but is still a well-known local landmark. Today, the travel scene is focused on Big Milly's Backyard, an admirably laid-back beach resort set right in the heart of the village and known for its 24-hour bar and weekend parties featuring live music. All in all, Kokrobite is a great chill-out venue for those seeking a bit of a party atmosphere, conveniently close to Accra, and dominated by a beach that would be thoroughly idyllic were it not for the potentially dangerous undertow (do ask before you swim). However, two other nearby beaches – Bojo, about 4km to the east, and Langma, some 3km to the west – are better suited to those looking for a more peaceful (and upmarket) beach location close to Accra.

GETTING THERE AND AWAY In a private vehicle, follow the Winneba road west out of Accra for approximately 15km past Kaneshie Market, through what feels like interminably chaotic suburbia, to Aplaku Junction (also known as the Old Police Barrier). At Aplaku, turn left, towards the coast, passing Bojo Beach to your left after about 4km, then shortly afterwards passing through the village of Bortianor, from where it is another 3km or so to Kokrobite, and about 3km further to Langma. A direct taxi from central Accra or Kotoka International Airport will cost around US$20–30 (contact Big Milly's in advance – see below – and they will arrange for you to be met by a tried and trusted driver). Using public transport, trotros leave Accra from Dansoman Station in Kaneshie, and charge less than US$1, but they can take ages to fill up. Alternatively, any other vehicle heading towards Winneba from Kaneshie Station can drop you at Aplaku Junction, from where you can pick up a shared or charter taxi to Kokrobite. However you travel, traffic along the Winneba road between Kaneshie and Aplaku Junction can be very heavy, so allow at least 2 hours to get there.

Coming from the west, there's now a surfaced road branching south from the Winneba–Accra Road at Tuba Junction (also known as New Barrier – 6km west of Aplaku/Old Barrier), which passes through Tuba village after 3.5km, and reaches Kokrobite after another 3km or so. Shared and charter taxis can be found at Tuba Junction.

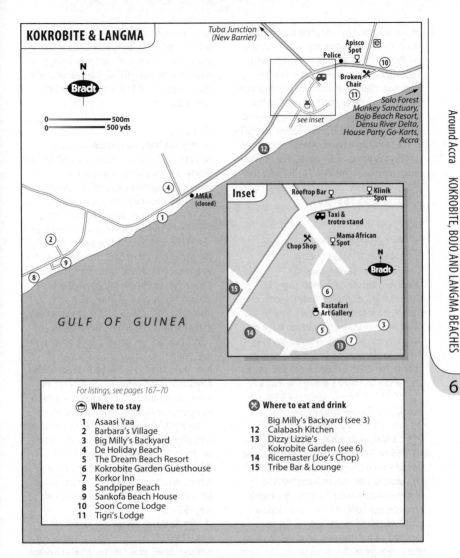

KOKROBITE & LANGMA

Tuba Junction
(New Barrier)

Apisco
Spot

Police

Broken
Chair

N

Bradt

0 _____ 500m
0 _____ 500 yds

see inset

Solo Forest
Monkey Sanctuary,
Bojo Beach Resort,
Densu River Delta,
House Party Go-Karts,
Accra

AMAA
(closed)

Inset

Rooftop Bar

Klinik
Spot

Taxi &
trotro stand

Mama African
Spot

Chop Shop

N

Bradt

Rastafari
Art Gallery

GULF OF GUINEA

For listings, see pages 167–70

Where to stay

1 Asaasi Yaa
2 Barbara's Village
3 Big Milly's Backyard
4 De Holiday Beach
5 The Dream Beach Resort
6 Kokrobite Garden Guesthouse
7 Korkor Inn
8 Sandpiper Beach
9 Sankofa Beach House
10 Soon Come Lodge
11 Tigri's Lodge

Where to eat and drink

Big Milly's Backyard (see 3)
12 Calabash Kitchen
13 Dizzy Lizzie's
Kokrobite Garden (see 6)
14 Ricemaster (Joe's Chop)
15 Tribe Bar & Lounge

SAFETY Kokrobite Beach is one of the few crime hotspots in Ghana, and over the years we have received more reader reports of theft and muggings here than for anywhere else in the country, though the situation has improved greatly following Big Milly's initiative to pay former criminals to perform security patrols. So far as we can ascertain, the problem is more or less confined to the actual beach, particularly the stretch running east from the village towards Accra, so you should be fine if you make a point of not taking any valuables (money, jewellery, camera, mobile phone, etc) on to the beach with you.

WHERE TO STAY *Map, above, unless otherwise stated*

Exclusive

Bojo Beach Resort [map, page 152] (35 rooms) 03029 12946; m 0242 325169;

e bojo_beach@yahoo.com; www.
bojobeachresort.com. Situated at the Densu River
Delta close to Bortianor, 4km east of Kokrobite, this

lagoon-side resort has one of the most tempting beaches within a day-tripping radius of Accra, & excellent facilities including a swimming pool, 3 restaurants, canoe trips & various beach & watersports. The accommodation is set back from the beach, in a sturdily built but characterless block containing spacious & tastefully furnished rooms that come with AC, large-screen satellite TV, W-Fi & hot water. It seems to be growing into its considerable potential, & a recent price reduction means rooms are considerably better value than in years past. *US$159/198 B&B self-contained sgl/dbl; US$405 suite.* **$$$$$–$$$$**

Moderate

✴ 🏠 **Sankofa Beach House** (7 rooms)
m 0244 616081/311439; e info@ sankofabeachhouse.com; www. sankofabeachhouse.com; see ad, page 172. Situated in beautiful palm-shaded beachfront gardens in Langma, 3km west of Kokrobite, this smart owner-managed self-catering lodge looks like a very tranquil set-up, & for families there is the option of renting a 3-bedroom house in its entirety. The rooms & chalets are all different, but are stylishly decorated & mostly self-contained, with AC, W-Fi, flatscreen satellite TV & hot water. *From US$70–160 self-contained dbl; US$250 3-bedroom house.* **$$$$–$$$**

🏠 **Sandpiper Beach Hotel** (33 rooms)
m 0265 726980/0244 078922; e sandpipergh@ gmail.com or ishmael.norman@yahoo.com. Set on a glorious palm-shaded 5-acre beachfront plot immediately west of Sankofa, this recently renovated hotel offers the choice of standard rooms with tiled floor, dbl bed, AC, flatscreen satellite TV & hot shower, or larger deluxe rooms that have a queen-sized bed & jacuzzi. The rooms are clean & comfortable without being anything to write home about, but the grounds & beach more than compensate, & there is also a good restaurant & swimming pool. *US$50 B&B self-contained dbl; US$66 deluxe dbl.* **$$$**

🏠 **De Holiday Beach Hotel** (10 rooms)
☎ 03029 20710/1; m 0289 583767/8; e info@deholidaybeachhotel.com; www. deholidaybeachhotel.com. Set a few hundred metres back from the beach, this bright-blue 3-storey hotel lies in a cramped compound along a side road opposite the old AAMA site. The rooms are small & quite garishly furnished, but come

with flatscreen satellite TV, Wi-Fi & kitchenette with coffee & tea facilities. Other features include a small gym, massage room, business centre, games room, sparkling central pool, & restaurant serving good meals. *US$50/57 B&B self-contained dbl/twin.* **$$$**

Budget

✴ 🏠 **Big Milly's Backyard** (22 rooms)
m 0249 999330/0262 999330; e bigmilly2000@ hotmail.com; www.bigmilly.com. This perennially popular budget resort, owned & managed by an Anglo–Ghanaian couple, is one of the few places close to Accra – indeed anywhere along the Ghanaian coast – with the sort of laid-back sociable vibe associated with the myriad beachfront backpacker lodges dotted around southern Africa. An on-site restaurant & bar serves excellent b/fasts, as well as good seafood, fruit juices & cocktails, all at very reasonable prices. Since 2015, it's also been home to the renowned Mr Bright's Surf School (page 170). Other facilities include a book-swap service, safe, professional massages, & a number of hand-picked traders selling batik, beads & other handicrafts in the compound. Visitors can also enjoy cultural shows around a beach bonfire on Fri nights, as well as live reggae or highlife music on Sat nights. A wide variety of accommodation is on offer. *US$30/39/45 self-contained dbl/tpl/ quad with AC, fridge & hot water; US$26/31/34 self-contained dbl/tpl/quad with fan; US$16 sgl with fan & common showers; US$7 pp in an open loft-style dorm; US$5/8 sgl/dbl camping (own tent).* **$$–$**

✴ 🏠 **Barbara's Village** (13 rooms)
m 0244 957278; e barbarabizovicar@yahoo.com or barbarasvillage@gmail.com; www.barbarasvillage. com. Set in a shady compound about 200m from the beach at Langma, 3km west of Kokrobite, this sedate & rustic Slovenian owner-managed lodge is centred on a large thatched restaurant/bar serving a varied selection of seafood, vegetarian & meat dishes. For accommodation, you have the choice of a stilted bamboo dormitory, round dbl or twin huts or stilted bamboo huts using shared baths, or self-contained twins with a similarly organic feel. *US$37/42 self-contained sgl/twin; US$11–19 twin or dbl using shared bath; US$5 dorm bed.* **$$$–$.**

✴ 🏠 **Kokrobite Garden Guesthouse**
(6 rooms) m 0546 392850; e kokrobitegarden@

yahoo.com; www.kokrobitegarden.com. Best known as a restaurant, this central Spanish- & Italian-owned & managed haven also offers beautifully kept budget accommodation, ranging from a 1-person treehouse to a few cute 2- or 4-bed wooden cabins & new whitewashed self-contained rooms. It lies in a lovely art-filled garden with a swimming pool, where there's acoustic music on Fri. *Good value at US$45 dbl in new self-contained room; US$20 dbl in old bungalow using shared bath; US$40 for a room sleeping 4.* **$$**

🏠 **Asaasi Yaa** (10 rooms) m 0545 434440; e asaasiyaa@gmail.com; www.asaasiyaa.com. Situated on a lovely beach next to the old AAMA site about 1.5km west of the village centre, this attractive-looking lodge caters mainly to groups & although individual travellers are welcome, it can feel a bit empty & isolated if nobody else is staying there. Accommodation is in large rooms with tiled floor, queen-size bed, cane & batik furnishing, hot shower & fan, facilities include a beachfront restaurant/bar as well as drumming lessons & workshops by arrangement. *US$20/30/40 self-contained dbl/trpl/quad, not including 17.5% VAT.* **$$**

🏠 **The Dream Beach Resort** (20 rooms) m 0244 1266236/0246 903585; e info@thedreambeachresortgh.com; www. thedreambeachresortgh.com. This slightly rundown but pleasant enough lodge is situated just down from Big Milly's & accommodates a lot of its spillover. While it's certainly not as lively as its near neighbour, the rooms (all with fan & fridge) are fair value. *US$16/20/32 self-contained dbl/trpl/quad.* **$$**

🏠 **Korkor Inn** (5 rooms) m 0509 362518/0200 006033. This laid-back beachfront hotel a few doors up from Big Milly's is nothing special, but the large tidy rooms with queen-size bed & fan are pretty good value. *US$ 26 self-contained dbl with fan; US$40/53 self-contained dbl/twin with AC.* **$$$–$$**

🏠 **Tigri's Lodge** (4 rooms) m 0244 961185; e tigrislodge@hotmail.com. A few hundred metres up the beach heading east from Big Milly's, there's nothing special about the dbl rooms here, but they're cheap enough & it'd be hard to find fault with the beachfront location. *US$18.50 dbl with fan.* **$$**

Shoestring

🏠 **Soon Come Lodge** (6 rooms) m 0243 856765. This laid-back little lodge, set in large sandy gardens at the east side of the village, consists of a colourfully decorated thatched restaurant (serving local dishes for around US$4) at the front, & a cluster of small but brightly decorated huts at the back. *US$7 dbl using shared bath.* **$**

✗ WHERE TO EAT AND DRINK *Map, page 167*

The social hub of Kokrobite is **Big Milly's Backyard**, which has a 24-hour bar, a good restaurant, and parties with live music on Friday and Saturday nights. Other good eateries are as follows:

✳ ✗ **Kokrobite Garden** m 0546 392850; www.kokrobitegarden.com; ⊕ 08.00–20.00 daily, later at w/ends. Real Italian coffee, delicious pasta dishes & thin-crusted pizzas are the specialities at this relaxed Italian-owned & -managed garden restaurant in the village centre, but it also serves a diversity of international dishes (from Morocco, Mexico, Tunisia, etc) & has a good cocktail & dessert menu. Most mains are in the US$8–12 range. **$$$–$$**

✗ **Dizzy Lizzie's** m 0205 600990/0268 070560; e dizzylizziesbeachside@gmail.com; www. dizzylizzies.com/blog; ⊕ 07.00–late daily. This cheerful Rasta-chic beach bar & restaurant was rather new & still under construction when we checked in in 2016, but looked quite promising. Plans include several self-contained dbl rooms for US$20 a pop (2 of which are now complete), as well as live music on Fridays, drumming on Sundays, bonfires, dancing, & a daily menu of Ghanaian & seafood dishes. **$$**

✗ **Ricemaster (Joe's Chop)** m 0556 585243; ⊕ 07.00–22.00 daily, later at w/ends. With a new location about 300m up the road from Big Milly's, this increasingly popular kiosk has been praised by several readers for its charmingly garrulous owner & great street food, including tasty egg or cheese sandwiches, pizzas, & fried rice or Chinese noodles with vegetables, beef or chicken, all for between US$2–7. **$**

✕ Calabash Kitchen m 0244 561795; ⏰ 08.00–22.00 Wed–Mon. Situated about 500m southwest of the village centre, this locally owned restaurant, also known as Mada's Place after the delightful owner-manager, serves a selection of soups, salads, sandwiches & b/fast dishes in the US$3–5 range, as well as more substantial seafood & pasta dishes for US$4–9. $$–$

☆ Tribe Bar & Lounge m 0279 673232/0506 614921; ◻ fb.me/tribe.bar.and.lounge; ⏰ evenings daily. This surprisingly stylish nightspot on the main road through town is a good bet for DJs & occasional live music – check their Facebook page to see what's on.

WHAT TO SEE AND DO For most visitors, Kokrobite is about chilling out, spending some time on the beach, eating and drinking, and maybe doing a little shopping at any of several locally owned craft and art stalls dotted around the town. But if you get restless, a few activities can be undertaken a little further afield.

Surfing Owned and managed by Brett Davies, a highly qualified professional British surf coach and lifesaver with 30 years' experience, **Mr Bright's Surf School** [241 C2] (m *0264 316053/0543 320978;* e *mrbrights@hotmail.co.uk; www. mrbrights.com*), inside Big Milly's Backyard, offers lessons both to beginners and to more experienced surfers (*US$16/26pp for group/private lessons*), as well as stand-up paddleboard, bodyboard and kayak hire. Full weekend packages are also available. The affiliated West African Surfing Association (WASA) is dedicated to the promotion of a local surfing culture and assisting talented kids of West Africa through donations of surfing equipment.

Cycling The new **Ahunu Bike Tours** (m *0542 436650/0240 025792*; e *ahunubiketours@gmail.com*; ◻ *fb.me/ahunubiketours*) works closely with Big Milly's Backyard (trips can be booked directly or through Big Milly's reception) and offers 2–3-hour bicycle tours through Kokrobite and the Solo Forest Monkey Sanctuary, which can be combined with a canoe trip through the Densu River Delta as well. Tours officially depart at 08.00 and 16.00, though this is definitely flexible, and depending on which destinations you take in, tours cost between US$9–17 per person. It's also possible to hire the bikes without a guide and go exploring on your own.

Go-karting Apropos of nothing much at all, **House Party Go-Karts** (m *0261 714515/0502 169665; www.housepartykarts.com;* ⏰ *noon–22.00 daily*) in Bortianor (clearly signposted about 5km towards Aplaku Junction) offers high-speed go-karting at US$10 per 8 minutes, along with an attached bar and video arcade.

Solo Forest Monkey Sanctuary Of particular interest to travellers who won't have the opportunity to visit Tafi Atome or Boabeng-Fiema, this community-run sanctuary at Bortianor, 4km from Kokrobite, comprises a sacred grove of tall trees bisected by a small stream. A troop of semi-habituated spot-nosed monkeys that live in the area, and regularly come to the stream to drink, are most easily seen in the early morning. To visit the sanctuary, ask any transport heading between Kokrobite and Aplaku Junction to drop you at Bortianor, where the entrance fee of US$7.50 must be paid and a guide arranged at the **Tsokomey Nature Centre**, 100m from the road. The walk from here to the sanctuary takes no more than 5 minutes.

Densu River Delta Situated about 4km east of Kokrobite, this delta, which comprises around 100km² of palm-fringed dunes, freshwater lagoons and mangrove swamps, was declared a Ramsar Wetland Site in 1992, though much of the area is mined commercially for salt. Ecologically, the delta is of significance both as a turtle breeding site and for supporting immense seasonal colonies of marine birds, most notably the rare roseate tern (flocks of 500 have been recorded), but also the likes of common tern, sandwich tern, little tern, black tern, royal tern and spotted redshank. For birdwatchers, a good access point to the delta is the bird observation post 3km away and signposted from the small town of Mendkrom on the main Accra–Cape Coast road, a short distance east of Adaklu Junction. Alternatively, canoe trips into the delta can be arranged through the Tsokomey Nature Centre in Bortianor for US$20 per person.

Bojo Beach Resort For a complete change of scene, this resort on the western edge of the Densu River Delta, near Bortianor, is reputedly safer for swimming than Kokrobite, and it also has more upmarket facilities, ranging from golf and a swimming pool to various watersports and three restaurants. Day entrance costs US$5 per person.

GOMOAH FETTEH AND SENYA BERAKU

Another 20km southwest of Kokrobite, and connected to each other by a 6km road covered by regular shared taxis, the rather isolated twin ports of Gomoah Fetteh (also spelt Fete) and Senya Beraku form a worthwhile weekend goal from Accra, as well as being a worthwhile diversion for unhurried travellers heading west along the coast. The main point of interest in Senya Beraku is the 18th-century **Fort of Good Hope** (*entrance US$1*), which boasts a dramatic clifftop position overlooking a beach covered in colourful fishing boats and now doubles as a guesthouse. By contrast, the smaller town of Gomoah Fetteh, which sprawls over a low hill down to two attractive sandy beaches, is prime sun 'n' surf territory, serviced by a couple of long-serving and highly regarded resort hotels.

HISTORY Senya Beraku first attracted the interest of Holland in the 1660s when a small trading lodge was built there, only to be abandoned shortly afterwards. In 1704, the Dutch returned to the site, and with the permission of the Queen of Agona they started work on what would turn out to be the last fort they were to build in West Africa. Originally a very small, triangular construction designed to facilitate a low-key trade in gold, the Fort of Good Hope – would it be too heavy-handed to note the irony? – ended up serving almost exclusively as a slave-trading centre. In 1715, the fort was extended to cover more or less its present area, and large male and female slave prisons were built into the southwest bastion. Handed to Britain as part of the 'fort exchange' treaty of 1868, it fell into disuse at some point during the colonial era, and by the time of independence had become a partial ruin. In the 1980s, the Fort of Good Hope was restored as a joint historical monument and resthouse.

GETTING THERE AND AWAY Situated some 6km apart, the two towns are connected to the main road between Accra and Winneba by a 15km surfaced road that splits after about 10km at Bonsuoku, with the western fork heading to Gomoah Fetteh and the eastern to Senya Beraku. The best place to pick up public transport or to charter a taxi from the main Cape Coast road is not at the junction itself, but at Awutu Beraku, 2km further east. If you are coming direct from Accra, trotros to Senya Beraku leave reasonably regularly from Kaneshie Station.

WHERE TO STAY AND EAT *Map, page 152*

Luxury

🏠 **White Sands Beach Resort** (13 rooms)
m 0263 050504/6; e info@whitesands.com.gh;
www.whitesandsholidays.com. The most luxurious
& costly resort in the country, White Sands in
Gomoah Fetteh operates much like an all-inclusive
members-only club. Those that can stomach the
price tag will be rewarded with Hopi architecture,
a private plunge pool overlooking the private
beach, a 24hr butler to fulfil your every whim & a
restaurant & bar that could compete for culinary
& interior decoration prizes anywhere. *From
€1,000–1,300 dbl; €1,700 family unit sleeping 4
US$30 day use.* **$$$$$**

Moderate

🏠 **Till's Beach Resort** (16 rooms)
m 0242 855035; e tillsbeach@yahoo.com; www.
tillsbeachhotel.com. Set on a beautiful beach 500m
from Gomoah Fetteh, Till's is not quite as plush as it
once was, but it nevertheless offers very good value
for money in its price bracket. The restaurant serves
excellent seafood & grills, while facilities & activities
include beach & indoor games, mini-golf, drumming
& dancing lessons, as well as minibus excursions
with a driver. Rooms all have queen-size bed, fan,
satellite TV, fridge & private balcony with sea view.
*US$55/65 B&B self-contained std/exec dbl with AC;
US$92 family room.* **$$$**

Budget

🏠 **Fort of Good Hope** (5 rooms) m 0243
184766. One of the few remaining Ghanaian forts
to serve as a guesthouse, & the best of those that
do, this well-organised set-up has a communal
lounge, clean shared toilet & shower, gift shop, bar
with fridge, & restaurant serving chicken or fish
with fried rice or chips for around US$6. The freshly
painted rooms are surprisingly pleasant & all
come with ceiling fans. A tour of the fort is free to
lodgers, or US$1 to other visitors. *US$13 twin with
fan using shared bath.* **$**

🏠 **Emily's Place** (2 rooms) m 0242 573420.
This homely little B&B about 300m from Till's has
1 dbl & 1 twin room attached by a cosy communal
kitchen & living room. In the backyard there's a
garden with a lazy hammock & stairs that lead
to a 2nd-level deck with fantastic views of the
surrounding area. Meals are also available on
request. *US$15–20 B&B dbl/twin.* **$$**

🏠 **Sunflower Beach Resort** (4 rooms)
m 0245 891731/0542 522025. This family-run
beach resort sits in expansive grassy grounds down
a well-signposted turnoff some 2.5km to the west
of Senya Beraku. Accommodation is in clean &
spacious duplex chalets with fan, TV, & terraces
overlooking the water. Meals on request. *US$25
self-contained dbl.* **$$**

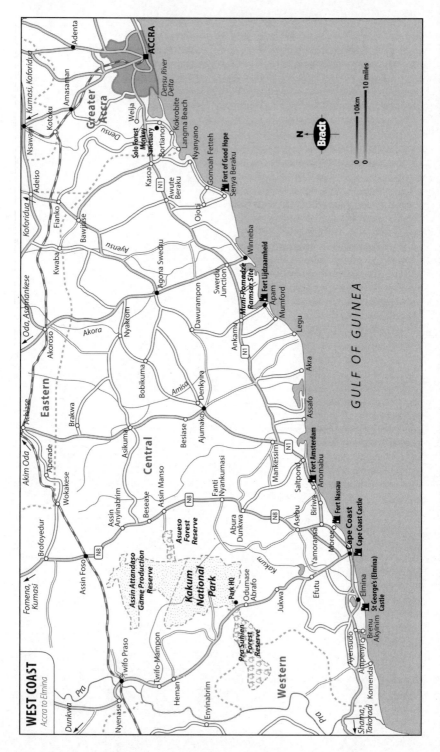

Part Three

THE COAST WEST OF ACCRA

It is hardly surprising that Ghana's coast lies at the centre of its tourist industry. But what is remarkable is that such a magnificent chunk of tropical coastline should support a tourist industry based largely around historical sightseeing. This is not because the beaches fail to live up to every archetype of white-sanded, palm-fringed tropical nirvana – many of them do, even if rip tides and currents pose a potentially fatal threat to swimmers in several places. No, it is that Ghana, alone in Africa, bears tangible physical evidence of an episode as barbarous and shameful as any in the recorded history of the continent: the transatlantic slave trade.

For the sake of historical accuracy, we think it important to stress that Ghana is scarcely unique in having supported a substantial slave trade before 1850. But unlike other parts of West Africa, where the trade was generally conducted out of makeshift buildings, the Ghanaian slave trade was run out of a string of solidly built forts and castles, many constructed at the height of the gold-trading era and later adapted to include slave dungeons. The most substantial of these castles and forts are still standing today, from the Fort of Good Hope in the east to Fort Apollonia in the west, via the imposing whitewashed castles that dominate the beachfronts of Cape Coast and Elmina.

The west coast of Ghana is neatly divided in two by the twin towns of Cape Coast and Elmina, which lie 15km apart, roughly halfway between Accra and the Ivory Coast. Both towns warrant a visit, as in different ways they each retain something of the mood of an older Africa, not merely in terms of historical buildings, but also in their tangible sense of community.

While the immediate vicinity of Cape Coast and Elmina could hardly be described as heaving with tourists, the area does support a perceptible tourist industry, and it is thus accorded its own chapter. Other chapters in this section cover the relatively untrammelled stretches of coast between Accra and Cape Coast, the rather mundane port city of Takoradi, the thriving backpacker scene around Busua, and the truly magnificent coastline running further west towards the Ivorian border via Axim, Beyin and Nzulezo stilt village.

BEST OF THE WEST COAST

MUNI-POMADZE RAMSAR SITE This Ramsar wetland bordering Winneba is the only official turtle-tracking site along the coast west of Accra. Pages 182–3.

ANOMABU This historic village near Cape Coast supports Ghana's largest collection of bizarre posuban shrines. Pages 188–93.

CAPE COAST Steeped in history, the first capital of the Gold Coast colony is dominated by the hulking Cape Coast Castle, nerve centre of the 18th-century transatlantic slave trade. Pages 195–207.

ELMINA Bisected by the Benya Lagoon, its mouth seething with colourful pirogues, Elmina and its castle are the equal of nearby Cape Coast in terms of historical sightseeing. Pages 213–23.

KAKUM NATIONAL PARK Africa's oldest canopy walkway is the highlight of this vast national park, which protects a tract of rainforest teeming with birds and other wildlife. Pages 207–13.

BUSUA Arguably the ultimate Ghanaian beach chill-out venue, this backpacker-friendly village is also the centre of a growing surfing scene. Pages 240–8.

AKWIDAA/CAPE THREE POINTS Dotted with isolated budget resorts, a series of absolutely stunning beaches runs westward from Busua towards Cape Three Points, the most southerly protrusion in Ghana. Pages 250–5.

AXIM The town might not offer much to tourists, but it is flanked by a trio of breathtaking beach resorts, including the peerless Lou Moon Lodge. Pages 258–62.

NZULEZO This unique stilted village in the Amansuri Wetlands can be visited by canoe from the beachfront village of Beyin. Pages 265–6.

ANKASSA PROTECTED AREA One for off-the-beaten-track adventurers, this vast but underdeveloped forest boasts the greatest biodiversity of any reserve in Ghana. Pages 266–8.

UPDATES WEBSITE

Go to www.bradtupdates.com/ghanafor the latest on-the-ground travel news, trip reports and factual updates. Keep up to date with the latest posts by following Philip on Twitter (🐦 @philipbriggs) and via Facebook: 📘 fb.me/pb.travel.updates. And, if you have any comments, queries, grumbles, insights, news or other feedback, you're invited to post them directly on the website, or to email them to Philip (e philip.briggs@bradtguides.com) for inclusion.

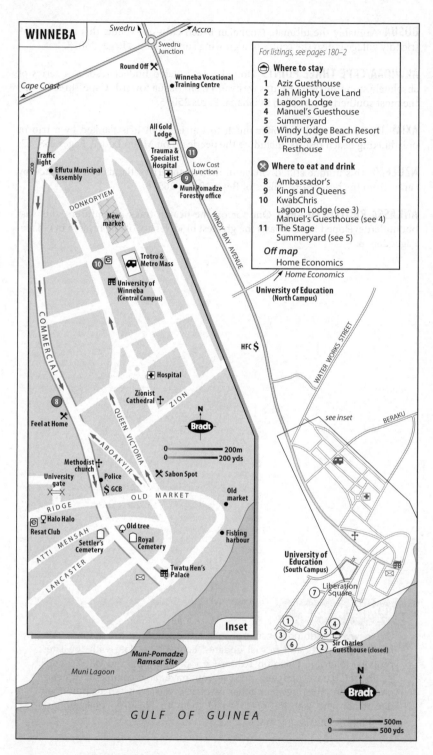

WINNEBA

Swedru ↑
→ Accra
Swedru Junction

Round Off ✕

Cape Coast

Winneba Vocational Training Centre

All Gold Lodge

Trauma & Specialist Hospital

11

Low Cost Junction

9

Muni Pomadze Forestry office

Traffic light

Effutu Municipal Assembly

DONKORYIEM

New market

10

Trotro & Metro Mass

University of Winneba (Central Campus)

COMMERCIAL

WINDY BAY AVENUE

8

Feel at Home

Hospital

Zionist Cathedral

ZION

N
Bradt

QUEEN VICTORIA

ABOAKYIR

Methodist church

University gate

Police

GCB

RIDGE

OLD MARKET

Old market

Halo Halo

Resat Club

ATTI MENSAH

LANCASTER

Settler's Cemetery

Old tree

Royal Cemetery

Twatu Hen's Palace

Sabon Spot

Fishing harbour

Inset

0   200m
0   200 yds

For listings, see pages 180–2

🏠 **Where to stay**

1 Aziz Guesthouse
2 Jah Mighty Love Land
3 Lagoon Lodge
4 Manuel's Guesthouse
5 Summeryard
6 Windy Lodge Beach Resort
7 Winneba Armed Forces Resthouse

✕ **Where to eat and drink**

8 Ambassador's
9 Kings and Queens
10 KwabChris
   Lagoon Lodge (see 3)
   Manuel's Guesthouse (see 4)
11 The Stage
   Summeryard (see 5)

Off map
   Home Economics

↗ *Home Economics*

University of Education (North Campus)

HFC $

WATER WORKS STREET

see inset

BERAKU

University of Education (South Campus)

7

Liberation Square

1   4
3   5
6   2   Sir Charles Guesthouse (closed)

N
Bradt

Muni-Pomadze Ramsar Site

Muni Lagoon

G U L F   O F   G U I N E A

0   500m
0   500 yds

7

Winneba and the Cape Coast Road

Many visitors to Ghana experience the coastal belt between Accra and Cape Coast as little more than a blur of small junction towns and erratically weaving taxis framed by the window of a trotro or coach. This is because, for most of its length, the main road connecting Accra and Cape Coast lies far enough inland that it offers few obvious indications that it follows the Atlantic coastline. And yet this stretch of coast is scattered with time-warped small towns, rundown forts and palm-fringed beaches, all of which can be reached along short feeder roads, but are bypassed by the overwhelming majority of visitors to Ghana.

Whether one chooses to explore this area slowly or in a straight whizz through is largely a matter of temperament. None of the forts is built on the scale of the castles at Elmina or Cape Coast, and neither do the beach resorts fully compare to their counterparts further west. Nevertheless, the area is rich in off-the-beaten-track pickings. For the historically minded, obvious highlights include Apam, Saltpond and Anomabu. Also of interest is Winneba, a relatively substantial town that hosts the country's most accessible turtle-tracking project.

WINNEBA

The largest coastal settlement between Accra and Cape Coast, Winneba feels far more substantial than the 2012 census result of 70,000 would suggest, sprawling as it does along the 4km road that separates the old town centre from Swedru Junction on the main Accra road. With its winding alleys, chaotic market, malodorous fishing harbour and fading colonial façades, the compact town centre has the feel of an antiquated port. However, aside from the late 19th-century Methodist church, and the old European and Royal cemeteries that face each other on Liberation Square, the town has very few sites of historical interest. Far more attractive is the expansive beach immediately to its west, and the Wildlife Department's official turtle-tracking ecotourism project, which is centred upon the Muni-Pomadze Ramsar Site, a couple of kilometres west of town.

The one time of the year when Winneba's status is upgraded from diverting backwater is the first weekend of May, when it hosts a famous 300-year-old hunting festival known as the **Aboakyir**. The festival's centrepiece is the deer (or, more accurately, antelope) hunt, wherein the town's two oldest asafo companies, dressed in full traditional regalia, compete to hunt down and capture a bushbuck using only their bare hands. The colourful festival carries on throughout the weekend, climaxing twice: early on Saturday morning, when the deer hunt takes place amid much noise and colour until one or other company wins; then at 14.00 on Sunday when the captured animal is sacrificed to the oracles at the Penkye Otu fetish shrine.

HISTORY Oral tradition has it that Winneba was founded before or during the early 16th century by an Efutu chief called Osimpa, and was originally known as Simpa in his honour. It has long served as the traditional capital of the Efutu, but its inhabitants also have a strong Akan heritage, for which reason they are often referred to as the Simpafo ('mixed people'). A British fort was built there in 1673, and its modern name, thought to be a bastardisation of the English phrase 'windy bay', was probably coined at around this time. The British settler community evacuated the town in 1812 following an Ashanti invasion in which their commander was tortured to death (for decades afterwards, British ships would fire a broadside when they passed by). Traces of the old fort can be seen in the Methodist church, which was built on the same site by missionaries who settled there in 1883.

The most important historical figure in Winneba's recent history is King R J Ghartey IV, who was the prime initiator behind the creation of the Fante Confederation in 1868–73, and served as its president until its dissolution in 1873. A Methodist convert who was strongly opposed to the palm-wine consumption and female toplessness that were customary among his people at the time, Ghartey established a temperance society nicknamed the Akonomnsu (literally, 'Water Drinkers') in Anomabu. He is also credited with designing the *kabasroto* (or *kaba*) 'shoulder-cover', a variation on a typical European blouse that he first issued to female members of his household and staff, and which later became fashionable throughout Ghana and elsewhere in West Africa. Following the death of Ghartey IV in 1897, his son and chosen successor Prince Ghartey was overlooked as paramount chief in favour of a matrilineal nephew, Kojo Aberka, who was installed under the name Nana Ayirebi Acquah II in 1998. Ever since, the throne has been contested between the Ghartey and Ayirebi Acquah factions. Indeed, while the incumbent Nana Ayirebi Acquah V was enstooled as paramount chief of Winneba in 1993, his position only received full legal affirmation when the Court of Appeals ruled in his favour in 2011, and it is still disputed by Kobena Bortsie Ghartey VII, who was enstooled in a separate ceremony in 1996.

GETTING THERE AND AWAY The town centre lies about 4km south of Swedru Junction on the main road between Accra and Cape Coast. About 20 Metro Mass buses cover this route daily, leaving from Kaneshie Station in Accra as they fill up, and charging around US$1. There are also regular trotros between Kaneshie and Winneba. Coming from elsewhere, it's easiest to catch a bus or trotro to Swedru Junction, from where regular shared taxis make their way to the old town. Note that the main trotro station is about 1km north of the old town centre, and further still from most of the accommodation, so you might want to charter a taxi to your hotel when you arrive.

WHERE TO STAY *Map, page 178*

Winneba boasts a particularly attractive selection of budget and shoestring lodges, most of it set close to the beach west of the town centre, while the neighbouring Windy Lodge Beach Resort is the most upmarket option in town.

Mid range

Windy Lodge Beach Resort (90 rooms) 03323 22479; m 0501 282387/0245 164034; e windy.lodge@yahoo.com; fb.me/windylodgehotel. Far & away the largest hotel in Winneba, this new 3-storey property across the street from the beach & under the same management as the Windy Lodge near Swedru Junction is firmly on the bland side, but perfectly functional & well priced. Rooms come with AC or fan, along with fridges & flatscreen TVs, & some have private balconies. There's a swimming pool (though this was half-full when we visited) & restaurant attached. *US$17/21 dbl with cold water & fan/AC; US$24–34 executive rooms with AC & hot water.* **$$**

Budget

✳ 🏠 **Lagoon Lodge** (20 rooms) 📞 0332 322434/5; **m** 0208 162031/4; **e** lagoon_lodgegh@ yahoo.com. Situated 1.5km west of the town centre in the direction of the lagoon, & reached via the southern campus of the University College of Education, Lagoon Lodge is routinely praised by readers as one of the best-value & friendliest town hotels on the coast. The self-contained rooms are large, bright & spotless, while 4 connecting rooms are available upstairs for families & groups. A good restaurant serves seafood & local dishes in the US$4–6 range. The energetic & friendly Ghanaian owner is an excellent source of local travel advice, & can direct you to the beach. Booking is recommended. Brilliant value at *US$10/13 self-contained sgl/dbl with fan.* **$**

Shoestring

🏠 **Winneba Armed Forces Resthouse** (6 rooms) 📞 03323 22208; **m** 0200 162824/0540 943249. Set within the southern campus of the College of Education about 1km west of the town centre, this time-warped hilltop lodge has a great view over the beach & hill where the antelope is caught during the Aboakyir. The bright & airy dbl rooms are also fantastic value, & while 1st priority is given to military personnel, it is seldom full. Food is available on request. *US$7/10 self-contained dbl with fan/AC.* **$**

🏠 **Summeryard** (4 rooms) 📞 03323 21790; **m** 0202 122223; **e** summeryard@live.com. Well signposted directly next door to Manuel's (& run by his brother!), this welcoming new place is best known for its superb smoothies, fresh juices & commendable vegan & vegetarian meals (for which pre-ordering is recommended), but they've got a handful of clean cabin-style rooms on stilts tucked into their leafy compound as well. Drum lessons, canoe trips, & hikes in the area can all be easily arranged, & there's Wi-Fi for guests & diners. *US$11/16 sgl/dbl using shared bath; US$16/21 self-contained sgl/dbl.* **$$–$**

🏠 **Manuel's Guesthouse** (16 rooms) **m** 0244 422684/0247 001728; **e** manuelsguesthouse@yahoo.com. This justifiably popular owner-managed backpackers' haunt lies close to the beach about 1km southwest of the town centre. The attached restaurant serves a limited selection of tasty dishes for around US$4, & there's a neat grassy garden at the back, shaded by palm trees. Wi-Fi. *US$7 dbl with fan & shared bath; US$9/18 self-contained dbl with fan/AC.* **$$–$**

🏠 **Jah Mighty Love Land** (5 rooms) **m** 0267 083244; **e** cburghard@whippersnappers. org; www.jahmightyloveland.com. With several comfortable en-suite rooms, a colourful beach bar, plenty of thatch palapa huts on the beach, & a stage for the occasional live bands, this Rastafied retreat is a solid bet for a well-priced weekend on the water. Meals on request. *From US$8 dbl; US$22 2-bedroom flat.* **$$–$**

🏠 **Aziz Guesthouse** (8 rooms) **m** 0274 906155/0548 740044. Set in a grassy compound behind Lagoon Lodge, this is another well-run & good-value option, with the cheapest twin rooms in town, though it's rather lacking in charm by comparison with its competitors. It has a bar, but no restaurant, though food is available at Lagoon Lodge around the corner. *US$10 self-contained twin with fan, fridge & TV.* **$**

✕ WHERE TO EAT AND DRINK *Map, page 178*

Lagoon Lodge has a very popular restaurant, and is particularly recommended if you are after seafood. The food at Manuel's Guesthouse is also reliable and affordable, while the vegan and vegetarian menu at Summeryard is Winneba's new culinary star. Other good local eateries include the following:

✕ **The Stage** **m** 0244 279068; ⏱ 08.30–midnight daily. This relatively smart bar & restaurant serves a good selection of mains with rice or chips for around US$5, & it also hosts Winneba's most popular nightclub on Fri & Sat, staying open until 05.00 the next morning. **$**

✕ **Home Economics Restaurant** ⏱ 08.00–17.00 Mon–Fri. This popular lunch venue in the North Campus of the University of

POSUBANS

Unique to Ghana's central coastal region, posubans – a name deriving from the English word 'post' and Fante '*ban*' (fortification) – are the eye-catching and often elaborately decorated concrete shrines that dot the urban landscape of many Fante settlements, reaching something of a garish zenith in such ancient trading centres as Elmina, Anomabu and Mankessim.

These shrines are the work of asafo companies, the patrilineal military units that are a feature of most Akan societies. Asafo companies are traditionally responsible for the defence of their town, but these days they are perhaps more significant for their ceremonial function and for their activity and influence in the arts and local politics. Most towns in the region have between five and 12 rival asafo companies, each identified by a number, name and location. Generally, the lower the number of the unit, the earlier it was established, and the more influential it is on the chieftaincy. In Anomabu, for instance, a new paramount chief is always sworn in at Company #1's posuban, which is adorned with a symbolic padlock and key.

Many posubans originated as storage houses, used to hold not only arms, but also the company regalia, and they are often decorated in a manner that is both richly symbolic and – to the outsider – decidedly cryptic. The extent of this decoration varies enormously from town to town. You could easily walk right past most of Cape Coast's posubans without noticing them, since at best they are decorated by one small mural. In Elmina and Mankessim, by contrast, the most important shrines are multi-storey affairs decorated with up to ten life-size human forms, and complex enough in their symbolism to keep you guessing for several hours.

Perhaps the most surprising thing about posubans is that, despite their antiquity and uniqueness to the Ghanaian coast, they owe little to any other African artistic tradition. Indeed, were you to show a photograph of a typical shrine to most outsiders, they would be hard pushed to guess in what continent it had been taken. One renowned shrine in Anomabu just about conjures up Africa by

---

Education serves tasty fufu, banku and plain or jollof rice with fish or chicken, as well as boiled yam with *kontomire* (spinach) stew prepared by the Home Economics Department. *US$3*. $
✖ **Kings and Queens Restaurant** m 0244 279068/0240 737785; ⊕ 09.00–22.00 daily, later at w/ends. Situated close to the Wildlife Department office, this place sits in a large courtyard with pool tables & serves the usual staples in the US$2–3 range, but is best known for tilapia (served with banku) for around US$6. $$–$

✖ **Ambassador's Restaurant** m 0244 574850/0207 302845; ⊕ 07.30–20.00 daily. Another popular central eatery, top choices here include fried rice & chicken or banku with okra. *US$2.50–3.50*. $
✖ **KwabChris Restaurant** m 0545 648448; ⊕ 09.00–22.00 daily. A simple but surprisingly artistic eatery around the corner from the new market & trotro station, this is a good place to try fufu & rice balls on Sun. *US$2–3*. $

AROUND WINNEBA

Muni-Pomadze Ramsar Site Designated in 1992, this 95km² reserve to the immediate west of Winneba is listed both as a Ramsar Wetland and an Important Bird Area. It is dominated by the vast Muni Lagoon, which extends over 30km² when full, but also incorporates two forest reserves as well as the traditional hunting ground used in the Aboakyir festival. The marine birdlife includes large seasonal colonies of black, roseate, common, royal and little tern, which can usually be seen from a bird observation post with good binoculars, and Yenku Forest Reserve is the

depicting lions and leopards (sitting somewhat incongruously alongside a whale and several surreal antelope-like creatures), but the same cannot be said for the town's best-known posuban, which is several metres long and built in the shape of a European warship. Others depict European sailors and overgrown clocks, while one startling example in Elmina recounts the story of Adam and Eve. This strange melding of exotic and indigenous influences is a fascinating reflection of a full five centuries of European and African interaction in coastal ports such as Elmina and Anomabu.

Despite vigorous questioning of local elders, we were unable to establish when, why and how these elaborate posubans were constructed. Most of the shrines we saw look as if they took their present form in the post-independence era, and we've been told that the 'Adam and Eve' posuban in Elmina was first made public in the mid 1960s. Another shrine that can be aged is the one in Saltpond, which, somewhat contradictorily, is dated to 1685. Our understanding (open to correction) is that this apparent anomaly reflects the fact that while the actual posuban sites are often centuries old, the exterior is re-sculpted every few decades, to reflect changes in fashion, and to incorporate any important recent additions to the long list of symbols and proverbs associated with the individual asafo.

Details of important individual shrines are given under the town where they are found. For most short-stay visitors, the obvious place to go posuban viewing is Elmina, though the selection found in Anomabu is arguably more varied and interesting. The main shrine in Mankessim (traditionally regarded as the first capital of Fante) is probably the largest and most elaborate in the country, and the one in Saltpond among the most bizarre. Most of the shrines lie on main roads so viewing them is free, but a donation of around US$1–3 will be expected if you want to take photographs.

only known Ghanaian haunt of the localised Puvel's illadopsis. Guided birdwatching excursions can be arranged through the Wildlife Division (see below).

The palm-fringed beach that divides the lagoon from the open sea regularly hosts breeding turtles between September and March, primarily leatherback and olive ridley turtles. During this season, nocturnal guided turtle-tracking tours are offered for US$12.50 per person as part of an ecotourism project developed by the Ghana Wildlife Division. The fee includes an introduction to turtle ecology in Ghana and Winneba, and the guide will pick you up from your hotel and return you there after the walk. For further details, visit the Wildlife Division/Forestry Commission office, opposite the Trauma and Specialist Hospital near Low Cost Junction, or contact them (m 0242 580606/0207 488382/0243 251568; e turtlewatch. winneba@yahoo.com).

APAM

This small seaside town south of the main Cape Coast road is best known as the site of **Fort Lijdzaamheid** ('Patience'), which now doubles as a rather rundown resthouse. Built in 1697 to protect a sliver of Dutch territory sandwiched between British-held Fante and Agona, the fort was captured by the British in 1782, returned to the Dutch three years later, then finally handed back to Britain in 1868. It must be the smallest extant fort on the Ghanaian coast, and the cramped dimensions of the prison cell suggests that it was never used to store slaves to any serious extent. The most impressive thing about the fort is its position, perched on top of a sharp little hill overlooking a picturesque fishing harbour laden with colourful pirogues. Entrance costs US$1.50.

Also of interest is the late 19th-century Methodist church, and a timeworn three-storey posuban (opposite the trotro station) that depicts a few biblical figures – some accidentally decapitated! Sadly, the beach leaves much to be desired, since it doubles as a toilet, with one part set aside for men and another for women.

GETTING THERE AND AWAY Apam lies about 6km south of the main Accra–Cape Coast road. Regular shared taxis run there from Ankamu Junction, which is easily reached by trotro from either direction.

WHERE TO STAY AND EAT
Shoestring
⌂ **Fort Patience Resthouse** (7 rooms) m 0243 117675. The dirt-cheap bedrooms on the top floor of the fort offer stunning views over the harbour but are uncomfortably cell-like & musty, & the only facilities are bucket showers. No food is served, but a fair selection is available around the market. *US$4pp.* $

✗ **Sankofa Square** m 0247 878655/0542 946294; www.sankofasquare.com; ⊕ 09.00–

23.00 daily. Set 1.5km south of Ankamu Junction on the road to Apam, the jerk chicken, curry goat, oxtails & beef patties (the last only at w/ends) at this new Jamaican-owned restaurant would make a worthwhile diversion whether you're headed to Apam or just passing along the coastal road. It gets lively with reggae on the weekends, & most main dishes come in around US$4. Rooms are planned. $

MANKESSIM, SALTPOND AND SURROUNDS

Situated about 8km apart along the main road between Accra and Cape Coast, the twin towns of Mankessim and Saltpond, each of which supports a population of around 20,000, lie in an area steeped in Fante history. A significant junction and market town situated about 5km inland as the crow flies, Mankessim is the busier of the two towns – indeed, on market days (Wednesday and Saturday), the atmosphere can be positively frantic. Saltpond, with its narrow roads and colonial architecture reminiscent of a scaled-down version of Cape Coast, is altogether more subdued in character, belying its status as the capital of Mfantsiman Municipal District. Saltpond is also the more useful and attractive base for tourists, thanks to its pretty palm-lined beach and scattering of decent lodgings. Both towns host exceptional posuban shrines, and the hilltop Fort Amsterdam, a short walk or drive east of Saltpond, is also worth a visit, if only for the lovely views.

HISTORY Mankessim is the focal point from which the Fante expanded into much of what is now south-central Ghana, following a southward exodus from Techiman by their ancestors (an offshoot of the Akan people who eventually became the Ashanti) some time between the mid 13th and mid 15th centuries. According to oral tradition, the migrants were led south by a trio of powerful warriors, Obrumankoma, Odapagya and Oson, who are respectively associated with, and frequently represented by, a whale, an eagle and an elephant. Legend has it that the migrants initially settled at a rocky grove 3km south of present-day Mankessim (close to the village of Obidan), after the fetish priest Komfo Amona drove his spear into the ground there and, in keeping with Akan tradition, was unable to remove

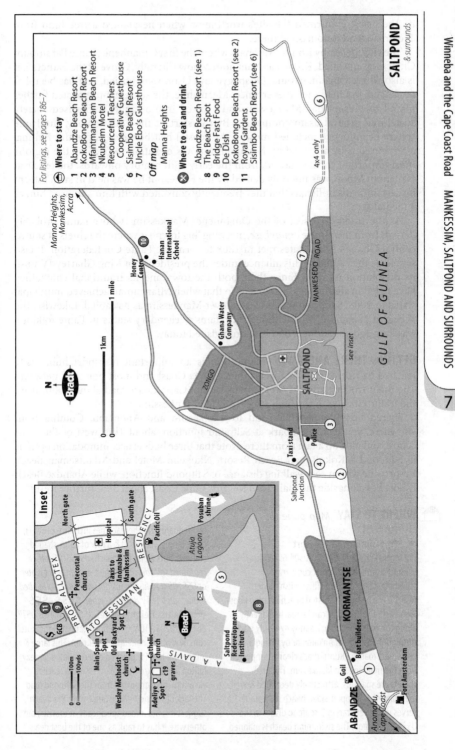

SALTPOND
& surrounds

For listings, see pages 186–7

Where to stay
1 Abandze Beach Resort
2 KokoBongo Beach Resort
3 Mfantmanseam Beach Resort
4 Nkubeim Motel
5 Resourceful Teachers
   Cooperative Guesthouse
6 Sisimbo Beach Resort
7 Uncle Ebo's Guesthouse

Off map
   Manna Heights

Where to eat and drink
   Abandze Beach Resort (see 1)
8 The Beach Spot
9 Bridge Fast Food
10 De Dish
   KokoBongo Beach Resort (see 2)
   Royal Gardens
11 Sisimbo Beach Resort (see 6)

it. The priest confirmed the site's worthiness when he planted a tree limb from Techiman, and it flourished there.

The site chosen by Komfo Amona is where the first Omanhene (Fante Paramount Chief) was installed. Known as Nananom Mpow (literally 'Grove of the Fathers'), it is also where Obrumankoma, Odapagya and Oson were buried, and has been left uncleared and held sacred ever since. Meanwhile, the settlement relocated further inland to present-day Mankessim and evolved into a highly militarised society structured around asafo companies. By the start of the 18th century, the Fante sphere of influence included most of the coastal belt between Accra and Elmina, a territorial gain mirrored by Nananom Mpow's elevation to become the region's most important shrine. Indeed, from the early 18th century onwards, the oracle at Nananom Mpow was not only deified by the Fante, but he was held in such esteem by certain British officials that they frequently consulted with him and used him as a mediator.

As the traditional seat of the Omanhene, Mankessim (whose name probably derives from the phrase *oman kese*, meaning 'big town') is where the chiefs of south-central Ghana's Akan states met in 1868 to form the Fante Confederation. It also served as the capital of this alliance under the presidency of King Ghartey IV until its dissolution in 1873. Since then, both the town and its traditional chieftaincy have faded in significance – so much so that when Mfantsiman achieved municipal status in 2008, Saltpond was preferred over Mankessim as its capital. Likewise, the shrine at Nananom Mpow, though it retains a legendary status in Fante folklore, was long ago abandoned, and is seldom visited today.

GETTING THERE AND AWAY Mankessim is an important transport hub, easily reached by trotro from Accra, Winneba, Cape Coast and most points in between. The main trotro station is on the main Accra–Cape Coast road about 100m from the traffic circle with the high street through Mankessim.

Shared taxis connect Saltpond to Mankessim and Anomabu. Coming from elsewhere, you can disembark at Saltpond Junction, about 1km west of the town centre, and pick up a taxi from there. Note that three budget accommodation options in Saltpond – KokoBongo Beach Resort, Nkubeim Motel and Mfantseman Beach Resort – lie within easy walking distance of Saltpond Junction, while Abandze Beach Resort lies alongside the main road towards Cape Coast about 3km further west.

WHERE TO STAY *Map, page 185*
Upmarket
Sisimbo Beach Resort
(12 rooms) m 0269 256620/0504 698614;
e info@sisimbobeachresort.com; www.
sisimbobeachresort.com. This stylish modern resort has a beautiful isolated beach location about 3km east of Saltpond. It can be reached directly along the coast following a sandy 4x4-only track through the village of Ankafor, or by taking a better dirt road via Kuntu that's clearly signposted from the main road to Mankessim. The tiled chalets are spacious, attractively decorated & well maintained, & an open-sided beach restaurant serves meat, vegetarian & seafood dishes in the US$10–20 range. The swimming beach is manned

by lifeguards, & other facilities include free Wi-Fi, table tennis, volleyball & a row of palm-shaded summer huts along the beach. *US$85/95 self-contained sgl/dbl with dbl bed, AC, fan & hot water or US$105/120 luxury sgl/dbl with queen-sized bed, fridge, satellite TV & coffee corner.* **$$$$–$$$**

Manna Heights Hotel (50 rooms) m 0577 661111/0208 110400; e info@mannaheightshotel.com; www.mannaheightshotel.com. This large & impressive hotel is perched on an isolated, breezy hilltop about 3km from Mankessim, & reached via a turn-off signposted from the Saltpond road. The lack of sea views & distance from the beach suggest it is not aimed specifically at tourists, but otherwise it has to rank as one of the best deals in its range near the Ghanaian coast, & would make a useful base from which to explore the area. Facilities include a swimming pool, tennis courts & excellent restaurant. *US$80–120 large, smart self-contained rooms with DSTV, AC & a hot bath, inc b/fast.* **$$$$–$$$**

Moderate

⌂ **Abandze Beach Resort** (10 rooms) m 0244 576439; e info@abandzebeach.com; www.abandzebeach.com. Flanked by the crashing Atlantic Ocean & tranquil Etsi Lagoon & shadowed by Fort Amsterdam, this family-friendly beach resort 3km west of Saltpond Junction couldn't want for a better location. The comfortable chalets have attractive wood & bamboo furnishing, & they all face the sea, so you'll be lulled off to sleep in no time; plus they were all getting a fresh lick of paint when we checked in. The huge thatched-roofed restaurant & friendly beachside bar are atmospheric & the food excellent, with snacks & meals in the US$6–15 range. The hotel is located off the main Accra–Cape Coast road just before Abandze – from Saltpond catch any of the shared taxis towards Anomabu. *US$53 dbl semi-detached room with queen-sized bed, fan, AC & satellite TV.* **$$$**

Budget

⌂ **KokoBongo Beach Resort** (6 rooms) m 0241 771164. Boasting a wonderful beachfront location about 5mins' walk from Saltpond Junction, & only 50m from the crashing waves, this wallet-friendly setup lies in a small palm-shaded compound littered with hammocks, though it feels a bit disorganised today & we suspect that standards have taken a plunge after a recent change in management. The raised bar & restaurant are positioned to catch the sea breeze,

& serve local dishes in the US$6–8 range. The light, airy & brightly coloured rooms come with fans, & there's also space for camping. *US$13 self-contained dbl.* **$**

⌂ **Mfantmanseam Beach Resort** (4 rooms) m 0237 808618/0555 393318; mfantmanseam1@gmail.com. Just opened as this book was going to print, this new beachfront place sits in colourful, palm-studded grounds behind the police station near Saltpond Junction, & comes warmly recommended by readers for the food & ambiance. The British owner-managers are an excellent resource on the region, & the tiled rooms are well kept. *US$25 self-contained dbl.* **$$$**

⌂ **Resourceful Teachers Cooperative Guesthouse** (6 rooms) \ 03321 97864; m 0547 553967; e mmtccu@yahoo.com. Situated on the verge of Saltpond's small town centre, perhaps 100m from the beach, this well-managed & pleasant new guesthouse occupies the 1st floor of the same building as the Teachers Cooperative Bank. The clean rooms all come with fan, AC & writing desk. *US$11/13 self-contained dbl/semi-suite.* **$**

Shoestring

⌂ **Uncle Ebo's Guesthouse** (4 rooms) m 0249 757411/0546 103532. A bit of a walk east of the town, but close to the beach, this small & friendly village guesthouse has clean but no-frills rooms with a dbl bed & fan. Meals can be arranged on request. *Good value at US$9 self-contained dbl.* **$**

⌂ **Nkubeim Motel** (20 rooms) m 0244 758558/0243 217976. Situated perhaps 100m from Saltpond Junction, this friendly but characterless family-run guesthouse has tidy, reader-recommended rooms with king-sized beds, fridge & TV. *US$11/13 self-contained dbl with fan/AC.* **$**

✖ **WHERE TO EAT AND DRINK**   Map, page 185

There are good restaurants at the Sisimbo and Abandze beach resorts, as well as the more affordable and central KokoBongo Beach Resort. In central Saltpond, the **Royal Gardens Restaurant** (m *0244 453700*) and **Bridge Fast Food** (m *0244 532566*), situated opposite each other on Prof Allotex Road, both serve adequate local fare. On the main Accra–Cape Coast road, the **Honey Centre** (m *0209 928143/0244 778823*) sells raw honey, pollen, propolis, and a variety of other medicinal and cosmetic products derived from bees, and it's situated right next to **De Dish**, where you can chop the usual range of local dishes in pleasant surroundings. There are also plenty of bars dotted around town, the pick – if only for its beachfront location – being **The Beach Spot**, which is open daily.

WHAT TO SEE AND DO

Mankessim The most famous landmark in Mankessim is the three-storey posuban built by Asafo #2. The ground floor of this elaborate shrine incorporates a diverse collection of life-size sculptures, including two male lions, a cannon, a drum, and about seven human figures, one of which is on horseback and another on the back of an indeterminate spotted carnivore. The first floor is dominated by three human figures depicting the town's founding fathers, Obrumankoma, Odapagya and Oson, while the top floor bears a coat of arms flanked, by cannons and what appears to be a pair of reindeer. There is no charge for looking at the posuban, but you will be expected to make a donation for upkeep if you photograph it or have the caretaker show you around and explain the symbolism.

To get to the posuban from the traffic circle on the Accra–Cape Coast road, turn north into the high street, passing the Ghana Commercial Bank and Methodist church to your right, then the taxi park to your left, and you'll see it to the left after about 600m. The traffic circle itself is adorned with a trio of modern statues representing Obrumankoma, Odapagya and Oson as a whale, eagle and elephant.

Saltpond Aside from its beach, which is long, sandy, lined with palms and (like many urban beaches in Ghana) doubles as a public defecation site, the main attraction of Saltpond is another fine posuban built by Asafo Company #2 and dated to 1687. The shrine is adorned with an elaborate assemblage of sculpted concrete figures, including what appears to be a multi-headed dragon behind the main building. The central drama depicts a local soldier pointing a gun at the disembodied head of an (European?) enemy, while another soldier raises the machete that was presumably used to decapitate the victim. To get to the posuban, follow the coastal road east out of the town centre until, after about 300m, you come to the south gate of the hospital, then turn right towards the lagoon and you'll see it, almost totally obscured by a tall tree, to your left after another 300m or so. The caretaker charges a flat fee of US$2.50 per person to look at the shrine, and another US$2.50 to take photographs.

Fort Amsterdam Overlooking Abandze, on the Cape Coast road about 3.5km west of Saltpond Junction, Fort Amsterdam evolved from the very first structure that the British built on the Gold Coast, a small lodge constructed in 1631 and fortified seven years later. The original fort was attacked and destroyed by an asafo from Anomabu in 1811, but was restored by the Ghana Museums and Monument Board in 1951. Perched on a hilltop, Fort Amsterdam affords excellent views over Abandze's busy fishing beach and the Etsi Lagoon to the village of Kormantse, from which its alternative name of Fort Cormantine derives. The slaves held in Fort Amsterdam, sold mainly to the Caribbean plantations, became known as Cormantines – a name that reportedly travelled to the West Indies. Among the prominent Afro-Americans to have traced their roots to Kormantse is Louis Armstrong. Entrance costs US$2.50 per person. Be warned that the gaggle of aggressive kids who hang around the fort trailing behind visitors can make for a rather unpleasant experience.

ANOMABU AND BIRIWA

Situated about halfway between Mankessim and Cape Coast, the small and rather sprawling fishing town of Anomabu (sometimes spelt Anomabo) has more to offer visitors than first impressions might suggest. One of the oldest trading centres in

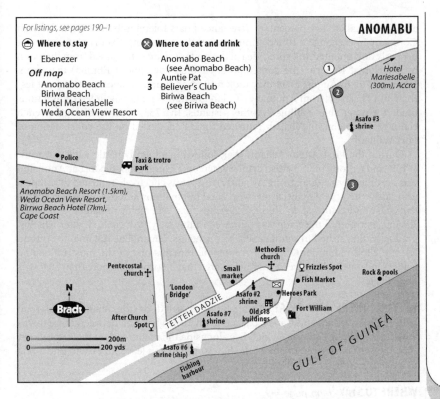

For listings, see pages 190–1

ANOMABU

🏠 **Where to stay**

1 Ebenezer

Off map
Anomabo Beach
Biriwa Beach
Hotel Mariesabelle
Weda Ocean View Resort

❌ **Where to eat and drink**

Anomabo Beach
(see Anomabo Beach)
2 Auntie Pat
3 Believer's Club
Biriwa Beach
(see Biriwa Beach)

the Fante region, it is the site of Fort William, which first opened to tourism in 2007, as well as the most impressive collection of posubans anywhere along the coast. And while the main beach in front of the town is (predictably) turd-laden at low tide, the clean beach in front of Anomabo Beach Resort, about 2km west of town, is one of the finest between Accra and Cape Coast. Another 5km west of Anomabu, the small fishing village of Biriwa is best known for its superb beach, a popular hippy hangout in the 1970s, but these days used almost exclusively by patrons of the clifftop Biriwa Beach Hotel.

HISTORY Anomabu has a strong history of independence, despite having been settled intermittently by various European powers over the centuries. First documented in 1602 by the Dutch merchant Pieter de Marees (who called it Fantijn), Anomabu is thought to have been the main coastal trade centre for the Fante of Mankessim long before the earliest earthwork European lodge was built there in 1640 by the Dutch. This lodge changed hands several times – going to the Swedes, then the Danes, then back to the Dutch – before it was abandoned c1665 due to pressure from the newly installed British at nearby Cape Coast. The lodge later served as the palace of Omanhene Nano Eno, the first recorded paramount chief of Anomabu, who died c1708. In 1674, the British occupied Anomabu, and built a small fort they named after King Charles II. Shortly afterwards, they abandoned Anomabu to focus on the development of Cape Coast, and trashed the fort to prevent it falling into the hands of another European power.

Over subsequent decades, Anomabu grew to become perhaps the largest slave emporium on the Gold Coast, with most trade taking place between the local Fante and the so-called 'ten-percenters' (freelance boats tolerated by the Royal African Company in exchange a 10% commission on their custom). Export figures are not properly documented, but some idea of the trade's scale can be gained from the claim by Engelgraaf Roberts (the contemporary Dutch governor at Elmina) that 'from January 1702 to August 1708 they took to Barbados and Jamaica a total of not less than 30,141 slaves [from Anomabu] and in this figure are not included transactions made for other ships sailing to [other] islands'. In 1753, after thwarting a French claim to Anomabu, the British returned there and started on the construction of Fort William.

During the First Anglo-Ashanti War, following a bloody battle with Governor White and a group of 25 British artillerymen on 15 June 1806, the fort at Anomabu was occupied by a 2,000-strong Ashanti army. It was effectively returned to Britain a year later when the Ashanti army, weakened by smallpox and dysentery, evacuated the coast and returned to Kumasi. Despite this, Anomabu remained a thriving slaving centre until the trade was outlawed in the early 19th century, after which it gradually diminished in significance. Nevertheless, Omanhene Katamanto Amonu XI, the 22nd paramount chief of Anomabu, remains one of the most influential leaders in Fante, ruling over a traditional area that incorporates more than 50 towns and villages.

GETTING THERE AND AWAY Anomabu is bisected by the main coastal road between Mankessim and Cape Coast, and any trotro heading between these towns will drop you at the station (which lies alongside the main road on the Cape Coast side of town) or in front of any of the hotels. When you leave it's easy to find a seat in a passing trotro in either direction.

WHERE TO STAY *Map, page 189*
Moderate

Biriwa Beach Hotel (7 rooms) m 0244 446277/767115; e mail@hotelbiriwabeach.de; www.hotelbiriwabeach.de. Positioned on a high bluff overlooking Biriwa's fantastic beach, this stalwart hotel started life more than 30 years ago as a restaurant, since when it has expanded to become one of the most cosy beachside retreats in Ghana, all the while owned & managed by the same German family. Architecturally it is a little dated, but the brightly decorated rooms are comfortable, clean & reasonably priced, & all come with AC, satellite TV, writing desk & tea/coffee corner. With a varied menu that reflects not only the proximity to the sea, but also the owner's nationality, the garden restaurant remains sufficiently outstanding that it attracts frequent day custom from Cape Coast, and most selections are in the US$9–13 range. Other facilities include free internet access for guests, a good souvenir shop filled with curios from across West Africa, & a well-maintained circular swimming pool overlooking the beach. *US$53 self-contained twin without view; US$65/92 similar room with garden/sea view.* **$$$**

Anomabo Beach Resort (50 rooms) m 0501 286213, 0244 331731/2; e anomabo@ hotmail.com; www.anomabo.com. Strung out along a palm-lined beach to the west of the town centre, this popular resort combines comfortable accommodation with an appealing organic aesthetic, making it very popular with expats from all over West Africa. It has a relatively safe swimming beach with lifeguards, & free body-board hire. In the evening, the raised wooden restaurant is a great place to catch the breeze & serves excellent meals priced at around US$6 for Ghanaian fare or upwards of US$15 for seafood. The accommodation is arranged in 2 'villages', both of which now offer smart self-contained units with AC. Day visitors are welcome for US$1.50/2.50 weekday/weekend. *US$60/80 sgl/dbl self-contained bungalow with AC; US$80/100 sgl/dbl exec bungalow; US$100/120 sgl/dbl beachfront; US$20pp standing tent; US$15pp camping.* **$$$$–$$**

Weda Ocean View Resort (11 rooms) m 0208 140435/0244 806958. Coming in a poor third to the alternatives listed above, this hilltop villa overlooking Anomabo Beach Resort has comfortable albeit rather bland rooms & a rather unattended feel, but the staff is welcoming. *US$23 self-contained dbl with fan, fridge, & TV; US$25–30 self-contained dbl with AC, fridge, & TV.* **$$$–$$**

Budget

🏠 **Hotel Mariesabelle** (27 rooms) 🔌033 2192024; 📱 0249 448510. To the right of the main road as you approach the town coming from Accra, this friendly hotel offers decent self-contained dbls with fan or AC. The restaurant serves adequate

meals & ice-cold drinks, best enjoyed on the breezy rooftop balcony. *US$15/19 dbl with fan/AC; US$22 suite.* **$$**

🏠 **Ebenezer Hotel** (9 rooms) 📱 0204 721598/0242 665525. Situated along the main coastal road through the centre of Anomabu, this well-established hotel offers large self-contained rooms with hot water & private balcony. The ground-floor restaurant serves adequate chop. *US$9/13 self-contained sgl/dbl with fan; US$14–17 dbl with AC.* **$$–$**

✗ **WHERE TO EAT AND DRINK**   *Map, page 189*

Biriwa Beach Hotel has one of the finest restaurants in the area, and the food at the Anomabo Beach Resort isn't far behind. For cheaper (and credulous) eats, the new **Believer's Club**, on the east side of the road between Fort William and the Ebenezer Hotel, has been recommended by locals, and **Auntie Pat** also does meals further north, at the junction with the main road.

WHAT TO SEE AND DO

Fort William   Anomabu's seafront is dominated by Fort William, which the British built over 1753–57 on the foundations of the older Fort Charles, a site chosen for its sheltered anchorage. Originally known as Annamaboe Fort, it was designed by the military engineer John Apperley, who served as its first governor prior to his death in 1756, and completed by his successor, Richard Brew. The fort is widely regarded as one of the most elegant and solidly constructed on the Ghanaian coast, built with bricks fired in a purpose-built kiln operated by slaves trained in the craft of brickmaking, and cement made with limestone imported from Barbados. It survived a French bombardment in 1794 and an attack by the Fante of Anomabu in 1801, but its cannon power was insufficient to repel an attack by the Ashanti, who occupied it over 1806–07. In the early 1830s, during the governorship of Brodie Cruikshank, the original building was extended upwards by one storey and renamed Fort William in honour of King William IV.

Built at the height of the slave trade, Anomabu's fort is the only one in Ghana whose original structure included a large prison built specifically to incarcerate captives prior to their shipment overseas. There are six dungeons in total. Three were used for male captives, and three for females, who were further segregated by age, with one of the women's dungeons being reserved for potential concubines. It has been estimated that a total of 280,000 slaves passed through the fort *en route* to the Americas (in particular Barbados). Most would have exited through the Gate of No Return, which leads to a beach where small vessels, not dissimilar to the fishing boats that still moor there today, ferried them to slave ships anchored 1km offshore.

In more recent decades, Fort William served as a resthouse and post office, then as a state prison. The prison closed in 2001 and the fort reopened as a museum in 2007. The entrance fee of US$2.50 per person includes a guided tour with the knowledgeable and articulate caretaker, Philip Atta (📱 *0275 429543/0245 538805*), and photography costs an additional US$1. Opposite the fort is the substantial ruin of a double-storey building constructed by Governor Brew in the 1770s, reputedly as a venue for parties and to house concubines. There was some restoration going on here when we dropped by in 2016, but we're told this could yet prove to be abortive. About 100m further east, there's a sanded-up swimming pool in the rocks, also probably dating to the 18th century. Look out to sea from here, and you'll also see the Obonoma ('Rock of Birds') from which derives the name Anomabu – and, seasonally, the small rocky outcrop still hosts a breeding colony of gulls.

Heroes Park The centrepiece of this small park, situated directly opposite Fort William, is a trio of bronze statues cast in 2007 and depicting three of Anomabu's most celebrated sons: George Ekem Ferguson, Nana Amonu Katamanto IV and Dr James Kwegyir Aggrey. The famed surveyor George Ekem Ferguson (born Ekow Atta in 1864), a trained geographer and gifted linguist, was perhaps the single most important pioneer in expanding Britain's knowledge of the Ghanaian interior before his death in battle near Wa in 1897. Nana Amonu Katamanto IV, the Omanhene of Anomabu from 1868 to 1873, was an important figure in the creation of the Fante Confederation. Dr James Emmanuel Kwegyir Aggrey, born in 1875, was a brilliant and far-seeing theologian, scholar and politician best known today for his pioneering role in female education in Africa (his most famous quote, delivered in an address to Governor Guggisberg, is, 'The surest way to keep people down is to educate the men and neglect the women. If you educate a man you simply educate an individual, but if you educate a woman, you educate a family'.).

Posubans Anomabu is studded with posuban shrines, one for each of its seven Asafo companies, and they are all quite easy to find. There are two main clusters, with the posubans built by Asafo #3–5 all lying to the east of the feeder road linking the Ebenezer Hotel to Fort William, while the remainder are in the old town centre, within 200m of Fort William. Visitors are free to wander around Anomabu and look at the shrines, but expect to be asked for a donation of US$1–3 if you want to take a photo of any individual shrine. The posubans are as follows:

Eastern cluster Oral traditions state that the three asafo companies based in the alleys east of the town centre are the oldest in Anomabu, having been founded under Omanhene Nano between 1690 and 1708, and charged to protect the village against attacks by the Ashanti and other enemies. If this is true, it would suggest that the original site of the village, and of the first Dutch lodge built there, was a few hundred metres east of the modern town centre.

Asafo #3 (Dontsin) The most impressive of the eastern posubans hosts an improbable assemblage of sculpted animals, including two lions, a whale, a miniature elephant, a blue giraffe and a pair of spotted carnivores that look like a cross between a hyena and a cheetah. It is situated about 50m east of the feeder road, not far south of the Omanhene's Palace, and close to a contorted strangler ficus tree that's one of the most impressive of the town's 70-plus gods. Its Dontsin builders are regarded as the central asafo group and a new Omanhene, irrespective of his original company, automatically switches to it.

Asafo #4 (Iburon) This small shrine a short walk further east comprises a tortoise (signifying patience) on top of a small block. Though rather plain, the sculpture is said to be around 200 years old, making it the oldest shrine to have taken its present form.

Asafo #5 (Ebiram Wassa) The most easterly of the seven posubans is also the plainest, consisting of a circular concrete block, representing an oven, built in 1992 over what was formerly a tree stump surrounded by stones. Ebiram Wassa claims to be the original asafo #1, but although it was later usurped by Tuafo, the two still coexist peacefully.

Central cluster The two oldest shrines here flank the main road running west alongside the sandstone Methodist church, but the more interesting shrines are those built by asafo #6 and #7 about 200m west of Fort William.

Asafo #1 (Tuafo) Built in 1919, the posuban associated with Tuafo (the oldest of the central companies) is not much to look at, but it is of special significance as the site where a new Omanhene is sworn in, a role symbolised by the lock and key depicted on one side of the shrine.

Asafo #2 (Etsiwa) A relatively modern shrine, built in the 1970s, this comprises a barrel flanked by a pair of large predators (probably leopards) and decorated with several other small surrealistic mythical creatures

Asafo #6 (Kyirom) Probably the most famous of Anomabu's posubans, this replica of a European steamship, adorned with cannons and naval figures, is the size of a small house. Built in 1955, it reputedly refers to a much earlier naval battle with the Etsiwa, wherein the Kyirom victors decapitated their foes and sent their heads home to their families in fish bags. Their reputation as bloodthirsty fighters has led to the Kyirom being personal bodyguards to the Omanhene in times of war.

Asafo #7 (Akomfodze) Built in 1965 around the corner from the Kyirom shrine, this large but rather plain posuban is most notable for including a small figure of a three-headed dragon.

MOREE

This small town 5km northeast of Cape Coast is the place where the Dutch gained their first legal foothold on the Gold Coast, with the signing of the Treaty of Asebu (the name of a defunct Fante chieftaincy) in 1612. Moree (then known as Moury) was also the site of their first fortress in the region. This was Fort Nassau, which was built in 1612 with bricks shipped over from Holland, and went on to serve as the Dutch headquarters in West Africa until the capture of Elmina Fort in 1637. Now a substantial ruin, Fort Nassau is clearly visible on a hill above the town, where the standing walls are interspersed with the circular, mud fish-smoking ovens so characteristic of this part of the coast. More engaging than the ruined fort, however, is the view from the hill: on one side, Moree stretches out in all its corrugated-iron-roofed glory; on the other side is a beach as beautiful as any in Ghana, dotted with typically colourful fishing boats.

GETTING THERE AND AWAY Moree lies about 3km from the main Accra road (though it feels so isolated that it could be 200km). At the junction, you'll find some of the most dilapidated taxis in Ghana waiting to trundle down to Moree in blissful, pot-hole-dodging lethargy. Alternatively, direct shared taxis between Moree and Cape Coast take about 15 minutes.

⌂ WHERE TO STAY AND EAT

⌂ **Moree Beach Resort** (13 rooms) m 0244 216411/0208 135160; e info@moreebeachresort. com; www.moreebeachresort.com. Moree's only accommodation option, about 1km from the main road along a poorly signposted fork to the left as you enter town, is this owner-managed resort that sits on well-manicured lawns running down to an idyllic beach. The comfortable & nicely decorated sea-facing thatched chalets come with AC, fan & writing desk, & are very reasonably priced, though we've had reports that maintenance standards aren't what they used to be. The open-air restaurant-cum-bar serves a varied selection of vegetarian dishes at around US$3–4 & meat & fish dishes in the US$5–7 range. *From US$33 self-contained dbl; US$50 family chalet.* **$$$–$$**

8

Cape Coast and Elmina

Although Ghana has a comparatively ill-defined travel circuit, it does boast one obvious touristic focal point in the form of the twin ports that adorn the coast 150km west of Accra. These are Cape Coast and Elmina, centuries-old trade and military rivals protected by two of the oldest, largest and best-preserved European-built castles in West Africa, yet only 10km apart as the cannonball flies. Due to their great antiquity and nefarious role in the Atlantic slave trade, the castles at Cape Coast and Elmina are of global significance as the centrepieces of a UNESCO World Heritage Site embracing all the fortified buildings along the Ghanaian coast. Yet the towns over which they stand sentinel, far from being stuffy period pieces, are lively modern ports, steeped in Fante tradition and history, but also reflecting the contradictions and intricacies of 21st-century urban Africa. Further afield, there are some great beaches running westwards from Elmina, while Kakum National Park, inland of Cape Coast, which is renowned for its 40m-high canopy walkway, is also the most accessible place to seek out some of Ghana's elusive forest wildlife.

CAPE COAST

The attractive fishing port of Cape Coast, set on the east bank of the Fosu Lagoon, is steeped in history. Settled at various points by Portuguese, Danish, Swedish and Dutch traders, it became the coastal headquarters of Britain's Royal African Company in 1664, and later served as the first capital of the Gold Coast colony. The town's antiquity is reflected in a varied range of architectural relicts spanning four centuries, most notably the hulking seafront presence of Cape Coast Castle, but also in its organic shape of tangled roads hugging the curves of low hills.

Cape Coast is a fascinating town to explore. In some respects, the streets and alleys of the old town centre, with their comfortable lived-in feel, genuine sense of community, and blurred boundaries between administrative, business and residential districts, recall the older ports of East Africa's Swahili Coast. And yet the administrative capital of Central Region is also, emphatically, a very modern town, supporting a population of 215,000, of which something like 15% are in some way associated with the respected University of Cape Coast on the town's northwestern outskirts.

A popular base with backpackers and volunteers, central Cape Coast is well endowed with budget accommodation and eateries catering to Western palates, as well as with banks, internet cafés, bookshops and other tourist amenities. The main central attraction is the castle, now a museum dedicated to the history of the transatlantic slave trade, but it is also a good base for exploring nearby Elmina and Kakum National Park.

HISTORY Settled at least since the early 15th century, Cape Coast is also known by two older traditional names: Kotokuraba and Oguaa. Kotokuraba means 'River of Crabs'

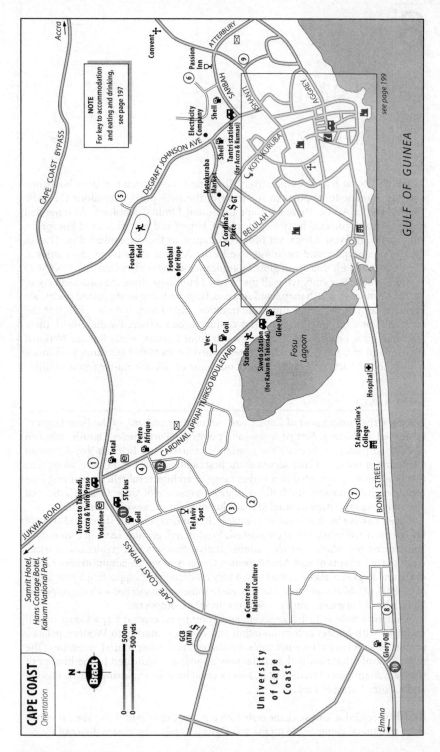

or 'Village of Crabs', and it refers to the abundance of these creatures – reputedly the favourite food of an early chief – in the vicinity. Two contradictory traditions relate to the origin of the name Oguaa. One holds that it derives from the Akan word *gua* (market), suggesting that Cape Coast was an important centre of trade even before it was settled by Europeans, while the other states that it was founded by a hunter from Efutu called Egya Oguaa. The region ruled by the Omanhene (paramount chief) of Cape Coast is today known as Oguaa Traditional Area, while Kotokuraba is the name of the town's largest market and one of its main roads.

In 1471, the Portuguese navigators João de Santarém and Pedro Escobar sailed past Oguaa, naming it Cabo Corso (Short Cape), which was later bastardised to Cape Coast. The earliest written descriptions of Oguaa, penned in the 1550s by the British captains John Lok and William Towerson, portray a fishing village of roughly 20 small houses, enclosed within a reed fence, and presided over by a chief who went by the rather intriguing name of Don Juan. Nothing more is heard of Oguaa for two generations, until 1610, when a Portuguese lodge was built at an undetermined site on the outskirts of the village, which at that time probably extended north from the beach to what is now Jackson Street.

Oguaa grew rapidly and changed hands several times during the second half of the 17th century. In 1652, the Swedes occupied the abandoned Portuguese lodge. Only six years later, it was captured by the Danes, who signed a treaty with the paramount chief of Efutu (the inland village under whose rule Oguaa fell) allowing them to construct a larger, triangular fort at nearby Amanful. This new fort was held briefly by the Dutch – then the dominant European power in the region – before Britain took over in the wake of the Anglo–Dutch War of 1664–65. From then on, Cape Coast was the key British outpost along the Gulf of Guinea, a role cemented in the 1670s by the expansion of the fort to become modern-day Cape Coast Castle. By 1695, the number of houses in Cape Coast exceeded 500, and the town centre had more or less assumed its present shape.

The initial importance of Cape Coast had derived from its position as the link between the maritime trade routes of the European powers and the terrestrial trade routes through to the Sahel. By the early 17th century, however, its economy was dominated by the transatlantic slave trade, in which it played a key role (along with nearby Anomabu). At any given time between the early 17th century and 1807 (when the trade was abolished by the British parliament), the dungeons of Cape Coast Castle would have held up to 1,500 slaves awaiting shipment to the Americas.

Cape Coast experienced two significant domestic power shifts in the early years of British rule. The first occurred in 1693, when the paramount chief of Efutu, seeking to capitalise on the growing trade out of Cape Coast, relocated his inland capital to the site of what is now Emintsimadze Palace, opposite present-day Victoria Park, about 300m west of the castle. Then, in 1729, following the defeat of Efutu by the Fante of Mankessim, the first Omanhene of Oguaa was appointed in the person of Nana Brempong Codjo, a former messenger and translator for the Royal African Company. Codjo remained

Omanhene of Oguaa until his death in 1770, founding a patrilineal dynasty that produced a succession of respected paramount chiefs prior to the 1850s.

In January 1856, the unpopular eighth Omanhene of Oguaa, Kofi Amissa, was destooled in the aftermath of a palace revolution in which he and his supporters in asafo #4 were defeated by an alliance comprising the town's other six asafo companies. After this, it was decided to switch over to matrilineal descent, starting in March 1856 with the enstoolment of Kweku Atta as Kofi Amissa's successor. This matrilineal system has endured ever since, right up until the appointment of the incumbent, Nana Osabarima Kwesi Atta II, as Omanhene of Oguaa Traditional Area in 1996.

Following the abolition of the slave trade, legitimate commerce was re-established along the Gulf of Guinea, and all the forts and castles owned by the Royal African Company were formally taken over by the British crown, to be placed under the Governor of Sierra Leone in 1821. From 1828 onwards, Cape Coast Castle served as the administrative headquarters of these British possessions, and in 1874 it became the first seat of government of the Gold Coast colony. Three years later, this role was assumed by Accra, and although Cape Coast has hardly slid into backwater status since, one still senses that the town centre would be instantly recognisable to a time traveller from the Victorian era.

GETTING THERE AND AWAY Cape Coast is the biggest transport hub between Accra and Takoradi, but the most important stations are somewhat scattered. The Metro Mass terminus recently relocated to a new site at Aquarium Junction on Cardinal Appiah Turkso Boulevard. About 20 Metro Mass buses run from here to Accra daily, and at least a dozen head north to Kumasi. The much-diminished STC has a station next to the Goil garage on the Cape Coast bypass, but the only STC bus servicing Cape Coast today is a once daily run between Accra and Abidjan.

Ordinary **trotros to/from Accra or Kumasi** (*around US$4 to/from either destination*) or more comfortable air-conditioned Yutons/Stanbics (*US$6*) run solidly throughout the day out of Tantri Station, which lies at the northeast end of the town centre, on the junction of Sarbah and Tantri roads. More centrally, the Total filling station on the south side of the traffic circle at the junction of Market and Cardinal Appiah Turkso roads is the place to pick up comfortable air-conditioned Fords to/from Accra, which cost about the same as Stanbics.

Trotros to Takoradi (*around US$3*) leave regularly throughout the day from Siwdo (pronounced 'Sudu') Station, which lies at the northwest end of town, on Cardinal Appiah Turkso Boulevard, opposite the junction with Kotoku Road. Siwdo is also the place to pick trotros to Twifo Praso, which can drop you at the entrance gate for Kakum National Park. These usually leave every 45 minutes or so, and you'll need to pay the full US$1.50 fare to Twifo Praso even if you are dropping at Kakum. Vehicles to Takoradi and Twifo Praso can also be found at a separate, smaller station adjacent to Pedu Junction.

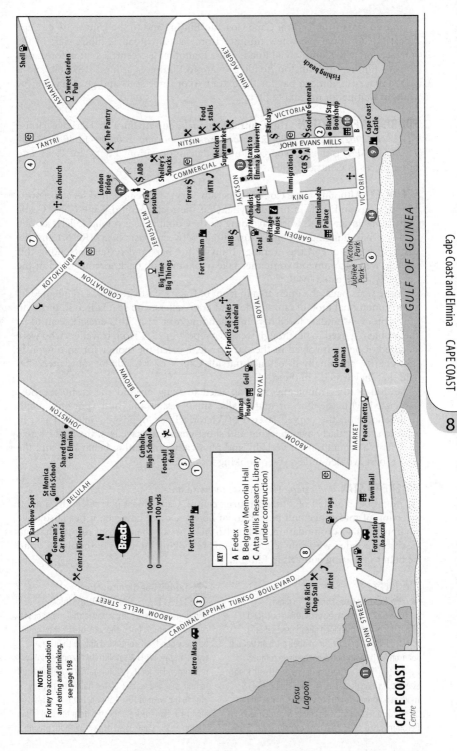

8

GULF OF GUINEA

CAPE COAST
Centre

NOTE
For key to accommodation
and eating and drinking,
see page 198

KEY
A Fedex
B Belgrave Memorial Hall
C Atta Mills Research Library
   (under construction)

Fosu
Lagoon

Bradt

N

0   100m
0   100 yds

Fishing beach

Cape Coast
Castle

Metro Mass

Shell

Sweet Garden
Pub

The Pantry

Zion church

London
Bridge

'Crab'
posuban

ADB

Shelley's
Snacks

Food
stalls

Melcam
Supermarket

Barclays

Victoria

Societe Generale

Black Star
Bookshop

NITSIN

COMMERCIAL

Forex

MTN

Immigration

GCB

JOHN EVANS MILLS

Shared taxis to
Elmina & University

JACKSON

Methodist
church

Heritage
House

Emintsimadze
Palace

KING

Total

NIB

Fort William

Big Time
Big Things

St Francis de Sales
Cathedral

ROYAL

Garden

Jubilee Victoria
Park   Park

Victoria

Global
Mamas

Kumasi
House

Goil

ROYAL

ABOOM

Market

Peace Ghetto

Town Hall

Catholic
High School

Football
field

Johnston

J P BROWN

BELULAH

Shared taxis
to Elmina

St Monica
Girls School

Rainbow Spot

Geoman's Car Rental

Central Kitchen

Fort Victoria

CARDINAL APPIAH TURKSO BOULEVARD

ABOOM WELLS STREET

Nice & Rich
Chop Stall

Airtel

Fraga

Total

Ford station
(to Accra)

Bonn Street

Total

KOTOKURUBA

CORONATION

JERUSALEM

ASHANTI

TANTRI

KING AGGREY

199

Shared taxis from central Cape Coast to Elmina and to the University of Cape Coast (UCC) leave every few minutes from Jackson Road, a block west of the intersection with Commercial Road. There is another less central station for shared taxis to Elmina on Johnston Road. The fare to Elmina is around US$0.60, and if you're in a rush you can pay for the extra two or three seats and go straight away without waiting for the taxi to fill up.

TOURIST INFORMATION The **Central Regional Tourist Office** in Heritage House (⋏ *03321 32062;* m *0277 412305;* e *gtbcentral@gmail.com;* ⊕ *08.00–12.30 & 13.30–17.00 Mon–Fri*) is the best source of up-to-date information about Cape Coast and other places in Central Region.

SECURITY Although Cape Coast is generally very safe, we have had several reports of muggings and theft in broad daylight on the rocks behind Cape Coast Castle (which are in any case worth avoiding as they double as a public toilet), as well as nocturnal muggings along Victoria Road between Oasis Beach Resort and the castle. If you're out in the evening at any of the bars and restaurants along this stretch, we'd recommend you either take a taxi or walk back to your hotel in the company of a trusted local.

Some years back, the open area in front of Cape Coast Castle was frequented by a confrontational mob of faux-guides and craft-sellers who specialised in trying to guilt-trip or intimidate foreigners into handing over cash. This doesn't seem to be the problem it used to be, though we had a report in 2011 from travellers who were 'accused of being involved in the slave trade, hassled for money for an obviously fake charity, and finally threatened outside Cape Coast Castle by some men who said that they would kill them'.

Several of the troublemakers who used to hang around the castle are now associated with the line of craft stalls, small restaurants and spurious 'youth foundations' on the curved stretch of Victoria Road opposite Victoria Park. In addition to regularly overcharging and short-changing travellers, the stall owners here have a reputation for verbally and physically threatening behaviour, and the area is best avoided unless you're looking for trouble.

WHERE TO STAY *Map, page 196, unless otherwise stated*
As might be expected of a major tourist centre, Cape Coast is serviced by a good selection of mid-range and budget town hotels. Oddly, however, it has absolutely no upmarket accommodation, and it also lacks for any beachfront resorts that can be recommended with conviction – if you are looking for either of the above, you'd be better off basing yourself in Elmina.

Moderate

⚹ 🏠 Kokodo Guesthouse (5 rooms)
m 0243 529191. We've heard nothing but good about this owner-managed guesthouse set on a forested hilltop opposite the football pitch on DeGraft Johnson Av, halfway between the town centre & bypass. Spacious & attractive rooms come with king-size bed, writing desk, fan, AC, satellite TV, Wi-Fi & modern bathrooms with hot water, & it also houses an excellent restaurant with indoor & garden seating. Recommended. *US$52 B&B self-contained dbl.* **$$$**

🏠 Fairhill Guesthouse (15 rooms)
⋏ 03321 33322; m 0244 148015; e info@ fairhillguesthouses.com; www.fairhillguesthouses. com. This homely but rather out-of-the-way hotel has very good self-contained dbls with AC, hot water, fridge, Wi-Fi & satellite TV, & comes highly recommended for its helpful staff. It is a bit difficult to find, perched on an isolated hill in the marshy area to the west of Fosu Lagoon, but is clearly along a 1.4km track signposted from the Goil filling station on the Cape Coast bypass. Without private

transport, you're advised to get a taxi to drop you off with your luggage, though once you know the way, it's only 10mins' walk from Cardinal Appiah Turkso Boulevard, where you can pick up shared taxis to the town centre. *US$23 self-contained dbl; US$31–39 B&B exec dbl.* **$$**

🏠 **Cape Coast Hotel** (30 rooms) ✆03321 32919; m 0208 169375; e capecoasthotel@gmail. com. Getting the negatives out of the way first, this multi-storey hotel overlooking Cape Coast bypass, opposite the junction with Cardinal Appiah Turkso Boulevard, has a location that could kindly be called indifferent, as well as a total deficit of character. If you can get past that, it is a pleasant enough set-up & the large dbls with AC, fridge, satellite TV, balcony & hot bath are very good value for money. There is an adequate restaurant & good outside bar, & you can easily pick up a shared or charter taxi into town at the junction opposite. *US$48 self-contained dbl; US$53 suite.* **$$$**

🏠 **Samrit Hotel** (36 rooms) ✆03321 33129; m 0266 675316; e info@samrithotelgh.com; www.samrithotelgh.com. Set just off of the Kakum Rd, about 700m north of Pedu Junction, this characterless new business hotel looks a lot fancier outside than it is inside, but the tiled rooms are nonetheless clean & come with AC, fridge, flatscreen TV & Wi-Fi. More unusually for Cape Coast, there's a swimming pool. *US$35/48/58 dbl/exec/suite.* **$$$–$$**

🏠 **Sanaa Lodge** (29 rooms) ✆03321 32788; m 0244 508841; e info@sanaalodge.com; www.sanaalodge.com. Once the priciest lodge in Cape Coast, the 3-star Sanaa has definitely seen better days, despite a few attempts at renovation, & the poor service & maintenance come in for regular criticism. That said, facilities include a large (half-full) swimming pool, hairdressing salon, gift shop, conference centre, restaurant & cocktail bar. It lies a couple of kilometres west of the bridge across the Fosu Lagoon, on a rise near the Ministry of Health, & rooms high enough to see over the utilitarian block in front have an attractive view over the beach in the distance. The rooms feel thoroughly dated, but they all come with AC, hot water, satellite TV, fridge & balcony. *US$32/41 sgl/dbl; US$67 family room.* **$$$–$$**

Budget

✳ 🏠 **Ewurafio Guesthouse** (7 rooms) ✆03321 35740; m 0245 645535; e infoewurafioltd@gmail.com. Hidden away at the end of a tangle of backroads west of Fosu Lagoon, this enjoyably retro-feeling family-run hilltop inn is well signposted about 1.2km off of Cardinal Appiah Turkso Boulevard & offers immaculately clean en-suite rooms with AC, hot water, fridge, satellite TV & Wi-Fi, some of which also come with private balconies. The uninterrupted views over the lagoon here might be the best in town, & there's a terrace bar & unfurnished roof terrace where you're free to soak it all in. Seafood & other meals are available at request, & the only real drawback here is that it's a bit of a hike if you don't have private transport. *US$19/26 B&B dbl/exec.* **$$**

🏠 **Mighty Victory Hotel** [map, page 199] (22 rooms) ✆03321 30135/42; m 0208 235387; e info@ mightyvictoryhotel.com; www. mightyvictoryhotel.com. Regularly praised by readers as one of the best budget deals in town, this owner-managed hotel has a friendly atmosphere, & an inexpensive restaurant serves meals in the US$4–6 range. It's an easy walk to the centre of town. The clean & airy rooms all come with crisp white sheets, hot water, TV & a powerful fan. *US$15/17/20 self-contained dbl/twin/trpl with fan; US$23 dbl with AC.* **$$**

🏠 **C-Lotte's Hotel** [map, page 199] (15 rooms) m 0265 599726; e maananwilson@ yahoo.co.uk. Located on Aquarium Junction on the corner of Cardinal Appiah Turkso Boulevard, this family-run hotel with its brightly decorated façade is a safe, albeit unexciting, budget bet. The neatly furnished rooms with satellite TV are spotlessly clean & there's a good ground-floor restaurant. Pick-ups from central bus stations can be arranged. *US$21/26 self-contained twin or dbl with fan/AC.* **$$**

🏠 **Sarah-Lotte Guesthouse** (7 rooms) m 0544 359070/0574 362051/0541 267710. This friendly, family-run out-of-town lodge lies in Ola Estate, opposite the beach & only 500m from the intersection with Cape Coast bypass. It seems that meals are no longer available, but you could eat a short walk away at Da Breeze or in town – all shared taxis & *trotros* between Cape Coast & Elmina run right past. *US$13 dbl with shared bath & fan; US$16/19 self-contained dbl with TV, fridge, & fan/AC.* **$$–$**

🏠 **Nana Bema Hotel** (16 rooms) ✆03321 32616; m 0577 709696/0508 707091; e bemahotel@yahoo.com. This bland concrete block located on the hill off Sarbah Road could not be described as beautiful, but with fantastic 360° views of the city it won't be the hotel you're looking at. There's an on-site terrace restaurant, clean & comfortable self-contained rooms, & a new block under construction that will soon see the hotel double in size. *US$25 self-contained dbl with AC.* **$$**

🏠 **Prospect Lodge** [map, page 199] (15 rooms) 📞03321 31506; m 0207 46746. Perched on top of Prospect Hill, this well-priced hotel, just off Coronation Road past Cornel internet café, is a deservedly popular central option. There's a good affordable restaurant & a terrace bar with live music most w/ends, both ideal for drinking in the view. *US$20 B&B self-contained dbl with AC, Wi-Fi, satellite TV.* **$$**

🏠 **Fespa Hotel** (40 rooms) 📞03321 35886; m 0208 114950; e fespahotel@yahoo.com; 🟦 fb.me/fespahotel. This multi-storey on Cardinal Appiah Turkso Boulevard seems decent enough, but it's quite a way from the town centre, the rooms are not noticeably superior to most other options in this range, & the rates are noticeably higher. *US$23 self-contained dbl with fan; US$29–40 with king-size bed & AC.* **$$**

🏠 **Oasis Beach Resort** [map, page 199] (10 rooms, 3 dorms) m 0244 089535/0243 022594/0245 128322; e info@oasisbeach-ghana.com; www.oasisbeach-ghana.com. The only beachfront option in Cape Coast doesn't quite live up to its ample potential. It could scarcely be more central, situated as it is alongside Victoria Park, about 200m west of the castle. The rustic rooms (some of which now have AC) seem pleasant enough, it has a good restaurant & bar with a varied menu, & there were renovations afoot in 2016. Unfortunately, however, we've had several complaints from readers, ranging from theft from the rooms, to aggro from the Rastas who often hang out there at night, to rowdy music making it difficult to sleep at w/ends. *US$20 dbl using shared bath; US$31/40 self-contained dbl with fan/AC; US$27 family room sleeping 4 & using shared bath; US$5pp in 10- or 16-bed dorm.* **$$–$**

Shoestring

🏠 **Baobab Guesthouse** [map, page 199] (5 rooms) m 0540 436130; e baobab.house@yahoo.com; www.baobab-children-foundation.de. The newish accommodation on the 2nd floor of the couldn't-be-more-central Baobab House is proving to be as popular with readers as the more established ground-floor restaurant. The simple but brightly decorated 2-, 3- & 4-bed rooms come with fans & free Wi-Fi, & use a shared bath. *US$11/13/16/18 sgl/dbl/trpl/quad.* **$$–$**

🏠 **Sammo Guesthouse** [map, page 199] (43 rooms) 📞03321 33242. A long-serving shoestring favourite, this pink 3-storey building, which lies conveniently close to the Ford Station for Accra, & only 10mins' walk west of Cape Coast Castle, receives mixed but mostly positive reviews. Although the rooms are a bit run down & cramped, they are also fantastic value. The rooftop bar is a pleasant spot for a drink & meal, & a good place to meet other travellers. *US$6/7 sgl/dbl with fan & shared bath; US$8 self-contained dbl; US$10–13 larger dbl with TV.* **$$–$**

🏠 **Savoy Hotel** (20 rooms) 📞03321 32805; m 0264 515223/0206 690549; e savoyhotel@yahoo.com. Built in 1971 in something approaching Art Deco style, & now sporting a bright red & yellow exterior, this time-warped hotel on Ashanti Road is a good compromise between comfort & cost, as well as being very convenient for the town centre & Tantri trotro station. The rooms are neither the cleanest nor the most modern, but they are more than adequate at the price. *US$15/24 self-contained dbl with fan/AC.* **$$**

🏠 **Haizel Guesthouse** [map, page 199] (9 rooms) m 0248 470646. With its central location just south of Tantri Station, this unfussy but clean guesthouse is a decent enough bet, though we have had reports of theft from a locked room. *US$8 sgl with shared bath & fan; US$11/13 self-contained dbl/twin with fan.* **$**

🏠 **Africa Best Resthouse** [map, page 199] (6 rooms) m 0244 932691. Situated next to the Mighty Victory Hotel, this clean little place is inexpensive & good value, but often full, so call first. *US$7 dbl with shared bath; US$10 self-contained dbl.* **$**

✕ WHERE TO EAT AND DRINK *Map, page 199, unless otherwise stated*

Although we highlight only those worth a special mention below, most of the hotels listed above have adequate restaurants. For street food, head to Ntsin Road, which positively buzzes at night, exuding the aura of sociability and community typical of Cape Coast. During the day, you can normally buy fresh coconuts for drinking from a vendor who stands in front of the Total filling station on Jackson Street, while pineapples and other fruits are sold by vendors along Ntsin Street near the castle.

Moderate

✳ ✖ **Kokodo Restaurant** [map, page 196] Attached to Kokodo Guesthouse; ⊕ 07.00–23.00. This hilltop restaurant, widely rated as the best in Cape Coast, has an attractive interior, shaded garden seating, & a varied menu of salads & sandwiches (*US$5–8*) as well as excellent seafood, steak & other continental dishes (*US$8–12*). **$$$–$$**

✖ **Castle Restaurant** m 0249 397964/406262; ⊕ 08.00–22.00 daily. This popular seafront restaurant, with its breezy location overlooking the waves crashing against Cape Coast Castle, is an excellent spot for a drink, & the extensive Ghanaian & continental menu is reasonably priced, with most dishes in the US$6–8 range (slightly more for fish). The food & service both get mixed reviews, but even on a bad day, the location compensates. **$$**

Budget

✳ ✖ **Baobab Moringa Restaurant** Ground floor of Baobab Guesthouse; ⊕ 07.00–19.00 daily. Universally praised by readers, this bright vegetarian snack & juice bar 100m inland of the castle is perfect for an inexpensive lunch, dinner or mid-morning/afternoon pick-me-up. The menu includes smoothies, organic juices, vegetable pies, & soya, tofu & wheat kebabs plus a range of fresh salads, & there is a pleasant outdoor seating with free Wi-Fi. Set up by Baobab Children Foundation, it also has a health-food shelf selling packaged goods such as tofu, powdered soy milk, brown sugar, honey & molasses. Most mains under US$5. **$**

✖ **Orange Beach Bar & Restaurant** m 0576 605250/0272 259034; ▪ fb.me/ orangebeachbarghana; ⊕ 07.30–01.00 daily. Opened in Sep 2015 & barely 200m from the castle, this bright & breezy new beach bar makes an excellent alternative to the rather dark Castle Restaurant. There's a good menu of breakfasts, seafood grills & pasta for US$4–6, along with fresh juices & smoothies, plus live drumming, dancing, & bonfires on Fri & Sat nights. **$$–$**

✖ **Hayford Lounge & Bar** m 0545 056807; e hayfordlounge@hotmail.com; ⊕ 10.00–22.00 Mon–Sat & 15.00–midnight Sun. Situated on Commercial Rd opposite the Melcom Supermarket, this modern & spacious Ghanaian-German 1st-floor restaurant/bar seems to have lost most of its Teutonic character after the recent death of the German co-proprietor, but it's still recommended for the mini-pizzas, cheeseburgers & salads, which cost around US$5. It's a comfortable, open space & the assortment of bottled drinks is very good, as is the service. **$**

✖ **Coast2Coast** m 0248 155459; ⊕ 08.00–20.00 daily. Conveniently located right opposite Cape Coast Castle, this brightly coloured new pavement restaurant serves good coffee & fruit juices, cocktails & beer, sandwiches & pancakes in the US$3–5 bracket, & seafood & other mains for US$8–12. It's a great spot to relax after a visit to the castle, but unfortunately the food doesn't quite match the ambience. **$$–$**

BARS AND NIGHTLIFE *Map, page 199, unless otherwise stated*

☆ **Ali Baba Seascape Nightclub** Situated at Oasis Beach Resort, this is a popular hangout for volunteers & locals alike, & it plays a varied selection of reggae, highlife & contemporary R&B, as well as hosting occasional live music. The beach bar also has a good music system & extensive cocktail menu, making it an excellent place to watch the sunset over a drink, & reasonable meals are available until 23.00.

☆ **Hacienda Plaza** This central nightspot next to the Crab Shrine & London Bridge can be relied upon for cold drinks & blaring reggae or highlife. It has a

bit of a reputation for attracting light-fingered types, so don't carry any unnecessary valuables.

♀ **Goil Spot** [map, page 196] A few inexpensive bars & restaurants are clustered at the Goil filling station on the Cape Coast bypass about 100m west of the junction with Cardinal Appiah Turkso Blvd. It's open daily but best on Fri, when there is usually live music.

♀ **Solace Spot** m 0245 099909; ⊕ 09.00–22.30 daily. This popular outdoor drinking spot at the turnoff for the Ewurafio & Fairhill guesthouses has draft beer & several different booths serving up brochettes, banku & tilapia, & the other usual suspects.

Ŷ Da Breeze m 0246 480234/0244 026434; ⊕ 10.00–late Tue–Sun. Though it's slightly out of town at the junction of the Cape Coast Bypass & Bonn St, the brilliant seaside location here is more than worth the trip. The main bar sits under a large palapa hut overlooking the water, & there are also

tables scattered under the palms running down to the water. The usual Ghanaian meals are served & DJs come to play at the w/end.

Ŷ Community Gardens m 0243 333572; ⊕ 07.00–midnight daily. Though the bar itself isn't much to talk about, the grassy grounds abutting the lagoon are, & the shady gazebos make for a good spot to sink a few beers.

SHOPPING

Bookshops The excellent and well-stocked **Black Star Bookshop** (m *0244 928737*; ⊕ *08.00–18.00 Mon–Sat*) on the south end of Commercial Street stocks an extensive range of mostly secondhand novels, which can be bought for around US$3–5 or exchanged for a nominal fee.

Crafts and clothes In the same building as Baobab Moringa Restaurant, the **Baobab Craft and Fashion Shop** sells an interesting selection of batiks, paintings, tie-dye clothing, kente cloth, recycled bags, jewellery, postcards, and vegetarian and other health products. The dressmaker here can turn around customised clothes in 24 hours. Most products are made by the Baobab School and, as with the restaurant and guesthouse, all proceeds go towards supporting it.

There are two main clusters of **craft stalls**, and though both tend to be overpriced compared with elsewhere in Ghana, the one between Cape Coast Castle and the Castle Restaurant has a better reputation than the cluster about 200m further west, opposite Victoria Park. Plenty of crafts can also be bought at the vast and sprawling **Kotokuraba Market**, which is enclosed by a triangle of roads to the northeast from Kotokuraba Road, but was undergoing a major facelift – making it even more chaotic than normal – in mid 2016.

OTHER PRACTICALITIES

Car rental Based on Aboom Wells Road, **Geoman's Car Rental** (m *0208 159453*; e *geomans2@gmail.com* or *geomens117@hotmail.com*) offers chauffeur-driven vehicles for rent at a cost of around US$30 per day for a saloon car or US$70 per day for a 4x4, excluding petrol and driver's expenses. Self-drive rental is available, but at a high premium due to the insurance costs. The company can also organise day trips to Kakum National Park as well as transfers to Takoradi, Busua, Accra and other towns and cities around Ghana. Reader feedback has been consistently positive, although it's worth agreeing an exact itinerary in advance, as well as who will be paying for the driver's lunch.

Foreign exchange All the major banks are represented in the town centre, and there are ATMs where you can draw local currency with a Visa card outside most of them (MasterCard should be accepted at GCB). There is also an ATM outside the Ghana Commercial Bank in the university campus of the Cape Coast bypass. There are a few forex bureaux dotted around town, mostly on Commercial Road.

Internet There are several internet cafés in Cape Coast. Among the most useful are Cedecom on Commercial Road, just north of Baobab House, Ocean View a bit further north on Commercial Road, Odas near the junction of Kotokuraba and Coronation roads, and Vodafone on the Cape Coast bypass opposite the Goil filling station. There's free Wi-Fi at the Baobab Moringa Restaurant on Commercial Road.

Tour operators Though they're based in Elmina, the dependable Ghana Ecotours now offers informative guided walking tours of Cape Coast in addition to their tours of Elmina. See page 220 for details.

WHAT TO SEE AND DO

Cape Coast Castle (03321 32701; *www.capecoastcastlemuseum.com*; 09.00–16.30 daily; entrance US$10.50 non-Ghanaians inc an emphatically recommended 45min tour) This World Heritage Site is reputed to have been one of the largest slave-holding sites in the world during the colonial era, where Ghanaians – many of them traded to the British by the Ashanti in return for alcohol and guns – were stored before being crammed into returning merchant ships and deported to a life of captive labour. Sited on the edge of town overlooking a rocky stretch of coast with crashing waves, this whitewashed building is far more attractive than you feel a place with its history ought to be. But once below ground, in the claustrophobic dungeons that saw tens of thousands of Ghanaians incarcerated during the peak of that barbaric era, it is a grim and sobering place indeed.

Once inside, the museum houses an absorbing sequence of displays charting the origin and mechanisms of the slave trade, the scale of the resultant diaspora, and its aftermath in the hands of inspirational black leaders such as Marcus Garvey and Martin Luther King. But, ultimately, it is the time you spend in the slave dungeons that cuts most closely, their stone walls still marked by the desperate scratching of those imprisoned within them. There are three dungeons in total, all grimly efficient in design. The oldest was built before 1790 on the southeastern bastion, and was followed with the male dungeon below Dalzel's Tower in 1792. The female dungeon is on the eastern wall, near the exit to the sea that bore the grim nickname 'Door of No Return'. A couple of years ago, a symbolic invitation was issued to two descendants of slaves that saw them return through the Door of No Return, thus effectively breaking the chain. There is a sign on the other side, now, that says 'Door of Return'.

The castle itself – a squat, solid fortress of ramps, stairs and parapets – is thought to stand on the site of the Swedish Fort Carolusborg, built from wood in 1653 and fortified with stone the following year (note that there is little foundation for the claim that the original Portuguese lodge at Cape Coast stood on this site). After Cape Coast was captured by Britain in 1665, the fort was expanded to be comparable in size and strength to the nearby Dutch fort at Elmina, and in the 1680s the slave dungeons were constructed in such a way that they were accessible only from the seaward side of the fort. A second phase of expansion, prompted in part by the notorious leakiness of the roof, took place roughly between 1760 and 1795. By the end of this period, the castle had assumed its modern, loosely pentagonal shape, and practically no traces of the original Swedish fort remained.

Those buried in the courtyard of the castle include the Reverend Philip Kwakwe (1741–1816), a native of Cape Coast who became the first Anglican priest of African origin. Also buried here are the novelist Letitia Elizabeth Landon (1802–38) and her husband George MacLean (1801–47), Governor of Cape Coast from 1830 until 1843 and Judicial Assessor of the town from 1843 until his death.

Around the old town Several of the hills in Cape Coast have been fortified at some point in their history. Only two such out-forts now survive, Victoria and William, both part of a chain of lookout posts that were used for signalling purposes, and both of which are still clearly visible from the governor's rooms at the castle. **Fort Victoria**, to the northwest of the castle, was constructed in 1837 on the site of a ruined fort built in 1712 and formerly known as 'Phipp's Tower'.

On Dawson's Hill, **Fort William** is now a lighthouse and has been since 1855, but it was constructed over the older Smith's Tower, built of mud and stone in 1820. Both forts are in good condition and welcome visitors.

Otherwise, the centre of Cape Coast may lack individual landmarks, but it is certainly well endowed with Victorian-era buildings, especially along Coronation and Jackson streets and Beulah Lane – and there is even a bust of Queen Victoria standing in her namesake park to prove it. Many of these old buildings are solidly constructed brick homes with an enclosed upper-floor balcony. The area around Dawson's Hill is one of the best-preserved parts of the old town, with Coronation Street in particular boasting several two- and three-storey buildings architecturally characteristic of Cape Coast in the mid to late 19th century. Particularly notable is the now derelict building near the junction with Coronation Street, built as a hotel in the 1880s and later a convent.

Possibly the oldest unfortified building in Cape Coast is the former **Government House**, opposite the Methodist church off Jackson Street. It is known that this building was leased to the government by one Caroline Jackson in 1850, but it is unclear how much older it actually is – it seems reasonable to assume it was built before or during the period 1817–22 (when John Hope-Smith was governor), and it may conceivably have been built in the late 18th century. Renamed **Heritage House**, the three-storey Government House has since been restored and now houses the tourist information office.

Near to this, on Royal Lane, the former **Convent of St Mary** is perhaps the best-preserved building of its kind in Cape Coast. Originally built by an Ashanti prince c1850, this building was bought by a community of nuns in 1891 and served as a convent until 1975, since when it has been only intermittently occupied.

There are a few **posuban** shrines in Cape Coast, but none is very impressive. At the centre of the traffic circle on the junction of Ashanti and Coronation roads there is a small posuban-like sculpture of a **crab**. Although comparatively recently placed there, this statue has a great significance, as the crab is the official mascot of Cape Coast (which used to be known as Kotokuraba ('Crab Village') because of the good crab meat available). Near the above junction, **London Bridge** is a rather odd and unimposing little bridge dating to the late 19th century and appropriately garnished with painted Union flags and the like – it's worth crossing if only for amusement's sake.

Gramophone Records Museum and Research Centre

Established in 1994 as a non-profit organisation by the late musicologist Kwame Sarpong, this comprises a uniquely vast collection of recordings made solely in Ghana by almost 750 Ghanaian artists between the first decade of the 20th century and the 1970s. The core collection consists of 19,000 78rpm shellac discs, but there are also more than around 3,000 old vinyl recordings. These were released on various international labels such as Decca, His Master's Voice and Zonophone. The core of this collection is the Ghanaian Highlife and Traditional Music Collection, and it includes the first ever recorded Ghanaian highlife music, by Jacob Sam and his Kumasi Trio, released on London's Zonophone Record Label in 1928.

With the aid of a grant from Montreal's Daniel Langlois Foundation for Art, Science and Technology (*www.fondation-langlois.org*) and the French Embassy in Ghana, the museum digitalised some 1,000 key recordings in 2004, and a further grant from the French Embassy in Accra has since made it possible to digitalise a further 500, the majority of which seldom appear in record shops and catalogues. Copies of these digitalised materials are lodged at the United States Library of

Congress and the National Library and Archives of Canada, and are available to researchers, and some 400 songs are now available on the Langlois Foundation's website for listening pleasure as well as research. It is eventually hoped that these recordings will form the basis of a collection for a future Highlife Music Museum to be opened in Cape Coast, though the death of founder Kwame Sarpong in July 2015 could throw the future of this project into jeopardy.

As things stand, we were told that activities at the centre were suspended following Mr Sarpong's death, and it's unclear how and when they might restart. If things do get going again, the research centre is located in the Central Regional Centre for National Culture Buildings in Cape Coast (opposite the Parks and Gardens Department of the University of Cape Coast on the main bypass highway). This facility is for the ongoing digitalising project, and prior to its suspension, visitors could see the processes as well as view the collections from 10.00 to 15.00 Monday, Wednesday and Friday. A scheduled second facility at New Abrobiano (nearly 3km from Komenda town on the main road from Komenda College) for those who wish to listen as well as research has yet to open. For further information, contact Dr Carmelle Bégin (m 0269 162462; e carmelle.begin@gmail.com).

Global Mamas Cultural Workshops (m 0544 323833/0244 530467; e workshops@globalmamas.org; www.globalmamas.org; costs range from US$17–25pp depending on group size) Formerly known as Women in Progress, this is an NGO developed by a former Peace Corps volunteer working with local women to improve their handicrafts for export and local sale. It has developed several different half- to full-day workshops – concentrating on batik-making, Ghanaian cuisine, dancing/drumming (run by the only woman master drummer in Ghana) and hair-wrapping. Workshops last for around 3 hours and should be organised at least two days in advance.

Assin Manso (⊕ 08.00–17.00 Mon–Sat; small entrance fee) This small town, which lies about an hour from Cape Coast along the Kumasi road, was formerly an important stop along the slave trade routes of the 18th and 19th centuries. It is located on the banks of the Ndonkor Nsuo ('Slave River'), where slaves were washed and checked for fitness before being taken to the coast for shipment out of Africa. As a symbolic gesture, the bodies of two slaves – Samuel Carson from the USA and a woman known as Crystal from Jamaica – were flown to Ghana in July 1998 to be reburied here. Visitors are welcome to see the graves along with the newly built Memorial Wall of Return, also known as the Pillars of Recognition, on which it's possible to have your name inscribed for a donation. The visitor centre, built in 2004 by the Ministry of Tourism, houses an interpretive display that builds on the stories told at Cape Coast Castle, as well as a small curio shop selling batik and other garments made by a local women's sewing co-op. No accommodation is available at the site, but there is a small guesthouse in Andoe, about 5 minutes' drive from Assin Manso. Regular trotros in this direction leave from Cape Coast's Tantri Station, and they will drop you outside the large building that serves as the seat of the traditional council, where it would be courteous to pay your respects before you look around.

KAKUM NATIONAL PARK

Extending over an area of 375km² inland of Cape Coast, Kakum National Park protects the core of Ghana's largest remaining tract of rainforest, parts of which also

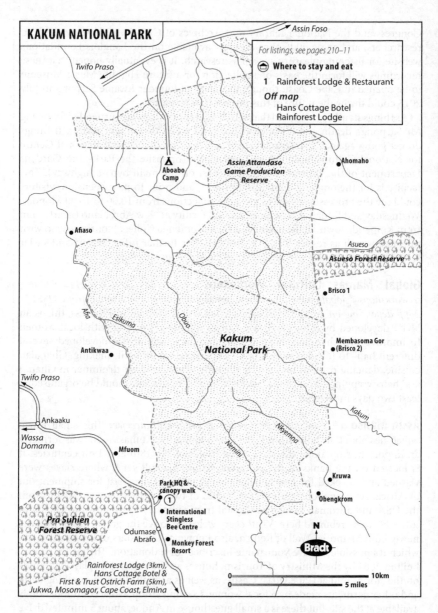

For listings, see pages 210–11

KAKUM NATIONAL PARK

Twifo Praso

Assin Foso

For listings, see pages 210–11

Where to stay and eat

1 Rainforest Lodge & Restaurant

Off map
  Hans Cottage Botel
  Rainforest Lodge

Aboabo Camp

Assin Attandaso Game Production Reserve

Ahomaho

Afiaso

Asueso

Asueso Forest Reserve

Brisco 1

Ano

Esikuma

Obuo

Antikwaa

Kakum National Park

Membasoma Gor (Brisco 2)

Twifo Praso

Ankaaku

Kakum

Wassa Domama

Mfuom

Nkyemna

Nemini

Kruwa

Park HQ & canopy walk

Obengkrom

International Stingless Bee Centre

Pra Suhien Forest Reserve

Odumase Abrafo

Monkey Forest Resort

N

Bradt

Rainforest Lodge (3km),
Hans Cottage Botel &
First & Trust Ostrich Farm (5km),
Jukwa, Mosomagor, Cape Coast, Elmina

0   10km
0   5 miles

lie within the contiguous Assin Attandaso Game Production Area and Pra Suhien Forest Reserve. In addition to harbouring an immense diversity of plants and animals, Kakum is an important watershed, named after one of several rivers that rise within its boundaries and collectively provide water to 130 towns and villages, including Cape Coast. One of the most popular and accessible wildlife destinations in Ghana, the national park is less than an hour's drive north of Cape Coast, whether you travel in a private vehicle or trotro. The main attraction for most visitors is a much-publicised canopy walkway that rises up to 40m above the forest floor, but birding walks and a limited range of other activities are also offered, albeit sometimes rather reluctantly.

FAUNA AND FLORA Originally set aside as a forest reserve in 1931, Kakum was gazetted as a national park in 1992, partly at the initiative of local communities. The predominant vegetation type is moist semi-deciduous close canopy rainforest, which is characterised by high rainfall figures (peaking between May and December) and an average humidity level of 90%. Parts of the park are ecologically compromised as a result of the extensive logging that took place in the 1970s and 1980s, but most of the forest remains in pristine condition, and logging has been outlawed within its boundaries since the national park was proclaimed.

The diversity of Kakum's flora is such that the number of plant species comfortably exceeds 200 per hectare in some areas. This vegetation is divided into five broad vertical layers. The sparsely vegetated floor of the forest interior is dominated by herbaceous plants, above which a layer of shrubs reaches up to about 4m. The upper three layers together form the canopy: the lowest consists of spreading trees reaching a height of around 18m, above which lies the main closed canopy of larger trees, typically around 40m high, and then finally there are the emergent trees, many of them very old, reaching a height of up to 65–70m.

The contiguous 600km² forest block centred on Kakum is home to around 650 species of butterfly, more than the whole of Europe, and it is the type locality of the genus *Kakumia* and two species, *Diopetes kakumi* and *Hypolycaena kakumi*. It also harbours around 100 different mammal species, including the country's densest population of forest elephant, estimated at around 250 individuals, as well as giant forest hog, six types of duiker, bushbuck, bongo, various flying squirrels, leopard, spot-nosed monkey, Diana monkey, mona monkey, and black-and-white and olive colobus. None of these mammals is likely to be seen by day visitors, but it is possible to arrange overnight camping trips to Antikwaa Camp, where elephants are encountered with some frequency.

Kakum supports an exceptional variety of forest-associated birds. The total bird checklist runs to around 320 species, around 50 of which await confirmation. This list includes at least eight species of global conservation concern, ie: white-breasted guineafowl, brown-cheeked hornbill, yellow-casqued hornbill, yellow-footed honeyguide, green-tailed bristlebill, yellow-throated olive greenbul, rufous-winged illadopsis and copper-tailed glossy starling. Other alluring Kakum residents include the secretive white-crested tiger heron, great blue turaco, Verreaux's turaco, rosy bee-eater, rufous-sided broadbill, and an additional seven forest hornbill species. Compared with somewhere like Mole National Park, however, the birding at Kakum is challenging, and visitors hoping to see a reasonable selection of forest birds would need to spend a couple of days in the area and do some early-morning guided walks – the Aboabo section is particularly recommended.

For the closest thing to a full checklist of the park's large mammals, birds and reptiles, together with detailed notes and line drawings of the more common and interesting species, try to get hold of Roell's, Helsen's and Nicolet's out-of-print *Field Guide to the Kakum National Park* – though do note that the bird checklist in this 124-page paperback is incomplete and includes several erroneous species.

TIMES AND FEES All activities must be arranged through the visitor centre (m *0243 413742/0501 291683;* e *kakumwd@yahoo.com* or *apassnaba@gmail.com* ☺ *06.00–16.00 daily*), which lies about 300m past the main entrance gate. The best time to be there is earlyish in the day, which is when wildlife is most active and other tourists are least so. Should you want to take a guided walk before 06.00, arrange it the day before. It is emphatically worth avoiding the park on weekends and public holidays, as it tends to be overrun with school and other coach groups.

A one-off entrance fee of US$0.50 per person is levied at the entrance gate. This gains you access to the museum and restaurants, but all activities are charged separately. The fee for the canopy walkway is US$14 per person for non-Ghanians (US$8 for students). Guided walks into the rainforest are charged at US$11 per person for the first hour (or US$7 for students) and US$2.50 per additional hour, while walks into the swampy area bordering the forest cost US$8 for the first hour (or US$5 for students) and US$2.50 per additional hour. Unguided walks beyond the short stretch of road connecting the entrance gate to the visitor centre are forbidden.

GETTING THERE AND AWAY The entrance gate and headquarters to Kakum National Park are clearly signposted on the east side of the (impressively potholed) Twifo Praso road at Odumase Abrafo, a tiny village situated roughly 33km north of Cape Coast. Using public transport from Cape Coast, your best bet is to pick up a trotro to Twifo Praso from Siwdo Station and ask to be dropped at Kakum. These leave when full, usually every 30–45 minutes, from around 06.30 to 17.00, so with an early start, you can be at the headquarters shortly after it opens. Note that you will be expected to pay the full fare to Praso (US$1.50). Another option is to charter a taxi, which should cost around US$20, depending on how long you want it to wait.

WHERE TO STAY AND EAT *Map, page 208*
Although most people visit Kakum as a day trip out of Cape Coast or Elmina, there are a few decent accommodation options close to the park for those who prefer to semi-immerse themselves in the Kakum experience. Confusingly, this shortlist includes two different places that bear the name Rainforest Lodge, one a budget government resthouse next to the visitor centre, the other a relatively upmarket private hotel back along the road to Cape Coast. Another good option is the mid-price Hans Cottage Botel, which actually lies closer to Cape Coast than Kakum, but still has much to offer wildlife enthusiasts. Camping at several sites in the park is also possible for self-sufficient travellers, the easiest of access being the **Afrafranto Campsite** (*US$11pp*) some 200m from the visitor centre in a section of previously logged forest on the park boundary. Further within the park and accessible by guided walk with a ranger, the **Hilltop Campsite** (*US$13pp*) and **Treehouse** (*US$14pp*) are both accessible to travellers with their own camping equipment. There are covered platforms & toilet facilities at each site, & there's theoretically a very limited number of mattresses & tents that can be hired, but this service may not be entirely reliable.

Moderate

🏠 **Rainforest Lodge** (17 rooms) ⏎03321 92499; m 0241 323948; e info@ rainforestlodgegh.com or rainforestlodge1@gmail. com; www.rainforestlodgegh.com. Set in grassy gardens without any forest in sight, this pleasant, modern but somewhat nondescript new hotel makes a useful base for those planning to spend a few days in Kakum, since it lies only 12km south of the park entrance, alongside the Cape Coast road. The spacious & attractively furnished rooms are the equal of anything in Cape Coast, & a cheerful restaurant with Wi-Fi & a view over the garden serves a cosmopolitan selection of meat & seafood dishes, as well as pizzas, in the US$8–15 range.

US$26/52 self-contained sgl/dbl with AC, TV & hot water; US$104 family suite with 2 bedrooms & sitting room. **$$$–$$**

Budget

🏠 **Hans Cottage Botel** (57 rooms) ⏎03321 91456; m 0244 322522; e hcottage@yahoo.com; www.hansbotelghana.com.gh. Situated about 8km north of Cape Coast on the road to Kakum, Hans Cottage Botel (pages 212–13) is a popular lunchtime stop with tour groups thanks to its platformed restaurant overlooking a pool dense with crocodiles. It has a discrete accommodation block, catering to most requirements & budgets, with everything from camping space & a 14-bed dorm to suites & family units. Standards are quite high, though feedback is variable, & it is definitely to be avoided at w/ends, when it attracts coachloads of schoolchildren. In addition to good birdwatching, it has a swimming pool, tennis court & internet café. *US$4pp camping; US$5 dorm bed; US$17 B&B dbl with fan using shared bath; US$20/25 B&B self-contained sgl/dbl with fan; US$29/36 B&B self-contained sgl/dbl with AC & TV; US$52–118 suites & chalets.* **$$$$–$**

Shoestring

🏠 **Rainforest Lodge & Restaurant**
(10 rooms) m 0243 413742/0501 291683. Boasting an unbeatable location about 100m from the visitor centre, this small lodge offers simple but comfortable (& very reasonably priced) accommodation to those who want to stay in the park proper. Kakum Rainforest Café, in the same building as the visitor centre, serves a variety of local & continental dishes in the US$4–7 range, as well as cold drinks & beer, but note that it closes at 16.00, so overnight visitors will need to arrange food in advance. *US$9/12 self-contained sgl/dbl with fan.* **$**

WHAT TO SEE AND DO

Canopy walk The main tourist attraction at Kakum, constructed in 1995 with the support of USAID, is the much-publicised canopy walk, which consists of a 350m-long, 40m-high wood-and-rope walkway suspended between seven trees and broken up by several viewing platforms. Though a little gimmicky, it is undoubtedly good fun, and offers a rare opportunity to actually look into the forest canopy, a breathtaking experience in itself, though emphatically *not* for those with a poor head for heights.

Feedback tends to be polarised, with some people rating it as a highlight of their trip to Ghana, and others being more dismissive (typical comments include 'a regular tourist-mill' and 'more of a tourist gimmick than an interesting sight'). Given the popularity of the attraction, you'll get the most from the experience by being at the headquarters as early as possible, and should avoid weekends if at all possible. Timing aside, the extent to which you'll enjoy the canopy walk will probably depend greatly on whether the fee (US$14 per person for non-Ghanaians and US$8 for students) is small change or relatively expensive within the context of your travel budget.

Disappointingly, it is less rewarding than you might expect for wildlife, partly because the rangers tend to frogmarch visitors across as quickly as possible. However, Adam Riley notes that 'an extended session on the walkway offers the possibility of a plethora of canopy dwellers including crowned and Cassin's hawk-eagles, the fabulous great blue, guinea and yellow-billed turaco, the giant black-casqued and yellow-casqued wattled hornbills, and the diminutive dwarf hornbills, as well as various cuckoos, wood-hoopoes, barbets, honeyguides, bush-shrikes, and weavers'. These can be arranged starting at US$18.50 per person for the first hour and US$1.50 for every hour after that, with the price oddly increasing on subsequent days should you want to come back (days two and three are $32 and $47 per person for the first hour, respectively).

Before heading out on the walk, it's worth spending a few minutes looking around the informative natural-history displays in the information centre.

Other guided walks Although the canopy walk dominates thinking at the visitor centre, this richly diverse forest has so much more to offer than one novelty, and those with the time and an interest in natural history are encouraged to think about doing a more general walk. This costs US$8–11 per person for the first hour (though a discount is offered to students) plus US$2.50 per extra hour. The early morning is the best time to see birds, and you can arrange a specific time to meet the following morning on the previous afternoon. The best birding guide is Robert Akwesi Ntakor, an ex-park guide who can be contacted through Ashanti Tours (*www.ashantiafricantours. com*). Otherwise, park guide James Biney comes highly recommended. If your main interest is butterflies, leave later, because these tend to peak in activity in the mid to late morning. Mammals are very unlikely to be seen at any time.

The best area for birding is generally regarded to be the Aboabo sector, which borders the Assin Attandanso Game Production Area about 25km north of the park headquarters, and is only a realistic goal with private transport, ideally a sturdy 4x4. Here, an excellent variety of forest birds might be seen from the roadside, among them such unusual species as Congo serpent-eagle, long-tailed hawk, black bee-eater, black dwarf hornbill, African piculet, hairy-breasted barbet, yellow-billed barbet, blue cuckoo-shrike, black-capped apalis and Preuss's weaver. Adam Riley adds: 'lower-storey bird parties are composed of greenbuls, sunbirds, flycatchers and warblers, while ground-dwelling species include the elusive Nkulengu rail, the white-spotted flufftail, no fewer than three illadopses, and several specialised ant-attending species'.

International Stingless Bee Centre (m *0200 859619/0267 839779*; e *isbcstinglessbeesgh@gmail.com*; f *fb.me/InternationalStinglessBeeCenter*; ⊕ *08.30–16.00 Mon–Sat, 13.00–16.00 Sun; US$6pp, US$2.50 for students*) Set on 8ha of land just outside the park boundaries in Odumase Abrafo and well signposted 800m off of the main road, this rather oddball attraction makes for a surprisingly worthwhile visit. Primarily an apicultural research facility, the centre is home to six different species of stingless bee out of the 12 that are present in Ghana. The hives here have been carefully translocated from the surrounding bush, & an informative tour introduces visitors to the various species of bee and the various types of hive they build. You can also take a short walk through the forested grounds and bamboo grove, where many trees and plants are identified and labelled. Honey, propolis, pollen, & other bee-made health products are on sale.

Monkey Forest Resort (m *0244 118313*; e *rubberaap@yahoo.com; www. monkeyforestresort.com*; ⊕ *08.00–15.30 daily; entrance US$6pp, camping US$4pp; photography is forbidden*) Situated on the Cape Coast road 2km before the entrance gate to Kakum, Monkey Forest Resort provides caged refuge to a few miserable-looking orphaned animals, including civet, genet and several species of monkey, along with some crocodiles borrowed from Hans Cottage Botel. A slightly more alluring prospect than the zoo itself is a short walk to a hilltop viewpoint that should eventually be transformed into a snack bar.

Hans Cottage Botel This attractive and original restaurant and hotel (see also details on pages 210–11) is situated about 10km from Cape Coast along the road to Kakum National Park. Its centrepiece is a double-storey wood-and-thatch restaurant, built on a stilted platform over a small lake, and connected to the shore by several wooden walkways. A dozen or so resident crocodiles are easily lured to the surface by throwing bread, which attracts the fish on which they feed, and you can also take a boat out on to the water. The lake supports varied avifauna. Aurally, things are dominated by the ceaseless chattering and swizzling that emanates from various weaver colonies around the lake (we identified village, orange and Vieillot's black weaver), but several types of kingfisher also appear to be resident, and herons and egrets are well represented – patient photographers with adequate lenses could find it very rewarding.

The 'botel' is well worth visiting as a day trip from Cape Coast, and also makes a convenient brunch stop after a morning walk at Kakum. It serves a good variety of reasonably priced meals, ranging from salads for US$3–4, to meat and seafood mains for US$8–11, as well as chilled drinks of every variety, though service can be a little slow, so allow at least 90 minutes. Another attraction is live music on Saturday and Sunday evenings. Coming from Cape Coast, Hans Cottage lies to the left of the main Kakum road at Efutu.

First and Trust Ostrich Farm (⏲ 07.00–18.00 daily; entrance US$2.50pp)
Situated about 1km west of the main road along a dirt track signposted 500m north of Hans Cottage Botel, this small farm is home to seven individual ostriches descended from stock transported from Zimbabwe in the 1990s. It provides quite a good opportunity to pet and feed the world's largest bird (which, incidentally, is not thought to occur naturally in Ghana), especially as it no longer seems to operate as a farm proper, just as a tourist attraction.

Wassa Domama Rock Shrine
Situated 28km west of Kakum by road, the shrine is a cool three-storey-high natural cavern formed by one large rock balanced on three others. A community-based ecotourist project has been set up in the area, offering both a guided visit up a near-vertical rock face to the sacred cavern, which is associated with a paramount deity known as Bosom Kese, and canoe trips on the 500m-wide, forest-fringed Pra River (except during the dry season or on Wednesdays). The river offers good birding and butterfly viewing. Accommodation in a basic four-room guesthouse with no electricity or running water costs US$4, and local meals can be prepared on request.

Domama is most easily visited as an extension of a trip to Kakum. From the national park entrance gate, drive north for about 8km to Ankaako Junction, where a left turn will lead to Wassa Atobiase after about 15km. Turn right here, and you will reach Wassa Domama after 5km. Using public transport from Cape Coast, head to Siwdo Station and ask for a trotro to Wassa Atobiase. The road from Wassa Atobiase to Wassa Domama is often in very poor condition during the rainy season. The site is open 08.00–17.00 daily and guided tours can be arranged on arrival, but accommodation should ideally be booked in advance (m 0246 616086).

ELMINA

Straddling the thin strip of land that separates the brackish Benya Lagoon from the crashing waves of the Atlantic, the strikingly attractive town of Elmina is the equal of nearby Cape Coast in terms of historical sightseeing, though it is often overlooked by tourists in favour of its larger neighbour. It started life as a fishing and salt-producing village at least 700 years ago and – despite having once formed the epicentre of the West African gold trade, first as the Portuguese and later the Dutch coastal headquarters – an overgrown fishing village is basically what Elmina remains today.

Much of this small town's fascination lies in the juxtaposition of its grandiose European architecture and modest African village roots. There is something decidedly odd about watching colourful pirogues sail in and out of the lagoon, much as they might in any other small Ghanaian port, except that here it all takes place in the shadow of the oldest European building in sub-Saharan Africa. Elmina also boasts an interesting collection of posuban shrines, second only in their variety to those at Anomabu, while the beach running west of the town centre supports a string of superb beach resorts catering to all tastes and budgets.

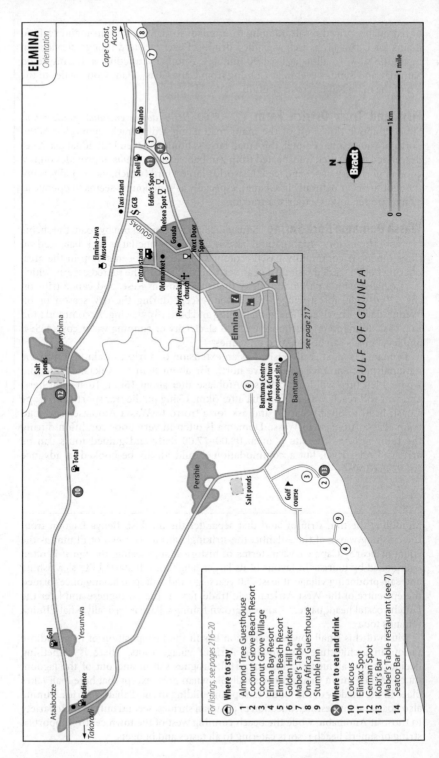

ELMINA
Orientation

Bradt

Cape Coast,
Accra

8

7

Qando

1

14

5

Shell

11

Eddie's Spot

Taxi stand

GCB

Chelsea Spot

Gouda

Next Door
Spot

GOUDAS

Elmina-Java
Museum

Trotro stand

Old market

Presbyterian
church

Elmina

see page 217

GULF OF GUINEA

Bronyibima

Salt
ponds

12

Bantuma Centre
for Arts & Culture
(proposed site)

Bantuma

Total

10

Pershie

Salt ponds

Golf
course

6

3

13

2

9

4

Goil

Yesuntwa

Ataabodze

Radience

Takoradi

N

0   1km

0   1 mile

above Women praying at the Cathedral of Our Lady of the Seven Sorrows in Navrongo, built in 1919 (AVZ) page 466

right The impressive St Joseph's Cathedral in Elmina (AVZ) page 222

below A posuban shrine in Elmina depicting Adam and Eve – built by Asafo companies, these shrines are unique to central Ghana and are a feature of most Akan societies (AVZ) pages 182–3

The Ghanaian coast was the West African epicentre of slave and gold trade in the 18th century and contains an impressive string of fortifications, including Fort Lijdzaamheid in Apam (*below left*), **Fort Amsterdam in Abandze** (*below right*), **Fort Metal Cross in Dixcove** (*bottom*) **and Cape Coast Castle in Cape Coast** (*left*) (all AVZ) pages 183, 188, 247 & 205

The Larabanga and Nakore mosques (*top and above inset*) are both examples of the West Sudanese mud-and-stick architectural style popular in northern Ghana (both AVZ) pages 445 –8 & 476

right Dating to the early 19th century, the Atia Kusia Kwame Shrine in Edwenase is one of the most elaborately decorated *abosomfie* in Ashanti

(AVZ) pages 394–5

above   Traditional dancers are often seen decorated in beads (AVZ) pages 300–1

left   A *kente* weaver at work in Kpetoe (AVZ) pages 382–3

below left & right   One of the most exciting markets in the country, Agomanya Market in Manya Krobo is known for its dizzying selection of beads, but you can also find everything from fabrics to *kenkey*, a Ghanaian specialty made from maize and wrapped in plantain leaves (both AVZ) page 302

A notable feature of Ghanaian culture, traditional dancing is often a central component of festivals and events — the Paga Cultural Dance Club in Kisseman, Accra, is a commercial dance troupe *(top and above left)* (both AVZ) pages 84–5

above right Revellers don elaborate masks for a Christmas celebration in Takoradi (AVZ)

right Colourfully painted pirogues are a common sight in fishing harbours across the country (AVZ)

above   An estimated 1,000 species of butterfly have been recorded in Ghana (AVZ) pages 48–9

left   Kob (*Kobus kob*) (AVZ)

below   Paga is known for its two sacred crocodile ponds (AVZ) pages 468–9

above left   **Blue-bellied roller**
(*Coracias cyanogaster*) (AVZ)

above right   **Flap-necked chameleon**
(*Chamaeleo dilepis*) (AVZ)

right   **Lesser spot-nosed monkey**
(*Cercopithecus petaurista*) (AVZ)

below   **African elephant**
(*Loxodonta africana africana*)
(AVZ)

Reputedly the tallest waterfall in West Africa, Wli Falls is a spectacular cascade in the heart of forested Agumatsa Wildlife Sanctuary (AVZ) page 329

HISTORY Traditional accounts suggest that Elmina has been settled at least since 1300, when it was chosen as the capital of Kwaa Amankwaa, the founder of the Edina State, originally a matrilineal chieftaincy, though its monarch was selected on patrilineal lines after 1680. The site was probably chosen because of the Benya Lagoon, an excellent venue for salt production. An important trade route developed in prehistoric times between the salt mines of Elmina and the goldfields of the Bono Empire (around what are today Tarkwa and Obuasi), which is why the Portuguese were able to buy gold with such ease when they first landed at Elmina in 1471.

Our best idea of Elmina's wealth and political set-up prior to the arrival of the Portuguese comes from a contemporary account of a meeting held in 1482 between the Portuguese captain Diogo de Azambuja and King Caramansa (probably an erroneous transcription of the common Edina royal name Kwamina Ansah). The narrator writes that Caramansa 'was seated on a high chair dressed in a jacket of brocade, with a golden collar of precious stones … his legs and arms covered with golden bracelets and rings … and in his plaited beard golden bars' and that 'his chiefs were all dressed in silk [and] wore rings and golden jewels on their heads and beards'. The same account goes on to describe the king as a man 'of good understanding, both by nature and by his dealing with the crews of the trading ships' and that 'he possessed a clear judgement … as one who not only desired to understand what was proposed to him, who not only listened to the translation of the interpreter, but watched each gesture made by Diogo de Azambuja; and while this continued, both he and his men were completely silent; no-one so much as spat, so perfectly disciplined were they'.

In 1482, with the permission of Caramansa, the Portuguese began work on the rather humble fort that formed the earliest incarnation of St George's Castle. Within five years, several Portuguese traders had settled around the fort, and Elmina had been elevated to city status by the King of Portugal. Elmina remained the Portuguese centre of operations for more than 150 years, though their grip on the fortress gradually waned towards the end of this period. In August 1637, St Jago Hill was taken by the Dutch and the castle was bombarded by cannons, forcing a Portuguese surrender that effectively ended their influence in West Africa.

Elmina probably acquired its modern name shortly after this Dutch takeover. The Portuguese had always known it as Aldea das Duas Partes ('Village of Two Parts'), a reference to the lagoon that still bisects it today. Nevertheless, the name Elmina is almost certainly derived from the Portuguese Da Costa de el Mina de Ouro ('The Coast of Gold Mines'), a term they used to describe the entire coast of present-day Ghana. It is also possible that the name Elmina is simply a bastardisation of Edina, but rather more unlikely, as some sources suggest without any apparent foundation, that it derives from the Arabic phrase *al mina* ('the harbour').

From 1637 until 1872 (when Holland sold all its Gold Coast forts to Britain), Elmina was in many respects the Dutch equivalent to Cape Coast. The Castle of St George was substantially expanded shortly after the Dutch took possession of it, and it was further renovated and expanded throughout their centuries of occupation. In 1665–66, a second fort was established on St Jago Hill, ensuring that no other rival power could take Elmina with the same ease as the Dutch had. A French trader, describing Elmina in the 17th century, wrote that it was 'very long, containing about twelve hundred houses, all built with rock stones [and] divided into several streets and alleys'. Old maps show that the small town centre had assumed its modern shape by the late 18th century, perhaps earlier. And it would appear that the town has seen surprisingly little development since being abandoned by the Dutch, partly because the British were already well ensconced at nearby Cape Coast, but more significantly perhaps because its very location between ocean and lagoon precluded the sort of expansion that has taken place in Cape Coast since the late 19th century.

GETTING THERE AND AWAY The town centre of Elmina lies about 2km off the main Takoradi–Accra road, only 12km west of Cape Coast, which is the larger town and more important transport hub, for which reason there is practically no long-haul transport to Elmina. In most circumstances, your best bet is thus to catch public transport to Cape Coast, which is connected to Elmina by a regular stream of trotros and shared taxis charging about US$0.60 for a seat. These leave Cape Coast from Jackson Road (a block west of the intersection with Commercial Road) or from a less central station on Johnston Road. If you are heading out to Stumble Inn, Coconut Grove or Elmina Bay Resort, a charter taxi from the town centre should cost around US$5–6. Alternatively, ask for a shared taxi to Edinaman Junction, from where it's a 10-minute walk to Coconut Grove or 20 minutes to Stumble Inn or Elmina Bay Resort.

When you are ready to leave Elmina, shared taxis to Cape Coast leave from Liverpool Street next to the Methodist church, though you can usually also pick them up anywhere along the main road connecting St George's Castle to the Elmina bypass via Elmina Beach Resort. Upon arrival at Cape Coast, if you are heading on to Accra, most taxis from Elmina will go straight past the Ford Station, which lies on the traffic circle at the south end of Cardinal Appiah Turkso Boulevard.

It is worth noting that the bridge across the lagoon in front of St George's Castle was closed to vehicular traffic and under renovation in early 2016. It can still be crossed by foot, and will most likely have reopened to cars by the time you read this, but until such time as it does, Elmina is once again a 'Village of Two Parts', with no road connecting the town centre to the castle and points further west.

SECURITY A few years back, dozens of pseudo-guides and children seeking sponsorship/addresses used to lurk around the grounds of St George's Castle playing 'guess the nationality' with passing tourists. And visitors who made the mistake of letting one such opportunist entice them into conversation would often be swarmed by his buddies, who might then engage in low-key verbal abuse and accusations of racism to guilt-trip them into handing over cash or a present. Thankfully, we saw no evidence of the latter sort of behaviour on our 2016 research trip, but 'guess the nationality' and unsolicited seashells and bracelets with your name on them still seem to be *de rigueur*. So simply be warned that, no matter how convincing the yarn you are spun, anybody who tries too hard to befriend you around the castle probably has cynical motives.

⌂ **WHERE TO STAY** *Map, page 214, unless otherwise stated*
In direct contrast to Cape Coast, Elmina has a limited choice of accommodation, especially when it comes to central budget options. However, the beaches immediately east and west of the town centre are serviced by a number of good lodgings, ranging from the backpacker-friendly Stumble Inn to a trio of genuinely upmarket resorts.

Upmarket

* ⌂ **Elmina Bay Resort** (24 rooms) m 0541 614812/0205 660670/0285 240202; e elminabayresort@gmail.com; www.

elminabayresort.com. Set on a beautiful sandy beach around 4km west of the town centre, this relatively new resort is currently the upmarket pick in the Elmina & Cape Coast area,

ELMINA
Centre

N

Bradt

0 ———————— 200m
0 ———————— 200 yds

GULF OF
GUINEA

Top View

Anglican
church

Cozy
Corner

St Joseph's
Cathedral

ST JOSEPH'S HILL

Steps

Asafo #4
posuban

Asafo #1
posuban

Cathedral
Square

GN

Obra
Spot

Dutch
Cemetery

DUTCH CEMETERY

Methodist
church

Shared taxis
to Cape Coast

Asafo #2
posuban

YARTEL

ANOWI

BENYA

Asafo #5
posuban

LAGOON

Fort St Jago

Seaview
Spot

Lagoon

(pedestrian only)

Fish market

Shell

Trotros to
destinations west

Market

St George's
(Elmina) Castle

Castle Bookshop
& Ghana Ecotours

Crafts &
arts market

LIME

LIVERPOOL

ATO QUARSHIE

For listings, see pages 216–20

Where to stay
1 Coconut Grove Bridge House
2 Nyansapow (Hollywood)

Where to eat and drink
Coconut Grove Bridge House (see 1)
3 Gramsddel JJ Beach
4 St George's Castle

comprising a semicircle of 6 dbl-storey lodges, each containing 4 individual self-contained rooms with quality pale hardwood furnishings, matching linen & fluffy towels, satellite TV, fridge, Wi-Fi, small dressing room, private balcony & sea view. Facilities at this top-notch resort include a sparkling free-form swimming pool, a breezy bar & a 1st-rate restaurant serving everything from pizzas & steaks to mouth-watering home-baked apple pie. The only negative is that the grounds are still quite undeveloped, & this doesn't seem to have changed much over several editions of this guide. *US$125/150 B&B self-contained sgl/twin; suites from US$260.* **$$$$$–$$$$**

Coconut Grove Beach Resort
(68 rooms) m 0263 006896/0244 333001; e beachresortreservations@

coconutgrovehotelsghana.com; www. coconutgrovehotelsghana.com. Set on a superlative palm-lined beach about 3km west of central Elmina, Coconut Grove is one of the country's premier beach resorts, set in spacious landscaped grounds, set around a large swimming pool, & running down to a lovely stretch of beach watched over by lifeguards. Other facilities include free Wi-Fi, an 18-hole golf course (free to hotel residents), horseback riding, & a quality restaurant serving meals for around US$10–18. The one flaw in an otherwise excellent set-up is the rooms, which are quite small & gloomy, & although they come with hot showers, AC, satellite TV & fridge, feel below par for a resort of this standard. *From US$125/140/180 B&B self-contained sgl/dbl/suite.* **$$$$$–$$$$**

⌂ Elmina Beach Resort (100 rooms)
m 0544 312370–5; e ebrres@gbhghana.net;
www.gbhghana.net. Part of the Ghanaian Golden
Beach Hotels group this international-standard
hotel lies about 1km northeast of the town centre,
near the Elmina bypass junction. Despite its
seafront location, it has no swimming beach, &
feels more like a business hotel than a resort, with
a great swimming-pool area, conference facilities,
a fitness centre, tennis & squash court, & a fair
restaurant. The comfortable rooms come with AC,
satellite TV, free Wi-Fi & hot water, but are starting
to look in need of refurbishment. *From US$125/160
B&B self-contained sgl/dbl; suites from US$215.*
$$$$$–$$$$

⌂ Golden Hill Parker Hotel (16 rooms)
m 0207 489578; e fir.tiebout@gmail.com; www.
goldenhillparkerhotel.com. Set on Bantuma Hill just
to the west of central Elmina, this new hotel had yet
to open when we were in town, but looks set to offer
high-standard accommodation in line with any of
the above hotels once it does. The en-suite rooms are
set in grassy gardens & come with private terraces,
many of which have views over the salt ponds &
shoreline. There's also a large swimming pool &
restaurant, & they ought to be open by the time you
read this. *Around US$110 B&B dbl.* **$$$$**

Moderate
✳ ⌂ Coconut Grove Village (20 rooms)
m 0263 018707/0245 125176; e village@
coconutgrovehotelsghana.com; www.
coconutgrovehotelsghana.com. Effectively a
budget annexe to the upmarket Coconut Grove
Beach Resort, this separate compound offers
accommodation in comfortable & spacious chalets
with AC & hot water. It lies a short distance from
the main gardens, & guests have access to all
hotel facilities including the swimming pool,
beach, restaurant & golf course. *US$55/65/75 self-
contained sgl/dbl/trpl.* **$$$**

⌂ Almond Tree Guesthouse (10 rooms)
m 0265 379798/0244 281098; e bookings@
almond3.com; www.almond3.com. This well-
thought-of family-managed guesthouse next to
Elmina Beach Resort has brightly decorated rooms
with simple but tasteful furnishings & Wi-Fi, &
a colourful garden & terrace restaurant serving
Jamaican & Ghanaian meat & vegetarian cuisine
in the US$5–8 bracket. Activities on offer include
African drumming & dancing, tie-dye & batik,

traditional storytelling & head-wrapping. *US$35 dbl
with shared bath & fan; US$43–53 self-contained
dbl with fan; US$68–72 dbl with AC & sea view.*
$$$–$$

⌂ Coconut Grove Bridge House [map, page
217] (10 rooms) m 0263 018743/0243 951282;
e bridgehouse@coconutgrovehotelsghana.com;
www.coconutgrovehotelsghana.com. Housed
in one of the old town's oldest buildings, with a
patio bar facing the fishing harbour & castle, this
is the top choice in Elmina for those who put a
high premium on characterful accommodation.
Comfortable rather than luxurious, the AC rooms
with satellite TV are good value, but the setting
– assuming you want to soak up the nocturnal
atmosphere of the old town – really is unbeatable.
The hotel runs a daily shuttle between Bridge
House & the beach resort, where residents have
free access to all facilities. There is a good ground-
floor restaurant with outdoor seating & Wi-Fi.
US$45/55/70 sgl/dbl/trpl B&B. **$$$**

Budget
✳ ⌂ Stumble Inn (9 rooms) m 0541
462733; e info@stumbleinnghana.com; www.
stumbleinnghana.com. Next to Elmina Bay Resort
about 4km west of the town centre, this popular
backpacker-orientated resort offers the winning
combination of a superb beachfront location,
chilled atmosphere, tasty food in the beach bar
& restaurant, & good-value accommodation in
well-ventilated 8-bed dorms or private rooms with
nets. Facilities include beach volleyball, a book-
swap service, & plenty of shaded seating at the
beach. Batik, carving & drumming workshops are
also sometimes offered. The varied b/fast menu is
mostly in the US$3–5 range, sandwiches & salads
cost around USA$4, & it usually has 3–4 dinner
choices in the US$6–10 range. A taxi from the town
centre will cost around US$5–6, or you can catch a
shared taxi to Edinaman Junction & walk the last
20mins to the resort. *US$14/17 sgl/dbl with shared
bath; US$18–21/21–24 self-contained sgl/dbl; US$5
dorm bed; US$2.50pp camping.* **$$–$**

⌂ One Africa Guesthouse (10 rooms)
m 0208 195483/0244 830451; e oneafrica_
ghana@yahoo.com; www.oneafricaghana.com.
Some 200m from the main Cape Coast road, this
friendly hotel, restaurant & wellness centre lies in
neat gardens overlooking an attractive stretch of
rocky coastline within walking distance of a safe

swimming beach. A pleasant & highly regarded garden restaurant serves a varied international selection (including several vegetarian dishes) in the US$6–8 range, though be warned that service is slow, because all meals are created to order. We like the pan-African theme of the small Wall of Remembrance Museum, and the clean airy chalets, which are daubed in bright Rasta colours, decorated with photographs of ethnic folk from all over the continent, & individually named in honour of eminent Africanist pioneers such as Yaa Asantewaa, Marcus Garvey & Malcolm X. Shame, then, that the unifying sentiment is undermined by a sign at reception dedicating the lodge to that divisive despot, 'His Excellency Robert Mugabe'! *US$46 B&B self-contained dbl or twin with fan.* **$$$**

🏠 **Mabel's Table** (12 rooms) m 0244 610009/0208 210027; e kohainh@gmail.

com. Situated next to One Africa, this popular restaurant, set in a large, green beachfront garden, also offers acceptable but rather dingy budget accommodation in spacious rooms & chalets with tiled floors, wood & cane furniture, & good beach access. *US$25 self-contained chalet with fan; US$32/42 dbl/suite with AC.* **$$$–$$**

Shoestring

🏠 **Nyansapow (Hollywood) Hotel** [map, page 217] (15 rooms) m 0244 458887. The only budget hotel in central Elmina is this long-serving central lodge set around a large, open courtyard about 10mins' walk north of the castle. It's rather basic, but priced accordingly & the rooms are quite clean. There is a bar on the ground floor but no restaurant. *US$11/14 self-contained dbl/twin with fan.* **$**

✖️ **WHERE TO EAT AND DRINK** *Map, page 214, unless otherwise stated*

Moderate

✳️ ✖️ **Coucous Restaurant** m 0573 420496/0540 494920; ⊕ 08.00–22.00 daily. Owned by a Ghanaian chef who learnt her trade in Switzerland, this excellent thatched restaurant set in a large, green garden on the Elmina bypass may have a rather out-of-the-way location, but it is worth the drive out for the simple but well-prepared French-influenced cuisine. Mains are in the US$8–15 range. **$$$–$$**

✖️ **Coconut Grove Bridge House** [map, page 217] ⊕ 07.00–22.00 daily. All terracotta tiles & cane furniture, the ground-floor restaurant at this attractively located hotel has a varied menu, but specialises in seafood, with most dishes falling in the US$6–10 range. Outdoor seating facing the lagoon mouth & castle is available. **$$**

✖️ **St George's Castle Restaurant** [map page 217] m 0231 965738/0546 318251; ⊕ 08.00–20.00 daily. With its historical setting inside the castle, & good selection of pasta dishes, sandwiches, seafood & Ghanaian fare in the US$4–6 range, this is a great central choice. Service is slow, but it does at least come with a smile. **$$–$**

✖️ **Mabel's Table** ⊕ 08.00–22.00 daily. This long-running beachfront bar & restaurant is a great place for a chilled sundowner. Seafood & other mains cost around US$5–6 for a large plate. **$$–$**

Budget

✳️ ✖️ **Elimax Spot** m 0244 973857; ⊕ 07.00–22.00 daily. A favourite with locally based volunteers, this local eatery across the road from the Almond Tree Guesthouse serves up some of the tastiest Ghanaian dishes around, including spicy red-red with fried plantains, yam balls & egg stew for around US$4–6 per plate. Genial owner Eli also cooks excellent burritos (chicken or vegetarian) & the best chips in town. All food is cooked to order, so allow 30mins for b/fast & ideally give her a few hours' notice for dinner. **$**

✖️ **German Spot** m 0262 191065/0242 225115; ⊕ 07.00–22.00 daily. If you've ever wanted to practice your *auf Deutsch* over a plate of red-red, this friendly spot on the Elmina bypass might just be the place to do it. The engaging proprietress spent 25 years in Germany, & while the food is decidedly Ghanaian, you can usually get a Bitburger or a Becks to wash it down with. **$**

BARS AND NIGHTLIFE *Map, page 214, unless otherwise stated*

🍸 **Seatop Bar** m 0242 542712; ⊕ 09.00–late Sun–Fri, 18.00–late Sat. Situated between Elmina Beach Resort & the Almond Tree, this popular & friendly bar serves the

cheapest & coldest beers in town. Popular with volunteers, it also now has satellite TV & a projector, making it a good place to watch major sports events.

♀Gramsddel JJ Beach [map, page 217] m 0508 011545; **f** fb.me/GramsddelJJ; ⊕ 07.00–midnight daily. On both sides of the coastal road just up from the town centre, this friendly stilted bar has the nicest location in town, on the beach with views across the water to the castle. They also do a good range of Ghanaian food for US$4–6, with an *omo tuo* special on Sun.

♀Kobi's Bar m 0243 609945; ⊕ 17.00–late daily. This stilted bar next to Coconut Grove Beach Resort has a great beachfront location, cheap beers, music at w/ends, often supplemented by live performances on Fri or Sat. Drumming & dancing workshops are also offered & there are a couple of basic rooms under construction.

OTHER PRACTICALITIES

Books Situated on the first floor of St George's Castle, next to Ghana Ecotours, the Castle Bookshop (m *0208 189462*; ⊕ *09.00–16.30 daily*), stocks the most comprehensive selection of books and maps about Ghana and West Africa we've ever seen in one place.

Car rental Eddiesac Car Rental (m *0208 169149/0249 705185*; e *eddiesac@yahoo. com; www.eddiesac.wordpress.com*) has an office in the lobby of the Elmina Beach Resort Hotel and is its official transportation agent.

Foreign exchange There is no international bank, ATM or forex bureau in the town centre. The closest is the ATM at the Ghana Commercial Bank on the Elmina bypass, about 1km north of the centre. If that isn't working, the closest facilities are in Cape Coast.

Golf The 18-hole golf course at Coconut Grove Beach Resort is free to hotel residents and charges US$15 per person per round to day visitors. Club hire is an additional US$10.

Horseriding The stables at Coconut Grove Beach Resort offer beach rides at US$5 per 20 minutes.

Internet The only internet café, so far as we can ascertain, is on Dutch Cemetery Road opposite Cathedral Square. There's Wi-Fi at the Bridge House Restaurant and most of the upmarket and moderate hotels.

Swimming The most central swimming pool is at Elmina Beach Resort, which charges US$5 per person for day usage (with a discount for volunteers). For more of a seaside setting, 3km west of town, try the beach or swimming pool at Coconut Grove Beach Resort, which charges a steep US$13 to day visitors. The quieter Elmina Bay Resort charges US$7.50 for day usage of its swimming pool.

Tour operators The highly regarded **Ghana Ecotours** (m *0208 159369/0242 176357*; e *info@ghanaecotours.com; www.ghanaecotours.com*; ⊕ *09.00–17.00 Mon–Sat, Sun by apt; see ad, pages 102 & 194*), based on the first floor of St George's Castle (visitable without paying the castle entrance fee), specialises in informative guided walking tours of Elmina. These take around 90 minutes, and cost US$8 per person, with discounts for students and volunteers. They've recently begun offering a similar tour of Cape Coast, and can also arrange canoe outings, trips to cocoa farms, and tours further afield in Ghana, Togo and Benin.

Boat tours of Benya Lagoon, run by **Frederick Kennedy** (m *0246 605034*; e *fkennedy82@gmail.com*), offer an unusual fish's-eye view of Elmina town or St George's Castle, as well as good birding in the salt flats and mangroves.

WHAT TO SEE AND DO
St George's Castle (✆ 03321 32701; ⏰ 09.00–16.30 daily; US$10.50/8 non-Ghanaians/students) Perched on a rocky promontory between lagoon and ocean, St George's Castle, founded in 1482, is the oldest extant colonial building in sub-Saharan Africa, though it has been so extensively rebuilt and extended over the centuries that even its mid-17th-century shape is radically different from its modern one. (You could convincingly argue that the 'oldest building' tag hangs more meaningfully on the small Church of Senhora Baluarte on Mozambique Island, barely altered in architectural terms since it was constructed in 1522.) Also sometimes called Elmina Castle, the whitewashed building, now maintained as a historical monument and museum, is perhaps even more impressive architecturally than its Cape Coast counterpart, much of it four-storeys high, and it offers excellent views across to the beach and over the town.

The original St George, a small rectangular fortress, was sufficiently substantial to withstand three Dutch naval bombardments, before it was captured as a result of the bombardment from the top of St Jago Hill. The modern fort must cover about ten times the surface area of the original; the only recognisable relic of pre-Dutch times is the former Portuguese chapel, converted by the Dutch to an auction hall for slaves, now a museum with displays that concentrate on local history rather than the slave trade.

Around town The original old town, depicted in several paintings and lithographs, stood immediately east of the castle, between lagoon and ocean, before it burnt to the ground in 1873 following a British naval bombardment. It is now the site of the pretty fishing harbour and fish market, best viewed from the small bridge across the mouth of the Benya Lagoon, especially in the early to mid morning, when dozens of colourful pirogues can be seen making their way in and out of the harbour. An entry fee of US$0.50 is levied to visit the fenced part of the fishing market, and the enterprising ticket collectors might also ask tourists for a 'photographic fee'. If this happens, insist on a receipt and be warned that, fee or no fee, photography is barely tolerated within the market – best perhaps to leave your camera behind!

To get from the castle and fishing harbour to what, we suppose, has to be termed the modern **old town**, you must follow Liverpool Street north over the bridge across the lagoon mouth. During Elmina's prime in the early 19th century, this area was where the wealthiest citizens lived, many of them mulattos or prosperous Dutch merchants who married Elmina women and settled in the town. Immediately after you cross the bridge, you'll see a cluster of these houses running up the right side of Liverpool Street, large double-storey buildings now trimmed of many of their more ornamental touches. Built in the 1840s, this cluster of buildings consists of Bridge House (partially destroyed during heavy rains in 1981, subsequently renovated as a hotel), Quayson House, the twin Viala Houses, and Simons House (now a complete ruin).

From here, turn left into Lagoon Road, which follows the north bank of the lagoon, and after no more than 20m, to your right you'll see the steep path to the top of **St Jago Hill**, which offers a wonderful panoramic view over the fishing harbour and the town centre to St George's Castle. This vantage point was exploited by the Dutch in 1637 when they dragged four cannons to its peak and bombarded the castle, forcing a Portuguese surrender. **Fort St Jago** was built on top of the hill in 1665–66, so that the Dutch could be certain that they wouldn't lose possession of the castle in a manner similar to the one they had used to gain it. The resultant relatively modest fortified garrison post was named Fort Coenraadsburg by its Dutch constructors, but for reasons that are unclear it is generally known today by the hill's older Portuguese name. Though several extensions were made after 1666, the essential shape of the fort is little changed since that time. The caretaker will happily show you around for a small fee. And watch out for bag snatchers and petty thieves in this quite isolated location.

When you walk back down to the base of St Jago Hill, turn right back into Lagoon Road, then right again into Benya Road, curving inland. Here, over the space of perhaps 200m, is Elmina's main concentration of **posuban shrines** (see also box, pages 182–3). The first two, on the left side of the road a few metres after it curves inland, belong to Asafo Companies #5 and #2. The shrine built by Company #5 is a double-storey affair with several life-size figures carved on the ground floor and – strikingly – a ship with three naval officers on the upper one. Company #2's shrine consists of four life-size carvings of people surrounding an older man in a bright-blue robe and flanked by two aeroplanes. Most impressive, however, is the shrine built by Asafo Company #4 at the junction with Dutch Cemetery Street, which depicts a variation on the story of Adam and Eve including several life-size figures (some decapitated in recent years as a result of poor maintenance). Unlike in smaller towns, it's normally fine to photograph the shrines in Elmina without being asked for a payment.

Turn left into Dutch Cemetery Street if you want to nose around the old **Dutch Cemetery**, inaugurated in 1802 and moved to its present site at the base of St Joseph's Hill four years later. Well maintained, the graveyard boasts several marble tombstones (one of which marks the grave of Governor Hagenblom, who was murdered in 1808), as well as a large, neoclassical cenotaph dating to 1806. The cemetery is normally padlocked, but if you ask around – and are prepared to offer a dash or two – then it shouldn't be difficult to locate the caretaker. Walk up this hill to see a clutch of buildings associated with the Catholic mission, including the impressive **St Joseph's Cathedral**, which dates from the 1880s. The hill also offers great views over the old town, and east across the salt ponds in Benya Lagoon.

From the cathedral, a steep road running to the right leads downhill into Lime Street. This is the site of **Dolphin House**, built in the late 19th century by the merchant Fred Dolphin at the foot of the road running to the top of St Joseph's Hill. Once distinguished by its multi-arched façade, Dolphin House had become very rundown prior to collapsing entirely in late 1999. Walk back to Dutch Cemetery Street, turn left and follow it to Chapel Square, at the intersection of Liverpool and High streets and marked by an attractive **Methodist church**. A left turn into High Street will bring you to what is perhaps the best-maintained building of its vintage in Elmina, the former **post office**. This stone construction was built sometime between 1825 and 1850 as the domestic dwelling and trading quarters of the merchant C H Bartels (son of Governor Bartels), and it later served as a hospital during the colonial era.

Elmina-Java Museum (m *0244 683599; www.elwininternational.com;* ☉*09.00– 16.00 Mon–Sat, noon–16.00 Sun; entrance US$5/2 adult/student*) Situated on the Elmina bypass, about 750m west of the Ghana Commercial Bank, this private museum focuses on the history of the Belanda Hitam or Zwarte Hollanders, the Indonesian or Dutch name (literally 'Black Dutchmen') given to the 3,080 Ghanaian men recruited from 1831 to 1872 to serve in the Royal Netherlands East Indies Army (KNIL). Exhibits include photographs, documents and other artefacts related to the lives of the soldiers and their descendants in Indonesia, the Netherlands and Ghana. The museum also has extensive displays about the history of Elmina itself, the story of two Ashanti princes sent to the Netherlands in the early 19th century, and on the genealogy of the Ulzen family for ten generations. Many interesting

aspects of the cross-cultural mixing are explored (like why batik is so common in Ghana) and the curator gives an excellent tour.

TOWARDS TAKORADI

BRENU AKYINIM AND AMPENYI Situated 15km west of Elmina, the village of Brenu Akyinim is known for its attractive beach, a substantial chunk of which has been fenced off (ensuring that villagers do their ablutions elsewhere) to form a compound shared by the Brenu Beach Resort and Brenu Paradise Beach Resort. As with so many beaches in Ghana, swimming is not advisable unless you check current conditions with the locals, but Brenu is a great place to lounge in palm-fringed, white-sanded perfection, and facilities are suited to those on a budget. Only 1km west of Brenu as the crow flies, the village of Ampenyi, site of the backpacker-friendly Ko-Sa Beach, lies on a beach that is not only as pretty as any on the Ghanaian coast, but also boasts a natural rock pool where swimming is usually safe. Both Brenu and Ampenyi form easy goals for a day trip out of Elmina, though it would be normal to stay overnight.

Getting there and away In a private vehicle, follow the Takoradi road for about 15km until you reach Ajensudo Junction, where the respective turn-offs to Brenu and Ampenyi are signposted about 500m apart. The distance between the main road and either beach is about 5km and the roads are in decent nick.

There is no direct public transport between Elmina and Brenu Akyinim (and note that 'Akyinim', pronounced 'Achinim', is also, rather confusingly, the name of a suburb in Elmina) or Ampenyi. This means you will first need to catch a trotro to Ajensudo Junction; any westbound transport from Elmina will oblige. Here you'll find a few shared taxis to Brenu and Ampenyi. These taxis can fill up a bit slowly, but since the full fare for four passengers works out at little more than US$1, you could always treat yourself. Expect to pay around US$5–10 to charter a taxi from Elmina or Cape Coast. Travelling between Brenu and Ampenyi, the alternatives are to charter a car back via the junction, or take a 20-minute walk straight from one to the other along the beach.

Where to stay and eat

Upmarket

Brenu Beach Resort (11 rooms) m 0244 158675; e contact@brenubeach.com; www. brenubeach.com. This totally gorgeous beach resort in Brenu started out as a restaurant, & it still serves excellent seafood, most in the US$8–12 range, as well as other meals, & minerals & alcoholic drinks. Accommodation, set back about 200m from the sea, is in a block of clean & spacious tiled rooms with queen-sized bed, fan, AC, satellite TV, fridge, hot water & private balcony with a sea view. Camping is permitted & the beach is supervised by a lifeguard. *US$66/79 self-contained sgl/dbl.* **$$$**

Moderate

Ayikoo Beach House (3 rooms) m 0262 626206; e: info@ghanavakantie.nl;

www.ghana-beach-cottage.com. Sleeping up to 6 people in 4 spacious self-contained rooms with fan, this beachfront house lies in a palm-shaded garden 10mins' walk east of Ko-Sa. It has a large palm tree garden at the ocean, a spacious living room & veranda, & an equipped kitchen with microwave & fridge, or you could eat at nearby Ko-Sa or Alberta's. Aimed mainly at groups, it must be rented out as one unit. *US$70–115 per party per night, depending on group size.* **$$$$–$$$**

Budget

Ko-Sa Beach Resort (14 rooms, 3 under construction) m 0244 375432; e reservation@ko-sa.com; www.ko-sa.com; see ad, 3rd colour section. Set in well-maintained gardens that run down to the wonderful palm-lined beach to Ampenyi, this Dutch owner-managed resort offers a variety of accommodation, ranging from local-style clay-&-thatch huts using clean communal showers & toilets & a 4-person family room with fan, to smarter self-contained rooms & bungalows with fan, sleeping up to 4 people. Facilities include a good book-swap service, solar electricity, drum & dance lessons, guided turtle spotting & beach walks to Elmina as well as excursions to Cape Coast & Kakum National Park. There's also an arts centre under construction next door, where tie-die, batik, & beadmaking should soon be on offer. The spectacular thatched restaurant & bar serves a range of local, continental & vegetarian dishes in the US$5–10 range, with seafood a bit more expensive. *US$13/16 sgl/twin hut with fan & shared bath; US$27 family room with 2 dbl beds & fan; US$29–32 self-contained dbl or twin with private balcony; US$40 self-contained bungalow with 2 dbl beds.* **$$–$**

🏠 **Twitter Paradise** (5 rooms) m 0243 288152/0236 828230; e twitter_paradise@yahoo.com; www.twitterparadise.com. Easily spotted about 300m inland from Ko-Sa & the beach, this low-key new guesthouse sits in lovingly kept gardens studded with flowers & palms, where the only tweeting going on is of the avian variety. The tidy self-contained rooms come with ceiling fan & sitting area, & there's plenty of camping space as well. The garden restaurant & bar serves seafood, Ghanaian meals & fresh juices at US$5–8, & the engaging owner-manager can arrange tours around Ampenyi, Komenda, Cape Coast, & beyond. Recommended. *US$21 dbl, US$8/13 sgl/dbl camping.* **$$–$**

🏠 **Alberta's Palace Beach Resort** (21 rooms) m 0266 700727/0277 202429; e albertaspalace@gmail.com. Situated in Ampenyi, right next to Ko-Sa, this beachfront resort might lack its neighbour's laid-back ambience & harmonious integration into its surrounds, but taken on its own terms it seems like an agreeable & sensibly priced set-up. The bungalows, set around an enormous bare courtyard, all come with fan, AC, minifridge, satellite TV & hot water. *US$24/27 self-contained sgl/dbl.* **$$**

🏠 **Brenu Paradise Beach Resort** (5 rooms) m 0240 902291; e brenuparadise@yahoo.com. This unassuming budget resort, which shares a beach & large compound with its near namesake, Brenu Beach Resort, might not be in the same league in terms of comfort or facilities, but seems pretty good value at the price. It also has a cheaper (though not nearly so good) restaurant. *US$17/22/40 self-contained dbl/trpl/quad with fan.* **$$**

🏠 **Kofi and Adjoa's Esteem Guesthouse** (8 rooms) m 0244 541288; e adjoachilds@yahoo.com; www.esteemguesthouse.com. Situated at Ajensudo Junction, this friendly guesthouse, named after its American owner-managers, is excellent budget value, offering a variety of self-contained rooms with dbl bed, tiled floor & sofa. A good open-air restaurant (🕐 08.00–20.00 daily) serves sandwiches, salads, burgers & generously portioned American/Ghanaian mains in the US$4–8 range. Just a shame that the roadside location has so little going for it! *From US$20 dbl with fan to US$40 semi-suite with AC.* **$$**

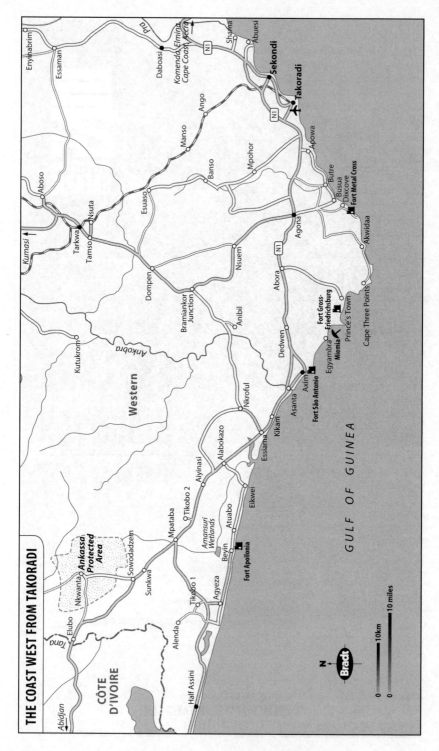

THE COAST WEST FROM TAKORADI

CÔTE D'IVOIRE

Abidjan

Tano

Half Assini

Elubo

Enyinabrim

Essaman

Aboso

Kumasi

Nsuta

Tarkwa

Tamso

Kutukrom

Ankobra

Western

Dompen

Bramiankor Junction

Esuaso

Manso

Banso

Mpohor

Ango

Daboasi

Komenda, Elmina, Cape Coast, Accra

Shama

Abuesi

Sekondi

Takoradi

N1

N1

Apowa

Butre

Busua

Dixcove   **Fort Metal Cross**

Akwidaa

Agona

Abora

N1

Nsuem

Anibil

Nkroful

Dedwen

Prince's Town

Cape Three Points

Fort Gross-Friedrichsburg

Egyambra

Mienla

Axim

Asanta

Fort São Antonio

Kikam

Essiama

Elkwei

Atuabo

Beyin

Agyeza

Alenda

Fort Apollonia

Amansuri Wetlands

Tikobo 1

Sunkwa

Sowodadzem

Nkwanta

Ankassa Protected Area

Mpataba

Tikobo 2

Aiyinasi

Alabokazo

Nsuta

GULF OF GUINEA

N

Bradt

0   10km

0   10 miles

226

9

Takoradi

Situated about halfway between Accra and the Ivorian border, the port city of Takoradi (often shortened to 'Taadi') serves as the joint administrative capital of Western Region, together with its twin city Sekondi (sometimes spelt 'Secondi'), which also lies on the coast about 10km to the southeast. Collectively, Takoradi and Sekondi form the fourth-largest urban conglomeration in Ghana, supporting a total population of around 400,000 according to the 2012 census. The more populous and industrialised of the two, Takoradi is also the most important transport hub in the southwest, and equally significant as an economic centre, a status recently boosted by the discovery of offshore oil and gas in the vicinity — so much so that the area's newest nickname is simply 'Oil City'.

The offshore fuel boom ensures that this sprawling coastal metropolis attracts plenty of business visitors. Indeed, the verdant and relatively affluent beachfront suburbs immediately south of central Takoradi support a burgeoning cluster of pricey hotels and restaurants – not to mention a well-maintained golf course – catering to those on expense accounts. For most other travellers, however, Takoradi serves as little more than a springboard for exploring the mouth-watering Atlantic beaches that lie further west. True, the compact and decidedly hectic city centre has the mark of unaffected authenticity one associates with towns that make few concessions to tourism. Equally, Takoradi offers little in the way of sightseeing, and with various 'stations' dotted around the city centre offering good road transport links in all directions, most travellers will choose to pass straight through.

HISTORY

Historically, Sekondi is a more significant settlement than its upstart twin. The Dutch established a trading post at the village they called Zakonde in the 1640s, and followed this up with the construction of Fort Orange in 1657. Captain Henry Nurse, a British agent, established a rival trading post there in 1682, and built Fort George close by. Neither fort was particularly imposing in its original incarnation, and both were destroyed in 1698 during altercations with the local Ahanta people. In 1726, the Royal African Company charged the surveyor William Smith with making plans of all their West African properties, and his drawing of the 'British and Dutch Forts at Secondee … pleasantly situated … within gun-shot' of each other, on a pair of hills flanking a small river inlet, demonstrates that both had been reconstructed by this time, though not necessarily on their original site. After capturing and destroying the British fort in 1782, the Dutch enjoyed supremacy at Sekondi until Fort Orange was transferred to Britain in accordance with a treaty signed in 1872. Since then, the fort has been used mainly as a lighthouse. Meanwhile, Sekondi evolved as an important naval base and administrative centre, particularly following the economic boost provided by the construction of a railway connecting it to Tarkwa and Kumasi between 1898 and 1903.

At this time, Takoradi was little more than an obscure fishing village, so low in ranking that it doesn't feature among 15 named coastal settlements west of Elmina on a map of the Gold Coast colony published in 1895. However, as early as 1895, British naval engineers had identified it as a potential site for a port, construction of which began in 1921 under Governor Gordon Guggisberg. The harbour started operations in 1928, and was the country's busiest port prior to the opening of Tema port, closer to Accra in the 1960s. Takoradi's fortunes took a long, slow dive over the following decades, only to be revived in the post-millennial era by a US$250 million dredging and modernisation project undertaken in 2004. Further rehabilitations and upgrades took place in 2009 in preparation for the export boom predicted when Ghana's offshore oilfields came online in late 2010. While subsequent oil production has fallen short of expected levels, Takoradi now handles around 70% of Ghana's export traffic, as well as transiting large amounts of cargo for its landlocked neighbour, Burkina Faso, and the local economy is visibly booming.

ORIENTATION

From a traveller's perspective, Takoradi is split into three main districts. The most important for public transport, shopping and budget accommodation is the **city centre**, which is focused on the circular central market, and is bounded by an upturned road triangle comprising Paa Grant Road to the north, Axim Road to the west, and Sekondi Road to the east. Important roundabouts (traffic circles) lie at all three points of the triangle. Kwame Nkrumah Roundabout at the northwest tip is where the main road east to Accra meets the main road west to Busua and Axim.

The Sekondi road emanates northwards from the Paa Grant Roundabout, on the northeast tip of the triangle. At the southern apex of the triangle is Shippers Council Roundabout, which you must head straight across to access **Beach Road** (the name of a suburb rather than a specific road). Located between the city centre and the beach, Beach Road is where you'll find most of Takoradi's more upmarket hotels and eateries. Finally, to the east of Beach Road, is the **old town centre** or **Harbour District**, which is the site of several buildings dating to the colonial era, among them the railway station, which is currently under renovation, as well as the main port. Though the old town centre is no longer of much significance to locals, it remains the main banking district in Takoradi, and the home of several shipping-related businesses.

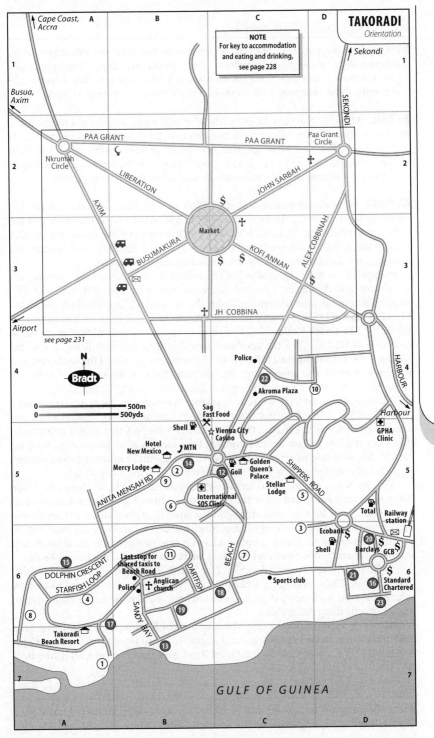

GETTING THERE AND AWAY

BY AIR Starbow (m *0245 000000;* e *info@flystarbow.com; www.flystarbow.com; online booking at www.ghanaticketservice.com*) operates two daily 45-minute return flights between Accra and Takoradi for around US$95 one way. The airport [229 A3] is only about 1km west of the Takoradi city centre, along Airport Road.

BY RAIL Although the colonial railway station still dominates the old town centre, passenger trains on the century-old line between Takoradi and Kumasi via Accra were suspended several years ago. The government secured a substantial loan from China to rehabilitate the line in 2011 and works on both the station and track were underway at the time of writing, but it's unclear when they'll be complete.

BY ROAD Sekondi-Takoradi lies about 230km west of Accra by road, a drive that normally takes around 3 hours in a private vehicle, at least once you've cleared the traffic on the outskirts of Accra. It lies about 80km west of Cape Coast, a drive that usually takes slightly longer than one hour. The road distance from Kumasi via Tarkwa is around 270km, and the drive takes upwards of 5 hours.

Takoradi is the main regional public transport hub, and several long-haul stations are clustered within a few hundred metres of each other along Axim Road (the western arm of the road triangle enclosing the city centre). These include the **Metro Mass Bus Station** [231 C3] on the northeast corner of the junction with Busumakura Road, the **STC Coach Station** [231 C4] directly opposite, the **Ford Station for Accra and Kumasi** [231 C3] on the southeast junction with Justmoh Road, the **trotro station for Accra and Kumasi** [231 C3] on the northeast corner of the same junction (where VIP buses also congregate), and the **main trotro station** [231 B2], covering all destinations west of Takoradi, north of the junction with Hayford Road.

The once dominant STC was only operating one daily service to Abidjan (*US$14 in cedi & US$12/7,000CFA that must be paid in Central African Francs*) when this seventh edition was researched. Otherwise, there were only two weekly departures: Mondays at 07.00 to Tamale, and Fridays at the same time to Bolgatanga, both for US$16. It's advisable to arrive at the STC station about 30 minutes before the bus departs to be sure of getting a ticket or, better still, to book a day ahead.

With the STC a shadow of its former self, a safer bet than buses these days is the air-conditioned Fords that cover the routes to and from Kumasi and Accra several times daily. Fares for the Fords are slightly cheaper than the buses, and they simply leave when they fill up. Cheaper still, but much less comfortable, are ordinary trotros to Kumasi and Accra. Another option includes the regular Metro Mass buses that connect Takoradi to Kumasi and Accra, as well as to Tarkwa, Obuasi and Tema.

Public transport to Agona Junction (for Butre, Busua, Dixcove and Akwidaa), Axim, Beyin, Elubo and most other points west of Takoradi is limited to trotros, which leave on a fill-up-and-go basis throughout the day from the main station further north along Axim Road.

Trotros also seem to be the only viable option for Elmina, Cape Coast, Winneba and other towns between Takoradi and Accra. These all leave from the **Cape Coast Station** [231 D1], which lies on Paa Grant Road near the junction with Justmoh.

GETTING AROUND

Plenty of transport to Sekondi can be picked up at the Sekondi **shared taxi station** [231 E2] on Mampong Road or the Sekondi **trotro station** [231 E1] off Amongo

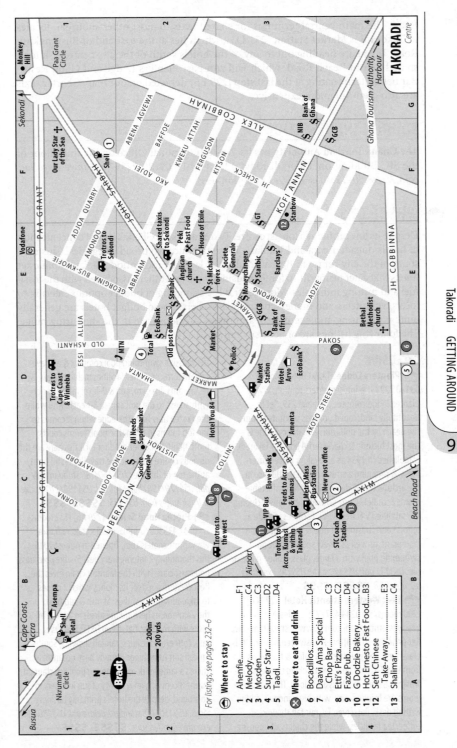

TAKORADI
Centre

Takeradi GETTING AROUND 9

For listings, see pages 232–6

Where to stay

1 Ahenfie.................F1
2 Melody..................C4
3 Mosden.................C3
4 Super Star.............D2
5 Taadi...................D4

Where to eat and drink

6 Bocadillos.............D4
7 Daavi Ama Special
   Chop Bar.............C3
8 Etti's Pizza............C2
9 Faze Pub...............D4
10 G Dodzie Bakery.....C2
11 Hot Ernesto Fast Food...B3
12 Seth Chinese..........E3
13 Shalimar...............C4

231

Road. The main central terminus for shared taxis to most other suburban locales in Takoradi is **Market Station** [231 D3], which lies at the east end of Busumakura Road. If you are heading out to any of the hotels south of the city centre, ask for a shared taxi to Beach Road, which will run past Planters Lodge and Gilou Resto-Bar before terminating at the **last stop** [229 B6] depicted on our map. Charter taxis are also plentiful and inexpensive.

TOURIST INFORMATION

The **Ghana Tourism Authority** has its Western Regional Office on the third floor of the SIC Building on Takoradi Ridge [231 G4] (✆ *03120 22357;* e *gtbwest@yahoo. com;* ⊙ *08.00–12.30 & 13.30–17.00 Mon–Fri*).

WHERE TO STAY

Despite its low profile as a tourist centre, Takoradi boasts Ghana's largest concentration of hotels outside Accra and Kumasi. These fall into two broad categories. Clustered south of the city centre in Beach Road are a dozen or more moderate and upmarket hotels that cater primarily to foreign businessmen and others associated with the fossil fuel and mining industries. More central is a scattering of budget options catering to locals, volunteers and money-conscious travellers. These budget hotels are generally quite uninspiring and overpriced, and there's precious little in the shoestring range. The following listings are of necessity rather selective.

EXCLUSIVE

Planters Lodge [229 C6] (44 rooms) 03120 22233; e info@planters.com.gh; www. planterslodge.com; see ad, page 239. Set in beautifully landscaped grounds separated from the beach by the golf course, Planters Lodge is the most historic & characterful hotel in Takoradi, established in 1934 as a Royal Air Force officers mess, & retaining a strong colonial influence in the architecture & décor. Stylish & comfortable rooms & chalets come with all mod cons including AC, satellite TV & free Wi-Fi. Facilities include a tennis court, business centre & excellent fusion restaurant, as well as a new spa & tempting swimming pool with a large, glass-walled poolside bar. *US$131 dbl; US$195 suite; US$295 exec suite; all rates B&B.* **$$$$$–$$$$**

Best Western Atlantic Hotel [229 C6] (200 rooms) m 0244 427777; e sales@ bestwesterntakoradi.com; www.bestwestern.com. Reopened in 2014 after extensive renovations, this place has been polished to a shine & the views from this 7-storey hotel overlooking the beach are worth the price of admission alone. The standard rooms are bright & airy, with big windows, fridge, writing desk, flatscreen TV, rainfall showers, & coffee/tea facilities, while the chalets sit opposite

the massive swimming pool complex & all have private terraces. Other facilities include 3 bars, 3 restaurants & a gym, spa & 2-level infinity pool with access to the golf course & beach. And while the Protea may have the edge when it comes to the top rooms in town, the pool, tennis courts, football pitch & other outdoor facilities here are the obvious choice for an active traveller & still firmly at the top of the pile. *US$160/180 standard sgl/ dbl; US$170/190 chalet sgl/dbl; US$190/210 deluxe sgl/dbl; suites from US$385.* **$$$$$–$$$$**

Protea Hotel Select [229 A6] (132 rooms) m 0242 435500; e info@phselecttakoradi.com; www.proteahotels.com. Opened in August 2015, this thoroughly contemporary new 5-storey business hotel associated with the Marriott chain gives the Best Western a run for its money when it comes to Takoradi's smartest digs. Stylish & subdued, the 24m² rooms here are the nicest in town & all come with minibar, flatscreen DSTV, hair dryer, safe, coffee/tea facilities, rainfall showers, South African soft furnishings & many have ocean views. There's a large outdoor swimming pool & restaurant, business centre, gym & plenty of sun loungers to go around, despite the hotel's primarily business focus. *US$150/175 standard/deluxe dbl; US$280/290 executive/garden suite.* **$$$$$–$$$$**

UPMARKET

✱ 🏠 **Africa Beach Hotel** [229 A7] (11 rooms) 📞03120 25148; m 0273 402140; e africa_beach@yahoo.co.uk; www. africabeachhotel.com. Surprisingly, this is the only proper beachfront hotel in Takoradi, for which reason alone it stands out as the first choice in this price range. The attractive hotel grounds, which run down to a small rocky beach, are dominated by a large round swimming pool surrounded by sunloungers, umbrella-shaded seating, & a neat hedge. The popular Body Clock Restaurant has indoor & outdoor seating & it's a popular w/end retreat for locally based expatriates & volunteers. The clean & spacious chalets, distinguished by high-quality furniture & fittings (a genuine rarity in Ghana), come with AC & DSTV. The hands-on owner-manager doubles as the Western Region warden for the British High Commission. *US$105/142 self-contained dbl with garden/ocean view; all rates B&B.* **$$$$**

🏠 **Casablanca Guest Inn** [229 A6] (16 rooms) 📞03120 23115; m 0243 364784/0553 005157; e casablancaguestinn@gmail.com; www.casablancainnghana.com. Converted from a gracious old colonial-era residence in a shady garden on a quiet section of Beach Road, this smart boutique-style hotel vies with Africa Beach as our top pick in this category, offering slightly superior accommodation at lower prices, but lacking the beachfront location. The spacious self-contained dbls have a queen-sized bed with netting, tasteful furnishing, ethnic décor, AC, satellite TV & a large bathroom. Facilities include a small swimming pool, thatched restaurant & bar, & free Wi-Fi. *Excellent value at US$66/80 B&B standard/exec dbl.* **$$$**

🏠 **Raybow International Hotel** [229 B5] (49 rooms) 📞03120 22072/25438/26829; e reservations@raybowhotel.com; www. raybowhotel.com. This smart high-rise hotel doesn't offer much in the way of character or setting, but it's an attractive & modern set-up, & particularly well suited to business travellers. The stylish mini-suites have a huge bed, sofa, DSTV & kitchenette. Facilities include a swimming pool, a good restaurant, Wi-Fi, & a gym is under construction. *From US$105/126 B&B self-contained sgl/dbl.* **$$$$**

🏠 **Hillcrest Hotel** [229 C5] (18 rooms) 📞03120 22277; m 0572 643301/06; e hillcrest.reservations@outlook.com; www. hillcresthotelandapartments.com. This bland international 3-star hotel, situated between the city centre & beach, lacks in character but has good facilities, including a business centre, free Wi-Fi, a swimming pool, AC & DSTV in all rooms, & a dependable restaurant. *US$125/139 B&B self-contained standard/exec dbl.* **$$$$**

MODERATE

🏠 **Hotel Alrose** [229 B5] (18 rooms) 📞03120 24230; m 0249 727300; e info@hotelalrose.com. Tucked away on a circular back road near the SOS Clinic, this unpretentious but pleasant little hotel has clean, reasonably spacious & agreeably furnished rooms with AC, satellite TV, fridge & hot tub/shower. There's a small garden & adequate restaurant. Good value. *US$40 self-contained dbl.* **$$$**

🏠 **Trust Lodge** [229 B6] (10 rooms) 📞03120 23923; e trustlodge@gmail.com. Set in pretty flowering gardens in Beach Rd, this agreeable lodge & restaurant doesn't quite nudge into the upmarket category, but the spacious tiled rooms with queen-size bed, Wi-Fi, AC, flatscreen satellite TV & a big bathroom with hot tub/shower seem like pretty good value at the price. *US$79 dbl.* **$$$**

🏠 **Animens Hotel** [229 B5] (31 rooms) 📞03120 24676; e animenshotel@yahoo.com. This utilitarian 3-storey block isn't exactly bursting with character but it's comfortable & reasonably priced. The attached restaurant offers good local & continental dishes, which can be enjoyed in the pleasant courtyard. The clean rooms have huge bathrooms, along with AC, DSTV, fridge & hot water. *US$32/40/48 B&B std/ deluxe/executive dbl.* **$$$–$$**

BUDGET

🏠 **Ahenfie Hotel** [231 F1] (59 rooms) 📞03120 21267/22966. This large, sludgy green block on Ako Adjei Av on the northern edge of the city centre, though slightly rundown, is probably the best budget deal in a town notable for its pricey accommodation. The small rooms are light, airy & clean, & most come with a TV. Facilities include parking, a good restaurant serving Chinese & Ghanaian dishes in the US$7–8 range, a garden bar, & a disco that no longer seems to function. *US$15 dbl with fan & shared bath; US$20/23 self-contained dbl/twin with AC. All room rates inc b/fast for 2.* **$$**

🏠 **Ridgeway Hotel** [229 D4] (12 rooms) 📞03120 32821; m 0241 847825. Set on a quiet back road not far from the city centre, this 2-storey hotel does suffer slightly from an isolated location, but the self-contained rooms with TV are about as good value as you'll find in this range. *US$19/25 dbl/twin with fan; US$30 dbl with AC.* **$$**

🏠 **Taadi Hotel** [231 D4] (15 rooms) 📞 03120 23778; e taadihotel@yahoo.com. This comfortable, friendly 1-star hotel has a convenient location on J H Cobbinah St, at the southern outskirts of the city centre, & clean spacious rooms with TV at sensible prices. Recommended. *US$15/16/18 self-contained sgl/dbl/suite with AC, all rates inc b/fast for 1 person only.* **$$**

🏠 **Melody Hotel** [231 C4] (19 rooms) m 0244 107144. Formerly one of the best places to stay in Takoradi, this pink hotel on Axim has gone downhill in recent years, but it remains above average in quality; reasonable value & very convenient for public transport. The large bright rooms come with queen-sized bed, fan, AC, fridge, satellite TV & en-suite cold shower. *US$21 dbl.* **$$**

🏠 **Super Star Hotel** [231 D2] (24 rooms) 📞 03120 23105; m 0206 574233. Inflated ego aside, this friendly set-up has large, clean self-contained rooms with satellite TV. The décor leaves something to be desired, but it's a good central compromise between cost & quality. *US$15/21 dbl with fan/AC; US$24 exec dbl.* **$$**

SHOESTRING
🏠 **Mosden Hotel** [231 C3] (17 rooms) 📞 03120 22266. This small hotel on the 1st floor of the Mankessim White House is very conveniently located both for exploring the city centre & for catching public transport. Rooms are comfortable & spacious, & come with a sitting area & satellite TV, but some are a little musty. *US$9.50 dbl with fan & shared bath; US$11–15 self-contained dbl with fan; US$17 self-contained dbl with AC.* **$$–$**

✕ WHERE TO EAT AND DRINK

Several of the restaurants below also double as bars, most obviously The Pub and Gilou Resto-Bar, and the Africa Beach Hotel is also a popular spot for a drink. All listings below are included on one of the two city maps; restaurants and bars in the city centre are mapped on page 231 and those located on Beach Road and environs are mapped on page 229.

RESTAURANTS
City centre
Upmarket
✳ ✕ **Bocadillos** [231 D4] 📞 03120 20366; m 0247 885801; ⏲ 07.00–18.00 Mon–Thu, 07.00–19.00 Fri–Sat. Don't let the Spanish name fool you: this fantastic little restaurant just south of Takoradi centre is known for its very good croissants, pains au chocolat & baguettes above all else. But the cosmopolitan menu also extends to tasty (if lurid) ice creams, as well as pizzas, continental dishes, hot paninis, & cuisine from all over West Africa. There's the choice of sitting on the shaded pavement or in a cool indoor restaurant that looks like it has been transplanted from France. Pastries up to US$2; mains are in the US$8–13 range. **$$$–$**

Budget
✕ **Hot Ernesto Fast Food** [231 B3] 📞 03170 90250; www.hoternesto.com; ⏲ 08.00–22.00 Mon–Sat, noon–22.00 Sun. Situated next to the trotro station for Accra & Kumasi, this superior chop

shop serves tasty jollof rice & chicken on the spot for US$4–6, while more elaborate dishes for around twice the price take 15mins to prepare. **$$–$**
✕ **Etti's Pizza** [231 C2] 📞 03120 93481; m 0244 532388; ⏲ 08.00–22.00 Mon–Sat, 13.00–22.00 Sun. This small corner shop serves tasty take-away pizzas for US$7–10. **$$**
🍴 **G Dodzie Bakery** [231 C2] ⏲ 06.00–21.30 Mon–Sat, 10.00–20.00 Sun. In addition to fresh white & wholewheat bread, this bakery next to Etti's Pizza serves pastries, filled rolls & other snacks to take away. **$**
✕ **Seth Chinese Take-Away** [231 E3] m 0244 280598; ⏲ 10.00–22.00 daily. This popular hole-in-the-wall Chinese has a varied meat & vegetarian menu, with most dishes in the US$7–8 range, as well as indoor seating & a cheap bar. **$$**
✕ **Shalimar Restaurant** [231 C4] m 0243 470041; ⏲ 09.00–19.00 daily. This old-school hole-in-the-wall Indian restaurant is hidden away in the STC depot, & the retro vibe makes sense

when you learn that the Indian proprietor has been managing restaurants in Ghana since the 1960s. The menu covers a welcome selection of curries for US$4–6, & vegetarians are well catered for. **$$–$**

✕ Daavi Ama Special Chop Bar [231 C3] **m** 0208 290688/0240 529219; ⏰ 08.00–22.00 Mon–Sat. The long queues alone should give you an idea that this is a fine place to chop. The menu covers Ghanaian staples including fufu, TZ, omo tuo, & konkonte, & you'll be out the door for under US$3. **$**

Beach Road and environs

✳ ✕ Captain Hook's [229 C5] ✆ 03120 27085; ⏰ noon–15.00 Mon–Sat & 18.00–23.30 daily. This German-owned restaurant on Beach Road is undoubtedly the smartest in Takoradi, specialising in top-notch seafood & grills. Although the prices seem steep if you've been in Ghana for a while, both the food & décor are good enough to see the restaurant packed at w/ends. Good wine list, too! Mains are mostly around US$20. **$$$**

✳ ✕ The Pub [229 D6] ✆ 03120 33091; ⏰ 09.00–01.00 daily. This German-owned restaurant lives up to its name in so far as it does have something of a sports-bar atmosphere, complete with gloomy lighting, large-screen TVs & dark-wood counters, tables & chairs. But it also doubles as a world-class French & continental restaurant, serving excellent meat & seafood dishes in the US$12–16 range, as well as cheaper bar fare – burgers, pasta, etc – for around US$8–10. The convivial atmosphere is completed by possibly the flashiest & cleanest bathroom facilities in all of Ghana. **$$$–$$**

✕ Body Clock Restaurant [229 A7] Africa Beach Hotel; ⏰ 06.30–23.00 daily. Popular as much for its beachfront location & swimming pool areas as its food, this is nevertheless one of the best eateries in Takoradi, particularly if you are after seafood or steak. Most mains are in the US$15–20 range, but cheaper grilled kebabs are also available. **$$$–$$**

✕ Han Palace [229 B6] ✆ 03120 21999; **m** 0203 921538; ⏰ 11.30–22.30 daily. Though rather lacking in character, this smart restaurant is widely regarded to serve the best Chinese in western Ghana, & the menu includes a varied selection of meat & vegetarian dishes. Around US$13–18 for a main with rice & there's a casino out back. **$$$**

✕ Gilou Resto-Bar [229 C6] **m** 0244 454359; ⏰ 08.00–23.00 Mon–Thu, 08.00–02.00 Fri–Sun.

Split into a sports bar with large-screen TV & a bright restaurant area with light wooden furniture (& another room currently under construction), this is a popular spot with expats, & the menu ranges from seafood & steaks in the US$14–20 range to Chinese dishes, burgers, & pizzas for US$8–10. **$$$–$$**

✕ Coffee Corner [229 B5] **m** 0508 419207; www.coffeecornerghana.com; ⏰ 07.00–17.30 Mon–Fri, 08.00–14.30 Sat, 08.00–13.00 Sun. Warmly recommended by readers, this new Dutch-owned café serves up real coffee, fresh bread, paninis, croissants, brownies, milkshakes & more. There's AC & Wi-Fi if you need to get some emailing done, & their daily lunch specials range from pulled pork to Indonesian soto ayam soup. **$$–$**

✕ Paragon Bar & Grill [229 D6] **m** 0202 3224835; ◼ fb.me/paragonbarandgrill; ⏰ 10.00–22.00 daily. Expanded from the nightclub next door, this thoroughly modern eatery sits across 2 floors of a new building in the harbour area & serves everything from piri-piri prawns to pork chops, pizza, pasta, burgers, Mongolian beef, & some local options as well for US$4–7. There's a full bar & cocktail menu, terrace seating, & the nightclub still gets going at w/ends. **$$–$**

✕ Classy Joint [229 D6] **m** 0207 077075/0203 194830; ⏰ 08.00–18.00 Mon–Fri. For a quick lunch in the harbour area, this popular & perfectly named canteen tucked behind the Cocobod building is a safe bet. There's a comfortable indoor dining area with flatscreen TV, & they dish up waakye, jollof, fufu, & more every weekday for US$4. **$**

✕ Country Club [229 A6] **m** 0556 150131/0503 323006; ⏰ 07.00–late daily. Though you can't actually golf here, the old wood & stone interior, pool tables, & big sofas feel comfortably clubby nonetheless. Outside, there's a swimming pool (US$5 day use), tennis courts, & plenty of shaded terrace & garden seating. The menu is continental with a few nods to Lebanon, & mains go for US$8–13. **$$$–$$**

BARS AND NIGHTCLUBS
City centre

♀ Faze Pub [231 D4] ⏰ 15.00–23.00 daily. This cosy central pub with blasting AC (& sometimes TV) on Pakos Rd has a good wine list, with most bottles falling in the US$6–13 range.

♀ Spike's Bar [229 C4] ✆ 0275 772058; ⏰ noon–late daily. Just south of the centre on

Alex Cobbinah Av, this new bar is a hotspot for music & a great place to chat with locals over a beer & popcorn or grilled meat. It also hosts an excellent regular happy hour.

BEACH ROAD AND ENVIRONS

✳ ♀Coconut Grove Bar [229 B7] ☺ daily. This no-frills beach bar is one of the few places in Takoradi where you can enjoy a cheap sundowner with the Atlantic crashing within eyeshot & earshot.

♀Vienna Beach Club [229 D6] m 0249 825924; ☺ 08.00–late daily. Boasting a great beachfront location in the old town centre, this glitzy spot offers a bit of everything: a swimming pool (*US$4pp/day*), a decent continental restaurant, 2 bars with a cocktail menu, pool tables & indoor & outdoor seating, a casino, & live music from 18.00 every Fri. The upstairs nightclub specialises in reggae on Fri night, & more chilled dance sounds on Sat & Sun.

♀Ebony Lounge [229 A6] m 0542 484647; ☺ 15.00–midnight daily. Situated around the corner from the Africa Beach Hotel, this oddball cocktail bar feels a bit like somebody's living room, except there are football shirts & women's panties pinned to the walls. They do mixed drinks in the US$6–8 range, plus the usual beers & soft drinks. There is also outdoor seating.

OTHER PRACTICALITIES

FOREIGN EXCHANGE All the major banks are represented, with the Standard Chartered [229 D6] usually offering the most favourable rates and Barclays head office in the old town centre [229 D6] able to change up to £250 per day (more than most other banks). St Michael's forex [231 E2] on Market Circle is one of several private forex bureaux in the town centre, and plenty of moneychangers hang around at the corner of Kofi Annan and Market Circle. There are ATMs where you can draw local currency against a Visa card outside most banks marked on the map (and GCB, GTBank and EcoBank take MasterCard).

INTERNET The super-fast **Vodafone Internet** [231 E1] (♦ *03120 24277/21113*; ☺ *07.00–23.00*) stands on the north side of Paa Grant Road, about 200m from Cape Coast Station. More pleasant if you've got your own device is the free Wi-Fi at Coffee Corner, just off Shippers Council Roundabout on Anita Mensah Road.

MEDICAL The best medical facility is the **International SOS Clinic** [229 B5] (♦ *03120 22024*; e *takoradi.clinic@internationalsos.com; www.internationalsos.com*), a private clinic situated 100m south of Shippers Council Roundabout, on the same back road as the Hotel Alrose. It offers 24-hour ambulance and emergency stabilisation, and has a small ICU as well as an in-house pharmacy, X-ray unit and laboratory. The **GPHA Clinic** [229 D5] (♦ *03120 22628*) near the harbour is also quite good.

SHOPPING Takoradi doesn't offer much in the way of craft shopping. There are gift shops or craft stalls at some of the smarter hotels, but they tend to be overpriced. If you're looking for reading matter, Elove Books [231 C3] on Busumakura Road has a few novels tucked away between the religious tracts and self-help manuals.

SWIMMING Day visitors will be asked US$5 to use the swimming pools at the Hillcrest Hotel [229 C5], Vienna Beach Club [229 D6], Africa Beach Hotel [229 A7], Protea Hotel Select [229 A6] and Country Club restaurant [229 A6].

WHAT TO SEE AND DO

There is not much in the way of sightseeing in Takoradi, though the central market area [231 D/E2–3] is a hive of commercial activity and can be quite exciting to explore. The old town centre has a few moderately interesting old buildings, and there are great views over the harbour about halfway along the main road connecting it to the city centre.

MONKEY HILL [231 G1] Though it is not formally protected as a nature sanctuary, Monkey Hill supports a 3ha patch of forest where tenacious populations of the localised olive colobus monkey and more widespread spot-nosed monkey survive practically within view of central Takoradi. A census in 1999 counted 12 colobus and 41 spot-nosed monkeys, and an anecdotal report in early 2013 suggests the total population is now around 50 pairs. It is easy to visit Monkey Hill informally, ideally in the early morning or late afternoon (17.00), when the monkeys are most active. The turn-off to the top of the hill lies on the west side of the Sekondi road, about 100m north of Paa Grant Circle.

SEKONDI Few travellers make the 20-minute trotro ride from Takoradi to Sekondi, but it's an interesting place. Those who do will be amply rewarded. The well-maintained **Fort Orange** is still in use as a lighthouse, and the caretakers will usually allow visitors to wander around the fortifications, which offer a great view over the town. The railway station is a fine piece of colonial architecture, while the harbour, with its backdrop of green hills, is bustling with colourful fishing boats. Above the harbour, the quarter still referred to locally as the 'European Town' is a compact jumble of crumbling turn-of-the-20th-century buildings, which make for interesting viewing.

AROUND TAKORADI

SHAMA The small coastal town of Shama (sometimes spelt Chama), 25km east of Takoradi, makes a diverting goal for a day or overnight excursion, mainly thanks to the formidable presence of **Fort St Sebastian** (⊕ *08.00–18.00 daily; entrance US$2.50 inclusive of a guided tour*), the third-oldest fortified building in Ghana. Looming imposingly above the main square and central market, the fort was originally built and named by the Portuguese in 1523. Roughly star-shaped, and protected by an inner and outer wall, the fort today has a ground plan almost identical to the Portuguese prototype, despite having been close to dereliction when it was captured by the Dutch in 1640. Following a brief British occupation in 1664, it was completely rebuilt by the Dutch, who added an extra storey to the central buildings. Later in its career, strong seaward buttresses were constructed to prevent the soft foundation rock from being washed away – hence the steep semicircle of stairs leading to the main entrance.

So far as we could see, Shama's only other building of any great vintage is the Methodist church, built opposite the fort in 1893. Also of interest is the fish market on the mouth of the Pra River, a short walk to the east of the town centre. During the gold-trading era, Shama was renowned for the seaworthy canoes that were crafted on an island a short distance upstream of the Pra mouth, and even today it is possible to organise a canoe ride up the river from near the market. The philosopher Anton Wilhelm Amo, who was born in the vicinity of Axim in 1703, taken to Amsterdam by a preacher at the age of four, and later studied at the University of Halle (making him the first African known to have attended a European university), died in Shama c1759, and is buried in the fort's cemetery.

Getting there and away From Takoradi, follow the Cape Coast road for about 20km to Shama Junction, then turn right on to the 4km feeder road. Several trotros run between Takoradi and Shama daily, or you could pick up a vehicle bound for Cape Coast, drop at the junction, then hop into one of the regular shared taxis into town.

🏠 Where to stay and eat

🏠 **Hotel Applause** (19 rooms) ✆03120 96402/03170 81232. The best feature of this 3-storey hotel is the rooftop bar & restaurant, which offers great views over the town & decent meals for around US$5. The rooms all have a balcony & seem fair value. *US$22/27 self-contained dbl with fan/AC.* **$$**

🏠 **Abuesi Resort** (8 rooms) ✆03120 91708; m 050 5838582/0244 359100; e info@ abuesibeachresort.com; www.abuesibeachresort. com. Set on a hill 5km southwest of Shama, this well-signposted resort offers stunning views of the beach from the thatched-roofed restaurant & bar, & the rooms with queen-sized bed, cane & wood furnishing, satellite TV, AC, fan & hot water are very good value. All of which sounds better on paper than it comes across in reality, as the overwhelming impact of the resort for some years has been its unfinished appearance & aura of forlorn isolation. *US$40 self-contained dbl.* **$$**

🏠 **Shama Beach Resort** m 0208 957262/0241 524494/0243 375073;

e shamabeachresort@gmail.com. Around 4km southwest of Shama along the road to Abuesi, this was billed in the 5th edition of this guidebook as potentially the biggest thing to happen to Shama since the Portuguese built their fort there. Development stalled shortly after that, but happily things have gotten off the ground since then, & today the resort offers well-equipped thatch-roof bungalows. It is also home to the 9-hole Pra River Golf Links (a round costs around US$20) & their thatched restaurant serves simple meals and local drinks. It remains something of a work in progress, so it seems the Portuguese don't have to worry about their legacy being overshadowed just yet, but it's a considerably more welcome addition to the town. *US$40 dbl.* **$$**

🏠 **Beach Gardens Lodge** (6 rooms) m 0277 683844. There's no beach, no garden, & the lodgings look pretty dismal. Still, this small out-of-town lodge is the cheapest option around Shama. *US$11–14 dbl.* **$**

OLD KOMENDA The mouth of the Komenda River was a focal point of Anglo–Dutch rivalry in the 17th and 18th centuries, as testified by two ruined forts on the opposite banks. **Fort Vreedenburg** was built by the Dutch in 1682, and **Fort English** by the British five years later. The substantial remains of the British fortress can still be seen in Old Komenda, a sleepy, small fishing port that also boasts an attractive old Wesleyan church and lies 5km south along a signposted turn-off from the main Cape Coast–Takoradi road. The fort aside, there is nothing to Old Komenda that couldn't be seen or done at dozens of other small ports along the Ghanaian coast, but it's an attractive enough backwater, practically unvisited by tourists, and in the right frame of mind it could be a worthwhile place to hang out for a few days.

Regular shared taxis run to Komenda from Takoradi, as do trotros from Cape Coast. The only accommodation, 300m and signposted from the west side of the feeder road, about 500m before the trotro station, is the clean but rather gloomy and overpriced three-storey **Grace Hotel** (*26 rooms;* m *0244 861720/838958*), which charges US$18/22 for a self-contained single/double with fan, and US$42 for a double with air conditioning.

TARKWA Set in the forested interior 50km northwest of Takoradi as the crow flies, this substantial town is the commercial hub of a region renowned for its gold and manganese mines. Despite its lush surrounds and a smattering of colonial architecture, it is of greater interest to business travellers than tourists, though the artificial lake at Tarkwa Banso, 45 minutes' walk from the town centre, has an attractive green setting, and there's a small local bar on the lakeshore. Tarkwa used to be an important stage on the passenger train service between Takoradi and

Kumasi, but access is now only by road, an 85km route via Agona plied by a few Metro Mass buses and several trotros daily.

↥ Where to stay and eat There is no shortage of accommodation in Tarkwa. The top address is the three-star **Hotel de Hilda** (*40 rooms;* \ *0249 522416/0540 121031;* e *reservation@hoteldehilda.com; www.hoteldehilda.com*), which charges from US$20 for a budget room, or US$46 for self-contained doubles with air conditioning, and has good facilities including a restaurant, car rental desk, salon, gym and infirmary. Cheaper options include the two-star **Hotel Lynka** (\ *03123 20412;* e *lynkahotel@yahoo.com*), 1km from the town centre, the budget **Morning Star Lodge** (\ *03123 20355;* m *0242 214305*) and very central **Rail View Hotel** (\ *03123 20136*).

Busua and Surrounds

Situated 20km west of Takoradi as the crow flies, the colourful fishing village of Busua (population 5,000) is the traditional capital of the historically important Ahanta Kingdom. It is also perhaps the country's most important beach resort, one whose friendly backpacker-orientated atmosphere and dense concentration of affordable lodgings/restaurants make it tempting to label it West Africa's answer to Malawi's Nkhata Bay. The idyllic stretch of coast flanking Busua has also seen plenty of recent tourist development, with at least half a dozen low-key eco-friendly resorts now lining the beaches around Butre (3km east of Busua) and Akwidaa/Cape Three Points (15–20km to the southwest). Important historical sites in the vicinity include the village of Dixcove and Fort Metal Cross (about 2km west of Busua), the hillside Fort Batenstein at Butre, and the lighthouse at Cape Three Points, the most southerly point in Ghana.

BUSUA

Strung along a wide sandy beach for about 1km, Busua has long rivalled Kokrobite (pages 166–71) as the ultimate Ghanaian beach chill-out venue, though its relative distance from Accra and less densely clustered facilities mean that it generally comes across as quieter and less overtly touristy than its eastern counterpart. Flanked on the west by the Busua Lagoon, the beach is generally regarded to offer some of the safest swimming in the country, though (as with anywhere along the Ghanaian coastline) tides and currents can be unpredictable, so take local advice before you swim, and don't venture out deeper than the locals do. Having attracted a steady influx of budget travellers to its beach since the 1960s, Busua has also emerged as a focal point of

BUSUA & surrounds
For listings, see pages 243–5, unless otherwise stated

Where to stay

1	African Rainbow Resort	C1
2	Akwidaa Inn *p252*	B4
3	Alaska Beach Resort	C1
4	Arena Beach Lodge	B1
5	Busua Beach Resort	C1
6	Busua Inn	B2
7	Ceto House *p252*	D4
8	Dadson's Lodge	B2
9	Elizabeth's Inn	A2
10	Escape3Points *p252*	A4
11	Ezile Bay Village *p252*	A4
12	Fanta's Folly *p249*	F3
13	Green Zion Garden *p249*	F3
14	Hideout Lodge *p249*	F3
15	Johannesburg Beach House *p249*	F3
16	Kangaroo Pouch Beach Resort *p249*	C2
17	Sabina's Guesthouse	B1
18	Scorpion Hill Lodge	A3
19	Stone Wonderland Lodge	E4

Where to eat and drink

	African Rainbow Resort	(see 1)
	Busua Inn	(see 6)
20	The Café	B1
21	Daniel the Pancake Man	B1
	Ezile Bay Village *p252*	(see 11)
	Fanta's Folly *p249*	(see 12)
	Green Zion Garden *p249*	(see 13)
	Hideout Lodge *p249*	(see 14)
	Johannesburg Beach House *p249*	(see 15)
22	Juliedan's Kitchen	B2
	Kangaroo Pouch Beach Resort *p244*	(see 16)
23	Okoreye Tree	C2
	Scorpion Hill Lodge	(see 18)

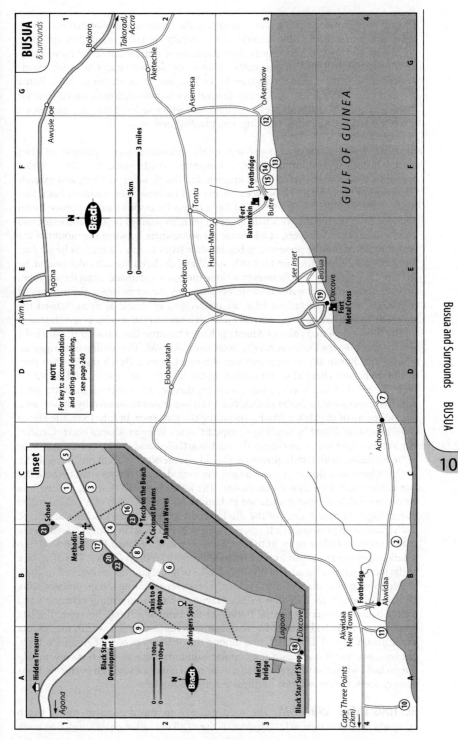

BUSUA
& surrounds

Takoradi,
Accra

Bokoro

Awusie Joe

Aketechie

Asemesa

Asemkow

Agona

Tontu

Boerkrom

Huntu-Mano

Butre

Fort
Batenstein

Footbridge

GULF OF GUINEA

Elobankatah

Achowa

BuSua

Dixcove

Fort
Metal Cross

Cape Three Points
(2km)

Akwidaa
New Town

Akwidaa

Footbridge

N

Brⱥdt

0 ————— 3km
0 ————— 3 miles

NOTE
For key to accommodation
and eating and drinking,
see page 240

Inset

Agona

Hidden Treasure

School

Methodist
church

Teec on the Beach

Coconut Dreams

Ananta Waves

Black Star
Development

Taxis to
Agona

Swingers Spot

Metal
bridge

Black Star Surf Shop

Dixcove

Lagoon

N

Brⱥdt

0 ——— 100m
0 ——— 100yds

Ghana's ever-growing surfing scene, following the recent opening of two surf shops along the beach. And while facilities are generally geared towards low-spending volunteers and backpackers, Busua does also cater to a more upmarket crowd, with the Busua Beach Resort in particular being a popular weekend retreat for expats associated with the mining industries in Tarkwa and Takoradi. Since 2011, Busua has also been home to the Asa Baako Festival (*www.asabaako.com*), which runs for three days every March and takes over the village with a series of concerts, parties, art exhibitions, sporting events, trekking, tree planting and more.

HISTORY Busua is the traditional seat of the Ahantamanhene, paramount chief of the historically important Ahanta Kingdom, which made its first recorded appearance on a map drawn by an anonymous Dutch sailor in 1629, and extends over most of the coastal belt between Shama and Essiama. Oral tradition has it that Ahanta was founded by a leader called Badu Bonsu (also spelt Baidoo Bonsoe), who emerged from the mouth of a whale, together with his younger brother and sister, and hundreds of other followers, at a landing site somewhere between the mouth of the Ankobra River and the present-day border with Ivory Coast. As soon as he set foot on land, Badu Bonsu took up his battle sword and declared himself ruler over all he surveyed. He then led his followers east along the coast and inland along the Ankobra River, to settle at a well-watered site remembered by the name Bresu, the first capital of Ahanta. A few generations later, an unspecified epidemic at Bresu caused the survivors to evacuate to the coast and establish a new capital at what is now Busua.

The most celebrated ruler of Ahanta is King Otumfuo Badu Bonsu II, who led a rebellion against the Dutch at nearby Butre over 1837–38. The conflict was triggered when Badu Bonsu seized a gunpowder shipment from a Dutch trader, then shot dead two envoys charged with negotiating the return of the goods, and displayed their decapitated heads as ornaments on his throne. The governor at Butre led a punitive expedition to Busua in October 1837, but it was ambushed by the Ahanta, who killed 45 of the Dutch troops, including the governor. In July 1838, the Dutch government retaliated by sending an expeditionary force to Ahanta under General Jan Verveer. The king was captured, court-martialled and – despite attempting to bribe his judges with lavish quantities of gold – sentenced to death on 26 July 1838.

Otumfuo Badu Bonsu II was hanged the next day, on the very spot where the two envoys had been shot a year before. The king's head was cut off, pickled in a jar of formaldehyde, and dispatched to Europe for the attention of a Leiden-based phrenologist (a practitioner of the discredited pseudo-science linking skull shape to character and personality). It was not seen or heard of again until 2002, when the Dutch novelist Arthur Japin, author of *The Two Hearts of Kwasi Boachi*, traced it to a dark and dusty cupboard in the Leiden University Medical Centre. The discovery of the long-lost royal head, still preserved in its original jar, was announced in 2005, and following four years of negotiations, a team representing the incumbent King Otumfuo Badu Bonsu XV flew to The Hague to stage a mourning ceremony and take it back to Busua for formal burial. At the time of writing, however, the late king has yet to be laid to rest, due to ongoing factional disputes within the Ahanta Traditional Council. Dissatisfaction among the ordinary people of Ahanta is high, not least because it has meant the popular Kundum Festival, which is customarily put on hold when the funeral rites of a dead royal have not yet been performed, has been cancelled every year for multiple successive Augusts.

GETTING THERE AND AWAY The road gateway to Busua (and to pretty much everywhere else covered in this chapter) is the small but rather chaotic junction town of Agona, which lies about 20km from Takoradi along the main road to Axim and Elubo. From Agona, the road running south to Busua and Dixcove splits after about 6km at the village of Asane (also known as Boerkrom), with the left fork reaching Busua after another 4km and the right fork reaching Dixcove after about 5km.

There is no direct public transport between Takoradi and Busua. Instead, you must first catch a shared taxi or trotro to Agona (these leave Takoradi from the main station on Axim Road), from where regular shared taxis continue on to Busua, Butre, Dixcove and Akwidaa. Alternatively, a charter taxi from Takoradi to most places covered in this chapter will cost around US$20–30.

SECURITY There are occasional incidents of robbery, typically at machete-point, on the paths running between most of the villages in this chapter (between Butre and Prince's Town, more or less). If you intend to hike between towns, we recommend you bring a guide along if possible (any hotel in this chapter can arrange this), and don't carry any valuables.

WHERE TO STAY
Upmarket
Busua Beach Resort [241 C1] (62 rooms) \03120 93307/8; m 0206 388029/0577 665958; e busua@gbhghana.net; www.gbhghana.net. This popular resort is set in large landscaped grounds running down to the beach at the east end of the village. It is easily the smartest option in Busua, with a wonderful location & excellent facilities, including a swimming pool, gym, spa, nightclub, curio shops, tennis court, 3-hole golf course & Wi-Fi throughout. There is also a good & quite reasonably priced restaurant specialising in seafood. Comfortable rather than luxurious, the semi-detached dbl/twin chalets are starting to look in need of refurbishment, but they do come with private balcony, ocean view, AC & satellite TV. *US$145/175/210 self-contained sgl/ dbl/suite with AC.* **$$$$$–$$$$**

Moderate
African Rainbow Resort [241 C1] (12 rooms) \03120 32149/91357; m 0270 246269/0206 557879; e africanrainbow@gmail.com; www. africanrainbowresort.com. Owned & managed by a hospitable & attentive Canadian-Ghanaian family, this 3-storey block is designed with a view to being naturally ventilated. The spacious & well-maintained rooms, each with its own private balcony looking over the road to the sea, are attractively decorated with colourful local fabrics & wooden furniture, & come with satellite TV, minibar, fan & hot water. Facilities include an excellent bar & restaurant, table tennis, pool table, & a well-stocked curio shop. The only real drawback is the lack of a private beach, but the Alaska Beach Resort & Busua Beach Resort both lie

within metres of the gate. Good value at *US$38/44 self-contained sgl/dbl with fan; US$50/58 sgl/dbl with AC; US$66/79 4-person room with fan/AC; all rates inc a good b/fast.* **$$$**

Busua Inn [241 B2] (4 rooms) m 0207 373579/0243 087354; e busuainn@yahoo.com; www.busuainn.com. Best known perhaps for its excellent wooden-terrace restaurant overlooking the beach, this French-owned/managed hotel in the heart of the village also has a few large, airy & exceedingly comfortable twin rooms, all of which come with fan & en-suite shower. The most expensive room also enjoys a terrace overlooking the sea, which is available for use by the other guests. *US$26–40 self-contained twin with cold shower; US$70 dbl with AC & hot shower.* **$$$–$$**

Arena Beach Lodge [241 B1] (14 rooms) m 0205 857178; e arenabeachlodge@gmail.com; www.arena-lodge.com. This new whitewashed multi-storey hotel right in the centre of the village was still a bit of a work in progress when we dropped in, but construction seemed to be nearing completion. Rooms here are simple but well kept, with modern bathrooms & some come with AC, fridge, & screened-in terraces. The Italian owner-manager's influence is especially felt on the outdoor restaurant's menu, where pizzas & seafood dishes go for US$4–8. *Dbl/trpl/quad rooms available for US$23–68.* **$$$–$$**

Budget
Alaska Beach Resort [241 C1] (12 rooms) m 0207 397311. Boasting an idyllic beachfront location adjacent to Busua Beach Resort, this

is the most inherently attractive budget option in Busua, & the brightly decorated huts & lively atmosphere have made it a perennially popular hangout for volunteers & budget travellers, though reader reports indicate maintenance & other standards have gone downhill in recent years, & we've also been told of a recent problem with theft from the rooms. The attached restaurant serves sandwiches, salads & Ghanaian dishes in the US$4–6 range. *US$12 sgl with fan & net using common bath; US$20 self-contained dbl; US$4pp camping.* **$$**

🏠 **Dadson's Lodge** [241 B2] (13 rooms) m 0503 591280. This long-serving double-storey budget lodge is nothing if not unassuming, but it gets glowing reviews from budget travellers & volunteers, & it's the first place you'll pass on your right when walking from the trotro park towards Busua Beach Resort. The building itself is fairly uninspiring, but the management is friendly & engaged, & the rooms invitingly priced. *US$11 sgl using shared bath; US$13/16 self-contained dbl/ twin with fan & TV; US$26/33 family room sleeping 4/5.* **$$–$**

🏠 **Stone Wonderland Lodge** [241 E4] (2 chalets) m 0249 151469/0247 837950. Formerly Black Mamba Corner, this isolated lodge lies in lush gardens on a peninsula on the western outskirts of town. The chalets are quite basic but the location is stunning. Camping is permitted. *US$19 dbl chalet; US$8 camping.* **$$**

🏠 **Scorpion Hill Lodge** [241 A3] (5 rooms) m 0209 169888; e scorpionhilllodge@hotmail. com; f fb.me/scorpionhilllodge. Set in a sandy grove of coconut & banana trees facing the inlet

at the southern edge of the village & just across the metal bridge, this Danish-owned backpacker haunt has quickly become a budget traveller favourite. The high-ceilinged tiled rooms with mozzie nets, reading lamps & ceiling fans are not long on décor, but they're a great deal, & one comes with hot water & a private terrace for the same price – ask if it's free. The new Black Star Surf Shop is based here, & there are bonfires & a slackline to entertain you on land. *US$13 dbl bed only; US$21 HB dbl.* **$**

🏠 **Kangaroo Pouch Beach Resort** [241 C2] (13 rooms) ☏ 03121 99767; m 0207 329260; e info@beachresortkangaroo.com or theglobe@ hotmail.com; www.beachresortkangaroo.com. This newish beachfront resort, owned by Ghanaians who lived for a while in Australia, has clean but small rooms & an especially central location. *US$17/23 self-contained dbl/trpl with fan & satellite TV; US$34 dbl with AC & balcony.* **$$**

Shoestring
🏠 **Sabina's Guesthouse** [241 B1] (10 rooms) m 0546 855891/0556 26616. This simple family-run guesthouse opposite the Methodist church has basic but reasonably clean cell-like rooms with fans, as well as equally rudimentary dormitory accommodation. *US$2.50pp dorm bed; US$6/8 sgl/dbl with shared bath; US$11/14 self-contained sgl/dbl.* **$**

🏠 **Elizabeth's Inn** [241 A2] (3 rooms) m 0502 124659. This agreeable but no-frills homestay-like set-up is favoured by several volunteer organisations. *US$8 dbl with fan.* **$**

✕ WHERE TO EAT AND DRINK
Restaurants
Moderate
✕ **Busua Inn** [241 B2] ⊕ 07.00–21.00 daily. Set on a spacious wooden terrace overlooking the beach, this top-notch restaurant has a menu reflecting the nationality of its French owner-manager, with vegetarian selections in the US$6–7 range, seafood & meat dishes at US$10–13, & a good selection of desserts. In addition to the standard menu, it usually has a few daily specials. There's also fresh coffee & a good wine list & cocktail menu. **$$$–$$**

✕ **African Rainbow Resort** [241 C1] ⊕ 07.00–22.00 Mon–Fri, 07.00–midnight Sat–

Sun. Specialising in delicious pizzas in the US$11–15 range, the ground-floor restaurant at this hotel also serves good b/fasts (*US$5–8*) & a varied selection of meat & seafood dishes (*US$8–13*). You can eat on the terrace, indoors or (when it's open) at the rooftop bar. **$$$–$$**

Budget
✳ ✕ **Okoreye Tree Restaurant** [241 B2] m 0544 525229; ⊕ 07.30–20.00 daily, later if they're busy. It's difficult to fault this breezy beachfront eatery operated by Black Star Surf Shop. The good-value menu features a mouth-watering

range of international dishes, including Thai, Indian & Mexican (the fiesta burrito is superb!) as well as Western-infused Ghanaian specialities such as the Black Star red-red, cheesy pizzas & hearty b/fasts. Vegetarians are well catered for, beers are cheap, & it also serves smoothies, cocktails & fruit juices. Most dishes cost US$3–7. $$–$

✗ **Daniel the Pancake Man** [241 B1] m 0503 687125; ◷ 07.00–20.00 daily. Hidden away in an unmarked, coral-coloured house behind the Methodist church & school, Daniel's friendly restaurant prepares 'world-famous' pancakes, great fruit juice & a small menu of mains at very reasonable prices. It's best to order mains other than pancakes a few hours in advance. Most mains US$1–3, lobster US$6. $$–$

✗ **Juliedan's Kitchen** [241 B2] m 0248 985026; ◷ 06.30–21.30 daily. Situated opposite Dadson's Lodge, this warmly recommended local eatery serves the usual Ghanaian chop, plus a few surprises like pizza, Senegalese *yassa poulet* (lemon chicken) & burgers. Great value at US$3–4. $

✗ **The Café** [241 B1] m 0269 675266/0266 604628; ◷ 07.00–19.00 Mon–Thu, 07.00–21.00 Thu–Sun. This new English-owned & reader-recommended café on Busua's main drag serves up real coffee, tea & smoothies, along with home-baked cakes, muffins & brownies. There's a rotating daily menu of light meals & sandwiches, & some well-priced rooms to let as well. $$–$

Bars and nightclubs Most of the restaurants listed above serve drinks, with the **Okoreye Tree Restaurant** [241 C2] being a particularly congenial spot serving beers, cocktails and wine by the glass, and usually staying open until the last customer is sated. Also worth a mention is the beachfront bar at the **Kangaroo Pouch Beach Resort** [241 C2], which is open 24 hours daily. For something more sophisticated, the breezy rooftop bar at **African Rainbow Resort** [241 C1], usually open evenings only, is a wonderful spot to sip cocktails or beers under the sparkling African night sky, accompanied by chilled music played through a great sound system and more occasional live jazz. At the south end of the village, **Scorpion Hill Lodge** [241 A3] throws occasional parties.

OTHER PRACTICALITIES

Internet There's Wi-Fi at African Rainbow Resort [241 C1] and Busua Beach Resort [241 C1], both of which should be available to restaurant or bar customers.

Surf shops There are now two surf shops in Busua, both of which charge around US$25 for a 90-minute private lesson. For altruistic shredders, the Surf & Impact programme (m *0245 946799/0209 352188*; *www.surfnimpact.org*) might be a good option for those who want to spend an extended period in Busua combining surfing in the morning with volunteer work in the afternoons. The well-loved Mr Bright's Surf School recently decamped to a new location in Kokrobite (pages 168 and 170).

Ahanta Waves [241 B2] (m *0269 197812/0272 492100*; e *info@ahantawaves. com; www.ahantawaves.com*) Once a manager at Black Star himself, Busua native and surf pro Peter Ansah struck out on his own in 2014 and opened Ahanta Waves at Black Star's former location on the beach next to Coconut Dreams, renaming the shop after the Ahanta people native to Busua. They do private and group lessons, week-long surf camps, and can also arrange surfing excursions all along the Ghanaian coast. Free all-day board use is included when you take a private lesson, otherwise boards are available at US$20/hour or US$24/day (with cheaper pro rata weekly and monthly rates available). In addition to surfboards, it also rents out snorkels/fins by the hour or day.

Black Star Surf Shop [241 A3] (m *0556 267914*; e *surfcampghana@gmail.com*; ⓕ *fb.me/blackstarsurfshop*). Tracing its origins to a couple of Peace Corps volunteers

If you are looking to explore uncrowded surf with loads of curious and friendly local spectators, then Ghana is the place for you. Although the 1960s movie *Endless Summer* placed Ghana on the surfers, world map, up until a few years ago there was only the occasional intrepid surfer in the country. Even today, you can generally surf anywhere with absolutely no-one else in the water. There are now professional surf shops in both Kokrobite and Busua that offer private and group surfing lessons along with equipment rental and sales.

Although the majority of breaks in Ghana suit beginner to intermediate-level surfers, they are attractive to all levels for the lack of crowds, the warm water, absence of sharks, ease of travel and the friendly locals. The hazards are minimal, with the biggest annoyance being the pollution (rubbish and human waste) and the occasional sea urchin. There is always a break working somewhere in Ghana, although the swell is consistently best (2–3m) from August to October.

You can effortlessly spend a couple of weeks working your way west along the coast from Accra. Kokrobite is becoming a popular surfing spot close to Accra, with a fast beach break that's best at mid-to-high tide. Just 10 mins walk from Big Milly's Backyard in Kokrobite, a spot called Joshua's is possibly the best intermediate wave in Ghana, with 400-yard rides breaking left and right. A short hop further west are Fete and Senya Beraku, where, depending on conditions, there are three breaks. The first is a long right-hand point break in front of White Sands Resort. The second is a beach break five minutes' walk east of Till's Resort. The third is a fun point break that curls into the bay directly beneath Fort Good Hope at the fishing village of Senya Beraku. Here you can jostle with local kids for waves as they surf (with incredible agility) on planks of wood that have literally been ripped straight from discarded fishing boats. If the swell is really pumping, the nearby village of Apam produces a long right-hander that breaks on a sandy bottom all the way into the protected bay.

West of Takoradi, Busua Beach offers a base to explore a number of breaks. The beach break can provide some fun hollow rides. A longer paddle out to Black Mamba (a right-hand point break over rocks) is arguably the best adrenalin-fuelled ride in Ghana. A little further west over the hill, Dixcove provides a long fat ride for the more adventurous long board rider.

For a mix of absolute pristine beach and guaranteed surf in the smallest of swell, make the trip out to Cape Three Points. This isolated area of coast offers short right- and left-hand breaks.

A spot you won't find in any surf guide but a must for any beginner surfer is Beyin, which, on swell less than 4ft, presents A-frames that will have you wishing for more daylight and less sunburn.

Regardless of your experience level, surfing in Ghana is a great way to engage with the locals in a tropical paradise.

back in 2006, this is Busua's oldest and best-known surf shop, and has been managed as a British-Ghanaian partnership since 2013. It changed location in 2014 and today operates out of the Scorpion Hill Lodge at the south end of town, where the enthusiastic manager and staff can set up customisable private or group lessons, plus longer surf camps. Boards are available at US$6/hour or US$12/day.

Bike tours Ebenezer at Busua Bikes (m *0245 946799/0209 352188/0275 283759*; e *ebenezerbusua@gmail.com*) offers mountain-bike rentals and fully customisable guided tours throughout the Western Region, including Busua, Butre, Dixcove, Akwidaa, Cape Three Points and beyond.

AROUND BUSUA Almost everywhere mentioned in this chapter is easily visited as a day trip out of Busua, and vice versa. See map on page 226 for orientation.

Nunu Busua Island The deserted Nunu Busua Island, in the bay below the village, can be visited by boat from Busua. There isn't a lot to see on the island, but there's nothing stopping you from camping overnight and peering at the mainland if the mood takes you. Swimming out cannot be recommended – even if the tides don't put you off, the proliferation of stinging jellyfish should! If you want to boat to the island, arrange it from the village itself – first visiting the chief (with the customary bottle of schnapps) if you want to camp overnight – as arrangements made via the hotels are very costly.

Dixcove Twenty minutes' walk west of Busua, this compact settlement of rundown alleys and crumbling colonial-era buildings imparts a strong sense of historical continuity. Nothing is known about the site prior to the mid 16th century, when the Ahantamanhene at Busua permitted a group of Fante migrants from the interior to settle here, in exchange for which he took the most beautiful of their women as his wife. The leader of these settlers was one Nana Dekyi, who named the settlement Mfuma.

When the British first landed at Mfuma in 1692, Nana Dekyi (or possibly one of his descendants) allowed them to build a fort on a small hill overlooking the bay. The British originally referred to Mfuma as Dekyi's Cove, which was later bastardised to Dickie's Cove, and eventually to Dixcove. For a full two centuries after its completion in 1696, Fort Dixcove was the only British property in the Dutch-controlled part of present-day Ghana, for which reason it suffered, and survived, more attacks than any other fortress on the Gold Coast. Captured by the Dutch in 1868 and renamed Fort Metalen Kruiz, it was returned to Britain in 1872 along with all other Dutch forts on the Gold Coast. Oddly, however, the Dutch name has stuck, and it is known as Fort Metal Cross today.

The obvious focal point for visits to Dixcove, Fort Metal Cross was leased to an English businessman several years ago with a view to renovating it as an upmarket hotel. Unfortunately, however, work on this project has been indefinitely stalled (linked, we are told, to local political shenanigans following the death of the chief who authorised the project in 2006). As a result, the Dixcove skyline is now uglified by a half-built hotel, complete with grungy swimming pool, that may never be completed. The whitewashed fort is still well maintained, however, and the caretaker will guide an informative tour by request, once you have paid the fixed entrance fee of US$1.50 per person (plus US$1 if you want to take photos). The elevated courtyard outside the fort is a good place to watch the colourful fishing boats on Dixcove's busy beach.

For the time being, there is no accommodation in Dixcove, but it is easy to visit the town as a day trip out of Busua. A rough 1.5km road, recommended only to high-clearance vehicles, connects the two, leaving Busua from the metal bridge across the lagoon on the west side of the village, and arriving at Dixcove a few hundred metres north of the fort. There is no public transport along this road. Either you must catch a trotro back to Agona and change vehicles there, or charter a private taxi between the two. You could instead walk; it only takes 15–20 minutes, but be warned that we periodically receive reports of robberies along this road. We've heard nothing like this in a while, but still we would advise against walking unguided between Busua and Dixcove with luggage or any valuables on your person. And if you do take a guide, make sure it is one recommended to you by another traveller or a hotel/restaurant owner.

BUTRE

Situated only 3km east of Busua, the tiny fishing village of Butre – beautifully sited on a wide sandy beach in a bay protected by a hilly, forested peninsula – provides access to several popular beach resorts via a footbridge over the mouth of the Butre River. Small though it may be, Butre is traditionally the second most important chieftaincy in Ahanta, after Busua. It has also played an important role in coastal history. It was here, on 27 August 1656, that the Dutch West India Company and four prominent Ahanta chiefs (who gave their names as Cubiesang, Aloiny, Ampatee and Maniboy) signed the Treaty of Butre, placing the area, then known as Boutry, under a Dutch protectorateship that endured for more than 200 years.

Perched on a tall hill above the village, the main point of historical interest at Butre is Fort Batenstein, which was built by the Dutch in 1656, abandoned between 1818 and 1829 on account of slow trade, then handed over to Britain in 1872. It fell into disuse shortly afterwards, and is now a substantial but somewhat overgrown ruin, reached via a short, steep footpath from the village, and offering exceptional views over the bay. Though the fort is easy enough to reach unguided (you can see it clearly from the village), prospective visitors must first check in with the **Tourist Services Centre** (m 0205 187763) at the trotro station opposite the church, and pay a community fee of US$2.50, though this seemed to be quite loosely enforced when we dropped by in 2016.

The Tourist Services Centre and various resorts around Butre can also arrange canoe trips up the Butre River, east of the village, to look for birds and crocodiles, and to visit a derelict British palm-oil factory a few kilometres inland near Sesse. These cost US$7.50 per person, with a discount offered to volunteers and students, and are best done at around 07.00 or 16.00.

GETTING THERE AND AWAY From Busua, Butre can be reached along a fairly direct 3km footpath from Busua Beach Resort. The path follows the beach for about 500m before ascending into low cultivated hills that offer lovely views over the ocean. It takes about 45 minutes to walk between Busua and Butre, and recent robberies along this path mean you are advised to take a recommended guide with you and not to carry valuables.

In a private vehicle or taxi, the quickest route between Busua and Butre entails following the Agona road back for about 4km until you see a dirt road forking to your right just before Asane (the junction for Dixcove). Head along this road for about 3km, then turn right at Tontu (aka Tentum) and you will reach Butre after another 4km.

Otherwise, public transport to Butre can be picked up at Agona (the junction village where the road for Busua runs south from the main road between Takoradi and Axim) in the form of shared taxis that charge less than US$1 per person.

The resorts listed below lie to the east of the Butre River, and are reached from the village via a makeshift footbridge across the shallow mouth. Johannesburg Beach House stands right next to this footbridge, and the Hideout and Green Zion Garden are only a couple of hundred metres away. It is more like 2.5km from the bridge to Fanta's Folly, however, so travellers heading that way might be better off picking up a shared taxi from Bokoro (which lies about halfway along the 20km road between Takoradi and Agona) to the more close-by village of Asemkow. Alternatively, a charter taxi from Bokoro to Fanta's Folly should cost around US$8.

Self-drivers should take note that cars *cannot* cross the river at Butre. This means that in a private vehicle, you can only approach Fanta's Folly or the Hideout from the northeast. The best route at the time of writing runs south from the main Takoradi–Agona road at Bokoro (⊕ *N4 53.566 W1 52.948*). From here, continue for about 2km before turning right at the signpost for Fanta's Folly, then turn left after another 2–3km, and right again just before you enter the beachfront village of Asemkow. Fanta's Folly is about 1km west of Asemkow and the Hideout is another 2km.

WHERE TO STAY AND EAT

Moderate

* 🏠 **Fanta's Folly** [241 F3] (8 rooms)
⊕ N4 49.709 W1 53.929; m 0243 213677/0208 304620; e pbreuillot@hotmail.fr; www.fantasfolly. com. Owned & managed by a charming French-Nigerian couple, this laid-back lodge, just above the beach 1km west of Asemasa, has been widely praised for its delicious home cooking. The comfortable, colourful, individually designed thatched chalets are built on stilted wooden platforms & have quality furnishings. Monkey-spotting canoe trips can be arranged into the mangroves behind the resort. A good on-site restaurant offers a range of French-based seafood dishes with an African twist, as well as delicious fresh pastas, pizzas & salads, with most mains in the US$6–10 range. There is also an outdoor spa with a jacuzzi. Together with Hideout Lodge, it runs a turtle-hatching project covering the 3.3km stretch of beach from Asemkow to Butre. *US$16 dbl with shared bath; US$35 self-contained dbl; US$40 family room sleeping 4.* **$$**

Budget

* 🏠 **Hideout Lodge** [241 F3] (14 rooms)
⊕ N4 49.566 W1 54.788; m 0207 369258/357039; e reservations@hideoutlodge.com; www. hideoutlodge.com. Boasting a superb location on a forest-fringed sandy beach on the opposite side of the river to Butre village, this excellent & well-established lodge is one of the most attractive hangout spots anywhere in Ghana. Accommodation is in low-ceilinged dbl & family huts with fan, net, private bathroom & porch, an 8-bed dormitory, spacious beachfront bungalows, & even a rustic treehouse. For most visitors, the main attraction is the opportunity to chill out

on a beach as remote & pristine as any in Ghana, but it's also worth arranging an early-morning canoe trip 45mins upriver to look for monkeys, birds & crocodiles. A beachfront bar/restaurant serves a good selection of pasta, seafood & vegetarian dishes in the US$4–12 range, but you could also eat at the Green Zion Garden (see below). *US$16/26/32 self-contained sgl/dbl/trpl; US$21/32/40 sgl/dbl/trpl beach bungalow; US$11/16 sgl/dbl treehouse; US$53 5-bed family house; US$8pp dorm bed.* **$$$–$**

Shoestring

🏠 **Green Zion Garden** [241 F3] (3 rooms)
m 0202 949398/0264 625900; e ellisannan@ yahoo.com; 🗗 fb.me/GreenZionGarden. Set just off the beach & about 200m behind Hideout Lodge, this long-serving vegetarian restaurant now offers rooms in addition to the Indian-style curries it has become well known for (US$3–5). The rustic rooms all come with fans & mozzie nets, & some of them are self-contained. Thai yoga massage treatments & drumming lessons are on offer, & there are hammocks aplenty scattered throughout the appropriately emerald-hued gardens. *US$8pp; US$2.50pp camping.* **$**

🏠 **Johannesburg Beach House** [241 F3] (3 rooms) m 0209 232576; e johnabban102@ yahoo.com. Situated right next to the footbridge across the Butre River, this simple locally run bar, restaurant & lodge offers accommodation in stilted wooden rooms with dbl bed, net & standing fan. Smoothies, cocktails & beers are served, as is a limited selection of meals in the US$2.50–3.50 range. *US$7/11 sgl/dbl.* **$**

The coastline immediately west of Dixcove, arguably the most scenic in the country, is of great natural, historical and cultural importance, despite having stagnated since the 1970s, when a crippling outbreak of a disease known as Cape St Paul's Wilt struck the extensive coconut plantations on which the local economy was based. It terminates about 20km southwest of Busua at the dramatic Cape Three Points, which is the most southerly point in Ghana, and the site of a historic clifftop lighthouse. Inland, the little-visited Cape Three Points Forest Reserve supports the country's largest tract of coastal forest and a wealth of associated wildlife.

The regional centrepiece is Akwidaa (also sometimes called Akodaa or Ezile), a quite substantial and very beautiful fishing village situated around 15km southwest of Busua and 5km northeast of Cape Three Points as the crow flies. Bisected by the Ezile River/Estuary, Akwidaa is a village of two parts. The more rustic 'old' village, usually referred to as plain Akwidaa, lies on the southeast side of the Ezile Estuary, at the terminus of a 12km road running east from Dixcove, while the more modern village of New Akwidaa lies on the northwest side of the river, along an entirely different road connecting Agona to Cape Three Points.

Hemmed in by a succession of clean, quiet and beautiful palm-lined beaches, the coast around Akwidaa supports several of the most attractive and popular budget beach resorts in Ghana. These include: the new and lesser-known Akwidaa Inn, which lies 2km east of old Akwidaa along the road back to Dixcove; Ezile Bay Village on the west side of the estuary about 2km past New Akwidaa; and Escape3Points another 5km along the road between New Akwidaa and Cape Three Points.

GETTING THERE AND AWAY
By private vehicle To get to 'old' Akwidaa (or to Ceto House and Akwidaa Inn) in a private vehicle, turn right at the taxi station as you enter Dixcove and follow this road westwards. You'll pass Ceto House to your left after 4km, just before you pass through Achowa, and Akwidaa Inn to your left after another 6km, about 1km before entering the village. The road is in very poor condition, and some stretches must be taken painfully slowly, even in a vehicle with high clearance.

Heading from Agona to Cape Three Points (or to Ezile Bay Village or Escape3Points) in a private vehicle you need to drive south to Asane Junction, take the right fork (as if you are heading to Dixcove) then keep going for another 1km. Here, a signposted dirt road to the right leads directly to Cape Three Points, passing Ezile Bay Village to the left after 20km (just after you drive through New Akwidaa) then Escape3Points after another 5km.

By trotros and taxis A few trotros run daily from Agona Junction to 'old' Akwidaa via Dixcove. These cost around US$2, take up to 90 minutes (due to the poor road), and they can drop passengers at Ceto House or Akwidaa Inn by request.

To get to Ezile Bay, you could also catch a trotro to Cape Three Points and drop at the junction, from where it is a five-minute walk to the lodge. However, only two or three trotros do this run daily, so it may be more expedient to catch a trotro to 'old' Akwidaa then walk along the beach (about 15 minutes), or catch a trotro to new Akwidaa then walk along the road (also 15 minutes).

To get to Escape3Points on public transport, your only option is to wait for the next trotro from Agona to Cape Three Points and drop. Alternatively, you could catch one of the more regular trotros to New Akwidaa, and then charter a taxi from there for around US$10.

Another possibility is a direct charter taxi, which should cost around US$20 from Agona or US$30 from Takoradi to any one of the above lodges, the exception being Escape3Points, which will most likely cost around US$5 more.

On foot It is possible to hike between Dixcove and Akwidaa. The more straightforward route is to follow the 12km main road via Achowa, but this runs inland and offers little in the way of scenic interest or shade. An alternative but slightly longer route passes through Mediya, an ancient and interesting village, dotted with the clearly visible remains of many old buildings, which lies about 4km from Dixcove by road. Onwards from Mediya, an interesting bush track leads to Chavane across thick, overgrown farmland and a series of small and rather precarious bamboo bridges, as well as a dark, shaded passage where many butterflies and birds can be seen and heard. From Chavane, the road continues to Kwamanfokrom through a rubber plantation, the management of which is willing to offer information on request. From Kwamanfokrom, it is a further 5km to Akwidaa by road. As with most of the paths between Butre and Cape Three Points, it's recommended you don't carry valuables on this route, and take a trusted guide if possible.

WHERE TO STAY AND EAT Of the four resorts in the area, Escape3Points is slightly more geared towards a younger crowd looking for a beach party atmosphere, while Ezile Bay and Akwidaa Inn have a quieter vibe suited to those seeking a more tranquil retreat. Less well known is Ceto House, which is aimed at small private parties.

Moderate

✴ 🏠 Ceto House [241 D4] (2 rooms)
⊕ N4 46.378 W1 58.108; m 0272 925633/0242 878818; e email@cetoghana.com; www. cetoghana.com. Situated 50m from a beautiful sandy beach near the village of Achowa, this circular thatched house was built in 2008 by a British couple. It is now run as a self-catering guesthouse, rented out in its entirety for up to 4 people, with what is effectively a secluded private beach. It comprises 2 dbl bedrooms, a shared bathroom, an open-plan kitchen & living area, & a 1st floor offering spectacular views of the sea & beach. The owners can arrange for the kitchen to be stocked with food & drink. *US$125 per night for up to 4 people & up to 3 nights; US$100 for 4 or more nights.* **$$$$–$$$**

Budget

✴ 🏠 Ezile Bay Village [241 A4] (11 rooms, 1 dorm) ⊕ N4 45.387 W2 02.323; m 0243 174860/0267 993131/0207 373579; e ezilebay@ yahoo.com; www.ezilebay.com. Owned & managed by the same friendly Frenchwoman as Busua Inn, this rustic resort has a captivating location on a sheltered swimming beach on the same bay as 'old' Akwidaa. Accommodation is in traditional square clay huts flanked by the

rainforest on one side & the palm-fringed Atlantic Ocean on the other. Camping is also permitted. There is now mains electricity, but the huts all have solar power. The sheltered bay with its white sandy beach is ideal for swimming. A feature of the lodge is the large open-air restaurant & French-influenced cuisine, with snacks for around US$5 & mains in the US$6–12 range. It can organise a number of local excursions, including tours of the nearby village. Discounts are available for students & volunteers. *US$23/29 dbl/trpl using shared bath; US$29 self-contained dbl; US$8pp dorm bed; US$6pp camping.* **$$–$**

✴ 🏠 Escape3Points [241 A4] (10 rooms)
⊕ N4 44.998 W2 04.683; m 0267 218700; e email@escape3points.com; www.escape3points. com. Located immediately east of Cape Three Points on an absolutely stunning beach hemmed in by 2 rivers & a backdrop of lush forest, this idyllic new eco-lodge is truly the stuff of tropical-island fantasies. It is owned by a dynamic young Canadian-Ghanaian-French couple who live in Ghana and play a large role in the day-to-day management. The owner is an architect specialising in low-cost natural construction techniques, & the characterful bamboo & earthen rooms combine a jungle-cabin character with natural ventilation & ocean views. Communally served meals, which

cost around US$5–8, are created from a fusion of Ghanaian & international dishes, with an added French twist using fresh produce from an organic garden. Flippers & surfboards are available for hire, there's football, billiards, & table tennis at the bar, & there are volunteer opportunities for those interested in turtle conservation. *US$19–23 self-contained dbl; US$24–32 self-contained family suites; US$7 dorm bed.* **$$–$**

🏠 **Akwidaa Inn** [241 B4] (8 rooms) e theakwidaainn@gmail.com; www.akwidaainn. com; see ad, page 255. With an enticingly isolated location just a few hundred metres from the former Green Turtle Lodge, this quiet new beachfront lodge offers pleasant accommodation in large standalone thatch bungalows with high ceilings, mozzie nets, fans, sitting area & en-suite facilities. The open-sided restaurant & bar feels a bit underfurnished for its ample size, but the Ghanaian & continental meals (*US$4–8*) are good, & so are the ocean views. There's a 4-bed dorm, organic gardens, & plenty of room to camp in the sandy compound. There's not much going on in terms of activities, but if your primary interest is kicking back on the beach, you won't go wrong here. *US$24 self-contained dbl; US$32 large dbl (can sleep 4); US$5.50pp dorm; US$5.50 per tent camping.* **$$–$**

WHAT TO SEE AND DO

Akwidaa The main attraction of the lodges around Akwidaa is the opportunity to chill out in an idyllic tropical beach location. But it is also possible to arrange canoe trips with local fishermen into the mangrove swamps upstream of the village on the Ezile River, where a large variety of birds, as well as monkeys, are likely to be encountered, especially towards dusk and shortly after dawn. Any of the lodges in the area can put you in touch with good self-taught local guides, some of whom are really impressive on birds. Of minor historical interest, the ruined Fort Dorothea

---

RESPONSIBLE MARINE TURTLE ECOTOURISM   *Phillip Allman PhD*

Ghana is home to five species of marine turtle, all of which are threatened with extinction due to global threats such as habitat destruction, direct harvesting for food, incidental capture by fishermen, and eggs being preyed upon by domestic animals. People seldom have an opportunity to observe turtles in the wild because they are so rare and difficult to find. However, tourists that visit Ghana during the nesting season of October through March are provided with a unique chance of watching a sea turtle come ashore to nest.

In Ghana, all sea turtles are protected by the Wildlife Regulations Act of 1974. This made it illegal to approach, touch or alter the behaviour of a turtle unless you are in the company of a person issued with an appropriate Ghana Wildlife Division (GWD) permit. Signing up for a sea turtle walk through a hotel without such a permit is thus illegal, and could potentially result in your being arrested if caught. In addition, for the highest level of safety, especially in the face of a poacher, it is advisable to do any 'sea turtle walk' with a trained GWD officer.

Participating in a properly organised 'sea turtle walk' will give you a unique opportunity safely to witness a nesting event. It will also help to support the communities that are trying to protect sea turtles. You should only search for nesting sea turtles with a trained professional guide who can teach you about turtles and ensure your safety as well as that of the turtles. Remember that sea turtles are endangered wild animals that are very sensitive to disturbance. Seeing one is never guaranteed but following the below guidelines will maximise your chances of having a great experience:

Sea turtles are very sensitive to light and a photographic flash can damage their eyes. For this reason, flash photography is prohibited in most turtle breeding

(or Fort Akodaa), a triangular trading post built for the Brandenburg Company in the 17th century, is situated on a rock promontory (which becomes an island at high tide) in Ezile Bay, immediately south of the old town centre.

Cape Three Points Lighthouse
A tall, forested peninsula situated about halfway between Akwidaa and Prince's Town, Cape Three Points (✪ *N4 44.441 W2 05.486*) is the most southerly land point in Ghana, and also the closest slice of terra firma to the oceanic intersection of the Equator and Prime (Greenwich) Meridian, about 500km to the southeast. Appropriately, it is also one of the more dramatic points along the Ghanaian coast, with cliffs rising 30m from the rocky shore, below a lighthouse constructed in 1925 alongside an older ruin built 50 years earlier. There is also a milestone showing the direction and distance to remote sites with slave trade connections, for instance New York, Brasilia and Trinidad.

To get to Cape Three Points, follow the road from Agona past Escape3Points for another 2km to the small village of Atinkyin (also known as Cape Three Points). It's a 20–30-minute walk to Atinkyin coming from Escape3Points, and around 2 hours in either direction from Akwidaa Inn, Ezile Bay or the other resorts around Akwidaa. Once at Atinkyin, an entrance fee of US$1 must be paid at the tourist service centre before continuing uphill for another 500m or so to the base of the lighthouse. Even if the caretaker isn't there, the panoramic views from the cliffs more than justify the effort of getting there, doubly so between November and January, when whales sometimes come close to the shore. If the caretaker is there, he will most likely show you around for a small fee.

sites globally, and you are urged not to use a flash even if your guide permits or encourages it.

Use a flashlight or headlamp with a red filter. Sea turtles are less sensitive to red light. But avoid shining any light in the turtle's eyes or near its head.

Wear dark clothing to reduce the chances that a turtle will see you approaching.

Wear closed-toed shoes with socks. Although sandals are fun to wear on the beach, they can cause blisters when walking for a long time. Also, Ghana's beaches are covered with rubbish that you may not want your feet exposed to!

While walking, always stay with your guide and feel free to ask lots of questions about turtles and their conservation needs.

It is best to walk on the wet sand close to the waterline, but do watch out for waves.

Talk softly and move slowly when you are around the turtle to avoid disturbing her. Too much disturbance will cause her to return to the sea without nesting.

Always stay behind the turtle's front flippers. Stay about 3m behind the turtle when she is covering her nest, or the powerful flippers will cover you with sand.

When she begins returning to the ocean, shift your position so that you stay behind her and on the landward side, giving her a clear path and view of the ocean. When she is crawling back to sea, do not get between her and the ocean.

Remember that sea turtles are endangered so you should feel very lucky if you are able to observe one in the wild. No-one can predict when or where a sea turtle will come ashore, so do not become frustrated if your guide is unable to find one. Not finding a turtle only illustrates the need to provide better protection for these amazing but endangered animals. With or without an observation, you should consider tipping your guide if they were knowledgeable and sincere.

TURTLE CONSERVATION   *Jo Miles, Green Turtle Lodge*

Marine turtles are ancient reptiles, or 'living dinosaurs', that have been swimming through the oceans for 100 million years. Marine turtles survived while dinosaurs became extinct. However, since their decline in the 20th century, turtles are now on the brink of extinction themselves, with all but one of the world's seven species now listed on the IUCN (International Union for the Conservation of Nature and Natural Resources) Red List, three of them being classified as Critically Endangered. Five of the seven species of marine turtle exist in Ghana and can be found nesting on many of the country's beaches. These are the leatherback, green turtle, olive ridley, hawksbill and loggerhead. The leatherback is the largest of all the sea turtles: the length of its shell can be up to 178cm and it can weigh up to 900kg.

In the 20th century, there became a global market for turtle meat and eggs, which were seen as a delicacy in the West and thus valued highly, along with turtle shells. This demand led to mass hunting of the sea turtles and their eggs. However, the biggest cause of death to sea turtles and, therefore, the biggest threat to them becoming extinct is commercial fishing. Huge boats, far out at sea with enormous nets, trawl the ocean for shrimps and fish. Unfortunately, sea turtles get caught and trapped in these nets. Thousands of turtles can be killed in only a few weeks when the trawling occurs in nesting season. These international threats to turtles are being mirrored in Ghana, where fishermen using nets can accidentally catch a turtle that becomes entangled in the net. There is also hunting of turtles nesting on the beaches and poaching of eggs, both of which are seen as a rich source of protein. In Ghana during the nesting season, from October to March, about 1,300 sea turtles venture on to the beaches to lay their eggs. Unfortunately, about 60% of these turtles are caught by fishermen and more than one million of their eggs are destroyed by man and domestic animals. In recognition of and co-operation with international efforts at turtle conservation, Ghanaian law states that it is illegal to catch or kill sea turtles and to sell their meat or eggs.

Attitudes are changing towards marine-turtle conservation. In many areas, the Ghana Wildlife Division now runs highly active conservation projects protecting important nesting sites such as the Muni-Pomadze Ramsar Wetlands on the outskirts of Winneba, and Songar Ramsar Site near Ada Foah. More informally, on the west coast of Ghana, the like of Escape3Points, Fanta's Folly and Beyin Beach Resort have implemented conservation projects resulting in the successful release of tens of thousands of hatchlings back into the sea at Beyin. At Ampenyi (Elmina), Winneba, Ada Foah and several lodges on the west coast, ecotourism projects offer night hikes to observe nesting turtles, the payment for which goes directly back into turtle conservation. These programmes involve and employ local people in the monitoring and management of marine turtles, whilst educating the local population about the importance of protecting them.

To change long-standing beliefs and behaviours is a process that takes time. Introducing the idea of conservation requires a major shift in beliefs and behaviours. This is not something that will happen overnight. Tourists play an important role in supporting and helping to sustain these projects and by adhering to good practices such as never touching a turtle and not using flash photography, both of which can stop the turtle nesting. See also the box on *responsible marine turtle ecotourism* on pages 252–3.

Cape Three Points Forest Reserve Demarcated in 1949, Cape Three Points Forest Reserve extends over 51km² of low hills, starting about 2km inland of Akwidaa and stretching north almost as far as the main road between Agona and Axim. Drained by the Nyan River and bordered by rubber plantations to the west, it protects what is probably Ghana's most extensive remaining patch of near-pristine coastal forest, with a biodiversity rating as high as that of the larger and better-known Ankassa Resource Reserve to its west. The reserve is reputedly still home to small populations of several localised large mammal species, including the endangered Diana monkey, white-crested sooty mangabey and bongo antelope. More than 160 bird species have been identified, including crowned eagle, chocolate-backed kingfisher, great blue turaco, yellow-billed turaco, blue cuckoo-shrike and seven hornbill species (including the rare yellow-casqued hornbill), and possibly the rare white-breasted guineafowl. A few years back, Cape Three Points was regarded to be among the least ecologically compromised forest reserves in Ghana, but recent reports suggest that encroachment is severe, with much of the interior having fallen victim to logging and cultivation.

Practically undeveloped for tourism, Cape Three Points Forest Reserve can be visited as a day trip from Akwidaa Inn, Ezile Bay or Escape3Points. It is essential to be accompanied by a knowledgeable local guide, as there are many tracks in the forest and one can get lost. This will cost around US$7.50 and the hike takes up to 4 hours, depending on your energy and level of interest. It is best to hike in the early morning and to wear closed shoes. The normal access point is a track leading from the Cape Three Points road about 500m from the entrance to Ezile Bay, and on the opposite side of the road. From here it is around 30–60 minutes' walk to the reserve boundary.

It is also possible to hike between Akwidaa and Prince's Town through the Cape Three Points Forest Reserve. Again, a guide is vital, or you risk getting lost or robbed. The first part of the hike involves a 3–4km walk through cultivation to the forest boundary. The second follows a shady trail within the reserve for about 8km, and is of great interest to butterfly and bird enthusiasts. This trail leaves the forest close to Aketechi, from where you can follow the coastal footpath on the dunes alongside the lagoon to Prince's Town, or arrange a canoe to take you.

10

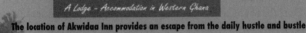

11

Axim and the Far Southwest

The coastline west of Cape Three Points sees relatively few tourists compared with Busua, Cape Coast or Elmina, but it still has plenty to offer. The palm-lined slices of tropical nirvana at the blissfully isolated LouMoon Lodge and Ankobra Beach Resort near Axim rank among the most stunning beaches in Ghana. For the historically minded, Nkroful is the birthplace of former president Kwame Nkrumah and the site of his original mausoleum, while a trio of old colonial forts stand sentinel over Axim, Beyin and Prince's Town. Beyin is also a wonderful beach retreat in its own right, as well as being the normal base from which to visit the unique stilted village of Nzulezo. And for nature lovers, while the coast around Prince's Town presents some interesting rambling opportunities, the sadly underdeveloped Ankassa Resource Reserve, protecting a vast tract of rainforest near the Ivorian border, has the potential to be one of the country's prime hiking and birding destinations.

PRINCE'S TOWN

Set on the attractive and largely unspoilt coastline flanking the east bank of the Nyan River mouth, Prince's Town is notable not least for having acquired a list of aliases worthy of the most notorious of gangsters – among them Prince's Terre, Princess Town, Kpokezoe, Pokesu and Prusi. Limited tourist development and a rather isolated location, almost 20km south of the main road between Agona and Axim, ensure that the small town (population 5,000) is visited by very few travellers. Its urban centrepiece is Fort Gross-Friedrichsburg, a near ruin at the time of independence, but now fully restored and functioning as a resthouse. Prince's Town also forms the base for several interesting day trips, notably to the Egyambra Crocodile Pond, about 2 hours' walk away, and the beautiful Ehunli Lagoon, which can be explored by boat.

HISTORY Fort Gross-Friedrichsburg has a rather unusual history, being one of only two Ghanaian forts with Germanic associations (the other being the ruinous Fort Dorothea at nearby Akwidaa). It was built by the Brandenburg Africa Company (BAC), a latecomer to the European struggle for dominance of the Gold Coast, formed as a representative of Prince Friedrich Wilhelm I (Elector of Brandenburg and Duke of Prussia from 1640 to 1688). A BAC expedition of two ships landed at the village then known as Pokesu or Kpokezoe, and its commander, the Prussian explorer Otto Friedrich von der Groeben, was ceded the promontory on which the fort now stands, in exchange for agreeing to protect the village against the Dutch and other slave raiders.

In 1681, von der Groeben started work on a strong stone fort that was completed two years later and named Fort Gross-Friedrichsburg in honour of the prince.

By the 1690s, this Brandenburger stronghold had become the most important smuggling centre on the coast, simply because the officials received so few ships from home that they were forced to trade illicitly with other nations to make a profit. Eventually, in 1716, the struggling BAC abandoned the Gold Coast, and Fort Gross-Friedrichsburg became the headquarters of John Kanu (also known as John Connie), an Ahanta chief who had already acquired the nickname 'King of Prince's Terre' for his role at the centre of a trade network so powerful that it caused a temporary economic slump at nearby Dutch-controlled Dixcove and Axim.

Over the next decade, the fort was the centre of a series of military clashes, and word of the Ahanta chief's victories over the Dutch made him something of a folk hero in the slave plantations of the Caribbean (John Kanu is evidently the source of the John Canoe festivals that have been celebrated in the region ever since). Prince's Terre was captured by the Dutch in 1724, and John Kanu vanished into obscurity – some oral sources claim that the Dutch sold him into slavery, while others that he escaped to Kumasi, where he eventually died a natural death and was buried. Renamed Fort Hollandia, Gross-Friedrichsburg remained under Dutch control for almost 150 years before being handed to Britain as part of the treaty signed in 1872.

GETTING THERE AND AWAY Prince's Town lies 18km south of Abora Junction on the main road between Takoradi and Axim. Any vehicle heading between Agona and Axim can drop you at the junction, which is signposted. You'll probably be in for a long wait at Agona, as there's not a lot of transport, but you should get through eventually, except perhaps after very heavy rain.

WHERE TO STAY AND EAT
Budget
* 🏠 **Yellow Rose** (5 rooms) m 0263 252664/0266 428482; e yellow-rose@hotmail.de; www.yellow-rose.bplaced.net. Owned & managed by a friendly & flexible German couple, this restaurant & lodge, set in large green grounds on the edge of the mangrove-lined lagoon, attracts plenty of monkeys & is a haven for birdwatchers. Boats are available to head out on to the lagoon. Signposted to the left as you enter the outskirts of town, the lodge (also known as Princess Guesthouse) lies about 2mins' walk from the main property & restaurant, & consists of a neat, clean house with 5 self-contained rooms, all with TV & fan, as well as a lounge with internet facilities. The restaurant, complete with balcony facing the

lagoon, has no formal menu, but it specialises in German cuisine, & they will prepare anything you request if they can locate the ingredients. Mains US$8–12. US$16 self-contained dbl. B/fast an additional US$5.50pp. **$$**

Shoestring
🏠 **Fort Gross-Friedrichsburg** (4 rooms) m 0243 269469. The fort contains 4 dbl rooms with fans & mozzie nets, & a communal bucket shower is available. We've had mixed reports as to the cleanliness of the rooms, & bugs seem to be an ongoing issue, as well as (in one report at least) nocturnal visits by drunken locals! Meals can be prepared with advance notice, or there are a couple of chop shops in the village. US$11 dbl. **$**

WHAT TO SEE AND DO
Fort Gross-Friedrichsburg (*entrance US$2pp*) Nominally, the main attraction in Prince's Town, this is the only surviving German fort in Ghana, built with stone transported by sea over 1681–83. It has been estimated that something like 300,000 African slaves were held captive in this fort before being shipped to the Americas. Despite this, the most striking thing about the fort today is how little it looks like a military building – on first glance, it could easily be mistaken for an old colonial governor's residence or something like that. Because it doubles as a guesthouse and bar, there are no formal opening times.

Ehunli Lagoon This inky 2km² expanse is separated from the ocean by a narrow, sandy – and practically uninhabited – beach that is reputedly safe for swimming. Canoe trips on the lagoon can be arranged through the staff of Gross-Friedrichsburg or Yellow Rose, except on Thursday, when taking a boat on to the water is taboo. Birdlife is prolific, and there is a good chance of seeing black-and-white colobus monkeys, as well as crocodiles, especially in the early morning. You can also ask to be taken to a bamboo forest and a traditional palm-wine distillery. More ambitiously, one could walk from the lagoon into the Cape Three Points Forest Reserve (page 255), which borders it at the village of Aketechi on the eastern shore.

Miemia Beach The most attractive beach in the vicinity, Miemia lies only 4km northwest of Prince's Town as the crow flies, and is usually good for swimming, as the sea tends to be calm (but do check conditions before taking the plunge). You can walk along the beach from Prince's Town to Miemia, which will take about one hour, passing Mutrakni Point *en route*, with views over the sea, the river and the mangroves. Another more appealing option is to arrange a canoe to take you there along the Kpani River, passing through mangrove swamps teeming with birds. It is possible to stop off at the akpeteshie distillery on the riverbank between Prince's Town and Miemia to observe the distilling process.

Egyambra Situated about 6km west of Prince's Town as the crow flies, and not quite 2km from Miemia, this small seaside village, also known as Agyembrah, is of interest mainly for its sacred crocodile pond, which offers a similar but less publicised experience to the one at Paga on the Burkina Faso border. For a negotiable fee of around US$5–10, plus the cost of two chickens and two bottles of Coke, the fetish priest at the pond will call a crocodile to be fed on the shore, offering a good but usually quite brief photo opportunity before it disappears back into the water.

A rough 15–20km road connects Egyambra to the main Takoradi–Axim road at Anyame. Public transport along this road leaves from Axim and Agona, and is reasonably frequent. Since the crocodile ceremony takes place only in the morning, travellers wanting to experience it should get an early start.

A more popular option is to visit Egyambra by foot or canoe as a day trip from Prince's Town. From there, walk or take a canoe to Miemia, from where a footpath of roughly 1.5km continues to Egyambra via the beach and then around a rocky outcrop seasonally surrounded by brightly coloured flowers.

Keen hikers could think about continuing westwards on foot from Egyambra to Axim, roughly a 10km beach walk, with the option of popping in for a drink at the upmarket LouMoon Lodge after about 3km, then staying overnight at more affordable Axim Beach Hotel after another 5km. The trail towards Axim follows a lovely coastline of palm-lined beaches, shady lagoons, interesting rock formations and small fishing villages (where one should greet the locals). It would be advisable to take a guide along this route, which is currently used by few tourists.

AXIM

The largest coastal town west of Takoradi, with a population estimated at 25,000, Axim (pronounced more like 'Azsim') is also the site of Fort St Anthony (Forte São Antonio), the second-oldest building on the Ghanaian coast, and one of the most impressive. This one building aside, there is little about Axim today that betrays its historical significance, though the streets close to the fort are lined with several crumbling mansions erected by timber magnates and other businessmen during the colonial era,

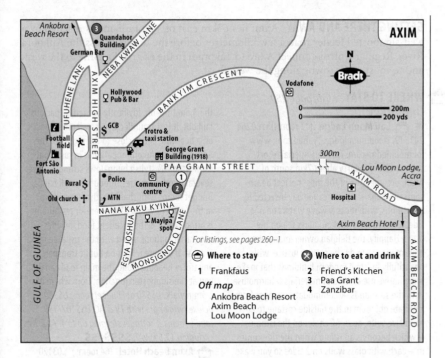

For listings, see pages 260–1

Where to stay

1 Frankfaus

Off map

Ankobra Beach Resort
Axim Beach
Lou Moon Lodge

Where to eat and drink

2 Friend's Kitchen
3 Paa Grant
4 Zanzibar

while the offshore Boboewusi (or Bobo Yesi) Island is the site of a historic lighthouse, still in use today. In the first edition of this guide, Axim was described as 'the most characterless port in Ghana, chronically run-down and rather unwelcoming', an assessment that, in hindsight, seems unduly harsh. All the same, most visitors would agree that the best thing about Axim is not the town itself, but a trio of nearby resorts – LouMoon, Axim Beach and Ankobra Beach – set on beaches of breathtaking near-perfection. There's now a GCB bank with ATM at the centre of town if you need cash.

HISTORY Axim was the site of one of the region's earliest Portuguese trading posts, established in the late 15th century. The most significant relict of this era, built in 1515, is the triangular Forte São Antonio, which stood sentinel on a prominent outcrop whose excellent natural protection, in the form of a few small rocky islands and a reef, was bolstered by a 3m-deep trench cut into the rock. After Elmina Castle fell to the Dutch West India Company in 1637, Axim was the last remaining Portuguese stronghold along the Gold Coast, and the defensive capacity of Forte São Antonio was tested to the full prior to being captured by the Dutch in February 1642. The Portuguese were allowed a free passage out of the port, effectively ending their long period of trade dominance in the region, while the Dutch went on to negotiate the Treaty of Axim with the paramount chiefs of the upper and lower towns.

Under Dutch rule, Axim was one of the busiest trading posts anywhere on the West African coast. In the late 17th century, more gold was traded through Fort St Anthony than any other Dutch outpost, much of it supplied by traders from Adanse and Denkyira. In the 18th century, the area around Axim became an important producer of cotton and timber. The fort was handed to Britain in 1872 and its name was anglicised to Fort St Anthony. It was used as a regional administrative centre in the colonial era, and it continued to house government offices until early 2000, when it was transferred to the Ghana Museums and Monuments Board and restored as a tourist site.

GETTING THERE AND AWAY Axim lies 65km east of Takoradi and is reached by a well-signposted feeder road a few kilometres before the bridge across the Ankobra River. Regular trotros connect Axim to Takoradi in the east, to Essiama to the west, and to most other towns along the west coast.

WHERE TO STAY *Map, page 259*
Upmarket

✳ 🏠 Lou Moon Lodge (11 rooms) m 0264 241549; e loumoonlodge@yahoo.com; www. loumoonlodge.com. This very special resort, set in a 12ha property about 7km south of Axim, occupies one of the most perfect beach spots in Ghana – a picturesque bay bisected by an isthmus, with rocks & wavy waters on one side, & a turquoise-looking glass sea on the other. Happily, the Belgian owner-managers have managed to do the setting justice, with beautifully finished modern buildings that make imaginative use of natural materials & harmonise with the surrounds. Accommodation ranges from a private dbl room in the hillside cottage to an executive suite, or an AC chalet on the isthmus – which becomes an island when the tide comes in – each with glass walls on 2 sides so you wake up looking out on to the sea. In 2015, 2 designer island cape suites were added on the isthmus, both of which come with private swimming pools, vaulted ceilings & canopy beds, & make for one of Ghana's most indulgent & luxurious retreats. At the centre of the lodge is a large, airy loft-style bar & restaurant, where the owners offer a daily à la carte menu of freshly prepared French- & Italian-inspired dishes. Expect to pay US$6–8 for a starter & US$15–30 for a main. Facilities include free Wi-Fi, volleyball, canoeing, & massages by appointment. To get there, follow the signposts for 6km from the main feeder road connecting Axim to the main road between Takoradi & Elubo. Occasional trotros run from Axim to the small fishing village of Agyan, a few hundred metres before the lodge. *€85 hillside dbl; €125–150 bay-view suite; €175 island chalet; €350 island cape exec suite; all rates B&B.* **$$$$$–$$$**

🏠 Ankobra Beach Resort (20 rooms) ☎03120 92321/3; m 0240 969789/0541 221491/0543 287926; e info@ghana-resorts. com; www.ghana-resorts.com. This German-owned & managed resort is situated about 500m south of the main Takoradi–Elubo road, from where it is clearly signposted about 5km west of

the Axim turn-off. Idyllically located & spaciously laid out, it is surrounded by a small pine wood on a beautiful beach close to the mouth of the Ankobra River. Accommodation is in rustic but comfortable & stylish bungalows strung out over several hundred metres through the tall palms. Budget rooms with shared bath are available in the workers' village. The open-air restaurant is atmospheric & the excellent food includes vegetarian options along with the usual seafood & meat. If you are reliant on public transport, any trotro heading along the main road can drop you at the signposted junction, from where it's a 5min walk. *US$30 dbl budget room; US$80 deluxe twin or dbl with TV & AC; US$107/159 family rooms & cottages sleeping up to 4. All prices excluding 17.5% VAT.* **$$$$–$$**

🏠 Axim Beach Hotel (64 rooms) ☎03120 92397; m 0244 885920; e info@aximbeach. com; www.aximbeach.com. Planted on a rocky promontory to the southeast of Axim, this well-established resort overlooks a pristine expanse of sandy palm-fringed beach stretching eastwards towards the Awangazule Lagoon. In many respects, it's the stuff of desert-island fantasies, though the swift expansion of the resort over recent years, & the addition of TVs in every room, neutralises the impact to some extent; works are ongoing on a sizeable new swimming pool & restaurant downhill from the main lodge. Decorated tastefully in African style, accommodation ranges from budget rooms with fan, honeymoon chalets & family villas with AC. Facilities include a wellness centre & a good open-air restaurant overlooking the bay. The resort is about 2km south of the feeder road between Axim & the Takoradi–Elubo road, and well signposted about 1km out of central Axim (close to the hospital). Walking along the bush path between the town & the resort is not recommended due to reports of robbery. If you don't have private transport, charter a taxi. *US$25/50 self-contained sgl/dbl with fan & satellite TV; US$80/130 self-contained standard/honeymoon dbl with AC; US$180–240 4–6 person villa.* **$$$$$–$$**

Budget

Far better value than the only hotel in town are the budget rooms described above at the Ankobra and Axim beach resorts.

🏠 **Frankfaus Hotel** (15 rooms) m 0207 073435/0542 859606. The only accommodation in Axim town, this reasonably comfortable 2-storey building lies roughly 200m uphill from the trotro station & main traffic circle. *US$13/21 self-contained sgl/dbl with fan; US$22/26 sgl/dbl with erratic AC.* **$$$–$$**

✖ WHERE TO EAT AND DRINK *Map, page 259*

The upmarket lodges listed above all serve good continental-style food. The open-air **Zanzibar Restaurant**, near the junction for LouMoon Lodge and Axim Beach Hotel, is a local favourite, though it seems to open and close rather erratically. More reliably, the best local eatery is **Friend's Kitchen** (m *0276 340498*), around the corner from the Frankfaus Hotel, and there are also a couple of good chop kiosks next to the trotro station. There's no shortage of places to sink a beer or two, with the stilted **Paa Grant Garden** (m *0204 075071*) looking a particularly attractive option.

WHAT TO SEE AND DO

Fort St Anthony/Fort São Antonio (03321 32529; m 0241 598411; ☺ 07.30–16.30 Mon–Sat, noon–16.30 Sun; entrance US$3, US$1 photography fee)

The most significant tourist attraction in Axim is this Portuguese fort, whose basic shape and bastions – unlike those of Elmina Castle, nominally the only older European building in sub-Saharan Africa – have changed little in the 500 years since its foundations were laid. The three-storey building that rises above the main fortifications was added later, presumably in the early years of the Dutch occupation, since it is recognisable from an etching dated to 1682. Some of the panelling is also unchanged since the 17th century. It is now a museum, and in addition to its great architectural interest, it affords a thoroughly arresting vantage point over the dramatic Axim beachfront. Plans to transform the fort into a six-bedroom guesthouse and restaurant have been in the air for so long now that it would be outrageously optimistic to suggest that they might translate into reality any time soon, but one can only hope!

Boboewusi Island About 500m offshore and clearly visible from the fort, Boboewusi Island is home to a 1915 lighthouse that lay dormant for several decades after independence until it was restored in the early 2000s, and we're told it's possible to hire a boatman to ferry you over there for a negotiable fee, though you'd be one of a very few people to make this trip.

Ankobra River One of the largest rivers in southern Ghana, the mud-brown Ankobra is almost 200km long, rising in the interior near Wiawso and spilling into the Gulf of Guinea about 6km west of Axim. Navigable by small crafts for the first 80km upriver of its mouth, the Ankobra is also of historical note as the main channel used to carry timber and other goods to Axim in the 18th and 19th centuries. Indeed, it is still an important trade conduit between the coast and the interior, plied by large canoes that carry cargoes of salt, fish, clothes, gold and timber. Canoe trips on the river, which is flanked by mangrove and riparian forest, can be arranged through any of the resorts around Axim, and usually leaving from the bridge near the Ankobra Beach Resort. The river is of particular interest to birdwatchers for specialities such as Cassin's flycatcher, Eurasian curlew, African finfoot and various kingfishers.

Nkroful This small town 4km north of Essiama (a sprawling junction town on the main Elubo road 15km west of Axim, with an EcoBank ATM) was the birthplace of Kwame Nkrumah, Ghana's first president, and is the site of the small mausoleum where he was buried after his death in 1972. Though rather underwhelming by comparison with the newer Nkrumah Mausoleum in Accra (which is where Nkrumah's body is now interred), the original mausoleum is now the centrepiece of the diverting **Nkrumah Museum** (m 0544 109750/0244 848560; e hyawson@gmail. com; ⏲ 07.00–18.00 daily; entrance US$2.50pp inc guide & photography), situated about 100m left of the main road as you enter town coming from Essiama. In addition to the old mausoleum, an informative guided tour takes in a few restored buildings in the Nkrumah family compound, and a short walk to the 'mysterious river' where Nkrumah swam as a child and, it is said, his miraculous ascent to presidency started. Long-term plans include the construction of a library and a formal museum containing artefacts relating to the former president's life. There is plenty of trotro traffic between Axim and Essiama, from where regular and inexpensive shared taxis go directly to Nkroful, and can drop you at the junction for the mausoleum as you enter the town centre. There is no reason to spend a night in Nkroful, and since the only hotel in town has been long-term rented by a mining firm, you'd have to try one of the numerous accommodation options in Essiama if you wanted to stay nearby.

BEYIN, NZULEZO AND THE AMANSURI WETLANDS

Situated about halfway along the relatively undeveloped 60km of coastline separating Axim from the Ivorian border, the seaside village of Beyin is the most important tourist focus in the far west of Ghana. This is mainly thanks to its proximity to the unique Nzulezo Stilted Village, which lies about 5km inland amidst the bird-rich Amansuri Wetlands, but Beyin is also the site of the compact but well-maintained Fort Apollonia, which now operates as a museum. As for the beach, in November 2012 CNN Travel listed this 'beautiful sandy arc [edged by] tall, soaring palms' as one of Africa's top 25 beaches, noting that it is a 'classic African working beach [where] you can expect to watch about 100 men pulling in enormous seine nets filled with fish'. It is also one of the few sites in Ghana where the spectacular European oystercatcher is regularly observed.

When the first few editions of this guidebook were researched, tourist facilities in Beyin were limited to a few basic rooms in Fort Apollonia, which then doubled as a no-frills resthouse. This situation has changed dramatically since then, starting with the opening of Beyin Beach Resort in 2007, and the village now boasts a surprisingly good range of accommodation and eateries aimed at travellers. Further development is on the cards, too, as Beyin stands to cash in from the influx of foreign capital associated with the construction of the US$850m National Gas Processing Plant at Atuabo, a mere 5km to its east. Opened at the end of 2015, the plant can process up to 150 million cubic feet daily of gas piped from offshore wells, a figure that should double when the second phase of development is completed in 2017. Unfortunately, the presence of hydrocarbon processing in the neighbourhood also means that pollution may be starting to become a concern, and we've had at least one reader report that the water isn't as clean as it used to be.

GETTING THERE AND AWAY Driving from Axim, follow the main road west towards Elubo for about 15km past Essiama to Alabokazo Junction, where you need to turn left on to the recently surfaced coastal road that branches southwest from here and follow it for another 20km to reach Beyin. Coming from the west, you need to branch right from the Elubo–Axim road at Mpataba Junction, then turn left at Tikobo #1 (also known as 'T1'), from where it is another 15km on a

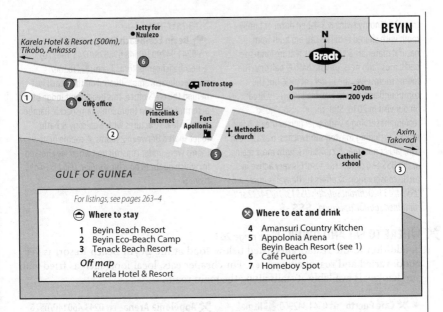

BEYIN

Karela Hotel & Resort (500m),
Tikobo, Ankassa

Jetty for
Nzulezo

N

Bradt

⑥

⑦

Trotro stop

0 ——————— 200m
0 ——————— 200 yds

① ④ GWS office

Princelinks
Internet

②

Fort
Apollonia

Methodist
church

Axim,
Takoradi

⑤

Catholic
school

③

GULF OF GUINEA

For listings, see pages 263–4

🏠 **Where to stay**

1 Beyin Beach Resort
2 Beyin Eco-Beach Camp
3 Tenack Beach Resort

Off map
Karela Hotel & Resort

✖ **Where to eat and drink**

4 Amansuri Country Kitchen
5 Appolonia Arena
Beyin Beach Resort (see 1)
6 Café Puerto
7 Homeboy Spot

fair surfaced road to Beyin. Using public transport, a few direct trotros connect Takoradi to Beyin, taking around 2 hours in either direction, and depart from Takoradi's Nzema Station between 07.00 and 15.00, and from Beyin at around 04.00–05.00. At other times of day, you can catch a trotro from Takoradi or Axim to Essiama, then a shared taxi to Eikwe, and another shared taxi to Beyin.

There are also a few shared taxis daily between Beyin and Tikobo #1, from where plenty of transport runs in the direction of Mpataba. If you are travelling at night, we recommend you take a trotro to Essiama and then hire a private taxi to Beyin (*US$15–20*).

WHERE TO STAY *Map, above*

Moderate

🏠 **Tenack Beach Resort** (32 rooms)
m 0205 004685/0269 416629/0545
661520; e tenackbeach@gmail.com; www.
tenackbeachresort.com. This newish hotel on
the east side of the village offers comfortable
accommodation in rather ugly whitewashed blocks
whose angular austerity undermines the otherwise
luxuriant beachfront location. The rooms are very
pleasant inside, however, & all come with nets,
fan, fridge & satellite TV. There is also a good beach
restaurant specialising in seafood. *US$40/65/80
std/beachfront/exec dbl.* **$$$**

🏠 **Karela Hotel & Resort** (36 rooms)
m 0545 293251; e info@karelahotelandresort.
com; www.karelahotelandresort.com. Set about
500m west of town, this business-orientated
option is definitely a little heavy on the concrete
& sea-foam green paint, but the rooms & grounds

are smart nonetheless. Rooms are organised into
triplex chalets, & all come with flatscreen TV, AC,
bathtub & fridge. There's a swimming pool with
adjacent bar, plus 2 restaurants & a business centre,
& it's all facing a nicely maintained stretch of beach
punctuated with serviced gazebos. *US$66/92 std/
deluxe dbl; US$118 suite.* **$$$–$$$$**

Budget

✳ 🏠 **Beyin Beach Resort** (8 rooms)
m 0242 188240/0245 433790;
e beyinbeachresort@yahoo.com. Conveniently
located on a superb beachfront plot next to the
Ghana Wildlife Society (GWS) office (where you
arrange visits to Nzulezo) at the west end of
the village, this popular owner-managed resort
consists of 4 big thatched-roofed luxury wooden
chalets set under a swaying grove of coconut
palms, while the budget-conscious can choose

11

from 2 economy twins & 1 4-bed dorm or family room with shared facilities. All are built from natural materials & the chalets feature king-size beds, mosquito nets, private bath & balcony. The rooms themselves are in decent nick, but the compound as a whole was feeling pretty tired on our visit in 2016. Still, there's also a good restaurant serving a wide selection of meals & light snacks, including toasted sandwiches, pizzas, fresh fish, jacket potatoes & croissants, with most mains in the US$4–6 range. The resort is very active in turtle conservation, & offers turtle walks in season. *US$34/43 beachfront sgl/dbl; US$13/16/24/32 self-contained sgl/dbl/trpl/quad..* **$$$–$**

Shoestring

⌂ **Beyin Eco-Beach Camp** (6 rooms) m 0241 947903/0548 696628/0244 186770; e becobeachcamp@gmail.com; f fb.me/beyinecobeachcamp. Situated on the beach just behind the GWS office, this beachfront lodge offers accommodation in thoroughly ramshackle bamboo & palm-leaf structures with a balcony & bath/toilet shared between 2 rooms. A couple of new rooms were under construction when we checked in, which ought to be a bit sturdier. *US$11/14 dbl/twin.* **$**

✖ WHERE TO EAT AND DRINK *Map, page 263*

In addition to the restaurants listed below, food at the Beyin Beach Resort is very good, varied and reasonably priced. For cheaper eats, local food such as fried yam and kenkey is available at stalls along the main road.

✳ ✖ **Café Puerto** m 0544 342960; f fb.me/cafepuertobeyin; ⊕ 09.00–22.30 or later daily. This superb stilted outdoor restaurant & bar opened in 2012 on the jetty where boats leave for Nzulezo in the rainy season. The menu reflects the nationality of the friendly Spanish owner-manager couple, and includes the likes of paella, chilli con carne, various seafood dishes, & imported steak, along with various local dishes. Prices range from US$3–6 for a snack or simple dish, to US$10–15 for the more specialised dishes. Facilities include satellite TV & a very well-stocked bar, & there's good in-house birding in the wet season. **$$$–$$**

✖ **Homeboy Spot** m 0546 911209/0503 515040/0570 803623; ⊕ 07.00–22.00 daily. This cheerful spot serves up the usual array of local meals & cold drinks in an open-sided building right in front of the GWS office. **$**

✖ **Appolonia Arena** m 0243 460140/0576 879140/0503 591930; ⊕ 07.30–21.00 daily. Just opposite the fort, this well-signposted new restaurant is an eminently attractive option, & there's even a little beach bar maybe 50m from the main building towards the water. The menu offers Ghanaian & continental dishes for US$2–6, though the fact that 'Octopus Africa Hot Pepper Soup' is categorised under 'continental' may give you an idea as to where their strengths lie. A few rooms are planned in the near future. **$$–$**

✖ **Amansuri Country Kitchen** m 0243 223951; ⊕ 08.00–17.00 daily. Situated next to the GWS offices, this agreeable outdoor restaurant serves Ghanaian mains in the US$4–6 bracket, as well as pizzas for US$8–10. **$$–$**

WHAT TO SEE AND DO

Fort Apollonia (m *0244 528935;* ⊕ *08.00–17.00; entrance US$3pp, nominal photography fee*) The only permanent fort built along the coast west of the Ankobra River, and the last one to be built by Britain anywhere on the Gold Coast, Apollonia was constructed in 1770 with the permission of the Nzema chief Amenihyia. The name Apollonia is much older, however, and was coined by a Portuguese ship that sailed past Nzema on St Apollonia's Day (9 February) some time in the late 15th century. Fort Apollonia was built in a different manner from any other fort in the country, with a substantially stronger seaward bastion that not only served a defensive purpose, but also contained the cells used to store slaves. And being built to endure, it has retained its original shape, despite having been shelled during the war between the British and the French, and having been abandoned for long periods of time. It was renovated in the late 1950s, and converted to a resthouse in the 1970s. Following an agreement reached between the Ghana Museums and Monuments Board and the University of Pisa in Italy, however, the resthouse closed in around 2002, and the fort now doubles as a historical and ethnographical museum dedicated to the Nzema people, with displays on their traditional musical instruments and fishing methods, plus an ecological display dedicated to the Amansuri Wetlands.

Nzulezo and the Amansuri Wetlands Arguably one of Ghana's travel highlights, the small village of Nzulezo (population about 500) lies on the freshwater Lake Tadane in the Amansuri Wetlands, about 5km north of Beyin. Nominated as a UNESCO World Heritage Site in 2000, Nzulezo comprises one solid construction raised above the water, consisting of a central wood-and-raffia walkway with a few dozen individual houses on either side of it. Architecturally, it is a fascinating place, and utterly unique in Ghana, but be warned that it can be quite disappointing in the dry season, when the water retreats and most of the village is on land. Photography of people is expressly forbidden unless you have their permission, and we have had a few reports from readers who found the villagers to be (understandably) jaded by tourists, and sometimes outright hostile.

Quite why the people of Nzulezo decided to build their village above the water is an open question – especially as they are not primarily fisherfolk but agriculturists, whose fertile fields lie about 1km north of the lake. One legend has it that it was built about 500 years ago by refugees from modern-day Nigeria, who were chased there by another tribe during a war. Another legend traces the villagers' origins to Walata, a city in the ancient Ghana Empire, and states that they were guided there by a snail. Traditionally, there is a taboo on most activities associated with the lake on Thursdays. These days, however, the village welcomes tourists daily, though it's probably worth trying to avoid setting up a visit on Sundays, as the boatmen may be at church.

Nzulezo can be reached by dugout canoe only and the one-hour ride there is immensely rewarding, passing as it does through the Amansuri Wetlands, the largest intact stand of swamp forest in Ghana. The canoes follow the Amansuri River through areas of marsh and open pools fringed by raffia-palm thickets and lush jungle until it opens out on to the reflective black water of the lake itself. It's a lovely trip, especially in the early-morning cool, and you should see plenty of birds. Pygmy geese and African jacana are abundant on the lily-covered pools, while purple and squacco heron are often flushed from the reeds; purple gallinule and black crake creep through the fringing vegetation; hornbills and plantain-eaters draw attention to themselves as they cackle and chuckle in forest patches; and a variety of colourful bee-eaters, rollers and kingfishers perch silently on low branches. Indeed, keen birdwatchers and photographers could happily spend an additional morning on the water without visiting the village, and might even visit the wetlands without stopping at Nzulezo at all.

Getting there and away All visits to Nzulezo and/or the Amansuri Wetlands must be arranged through the **Ghana Wildlife Society** (*GWS;* m *0241 152811/0243 223951; www.ghanawildlifesociety.org or* f *fb.me/TheVillageOnStiltsNzulezo;* ☉ *08.00–16.00 daily*), which has a well-signposted office next to Beyin Beach Resort. The total cost of the excursion is around US$9 per person (with a small discount for students and volunteers), and an additional photography fee of US$1 or a video fee of US$1.50 is levied (allowing you to photograph the village but not the people). These fees are split between six communities in the area. In addition, you'll need to bring a bottle of schnapps, or donate around US$5 per party, if you

11

want to meet with the chief, and will also be expected to tip your canoe poler/ guide. A number of travellers have reported feeling pressurised and one notes that 'the boat guides feigned disgust at my tip because it was "not large enough"'– but many travellers still write to say this was the highlight of their trip. During the rainy season, you can canoe all the way from Beyin to the Nzulezo, leaving from the jetty at the Café Puerto. During the dry season (roughly January–April), you will need to walk 25–30 minutes to a launch point nearer to Nzulezo. Note that it is hot out on the water, and there is no shade once on the lake, so take bottled water, wear a shady hat and liberally slap on the sunblock.

Where to stay and eat Most people visit as a day trip out of Beyin, but it is possible to overnight at two basic lodges in Nzulezo. These are the popular **Home Stay Bar and Resthouse** (*5 rooms;* m *0541 720397*), which consists of basic but clean stilted rooms constructed entirely from raffia-palm branches and fronds, and the **Kasapa Guesthouse** (*7 rooms;* m *0206 816866*), which offers rooms of similar design and quality. Basic rooms with bucket shower cost US$8–11 double, and inexpensive fish and other meals can be prepared with advance notice.

HALF ASSINI

The most westerly Ghanaian port of any substance is the brilliantly named Half Assini, which lies about 5km from the Ivorian border and was the main crossing point between the countries prior to the construction of the modern road to Elubo. Now something of a backwater – albeit one accessible from Beyin by a good surfaced road – Half Assini lies along a wide sandy beach flanked by a pair of lagoons, one of which is said to harbour an evil witch and the other a good witch. It was the battle for dominance between these witches that led to the tragic sinking of a British cargo vessel offshore of Half Assini in 1913 – a show of strength by the evil witch, or so legend has it. Today, the grave of Captain Williams, who went down with the ship, stands in bizarre isolation in the middle of a road running north of and parallel to the main surfaced road through town.

That minor curiosity aside, Half Assini has little in the way of tourist attractions, though you could do worse than spend a few hours exploring the attractive beach and busy fishing harbour. Should you decide to visit, there's plenty of public transport running along the surfaced road from Tikobo #1, aka 'T1', at the junction with the road to Beyin.

WHERE TO STAY AND EAT The new **Sunset Paradise** (m *0208 164217/0508 801938*; e *info@sunsetparadisegh.com*; *www.sunsetparadisegh.com*) sits about 1km west of Half Assini towards New Town and offers well-equipped round thatch huts with air-conditioning, fridge, satellite TV and Wi-Fi in a palm-studded compound for US$50–100, plus a well-stocked bar and restaurant with meals at around US$10– 13. Alternatively, the comfortable **Hotel Gracia** (*16 rooms;* m *0209 223967/0208 216422*; e *hotelgracia@gmail.com*) charges around US$16 for a clean, carpeted self-contained double with fan or US$22 for a double with air conditioning, and lies on the left side of the main road as you enter Half Assini.

ANKASSA PROTECTED AREA

One of Ghana's most potentially exciting but sadly underdeveloped ecotourist destinations, bounded by the Ankassa River to the south and the Nini River to the north, the Ankassa Protected Area is a 509km² chunk of wet evergreen rainforest comprising the contiguous Nini–Suhien National Park and Ankassa Resource Reserve. Ankassa is regarded as having the greatest biodiversity of any reserve in Ghana. Up to 300 plant species have been counted in 1ha, with over 870 vascular plant species so far on record for the reserve. The list of more than 70 resident mammal species includes forest elephant, bongo antelope, Ogilby's duiker, bay duiker, golden cat, giant forest hog and red river hog. All ten forest primates known from Ghana have been recorded in the past, including chimpanzee, mona monkey, spot-nosed monkey, black-and-white colobus and the localised Diana monkey and white-naped mangabey, but it is probable that some primate taxa are now extinct.

Ankassa's checklist of 190 bird species (a figure that excludes many savannah species found in the surrounding farmland) contains more than 100 forest-obligates, with spot-breasted ibis, grey ground thrush, white-breasted guineafowl and great blue turaco being of particular note. It is also a known site for the rare nocturnal Akun eagle-owl, and a trio of waterholes near Nkwanta Camp often hosts localised forest-associated waterbirds such as Hartlaub's duck, white-crested tiger-heron and white-bellied, blue-breasted and shining blue kingfisher. A full bird checklist is sold at the gate for a nominal fee. The reserve also protects a prodigious variety of butterflies (some authorities estimate more than 600 species), reptiles and amphibians.

Several years back, Ankassa was targeted for tourist development by an EU-funded project that built two hutted camps, opened up an 'exploration centre' at the main entrance gate, cut two campsites and several hiking trails in the forest, and planned to open up mountain-bike and canoeing trails, as well as a small restaurant near the park office. However, these facilities have gone backwards in recent years, and all that is really offered is guided walks from the exploration centre, which are worthwhile but scarcely do credit to the forest's immense biodiversity. In part, this seems to be due to a communication breakdown between the forestry headquarters 17km away at Elubo, and the staff working on the ground. Furthermore, much of the reserve was for some time inaccessible by road due to an 'obstacle' along the 8km stretch between the main gate and Nkwanta Camp, though we're told the mysterious obstruction has been dealt with and the reserve can today be approached in a 4x4.

FEES Entrance costs US$5/2.50 per person for non-Ghanaian adults/students, and US$1.50 per vehicle. In addition, all walks attract a guide fee of US$2.50 per person per hour, though special birding fees of US$10 for one day or US$30 for two days (inclusive of guide fees) are charged to birdwatchers. Note, birding fees may soon be changed to US$13 per 2 hours, to bring prices into line with other parks and reserves.

GETTING THERE AND AWAY Ankassa Gate and the (now very run-down) Ankassa Exploration Centre lie 6km north of the main Takoradi–Elubo road along a signposted turn-off 21km east of Elubo, and can be reached in any vehicle. The best day to get to the reserve using public transport is Monday (local market day), when you can catch a trotro from Aiyinasi or Elubo to Sowodadzem, and then another trotro from Sowodadzem directly to the Ankassa Gate. On other days, your options are either to charter a taxi to the gate from Elubo or Aiyinasi (this shouldn't cost more US$20 one-way), or else to ask a trotro heading along the main road to drop you at the junction, from where you can hitch or walk the last 6km. If you go for

11

the latter option, it's a pleasant walk on gentle slopes and you can break the walk at a small bar in Amokwasuazo.

Do note that when you arrange transport to Ankassa, you should make it clear that you want to visit the reserve and not the eponymous town.

⌂ WHERE TO STAY AND EAT

⌂ **Frenchman's Farm** (10 rooms) m 0208 412085. Though the signposts have fallen down, this surprisingly smart place is still very much open, & reachable by taking a right turn about 500m before Ankassa Gate (at the Church of Pentecost–Old Ankasa sign), & following a rough dirt track for 1.5km. The thoroughly bucolic Frenchman's Farm is the only private accommodation in the vicinity of the forest reserve, & has both a homestay-like set-up with a row of small rooms on a stilted wooden platform & several new detached en-suite bungalows nearby, which are fastidiously clean & simply equipped with nets, fans & private terraces. Meals are available at around US$3 b/fast or US$5 lunch or dinner. The hands-on owner (not French, but a Ghanaian who lived in Ivory Coast for years) is very well spoken, friendly & helpful. *US$10/13/16 self-contained dbl/twin/trpl; US$40 2br-2bath suite with kitchen.* **$$–$**

⌂ **Nkwanta Camp** m 0209 545716/0249 182936. Situated 8km by road from the Ankassa Gate, this staff camp is named after the nearby village of Nkwanta, an ancient slave-trading post

mentioned in literature dating from 1640. The last inhabitants were compensated & moved out in the late 1990s. The camp lies near a fantastic stand of bamboo forest often referred to as the Bamboo Cathedral, an excellent site for black-&-white colobus monkeys in the morning & for potto at night (though you might need a spotlight or a strong torch to see the latter). The nearby forest regularly turns up fresh bongo spoor (though this elusive antelope is very difficult to see). Little more than 100m from the camp, the mango trees & plantains around the abandoned village are a favoured haunt of elephants during the fruiting season of Mar–May. Basic accommodation is theoretically available in 1 of 4 twin rooms. Camping is also permitted; the camp staff can provide you with a kerosene lamp, mosquito net & mattress for an additional cost. Note that the road there is 4x4 or foot traffic only, & the camp facilities aren't really functional in any meaningful sense, so visitors should be self-sufficient for food, drink, & ideally shelter. *US$7pp per room, US$5 per tent camping.* **$**

ELUBO

Everything about Elubo screams 'border town', from the exceptionally chaotic market spilling over on to the main street, to the hissing money changers and mandatory clowns who try to overcharge you for everything on the basis that you've probably just crossed into Ghana from Ivory Coast. As a result, Elubo is the sort of place you'll probably want to pass through as quickly as possible. Redeeming features include the street food – the beef kebabs on sale here are as tender, tasty and generous as any in Ghana – and a few adequate to good hotels. Market days here are Wednesday and Saturday, and there's an EcoBank ATM just after you enter Ghana.

GETTING THERE AND AWAY Regular trotros connect Elubo to Axim and Takoradi, as well as to Abidjan in Ivory Coast. There are also VIP buses and some Fords connecting directly to Accra, Kumasi, and Aflao from here, departing from a station about 200m from the border post. If you are travelling from Elubo to a point before Axim, you may have to change vehicles in Aiyinasi.

⌂ **WHERE TO STAY AND EAT** Both hotels are more or less 800m from the border, opposite the Total filling station.

Best Star Hotel (26 rooms) 📞 03122 22294; m 0271 387999; e beststarhotel@yahoo.com. This unexpectedly smart & very prominent 5-storey block offers comfortable modern accommodation with Wi-Fi, satellite TV, fan & AC in every room, plus a business centre, terrace bar & international restaurant. *US$23 self-contained dbl, US$48 VIP suite.* **$$$–$$**

Hotel Osamadi (16 rooms) m 0542 426556. This reasonably priced & vividly orange budget hotel is conspicuously signposted on the right side of the main road as you enter town from the east. There's a nicely situated terrace restaurant, but it wasn't functioning when we dropped in. *US$8/16 self-contained dbl with fan/AC.* **$–$$**

UPDATES WEBSITE

Go to www.bradtupdates.com/ghana for the latest on-the-ground travel news, trip reports and factual updates. Keep up to date with the latest posts by following Philip on Twitter (🐦 @philipbriggs) and via Facebook: 📘 fb.me/pb.travel.updates. And, if you have any comments, queries, grumbles, insights, news or other feedback, you're invited to post them directly on the website, or to email them to Philip (e philip.briggs@bradtguides.com) for inclusion.

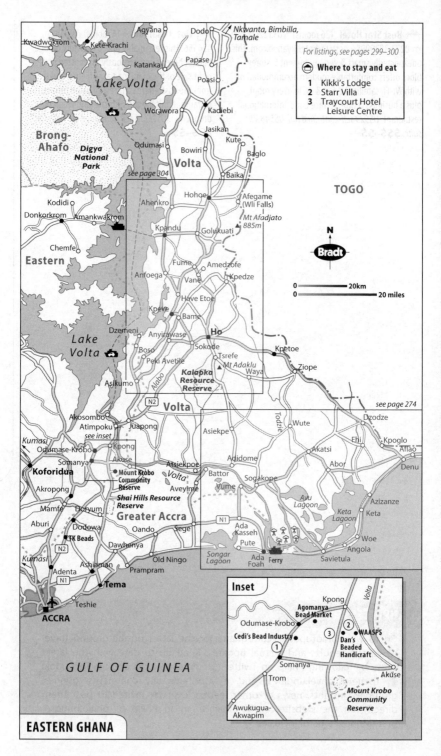

For listings, see pages 299–300

⊖ **Where to stay and eat**
1 Kikki's Lodge
2 Starr Villa
3 Traycourt Hotel
  Leisure Centre

TOGO

N

Bradt

0 _____ 20km
0 _____ 20 miles

see page 304

see page 274

GULF OF GUINEA

Inset

Kpong

Agomanya
Bead Market

Odumase-Krobo

Cedi's Bead Industry

③ ② **WAASPS**
Dan's
Beaded
Handicraft

①

Somanya

Trom

Akuse

*Mount Krobo
Community
Reserve*

Awukugua-
Akwapim

EASTERN GHANA

Part Four

EASTERN GHANA

OVERVIEW

The east of Ghana, though less geared towards upmarket tourism than the west coast, is a haven for independent travellers, rich in natural beauty and offering a wealth of low-key, low-cost travel possibilities to those with the initiative to take them up. For keen hikers and ramblers, the lush and relatively cool highlands around Ho and Hohoe are studded with the country's highest peaks, as well as a plethora of accessible waterfalls and an excellent little monkey sanctuary at the village of Tafi Atome. The east coast, too, is rich in isolated, out-of-the-way gems, most notably the small ports of Ada and Keta, while the area immediately inland of Accra is notable, among other things, for the tranquil Aburi Botanical Garden and impressive Akosombo Dam on the Volta River.

Travel conditions in eastern Ghana generally conform to those experienced in other parts of the country; a little cheaper perhaps, but no more arduous. Nevertheless, this region will appeal greatly to those travellers for whom travel means 'travel' in the chest-thumping, epic journey sense, rather than, say, soaking up the tropical beach atmosphere at Ada. Two exceptional ferry rides run through this part of Ghana: the twice-weekly trip from Ada north to Akuse along the Volta River, and the legendary overnight run from Akosombo to Yeji via Lake Volta. And there is also the bumpy overland trip from Hohoe through to the northern capital of Tamale, the closest thing in Ghana to those interminable bone-crunching trips for which many other African countries are renowned. A less obvious attraction of the east, but one that strikes us sharply whenever we revisit, is the almost total absence of hassle, particularly when compared, for instance, with the coast west of Accra – this truly is one part of Ghana where the country's reputation as the friendliest in Africa seems fully justified.

BEST OF EASTERN GHANA

ADA FOAH Stunningly located at the mouth of the Volta River, Ada Foah is the site of a few supremely chilled beach resorts, as well as being one of only two official marine turtle-viewing sites countrywide, and the terminus for a twice-weekly ferry upriver to Akatsi. Pages 275–81.

AKOSOMBO AND ATIMPOKU Lined with resorts catering to all budgets, the stretch of the Volta downriver of Ghana's largest dam exudes an aura of tropical languor – and for those looking to splash out, the opportunity to see it all from the air on a trial flight with West African Aviation Solutions and Provider of Services (WAASPS). Pages 289–98.

BEAD MARKETS The area immediately west of the Volta is renowned for its glass beads, which are sold at a vibrant twice-weekly market at Agomanya (close to Cedi's Bead Industry, where you can see traditional bead-makers at work) as well as a quieter daily market in Koforidua. Pages 300–1.

ADAKLU MOUNTAIN A community-based ecotourism project offers day hikes to the top of this striking inselberg, which dominates the skyline south of Ho, the capital of Volta Region. Pages 312–13.

AVATIME HILLS Centred on the historic old mission at Amedzofe, Ghana's highest town, these hills on the Togolese border offer some fantastic walking opportunities, and the Mountain Paradise Lodge in Biakpa is an excellent budget base for exploration. Pages 314–19.

TAFI ATOME MONKEY SANCTUARY An eastern counterpart to Boabeng-Fiema, this delightful forest-fringed village is the site of an excellent community project centred on a troop of habituated mona monkeys. Pages 319–21.

WLI FALLS The showpiece of Agumatsa Wildlife Sanctuary, which lies on the Togolese border east of Hohoe, the waterfall at Wli is reputedly the tallest in West Africa, and certainly among the most spectacular. Pages 329–30.

MOUNT AFADJATO Part of the tallest massif in Ghana, forested Afadjato, home to a wide variety of monkeys, birds and butterflies, is the focal point of two community projects offering affordable hikes and accommodation. Pages 330–32.

BUNSO ARBORETUM This lovely low-key stopover *en route* to Kumasi lies in a hillside arboretum that was established in the 1940s and still supports a wealth of birds and butterflies, plus a new canopy walkway. Pages 343–45.

KWAHU PLATEAU Situated between Lake Volta and the main road to Kumasi, this mountainous area is best known for the paragliding festival held there every Easter. Less seasonal attractions include the breezy Highland Mission at Abetifi, Ghana's first-ever zip-line at Obo, and access to the remote western Lake Volta shore. Pages 347–52.

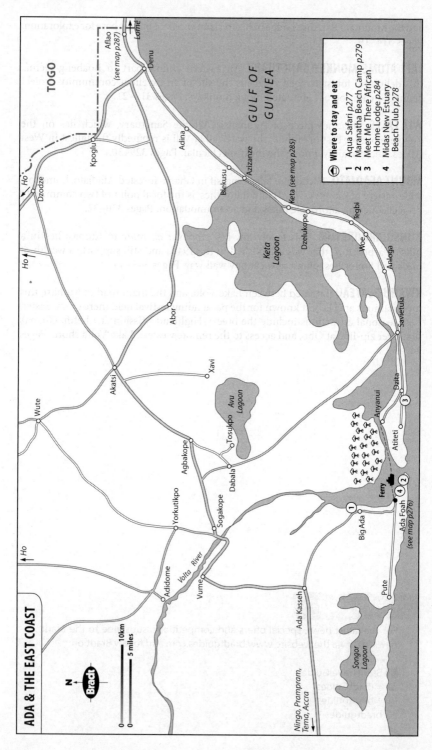

ADA & THE EAST COAST

Where to stay and eat

1 Aqua Safari *p277*
2 Maranatha Beach Camp *p279*
3 Meet Me There African
  Home Lodge *p284*
4 Midas New Estuary
  Beach Club *p278*

TOGO

GULF OF GUINEA

Lomé
Aflao *(see map p287)*
Denu
Adina
Kpoglu
Dzodze
Ho
Abor
Akatsi
Wute
Xavi
Tosukpo
*Avu
Lagoon*
Agbakope
Dabala
Sogakope
Yorkutikpo
Adidome
Vume
Ada Kasseh
Big Ada
Pute
Ada Foah
(see map p276)
Ferry
Atiteti
Atyanui
Dzita
Savietula
Anloga
Woe
Dzelukope
Tegbi
Keta *(see map p285)*
Azizanze
Blekusu
*Keta
Lagoon*
*Songor
Lagoon*
Volta River

Ningo, Prampram,
Tema, Accra

N

Bradt

0   10km
0   5 miles

12

Ada and the East Coast

The coast east of Accra remains surprisingly underdeveloped for tourism by comparison with the west coast, an anomaly best explained perhaps by a lack of substantial towns, and – with the exception of a small fort at Keta – a dearth of historic landmarks associated with the slave trade. Nevertheless, the east coast does boast two very attractive (and very different) beach resorts in the form of Ada Foah and the area around Keta (see below and pages 283–7 respectively), as well as a system of vast lagoons and estuaries that offer the country's finest marine birding, and (seasonally) the opportunity to see giant turtles laying their eggs on the beach.

ADA FOAH

Situated on the west bank of the Volta only a kilometre or two upriver of its sandy mouth, Ada Foah, the capital of Dangme East district, is something of a backwater today, but it was an important port prior to the 1960s, when the construction of Akosombo Dam closed a riverine trade conduit that had formerly been navigable for several hundred kilometres inland. A few faded colonial-era buildings aside, Ada Foah (literally 'Ada of the Fort') has little to show for its illustrious past, but the superb beach and riverfront scenery, combined with a range of activities and accommodation to suit all tastes and budgets, make it a worthwhile stop. Also of interest is the bordering Songor Lagoon, centrepiece of a Ramsar Wetland famed for its birdlife and turtle-viewing opportunities, the seasonal Asafotufiami Ceremony (held in Big Ada, a few kilometres further upriver), and the opportunity to explore the lushly vegetated lower regions of the Volta River, whether by chartered canoe or via the public ferry to Akuse and Anyanui.

HISTORY Ada is the traditional core of the Ada nation, one of the most important and cohesive empires on the pre-colonial Gold Coast. Oral tradition suggests that the Adali – the people of Ada – arrived in their modern homeland from somewhere to the east (probably Benin or Nigeria) prior to the late 17th century and eventually settled at Big Ada. The nation expanded in the early 18th century, as several lesser chieftaincies in territories along the Volta pledged their allegiance to the Ada Matse (king), who is today the paramount chief over ten major clans occupying an area of almost 20,000km² south and east of the Volta.

The wealth and influence of the Ada Empire was based on its strategic position at the mouth of the Volta River, from where it traded as far upriver as Yeji, and the limitless source of raw salt that is the Songor Lagoon. Both these assets were coveted by neighbouring powers, for which reason the empire spent much of the 18th and early 19th centuries fighting territorial wars, often with Danish backing. Despite Ada Foah's significance as a combined river and ocean port, and the allusion in its name, the only fort it ever hosted was the modest Fort Kongensten. This was

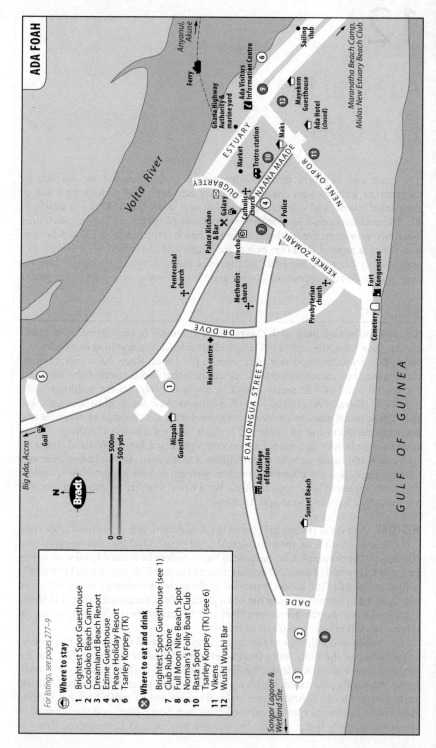

ADA FOAH

For listings, see pages 277–9

Where to stay
1 Brightest Spot Guesthouse
2 Cocoloko Beach Camp
3 Dreamland Beach Resort
4 Ezime Guesthouse
5 Peace Holiday Resort
6 Tsarley Korpey (TK)

Where to eat and drink
Brightest Spot Guesthouse (see 1)
7 Club Rub-Stone
8 Full Moon Nite Beach Spot
9 Norman's Folly Boat Club
10 Rasta Spot
Tsarley Korpey (TK) (see 6)
11 Vikens
12 Wushi Wushi Bar

constructed by the Danes in 1784, sold to the British in 1850, and now stands close to the Presbyterian church, looking more like a ruined warehouse than a fort, and threatened by sea encroachment.

Ada probably peaked in importance in the 19th century, but its autonomy became increasingly tenuous after the Danes sold their Gold Coast assets to the British in 1850. Following the Dutch evacuation of the coast in 1872 and the British victory over the Ashanti two years after that, Ada became an *ipso facto* crown colony. Among the most celebrated visitors to Ada at this time was Henry Morton Stanley, who sailed there from London in a Thames pleasure launch several months after his renowned 'discovery' of Livingstone on Lake Tanganyika. It was Stanley, in the company of Captain Glover, who took the first steamer across the perilous Ada Bar and up the Volta. British colonisation neutered the role of the paramount chief, so much so that all but one of the four Matse who were enstooled between 1876 and 1927 died in suspicious circumstances, and the stool was left vacant for 25 of those years. By contrast, only two Matse have ruled since 1927: Dake II (1927–77) and Nene Abram Kabu Akuaku III (1977–present day).

GETTING THERE AND AWAY Ada Foah lies 120km from Accra, about 20km southeast of the main road to Aflao, and is reached along a heavily pot-holed cul-de-sac that branches to the right at the junction town of Ada Kasseh and bypasses Big Ada after about 15km. Using public transport, regular trotros to Ada Foah leave from Tudu Station in Accra throughout the day, and take about 2 hours, depending on traffic. Coming from elsewhere, if you can't find direct transport to Ada Foah, just ask to be dropped at Ada Kasseh, from where regular trotros run up and down to Ada Foah.

In addition, the Ghana Highway Authority (GHA) operates a twice-weekly river ferry between Ada Foah and Akuse (near Akosombo), stopping at most villages and towns along the way. This boat leaves from the GHA marine yard (m *0243 154156/0248 926989*) in Ada Foah at 06.30 on Mondays and Fridays, arriving at Akuse at around 17.00, then starting the return trip from Akuse at 06.30 on Tuesdays and Saturdays, arriving back in Ada Foah at around 16.00. Tickets cost less than US$2 and it is a great way to travel most of the length of the Lower Volta downriver of Akosombo. The ferry also makes two return trips to Anyanui (for Keta, see pages 283–7) every Wednesday, when the market at Anyanui is in full swing. These leave Ada Foah at around 08.30 and 14.00, and Anyanui at around 12.30 and 18.00, take around 90 minutes in either direction, and tickets cost US$0.50. On other days of the week, motorised canoes usually run between Ada Foah and Anyanui.

TOURIST INFORMATION A semi-official tourist office is run by the **Ada Tourism Stakeholders Association (Ada Visitors Information Centre)** ((*03029 44676;* m *0244 565466/0570 767001;* e *adatourism@gmail.com; www.adatourism.com;* (*07.30–16.30 daily*), set in a signposted compound next to the GHA marine yard. In addition to maintaining a very useful website, it can arrange trips to all sites in and around Ada Foah, and also set up turtle-viewing tours to Songor through the Wildlife Division, though they keep rather whimsical opening hours.

WHERE TO STAY *Map, page 276, unless otherwise stated*

Luxury

Aqua Safari [map, page 274] (91 rooms, more under construction) (03022 41120; m 0540 110190/5; e res.aquasafari@gmail.com; www.aquasafariresort.com. About 5km north of Ada Foah as the crow flies, in Big Ada, this unprecedently large resort (for the area, anyway) has a fabulous riverside location, with a restaurant, 2 swimming pools, & several viewing decks overlooking the water & islands opposite. The architecture is decidedly unsubtle – think giant fountains, boat-shaped buildings, & lots of statues of horses, but the rooms are tastefully appointed & all come with wood floors & décor, satellite TV, tea/coffee facilities, fridge, & AC, while the riverfront units are set in standalone chalets. Jet-skis, pontoon boats & pedalos are all available for hire, & there's a gym under construction. *US$144/256/345/475 standard/ deluxe/waterfront/suite.* $$$$$–$$$$

Upmarket

✴ 🏠 **Tsarley Korpey (TK) Hotel**
(6 rooms) m 0274 218430/0207 898660; e info@tsarleykorpeybeachresort.com or akuarts@ yahoo.com. Nestled in the row of opulent w/end homes that line the riverbank southeast of the town centre, this comfortable & unusually tasteful boutique hotel has the feel of a private house. The spacious & airy rooms are dominated by light wood fittings & pastel shades, & come with satellite TV & AC. On the ground floor, there is a comfortable sitting room, whilst the garden has a gorgeous pool & floating deck on the river. The restaurant serves tasty meals. Boat tours can be arranged & jet-skis are available for hire. *US$105 self-contained dbl; US$183 family suite.* $$$$$–$$$$

🏠 **Peace Holiday Resort** (13 rooms) ☎03029 53077; m 0241 267450/0548 842723; e info@ peaceholidayresort.com; www.peaceholidayresort. com. This rather ostentatious lodge has a beautiful riverfront location about 2km out of Ada Foah along the road to Big Ada, as well as a tempting swimming pool, a wooden deck overlooking the river, & a restaurant serving varied international cuisine for around US$10 per main course. The small rooms are blandly decorated & come with dbl bed, satellite TV, AC, fan, minibar & hot water. The resort faces a tiny river island, which they'll punt you across to explore for US$8pp round-trip. *A bit overpriced at US$118/157 self-contained dbl/ deluxe or US$313 family suite with 3 bedrooms, living room & kitchen.* $$$$$–$$$$

Moderate

🏠 **Ezime Guesthouse** (5 rooms) m 0246 470083/0540 954486; e info@ezime-guesthouse. com; www.ezime-guesthouse.com. Situated in a restored 1933 house on the main junction in the town centre, this is easily the nicest of Ada

Foah's non-waterfront options. The bright, airy & attractively decorated rooms all come with writing desk, fan, AC, hot water & satellite TV, & there is a self-catering kitchen, though meals are also usually available for around US$5–8, with seating on a pleasant veranda at the back. They've also just opened Ada's very first pizzeria right next door, which is not to be missed. *Good value at US$28/32 self-contained sgl/dbl B&B; US$24 dbl bed only.* $$

Budget

🏠 **Midas New Estuary Beach Club** [map, page 274] (17 huts) m 0244 965078/0247 592970/0542 412889. Boasting a stunning location about 2km southeast of town with the Volta lapping on one side & Atlantic waves crashing on the other, this is less patronised than the neighbouring Maranatha, & it is generally a lot quieter at w/ends. Accommodation is in reed huts with natural ventilation, mosquito nets, concrete floors, & there are flush toilets, though showers are bucket-style. Cold drinks are available & basic meals cost US$4–5. To get there, you can either ring ahead & ask a boat to collect you from town (US$2.50 per person one-way) or walk out from the Wushi Wushi Bar, which takes around 40mins along a sandy footpath through the village of Azizanya. *US$13 dbl; US$21 twin (sleeps up to 4).* $$–$

🏠 **Cocoloko Beach Camp** (25 rooms) m 0244 885795/160409; e cocolokobeach@ gmail.com. This long-serving camp lies about 30mins' walk west of the town, within view of a rather dirty beach where turtles regularly come to nest in Nov–Dec. It lacks the rustic charm & perfect location of Midas & Maranatha beach camps, but the accommodation is comfortable & the vibe very relaxed. Renovations were under way in 2016, & the restaurant offers a large choice of food at around US$5 a plate. *US$13/18 self-contained dbl with fan/AC; US$5pp dorm bed.* $$–$

🏠 **Dreamland Beach Resort** (9 rooms) m 0244 766271/936892; e beate@ dreamlandghana.com; www.dreamlandghana. com. Situated about 500m past Cocoloko & overlooking the same scruffy beach, this small child-friendly resort, set in a rustic but rather cramped compound, is not as vibey as Midas & Maranatha, but it's still a very agreeable place with excellent facilities & good, clean amenities. It has a restaurant serving meals in the US$4–7 range & offers a variety of activities, including bike hire, boat trips in the Volta Delta & a visit to a local distillery. The nicely furnished bamboo huts are equipped with dbl bunks accommodating up to 4 people & include nets, fan, wardrobe & own private porch. *US$16/21 self-contained sgl/dbl; US$26 self-contained dbl with sea vies; US$11/16/18/21 for 1/2/3/4 people in room using shared bath.* **$$–$**

Shoestring

✴ 🏠 **Maranatha Beach Camp** [map, page 274] (34 rooms) m 0243 528248/0555 223323; e maranathabeaachcamp@hotmail.com; www. maranathabeachcampghana.com. Located 2km southeast of town, right next door to the Midas New Estuary Beach Club, this lusciously laid-back resort has an equally attractive location & is pretty similar in feel, though most of the reed huts, with mosquito nets above the beds & brightly painted world flags on the front doors, have sand floors only. There are currently compost toilets & bucket showers, but piped water is in the works. A portion of the proceeds is ploughed into local community projects such as turtle conservation & the maintenance of a school in the nearby village, at which there are plenty of volunteer opportunities. On w/ends there are bonfires with drumming & dancing. Basic meals are available for US$2–5. Directions are as for Midas, & boat pickups also available. *US$11/13 dbl with sand/concrete floor; US$21 family room sleeping 4; US$7pp dorm bed.* **$$–$**

🏠 **Brightest Spot Guesthouse** (16 rooms) m 0244 065760/0269 940822. If you don't mind a non-beachfront location, this clean guesthouse along the road back to Big Ada is recommended. Bright self-contained rooms with a fridge, TV & AC. A pleasant garden bar & restaurant serves some of the best food in town, mostly for around US$5. *US$17 dbl with AC & cold water; US$21–26 self-contained dbl with AC & hot water.* **$$**

✕ WHERE TO EAT AND DRINK *Map, page 276*

The standout restaurant, both for the riverfront setting and excellent food, is at the **Tsarley Korpey (TK) Hotel**, where mains cost US$8–10. Most of the other hotels and camps listed above serve adequate food for around half that price, with the garden restaurant at the **Brightest Spot Guesthouse** being recommended for grilled tilapia and banku. Several bars are dotted around town, including the Wushi Wushi Bar and Rasta Spot.

✕ **Vikens Restaurant** m 0204/0264 270630; ⏰ 08.00–22.00 daily. This pleasant garden eatery, about 500m southeast of the trotro station & market, has a well-stocked bar & serves pasta, salads & a selection of simple meat & fish dishes for around US$4–5. **$**

✕ **Norman's Folly Boat Club** m 0209 607633; 🅕 fb.me/ghwatersports.norman. Though it was locked up tight when we visited, this looks to be a promising address for coffee, cocktails & even cigars, should you catch them while they're open. They also hire watersports equipment including canoes, kayaks, waterskis, bicycles & more. **$$**

🍸 **Club Rub-Stone** m 0242 571508; ⏰ 08.00–late daily. Centrally located opposite the Ezime Guesthouse, this is primarily a bar, but it also serves a few tasty local dishes in the US$3-4 range. **$**

🍸 **Full Moon Nite Beach Spot** Situated opposite the affiliated Cocoloko Beach Camp, this sleepy out-of-town beach bar hosts reggae nights at w/ends, often with live music. Ring Cocoloko (page 278) for details of what's on.

OTHER PRACTICALITIES So far as we are aware, there is no bank, ATM, or forex bureau in Ada Foah, but **Arecho Internet** (⏰ *07.00–22.00 daily*) has a few computers near the centre of town if you need to get online.

The best **swimming** spot is out at the river mouth, in front of the Midas and Maranatha beach camps. However, the sea here is usually quite rough, so it is probably safer to swim on the river side of the estuary than in the ocean, but ask local advice before you take the plunge. Day visitors can use the swimming pools at the Tsarley Korpey (TK) or Peace Holiday hotels for US$5.

WHAT TO SEE AND DO

Around town The main point of interest in Ada itself is the beach and riverfront, but the town does boast a few minor historical landmarks, notably an attractive Presbyterian church built in 1918, the nearby 19th-century European cemetery, and the remains of the fort for which Ada Foah is named. The central market is worth visiting on the main market days of Wednesday and Saturday. An attractive stroll out of town takes you in a southeasterly direction from the Wushi Wushi Bar towards the estuary, through the fishing village of Azizanya. This very friendly village, on a turd-free sandy beach lined with colourful fishing boats and positioned below the tall palms, is a good place to watch rural activities such as smoking and sun-drying fish, and repairing boats and fishing nets. You could continue out past the village to Maranatha Beach Club, a great spot for a drink near the river mouth.

Boat trips Trips on the Volta River can be arranged through the Ada Visitors Information Centre or private boat owners (a pilot recently recommended by a reader is Isaac (m 02469 38510)) and typically cost around US$30 per hour for a group of up to 20. Maranatha Beach Camp and Dreamland Beach Resort are equally good places to set up boat trips. Popular goals within 5km of Ada Foah include Monkey Island, home to small numbers of spot-nosed and green monkey, which can often be seen from a custom-built viewing platform, generally only in the early morning. Pediatorkope Island, the largest in the chain, is also known as Crocodile Island, and while it harbours crocs on a regular basis, it is renowned for its basket-weaving industry, and forms a major breeding site for several species of egret, heron and cormorant between July and September. This island, in partnership with local government and NGOs, has also become a testing ground for renewable energy projects ranging from solar panels to electricity-generating swing sets and merry-go-rounds that can be seen at the school and clinic. Another good excursion is to the mouth of the estuary, about 2km from the town centre, or to Sugar Cane Island (Azikpe), where a group tour of the rum distillery costs the price of a bottle of its produce.

The river can also be explored using the inexpensive ferry services operated by the Ghana Highway Authority Marine Yard (page 277). The most interesting of these runs twice in either direction between Ada Foah and Anyanui on the eastern bank of the Volta on Wednesday (market day in Anyanui). The market here is among the largest in this part of the country, sprawling inland from the riverbank for almost 1km, and a great place to seek out anything from authentic local crafts to secondhand T-shirts to fishing nets. The ride across is also fun (if the ferry isn't operating, shared boat-taxis will be) with the option of either returning to Ada by boat, or – having crossed the Volta – continuing on the good tar road that connects Anyanui to Keta. Anyanui is also home to the Anyanui Tourism Information Centre (m 0248 448613; e bmadzagba@gmail.com; f fb.me/woezortrail; anyanui.wixsite. com/turism), who can arrange further boat trips along with kayak and bicycle hire.

Songor Wetland Site Centred on the 115km² Songor Lagoon, this Ramsar Wetland west of Ada Foah is one of two official turtle-viewing sites in Ghana. Three species of marine turtle breed here: green and olive ridley turtle are active between March and September, while the leatherback turtle comes to shore between September and January, with sightings most common over November and December. Formal guided excursions to look for nesting turtles can be arranged at the **Wildlife Division** (m 0246 429706; e songorwetlands@gmail.com; ☉ 08.00–16.00 Mon–Fri, w/ends by appointment), which has an office in Luhuase, on the east side of the main road between

Ada Foah and Big Ada, or indirectly through the Ada Visitors Information Centre or most of the hotels and camps around town. These cost around US$6 per person, and help fund the petrol and maintenance costs of the motorbike used to patrol the beach in search of illegal poachers. Wildlife Division officers have complained about tourists demanding a refund when they didn't see a turtle, so we should stress that sightings are not guaranteed and that those who do witness the nesting process are very lucky indeed. Turtles generally come ashore to lay eggs between 23.00 and 02.00, so these trips start at 21.00 or later, allowing time for the 5km walk to the nesting grounds. The best time to see nesting turtles is generally from August through to March, with big leatherbacks most likely from November to February.

The Songor Lagoon is also the country's second most important locale (after Keta Lagoon) for marine and other water-associated birds, with more than 90 species recorded in the saline marsh and open water, several of which breed around the lagoon or on islands in the Volta estuary. The area is most rewarding for birders during the European winter, when the number of waterbirds present has been known to exceed 100,000, with resident species such as egrets, herons and gulls joined by a host of Palaearctic migrants such as terns, sandpipers and other waders, and waterfowl. Mixed roosts of more than 50,000 terns – most commonly sandwich and black tern, but also royal, roseate and little tern – are frequently seen in September and October. Waders are also well represented, in particular black-winged stilt, avocet, ringed plover, curlew sandpiper, spotted redshank and greenshank. The wildlife office can also arrange birding trips to the area's two birdwatching platforms for US$5 per person, plus US$16 for a five-passenger vehicle to the platforms, should you need one. Boat trips around the estuary can also be arranged, starting at US$50 for up to eight passengers.

Songor is traditionally an important source of salt, which is still extracted on the west side of the lagoon near the village of Akplabanya, which can be reached from the main Accra–Aflao road by turning south at Sege, about 25km west of Ada Kasseh.

Asafotufiami Ceremony Ada's main festival, centred on Big Ada but spilling over to Ada Foah, is held every August in remembrance of the military achievements of Ada during the 18th and 19th centuries. The festival always begins on the first Thursday of August, when libation is poured at various ancestral shrines, but is far more colourful on Friday, when a succession of traditional military processions are held around the town, starting at dawn and carrying on until late at night. On Saturday, the festival climaxes with the durbar, during which the Matse (paramount chief) and various lesser chiefs are carried through the town on palanquins. Festivities continue until the next Thursday, though these are mostly less traditional and so of less interest to tourists. (As one local brochure puts it 'boat races, river cruises, football matches, and people greeting and bidding goodbye to each other'!)

SOGAKOPE

On the east bank of the Volta, some 25km upriver of Ada Foah, the small town of Sogakope forms something of a transport hub, since it lies adjacent to the most southerly bridge across the Volta, making it the sole funnel for road traffic crossing directly between Greater Accra and Volta regions. Sogakope is also the main port stopped at by the ferries between Ada and Akuse. The Vume area, on the opposite side of the river to Sogakope, is rightfully renowned for its painted ceramic pots, which are displayed for sale on the side of the road. Sogakope is the site of two large riverfront spa resorts popular with Accra weekenders, but of limited interest to travellers.

WHERE TO STAY AND EAT

Villa Cisneros Resort & Spa (80 rooms) m 0244 330624/578636; e info@cisnerosresort. com; www.cisnerosresort.com. This unexpectedly large & upmarket complex lies on the east bank of the river, about 1km downstream from the bridge. Facilities include a tennis court, swimming pool, internet café, health spa & 'goose garden'. River trips are also offered. Rooms are fair value, & come with AC & satellie TV. *US$37/42 sgl/dbl with AC; US$51 chalet; US$91 suite.* **$$$**

Holy Trinity Spa & Health Farm (39 rooms) ☎ 03620 91334/5; m 0260 311160/0244 311160/1; e holytrinityspa@yahoo.com; www. holytrinityspa.com. This destination spa next door to Villa Cisneros could be mistaken for a psychedelic hospital, with its main 5-storey building painted a decidedly unrestful shade of frog green. It offers a wide range of beauty & health treatments, starting at US$50, & other

facilities include tennis courts, gym, horseriding, & boat trips on the river, as well as a restaurant serving health-orientated food. The rooms are spacious & have AC but look a little tired at the asking price. They've also recently opened a similar-standard resort annex just north of the bridge. *US$102 self-contained dbl; US$157 chalet.* **$$$$**

Somewhere In Sogakope m 0200 246201/0248 531817; ⏰ lunch & dinner daily. Set in wide grassy grounds, this brightly painted new garden restaurant & bar is directly between Villa Cisneros & Holy Trinity Spa, making it an easy option if you're itching to get out of your hotel. The menu is a fairly usual selection of Ghanaian & continental dishes for about US$6–11, & they've got a reputation for their grilled tilapia. They also have 3 1st-floor dbl rooms with AC, TV & private terraces for US$52. **$$$–$$**

AVU LAGOON

Situated about 20km inland of the Atlantic coastline, the 10km-long Avu Lagoon, whose western tip almost spills on to the main road to Keta, is the second-largest of the shallow lagoons that comprise the 1,280km² Anlo-Keta Lagoon Complex, listed a Ramsar Wetland of International Importance in 1992. The freshwater lagoon is of considerable ornithological significance, since it hosts a long list of resident birds, including the massive Goliath heron, lily-trotting African jacana and various kingfishers, as well as being a seasonal breeding site for large flocks of red bishop and various marine species. Various monkeys and small carnivores are also present, while the lagoon's marshy shores are the last Ghanaian refuge for the sitatunga, a localised and rather elusive semi-aquatic antelope that was thought to be extinct in the country prior to being discovered at Avu in 1999.

Local communities have set aside an area of 150km² around Avu for the protection of the sitatunga, and the lagoon is also now the centrepiece of a community ecotourism project focused on two sites. The longer-serving of these, aimed mainly at birdwatchers, is Xavi (pronounced 'Havi', and often spelt the same way), which lies on the Lotor River a few kilometres east of the lagoon and about 10km south of Akatsi on the main Accra–Aflao road. More recently established is the site at Tosukpo, which lies on the northwest side of the lagoon, and is centred on a sitatunga-viewing platform from where these shy antelope are regularly seen, particularly by those who overnight there. A community entrance fee of US$1 is charged to all visitors, over and above the fees for individual activities.

GETTING THERE AND AWAY Tosukpo lies about 15km east of Sogakope as the crow flies. To get there, follow the Aflao road for about 10km to Dabala Junction, then turn right, as if heading to Keta. You will reach Dabala after 5km, and immediately after you pass through town, you will see Tosukpo signposted to the left. Turn to the right after another 1.3km, and then it is 2km to Tosukpo. A few shared taxis run from Dabala to Tosukpo daily, or you can charter a taxi for around US$3.

The springboard for visiting Xavi is Akatsi, a minor district capital and junction town on the main Accra–Aflao road about 30km northeast of Sogakope. The 10km feeder road running south to Xavi is clearly signposted on the Accra road about 1km west of Akatsi. Akatsi is well serviced by trotros to and from Accra, Ada Kasseh, Aflao and Ho. Once there, reasonably regular shared taxis to Xavi leave from Xavi Station, opposite the main lorry park, or you can charter a private taxi at the same station.

Confusingly, at least two other villages, Avuto and Bekpo, are signposted from the east side of the road from Dabala to Keta as part of the Avu Ecotourism Site. However, this evidently has more to do with local politics than with tourists: the villages are part of the board governing ecotourism at the lagoon, but in the words of one board member, they offer 'nothing to do, nothing to see'; they just hold the occasional meeting there.

WHERE TO STAY AND EAT There is no formal accommodation at the lagoon, but Xavi offers informal homestays for around US$5 per person. Many visitors to Tosukpo opt to stay overnight on the sitatunga-viewing platform, which costs an additional US$5 per person, and greatly improves the odds of seeing the antelope (but can also be quite hectic mosquito-wise, so bring repellent). In both cases, inexpensive food can be arranged, too. Alternatively, there are a few inexpensive hotels in Akatsi, including the **Magava Hotel** (*22 rooms;* ✆ *03626 44429*), signposted behind the telecommunications aerial on the Aflao road, or the reader-recommended **Dzifanor's Guest** (m *0268 218088/0248 633051;* e *dzifanorsguest@gmail.com*), which has clean and comfortable air-conditioned double rooms for US$12 and is located just off the Xavi road.

WHAT TO SEE AND DO
Tosukpo Ecotourism Site The most popular activity here is the trip to the sitatunga-viewing platform, which costs US$4 per person and involves a 30-minute canoe trip then an hour's walk. The antelope are very shy, so while you are almost certain to see their spoor, actual sightings are unlikely unless you stay overnight during the rainy season. Also worthwhile is a 90-minute canoe trip into the lagoon, which also costs US$4 per person, and can offer very good birding. Village and gin distillery tours are also available. It is advisable to call one of the guides – Jacob (m *0247 291741*) or Simo (m *0242 010318*) before heading out here, as they get very few visitors and may not always be around.

Xavi Ecotourism Site The main attraction at Xavi, costing US$2.50 per person, is a tranquil one-hour tour in a traditional dugout canoe on the small and quiet Lotor River, which lies 15-minutes' walk from the village and feeds into the Avu Lagoon to the south. Some 90 bird species have been recorded from the river, with some of the more conspicuous being malachite and pygmy kingfisher, Senegal coucal, emerald cuckoo, yellow-crowned gonolek, pin-tailed whydah, splendid sunbird, yellow-crowned bishop and white-throated bee-eater. Visitors can also observe traditional local fishing practices, and visit a stand of more than 60 baobab trees close to the river (US$3.50 per person). Another attraction is a cultural troupe, made up mostly of children, who perform traditional drumming and dancing routines accompanied by an English narration about the history and meaning of each of the dances, but this requires at least two days' prior notice. To make advance contact, call m 0249 738337.

KETA AND SURROUNDS

Probably the least-visited part of eastern Ghana, the 100km stretch of coast between the Volta River and the Togolese border is also one of the most rewarding to travellers with the inclination to spend a few days away from any established travel circuit. The defining feature of this region is the 40km-long Keta Lagoon, which is separated from the sea by a strip of sand less than 1km wide for much of its length. This narrow belt of land is dotted with small towns, the most important of which is Keta, a former Danish trade outpost and the site of Fort Prinzenstein. Like the smaller Avu Lagoon, Keta Lagoon – the country's largest such feature – forms part of the Anlo-Keta Lagoon Complex, and is an important breeding site for marine birds.

GETTING THERE AND AWAY Coming from the direction of Accra, you need to follow the main road east to Aflao as far as Dabala Junction. From Dabala, a surfaced road runs for 40km south to Savietula Junction, then 30km northeast towards Keta. Direct trotros to Keta leave Accra from Tudu/Aflao Station. Coming from Ho, you'll probably have to catch one trotro to Akatsi, then another to Keta. Coming from Ada, you may also have to do the trip in stages, changing vehicles at Ada Kasseh and Sogakope.

A more interesting approach from the west would be to take the Wednesday ferry across the Volta River from Ada Foah to Anyanui, from where the occasional trotro covers the 10km or so road to Savietula Junction. On any day other than Wednesday, the occasional motorised passenger canoe might cross from Ada Foah to Anyanui, but this is far from certain so check in advance in Ada Foah.

An excellent road now runs eastwards from Keta to Aflao as a result of a land reclamation project initiated after part of the old road was washed away by sea erosion. It is a wonderfully scenic route, passing through a few small palm-lined villages fringed by both lagoon and ocean, and notable for several large, modern burial shrines reminiscent in style of the posuban shrines of the Elmina area (see pages 182–3). There is a fair amount of transport between Keta and Aflao at all times, but it is most frequent on market day in Keta (every four days), when you'll rarely wait more than about 20 minutes for a trotro.

WHERE TO STAY AND EAT *Map, opposite, unless otherwise stated*
Note that accommodation in this area is very dispersed, with one of the most popular lodges, Meet Me There, situated 35km southwest of Keta in Dzita village. There are a few options within walking distance of central Keta, including the Keta Beach Lodge, Aborigines, Emancipation Beach Camp, Keta Lagoon Resort, and Wild Camp Ghana. Most of the hotels serve decent to good food, but for a meal out we recommend **Happy Corner Restaurant** (m *0243 135435*) in Woe. As for nightlife, there's usually some drinking and dancing going on at **Club 3T** in Dzelukope.

Moderate

Lorneh Lodge (67 rooms) m 0242 073255. Situated 7km south of central Keta on the ocean side of the main road back towards Savietula, this once-popular lodge closed down for renovation in May 2015, but no work had been done on it nearly a year later. The plan is still for it to reopen, but that could be a long way off. Prices will likely start around US$42 *self-contained dbl with AC.* **$$$**

Aborigines Beach Resort (17 rooms) m 0502 836368/0342 290220/0554 863747; e info@aboriginesbeachresort.com; www. aboriginesbeachresort.com. Though it was still something of a work in progress when we checked

in, this resort-like new place faces a particularly lovely stretch of beach in Dzelukope & now likely represents the most upmarket accommodation available near Keta. Rooms are modern & comfortable, with AC, flatscreen TV, fridge & ceiling fan. There's a large restaurant-bar & swimming pool under construction, & aquatic activities can be arranged. US$47/52 *queen/king dbl.* **$$$**

Budget

Meet Me There African Home Lodge [map, page 274] (10 rooms, 1 dorm) m 0541 838387/0543 670194; e dougaljc@hotmail.co.uk; www. ghanameetmethere.com; see ad, page 288. This relaxing beach lodge is located in the small village of Dzita around 5km west of Savietula Junction on the main road between Keta & Anyanui. Surrounded by swaying coconut palms & with waves crashing on the beach, time slips away easily here. Accommodation consists of traditional-style thatched-roofed dbl huts with cold shower & private balcony, along with larger 'chief's suites' that come with scenic outdoor showers. The attached restaurant cooks delicious local & continental dishes with an emphasis on fresh seafood & pizza on Sat. There are plenty of activities to keep you entertained, including swimming & canoeing on the saltwater lagoon, boat trips down the Volta River, tours to Fort Prinzenstein, dancing & drumming lessons, nocturnal turtle patrols, & getting involved with one of their many community projects. *US$16 self-contained dbl; US$32 dbl chief's suite; US$8 dorm bed.* **$$–$**

* 🏠 A&Y Wild Camp Ghana
(2 rooms) m 0541 574954/0241 624717; e wildcampghana@gmail.com; www. wildcampghana.com. Hidden away in a neighbourhood of fishing families just north of Keta, this happy little reed & thatch compound fits right in, & can be found about 200m from the beach & 200m northeast of Emancipation Road, which runs more or less between Emancipation Beach Camp and Keta Lagoon Resort. Lovingly managed by an Italian-Ghanaian couple, the no-frills thatch rooms here are immaculately kept & come with mozzie nets & either a concrete or sand floor. There's a central sitting area & library where the authentic Italian pizzas & pastas are served, bonfires, drumming, crafts, body boarding & other activities on offer, & they encourage guests to go out and meet the neighbours. *US$8 smaller dbl; US$13/18/24 larger room sleeping 2/4/5.* **$$–$**

🏠 Abutia Guesthouse (16 rooms) m 0246 984499/0248 204370/0544 836417. Among the best deals in this range, the Abutia is situated 500m from the centre of Woe in the direction of Savietula Junction, making it very well positioned for exploring the lagoon & walking out to the lighthouse. It lies in pleasant gardens, signposted 20m from the main road & not much further from the lagoon. There's no restaurant anymore, but Happy Corner (page 284) is close by. The clean dbl rooms with fans are great value. *US$10/12 self-contained dbl with fan/AC.* **$**

🏠 Keta Lagoon Resort (15 rooms)
☏ 03621 93423; m 0246 742929/0541 476914;

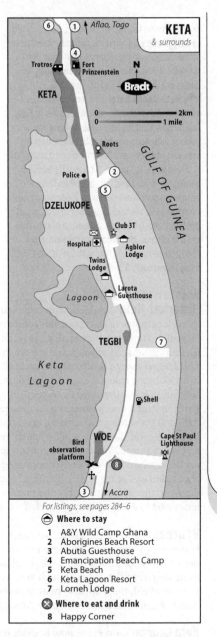

For listings, see pages 284–6

🛏 **Where to stay**
1 A&Y Wild Camp Ghana
2 Aborigines Beach Resort
3 Abutia Guesthouse
4 Emancipation Beach Camp
5 Keta Beach
6 Keta Lagoon Resort
7 Lorneh Lodge
✖ **Where to eat and drink**
8 Happy Corner

f fb.me/ketaLagoonResortsAndTours. If you've ever wanted to stay in a stilted lodge over the water but were scared off by the prices in Tahiti, the bargain bungalows here might just be your chance. Set over Keta Lagoon just north of town, the thatched cottages here are quite bare when it comes to furnishings, but all come with reed-mat

12

flooring, ceiling fan, running showers, & an en-suite camping loo. It's definitely the most unconventional accommodation in the region, & even if you don't stay here, it'd be eminently worth stopping by for dinner or a drink. *US$32/40 dbl/twin.* **$$**

🏠 **Keta Beach Hotel** (38 rooms) ✆03626 42288; m 0203 976327. The closest hotel to Keta, this rundown but likeable establishment was once popular with Accra w/enders, but these days it sees very little custom. Decent if unspectacular fare is served in the restaurant & pleasantly wooded garden bar, & cold beers are available. There's a swimming pool & net café as well. Coming by road from the west, ask the trotro driver to drop you at the hotel, which is clearly signposted next to the main road some 2km before central Keta. *From US$13/19 self-contained dbl with fan/AC; US$11 dbl using shared bath.* **$$–$**

Shoestring

🏠 **Emancipation Beach Camp**
(12 rooms) m 0202 841690/0543 510801; e emancipationbeach@yahoo.com. This fun new beach camp, under the same management as Maranatha Beach Camp in Ada Foah, is located right on the spectacular beach immediately east of Keta & Fort Prinzenstein. The set-up is almost identical to Maranatha, with the same reed huts adorned with brightly painted world flags & bucket showers. There's a good beach bar & restaurant serving a decent range of continental dishes priced from US$3–5, but meals must be ordered ahead as food is purchased from the market then cooked. Other facilities include beach football & volleyball. *US$5/7 dbl/twin using shared showers; US$2.50 per tent camping.* **$**

WHAT TO SEE AND DO

Historical Keta Studded with old warehouses and other time-worn buildings in various states of disrepair, the compact but rather bleak old town of Keta seems incredibly rundown, presumably as a result of the water erosion that threatens to engulf its foundations. Its focal point is **Fort Prinzenstein** (⊕ *08.00–17.00 daily; entrance US$2.50 per foreign adult*), which was built by the Danes in 1784 and sold to the British in 1850. In the colonial era, Fort Prinzenstein served as a prison, a role it continued to serve until it was damaged by waves during a storm in 1980. More recently, it has been partly restored and reopened as a museum, housing a limited selection of artefacts dating to the slaving and whaling eras. The caretaker will also take you to the old slave chambers, and show you a pile of dusty record books dating from the days when the fort was a prison. The other main historical landmark is the **Cape St Paul Lighthouse** on the seaward side of Woe (pronounced 'Wo-Ay'), 6km south of central Keta, and about 1km east of the main road. This is reputedly the oldest lighthouse in the country, dating to the 18th century, but the present building – a bizarre steel construction that looks a bit like a cartoon space rocket – only dates to 1901.

Beaches In Keta, the attractive beach immediately in front of Fort Prinzenstein is unsafe for swimming, mainly due to the large chunks of collapsed wall that jut out of the water, but it is reputedly usually safe to swim at Emancipation Beach, immediately to the north, though you are strongly advised to seek local advice first. Further afield, there are also swimming beaches, with resort facilities, at Aborigines Beach Resort and Meet Me There African Home Lodge.

Keta Lagoon A very shallow body of fresh or brackish water, flanked by extensive shallot farms (especially around Anloga), Keta Lagoon is the most important site for marine birds in Ghana, with 76 aquatic species recorded, and concentrations of up to 100,000 individual birds not unusual in the European winter. Among the more common species are great white and little egret, western reef heron, fulvous and white-faced duck, black-winged stilt, avocet and a similar range of terns to Songor Lagoon. Several of the islands are important avian breeding grounds. A good starting point for birdwatchers is the observation tower in Woe, which lies only 50m from the main road. Even in Keta town itself, birdlife is abundant, including seasonal concentrations of pied kingfisher and avocet. The lagoon could reward further exploration by boat, and you'll have no difficulty finding somebody to take you out on the water at Keta or elsewhere. Though it's a bit out of the way, the Anyanui Tourism Information Centre (page 280) is a good resource for setting up trips on the lagoon.

AFLAO

This typically chaotic border town is the third-largest urban settlement in Volta Region, with a population of approximately 66,000, and it must be a disconcerting introduction to Ghana coming from Togo. Aflao is practically a western extension of the Togolese capital Lomé, which lies immediately across the border, as evidenced by some unusual French-influenced street food, in particular crusty baguettes. For those travelling entirely within Ghana, the most likely reason you would pass through Aflao is if you'd followed the coastal road from Keta and wanted to pick up transport back towards Accra or Ho. Readers have passed on stories about 'unofficial officials' hanging around, and shifty 'guides' getting in the middle of things – but if you're alert, refuse any advances made by prospective guides or money changers, and walk straight from the lorry park to the border post (you can't miss it), then you shouldn't have any problems. There's now a GT Bank ATM accepting Visa and MasterCard just steps from the border post (so you can avoid the moneychangers altogether if you're just arriving), and Ghana Commercial and EcoBank ATMs further into town.

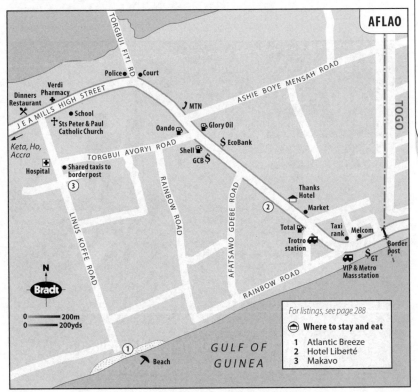

AFLAO

TORGBUI FITI RD

Police ● Court

Verdi Pharmacy
Dinners Restaurant

ASHIE BOYE MENSAH ROAD

J E A MILLS HIGH STREET

♪ MTN

TOGO

● School
✝ Sts Peter & Paul Catholic Church

Oando 🏪

🏪 Glory Oil

Keta, Ho, Accra

TORGBUI AVORYI ROAD

Shell 🏪

$ EcoBank

GCB $

✚ Hospital

● Shared taxis to border post

③

RAINBOW ROAD

AFATSAWO GDEBE ROAD

Thanks Hotel
②
● Market

Total 🏪

Taxi rank

Melcom

Trotro station

$ GT

Border post

N
Bradt

LINUS KOFFE ROAD

VIP & Metro Mass station

RAINBOW ROAD

0 ▬▬ 200m
0 ▬▬ 200yds

For listings, see page 288

🏠 Where to stay and eat

1 Atlantic Breeze
2 Hotel Liberté
3 Makavo

① 🏖 Beach

GULF OF GUINEA

GETTING THERE AND AWAY The main station, as crowded and chaotic as any in Ghana, is only 100m or so from the border post. Trotros from Accra leave from Aflao/Tudu Station and cost US$6, while direct transport from Ho costs US$2.50. There's a separate VIP and Metro Mass station right around the corner with direct buses to Kumasi, Ho, Accra, and even Elubo on the Ivorian border. The most interesting route in or out of Aflao, however, is the wonderfully scenic coastal road from Keta, as described on page 284.

WHERE TO STAY AND EAT *Map, page 287*

⌂ **Atlantic Breeze Hotel** (22 rooms) 📞03621 93470; m 0247 920368/0244 279797. Just the fact that this mosaic-heavy & colourful new place is Aflao's only beachfront hotel gives it an edge, but it's also clean, well kept, & conscientiously managed. The en-suite rooms don't have much of a view, but all come with fridge, flatscreen TV & ceiling fan, & there are plenty of views to be had from the shady resto-bar in the sand out front. *Good value at US$16/19 dbl with fan/AC.* **$$**

⌂ **Makavo Hotel** (21 rooms) m 0246 288640. This venerable hotel, situated about 1km from the border post, has clean rooms, a good restaurant, an attractive beer garden & a swimming pool (*US$2.50 for non-guests*). Shared taxis run between the border post & a taxi rank in front of the hospital 50m from here. *US$13/19 self-contained dbl with fan/AC.* **$$–$**

⌂ **Hotel Liberté** (33 rooms) 📞03625 31260; m 0249 056924. This characterless multi-storey hotel near the border post lacks a restaurant but the rooms are very respectable & well priced. *US$17/19 self-contained dbl with fan/AC.* **$$**

13

Akosombo and Krobo

The main focal point of this chapter is Akosombo Dam, Ghana's largest such construction, and the wide forest-fringed stretch of the Volta River immediately downstream of it. Situated in Asuogyaman District, about 80km northeast of Accra as the crow flies, the area makes for a popular weekend getaway from the capital, while for tourists it forms an enjoyable gateway to the town of Ho and elsewhere in Volta Region, on the east side of the river. Also covered in this chapter are various markets, factories and outlets for the traditional glass and other beads manufactured in the Manya Krobo District, an industry focused on the area between Kpong (on the Volta River south of Akosombo) and the small town of Odumase Krobo about 10km to its west.

AKOSOMBO, ATIMPOKU AND SURROUNDS

The area broadly referred to as Akosombo in fact comprises about half a dozen small towns and villages strung along the west bank of the Volta River for around 15km downstream of the Akosombo Dam, which lies in the Akwamu Traditional Area. These include the service town of Akosombo, purpose built a couple of kilometres below the dam to house the workers involved in its construction; the district capital of Atimpoku, which is also the site of Adome Bridge (one of only two to span the Volta downriver of the dam); and the near-contiguous village of New Senchi on the road towards Accra. An obvious place to stop over *en route* between Accra and Volta Region, the Akosombo area boasts three main attractions: the impressive dam wall (guided tours are available), the attractively forested stretch of the Volta River below, and the opportunity (temporarily suspended) to take a day cruise on the southern portion of Lake Volta. More adventurously, Akosombo Port, on a peninsula northwest of the dam wall, is the southern terminus of the weekly Lake Volta ferry to the northern ports of Kete Krachi and Yeji.

GETTING THERE AND AWAY Coming from further away, the main regional transport hub is Kpong, situated on the west bank of the Volta some 10km south of Atimpoku and 10km north of the river ferry terminal at Akuse. Kpong is bisected by the main Accra–Ho road, and is connected by regular trotros to Ashaiman (for Accra), Ho and Akuse. Regular trotros also run up and down from Kpong to Akosombo via Atimpoku and New Senchi, and you'll rarely wait more than five minutes for a seat between any of these places. In addition, Metro Mass and other coaches and minivans travelling between Accra and Ho will generally drop passengers on request at Atimpoku, provided that they don't mind paying the full fare.

If you're heading to Ho or elsewhere in Volta from Atimpoku, you could wait at the rest stop on the east side of the main traffic circle, but most vehicles stopping here are full when they come past, so it may be quicker in the long run to take a

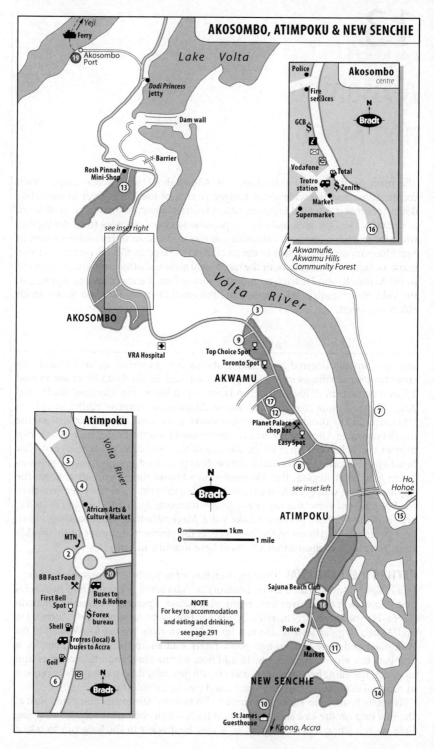

AKOSOMBO, ATIMPOKU & NEW SENCHIE

Lake Volta

→ Yeji
Ferry
Akosombo Port **19**

Dodi Princess jetty

Dam wall

Barrier

Rosh Pinnah Mini-Shop **13**

see inset right

AKOSOMBO

VRA Hospital

Volta River

3

Top Choice Spot **9**
Toronto Spot

AKWAMU

17
12
Planet Palace chop bar
Easy Spot

8

see inset left

ATIMPOKU

7

15

→ Ho, Hohoe

Akosombo centre

Police

Fire services

GCB $

Vodafone

Total
Trotro station $ Zenith

Market

Supermarket

16

↑ Akwamufie,
Akwamu Hills
Community Forest

N **Bradt**

Atimpoku

1
5
4

Volta River

African Arts &
Culture Market

MTN
2
20

BB Fast Food

First Bell Spot
$ Forex bureau
Buses to Ho & Hohoe

Shell

Trotros (local) &
buses to Accra

Goil

6

N **Bradt**

N **Bradt**

0 ————— 1km
0 ————— 1 mile

NOTE
For key to accommodation
and eating and drinking,
see page 291

Sajuna Beach Club
18

Police

11

Market

14

NEW SENCHIE

St James **10**
Guesthouse
↓ Kpong, Accra

trotro to Kpong and board a Ho-bound vehicle there. Likewise, while any Accra-bound vehicle with a spare seat will stop outside the station between the Shell and Goil filling stations a few hundred metres south of the main traffic circle, it might be easier to head to Kpong and change vehicles there. See also the box *The Akosombo–Yeji ferry*, page 292.

ORIENTATION AND GETTING AROUND The low-key district capital Atimpoku straddles the Accra–Ho road on the west side of Adome Bridge, a massive two-hinged steel arch suspension bridge that has spanned the Volta River since 1957. Atimpoku is the main disembarkation point for coaches and other transport passing through *en route* between Accra and Volta Region, and a good selection of lodges catering to most budgets can be found within a kilometre of the main roundabout on the west side of the bridge. Akosombo township lies about 8km northwest of this roundabout, along a good tar road that winds northwards for another 5km or so, passing Akosombo Dam to the right and the upmarket Volta Hotel to the left, before it terminates at Akosombo Port, the embarkation point for ferries further north. Other important travel focal points, both with several hotels, are the village of Akwamu about halfway along the main road between Atimpoku and Akosombo and New Senchi on the Accra road south of Atimpoku. Plenty of shared taxis and trotros connect Atimpoku to Akosombo, Akwamu and New Senchi. From the main stations in Atimpoku or Akosombo, ask for a taxi to 'Mess' for the Volta Hotel, and one to 'Marine' for the ferry jetty and ticket office.

WHERE TO STAY *Map, opposite*

Luxury

The Royal Senchi Resort Hotel
(84 rooms) 03034 09170/80; e info@
theroyalsenchi.com; www.theroyalsenchi.com.

AKOSOMBO, ATIMPOKU & NEW SENCHIE
For listings, see pages 291–5

Where to stay
1 Adi Lake Resort
2 Adomi
3 Afrikiko Riverfront Resort
4 Akosombo Continental
5 Aylos Bay Lodge
6 Benkum Motel
7 Black Star Lions
8 Hotel Rhozo
9 Joetina
10 Lakeside Motel
11 The Royal Senchie Resort
12 Sound Rest Motel
13 Volta
14 Volta Safari Guesthouse
15 Wadiva Waterfront Inn
16 Zito Guest Inn
17 Zito Guest Inn Annex

Where to eat and drink
Adi Lake Resort (see 1)
Afrikiko Riverfront Resort (see 3)
Aylos Bay Garden Restaurant (see 5)
Black Star Lions (see 7)
18 La Plus
19 Maritime Club
20 On The Bridge (Berima Nkwan)
Volta (see 14)

Opened in Sep 2013, this stylish 4-star riverside resort is set in vast grounds overlooking the forested Denkyenyam Island behind the New Senchi Market. Spaciously laid out, with plenty of curves & tall thatched roofs, it has a formal restaurant, a more casual terrace snack bar, tour desk, spa, gym, tennis court, children's playground, riverfront swimming pool, & free kayaks & pedalos for guests. All rooms have a river view and come with king-sized bed, Wi-Fi, AC, large-screen satellite TV, complimentary minibar, en-suite hot tub & shower, tea-/coffee-making facility & safe. Rooms for disabled travellers are also available. *US$240 self-contained dbl; US$560–3,000 suite.* **$$$$$**

Upmarket

Volta Hotel (35 rooms) 03430 20731/46;
m 0544 357703–5; e info@voltahotel.net; www.
voltahotel.net. The building may not be beautiful & the décor feels decidedly pre-millennial, but this 3-star hotel is very well run & the spectacular views over the dam are genuinely special. Facilities include an ATM machine, an internet café, a large swimming pool area, a good restaurant, snack bar & nightclub, as well as live highlife music in the bar on Sat. Sailboats, kayaks, jet-skis & more are all available for hire. The compact self-contained

The MV *Yapei Queen*, which has plied the length of Lake Volta from Akosombo to Yeji and back on a weekly basis since the late 1960s, is primarily a cargo vessel, but it also has limited cabin space and deck space for passengers. Its route is the longest followed by any boat in Ghana, and while it's anything but a luxury cruise, many adventurous travellers rank it to be a highlight of travelling around the country.

In theory, the full cruise between Akosombo to Yeji takes about 36 hours in either direction, but in practice it can take a lot longer, and we've had numerous reports from travellers who were on the boat for 60–70 hours in one or other direction thanks to a combination of engine failure, steering problems or interminable loading stops at villages along the way. For what it's worth, then, the boat is scheduled to leave Akosombo Port every Monday at 16.00, to arrive in Kete-Krachi Tuesday morning, and Yeji late on Tuesday evening. Southbound departures from Yeji are scheduled for every Wednesday morning at 05.00, stopping in Kete-Krachi Wednesday evening, and arriving in Akosombo late Thursday evening. Delays seem to be a greater problem on the southbound leg.

Only two first-class passenger cabins are available on the MV *Yapei Queen*, though the so-called Owner's Cabin will normally be made available to tourists if it is not being used by Volta Lake Transport Company staff. The cabins are quite comfortable, with air conditioning and two beds each, and pretty good value at US$21/26 per person from Akosombo to Keti Krachi/Yeji. Unfortunately, with cabin tickets being at such a premium, they can only be bought in person from the booking office in Akosombo Port (about 5km northwest of the Volta Hotel by road), which means you must either get yourself to Akosombo with a few days to spare to secure a cabin berth, or take your chances on the day. Although bookings cannot be made by phone or email, you could try to make advance contact to check availability (✆ 03430 20084; m 0206 777518; e akoport.vtc@yahoo.com). If the cabins are unavailable, second-class seating costs US$5/6 to Keti Krachi/Yeji, and booking is seldom necessary, but be quick off the mark to get a seat in the dining room, otherwise you'll end up out on deck as there is now no longer a third class. If you're embarking in the north, try ringing the harbourmasters in Yeji (m 0201 656388) or Kete-Krachi (m 0207 947788) for a status report.

There is normally plenty of food on the boat, but we've heard of travellers being stuck without food for 24 hours after it ran out. There does always seem to be plenty to drink at all times. If you arrive in Yeji in the late afternoon, don't let the touts convince you to cross to Makongo immediately, as there is nowhere to stay there and there will probably be no transport on to Salaga or Tamale until the next morning – better to overnight in Yeji.

---

rooms all have AC & satellite TV, & suites are also available. The hotel lies more than 1km north of Akosombo township off the road to the port; passenger taxis from the lorry station in the area known locally as 'Mess' pass by the bottom of its steep drive. *US$162/203 B&B self-contained sgl/dbl; US$355 suite.* **$$$$$–$$$$**

🏠 **Afrikiko Riverfront Resort** (30 rooms) ✆03422 90610; m 0242 625624/0503 130733; e afrikikoriverfrontresort@gmail.com; www.afrikikoriverfrontresort.com. Set in landscaped riverside gardens in Akwamu, this relatively smart resort is one of the most attractive retreats in the area, though the standard of service &

accommodation doesn't quite match the lovely setting. Rooms are comfortable & tastefully decorated, with restored colonial furniture & private flower-covered terraces, but definitely on the smallish side. Facilities include a 'wellness spa', which offers Western-standard treatments at Western prices, & a 15-man motorboat available for hire. There is also a tempting pool & an excellent bar & restaurant, which hosts cultural displays on Sat/Sun afternoons. *US$101/111 B&B self-contained sgl/dbl room with AC, satellite TV; US$105/120 sgl/dbl chalet.* **$$$$**

🏠 **Akosombo Continental Hotel** (37 rooms) 📞 03421 92450; m 0242 319070; e akoscontinentalhotel@gmail.com; www. akosombohotel.com. Boasting a superb riverfront location in Atimpoku, this hotel was award-winning once upon a time, but a change in management has seen standards slip considerably in recent years. Attractive grounds are set around a large swimming pool, but the once-fabulous Indian restaurant today serves a rather generic selection of Ghanaian dishes. The rooms are small & rather run-down, though all come with AC, satellite TV & fridge, & the larger chalets are set back away from the pool area. Overpriced at *US$79/92 sgl/dbl; US$131 chalet.* **$$$$–$$$**

Moderate

☀ 🏠 **Adi Lake Resort** (12 rooms) 📞 05036 72789; m 0245 298517; e info@adilakeresort. com; www.adilakeresort.com. This pleasant German-run resort set in landscaped riverfront gardens bordering Aylo's Bay is notable for its paddling pool & child-friendly atmosphere. The rooms are on the small side but all come with modern décor, satellite TV, AC, Wi-Fi, & executive rooms come with private balcony. The attached restaurant specialises in barbecued tilapia, but also serves chicken & seafood dishes, mostly in the US$6–10 range. Kayaks are available for exploring the river. *US$60/73 en-suite dbl/exec; suites from US$113* **$$$**

☀ 🏠 **Aylos Bay Lodge** (10 rooms) 📞 03430 20093; m 0243 374443; e infoaylosbay@ gmail.com or info@aylosbayghana.com; www. aylosbaylodge.com. Situated on the Akosombo road a few hundred metres north of Atimpoku, this long-serving family-owned & managed resort has a refreshingly unpretentious feel, a tranquil wooded setting in attractively

unkempt riverfront gardens, & a restaurant offering as good value as anywhere in Ghana. Accommodation is in a row of spacious chalets with kitchenettes & private wooden balconies stilted above the river. Budget travellers can pitch their tents onsite, or take a bed in the comfortable dormitory. Boat trips can be arranged & there are canoes for hire. *US$63/47 B&B self-contained dbl with/without river view; US$13pp dorm bed; US$8pp camping.* **$$$–$**

🏠 **Hotel Rhozo** (9 rooms) m 0244 047671/0208 417000/0546 475408; e rhozo. hospitable@gmail.com. If you're not fussed about staying on the water, this likeable new place is about 900m off the main drag on a clearly signposted side road branching west at the south end of Akwamu. Neatly carved into a small hillside, the terraced grounds are planted with bougainvillea & cacti & the quietude here lends itself to sitting back & soaking up the birdsong. Rooms all come with AC, fridge, bamboo furniture, ceiling fan, TV, & some wax-print décor, while the chalets are higher up on the hillside & come with private balconies. The breezy garden restaurant & bar does a menu of grills, pastas & Ghanaian dishes for US$6–10. *US$40 en-suite dbl; US$65–79 larger chalet.* **$$$**

🏠 **Black Star Lions** (5 rooms) m 0244 817459; e blackstarlions@gmail.com; www. blackstarlions.com. Long the only accommodation on the east bank of the river, set on a tall slope about 2km north of Adome Bridge along the road to Akwamufie, this quirky retreat is owned & managed by a laid-back, arty couple who hail from the US & UK via the Caribbean. Facilities include a recording studio, a good library aimed at local schoolchildren, kung fu & yoga lessons, & a restaurant serving Caribbean-style vegetarian dishes in the US$5–8 range (by advance order only). Accommodation is in cosy clay & thatch dbl or family rooms built in the local atakpame style, & set high on a slope (not suited to the elderly or very unfit) overlooking the river. It was closed for renovation in early 2016 but slated to reopen soon; either way, prospective visitors are asked to call a day or two ahead rather than just pitching up. *US$30 self-contained dbl; US$10pp dorm bed.* **$$–$**

🏠 **Volta Safari Guesthouse** (4 rooms) m 0245 397494/0208 128324; e voltasafari2010@yahoo.com; 📘 fb.me/volta.

safari. The most remote & southerly lodge in the Akosombo area, this quiet lodge is situated in large, green riverside grounds reached along a dirt road some 2km past the Royal Senchi. It has a restaurant & bar overlooking the river, & the smart tiled rooms all come with hot water, satellite TV & AC. *US$28–44 self-contained dbl depending on bed type & size.* **$$$–$$**

Budget

Lakeside Motel (14 rooms) m 0553 572562/0264 491749. Situated 2km south of Atimpoku in New Senchi, this likeably rustic hotel is the pick in this range, set in a rambling old house surrounded by shady, sloping gardens with a very distant view of the Volta River. A variety of meals is available on request & you can eat in the garden. The rooms are pretty good value but vary considerably in quality & price so it's worth checking a few before you settle. *US$10 dbl with fan & shared bath; US$14 self-contained dbl room with fan; US$16/18 dbl/twin with AC.* **$$–$**

Wadiva Waterfront Inn (6 rooms) m 0243 830982. This low-key new place has a unique location about 1km from the bridge on the east side of the river, but seems half-heartedly managed & unfortunately fails to take much advantage of its location. Still, the clean en-suite rooms are decent value if uninspired, set back 100m from the water & furnished with TV & fan. There's a small terrace bar overlooking the river, & meals are available at request. *US$19 dbl with fan.* **$$**

Zito Guest Inn (14 rooms) \03430 20474; m 0243 279520. The only hotel in central Akosombo is clearly signposted about 500m from the trotro station. It has a pleasant small garden & serves meals on request. The large, clean rooms have hot water, queen-sized bed & fan or AC & seem acceptable value for the standard & location. *US$17/25 self-contained dbl with fan/AC.* **$$**

Adomi Hotel (7 rooms) m 0554 035807. Situated on the 1st floor of a building overlooking the main traffic circle in Atimpoku, this just-about-OK hotel has few virtues other than its central location & (in theory – it's 'opening soon') an open-sided restaurant with great views over the bridge & river. *US$11/16 musty self-contained dbl with fan/AC.* **$$–$**

Shoestring

Zito Guest Inn Annex (5 rooms) \03430 21677; m 0251 216771. Situated in Akwamu, a few hundred metres west of the main road from Akosombo to Atimpoku, this newer, more rustic & less expensive cousin of the Zito Guest Inn has spacious & clean rooms with tiled floor & fan. *US$9/11 self-contained sgl/dbl.* **$**

Sound Rest Motel (21 rooms) m 0244 687317. Situated next to the Zito Annex, this long-serving hotel has an attractive setting, a relaxed & friendly atmosphere, & decent bar facilities, though there's no longer a restaurant. The rooms are set around a small shady courtyard & seem like good value. *US$7 sgl with shared bath; US$10/19 self-contained dbl with fan/AC.* **$$–$**

Joetina Hotel (7 rooms) m 0243 552510. This small family-run hotel in Akwamu has decent clean rooms. It sells drinks but no food, but lies close to the lovely Afrikiko Riverfront Resort. *US$9–13 self-contained dbl with fan; US$16 dbl with AC.* **$$–$**

Benkum Motel m 0245 864743. Only 50m from the main station in Atimpoku, this long-serving hotel looks like a dump from the outside, & the smelly rooms don't do much to dispel the notion. There's no restaurant, but plenty of street food around, & the large courtyard bar can be a lively place for a drink, with occasional live traditional music. *US$11/17 self-contained sgl/dbl rooms with fan.* **$$–$**

✗ WHERE TO EAT AND DRINK Map, page 290

In addition to the places listed below, the Volta Hotel, Adi Lake Resort and Afrikiko Riverfront Resort all have more than adequate restaurants and bars, while Black Star Lions serves excellent homemade vegetarian food with a Caribbean twist by advance order only. At the bottom end of the price scale, Atimpoku is a great place for street food: oyster kebabs and packets of smoked shrimp are two of the local specialities, both probably to be approached with some caution, as it takes only one dodgy chunk of shellfish to debilitate you with food poisoning. Several bars are also scattered around Atimpoku.

✕ Aylos Bay Garden Restaurant www.
aylosbaylodge.com; ⏱ 07.30–20.30 daily. This
family-run lodge started life as a restaurant
way back when, and it's still a great place to
eat, indoors, at a shady garden table, or on a
wooden pontoon floating out on the river. The
extensive & largely organic menu offers a good
range of chicken & fish dishes at around US$5–6
a plate, including grilled tilapia farmed on site, &
unbeatable golden fried shrimps direct from the
Volta. **$$**

✕ On The Bridge (Berima Nkwan) m 0245
188305; ⏱ 06.00–22.00 Mon–Sat, noon–22.00
Sun. Hidden down a set of stairs at the base of the
bridge, this unassuming chop bar has seating in a
bountiful & attractively haphazard garden shaded
in bananas & bougainvillea, with pithy slogans
('happy birthday my dear') painted on rocks
throughout. Chicken & sheep nonchalantly peck &
ruminate between the plastic tables, & while the
food runs to the usual Ghanaian favourites of fufu,

banku, rice & a variety of stews for US$2–4, the
setting is superb. **$**

✕ La Plus Restaurant m 0208 136825/0248
752158; e info@sajunabeachclub.com; www.
sajunabeachclub.com; ⏱ 07.00–19.00 daily.
Situated immediately outside the Sajuna
Beach Club (see page 296), but under the same
management, this smart dbl-storey restaurant
(with a 1st-floor gym) specialises in good-value
Ghanaian food, with most mains in the US$2–3
range. **$**

✕ Maritime Club m 0208 110817;
⏱ 07.00–20.00 daily. Operated by the Volta
Transport Authority, this affordable & stylish
lakefront restaurant & bar serves Ghanaian &
continental dishes for US$5–9 in pleasant shady
gardens about 500m from the ferry port. It's a
good place to hang out at any time, & especially
convenient when you are waiting for the ferry.
$$–$

OTHER PRACTICALITIES

Banking and foreign exchange There is a good forex bureau in Atimpoku,
opposite First Bell Spot. It accepts CFAs as well as the usual hard currencies.
The ATM outside the Ghana Commercial Bank in Akosombo township accepts
international Visa and MasterCard cards, as does the EcoBank ATM in the car park
of the Volta Hotel.

Internet The best option is the **Vodafone Internet Café** next to the post office in
Akosombo township. There is also an internet café in the Volta Hotel, and most of
the upmarket hotels offer Wi-Fi to guests.

Shopping The **African Arts and Culture Market** (m *0277 124322*) is a good
craft stall situated alongside the entrance to the Akosombo Continental Hotel.
Particularly for those with vehicles, the Akosombo area is a good base for exploring
the many bead factories and market situated a short distance to the southwest near
Kpong and Somanya (page 302).

Sport and fitness The only gym is upstairs at the La Plus Restaurant, next to
the Sajuna Beach Club. Foreign participants are welcome at the regatta involving
swimming and boat races held at Aylos Bay annually on 1 April to help raise local
awareness of issues relating to water pollution.

Swimming Plenty of people swim in the river, and so far as we can ascertain, it
is probably safe enough to do so from the perspective of dangerous currents and/
or dangerous wildlife in normal conditions. We'd be a lot less confident about
accepting local reassurances that bilharzia poses a minimal risk. So safer probably
to stick to swimming pools, either at the Sajuna Beach Club, or the (more sedate
at weekends) Volta Hotel, Akosombo Continental Hotel or Afrikiko Riverfront
Resort, all of which charge around US$5 for usage of the pool by people staying

13

Now submerged behind the eponymous dam, the imposing gorge known as Akosombo – a corruption of Nkonsonbo ('Chain of Rock') – was reputedly settled by the ancestors of the region's present-day Akwamu inhabitants in the 14th century. Incised through the base of the Akwapim and Togo ranges by the Volta River, the gorge offered a high level of security to the Akwamu, who farmed and fished there relatively undisturbed during a period when the Ghanaian interior was ravaged by the demand of the coastal slave trade. Historically, the most important settlement in the region is Akwamufie (on the little-visited west side of the river, about 6km north of Adome Bridge), which is also the traditional seat of the Akwamuhene, a lineage traced back by oral tradition to the paramount chieftaincy of Otumfuo Agyen Kokobo c1505–20. The 28th Akwamuhene, Nana Kwafo Akoto II died in 1992, instigating a heated and occasionally violent secession dispute resolved only with the enstoolment of Odeneho Nana Kwafo Akoto III in 2012.

The notion of damming the Volta at Akosombo to produce hydro-electricity goes all the way back to a 1915 proposal by the Australian geologist Sir Albert Kitson, but was taken no further until the 1940s, when the colonial administration drew up initial plans for the dam and plant. After independence, the construction of Akosombo Dam became a pet project of President Nkrumah, who formed the Volta River Authority (VRA) to that purpose in 1961, and contracted the work out to the Italian company Impregilo, which had finished work on the Kariba Dam (on the border of what is now Zambia and Zimbabwe) two years earlier. The main purpose of the dam was to create a domestic supply for the electricity required for Ghana's industrial development, in particular the Volta Aluminium Company (VOLCA) based at Tema. The project suffered several setbacks, notably a delay of longer than three months following heavy flooding on the Volta River in 1963, and at least 28 workers died during construction.

elsewhere. If you're feeling posh, non-guests can swim at the Royal Senchi for closer to US$13.

WHAT TO SEE AND DO In addition to the places listed below, almost all the attractions in Manya Krobo, including WAASPS, Krobo Mountain, Cedi's Bead Industry and Agomanya Bead Market, are possible day trips out of the Akosombo area.

Akosombo Dam Tours (03430 20658/20658) Guided tours of the dam wall and hydro-electric plant are arranged through the Tourist Information and Publicity Unit next to the Ghana Commercial Bank in Akosombo township. Tours last approximately 45 minutes, cost US$2.50 per person, and leave every hour on the hour between 09.00 and 15.00. The tours garners rave reviews from those with an interest in engineering. In 2016, we were told you needed your own vehicle to go on the tour (or to cover the 3.5km to the dam, anyway) and they were hiring cars at US$8 round-trip. Avoid public holidays and weekends when it is inundated with school parties.

Sajuna Beach Club (m 0208 136825/0248 752158; e info@sajunabeachclub.com; www.sajunabeachclub.com; ⊕ 09.00–18.00 daily; entrance US$3pp) This riverside complex in New Senchi consists of two swimming pools as well as a pleasant outdoor restaurant and bar serving a small menu of local and continental fare, and volleyball, trampoline and basketball facilities. Boat cruises for up to 4 passengers cost around

When, finally, Nkrumah inaugurated the clay-and-rock Akosombo Dam in 1966, it stood 114m tall, measured 366m across at the base and 660m at the top, and hemmed in what is generally cited to be the world's most expansive manmade reservoir, the 8,500km² Lake Volta, which accounts for 3.6% of Ghana's surface area. However, the social and ecological impact of losing more than 8,000km2 of land to the lake has been enormous. Some 700 subsistence farming and fishing villages, comprising a total of 80,000 people (or 1% of the national population), were relocated to resettlement villages under the direction of the VRA in the mid 1960s. Agricultural productivity in the region has subsequently declined as a result of the fertile seasonal floodplain flanking the Volta now being permanently submerged, forcing farmers to overwork the less adequate soils that lie above the waterline. Parts of the lake also suffer from a phenomenon known as eutrophication, a chemical imbalance, caused by fertiliser and sewage run-off, which encourages the spread of invasive aquatic weeds that provide ideal breeding conditions for malaria-bearing mosquitoes and bilharzia-carrying snails.

When the hydro-electric plant came online in 1966, it had an output of 912MW. Initially, however, some 80% of this output was reserved for VOLCA, while much of the rest was sold to neighbouring countries such as Togo and Benin, leaving a relatively small portion for general domestic usage. This situation has improved somewhat in recent years, due to the declining requirements of VOLCA and the upgrade of the hydro-electric plant in 2006 to produce 1,020MW. Nevertheless, Akosombo still cannot meet Ghana's growing domestic demands, as clearly evidenced by the regular rolling blackouts and power outages that have plagued the country in the past few years, a deficit that was considerably reduced when the 400MW hydro-electric plant at the new Bui Dam came online in 2013, though low water levels at both dams continued to cripple electricity production into 2016.

US$13 per party per hour and US$44 for a boat seating 14. The complex gets very busy over weekends and public holidays but is quite tranquil at other times.

Dodi Princess (03430 20731/46; m 0289 671313; e info@dodiprincess.com; www.voltahotel.net) Gutted by fire in May 2012, but currently being refurbished and likely to take to the water again before the end of 2017, the MV *Dodi Princess* undertakes a joyride from Akosombo to Dodi Island every Saturday, Sunday and public holiday. Prior to being suspended, the trip drew mixed reactions from readers – many complained that it was too touristy, but others reckoned it was tremendous fun, with the deciding factor probably being one's tolerance for the very loud live band. There's also a plunge pool and upper- and lower-deck bars to enhance the hedonistic pleasure inherent in sailing across this vast, hill-ringed lake on a sunny day. Assuming it resumes a similar schedule to its old one, it leaves Akosombo at 10.30 and gets back at around 16.00, mooring at Dodi Island for 45–60 minutes, when you can either splash around on the small beach or allow one of the gang of children who make up the boat's reception party to lead you across the island for a small fee. (There's also purportedly a rather depressing zoo under construction on the island.) Tickets are available from the Volta Hotel or online, and should cost around US$20 per person, inclusive of a good barbecue lunch. The jetty is on the right side of the road to Akosombo Port, about 3km past the Volta Hotel, and a shared taxi heading to 'Marine' can drop you there.

Akwamu Hills Community Forest (m *0244 329659;* e *info@akwamugorge.org;* *www.akwamugorge.org*) This 30km² community reserve was created in 2010 and placed under a 50-year lease to the Akwamu George Conservation Trust (AGCT), a joint project involving the Royal Senchi Resort Hotel and Akwamu Traditional Council. It extends over the steep forested hills that rise to around 400m above the eastern bank of the Volta between Adome Bridge and Akwamufie. Loosely protected by local tradition, it mostly comprises rare dry semi-deciduous forest types characterised by a dense canopy of relatively short trees – and, recently discovered, a critically endangered species of African hardwood, alive, well and thriving at Akwamu. Despite a recent threat of encroachment, it supports a diverse fauna including pied and olive colobus monkey, mona monkey, Maxwell's duiker, bay duiker, royal antelope and African golden cat. It is also a potentially superb birding site, with green and violet turaco, Narina trogon and white-throated greenbul among the 150 confirmed bird species. It also supports the most easterly recorded population of the threatened white-necked picathartes (see box, pages 406–7), an eagerly sought Upper Guinea Forest endemic that also features on the AGCT's logo. Planned tourist facilities include an interpretation centre about the flora, fauna and culture of the gorge, two separate botanical gardens designed in partnership with Kew Royal Botanical Gardens, a mid-range tented safari camp and restaurant supported by produce from local community market gardens, links to the new museum at Akwamufie, and activities such as canopy walkways, forest zip-lines and a self-guided interpretive nature trail through Akwamu Gorge. None of these is in place at the time of writing, but development should begin in earnest sometime in 2016-17, in association with the Royal Senchi Resort Hotel, which is likely to be your best local source of up-to-date information, and news will also (theoretically) be posted on the reserve's website.

Akwamufie Museum of Culture and History (e *info@akwamuman.org; www.akwamuman.org;* f *fb.me/akwamuhene*) Recently inaugurated in the presence of Akwamuhene Odeneho Nana Kwafo Akoto III following his enstoolment in 2012, this new museum is being developed in tandem with Akwamu Hills Community Forest. It lies in Akwamufie, the ancient capital of Akwamu, and is expected to house numerous historical relics, photographs, documents and artefacts reflecting the culture and history of Akwamu over its 500-year existence. These will include artefacts relating to a mutiny, led by Akwamu slaves bidding for their liberty, that caused a Norwegian ship called the *Fredenshborg* to be wrecked offshore of Copenhagen in 1768. The museum is still something of a work in progress, but if you are curious, it is only a few minutes' trotro ride from Atimpoku to Akwamufie.

MANYA KROBO AND YILO KROBO

Running west from the Volta River near Akosombo, the contiguous districts of Yilo Krobo and Manya Krobo (the latter split into its upper and lower components in 2008) are named after their Krobo inhabitants, who are best known today as Ghana's premier traditional bead-makers. Associated with a unique ceremony called Dipo, a (non-mutilatory) rite of passage and cleansing ritual for adolescent women still widely practised in the region today, Krobo beads are traditionally made by hand, and were originally family keepsakes, handed down from one generation to the next as a way of impressing potential suitors. The beads are still made using traditional methods today, but on a much larger scale, and mainly for export, both to other parts of Ghana and to other countries.

The bead-makers of Krobo are the region's main tourist attraction, and it is possible to see them at work at the likes of Cedi's Bead Industry, or to shop for beads at several dedicated shops, as well as at the famous Agomanya Market. Most of these sites are either centred around Kpong, a small port on the Volta River that also forms the main regional route focus and transport hub, or along the 20km road between Kpong and Somanya, which is lined with small towns that merge into each other, including Agomanya and Odumase. Other points of interest include the laudable WAASPS pilot training centre at Kpong, the historic Krobo Mountain overlooking the Accra Road 5km further south, and the port of Akuse, linked by a weekly ferry to Ada Foah. Using public transport, any of these sites makes a realistic goal for a day trip out of Akosombo/Atimpoku, while with a private vehicle, the area could be explored as a day trip out of Accra or Tema.

HISTORY The Krobo are a subgroup of the Dangme, whose origin is the subject of much academic debate. Some sources make the improbable claim that the Krobo share a common ancestry with the Zulu of southern Africa, but it is more likely they migrated to their present homeland from somewhere in present-day Benin or Nigeria. At some point prior to the 16th century, they settled on the flat summit of the isolated Krobo Mountain, which afforded them a high level of natural protection against Ashanti slave raids. Indeed, it was the Krobo defeat of one such attack in 1764 that triggered the forced abdication of Asantehene Nana Kusi Oboadum. The Krobo fared less well against a British punitive expedition that attacked their mountain stronghold in 1892, in retaliation for their refusal to pay poll tax, and forced them to resettle on the slopes below. Following this defeat, Emmanuel Mate Kole was enstooled as the Konor (paramount chief) of Manya Krobo (by this time a distinct political entity from Yilo Krobo to its south), and he relocated its capital to his birthplace Odumase, which had been the site of a Basel Mission since 1857. Today the region is divided between three administrative districts, Upper Manya Krobo, Lower Manya Krobo and Yilo Krobo, whose respective capitals are Asesewa, Odumase and Somanya.

GETTING THERE AND AWAY Good tar roads and regular trotros connect Somanya to Accra, Koforidua and Aburi, and there is also plenty of transport between Accra and Kpong. Once at Kpong or Somanya, it is easy to pick up transport to other towns in the region. In addition, the 20km road between Kpong and Somanya is serviced by a steady stream of trotros that can drop you at Agomanya Market (on the south side of the road 3km from Kpong) or Cedi's Bead Industry (about 1km south of the main road along a turn-off signposted 3km past Agomanya). There is a trotro park right next to Agomanya Market, and another at the junction 500m from Cedi's Bead Industry.

🏠 **WHERE TO STAY AND EAT** *Map, page 270*
Most people explore the region as a day trip out of Akosombo/Atimpoku or Accra. There is also quite a bit of budget accommodation scattered around the area, of which the following places are recommended.

Moderate

🏠 **Starr Villa Hotel** (12 rooms) m 0244 817452; e info@starvillahotel.com; www. starvillahotel.com. Set alongside a filling station next to Dan's Beads & Cedi's Annex on the Accra Rd 3km south of Kpong, this smart hotel incorporates an excellent restaurant & supermarket. The comfortable rooms with tiled floor, fan, hot water, satellite TV & AC are good value, too. *US$18/24/39 self-contained sgl/dbl/suite.* **$$**

For anyone interested in beads, Ghana is a treasure trove, with three interesting categories to be found: old trade beads, contemporary beads made in Ghana, and beads from elsewhere in Africa. The old trade beads, as their name suggests, were used for trading from pre-colonial times. Brought to Africa by mercantile ships from Europe, they were really treasured by the locals, and were accepted in exchange for everything from food and goods to – horror of horrors – slaves. Limited in number, these beads are getting ever harder to find and more expensive.

More modern Ghanaian-made beads include lost-wax brass beads, recycled glass beads and bauxite beads. These beads are still in production so you will find them both old and new. You will also find contemporary beads from Mali, Nigeria, Kenya, Morocco and various other African countries. Some examples that are easy to find in the markets are batik bone beads from Kenya and clay spindle beads from Mali.

All of these beads can be found in various bead markets. The most important is held in Koforidua on Thursday (page 341), where traders come from all over West Africa to set up stalls for the day. I would rank the Odumase/Agomanya bead market, every Wednesday and Saturday, as the second most important in Ghana. Next on our list would be central Accra's Agbogbloshie Market. Finally, bead lovers could also visit Kejetia Market in Kumasi where there are a few interesting stalls.

It is also worth scheduling a visit to see the actual craftsfolk making the beads. Recycled glass beads have experienced a real comeback thanks to Cedi Beads, a visit to which is easily combined with one to Odumase/Agomanya Market for a day's outing out of Accra. Other good glass bead factories in this area where you will be welcomed include TK Beads and Tet Beads. Glass bottles are used to make these gorgeous beads. Very eco-friendly!

Another bead particular to Ghana is the beautiful and incredibly labour-intensive bauxite bead. The main centre of manufacture for this bead is Akyem Abompe (pages 346–7), which used to be the site of an NGO specialised in bead-making and

Budget

🏠 **Kikki's Lodge** (6 rooms) m 0272 292245/0243 805158. Situated along the dirt side road to Cedi's Bead Industry, this clean & modern family-run lodge is both very good value & the most convenient option for serious bead enthusiasts. There's a TV lounge & garden bar in the carefully kept grounds, but no restaurant. *US$9 self-contained dbl with fan; US$13/16 dbl/twin with AC.* **$$–$**

Shoestring

🏠 **Traycourt Hotel Leisure Centre** (21 rooms) m 0244 531042/0243 160891. Diagonally opposite Starr Villa, this lodge is a touch rundown, but the clean rooms are very good value, & an attractive garden restaurant serves decent food & cold beer. *US$9–13 self-contained dbl with fan; US$18–21 dbl with AC.* **$$–$**

WHAT TO SEE AND DO

WAASPS trial flights (m *0285 075254/018028;* e *info@waasps.com; www.waasps. com*) Short for West African Aviation Solutions and Provider of Services, WAASPS is West Africa's premiere light aviation centre, based at Kpong Airfield, about 20km south of Atimpoku off the Accra Road. Run by a British pilot but staffed by local women, it has two main missions, which are teaching (mostly rural) young female Ghanaian females to build and fly light aircraft, and dropping medical supplies into accessible areas in outlying parts of Ghana (for more about the latter, see www. medicineonthemove.org). WAASPS also offers thrilling trial flights to tourists,

distribution. Sadly, it seems that this NGO is no longer functional and there are now only a couple of old people able to show you how the bead is made.

The lost-wax brass bead is another bead for which Ghana is famous. This uses a method similar to the method used to make brass statues, etc. All kinds of metals, from old taps to coins, are recycled to make these beads. Another eco-friendly bead! A good place to see these beads being made is the co-operative at Kofofrom, on the outskirts of Kumasi, close to Four Villages Inn. As with Akyem Abompe, bead-making at Kofofrom appears to be more of a dying craft than something thriving. You have to wonder why the government doesn't protect and encourage this national craft, which is an integral part of Ghana's heritage – and a viable trade to be passed on to the next generation.

If you are not inclined to make your own necklaces but would like to take some home, there are lots of local artisans making jewellery. You will find necklaces in all of the markets but there are also some other places worth mentioning. One fun place to visit and buy jewellery is Lady Volta in Ho (page 311). In Accra, Sun Trade Ltd (page 136) is a lovely store where you can buy beads, and also gorgeous local jewellery made with them.

Some pointers about buying beads. It is all cash, and preferably local currency (most traders will accept US dollars but this tends to create more confusion than anything). Also, the traders are usually ready to negotiate and deal with you. Depending on how green you look, the price could start at more than double what they will settle for, so do some research first. Find out how much the beads are worth before you arrive at the market. Or visit several stalls and find out what each of them is asking for one type of bead to get a feel for the range of prices. And there is a huge price difference between new beads and antique ones: a string of the former might cost as little as US$2, while the latter can fetch upwards of US$200. Finally, don't let the traders intimidate you – many are fun to deal with, but some can be whining bullies ... so stand firm but also remember that the beads are always great and worth every penny!

usually in light aircraft built on site, offering fantastic views over the Volta River between Kpong and Adome. There is plenty of trotro traffic between Atimpoku and Kpong. Standard 18-minute flights over the Volta cost US$175 per person, and run on Saturday or Sunday morning only. Longer flights are possible by arrangement.

Krobo Mountain This craggy 240m-high inselberg, which towers above the eastern side of the Accra–Akosombo road 5km south of Kpong, is the spiritual home of the Krobo people. Its flat top is studded with ruins of old Krobo villages, abandoned in the wake of defeat by the British in 1892, as well as the former chief's palace and the ceremonial 'Dipo Stone', which is still used to enact sacrificial rites. Natural attractions include the rare charcoal tree (*Talbotia genetii*), wild baboons, birds, caves and views across to Lake Volta. Sporadic attempts to develop the mountain as a community ecotourism reserve have never really taken off and the old tourist-related buildings have been derelict and overgrown for several years now. If you want to check it out yourself, follow the Akosombo road from Accra/Tema, past Shai Hills until you see the signposted junction to Krobo to your right (about 2km before Akuse Junction). It's about 10 minutes on foot from here to the disused reception area.

Akuse This small but scenic Ewe stronghold of around 3,000 people lies on the west bank of the Volta River about 10km south of Kpong. It is of interest to travellers primarily as the northern terminus of the inexpensive weekly ferry service that leaves Ada Foah twice a week, every Monday and Friday at 06.30 and arrives here around 10 hours later, starting the return trip at 06.30 on Tuesdays and Saturdays. Akuse is situated only 8km from the Accra–Ho road, and road transport to Kpong (and onwards) ties in with the ferry service. If you want to stay over, however, the unexpectedly smart and affordable Volta River Authority (VRA) Clubhouse (\ 03430 20705) has self-contained singles with AC, fridge and satellite television, set in large, green grounds with an inexpensive restaurant and bar, a swimming pool, and tennis courts.

Agomanya Market Reputedly the most important bead market in Ghana prior to the creation of its less organic but larger rival in Koforidua (page 341), the vast expanse of stalls at Agomanya – selling a huge selection of fabrics, basketwork, pottery, fruits and vegetables, etc – would place it among the country's most exciting markets even without the 50-odd bead sellers that gather there every Wednesday and Saturday (the former usually being the busiest day). To get there, ask any trotro heading between Kpong and Somanya to drop you at Agomanya station, which lies next to a conspicuous Total filling station. From here, it is just 200m downhill (south), through congested streets overflowing with stalls, to the main market.

Cedi's Bead Industry (m *0244 817457;* e *cedibeadindustry@yahoo.com; www. africancrafts.com;* ⊕ *06.00–18.00 daily*) The best place to see traditional bead-makers is Cedi's well-established bead factory, which, despite a rather humble appearance, exports its products as far afield as the USA, Europe, Australia and South Africa. The Nene Nomoda family, who run the factory, claim to have been bead-makers for more than 200 years. Here you can watch the centuries-old process from start to finish: to make new beads, the bead-makers first crush old bottles into small chips, then arrange them in glazed moulds, before placing them in what looks like a fiery pizza oven, made entirely from the mud of termite mounds, for about 45 minutes. They also restore worn beads – some of them many centuries old – by placing them intact in an appropriate mould, then baking them at low heat for about 15 minutes so that they come out shiny as new. Formal demonstrations take around 30 minutes and cost US$2.50 per person. A well-stocked showroom sells all sorts of bead-related products made *in situ*, with bracelets starting at around US$1 and necklaces at US$3. Recent plans for on-site accommodation seem to have been scrapped, but the leafy grounds are quite pleasant nonetheless. The factory lies about 1km along a well-signposted side road some 3km west of Agomanya in the direction of Somanya.

Dan's Beaded Handicraft/Cedi's Annex (m *0208 310640*) Lacking the full-on bustle of Agomanya Market or on-site manufacturing facet that makes Cedi's main outlet so fascinating, this pair of shops is still a great place to buy locally manufactured beads, and very convenient if you are shooting through *en rou*te between Accra and Akosombo or Volta Region. The two shops stand next to each other on the Accra road about 3km south of Kpong, opposite the Traycourt Hotel Leisure Centre and next to Starr Villa Lodge. Both of these places will let you look around with no pressure to buy.

TK Beads (m *0244 727853/862809;* e *tkbeadsgh@gmail.com; http://tkbeads1. weebly.com*) Also on the main road between Kpong and Accra, near the Christian University College, 10 minutes before Adenta Junction coming from the north, TK

Beads is a local set-up run by Florence Asare, reputedly the first woman in Ghana to run her own glass-bead business. Visits are welcomed at no charge, and Mrs Asare is happy to help you string any purchases into a bracelet or necklace.

Awukugua-Akwapim Situated about 10km southwest of Somanya, on the road towards Mamfe, Awukugua-Akwapim (usually just shortened to Awukugua) occupies a special place in Ghanaian legend as the birthplace of Okomfo Anokye, the priest who co-founded the Ashanti Empire together with Nana Osei Tutu, the first Asantehene. According to legend, Anokye was born c1670, with his palms closed tight around a sacred totem that was revealed only when he unclasped them at around two years old. This was taken as a sign that he was destined to be a great spiritual leader, confirmed as an adult when he attained priesthood, was given the title Okomfo, and was summoned to Kumasi to assist Nana Osei Tutu in defeating the Denkyira and establishing a united Ashanti Empire. Relicts of Okomfo Anokye's formative years in Awukugua include the house where he was born, which stands directly opposite the palace of the Awukuguahene (paramount chief), and a shrine comprising a palm tree (which he reputedly climbed on foot wearing his sandals) and a large rock with seven indentations made by his heel to denote the seven tribes that betrayed his gifts to Nana Osei Tutu before he became the king's advisor. Another stone beneath this is reputedly inscribed with his original secret, which was lost to the village forever after he smashed it with the top stone after his betrayal.

13

SEND US YOUR SNAPS!

We'd love to follow your adventures using our *Ghana* guide – why not send us your photos and stories via Twitter (🐦 @BradtGuides) and Instagram (📷 @bradtguides) using the hashtag #ghana. Alternatively, you can upload your photos directly to the gallery on the Ghana destination page via our website (*www.bradtguides.com/ghana*).

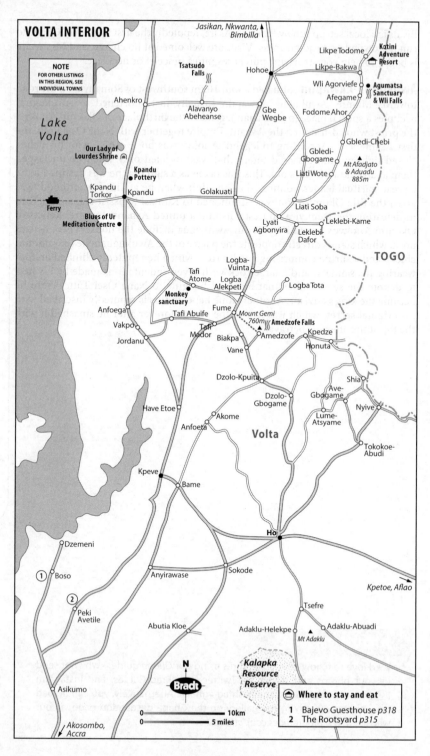

NOTE
FOR OTHER LISTINGS
IN THIS REGION, SEE
INDIVIDUAL TOWNS

Jasikan, Nkwanta,
Bimbilla

Tsatsudo
Falls

Likpe Todome

Katini
Adventure
Resort

Likpe-Bakwa

Hohoe

Wli Agorviefe

Agumatsa
Sanctuary
& Wli Falls

Afegame

Ahenkro

Alavanyo
Abeheanse

Gbe
Wegbe

Fodome Ahor

Lake
Volta

Gbledi-Chebi

Our Lady of
Lourdes Shrine

Gbledi-
Gbogame

Mt Afadjato
& Aduadu
885m

Kpandu
Pottery

Liati Wote

Kpandu
Torkor

Kpandu

Golakuati

Liati Soba

Ferry

Leklebi-Kame

Blues of Ur
Meditation Centre

Lyati
Agbonyira

Leklebi-
Dafor

TOGO

Logba-
Vuinta

Tafi
Atome

Logba
Alekpeti

Logba Tota

Monkey
sanctuary

Fume

Anfoega

Tafi Abuife

Mount Gemi
760m

Amedzofe Falls

Vakpo

Tafi
Mador

Biakpa

Amedzofe

Kpedze

Jordanu

Vane

Honuta

Dzolo-Kpuita

Shia

Have Etoe

Akome

Dzolo-
Gbogame

Ave-
Gbogame

Anfoeta

Volta

Lume-
Atsyame

Nyive

Kpeve

Bame

Tokokoe-
Abudi

Ho

Dzemeni

Kpetoe, Aflao

(1) Boso

Anyirawase

Sokode

(2)

Tsefre

Peki
Avetile

Abutia Kloe

Adaklu-Helekpe

Adaklu-Abuadi

Mt Adaklu

Asikumo

N

Bradt

Kalapka
Resource
Reserve

Akosombo,
Accra

0 ——————— 10km
0 ——————— 5 miles

Where to stay and eat
1 Bajevo Guesthouse *p318*
2 The Rootsyard *p315*

14

Ho and the Volta Interior

This chapter covers the interior of Volta Region, a lushly vegetated and relatively mountainous sliver of land bounded by Lake Volta to the west and Togo to the east. Administered from the regional capital Ho, the Volta interior is largely shunned by the package tourist industry, but it is increasingly popular with active independent travellers, for whom it offers a relatively inexpensive circuit of natural attractions within a compact area. These attractions range from the country's tallest waterfall and highest peak to a clutch of obscure but pedestrian-friendly nature reserves.

A noteworthy feature of tourism in this part of Ghana is the high concentration of well-run, community-based developments. These serve to ensure that virtually all of the revenue raised by tourism is retained locally, to be used for the development of communal resources such as schools and boreholes, while also creating a range of job opportunities at grass-roots level. Many of the community projects succeed in subverting the barriers that conventional tourism tends to create between visitors and local people; for instance, by offering travellers the opportunity to stay with families rather than in hotels or guesthouses. Perhaps related to this, the ceaseless catcalls of 'White man' or '*Obruni*' ('*Yavoo*' in Ewe) that are directed at travellers in areas such as the west coast are notable here by their absence, replaced by altogether more agreeable greetings such as '*Mia woezor*' or 'You're welcome'.

The main towns in this part of Ghana are Ho, Hohoe and Kpandu, all of which are useful travel bases with plenty of facilities for backpackers, but somewhat lacking in inherent interest. It is the area between Ho and Hohoe that provides the most rewarding travel circuit in the region, centred on the scenic hilltop town of Amedzofe,

> **VILLAGE NAMES**   *Gerard van de Garde and Sandra Smeets*
>
> It is worth drawing your readers' attention to the system of naming villages in Volta Region (and certain other parts of Ghana). Most villages have their own local chief and also form part of a cluster governed by a paramount chief, but although there is a main chief, there is not necessarily a main village. In some cases, the history of each village is traced back to separate groups of Ewe settlers, each of which chose its own spot when arriving in this area several centuries ago. Whatever the (pre)history of these clusters, villages of the same cluster now usually have a common first name (for instance Nyagbo, Tafi, Wli (pronounced 'Vlee'), Likpe, Fodome or Liati) and an individual second name. Thus, you get Tafi Atome, Tafi Abuife, etc. But when asking for directions, asking for trotro destinations, etc, people often only refer to the cluster: one asks for the road to Tafi, the trotro to Wli, etc. After we found out about that, we didn't have to remember long, complex Ewe names anymore. We also understood better where exactly we had to get out of the trotro.

a superb monkey-viewing community project at Tafi Atome, and the kente-weaving village of Tafi Abuife. Another very popular destination west of Hohoe is Wli Falls, reputedly the tallest waterfall in West Africa, while worthwhile goals for relatively off-the-beaten-track exploration are Adaklu Mountain, the little-known Kalapka Resource Reserve (see pages 312–14), the kente-weaving village of Kpetoe Agotime, and a half-dozen small waterfalls in the hills to the south of Hohoe.

HO

The former administrative centre of British Togoland and modern capital of Volta Region, Ho is the busiest town in Ghana east of Lake Volta, and the sixth-largest municipal area anywhere in the country, supporting a population of 275,000. It presents something of a mixed bag in tourist terms. A good selection of facilities and rather amiable character make it the obvious entry point to Volta Region for those coming from Accra on public transport. Once there, however, the town itself offers little in the way of compelling attractions, unless you count the Volta Regional Museum near the hospital, a couple of old colonial buildings (notably the old church and school) near the 19th-century Evangelical Presbyterian Mission, or the genuinely bustling market. Still, it remains a pleasant and well-organised place to take a day or two's break between exploring the many beauty spots that lie within a couple of hours' radius by trotro. It is especially worth spending time here over late September and early October, when the annual Asogli Yam Festival takes place, climaxing with a chief's durbar in the first week of October.

HISTORY Ho traditionally forms part of Asogli, which was founded by Ewe-speakers who, controversially, trace their roots back to Ethiopia, but more certainly migrated from Nigeria via Benin to the Togo-Ghana border area in the 12th century. Oral tradition has it that the ancestors of the Asogli settled at Notse, in present-day Togo, where they built a walled city that was taken over by a sadistic and tyrannical king called Agorkorli. Led by Togbe Kakla, the oppressed Asogli liberated themselves by using a sacred dagger called Gligbayi to breach the city walls, then walking backwards through the hole, a tactic that successfully confused King Agorkorli and his solders, who initially assumed the footprints were made not by escapees but by attackers trying to break into the city.

According to oral tradition, Togbe Kakla led his people to present-day Volta Region, settling at an unspecified site called Komedzrale, which proved to have poor soil for cultivation. After Togbe Kakla's death, Komedzrale was abandoned, and its inhabitants dispersed in four bands led by his four children, one of whom, Togbe Asor, settled at Ho after

HO
For listings, see pages 309–11

⊝ **Where to stay**
1	Buela Guesthouse	E1
2	Chances	A4
3	Hotel Stevens	E4
4	Kekeli	G4
5	Lord	G1
6	Malisel	B3
7	Rocklyne	E4
8	SkyPlus	C2
9	Tarso	B2
10	Tayco Lodge	G1
11	Woezor	D3
12	Volta Serene	C2

Off map
	Freedom	F1

✕ **Where to eat and drink**
	Chances	(see 2)
13	Club Fidele	B3
14	Hill View	E1
	Hotel Stevens	(see 3)
15	Mother's Inn	F3
16	Rebazzy Bar	B1
17	Prison Canteen	A2
	SkyPlus	(see 8)
18	White House Bar & Restaurant	B3

Off map
	Freedom	(see Freedom)

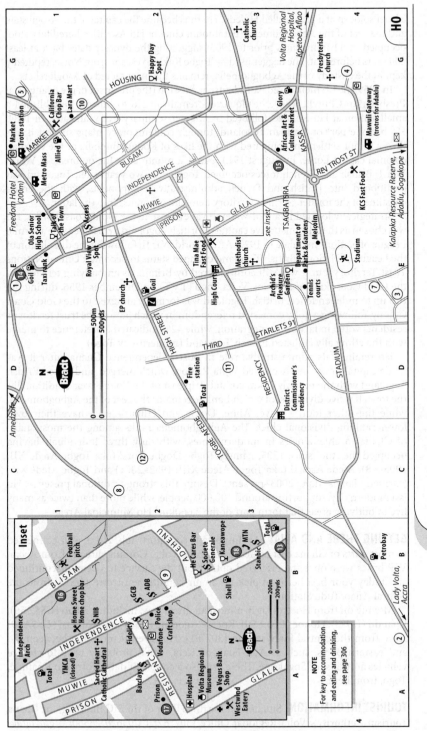

Inset

- Independence Arch
- Total
- YMCA (closed)
- Sacred Heart Catholic Cathedral
- Home Sweet Home chop bar
- NIB
- GCB
- ADB
- Fidelity
- Vodafone
- Police
- Craft shop
- Barclays
- Prison
- Hospital
- Volta Regional Museum
- Vegus Batik Shop
- Westwind Eatery
- He Cares Bar
- Societe Generale
- Kaneawope
- MTN
- Shell
- Stanbic
- Petrobay
- Total

BLISAM
INDEPENDENCE
MUWIE
PRISON
RESIDENCY
GLALA
ADEHENU

N   Bradt

0   200m
0   200yds

NOTE
For key to accommodation and eating and drinking, see page 306.

Lady Volta, Accra

Amedzofe

Freedom Hotel (200m)

- Market
- Trotro station
- California Chop Bar
- Lara Mart
- Allied
- Metro Mass
- Ola Senior High School
- Tail of the Town
- Access
- Taxi rank
- Goil
- Royal View Spot
- EP church
- Goil
- Fire station
- Total
- District Commissioner's residency
- Happy Day Spot
- Glory
- African Art & Culture Market
- Mawuli Gateway (trotros for Adaklu)
- KCS Fast Food
- Tina Mae Fast Food
- High Court
- Methodist church
- Archid's Pleasure Garden
- Department of Parks & Gardens
- Tennis courts
- Melkolm
- Stadium
- Catholic church
- Presbyterian church

HOUSING
MARKET
BLISAM
INDEPENDENCE
MUWIE
GLALA
PRISON
HIGH STREET
STARLETS 91
THIRD
RESIDENCY
TOGBE AFEDE
STADIUM
KASSA
TSAGBATSRA
REV TROST ST

Volta Regional Hospital, Kpetoe, Aflao

Kalapka Resource Reserve, Adaklu, Sogakope

N   Bradt

0   500m
0   500yds

see inset

HO

14

a brief sojourn at a place called Hofedo. Ho thus became the capital of the Asogli state and the seat of the Agbogbomefia (paramount chief of Ho Asogli), a hereditary stool occupied by 11 individuals prior to 1905, suggesting the dynasty dates back at least 200 years before that. The dagger used by Togbe Kakla to escape from Notse, reputedly kept in the custody of the Agbogbomefia, remains the most sacred of Asogli relics.

In 1859, the Bremen-based Norddeutsche Mission (the precursor of the Evangelical Presbyterian Church, whose headquarters remain in Ho to this day) established a small station at Ho-Kpodze, followed by a larger seminary five years later. In 1884, Ho became part of German Togoland, though contemporary maps suggest it was then a minor settlement compared with the likes of Kpong, Bimbilla or the German colonial capital Lomé. In August 1914, barely a month after the outbreak of World War I, British and French forces occupied Togoland. Two years later, Togoland was partitioned into British and French administrative components, with the entire coastline of the former German territory being incorporated into the latter.

Strategically located in a well-watered valley close to the Gold Coast border, Ho was chosen as the administrative capital of British Togoland, which became a formal League of Nations mandate in 1922. After World War II, following the dissolution of the League of Nations, British Togoland changed status to become a United Nations Trust Territory, but it was still administered by Britain, as an outlying territory of the Gold Coast known as Trans-Volta Togo (TVT). In December 1956, during the run up to independence, British Togoland was formally annexed to the Gold Coast Colony, following a hotly contested referendum in which 58% of the trust territory's residents voted in favour of integration, while 42% indicated a preference to merge with the ethnically affiliated French Togoland (modern-day Togo).

Ho retained its administrative role in post-independence Ghana, after it was made capital of the newly created Volta Region, which merged landlocked British Togoland with the roughly 70km coastal strip east of the Volta River. Traditionally, the town has five divisions, of which Bankoe remains the seat of the Agbogbomefia, while the other four – Heve, Ahoe, Dome and Hliha – each have their own lower ranking divisional chief. The Agbogbomefia ranks among the most stable of Ghanaian chieftaincies in modern times, with only three individuals having occupied the stool since 1905, namely Togbe Dogbe Korsi (aka Togbe Afede XII; 1905–48), Afede Asor II (aka Togbe Afede XIII; 1952–2001) and Togbe Afede XIV (formerly James Akpo; 2003–present). Despite this strong traditional presence, Ho is a modern city, supporting around 100,000 people, while more than twice as many live in outlying areas that form part of the 2,660km² Ho Municipal Area.

GETTING THERE AND AWAY An important transport hub, Ho is well connected to most parts of Ghana east of Accra and Lake Volta. Coming directly from Accra, VIP buses were once the preferred option, but the service has been discontinued and today your best bet is to pick up an air-conditioned trotro (US$6) from the central Aflao/Tudu Station.

Moving on from Ho, trotros in almost all directions, including Aflao (US$2.50), Kpandu (US$2), Hohoe (US$2.50), Kpetoe Agotime (US$1) and Kumasi (US$7.50) leave from the central lorry station [307 F1]. However, if travelling between Ho and eastern ports, such as Ada Foah or Keta, you'll probably have to change vehicles at Akatsi or Sogakope. There are also a couple of daily trotros to Kpalimé, Togo, from here.

TOURIST INFORMATION Situated on the third floor of the SIC Building, the **Ghana Tourism Authority's** Volta Regional Office [307 E2] (❩ 03620 26560; e gtavolta@

gmail.com; ⏱ *08.00–12.30 & 13.30–17.00 Mon–Fri*) is perhaps the most enthusiastic in the country, and well worth visiting for the latest information on developing tourist attractions throughout the area.

WHERE TO STAY
Upmarket

Chances Hotel [307 A4] (120 rooms) 03620 28344; m 0202 834444; e info@chanceshotel.com; www.chanceshotel.com. Set in attractive landscaped grounds off the Accra road, 3km west of the town centre, this 2-star hotel has deservedly won several regional & national awards, & has generally maintained high standards ever since the 1st edition of this guidebook was published, though it reputedly operates less well when the hands-on owner-manager isn't around. The smartly furnished self-contained dbl rooms & chalets all have AC, DSTV, Wi-Fi & hot water. Other facilities include a large conference centre, a good restaurant serving international & Ghanaian dishes indoors or in the garden, a children's playground, Wi-Fi & swimming pool (for hotel residents only), while the soundproofed generator & mechanised borehole ensure a 24hr supply of water & electricity. The adjacent Chances Mall was indefinitely closed in 2016. *US$34–53 self-contained dbl with AC; US$65 dbl chalet.* **$$$–$$**

Rocklyne Hotel [307 E4] (6 rooms) 03620 27531; m 0234 148805/31; e rocklynehotel@gmail.com; www.rocklyne.com. The closest thing to a boutique hotel in Ho, this brightly painted new dbl-storey lodge lies in a quiet & rather undeveloped part of suburbia a few hundred metres southwest of the stadium. The neat & well-equipped rooms come with queen-sized bed, fan, AC, Wi-Fi, flatscreen satellite TV, hardwood furniture including a writing desk, minibar & en-suite hot tub/shower. There is also a well-stocked residents' bar, TV lounge, summer house & smart restaurant serving mains in the US$6–10 range. *Good value at US$34/51 std/deluxe dbl; US$80 suite with 2 queen-sized beds & jacuzzi.* **$$$–$$**

Volta Serene Hotel [307 C2] (72 rooms) m 0205 038762/3; e info@voltaserenehotel.com; www.voltaserenehotel.com. Opened at the end of 2015, this new hillside hotel is easily the most luxurious option in town. Set into the same ridge as the SkyPlus & enjoying some of the same magnificent views, the 2 hotels are actually only about 250m apart, but much, much further by road since this is accessed from town, on a surfaced side road branching off of Togbe Afede High St. On first appearances, the mirror-sided main building & red-carpeted corridors feel a bit anachronistic, but the rooms themselves are fully up-to-date, with AC, flatscreen TV, desk, phone, tea/coffee facilities, private terraces, rainfall showers, & modern African décor. The chalets are slightly further up the hill near the brilliantly located swimming pool, & there's a breezy open-sided restaurant & bar atop the main building with views over Ho & mains are from US$8–11. *US$105/150 dbl/twin; US$120/155 dbl/twin with views; US$261 dbl chalet; suites US$355 & up.* **$$$$$–$$$$**

Moderate

✳ **SkyPlus Hotel** [307 C2] (25 rooms) 03620 91474; m 0289 000900/0208 113379; e info@skyplushotel.com; www.skyplushotel.com. Set at an altitude of 330m on a ridge overlooking Ho, this smart & fabulously located new hotel can be reached by following the Amedzofe road out of town for about 1km, then turning left at the signposted fork & following it for another 1km. The swimming pool & restaurant area offers fantastic views over the town centre towards Adaklu Mountain, while the smallish rooms all come with modern décor, fan, AC, Wi-Fi, satellite TV & fridge. *US$34/37 self-contained dbl; US$71 exec chalet.* **$$$–$$**

Hotel Stevens [307 E4] (16 rooms) 03620 27130/1; m 0234 448585. Located in the backroads southeast of Ho Stadium near the Ministry of Health Training Centre, this well-run hotel may not be bristling with character, but it has good facilities & seems well priced. The cosy tiled rooms come complete with queen-size beds, AC, free Wi-Fi, private balcony & hot water. There's also a good restaurant attached serving a varied menu of local & continental dishes (including several vegetarian options) in the US$5–10 range. *US$40/45 B&B self-contained dbl/chalet.* **$$$**

Freedom Hotel [307 F1] (52 rooms) 03620 28151/8; m 0247 766998/0209 792526; e freedomhotelgh@gmail.com; www.freedomhotel.com.gh. Formerly the Bob Coffie

Hotel, this popular, well-established & reasonably priced 2-star establishment has a friendly atmosphere & convenient location about 200m northeast of the main trotro station. The garden, centred on a swimming pool, is a relaxing place for a meal or a drink, though the rather sad caged monkey in the gardens lends a certain irony to the hotel's new name. All rooms have a queen-sized bed & satellite TV. *US$21/26 B&B self-contained dbl with fan/AC; US$45 chalet.* **$$$–$$**

Budget

🛏 **Woezor Hotel** [307 D3] (40 rooms) ✆ 03620 28339; m 0201 073062. Formerly the Government Catering Resthouse, the bright green Woezor Hotel, situated in large overgrown grounds on Third St, about 2km west of the town centre, is acceptably clean & comfortable, though a little frayed at the seams. It offers the option of self-contained dbls in the utilitarian main block, or slightly smarter stone chalets that are claimed to 'fascinate even the best of architects'. A cavernous banquet hall serves adequate Ghanaian & continental fare in the US$5–8 range. *US$22/25 dbl room/chalet with AC.* **$$**

🛏 **Malisel Hotel** [307 B3] (5 rooms) ✆ 03620 26161; m 0208 969622; e maliselhotel@gmail. com. Owned & managed by a well-travelled Ghanaian, this central hotel, set back off the main road, has large & reasonably clean rooms with hot water & satellite TV, & guests are welcome to help themselves from the mango tree outside. No other food is available at the moment (the restaurant was under construction in 2016), but it is so central, this doesn't really matter. *US$ 13/23 self-contained dbl with fan/AC.* **$$–$**

🛏 **Kekeli Hotel** [307 G4] (30 rooms) ✆ 03620 26670/26495; e epkeli@yahoo.com. The former Evangelical Presbyterian Social Centre, privatised in 2002, is situated in the pleasant, leafy grounds of Ho's historic & conveniently central Presbyterian

church, where it is surrounded by some fine examples of German colonial architecture. The clean & spacious rooms all come with AC & TV. *US$12 sgl using shared bath; US$23 twin or dbl with AC & hot water.* **$$–$**

🛏 **Buela Guesthouse** [307 E1] (5 rooms) ✆ 03620 25184; m 0208 919990. Boasting a reasonably central location at the north end of Independence St, this is a reasonably maintained & quiet lodge, marred a little by the tacky furniture, but the dbl rooms are comfortable , if a bit dingy, & all have fan, AC, satellite TV & fridge. *US$19–24 self-contained dbl, depending on bed size.* **$$**

Shoestring

🛏 **Tarso Hotel** [307 B2] (13 rooms) ✆ 03620 26732; m 0500 389045. Established in 1956, the amiable & centrally located Tarso proclaims itself to be the oldest hotel in Ho, & frankly it looks the part, but it still offers good value & the spacious but spartan rooms are often fully booked early in the day. It lies off Independence St but is poorly signposted & the smelly river next door can attract mosquitoes. There's a good chop shop attached serving traditional Ghanaian dishes from US$3 a plate. *US$6/7 sgl/dbl with fan & shared bath; US$9/12 self-contained dbl with fan/AC.* **$**

🛏 **Tayco Lodge** [307 G1] (7 rooms) ✆ 03620 25556/28893. Nothing special, but clean, quiet & conveniently close to the main trotro station, this place has adequate rooms with ceiling fan & satellite TV. *US$12–15 self-contained dbl with fan.* **$**

🛏 **Lord Hotel** [307 G1] (18 rooms) ✆ 03620 25240. This dbl-storey hotel, though a little more rundown than the Tayco, is very cheap & also conveniently close to the trotro station. *US$9–11 self-contained dbl with fan; US$17 larger room with queen-size bed & AC.* **$$–$**

✖ **WHERE TO EAT AND DRINK** For a town of its size, Ho is surprisingly poorly served with stand-alone eateries. The best options are generally the hotels listed in the upmarket and moderate categories above, with Freedom being the pick in terms of centrality and SkyPlus for its spectacular view, but Chances and Stevens hotels also have very good restaurants.

✖ **Freedom Hotel** [307 F1] www. freedomhotel.com.gh; ⏰ 06.30–22.00 daily. The garden of this landmark hotel, with its tempting

swimming pool, is a relaxing place for a meal, with a wide selection of local & international dishes available in the US$5–8 range. The open-walled bar on the upper floor is a good spot to catch the breeze or, when a Ghanaian football match is showing, to squeeze in with 200 roaring Ghanaians & watch it on the large-screen TV. $$–$

� **Hill View** [307 E1] m 0208 244862/149176; ⏰ 08.00–23.00 daily. Probably our favourite local eatery in Ho, this busy bar & restaurant at the north end of the High Street is known for its delicious grilled tilapia & banku, which starts at US$5, but cheaper dishes are available, too. It's especially popular on Sun. $

✕ **Mother's Inn** [307 F3] m 0542 123281; ⏰ 05.00–22.00 daily. A recommended & well-established establishment, where a plate of chicken with chips or fried rice costs around US$2, & you have the option of eating indoors or on the shaded balcony. $

✕ **Prison Canteen** [307 A2] ⏰ 08.00–20.00 daily. Right next to the central prison, this surprisingly welcoming spot is a good bet for lunch during the week or chilled drinks any other time. $

✕ **SkyPlus Hotel** [307 C2] www.skyplushotel. com. The restaurant at this out-of-town hotel serves a varied selection of salad, meat dishes, seafood & pizzas from US$5 to US$12, but its best feature is the swimming pool & indoor seating offering great views over the town centre & Adaklu Mountain. $$$–$

🍷**White House Bar & Restaurant** [307 B3] m 0202 701638/0208 233134; ⏰ 10.30–midnight daily. Once the most popular place to eat in the town centre, the White House now functions almost exclusively as a bar, serving a good selection of chilled drinks and draught beer. There is, theoretically, paid Wi-Fi.

☆ **Club Fidele** [307 B3] ⏰ 21.00–late Fri, Sat & (sometimes) Sun. The only nightclub in central Ho is situated on the top floor of KK House at the junction of Ahoe & High streets.

🍷**Rebazzy Bar** [307 B1] m 0244 409307/0208 400177; ⏰ 09.00–midnight daily. Spanning both sides of Blisam Rd, this likeable & popular local bar also does a good line in grilled sausages, kebabs & chicken, & it was officially recognised as Ghana's 'Drinking Bar of the Year' in 2014.

SHOPPING Ho has a busy market and many small supermarkets, including Lara Mart [307 F1]. The Chances Mall, next to the Chances Hotel, was previously the top shopping destination in town, but it was closed in 2016 and there's no indication of when it might reopen.

African Art & Culture Market Shop [307 F3] m 0277 124322/0202 094502. The Ewe, like the Ashanti, are skilled kente weavers, & good-quality work can be bought at this small shop opposite Mother's Inn Restaurant.

Lady Volta [307 B4] m 0208 187367; www. villageexchangeinternational.org; ⏰ 09.00–17.00 Mon–Fri. At a new site on the Accra road, 2km past Chances Hotel, this is a small but vibrant NGO where a group of women create & make their own batik fabric, then sew it into bags, aprons & all kinds of products. They also design & create necklaces, bracelets & earrings using local beads. Beading & batik-printing workshops are also offered.

Vegus Batik Shop [307 A3] ☎ 03620 25212; m 0208 171303; ⏰ 08.00–17.00 Mon–Sat. This good batik shop is on Glala Rd, right next to the museum.

OTHER PRACTICALITIES
Banking and foreign exchange The only bank offering a forex service to non-customers is Stanbic [307 B3], opposite the Total garage at the south end of the High Street. Barclays, Ghana Commercial and several other banks are also represented on Independence Street. Most of them have ATMs where you can draw cash against a Visa card, while GCB should accept MasterCard.

Internet There are a number of internet cafés around town, with the pick being **Vodafone Internet** [307 A2], behind the main post office. Other options include **Classic Internet Café** [307 F1], next to the trotro station, and the **Golden Gate Internet Café** [307 G4], near the Kekeli Hotel.

Swimming pool The swimming pool at the **Freedom Hotel** [307 F1] charges US$5 to non-residents and has a good poolside bar. You can also use the pools at the out-of-town **SkyPlus Hotel** [307 C2] for US$4 or the new **Volta Serene Hotel** [307 C2] for US$6, both of which offer stellar views over town.

WHAT TO SEE AND DO
Volta Regional Museum [307 A2] (\ *03620 26403;* ⊕ *08.00–17.00 daily; entrance US$2.50, US$1 camera fee*) Established in 1973 and situated in the former office of the Regional House of Chiefs, this odd little museum, though less-than-essential sightseeing, includes some interesting drums and other ethnographic artefacts, though sadly the display on the mud-and-stick mosques of the northwest has been removed, clearly not for lack of space. There is a contemporary art gallery at the back.

Kalapka Resource Reserve Situated no more than 10km south of Ho as the crow flies, this 325km² reserve, gazetted in 1975, has yet to see much in the way of tourist development. It protects an area of gently sloping land, dominated by dry savannah, but with a few patches of forest where illegal logging is unfortunately an ongoing problem. Large mammal populations are rather low, though kob antelope, baboon and green monkey are quite common and likely to be seen by most visitors, at least during the dry season when game concentrates around the palm-fringed Kalapka River, close to the park headquarters. Less conspicuous species include buffalo, bushbuck, waterbuck, Maxwell's duiker, patas monkey and a variety of nocturnal creatures such as bushpig and genet, along with one utterly unexpected lion sighting in February 2009 that's not likely to be repeated any time soon. The area has a reputation for good birding. Although few tourists visit Kalapka at present, and no roads run through the reserve, it is perfectly accessible and day walks can be arranged with the rangers – indeed, the small western sector open to tourists has several easy footpaths, wonderful views and much wildlife.

The only point of entry is through the village of Abutia Kloe, 18km from Ho by road, and connected to it by regular trotros, which take about 30 minutes. If you are driving from Ho, head out along the Accra road for 9km to Sokode Junction, where a left turn will bring you to Abutia Kloe after another 9km. The road to Abutia Kloe passes through some lush semi-forested scenery teeming with birds. On the way, it may be worth asking about the traditionally constructed former German governor's residence that lies on a mango tree-covered hillside near the village of Abutia Agove, also the site of a famous spring that used to draw people from far and wide during periods of drought. Look out, too, for the kente weavers who work in some of the villages around Abutia.

However you get to Abutia Kloe, you must first visit the Department of Wildlife office to pay the nominal entrance fee. A 2.5km side road branching left from here leads to the reserve boundary and a rangers' camp where you can arrange game walks. There is no formal accommodation, but it is possible to visit Kalapka as a day trip from Ho by trotro. In order to get an early start (game being most active in the early morning), it would be preferable for those using public transport to spend the night. Normally you can pitch your own tent, but long-standing talk of building formal tourist accommodation has yet to amount to more than verbiage.

Adaklu Mountain The dramatic inselberg that dominates Ho's southern skyline, Adaklu is one of the tallest free-standing mountains in Ghana, rising to an altitude of above 500m from a base below 100m. It is also a collective name for the 40-

odd settlements that lie around the mountain's base, including Adaklu Waya, the traditional stool of the Fiaga (paramount chief) of Adaklu and modern capital of Adaklu District (created by the split of the former Adaklu-Anyigbe District in 2012). Like their Asogli neighbours, the Adaklu are Ewe-speakers whose ancestors migrated to the area to escape the oppressive rule of King Agorkorli in present-day Togo. When the first refugees settled at the base of the mountain, they slaughtered a cow, roasted the meat and divided it out – an act of sharing to which the word Adaklu refers.

Adaklu Mountain is the focal point of a community ecotourist project based at the village of Adaklu-Helekpe, which lies at the western base about 12km south of Ho. Here, the Helekpe Visitor Centre (m 0249 737383) offers guided hikes to the mountain summit, a reasonably demanding walk that involves a steep 60–80-minute hike to the clifftop summit, passing through the quaint village of Adaklu Kodiaber *en route*, and a 30–40 minute descent, parts of which are sufficiently loose underfoot to justify taking a bamboo pole or similar as a walking stick. Although the mountain looks imposingly bare from the base, the plateau supports an extensive patch of forest where you are likely to see a variety of butterflies and birds, as well as giant snails (which are held sacred locally and may not be touched). Monkeys might also be present, but chimpanzees and buffalo, as suggested by our guide, seem rather unlikely. Either way, the views from the top are tremendous, stretching as far as Lake Volta on a clear day. The hike costs US$2.50 per person, and other similarly priced activities include drumming and dancing performances, a visit to the sacred bats of Avanyaviwofe, and bicycle tours.

Getting there and away Both Adaklu-Helekpe and Adaklu-Abuadi are connected to Ho by regular shared taxis (*US$1*) that leave from a station called Mawuli Gateway [307 F4] (just past KCS Fast Food on the Adaklu Road), except on market days (every five days) when they leave from the main trotro station. A charter taxi to either village should be around US$4.

Where to stay and eat The mountain is easy enough to visit as a day trip from Ho, but basic and inexpensive accommodation is available at both the **Helekpe Visitor Centre** for US$4 per person, and at a small **resthouse** (*US$8pp dorm, US$15 dbl*) at Adaklu Abuadi, on the eastern base of the mountain about 5km from Helekpe. This is run by the Help Our Village Foundation (m 0241 798791/0240 977503; f fb.me/ HelpOurVillageFoundation) a volunteer programme founded by the Queen Mother of Adaklu, Mamaga Afedima II, who passed away in 2016, and now carried on by her daughter. It's strongly affiliated to the ecotourist project at Helekpe. The foundation also oversees a co-operative of hand-weavers who make an off-white cloth using a naturally occurring local plant similar to cotton, and it also runs the Mount Temple Library and crèche in Abuadi, which is regularly seeking volunteers. In addition, the same family runs the Help Our Village B&B in Kumasi (page 367).

Kpetoe Agotime District capital of Agotime Ziope, the small town of Kpetoe, nestled close to the Togolese border about 30km east of Ho, is renowned throughout Ghana for the quality of its kente weavers, Indeed, while this craft industry is now largely associated with Ashanti, the weavers of Kpetoe claim that the style originated with them and was later adopted further afield after their best practitioners were captured during the Ashanti wars. Two types of cloth are made in Kpetoe: the light and popular Ashanti kente and the more durable Ewe *agbamevor* (for more details, see box, pages 382–3).

The focal point of kente weaving here is the **Agotime Ecotourism Centre** (m *0204 746580/0242 862119*; ☉ *06.00–17.00 Mon–Sat*), where a couple of dozen weavers work in a semi-open concrete construction on the left side of the main road coming from Ho, just behind the fire brigades. It's less than US$1 to enter, US$1 for a short weaving lesson, and some good-quality cloth is on sale. About 1km further down the road and also on the left (opposite CEPS Academy) is the newer **Dogbeda 'Vɔmawu' Kete Vocational Training Centre** (m *0242 965660/0245 125216*; e *pxkott@gmail.com*; ☉ *07.00–17.00 Mon–Sat*;), which offers weaving instruction to orphans and other vulnerable community members. It's free to look around and you can set up some informal kente lessons for yourself here should you be interested in learning the craft.

There are also plenty of places where individual weavers work out in the open, and tourists are still so infrequent that nobody is likely to object to you wandering around and taking it all in. If you are thinking of buying, prices are far lower than in Ashanti, and the atmosphere is more laid-back. **Desiadenyo Store** (✆ *03620 26878*) and **Israel Trading** (m *0244 562355*) have both been recommended. A great time to visit Kpetoe is over the last week in August, which is usually when the annual week-long Agbamevoza (Kente Festival) (*www.ewekente.com*) takes place, a lively event that incorporates a kente-weaving competition and the popular Miss Agbamevor (Kente) competition.

Kpetoe lies along the tarred road between Ho and Aflao, and there is plenty of transport in both directions. If you prefer to spend the night, decent rooms are available at the **Buggie Hotel** (*9 rooms;* m *0507 278721; US$8 dbl with shared bath, US$13/20 self-contained with fan/AC*), located behind a petrol station about 1km from town towards Ho, and at the more central **Pleasant Dreams Guesthouse** (*9 rooms;* m *0244 591791/0246 170085; US$8/13 old/new self-contained dbl with fan*) on a side road opposite the prominent CEPS Academy.

AMEDZOFE AND THE AVATIME HILLS

Spanning altitudes of 700–740m, roughly halfway between Ho and Hohoe, Amedzofe is the highest town in Ghana, perched below Mount Gemi in the beautiful and lushly vegetated Avatime Hills, which rise east from the Lake Volta hinterland towards the Togolese border. Though it supports a permanent population of fewer than 5,000, it is the largest town in Avatime, and a popular destination for enthusiastic hikers and other budget-conscious travellers, thanks to its relatively temperate climate, substantial stands of montane forest alive with birds and butterflies, inexpensive resthouses, and excellent opportunities for hiking and rambling to nearby beauty spots such as the Amedzofe Falls and the rounded peak of Mount Gemi. Further afield, other sites of interest in the hills include Biakpa, site of the wonderfully located Mountain Paradise Lodge at the base of the escarpment, and Logba Tota, closer to the Togo border.

HISTORY The Ewe of Amedzofe, like their counterparts at Ho, arrived in present-day Ghana from Togo, having fled the rule of the legendarily nasty King Agorkorli. Oral tradition suggests that they first diverted to Ketu in present-day Benin, then migrated to the Ahanta region of western Ghana, where they lived for the best part of a century before eventually being evicted for their warlike behaviour. They then headed eastwards in the direction of their homeland, but were waylaid in the cool, fertile and well-protected Avatime Hills, where they defeated a resident race of giants before settling down in the vicinity of present-day Amedzofe. This was probably in the late 17th century.

One of the nicest places to stay anywhere in Volta Region, the Rootsyard (see map, page 304) lies in a large semi-rural plot bordering Peki-Avetile on the main road between Accra/Akosombo and Hohoe. The lodge is owned and managed by a laid-back British-Ghanaian couple with a shining commitment to fair trade and the sourcing of local produce, and it will be particularly attractive to vegans for its imaginative, reasonably priced and totally vegan menu. For accommodation, there's a choice of two stylish self-contained mini-suites with screened windows and showers (*US$23 dbl*), more basic self-contained wooden family bungalows sleeping four (*US$37 per unit*), and a new dormitory (US$8 per bed with net). Camping costs US$7 per person in your own tent. Other facilities include a sociable bar, an open-air cinema, occasional live music, a well-stocked book swap and a stash of board games.

Peki-Avetile, though not close to any established tourist attractions, is an interesting and unaffected old town, best known as the birthplace and former home of the musicologist and composer Dr Ephraim Amu (1899–1995), whose image appeared on the old GHC20,000 notes and whose house still stands in the town centre. Guided tours of the old town are offered, or you can explore it yourself using a detailed map showing its best bars, eateries and other sites of interest. A 'Craft Village Complex' has been mooted in town, but progress seems to have frozen on this front. More cheeringly, the Rootsyard itself is behind an active reforestation project in need of hardy volunteers, and has brought skateboarding and a new skate park to the village school. With its roadside location *en route* to Hohoe, the Rootsyard makes for a great stopover between Accra and points further northeast, and it is also a useful base for exploring popular sites such as Tafi Atome (50km to the northeast) and Wli Falls (about 100km northeast), particularly for those with their own vehicle.

For further details, contact m *0549 747047 or* e *rootsyard@ymail.com, or browse their very detailed website: www.rootsyard.org.*

The main challenge to Ewe domination of the area came c1871 in the form of an assault by the expansionist Ashanti. That they were able to repel the better-armed and more militant Ashanti was partly because of their superior knowledge of caves and other hiding places in the mountains, and partly through the innovative tactic of rolling boulders down the steep approaches to Amedzofe to check the invaders' progress. It is said that the town was named Amedzofe – which roughly translates from Ewe as 'home of our soul' (and is also their name for Ketu) – in the wake of this historic victory over the Ashanti.

In 1889, Amedzofe was chosen as the site of a Bremen mission, which soon expanded to become one of the most important schools and hospitals in German Togoland. In 1939, a 4m-tall cross was erected on the grassy peak of Mount Gemi to mark the mission's 50th anniversary (a bizarre local legend says that the cross doubled as a communication device in World War II). The historic mission has since evolved to become the highly regarded Amedzofe Evangelical Presbyterian College of Education, which houses around 500 trainee teachers at any given time. The 19th-century church built by the missionaries, reached via a steep flight of stairs before the college gates, remains a prominent landmark, while the nearby Bremen Mission Cemetery was set aside in 1964 to mark its 75th anniversary.

GETTING THERE AND AWAY Amedzofe lies about 35km north of Ho by road. The most normal and direct route is the road that runs from Ho, through Akome, Vane and Biakpa, to the junction town of Fume on the main Akosombo–Hohoe road. This used to be quite a rough road, especially after rain, but it's recently been surfaced all the way through and is now the primary route for trotros between Ho and Hohoe. In a private vehicle, the smooth drive from Ho to Vane (the junction for the final ascent to Amedzofe) shouldn't take much more than 30 minutes. Allow another ten minutes for the final steep 3km ascent to Amedzofe, and be alert to daft drivers coming in the opposite direction (best to honk on your horn before taking any sharp corners).

Using public transport, there are a few vehicles that plod back and forth between Ho and Amedzofe daily, but any vehicle running between Ho and Hohoe can drop you off at Vane, from where you can get a shared taxi to Amedzofe for less than US$1. Coming from the north, if you end up on an Akosombo-bound vehicle you'll have to drop at the junction in Fume, which is only about 2km from Amedzofe as the crow flies, but more like 10km by road,

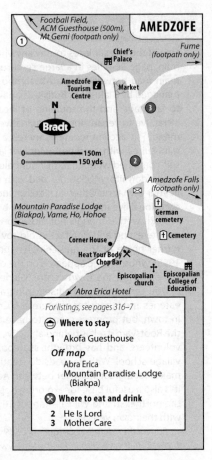

AMEDZOFE

For listings, see pages 316–7

🛏 **Where to stay**
1 Akofa Guesthouse
Off map
Abra Erica
Mountain Paradise Lodge (Biakpa)

❌ **Where to eat and drink**
2 He Is Lord
3 Mother Care

passing through Biakpa and Vane *en route*. Both Vane and Mountain Paradise Lodge in Biakpa are on the main road south to Ho, and it's simple enough to catch a passing lift to either one from here. For hikers, there is also a much shorter (about 3.5km) footpath between Fume and Amedzofe, but this is steep and slippery in parts, especially after rain, and may be tough going with a heavy backpack on.

TOURIST INFORMATION The helpful and well-organised **Amedzofe Tourism Centre** (m *0541 008334/0547 297493; www.amedzofe.com;* ⊕ *07.00–17.30 daily*) can be found in the central market square.

🏠 **WHERE TO STAY** *Map, above*
Moderate

🏠 **Abra Erica Hotel** (25 rooms) m 0547 752361/0208 132484; e abraericahospitalities@ yahoo.com; www.abraerica.com. This smart & scenically located new hotel, probably the country's highest at around 780m, is situated 500m south of the town centre, & reached by turning right (uphill) when you reach the main

junction at the top of the escarpment coming from Vane. Though slightly lacking in character, it offers wonderful views to Mount Gemi, as well as over the plains below, stretching to Lake Volta on a clear day, & it has a well-appointed restaurant/ bar serving Western fare in the US$5–8 range. The rooms, set in a large monolithic block below the restaurant, are comfortable enough, & come with hot water & TV. *US$16/18 self-contained sgl/ dbl with fan; US$23/27/80 dbl/twin/suite with AC.* **$$$–$$**

Budget

❋ ⌂ **Mountain Paradise Lodge** (8 rooms & 20-bed dorm) **m** 0208 137086/0244 166226; **e** fiakpui@yahoo.com; www.mountainparadise-biakpa.com. Located not in Amedzofe but at Biakpa, which lies at the base of the escarpment between Vane & Fume. This former government resthouse, run by an enthusiastic hands-on owner-manager, has a blissfully isolated & scenic location on a grassy knoll overlooking the Kulugu River, facing Mount Gemi, & encircled by lush tropical forest that still harbours small numbers of mona monkey & Maxwell's duiker, as well as a wide range of forest birds. In addition to several hikes, activities include volleyball & table tennis, & mountain-bike hire for US$1.50 per hour or

US$10 per day. A cosy patio restaurant serves fresh fruit juice, locally grown organic coffee, & a varied selection of mains (including vegetarian options by request) in the US$5–9 range. *US$11/13 dbl with fan & shared bath; US$15 self-contained dbl with fan; US$40 self-contained family room sleeping 4; $5.50pp camping.* **$$–$**

⌂ **Akofa Guesthouse** (4 rooms) **m** 0541 008334/0547 297493; www.amedzofe.com/ akofa-guest-house. Operated by the Amedzofe Tourism Centre, this attractive guesthouse has the feel of a family house & also offers stunning views across the valley, & down to the village of Biakpa. The rooms are large but cosy, & guests can use the self-catering kitchen & eat at the shared dining table. If it's full, don't fret: the tourist office can also arrange accommodation at a slightly inferior but identically priced mission guesthouse, or in a private home. *US$11 self-contained dbl with fan & TV; US$13 family room sleeping 4.* **$**

✕ **WHERE TO EAT AND DRINK** *Map, opposite*
The best place to eat in Amedzofe itself is **Abra Erica Hotel**, and good food is also available at **Mountain Paradise Lodge** in Biakpa, though in both cases you need to allow time for food to be prepared from scratch. Otherwise, a few chop stalls like **Mother Care** and **He Is Lord** are dotted around the town centre, but they tend to close in the late afternoon, or you can arrange simple meals cooked by local women a few hours in advance through the tourist office. There are a couple of bars next to the market; if you're luckier than us, then the one with the fridge and the one with the beer will be one and the same when you visit.

WHAT TO SEE AND DO In addition to the hikes described below, the monkey sanctuary at Tafi Atome and weaving co-operative at Tafi Abuife are both feasible targets for a day trip out of Amedzofe or Biakpa.

Hikes out of Amedzofe All hikes must be arranged through the **Amedzofe Tourism Centre** (page 316). Foreigners are charged US$2.50/1.50 for hikes to Mt Gemi/Ote Falls (discounts are available to students and volunteers, while an additional charge is made for a still or video camera), inclusive of a mandatory guide, who will most likely expect a tip. The most popular target for a short walk is Ote Falls (also known as Amedzofe Falls), which lies about 45 minutes from town following a dirt road and then a steep, muddy and slippery footpath, using ropes in parts, through lush forest to come out at the three knee-deep pools separating the upper and lower falls. More ambitiously, ask about visiting the valley at the base of the lower fall, said to harbour a population of black-and-white colobus monkeys. Another worthwhile local goal, offering tremendous views as far as Lake Volta, is the grassy peak of Mount Gemi, which lies about 30 minutes' walk from town, and is visible for miles around thanks to the cross erected there by the Bremen Mission in 1939. The tourist office also arranges guided walks further afield; for instance to Biakpa, Fume (on the main Ho–Hohoe road) and Tafi Atome.

Founded in the 18th century by Guan migrants fleeing human sacrifice and ill-treatment from other ethnic groups in the region, the small town of Boso's origin story leads back to the Mali Empire and Timbuktu, by way of a few stops over the centuries in what are now the Brong-Ahafo and Central regions of Ghana. Boso (marked on some maps as Dodi) sees few tourists, and while there are not exactly any prescribed attractions in the area, there's plenty to check out in the spirit of unstructured exploration.

To start with, the town itself sits on an escarpment above Lake Volta and is attractively ringed by a set of hills well suited for rambling. Heading towards the lakeshore, a rough road leads 4km downhill to the fishing village of Dodi Asantekrom, from where you can hire a boat (US$13) to nearby Dodi Island, where pleasure cruises from Akosombo on the *Dodi Princess II* are soon set to dock again (page 297). There's a tiny village on the island (do introduce yourself) and a couple of rocky beaches good for swimming, and what's reported to be a quite depressing zoo being built in connection with the *Dodi Princess*. Back on the mainland and about 10km north of Boso is the town of Dzemeni, whose Thursday market is packed with produce hauled over in canoes from all corners of Lake Volta.

The best place to base yourself to explore this tourist-free district is the **Bajevo Guesthouse** (*10 rooms;* ✆ *6.54158, 0.17608;* m *0554 036008/0541 040742;* e *info@bajevoguesthouseghana.com; www.bajevoguesthouseghana. com; US$11/13 dbl with/without TV; see map, page 304*) at the south end of Boso, which is run by an amiable British-Ghanaian-Latvian couple (who can take you to all the above-mentioned places) and has simple but spotless rooms set behind the reggae-fuelled terrace restaurant and bar, where excellent Ghanaian staples are served for US$2–5. To get here, head north for 1.5km from Asikumo Junction and make a left turn, continuing on the surfaced road for 14.5km, passing through Anum, hometown of the Ghanaian flag's designer, Theodosia Okoh (where she is honoured with a bust), and eventually arriving at Bajevo Guesthouse on your left. Trotros to Boso are easily found at Asikumo junction and can drop you right in front of the guesthouse.

Hikes out of Biakpa

Mountain Paradise Lodge in Biakpa is an excellent base for exploring the Avatime foothills, along a network of customised self-guided or guided walks. The most popular of these, charged at US$2.50 per person, is a 3-hour nature trail that follows the Kulugu River through riparian woodland teeming with birds (and possibly monkeys and duikers) and past five small waterfalls. More challenging is the steep but scenic 3-hour round hike to the peak of Mount Gemi, which also gives you the option of continuing for 30 minutes on foot to Amedzofe, where you can arrange a guided walk to Ote Falls. Another challenging option is a 6-hour round hike to Logba Tota. Biakpa is also a useful base for mountain biking, as these can be hired through the lodge.

Logba Tota

Set on a steep forested slope facing Mount Gemi, this attractive small town is the site of a community project offering guided walks to Apkonu Waterfall, which plunges into a pool where you can swim safely about 2km out of town. The cliff above the waterfall is riddled with small caves that house an impressive bat colony and one solitary stalagmite. Walks must be arranged, and a fee of US$2.50

per person paid, at the information office located on a small central square at the top end of the main road. You can hike to Logba Tota from Biakpa (a 6-hour round trip) but it is also easily reached along a signposted 7km turn-off running east from the main Hohoe road at Logba Alekpeti, about 3km north of Fume. This dirt road is initially quite flat, but after about 3km, where you must turn right, it becomes very steep and winding. Occasional shared taxis run between Logba Alekpeti and Logba Tota, but you could be in for a long wait – in which case it might be worth paying for the extra seats effectively to charter the vehicle.

TAFI ATOME MONKEY SANCTUARY

The small village of Tafi Atome, situated 5km west of the main Hohoe road, is the site of a thoroughly enjoyable community-based sanctuary inhabited by one of the most habituated monkey communities in Ghana. The sanctuary was created in 1993 to protect the mona monkeys that live in a small patch of forest adjacent to the village, and are traditionally sacred to its inhabitants, who reputedly migrated here from Brong Ahafo 200 years ago, carrying monkey and tortoise fetishes in a large pot that still exists today. For many years, this taboo protected the monkeys, who were believed to act as spokesmen for the slower tortoises, but numbers had dwindled badly by the late 1980s, largely as a result of the erosion of traditional beliefs by Christianity. Since the creation of the sanctuary, however, the monkey population has increased to about 350 individuals split across four troops.

Visiting the habituated monkeys is a highlight of any visit to Tafi Atome, but several other cultural activities are offered, and it is also a good base for visits to the kente-weaving village of Tafi Abuife. All activities must be arranged through the well-organised visitor centre, which is prominently signposted to the left as you enter the village coming from the main Hohoe road. It also has a minibus and driver for hire that you could use for exploring further afield. Funds raised from tourism go towards maintaining the monkey sanctuary or the development of the community. If you are in Ghana at the right time, it's worth knowing that Tafi Atome holds a fetish festival for the monkeys over the first or second week of February.

GETTING THERE AND AWAY Tafi Atome lies 5km along a newly surfaced road that leaves the main Hohoe road at Logba Alekpeti, about 3km north of Fume. There is plenty of transport to the village on Logba Alekpeti's market day, which is on a five-day cycle. On other days, there is the occasional shared taxi, and the fare is so low you might consider chartering the whole vehicle. Alternatively, you can charter a motorbike, or walk out from Logba Alekpeti (an easy hour's trip along a flat road through lush scenery).

WHERE TO STAY AND EAT

Tafi Atome Guesthouse (5 rooms) m 0245 458170/0245 457979/0571870004; e tamonkeysanctuary@gmail.com; f fb.me/ tafiatomemonkeysanctuary. This basic but serviceable community-run guesthouse is set in a forest clearing on the edge of the village behind the visitor centre (through which bookings must be directed). The thatch- or zinc-roofed rooms are clean but sparse – furnished with just beds, nets & a fan – & share a clean communal ablution block with sit-down toilets & cold showers. Meals can be arranged for around US$4–5 per plate, & a couple of shops in the village sell warm minerals, beers & pure water. Best to call in advance, as they had a hard time locating the man with the key when we last visited in 2016. *US$12pp, US$22pp package deal inc accommodation, food & sanctuary entrance; US$3pp to camp.* **$**

WHAT TO SEE AND DO

Monkey Sanctuary Tours Arranged through the visitor centre (m *0245 458170/0245 457979/0571870004*; e *tamonkeysanctuary@gmail.com;* ⓕ *fb.me/ tafiatomemonkeysanctuary.;* ⏲ *07.00–18.00 daily*), tours of the monkey sanctuary cost US$5.50 per person for foreigners (US$4 for volunteers and students), including the mandatory guide who will expect a small tip. The monkeys here are now almost as well habituated as their counterparts at Boabeng-Fiema, and generally most active before 08.00 and after 16.00, when they often descend to the ground and can be approached very closely, though they are usually also quite easy to locate at other times of day. As with Boabeng-Fiema, they are usually classified as mona monkeys, but they are more significant in conservation terms as they represent Ghana's only habituated population of the nominate race *Cercopithecus mona mona*, which is distinguished from the more widespread Lowe's mona (*C. m. lowei*) by its two white hip discs, and some authorities maintain should be treated as a discrete species.

Other activities Several other activities are available to visitors spending a night or two at Tafi Atome. These include a guided walk through the village, drumming lessons, forest walks, an evening session of storytelling around the bonfire, and drumming and dancing performances – the last particularly enjoyable judging by the visitors' book. For groups staying overnight, it is worth knowing that the sanctuary offers package deals inclusive of accommodation, food, monkey visits, drumming and dance performances, and bonfire storytelling. These range in price from US$70 per person for one to US$32 per person for groups of six or more. Another worthwhile project is to plant a tree in return for a donation that will be directed towards the building of a clinic. The idea is that after the facility is built, the trees will eventually mature and bring in revenue a second time round to help sustain the project. The guides can also organise inexpensive bicycle hire to explore further afield.

Tafi Abuife This small village to the southwest of Tafi Atome is one of Ghana's major kente-weaving centres, and one of the most enjoyable to visit, as in addition to the covered weaving centre, many of the craftsmen work outdoors, which gives it a far more organic and aesthetically pleasing atmosphere than similar villages in Ashanti. Outside almost every house in the village you'll see a few weavers at work – they are amazingly quick and dexterous – and there is very little hassle factor or pressure to buy. Having said that, if you are thinking of buying kente cloth, starting prices here are almost half of what you'll be asked in Ashanti or Accra, although you will have to allow extra time and possibly money to have the woven strips sewn together into full cloths. The visitor centre (m *0542 680056/0205 269255;* e *tourkenteta@gmail.com;* ⏲ *06.00–18.00*) at the main junction charges US$4 per person for entry (which includes an enthusiastic 30-minute tour), and also offers kente-weaving lessons for US$2.50 per hour, drumming and dancing performances for US$4, and homestays for US$7 per person excluding meals (which are available by arrangement). If there's no one there, the weaving centre is 300m north of the main junction, on the right-hand side.

Tafi Abuife lies at the midpoint of a recently surfaced 10km road connecting Tafi Mador (on the Accra–Hohoe road) to Jordanu (on the Kpandu road). It is an easy one-hour walk coming in either direction, or you could hop on a motorbike for US$1 per person. Tafi Abuife can also be visited from Tafi Atome on foot or using a rented bicycle following a 7km footpath. By road, the distance between the villages is about 14km – follow the Kpandu road out of Tafi Atome for 3–4km, turn left at the first junction, then left again at a small village about 7–8km further on, then continue straight ahead through the last junction, which you'll cross after another 1km or so.

KPANDU

This town of 29,000 is also sometimes known as Kpando, the name of the municipal district of which it has been the administrative centre since German colonial times. It is set back 4km east of the small ferry port of Kpandu Torkor on Lake Volta, but stands atop a steep scarp about 100m higher than the water. The compact centre boasts a few century-old buildings, part of a Basel Mission founded there in 1904, and it has a bustling central market, but otherwise there is little to distinguish it from any other medium-sized Ghanaian town. The area is known for its pottery, which can be seen at Kpandu Potters, 4km out of town at Fesi, and while tourists are an infrequent sight, the same cannot be said of the Virgin Mary, who evidently makes regular appearances and has two grottoes dedicated to her within 10km of the town centre. Note that the 'K' in Kpandu (and in other place names that begin with 'Kp') is silent – locals pronounce 'Kp' as a slightly more explosive 'P'.

GETTING THERE AND AWAY Kpandu is connected to Ho, Hohoe and Accra by regular trotros. Ferries, when they are running, arrive and depart from Kpandu Torkor 4km west of the town centre and connected to it by regular shared taxis. The main Lake Volta ferry between Akosombo and Yeji hasn't stopped at Kpandu for years because the harbour is too shallow, and the daily motor ferry to Donkorkrom on the Afram Plains (see box, pages 348–9) has not been operational since the end of 2011. Thus, inexpensive private passenger boats are your only option for crossing the lake from here, and these make the trip between Kpandu Torkor and Donkorkrom once or twice daily, with departure times and regularity being dependent on demand.

🏠 **WHERE TO STAY** *Map, page 322*

Moderate

🏠 **Johnson's Inn** (13 rooms) ☎03620 95269; m 0249 886561. Tucked away on a hillside about 1km north of the town centre, this modern hotel offers little in the way of character, but the clean, comfortable rooms are the best in town, & come with AC, satellite TV & hot water. A decent restaurant is attached. *US$16 B&B self-contained dbl; US$21 larger room with king-sized bed; US$32 suite.* **$$**

Budget

🏠 **Same Sisters Guesthouse** (7 rooms) m 0208 138742. Situated about 300m west of the hospital, this well-priced new guesthouse has spacious rooms with queen-size bed, fridge, modern wooden furniture, en-suite hot tub/ shower & fan. There is a TV lounge, & meals on request. *US$13 self-contained dbl with fan; US$20–26 self-contained dbl with AC.* **$$**

🏠 **Catherine's Lodge** (10 rooms) ☎03039 66882; m 0200 697750. This likeable set-up, tucked away in the backroads southeast of the

town centre, has a beautiful garden where you can enjoy a drink, but you will have to trek back towards town for food. The rooms are only so-so, but will seem good if AC is important to you. *US$13 self-contained dbl with AC; US$19 for larger room with queen-sized bed.* **$$–$**

🏠 **First Class Guesthouse** (5 rooms) ☎03623 50230; m 0573 819950/0548 510377. The most central lodge in this range, situated just off the road to the hospital, this pleasant & well-established lodge, though a little more worse for wear than its name might suggest, has very spacious & reasonably priced rooms with TV & AC. Meals are available to residents only. *US$11 dbl using shared bath; US$13–16 self-contained dbl with AC.* **$$–$**

Shoestring

🏠 **Desh Guesthouse** (11 rooms) m 0243 607952/0207 813893. This friendly hotel on the hospital road has clean, spacious & quiet self-contained rooms, some with a balcony. Their

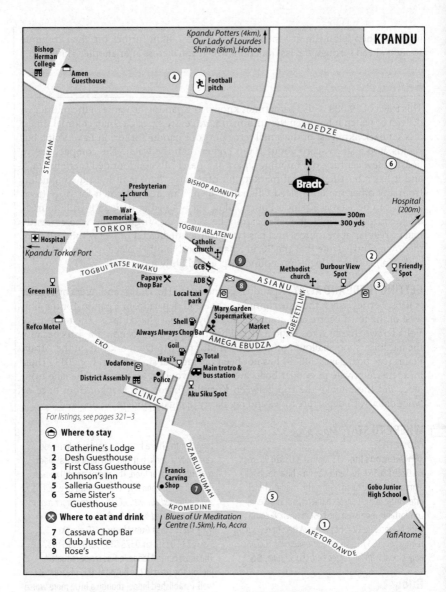

KPANDU

Kpandu Potters (4km),
Our Lady of Lourdes
Shrine (8km), Hohoe

Bishop
Herman
College

Amen
Guesthouse

Football
pitch

ADEDZE

STRAHAN

Presbyterian
church

BISHOP ADANUTY

War
memorial

TORKOR

TOGBUI ABLATENU

Hospital
Kpandu Torkor Port

Catholic
church

TOGBUI TATSE KWAKU

GCB

Papaye
Chop Bar

ADB

Methodist
church

Durbour View
Spot

Friendly
Spot

Green Hill

Local taxi
park

ASIANU

Refco Motel

Shell

Mary Garden
Supermarket

Always Always Chop Bar

AMEGA EBUDZA

Market

AGBETETI LINK

Goil

EKO

Maxi's

Total

Vodafone

Main trotro &
bus station

District Assembly

Police

CLINIC

Aku Siku Spot

Hospital
(200m)

N

Bradt

0   300m
0   300 yds

For listings, see pages 321–3

🏠 **Where to stay**
1 Catherine's Lodge
2 Desh Guesthouse
3 First Class Guesthouse
4 Johnson's Inn
5 Salleria Guesthouse
6 Same Sister's
    Guesthouse

❌ **Where to eat and drink**
7 Cassava Chop Bar
8 Club Justice
9 Rose's

DZABLUI KUMAH

Francis
Carving
Shop

KPOMEDINE
Blues of Ur Meditation
Centre (1.5km), Ho, Accra

Gobo Junior
High School

Tafi Atome

AFETOR DAWDE

restaurant is no more, but the appropriately named
Friendly Spot is right across the street. *US$14/16
self-contained dbl with fan/AC.* **$$–$**

🏠 **Salleria Guesthouse** (11 rooms) m 0506
417114. Hidden away in the backroads of the

maze-like suburb known as Angola, this well-
signposted guesthouse has a variety of very clean &
comfortable-seeming rooms with fan or AC. No food
is served, but it's only about 300m to the nearby
Cassava Chop Bar. *US$12/21 dbl with fan/AC.* **$$–$**

❌ **WHERE TO EAT AND DRINK** *Map, above*
❌ **Rose's Restaurant** \ 0241 517406/0503
949878; ⏰ 06.00–20.00 daily. Poorly signposted but
easily located down a short alley opposite the post
office, this central restaurant is popular with volunteers

& it serves a varied selection of local & foreign dishes,
including red-red, jollof rice, fillet steak & vegetables
with couscous. Allow time for them to prepare the
dishes. Mains in the US$5–6 range. **$$**

✗ **Club Justice** m 0208 291789/0265 438990; ⏱ 08.00–22.00 daily. With the longest hours in town, this popular central eatery & bar next to the post office dishes up reasonably fast Ghanaian staples like an (excellent) groundnut soup & fufu for US$3, with seating in a functional concrete courtyard. $

✗ **Cassava Chop Bar** ⏱ daily. Well-loved by local volunteers, this low-key chop bar serves the usual array of Ghanaian favourites for US$2–4 & is a good option if you're staying in the Angola neighbourhood at the south end of town. $

AROUND KPANDU

Kpandu Torkor One of the most accessible parts of the eastern Lake Volta shore, the port of Kpandu Torkor is connected to the town centre by a scenic 4km road descent, and a steady stream of shared taxis. It isn't the most scenic stretch of lakeshore, however, but the port hosts a bustling market selling fish along with all manner of cloths, garments and other foodstuffs.

Kpandu Potters Kpandu District is known for its fine hand-moulded pottery, which is often claimed to be the best in Ghana and traditionally made by women only. The best place to check it out is the Fesi Shed of Kpandu Potters (m *0285 346797*), a women's co-operative that exports its work throughout Ghana as well as into some neighbouring countries. To get there, follow the surfaced Ahenkro road north out of town for 4km to the suburb of Fesi, where a dirt track, clearly signposted to the right, leads to the shed after about 500m. The women who work here seem very friendly and will gladly let travellers watch them at work and look at some of the finished products – which include hand-modelled sculptures of animals such as tortoises, pigs and snails, as well as pots with designs based loosely on Adinkra symbols. If you're thinking of buying, fist-sized models start at around US$2.

Our Lady of Lourdes Shrine Situated at Agbenoxoe, some 8km north of Kpandu on the surfaced Ahenkro road, this unusual hillside shrine to the Virgin Mary – reputedly the third-biggest Christian grotto in the world – was founded by the Dutch Father Van Dyck in the 1950s in homage to the shrine at Lourdes. The grotto consists of 14 life-size sculptures of scenes related to the crucifixion of Christ, as well as a huge sculpture of the Virgin Mary that attracts Christian pilgrims from all over Ghana. A few years ago, some children allegedly saw the blue robe on this statue blowing in the wind and called the local priest, who decided that the Virgin was pointing towards one specific palm tree. Rumour got around that this palm had healing powers, and so many pilgrims cut off pieces of the sacred tree for medicinal purposes that it eventually died! An all-day vigil and service is held at the open-air church next to the grotto on the first Friday of every month, and there's also a large ceremony there every 11 December. No fee is charged, but expect to be asked for a donation towards the shrine's upkeep.

Blues of Ur Meditation Centre Located 2km south of the town centre on the right side of the Accra road, this bizarre meditation centre was founded in May 1964 by Kwame Linus Appaw, who saw a blue star in the sky above Kpandu and followed it into the bush until it landed on a large rock outcrop. There it transmitted a message from the Virgin Mary that the surrounding area should be used as a centre for meditation, prayer and tourism dedicated to her name. Thus were born the mysterious Blues of Ur (Ur being the name of the town where Abraham was born), a 200-strong cult centred on the meditation centre, which is owned by the Virgin Mary, and that prays to Mary more than to Jesus because the mother created the son. Though rather run-down, the centre is open to all comers (provided that they adhere

14

to a few prominently signposted rules, ie: 'don't pluck fruits or hunt for games, no shooting of birds nor picking of flowers, don't throw any missiles into trees and avoid sexy appearances') and is not without a certain offbeat charm, with its cement reliefs of nativity and other biblical scenes (categorised under the 'five sorrowful mysteries' and 'five joyful mysteries') and plentiful statues of Mary and Jesus.

HOHOE

The eponymous capital of Hohoe Municipal District is the second-largest town in Volta Region, supporting a population of almost 60,000. Much like the regional capital 60km to its south, the town is decidedly amiable and has decent amenities for budget travellers, but it boasts little in the way of tourist attractions. An outbreak of violence between local Muslim and Christian factions led to a dusk-to-dawn curfew being imposed on Hohoe in the latter months of 2012, but things subsequently calmed down and the restriction has been lifted. It used to be a popular overnight stop back when it formed the best base for visits to the Agumatsa Wildlife Sanctuary, site of the spectacular Wli Falls, but these days most people just pass through *en route* to the village of Wli Agorviefe, which borders the sanctuary and offers plenty of accommodation options more attractive than Hohoe's rather scruffy selection. The other big geographic landmark in the vicinity is Mount Afadjato/Aduadu, the highest point in Ghana, but this, too, is quite easily visited without actually basing yourself in Hohoe.

GETTING THERE AND AWAY Hohoe is connected to Accra by regular trotros and Fords (leaving from Aflao/Tudu Station) as well as by trotro to Ho, Kpandu, Wli, Nkwanta, and most other towns in the region (including Kpalime across the border in Togo). There is no direct transport to Amedzofe, but any Ho-bound vehicle can drop you at Vane, from where you can walk the last 3km or catch a shared taxi.

TOURIST INFORMATION AND GUIDES The district tourist information office [325 A5] (m *0249 150683;* ◷ *09.00–15.30 Mon–Fri*) opposite the main trotro station is of decidedly limited use, but might be worth a look in if you have specific questions. Freelance guides in Hohoe – even those with government cards – have a reputation for misleading travellers to suit their own agenda, for instance claiming that it's not permitted to visit Wli without a guide from Hohoe, or that the waterfall is off-limits due to flooding and offering an alternative guided trip.

🏠 WHERE TO STAY
Moderate

🏠 **Hampton Resorts** [325 D4] (28 rooms) m 0200 141516/104050. Though it wasn't quite finished when we checked in, this new place 2km along the road to Wli seems easily set to be Hohoe's smartest accommodation when it's complete. The pink exterior looks a bit overdone at first glance, but the rooms are spacious, bright, & tastefully decorated, with AC, fridge, flatscreen TV & writing desk. The sizeable grounds are slated to have a swimming pool & tennis court, & as of now there's a pleasant garden bar & restaurant at the edge of the grassy compound. *US$52/65 std/exec dbl.* **$$$**

Budget

🏠 **Greater Grace Guesthouse** [325 A6] (9 rooms) m 0244 235014. This pleasant guesthouse, situated about 5km south of Hohoe at the junction village of Gbe Wegbe, is superior to any of the more central options discussed below. The smartly furnished rooms with satellite TV & large bathrooms are good value, & a limited selection of food is available, including tasty grilled tilapia. *US$13–16 B&B self-contained dbl with fan; US$18–26 dbl with AC.* **$$–$**

🏠 **Evergreen Lodge** [325 B2] (6 rooms) ☏03627 22254; m 0274 511569. This smart 2-star

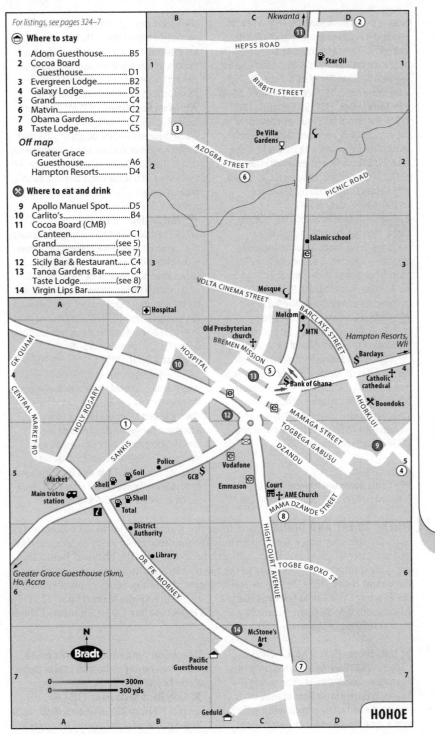

For listings, see pages 324–7

Where to stay

1 Adom Guesthouse..............B5
2 Cocoa Board
    Guesthouse.....................D1
3 Evergreen Lodge.................B2
4 Galaxy Lodge....................D5
5 Grand...................................C4
6 Matvin.................................C2
7 Obama Gardens................C7
8 Taste Lodge........................C5

Off map

Greater Grace
    Guesthouse.....................A6
Hampton Resorts..............D4

Where to eat and drink

9   Apollo Manuel Spot..........D5
10 Carlito's..............................B4
11 Cocoa Board (CMB)
     Canteen...........................C1
     Grand..............................(see 5)
     Obama Gardens...........(see 7)
12 Sicily Bar & Restaurant.....C4
13 Tanoa Gardens Bar............C4
     Taste Lodge..................(see 8)
14 Virgin Lips Bar.....................C7

Nkwanta

HEPSS ROAD

Star Oil

BIRBITI STREET

De Villa
Gardens

AZOGBA STREET

PICNIC ROAD

Islamic school

VOLTA CINEMA STREET

Mosque

BARCLAYS STREET

Melcom

MTN

Hampton Resorts,
Wli

Barclays

A

Hospital

HOSPITAL

Old Presbyterian
church
BREMEN MISSION

Catholic
cathedral

AHORKLUI

Boondoks

GK QUAMI

CENTRAL MARKET RD

HOLY ROSARY

SANKIS

Grand

Bank of Ghana

MAMAGA STREET

TOGBEGA GABUSU

DZANDU

Market

Main trotro
station

Shell

Goil

Police

GCB

Total

Shell

Vodafone

Emmason

Court

AME Church

MAMA DZAWDE STREET

District
Authority

Library

HIGH COURT AVENUE

TOGBE GBOXO ST

Greater Grace Guesthouse (5km),
Ho, Accra

DR FK MORNEY

McStone's
Art

N

Bradt

0   300m
0   300 yds

Pacific
Guesthouse

Geduld

A   B   C   D

HOHOE

14

hotel on the northern edge of town may be a bit bland but it is above average in quality & quite well priced. There's a bar attached, but no food. The quite attractively furnished & tiled rooms have hot shower & bath, satellite TV, AC & fridge. *US$9 sgl using shared bath; US$19 self-contained dbl.* **$$–$**

🏠 **Taste Lodge** [325 C5] (5 rooms) 📞03627 22023. This central family-run set-up has good but ever so slightly overpriced rooms in a carefully tended little compound, with satellite TV, fridge, fan & AC, & about the best restaurant in town. *US$13/24 self-contained dbl using fan/AC.* **$$–$**

🏠 **Galaxy Lodge** [325 D5] (16 rooms) 📱0244 046041/0542 645441; e visitgalaxylodge@gmail.com. This relatively central hotel lies about 400m south of the road towards Wli. Rooms are quite spacious & attractively furnished, & all come with satellite TV, fridge & hot shower. There is an agreeable garden bar & summer hut restaurant. *US$21/24/26 self-contained dbl with dbl/queen/king bed.* **$$**

🏠 **Obama Gardens** [325 C7] (9 rooms) 📱0556 824068/0205 507346. Set just behind the excellent restaurant & bar of the same name, the high-ceilinged rooms here are very clean & well kept, & seem like they're set far enough away from the action that bar noise won't be a major problem. The self-contained rooms seem decent value, but the ones using shared facilities are a bit overpriced. *US$16 dbl with AC & shared bath; US$18–21 self-contained dbl.* **$$**

Shoestring

🏠 **Cocoa Board Guesthouse** [325 D1] (4 rooms) 📱0245 702188/0265 504780. This low-key but very cosy gem is situated about 2km north of the town centre on the Nkwanta road. It has 2 spacious twin rooms with fan, fridge & hot showers, as well as a shared lounge & a large self-catering kitchen. *Superb value at US$5 dbl using shared bath; US$8 self-contained twin.* **$**

🏠 **Adom Guesthouse** [325 B5] (15 rooms) 📞03627 20829; m 0249 039621; e adombusinessventures@gmail.com. This clean & quiet lodge is on the basic side, but conveniently close to the trotro station & pretty good value. All rooms come with ceiling fans & there are meals & drinks at request. *US$11/14 self-contained sgl/dbl with fan & TV; US$26 suite with AC.* **$$–$**

🏠 **Matvin Hotel** [325 C2] (29 rooms) 📞03627 22134. The decaying old Matvin was once Hohoe's most upmarket hotel, & has the grounds to prove it, complete with a garden bar overlooking a stream about 1km north of the town centre. The rooms, though shabby, are very reasonably priced, but the restaurant recently closed down (although this is no great loss). *US$9 dbl with fan using shared bath; US$11/14 self-contained twin with satellite TV & fan/AC; US$20 semi-suite.* **$$–$**

🏠 **Grand Hotel** [325 C4] (10 rooms) 📞03627 22053; e godanq@yahoo.com. The most central hotel in Hohoe, situated on the main road opposite the prominent Bank of Ghana, is a good place to stay if you want to be close to the action, with a courtyard bar serving cheap draught beer & sensibly priced meals, but it can be quite noisy otherwise. The no-frills rooms are small but adequately clean. *US$11 dbl with fan using shared bath; US$13 self-contained dbl or twin; US$18–21 self-contained dbl with AC.* **$$–$**

✖ WHERE TO EAT AND DRINK Aside from the formal eateries listed below, a stall opposite the post office serves delicious kontomire stew (a spicy local speciality) and a cluster of good breakfast stalls can be found near the National Bank. There are quite a number of good bars in the town centre, including the courtyard bar at the **Grand Hotel** [325 C4] (where stalls outside also sell good spicy meat kebabs in the evening), the **Tanoa Gardens Bar** [325 C4] and the **Apollo Manuel Spot** [325 D5]. Also worth a look is the bizarrely named **Virgin Lips Bar** [325 C7], located about 1km southeast of the main trotro station.

✖ Taste Lodge [325 C5] 📞03627 22023; 🕐 06.30–23.00 daily. Assuming you can get past the macabre connotations of a sign reading 'This Business is Covered in the Blood of Jesus', this is probably the best eatery in town, with friendly service, good ventilation & a varied selection of Chinese, Ghanaian & Western dishes for around US$4. Meals are prepared to order so allow plenty of time for your food to arrive. **$**

✖ Sicily Bar & Restaurant [325 C4] 📞 03627 20377; m 0244 186076; 🕐 08.00–21.30 Mon–Sat. There's not much variety at this central eatery, but the tasty chicken & jollof rice (around US$3–4), breezy fans & fridge full of cold beers & sodas make it a very convenient option. $

✕ Obama Gardens [325 C7] ⏰ 10.00–01.00 daily. In a big grassy garden at the south end of High Court Av, there are a bunch of grills here that get fired up in the evening, & excellent plates of chicken & rice for US$3–5 at other times. Not to mention they were the recipients of 2015's 'Drinking Bar of the Year' award. $

✕ Carlito's [325 B4] m 0203 745196; ⏰ 10.00–late daily. It seems pretty dead during the day, but this new semi-outdoor restaurant & bar might have the most diverse menu in town – think hummus, pizza, burgers & more for US$4–7– along with a full bar, snooker, shisha pipes, & a DJ at w/ends. $$

✕ Cocoa Board (CMB) Canteen [325 C1] m 0205 168697/0244 501963; ⏰ 09.00–17.00 Mon–Fri. Popular with office workers on their lunch break, this clean & friendly chop bar is a good bet for rice, fufu, banku & the like at the north end of town. $

OTHER PRACTICALITIES

Foreign exchange The **Ghana Commercial Bank** [325 B5] on the main road and **Barclays Bank** [325 D4] next to the Catholic cathedral on the Wli road both have a Visa-only ATM.

Internet For internet access, the best service is available at **Emmason Internet** [325 C5], on the High Court Avenue just south of the post office. There is also a more central internet café opposite the Sicily Restaurant.

AGUMATSA WILDLIFE SANCTUARY

This 35km² sanctuary, which lies astride the Togolese border in the Wli Traditional Area directly east of Hohoe, was originally set aside to protect a cliff-nesting colony of the straw-coloured fruit bat (*Eidolon helvum*). The reserve is better known, however, as the site of Wli Falls, reputedly the tallest waterfall in West Africa, and one of the most popular tourist attractions in Volta Region. Formed by the Agumatsa River, 25km downstream of its mountainous source in Togo, Wli actually comprises two discrete waterfalls, the very accessible lower falls, which tumble around 70m over the same cliff that houses the fruit bat colony, and the slightly smaller and more difficult to reach upper falls. The entrance gate to the sanctuary, and start of the footpath to the lower falls, is in the village of **Wli Agorviefe**, readily accessible from Hohoe on public transport, and also now boasts a number of attractive mid-range and budget lodges. The waterfall is an important fetish to the 4,000-odd inhabitants of the Wli Traditional Area (which comprises the villages of Agorviefe, Afegame, Todzi and Dzogbega), who claim that its water can make barren women fertile, and who hold an annual festival below the waterfall, usually on the last Saturday of October.

GETTING THERE AND AWAY Wli Agorviefe lies about 25km from Hohoe along a surfaced road that runs directly east past the Catholic cathedral, then forks right at the T-junction at the village of Likpe Bakua. Trotros and shared taxis run from Hohoe, cost around US$1.50 and leave every hour or two throughout the day, with more on Wednesdays, which is the market day in Wli. They stop and leave from in front of Godsway spot at the main traffic circle in Wli Agorviefe, which is little more than 100m from **Wli Tourist Reception Office** (m *0202 572400/0200 292264/0201 401581*; e *wliagumatsawaterfalls@yahoo.com*; ⏰ *08.00–17.00 daily, latest departure time 16.00*) and entrance to Agumatsa Wildlife Sanctuary.

Coming from the south, Wli can also be reached from the Ho–Hohoe road via the scenic side road from either Golokwati or Logba-Vuinta, passing through

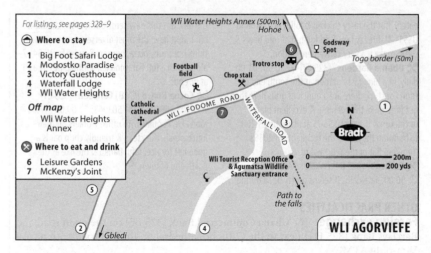

For listings, see pages 328–9

Where to stay

1 Big Foot Safari Lodge
2 Modostko Paradise
3 Victory Guesthouse
4 Waterfall Lodge
5 Wli Water Heights

Off map
Wli Water Heights
Annex

Where to eat and drink

6 Leisure Gardens
7 McKenzy's Joint

Wli Water Heights Annex (500m),
Hohoe

Godsway
Spot

Togo border (50m)

Trotro stop

Football
field

Chop stall

Catholic
cathedral

WLI - FODOME ROAD

WATERFALL ROAD

Bradt

N

Wli Tourist Reception Office
& Agumatsa Wildlife
Sanctuary entrance

0   200m
0   200 yds

Path to
the falls

Gbledi

WLI AGORVIEFE

Liati Agbonyira, Liati-Wote, Gbledi-Gbogame, Gbledi-Chebe and Fodome-Ahor. In a private vehicle, this mostly dirt road can be covered in about one hour, but public transport is thin on the ground and may involve multiple changes and long waits.

WHERE TO STAY *Map, above*
Moderate
Big Foot Safari Lodge (16 rooms) m 0207 882334/0204 431744; e info@bigfootsafarilodge. com; www.bigfootsafarilodge.com. The newest & smartest lodge in Wli Agorviefe, set in lush gardens just north of the main traffic circle, Big Foot offers accommodation in thatched semi-detached cottages with stylish ethnically inspired décor, tiled floor, queen-sized bed, fan, AC, satellite TV, private balcony & hot water. The restaurant serves a good variety of mains (including several vegetarian selections) in the US$6–8 range. Budget rooms are in the works & camping space is available. *US$42/53 self-contained sgl/dbl; camping US$10pp; tent rental US$15.* **$$$–$$**

Budget
Waterfall Lodge (8 rooms) m 0205 115388/0541 359872; e bernhard.hagspiel@web. de; www.ghanacamping.com. The oldest lodge in Wli Agorviefe, owner-managed by the same relaxed German couple since it opened in 2003, this has a superb location about 500m from the tourist reception centre in a large green garden that's alive with birdsong & offers a distant view of the upper falls. The large outdoor bar is a great place to enjoy a drink, or a tasty meal from the restaurant. Rooms are simple but very comfortable

& camping is possible. It is closed on Tue, when no b/fast or other meals are served, & no new arrivals are accepted. However, visitors who have slept here on Mon can stay on for Tue, though they will need to eat elsewhere. *US$18/21 self-contained dbl room/chalet; US$30 family chalet (sleeping 4); US$4pp camping.* **$$**

Wli Water Heights Hotel (7 rooms) m 0209 119152/387176; e wliheights@yahoo.com; www.wliwaterheightshotel.com. A few hundred metres past the turn-off for the tourist reception office, this friendly hotel lacks the organic feel of Waterfall Lodge, coming across more like a refugee from suburbia, but it is a well-organised & agreeable set-up, with smart well-maintained rooms, a patio restaurant serving an imaginative selection of dishes in the US$5–8 range, & drumming & dancing displays by local schoolchildren every Fri/ Sat evening. *US$21/23 dbl/twin using shared bath; US$26–31 self-contained dbl with fan; US$47 dbl with AC.* **$$$–$$**

Wli Water Heights Annex (13 rooms) m 0209 119152/387176; e wliheights@yahoo. com; www.wliwaterheightshotel.com. On your right-hand side as you enter Wli & about 500m from the main roundabout, this new branch of the Wli Water Heights Hotel has a lovely bush location & feels considerably woodsier than its counterpart across town, but the clean en-suite rooms are all kept to the same high standards. Wood flooring & walls in the 1st-floor rooms also gives them a pleasantly rustic feel. The restaurant menu, prices, & other offerings are all identical to their older counterpart. **$$$–$$**

Shoestring

⌂ Victory Guesthouse (4 rooms) **m** 0244 729286, 0200 723306/774461. Situated right opposite the tourist reception office, this cheap &

convenient lodge is somewhat on the functional side, but pretty good value all the same. *US$13–21 self-contained dbl with fan.* **$$–$**

⌂ Modostko Paradise (2 rooms) **m** 0207 591875; **f** fb.me/vincent.mokli1. In a haphazard compound at the south end of town, this Rastafied abode is primarily a place to go for reggae parties at the w/ends, but they've also got a couple of rather rickety & dishevelled (though undeniably cheap) rooms, & can arrange meals & drinks at request. *US$7 dbl; US$2.50pp camping.* **$**

✗ WHERE TO EAT AND DRINK *Map, opposite*

All the moderate and budget options listed above have good mid-range restaurants. A cheaper alternative is **McKenzy's Joint**, a pleasant little bar on the main road that can cook local dishes for groups for around US$3 per head by advance request, or the more reliable **Leisure Gardens** (**m** *0208 825609/0549 868618*), near the roundabout, which costs about the same.

WHAT TO SEE AND DO

Wli Waterfall Trail A relatively undemanding 45–60-minute footpath through the Agumatsa Wildlife Sanctuary leads from Wli Agorviefe to the base of the lower Wli Falls. This must be arranged through the Wli Tourist Reception Office (page 327), where non-Ghanaians need to pay the entrance fee of US$5/4 adult/volunteer, plus an optional camera/video fee of US$1/2.50. You'll be assigned a mandatory guide, who will expect a tip. The flat footpath leads through thick, semi-deciduous forest for 45 minutes, fording the Wli and Agumatsa rivers (the former reputedly warmer than the latter) a total of nine times on small footbridges that have sometimes been washed away in the past in heavy flooding. Once you reach the falls, there's a large and rather shallow pool where you can take a refreshing dip, though the water is chillier than you might expect, since it originates much higher up in the mountains. You're unlikely to see any large mammals on the waterfall trail, though mona monkeys and various small antelope reputedly still inhabit the forest. Birds are less noticeable than might be expected, but the checklist of around 200 species includes several greenbuls, barbets and hornbills. More conspicuous and impressive are the forest's dazzling butterflies, of which around 400 species have been recorded. The reserve's most memorable wildlife phenomenon, however, is the straw-coloured fruit bat colony that lives on the cliffs next to the waterfall. As you approach the waterfall, the roar of plunging water often vies with their high-pitched chirping, and it's awesome to be there towards dusk, when tens of thousands of these ecologically important creatures take wing to start their nocturnal foraging.

Solo female travellers should be aware that we received two reports of physical/verbal harassment and sexual assault perpetrated during hikes by guides assigned by the tourist office in mid 2015. We brought this up with the office during our inspection tour in early 2016 and were assured that they were aware of and had investigated the problem, found that one individual was responsible, and sacked him (though no mention was made of any legal consequences for the lecher). So, on the face of it, the problem seems to have been addressed (and we haven't had any subsequent reports), but it's something to be aware of nonetheless, and concerned hikers may want to consider pairing up with other visitors, particularly if you'll be heading to the upper falls.

Upper Falls Hike Tough at the best of times (one US reader declared 'it makes the Bright Angel Trail in the Grand Canyon look like a lazy afternoon walk'), the hike to the upper falls can only be undertaken between January and June, as it closes for safety reasons during the main rainy season, from 1 July to 31 December. Parts of the trail are very steep, with a knee-to-chin incline, and one wrong step on certain narrow stretches could cause you to fall or slide 10–20m. As with the hike to the lower falls, it must be arranged through the Wli Tourist Reception Office, which charges US$11/16 depending on the route taken (return or loop trail). A guide is mandatory, a walking stick is strongly recommended, and you should allow 3 hours in either direction or 8 hours for the loop trail. A recommended contact for hikes to the upper falls is **Francis Kludze** (m *0201 870706;* e *kludzefrancis@gmail.com*), who can organise overnight camping excursions there, as well as day hikes.

Likpe Todome Situated about 2km north of Likpe Bakwa (the junction village you pass through between Hohoe and Wli Agorviefe), the village of Likpe Todome is of interest primarily for a network of six caves that runs through the hills to its east. Some of these caves support large colonies of bats, while one contains the ancient stool of the first Likpe chief. The caves can be explored over a total of up to five hours, including a side trip to a beautiful waterfall. Guided hikes (*US$2.50*) are best arranged at the village's well-signposted **tourist centre** (m *0246 666458/0202 6798600540 941664*). Note that the hike up through the mountains is physically demanding, and the final ascent path to the caves involves a vertigo-inducing near-vertical climb using ropes whose safety is open to question. A less-demanding (and less atmospheric) option might be to walk up the recently cut road up the mountain (see below). If you decide to give it a go by either route, wear strong walking shoes and carry plenty of food and water.

The biggest tourist development to hit Todome in recent years, however, has to be the **Kɔtini Adventure Resort** (m *0244 379378/0208 153345*; e *onipaba@ gmail.com*; *www.flylikpe.com*), perched at nearly 705m near the caves on the ridge overlooking the village. As things stand today, the huge pointy-roofed and open-sided restaurant is easily visible for miles around, but it only operates for festivals and special occasions, like the associated **Likpe Paragliding Festival** (*www. flylikpe.com*), a three-day event filled with hiking, food, live music and traditional ceremonies that's taken place here every New Year since 2014. It's unclear if and when the restaurant might begin full-time operations and rooms up here still seem to be a long way off, but it's a stunning location regardless, and the expansive views from the top are as good as any in Ghana.

Kɔtini is accessed by a new, very steep, and *very* 4x4-only 2.5km access road signposted from Todome, which continues on to the Togo border and Danyi-Dzedrame, the nearest community in Togo, only 3.3km beyond the resort. Though it's not (yet) a legal border crossing, this construction realised a decades-long ambition of the two villages, who tried to cut a road of their own (with no government assistance!) in the late 1950s, but were eventually stymied by inadequate tools to demolish the hard rock in their path, along with infighting between the Likpe villages as to which one the new road would pass through.

MOUNT AFADJATO

An attractive and underrated goal for hikers, Mount Afadjato (aka Afadzato) – widely cited as the highest mountain in Ghana – lies on the Togolese border southeast of Hohoe, where it forms part of the Agumatsa Range along with

Wli Falls a short distance to the north. Although this range is undoubtedly the country's highest, Afadjato itself is rather embarrassingly surrounded by higher peaks, most of which actually lie in Togo, though at least one, Aduadu, reputedly falls within Ghanaian territory, and seems like the most likely candidate for the country's 885m highpoint.

Either way, the mountain offers spectacular views, with distant Lake Volta being visible on a clear day. The forested slopes also host a remarkable diversity of wildlife, including more than 100 butterfly species (several of which are endemic), as well as around 30 types of mammal, including mona and spot-nosed monkeys, Maxwell's duiker, bushbuck, cusimanse mongoose and golden cat. Afadjato is listed as an Important Bird Area, and although no full checklist has been compiled, a recent four-day expedition identified almost 90 species, of which ten are uncommon in Ghana, including brown snake eagle, Afep pigeon, green-tailed bristlebill, leaflove and olive-green cameroptera. Some say the name Afadjato derives from an Ewe word meaning 'at war with the bush', a reference to a common plant that causes severe skin irritation, others that it refers to the leaves of the water yam, which look similar to the leaves of a plant that grows wild there.

Confusingly, and rather counterproductively from a visitor's perspective, Mount Afadjato is the focal point of two rival community projects that make no secret of their mutual hostility. The forested northern slopes are protected within the 13km² Afadjato Agumatsa Community Reserve, which was established in association with the Ghana Wildlife Society in 1998, and is now run by the local communities in the Gbledi Traditional Area and Fodome Ahor. The main office for this reserve, situated a few hundred metres south of Gbledi-Gbogame, is the **Afadjato Agumatsa Conservation and Ecotourism Centre** (*AACEC*; m *0245 597293/0508 784428/0548 642712;* ⊕ *07.30–15.00 Mon–Sat, 10.30–15.00 Sun*), which offers a range of hikes as well as accommodation at the base of the mountain. Only about 2km south, at Liati Wote, similar activities and facilities are offered by the **Liati Wote Visitors Centre** (m *0240 488463;* ⊕ *07.30–17.00 daily*), a community tourism project originally established in association with the Peace Corps.

GETTING THERE AND AWAY Trotros to Liati Wote via Gbledi-Gbogame and Fodome Ahor leave Hohoe from the main trotro station, and take about one hour. The trotros run every day, but are most regular on market days (Monday and Friday), when you shouldn't wait longer than an hour for something to leave. The best time for transport on other days is generally between noon and 14.00.

Coming from the south in a private vehicle, you don't need to go all the way to Hohoe, but could branch right at either Logba-Vuinta or Golokwati Junction and follow side roads to Liati Wote and Gbledi-Gbogame. From Golokwati, head about 6km along the surfaced road to Liati Agbonyira where you'll turn left, then after 4km turn right at Liati Soba, from where it's another 4km to Liati Wote. From Logba-Vuinta, follow the surfaced road 8km to the junction at Leklebi-Dafor, turn left and carry on another 2km to Liati Agbonyira, where you'll make a right. From here the directions are the same. There is also some public transport along these routes, but it is slow and erratic, so you would be better chartering a taxi or moto from Golokwati, which should cost around US$10 or US$3 respectively.

Note that it is only about 12km from Wli Agorviefe to Gbledi-Gbogame via Fodome Ahor. This road will take no longer than 20 minutes to cover in a private vehicle, but will be slower going on public transport, as trotros are few and far between, and you will probably need to change vehicles at Fodome Ahor.

WHERE TO STAY AND EAT

AACEC Guesthouse (5 rooms) m 0245 597293/0508 784428. The ecotourism centre in Gbledi-Gbogame operates a new guesthouse just across the street with surprisingly smart self-contained dbl rooms that come with ceiling fan, flatscreen TV & AC. Somewhat bafflingly, they claimed no longer to organise meals, but guests can still pay a small fee to use a self-catering kitchen equipped with a gas stove & oven, running water & fridge, or try to scrounge up some chop in the village. *US$16 self-contained dbl.* **$$**

Nubui Guesthouse (10 rooms) m 0202 891226. Also operated by the AACEC, this renovated guesthouse in Fodome Ahor,

about 8km north of Gbledi-Gbogame, has a very friendly caretaker, as well as fastidiously kept rooms with ceiling fan, & meals & drinks available upon request. Camping is permitted, too, & it's a convenient base for visiting Afadjato & Wli, as it lies between the 2. *US$8 dbl with shared bath; US$9 self-contained dbl.* **$**

Afadjato Community Guesthouse (6 rooms) m 0547 214100/0247 498259. Set in a forest glade on the left side of the road at the entrance of Liati Wote coming from the south, this has basic but clean rooms with nets & fans. Camping is permitted & meals can be arranged with the community project staff. *US$5/7 sgl/dbl.* **$**

WHAT TO SEE AND DO

From Gbledi-Gbogame The most established trail here leads to the top of Afadjato, via a steep and well-shaded footpath through the Afadjato Agumatsa Community Reserve. The ascent takes about 90 minutes and the descent around an hour, and you should see plentiful butterflies and birds *en route*, though mammals are both scarce and shy. The guided walk costs US$5/4 for non-Ghanaian adults/volunteers. In addition, there's a newly accessible trail to the higher peak known as Aduadu (meaning 'tooth on tooth'), and plans exist to cut a trail to the Ahase Waterfall eventually as well. There's currently no additional charge to hike to the next peak.

From Liati Wote Afadjato can be ascended from the southeast as a roughly two-hour round trip, along slopes that are rather more open and less shady than those protected within the community reserve. The fee is only US$2.50 from here, and a guide is supplied but not paid, so he will need to be tipped. Another worthwhile attraction, reached in 45 minutes along a reasonably flat path through cocoa fields, is the impressive Tagbo Waterfall, which is surrounded by semi-deciduous forest, and has a refreshing plunge pool at its base. The charge for this walk is the same as to the mountaintop. All guided hikes must be arranged through the Liati Wote Visitors Centre, which also offers an exciting 20km overnight 'expedition walk' to Wli Falls at US$16 per person to hikers able to provide their own tent.

NKWANTA

The most remote town of substance in Volta Region, Nkwanta lies around 150km north of Hohoe along a route seldom taken by travellers unless they have opted to use the adventurous easterly backroad to Tamale and northern Ghana via Bimbilla. It's not the most beautiful or compact town, sprawling as it does for several kilometres along the main road from Hohoe, but you'll probably want to stop overnight if you are headed up to Bimbilla on public transport. With a couple of hours to spare, it is worth walking uphill for about 1km past the primary school and forestry office to a 300m-high ridge offering splendid views over the plains west of town. Nkwanta is also noted for its colourful annual Yam Festival, which takes place in November, and it offers ready access to the recently

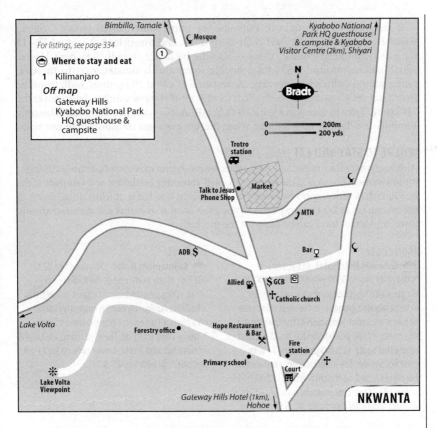

For listings, see page 334

⊖ **Where to stay and eat**

1 Kilimanjaro

Off map
    Gateway Hills
    Kyabobo National Park
    HQ guesthouse &
    campsite

Bimbilla, Tamale

Mosque

Kyabobo National
Park HQ guesthouse
& campsite & Kyabobo
Visitor Centre (2km), Shiyari

Bradt

0   200m
0   200 yds

Trotro
station

Market

Talk to Jesus
Phone Shop

MTN

ADB

Bar

Allied   GCB

Catholic church

Lake Volta

Forestry office

Hope Restaurant
& Bar

Fire
station

Primary school

Court

Lake Volta
Viewpoint

Gateway Hills Hotel (1km),
Hohoe

NKWANTA

gazetted and little-visited Kyabobo National Park, which lies on the Togolese border east of town, as well as being the springboard for visits to the unusual terraced village of Shiyari.

GETTING THERE AND AWAY The last stretch of the 150km road between Hohoe and Nkwanta was surfaced in April 2016, though parts of the road are still in poor repair and it should take around 2 hours to cover in a private vehicle. Several trotros run back and forth between Hohoe and Nkwanta daily, charging US$5 and ordinarily taking up to 3 hours. The trotros depart throughout daylight hours, from around 06.00 to 18.00, but we would recommend against leaving after midday, as breakdowns and delays are not unknown.

Heading north from Nkwanta, the 120km road to Bimbilla is in quite poor condition (dusty in the dry season, muddy during the rains, and bumpy at all times, particularly past Damanko) and you should allow at least three hours in a private vehicle. Using public transport, there are usually a couple of direct trotros to Bimbilla, leaving at 05.30–06.00 and taking around 5 hours. Failing that, you may need to do the trip in stages, possibly changing vehicles at Kpasa and Damanko, and should allocate a full day to allow for delays associated with waiting for vehicles. This road is scheduled to be surfaced during the lifespan of this edition as part of the Eastern Corridor Road project, which will eventually (sooner rather than later, supposedly) mean a fully surfaced route from Tema's port in the south to the Burkina Faso border crossing at Kulungugu.

If you need to overnight in Bimbilla, the improbably named Junior Original Guest House (m 0245 285545) is far from clean, and overpriced at around US$18 for a self-contained double. There is also the basic but friendly Teacher's Hostel, which charges around US$8 for a double room and is situated next to the Goil filling station (which has an adequate restaurant) about 20 minutes' walk from the trotro station. Continuing northwards from Bimbilla, allow another day to cover the 220km to Tamale, changing vehicles at Yendi. Avoid travelling between Nkwanta, Bimbilla and Tamale on a Sunday, when there is even less transport than normal.

WHERE TO STAY AND EAT Map, page 333

Although there is a limited selection of accommodation in Nkwanta, a more attractive option in most respects is the inexpensive **self-catering guesthouse** and **campsite** at the headquarters of Kyabobo National Park, only 2km northeast of town. In addition to the restaurant at the Gateway Hills Hotel, a few local restaurants are scattered around town, and street food can be found at the market.

Moderate

Gateway Hills Hotel (16 rooms)
\03029 48101 m 0509 769490/0246 380058; e gatewayhillshotelnkwanta@gmail.com. Set in large wooded grounds on the west side of the Hohoe road, about 1km south of the town centre, this unexpectedly plush hotel has small but neat rooms that come with fridge, satellite TV & en-suite hot shower. The indoor/outdoor restaurant/ bar serves local & continental dishes in the US$4–6 range. *US$21 self-contained dbl with fan; US$26 dbl with AC; US$31 dbl chalet with AC.* **$$**

Budget

Kilimanjaro Hotel (36 rooms) m 0242 002906. At the north end of the town centre, about 500m past the trotro station & market, this affordable family-run hotel is currently centred on a pleasant green courtyard, & there's a new 3-storey wing attached. The tiled rooms are large & en suite but with a cold shower only. *US$8/13 self-contained dbl with fan/AC.* **$**

OTHER PRACTICALITIES There are ATMs accepting Visa cards outside the **Ghana Commercial Bank** and **Africa Development Bank**. There is a nameless **internet café** about 100m east of the Ghana Commercial Bank. For other pressing matters, you could always try the wonderfully named **Talk To Jesus Phone Shop** next to the central market.

WHAT TO SEE AND DO
Kyabobo National Park Extending over some 218km² along the Togolese border, Kyabobo National Park protects a series of wooded ridges and slopes where – unusually – the closed canopy forest is currently expanding into what was formerly open woodland at a rapid rate, presumably as a result of increased rainfall. It is named after the 873m Kyabobo Peak (pronounced like 'Chabobo', and also spelt Djebobo or Dzebobo), which is Ghana's second-highest massif, but actually lies outside the park's southern border. Kyabobo supports a varied checklist of mammals, but most species are very shy, the exceptions being a few bushbuck and red-flanked duiker that haunt the immediate vicinity of the park headquarters. Elsewhere, the most commonly seen terrestrial mammal is the red river hog, while other resident species include buffalo, kob and at least four monkeys, and elephants might occasionally stray across the border from Fazao Malfacassa National Park in Togo. Given its small area, Kyabobo supports an impressive diversity of birds, with 235 species, including the little-known Baumann's bulbul and Lagden's bush-shrike, having been recorded during a pioneering expedition by the Dowsetts in 2005.

Hiking is the main activity and this can only be done in the company of a guide. Options range from a moderate 2-hour meander along the Kue River and slightly more demanding 2-hour round walk to the top of Breast Mountain to the quite arduous 4-hour climb to Laboum Falls. Note, however, that the trailhead for all these hikes is not within realistic walking distance of the park headquarters, so unless you have private transport, you'll need to cycle there (bicycles can be hired for US$2.50 per day) or arrange a taxi out of Nkwanta. A good target for birdwatchers is the Laboum Basin, which lies about one hour on foot from the park headquarters within walking distance of the main entrance gate, and hosts an excellent selection of forest birds. The riparian forest near Pawa Satellite Camp also offers excellent birding but requires an overnight stay. Brochures for the park state that other activities such as tubing and mountain-biking trails are available, but this doesn't seem to be the case on the ground.

All activities must be arranged though the **Kyabobo Visitor Centre** (m *0244 505192, 0243 202929/406002;* e *apassnabapatience@yahoo.com or aaboampong@ gmail.com; www.kyabobo.com;* ☉ *06.00–18.00 daily*), which lies at the park headquarters only 2km northeast of Nkwanta (a 25–30-minute walk or short taxi ride). There is also a six-room **guesthouse** at the visitor centre, charging US$11 for a double with shared bath or US$14 for a self-contained double, as well as a campsite with a few standing tents for US$5 per person. Beers and sodas are sold at the headquarters, and the guesthouse has a fully equipped kitchen with a gas cooker and fridge, but you need to bring all your food yourself. An entrance fee of US$5 is charged to non-Ghanaians, while the fee for a mandatory guide is US$2.50 per person per hour. Kyabobo has a terrible reputation for biting insects, so hikers are advised to wear long sleeves and long trousers, with socks pulled over. It can be visited throughout the year, but hiking conditions can be challenging during the height of the rains (June–October).

Shiyari Situated at an altitude of 600m on the slopes of Mount Kyabobo some 13km from Nkwanta along a very poor road, the Akyode (Guan) village of Shiyari is known for its picturesque terraced houses, cool misty climate, and a pair of nearby waterfalls and fetish shrine. The car park below the village can be reached by bus from Nkwanta on Monday, the local market day. On other days you'll almost certainly have to charter a taxi. Either way you must be prepared to walk the last steep uphill stretch to the village, which takes about one hour. Before visiting the waterfalls, you must visit the local chief, who may help arrange a guide if he takes a shine to you, but has also been known to refuse access to tourists for no obvious reason. One of the waterfalls can be seen only from a distance, while the other is approachable only via a narrow and rather dangerous (but also very beautiful) 30-minute footpath flanked by a slippery hill to the left and a wooded abyss to the right.

Also somewhat nearby, the profoundly isolated village of **Kyilinga** is reachable by another 8km of winding footpaths heading east from Shiyari towards the Togolese border. It is possible to visit independently, but you could also arrange a guide through the Kyabobo Visitors Centre.

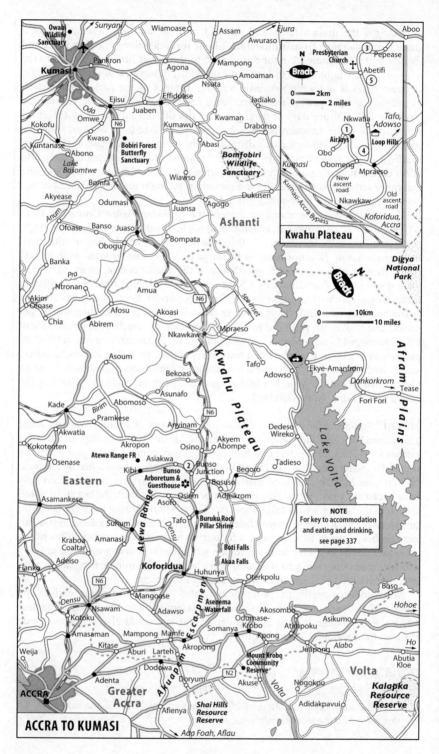

Kwahu Plateau

Presbyterian Church

N

0 — 2km
0 — 2 miles

Pepease
Abetifi
Nkwatia
Tafo, Adowso
Airleys
Loop Hills
Obo
Kumasi
Obomeng
Mpraeso
New ascent road
Nkawkaw
Koforidua, Accra
Kumasi-Accra Bypass
Old ascent road

Owabi Wildlife Sanctuary
Sunyani
Wiamoase
Assam
Ejura
Aboo
Awuraso
Kumasi
Pankron
Agona
Mampong
Amoaman
Nsuta
Effiduase
Jadiako
Ejisu
Juaben
Kwaman
Drabonso
Kokofu
Omwe
Oda
Juaben
Kumawu
Abasi
Kwaso
Kuntanase
Abono
Bobiri Forest Butterfly Sanctuary
Wiawso
Bomfobiri Wildlife Sanctuary
Lake Bosomtwe
Bomfa
Akyease
Odumasi
Juansa
Agogo
Dukusen
Ashanti
Ofoase
Banso
Juaso
Bompata
Obogu
Banka
Pra
Ntronan
Amua
Digya National Park
Akim Ofoase
Afosu
Akoasi
Chia
Abirem
Nkawkaw
Mpraeso
N
Asoum
Bekoasi
Tafo
Adowso
Ekye-Amanfrom
Donkorkrom
Tease
Kade
Birim
Abomoso
Asunafo
Fori Fori
Akwatia
Pramkese
Anyinam
Akyem Abompe
Dedeso Wireko
Kwahu Plateau
Kokotenten
Akropon
Osino
Osenase
Atewa Range FR
Asiakwa
Bunso Junction
Tadieso
Kibi
Bunso Arboretum & Guesthouse
Bosuso
Begoro
Lake Volta
Eastern
Osiem
Adjeikrom
Asamankese
Asofo
Tafo
Buruku Rock Pillar Shrine
NOTE
For key to accommodation and eating and drinking, see page 337
Sukum
Amanasi
Boti Falls
Kraboa Coaltar
Adeiso
Akaa Falls
Koforidua
Fianko
Huhunya
Oterkpolu
Baso
Densu
Nsawam
Mangoose
Asenema Waterfall
Hohoe
Kotoku
Adawso
Akosombo
Asikumo
Amasaman
Mampong
Mamfe
Somanya
Odumase-Krobo
Atimpoku
Alabo
Ho
Weija
Kitase
Aburi
Larteh
Akropong
Kpong
Juapong
Abutia Kloe
Dodowa
Mount Krobo Community Reserve
Volta
Adenta
Doryum
Akuse
Nogokpo
Kalapka Resource Reserve
ACCRA
Greater Accra
Afienya
Shai Hills Resource Reserve
Adidakpavui

ACCRA TO KUMASI

Ada Foah, Aflau

Koforidua and the Kumasi Road

Two main routes, both around 270km in length, link Accra to Kumasi, connecting at Bunso Junction (also known as Linda Dor after the restaurant and rest stop there) slightly less than halfway to Kumasi. Most coaches and other direct public transport prefer the more direct western route through the unremarkable towns of Nsawam and Suhum, while the eastern route through Aburi and Koforidua is typically a more engaging ride for those with private transport.

The route through Koforidua (capital of Eastern Region) is also of greater inherent interest for those who want to bus through in stages. And while most travellers shoot between Accra and Kumasi in a day, there are some worthwhile diversions for those who prefer to take things easy, notably the lovely Bunso Arboretum and a few other sites in the vicinity of Bunso Junction, and the Kwahu Plateau east of Nkawkaw. The region has also seen an unprecedented mushrooming in recreational facilities — there are now canopy walkways at both Bunso Arboretum and Obo village on the Kwahu Plateau, as well as Ghana's first ever zipline, also up on the plateau.

A more obscure route to Kumasi – but still doable in a day's travel and worth looking at if you are coming from Volta Region – involves using a combination of motor ferries and road transport from Kpandu on the eastern lakeshore via the Afram Plains to Nkawkaw on the main Accra–Kumasi road.

KOFORIDUA

Koforidua (or Koff-town, as it's often called locally), set at an altitude of 200m some 60km north of Accra as the crow flies, is the focal point of the 110km² New-Juaben Municipal District, which supports a population of 185,000. Though short on identifiable tourist attractions, Koforidua has a lively atmosphere and a good range of hotels, restaurants and other facilities, making it a pleasant enough place to spend a night or two. It is of specific interest to craft enthusiasts for its celebrated bead market, which is now open daily except Sundays, while other local attractions include the Boti Falls, about 15km northeast of town, and the Bunso Arboretum about 30km north along the Kumasi road.

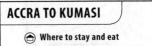

ACCRA TO KUMASI

🛏 **Where to stay and eat**

1 Jays Lodge *p350*
2 Linda Dor Rest Stop *p342*
3 Modak Royal *p351*
4 Ohene Nana Classic *p349*
5 Top *p351*

HISTORY Koforidua as we know it is a relatively modern settlement. It was established in the 19th century by refugees from the Juaben district of Ashanti, led by Nana Kwaku Boateng, who were forced into exile after they staged an unsuccessful revolt against the Asantehene, and granted land by

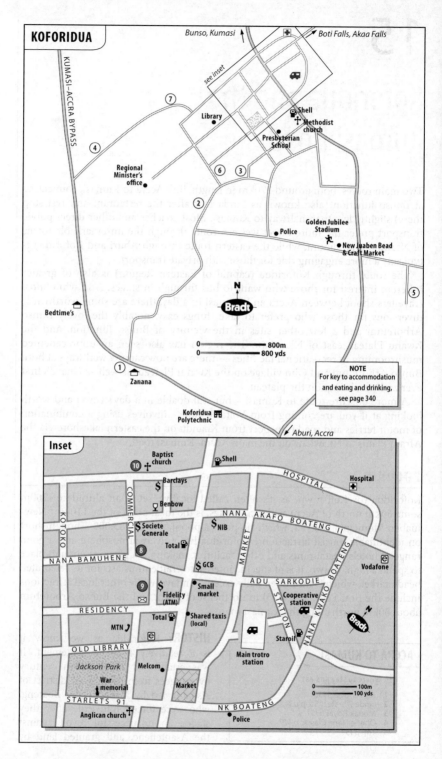

KOFORIDUA

Bunso, Kumasi

Boti Falls, Akaa Falls

KUMASI–ACCRA BYPASS

see inset

⑦

Library

Shell

Methodist church

Presbyterian School

④

⑥ ③

Regional Minister's office

②

Police

Golden Jubilee Stadium

New Juaben Bead & Craft Market

⑤

Bedtime's

N

Bradt

0 ____ 800m
0 ____ 800 yds

①

Zanana

NOTE
For key to accommodation and eating and drinking, see page 340

Koforidua Polytechnic

Aburi, Accra

Inset

Baptist church

⑩

Shell

Barclays

$

Benbow

HOSPITAL

Hospital

KOTOKO

COMMERCIAL

Societe Generale

⑧

Total

$ NIB

NANA AKAFO BOATENG II

MARKET

NANA BAMUHENE

$ GCB

ADU SARKODIE

Vodafone

⑨

$

Fidelity (ATM)

Small market

NANA KWAKO BOATENG

Cooperative station

STATION

RESIDENCY

Total

Shared taxis (local)

Staroil

MTN

N

Bradt

OLD LIBRARY

Jackson Park

Melcom

Main trotro station

War memorial

Market

0 ____ 100m
0 ____ 100 yds

STARLETS 91

Anglican church

Police

NK BOATENG

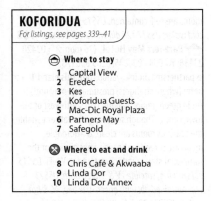

KOFORIDUA
For listings, see pages 339–41

⌂ **Where to stay**
1 Capital View
2 Eredec
3 Kes
4 Koforidua Guests
5 Mac-Dic Royal Plaza
6 Partners May
7 Safegold

✗ **Where to eat and drink**
8 Chris Café & Akwaaba
9 Linda Dor
10 Linda Dor Annex

Okyehene Nana Dokua of the Akan state of Akyem Abuakwa. Also known as New Juaben, Koforidua was founded at the base of Mount Obuotabiri, a prominent outcrop that traditionalists still regard as home to the town's gods. However, oral tradition suggests that the town's name, a condensation of 'Kofi Ofori Dua', predates the arrival of the Ashanti refugees, referring as it does to a large mahogany tree – 'dua' in the Akan language – that once stood on the land of a local farmer called Kofi Ofori and provided a shady respite for passing travellers.

Although it lies at the heart of one of Ghana's oldest cocoa production regions, Koforidua was evidently an insignificant settlement in the early colonial era (unlike, for instance, nearby Tafo, Odumase and Aburi, it doesn't feature at all on a detailed map of the Gold Coast published in 1896). However, it has been an important economic hub and route crossroads since 1915, following the completion of the railway line from Accra, which runs past the northern end of the modern town centre, and connected it as far north as Kumasi by 1923. Although Koforidua is not part of Ashanti today, it retains strong traditional links to Juaben, and the Omanhene (Chief) of New Juaben (a position occupied by Professor Daasebre Oti Boateng) remains subservient to the Asantehene.

GETTING THERE AND AWAY Coming from Accra, head out along the Legon road towards Aburi. About 15km after bypassing Aburi, turn left at Mamfe, then after a similar distance turn right at Adowso, from where it is about 20km to the southern outskirts of Koforidua. Using public transport, the most comfortable option will be one of the air-conditioned Stanbic minibuses that leave Accra from Medina Station and cost US$2.50. Ordinary trotros are slightly cheaper and leave more centrally, from both Neoplan and Tudu stations, but they are a lot less comfortable, so coming from the city centre it is probably worth getting a taxi or trotro to Medina to pick up a Stanbic.

Koforidua is an important transport hub with regular trotros and shared taxis heading in and out in most directions, for instance north to/from Bunso, Nkawkaw and Kumasi, or east to/from Somanya, Atimpoku and Akosombo. Note that when coming to or from Aburi, you will most likely need to change vehicles at Mamfe.

TOURIST INFORMATION The **Ghana Tourism Authority** office (✆ 03420 23209/32128; e eastourism@yahoo.com; ⊕ 08.00–12.30 & 13.30–17.00 Mon–Fri) for the Eastern Region is located on the third floor of the Social Security and National Insurance Trust (SSNIT) building.

WHERE TO STAY Map, opposite
Upmarket
Mac-Dic Royal Plaza Hotel (40 rooms) ✆ 03420 26476/7; m 0244 343012; e info@macdicroyalplazahotel.com; www. macdicroyalplazahotel.com. This well-run 3-star hotel is probably the pick of Koforidua's smarter

lodgings, with a pleasant peri-urban location on a 2ha plot near the Medical Village, 3km southeast of the town centre. The comfortable en-suite rooms come with Wi-Fi, AC, satellite TV, fridge, minibar & balcony. Facilities include large swimming pool, tennis court, restaurants, nightclub, conference centre & hair salon. *US$78 B&B self-contained dbl; US$87/90 deluxe dbl/twin; US$186 suite.* **$$$$$–$$$**

⌂ **Capital View Hotel** (112 rooms) ☎03420 26820–2; m 0542 504263; e cvhfrontofficegh@ gmail.com; www.capitalviewhotelgh.com. Another reliable 3-star option, the misleadingly named Capital View lies to the southwest of the town centre on the Kumasi–Accra bypass. Clean tiled rooms seem a little old-fashioned but come with king-sized bed, fan, AC, satellite TV & en-suite tub. There's a large swimming pool, & the restaurant attracts a well-heeled local crowd, with wine & a good range of tasty local, vegetarian & international dishes – although some of them won't bear much resemblance to their namesakes back home. *US$68/76 B&B self-contained sgl/dbl; suites from US$120.* **$$$$–$$$**

Moderate

⌂ **Koforidua Guests Hotel** (32 rooms) ☎03420 21112; m 0554 397149; e kduaguestshotel@gmail.com; www. koforiduaguesthotels.com. This newish & very reasonably priced hotel, set about 3km west of the town centre along a feeder road to the Kumasi bypass, is short on character but strong on service, & facilities include a good restaurant, a summer hut serving cocktails & a well-stocked gift shop. All rooms have Wi-Fi, AC, satellite TV & fridge. *US$37 self-contained dbl; US$66 executive dbl.* **$$$–$$**

Budget

⌂ **Safegold Hotel** (20 rooms) m 0244 716695. Though the rooms don't quite match up to the funky exterior decorated with traditional Ghanaian reliefs, this comfortable & reasonably priced hotel lies about 1.5km west of the town centre & has a decent restaurant attached. All

rooms are self-contained. *US$15 sgl with ¾bed & cold water; US$17–28 dbl with AC & hot water.* **$$**

⌂ **Partners May Hotel** (26 rooms) ☎03420 23138; m 0549 000845/0205 830178; e partnersmayhotel@yahoo.com. This bland 1-star hotel (where strangers, presumably, may not!) is set in green grounds about 1km southwest of the town centre. Though service can be rather variable, the spacious rooms are clean, & affordable meals are served in the well-kept garden or the somewhat starker indoor restaurant. Wi-Fi. *US$15 dbl with fan, satellite TV & shared bath; US$21 self-contained dbl with queen-size bed, AC & hot water; US$22–28 dbl with flatscreen TV & king-sized bed.* **$$**

Shoestring

⌂ **Eredec Hotel** (40 rooms) ☎03420 24265; m 0262 444244/0246 164134. Fashion hasn't been kind to this self-consciously modernist 1970s hotel, which still proudly displays its 2003 Budget Hotel of the Year award at reception. Get past the starkly angular architecture, however, & it seems a pleasant enough place, with an out-of-town location just past Partners May Hotel, reasonably priced self-contained chalets with TV & fan, an adequate restaurant, & large green & (like everything else) poorly tended gardens. *US$7/10 self-contained sgl/dbl with fan; US$12 dbl with AC.* **$**

⌂ **Kes Hotel** (25 rooms) m 0279 244555/0242 651721. This brightly painted 3-storey cheapie has prompted excellent feedback from readers, & while it is the closest lodging to the town centre, it's still quite a walk from the trotro station. There's now an on-site restaurant. *US$13 dbl with fan & shared bath; US$16 self-contained dbl with AC.* **$$–$**

✖ WHERE TO EAT AND DRINK *Map, page 338*

The hotels listed above all have restaurants and bars, but there are also some good stand-alone eateries in the town centre, along with the usual scattering of undistinguished but serviceable drinking spots. A pastry shop next to the Linda Dor Restaurant sells inexpensive fresh bread, pies, cakes and burgers.

✖ **Chris Café & Akwaaba Restaurant** ☎03420 22706; m 0244 450214; e chriscafe@ ymail.com; ⊕ 06.00–23.00 daily. Spanning 2 floors of the central SSNIT building, this popular venue comprises an airy formal restaurant serving

a selection of Ghanaian, Chinese & European dishes (including unusual accompaniments like mashed & boiled potato) for around US$5–6, as well as a cheaper café & an outdoor 'tilapia spot' serving tilapia & banku. It's good for b/fasts, too. **$$–$**

✗ Linda Dor Restaurant ☎ 03420 24236;
⊕ 06.30–23.00 daily. Assuming you aren't
dazzled by the excessive décor or above-average
prices, this long-standing AC restaurant, at the
north end of the town centre diagonally opposite
Barclays, is highly recommended. It has a varied
menu ranging from steaks & pizzas to spaghetti &
Chinese dishes, with most costing US$7–10. **$$**

✗ Linda Dor Annex ☎ 03420 22875;
⊕ 06.30–22.00 daily. The older & more central the
2 restaurants run by Linda Dor is also more down
to earth, with enthusiastically whirring fans rather
than AC, & it serves a good selection of local &
exotic dishes for around US$5. **$**

OTHER PRACTICALITIES
Foreign exchange There are several banks in the town centre, including **Barclays**
and **Ghana Commercial**, both of which have a forex desk and a 24-hour ATM where
local currency can be drawn against a Visa (and MasterCard in the case of GCB).

Internet Several internet cafés are dotted around town.

Shopping Less celebrated than the suburban bead market, the **Central Market**
at the main intersection at the south end of the town centre is chaotic and fun to
explore. The Melcom just opposite the market sells a good selection of packaged
food and household goods.

WHAT TO SEE AND DO
New Juaben Bead and Craft Market Koforidua's main tourist attraction is its
long-standing bead market, which relocated from Jackson Park to a customised
site that lies next to the Golden Jubilee Park, about 2km south of the town centre,
and was formally opened in May 2011 by the late President John Atta Mills. It vies
with Odumase Krobo (page 302) as the country's best bead market, but is perhaps
more attractive to serious buyers as it has a less chaotic atmosphere and is open
daily except Sunday. Traditionally, however, it has always been busiest on Thursday,
which is when craftsmen and -women from all over Ghana descend on Koforidua,
as well as the occasional merchant from Burkina Faso, Mali, Togo or further afield,
to trade in beads both antique and modern. Strings of new beads are often very
inexpensive, but expect to pay considerably more for older pieces, which are often
sold individually. There is also a small trade in ready-made pieces of jewellery,
which can make good gifts, but steer clear of any ivory for obvious reasons. In
theory, the market is open from 07.00–17.30 daily, but it tends to be busiest and
have the biggest choice of goods for sale from mid morning to mid afternoon. A
taxi from the town centre to the market costs around US$3, and facilities include
public toilets in the government building next door, and a small café where you can
get a cold drink. There is no ATM close by, so bring enough cash.

Boti Falls (m 024 3144912; ⊕ 08.00–17.30 daily; entrance US$3) The 30m-high
seasonal Boti Falls, on the Pawnpawn River in the Boti Forest Reserve to the
northeast of Koforidua, is one of the most attractive in Ghana. It is most impressive
during the rains, but the flow decreases greatly during the dry season, when the
waterfall usually splits into two separate streams before drying up altogether. The
pool at the base, reached by a sequence of 250 concrete steps, is safe for swimming,
provided that you keep clear of the waterfall itself, especially in the rainy season.
The scene is made by the surrounding forest, which boasts many enormous trees,
including flamboyants with their striking red flowers. Do watch out for army ants
on the way down – on a bad day they are everywhere, and it might be worth tucking

your trousers into your socks to keep them at bay! The Boti Falls is a sacred site, and the setting for a celebration every year on 1 July. Many thousands of Ghanaians visit the waterfall on this day, but foreign visitors are welcome to participate.

The rainforest around the waterfall once harboured chimpanzees and various monkey species, and although these have been hunted out, it still supports many different birds and butterflies. It's no problem to arrange a guided walk along other forest paths for a negotiable fee, or to explore the forest fringing the Agogo road on your own. Further afield, you can arrange guided walks to the so-called Umbrella Stone, known locally as Akataman, and a three-headed palm tree more than 3m tall. The round trip to these two sites takes around 2 hours, and is tough going in parts (you'll need proper walking shoes), but worth it for the great views and atmospheric jungle setting.

Getting there and away Boti Falls lies 21km from Koforidua, a 30-minute drive. To get there, follow the surfaced road northeast to Huhunya via Kurakan, then take the signposted fork to the left, a 7km dirt road that can be driven in any vehicle. If you're using public transport, a trotro from Koforidua to Agogo, a small village seldom shown on maps, will drop you at the entrance to the falls.

Where to stay and eat If you want to stay the night, a basic **self-contained chalet** overlooking the waterfall can be rented for around US$8–10, and camping is permitted. The caretaker will bring water for washing and can arrange for somebody to do your cooking. He keeps two fridges loaded up with ice-cold mineral water, soft drinks and beer, as well as a supply of biscuits and tinned sardines. You can buy other basic foodstuffs at a village 1km up the road, or arrange for the caretaker (who has a car) to run into Agogo to buy you meat or chicken.

Akaa Falls Cascading into a narrow forest-fringed canyon about 2km from Boti Falls, and along the same river, the less publicised Akaa Falls feel rather quiet and undiscovered by comparison, and some Koforidua locals prefer them. They can be visited as an alternative to Boti, or as part of the same outing. Coming from Koforidua, Akaa lies on the left side of the road about 2km before Boti Falls. The fee is US$1.50 per person, and the base of the waterfall is reached via a scenic set of 250 concrete steps. There is also some old playground equipment for kids. After seeing the waterfall, ask the caretaker to take you to the flat-topped Lookout Rock, which is reached via a rather unstable bamboo ladder, but offers amazing views over the forest below.

BUNSO AND SURROUNDS

The intersection of the main Accra–Kumasi road and the alternative route via Aburi and Koforidua – though officially called Bunso (or Bunso Junction) – is now almost universally referred to as 'Linda Dor' after the iconic Linda Dor Highway Rest Stop restaurant that opened there in 2006. This is the main rest stop for coaches, Stanbics and trotros between Accra and Kumasi, and it consists of numerous stalls selling fresh and packaged food, a canteen-like rest stop, and the classy restaurant at the **Linda Dor Rest Stop** (m *0542 377435/0543 990554; map, page 336*), a branch of its popular namesake in Koforidua serving a varied selection of mains for around US$8.

Stalls and restaurants aside, there's not much else to see at the actual junction that marks the convergence of the two main routes between Ghana's two largest cities. But Bunso Junction does lie at the epicentre of several low-key but worthwhile

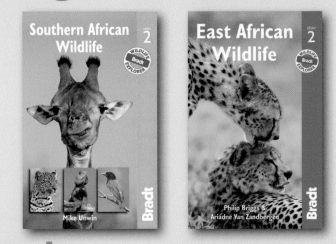

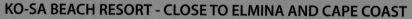

attractions. The best known of these, situated alongside the Koforidua road only 4km south of Linda Dor, is the Bunso Arboretum. Another 5km south of this, the small town of Osiem lies at the junction of a side road east to the cocoa-growing centre of Adjeikrom and pretty highland town of Begoro. In the opposite direction, rising to the west of the Accra road, and accessible from the small town of Asiakwa 6km from Linda Dor, the forested Atewa Range is of particular interest to birders. Finally, heading in the direction of Kumasi, the village of Akyem Abompe, reached along a side road branching east at Osino, 6.5km north of Linda Dor, is an important traditional centre of bauxite bead production.

BUNSO ARBORETUM (m *0244 527418*; ⏰ *07.00–17.00 daily*; *entry US$1pp*) Located on the west side of the surfaced road from Koforidua, only 4km south of Bunso Junction, the Bunso Arboretum is set amidst the lushly vegetated hills drained by the Birim River and its tributaries. It lies on land leased by a local chief to a gold-dredging company in 1905, and converted to an arboretum after being acquired by Achimota College in 1937. Having been taken over by the Ministry of Agriculture in 1946, the hillside arboretum is now managed by the Plant Genetic Resources Centre (PGRC). Its 16.5 hectares are split evenly between indigenous semi-deciduous forest and stands of introduced trees and herbs maintained for research purposes, including 70-year-old palms and the country's only Brazil nut trees.

Developed for tourism with the assistance of the Nature Conservation Research Centre (NCRC) and Peace Corps, the arboretum is traversed by a network of nature trails allowing visitors to learn more about uses for the various indigenous and exotic crop plants, fruit trees, timber species and herbs, around 70 of which are labelled for ease of reference. More than 130 bird and 300 butterfly species have been recorded, and there's a butterfly sanctuary within the grounds. Worthwhile guided tours lasting about 45 minutes are available for US$4, or you can explore the trails through the gardens and forest yourself.

Since 2014, the arboretum has also been home to Ghana's second **canopy walk** (*US$5/9 foreigners/students*). Set 38m into the treetops, the five spans run for a total of 210m, making it nearly two-thirds the length of its counterpart at Kakum National Park (pages 207–13). Rather frighteningly, it was closed due to an accident in 2015 in which a visiting school group is said to have overloaded one of the spans, leading to 20 injuries. The next months were spent repairing and re-engineering the affected areas, and the walkway reopened for business — with the inspection and blessing of the Ghana Institution of Engineers — in February 2016. Provided the capacity limits are strictly observed, we'd be happy to make the crossing ourselves.

Getting there and away The prominently signposted entrance gate, on the main Koforidua–Kumasi road, about 5km north of Osiem and 4km south of Bunso Junction, is difficult to miss. Coming from Koforidua, any transport heading towards Nkawkaw or Kumasi can drop you there. There is also a pretty steady stream of transport coming south from Bunso Junction towards Osiem.

🏠 **Where to stay and eat**

🏠 **Bunso Arboretum Guesthouse**
(5 rooms) m 0244 527418; e peprahbaffoe@ yahoo.com. Situated about 1km from the entrance gate on a hilltop offering great views, this pleasant guesthouse was closed for renovations in early 2016, but plans exist to reopen it before year's end.

If so (perhaps call ahead), guests can expect self-contained rooms, a patio, & a self-catering kitchen, but visitors must either bring their own food or drive/catch a trotro to eat at Linda Dor, 4km north of the entrance gate. *US$16 self-contained dbl, US$8pp to rent a tent.* **$$–$**

🏠 Cocoa Research Institute Guesthouse (12 rooms) 🅜 0277 609900/15. Situated in New Tafo about 25km north of Koforidua & 15km south of Bunso, this smart guesthouse in large well-tended grounds has immaculate rooms with AC. Preference given to researchers & booking is advised. *Around US$20/35 self-contained dbl/chalet.* **$$**

🏠 Echo Guesthouse (10 rooms) 🅜 0243 805921. Also situated in New Tafo, in the small housing estate behind the hospital, Echo has clean rooms & serves meals & drinks on request. *US$9 self-contained dbl.* **$**

ADJEIKROM Developed in association with Peace Corps, **Adjeikrom Cocoa Tours** (🅜 *0243 412016*) is based in the eponymous village, which lies at an elevation of around 270m and is unusual in that its inhabitants are all Ga even though the area is part of Akyem Abuakwa. Adjeikrom was the birthplace of Dr Ebenezer Ako-Adjei, a member of Ghana's 'Big Six', the name given to the core band of freedom fighters, including former president Kwame Nkrumah, who plotted Ghana's independence (and who now appear on all cedi notes except GHC2).

Based in a visitor centre on the left as you enter the village, Adjeikrom Cocoa Tours offers a guided demonstration of the ins and outs of cocoa harvesting, from pod-breaking to fermentation and drying process, for US$2.50 per person. Guided mountain and forest walks are also available for US$3 per person. The village lies 7km east of Osiem Junction; any trotro or bus heading from Koforidua to Begoro can drop you there. A budget **guesthouse** attached to the visitor centre offers basic rooms without electricity for US$4/6 single/double with shared bucket shower. Meals are available for around US$3 by prior arrangement.

BEGORO This town of 30,000, capital of Fanteakwa District, lies at a relatively refreshing altitude of 465m in the Akwapim Hills, at the southern end of the Kwahu Plateau. Though something of a backwater today, it was chosen as the site of a pioneering Presbyterian mission in 1875 (look for the arch near the Presbyterian church reading 'Presbyterian Boarding School 1885'), a decision influenced by its pleasant and relatively disease-free mid-altitude climate. Also worth a look is Fanteakwa's Palace, with its distinctive colonial architecture and the large murals of musicians on the outer wall. About 20 minutes' walk from the old mission site, Begoro Falls, dropping about 15m from a large overhang, is little more than a trickle in the dry season (though you can still wade knee-deep into the pool below for a refreshing natural shower), but more impressive during the rains.

Getting there and away Begoro lies 21km east of Osiem, a small town straddling the main road between Koforidua and Kumasi about 9km south of Bunso Junction. Coming from Koforidua, there are direct trotros and Metro Mass buses to Begoro. From elsewhere, ask any Koforidua-bound vehicle to drop you at Osiem and wait for transport there.

An adventurous onward option from Begoro follows the road descending from the Akwapim Hills via Abuoso to Dodeso on the Lake Volta shore. A good unsurfaced road as far as Abuoso is covered by regular shared taxis. Road conditions deteriorate on the descent to Dodeso, and public transport is often non-existent, but this is compensated for by some fantastic scenery in a rock-strewn valley offering occasional views across the western arm of Lake Volta to the Afram Plains.

From Dodeso, a rough road follows the lakeshore to Adowso, which has regular trotro connections to Nkawkaw (on the main Accra–Kumasi road) and is also the site of the ferry crossing to the Afram Plains. The road between Dodeso and Adowso is very little used, but there is occasional public transport on most stretches, and you could walk the other parts. The road is punctuated by fishing villages, notably Mpaem, Kwahu Amanforum, New Worobon, Nketepa (very large market with much fresh produce), Asuboni and Okragyei. Formal accommodation is not readily available, but requests to village chiefs or people you meet along the way may well lead to a room being offered, or church or school buildings being made available.

Where to stay and eat

Hillside Hotel (19 rooms) m 0244 379595/0204 379595; e charlesparry@hotmail.com. About 2km out of Begoro back along the road to Osiem, this agreeable & well-liked lodge has a small garden & offers views across a valley to forested hills. A comfortable restaurant with tiled floors & wooden chairs serves meals for around US$5. *US$11 sgl with shared bath; US$22 self-contained dbl with hot water; AC & satellite TV.* **$$–$**

Dorcas Hotel (7 rooms) \0342 022534; m 0243 357497. Situated right in Begoro town centre next to the junction leading uphill to the mission, this is a step down from the Hillside & has received some negative reader feedback, but there's a ground-floor restaurant & rather dingy rooms with fans upstairs. *US$8/11 sgl/dbl using shared bath; US$14 self-contained dbl.* **$**

ATEWA RANGE FOREST RESERVE Rising to the west of the main Accra–Kumasi road, the little-known 236km² Atewa Range Forest Reserve, which reaches an elevation of 770m, is listed as a Globally Significant Biodiversity Area in recognition of its unusually rich fauna. The reserve was set aside in 1926 to protect one of only two upland evergreen forests in Ghana, and it remains the country's best-preserved example of this habitat, despite extensive logging activity in recent years. It is also an important watershed, forming the source of the Ayensu and Densu rivers, both of which flow south into the Atlantic, as well as the Birim, which runs north and then southwest around the Atewa Range before becoming a tributary of the Pra River. Though it's still reasonably well-preserved, Atewa remains threatened by a combination of illegal logging, hunting, artisanal gold mining and land clearance for farming. In response to this, 2013 saw the launch of the Save Atewa Forest campaign (*www.saveatiwa.com.gh*) in partnership with the London-based conservation NGO A Rocha International (*www.arocha.org*), which hopes to both involve surrounding communities in the forest's maintenance, as well as improve the reserve's more or less non-existent tourism infrastructure.

A remarkable total of 400-plus butterfly species, including six endemics, has been recorded within this relatively small area of forest. These include the spectacular African giant swallowtail (*Papilio antimachus*), whose 20cm wingspan makes it a contender for the world's largest butterfly. Mammals include black-and-white colobus, olive colobus and Campbell's mona monkey, but half a dozen other monkey species are known to occur, along with four types of duiker. The spectacular bongo antelope used to be common but has been hunted close to extinction. It is one of the last strongholds of the critically endangered frog, *Conraua derooi*.

The birding is extremely productive – indeed, some experts rank it as highly as Kakum and Ankassa national parks, with the advantage that you don't need to pay the fees. A checklist of 200-plus species includes several highland forest dwellers with a limited distribution elsewhere within Ghana, for instance long-tailed hawk, crowned eagle, Afep pigeon, olive long-tailed cuckoo, African broadbill, Western least honeyguide, spotted honeyguide, yellow-throated olive greenbul, bristlebill and blue-headed crested flycatcher. Adam Riley adds 'Atewa is also a good site for the endangered rufous-winged illadopsis, dazzling but elusive blue-headed bee-eater, and the impressive great blue turaco, as well as Narina trogon, little green woodpecker, square-tailed saw-wing swallow, black-capped apalis, olivaceous and dusky crested-flycatcher, chestnut and red-cheeked wattle-eye, Bates's sunbird, many-coloured bush-shrike and green-backed twinspot.

Getting there and away Best visited during the drier months, the forest reserve is not formally organised for tourism, but keen birdwatchers and walkers are welcome, though they should be prepared for sweaty conditions. From Bunso Junction, the unsignposted main entry point lies 12km back along the Accra road. Coming from the direction of Accra, it is 8km past the quite substantial town of Kibi.

Noëlle and Hervé Jacob, who spent several days at Atewa in 2012, write that: 'Here, coming from Kibi, is a small trail to the left on an ascent just before a right bend. Park here, or a few meters further on the trail (there is a pink house on the right), and always go straight. The trail starts in plantations with many birds, then ascends past a blue gate to a small clearing with a trail on the right going to a stream. Further on is another clearing, which seems to be at the top, as a trail continues and turns right onto a plateau (where we saw the blue-headed bee-eaters).' If all this sounds too uncertain, visit the Forestry Office in Kibi, where a guide can be organised to direct you along the forest trails – no fee is charged but a decent tip will be expected.

Where to stay and eat The most attractive option, even though it is a bit of a drive away (and assuming it's reopened), is the **guesthouse** at Bunso Arboretum (page 343). There are also a few quite basic hotels in Kibi, including the **Hotel Asonaba** (m *0244 937656*) and **Ankobea Guesthouse** (m *0242 051563*), both charging around US$10 for a double room. Similar no-frills options in Asiakwa, a small town about 4km past the entry point for the forest and only 5km before Bunso Junction (and excellent Linda Dor Restaurant!) include the **Alexco Hotel** (m *0244 813303*) and **Hilltop Hotel** (m *0242 867716*).

AKYEM ABOMPE Ghana's main centre of bauxite bead production, the sprawling village of Akyem Abompe lies below the Abompe Hills, a tall, forested scarp whose striking cliffs are where the rock used to make the beads is quarried. Unfortunately, the Abompe Traditional Beadmaking Tours once offered here by a community-based ecotourism project seem to be no more. It still may be possible to witness the labour-intensive process by which these rough brown beads are made, but purely in an informal capacity.

This is confirmed by Anita Low, who writes: 'The NGO once operating here at Akyem Abompe is closed. There are only a couple of old people able to show you how the beads are made. We met one old man who was working away on beads when we arrived, and he seemed delighted to show us the process. It was very interesting but you had the feeling you were seeing a good and viable way of life disappearing. The old man told us the young people were leaving to work in the gold mines, and that there is also a lot of illegal mining, which causes tension in the area. All in all, it is a very sad situation.'

A more recent – and still viable – project at Akyem Abompe is **Bamboosero** (m *0246 427438;* e *peasahfelix@gmail.com; www.bamboosero.com*), a small team of bike-builders who make mountain and cargo bikes from bamboo. Hand crafted from locally harvested bamboo and using a robust Taiwanese parts kit, the completed bikes are exported to California with profits then ploughed back into the local community. Visitors are welcome to watch the workers and can even learn how to make their own bikes.

Getting there and away Akyem Abompe lies about 5km east of the Kumasi road, along a side road signposted to the right at the village of Osino, 6.5km north of Bonsu Junction. While you are in the area, there is also a batik and tie-dye workshop and a professional woodcarving factory at Osino. And if you are interested in buying bauxite beads (rather than seeing them being made), they are sold at a stall on the main road through the junction town of Osino.

THE KWAHU PLATEAU

Stretching some 250km from northwest to southeast, the Kwahu (or Kwawu) Plateau is arguably the most important watershed in Ghana, separating its two major river networks, as well as forming a seldom-traversed mountainous divide between the main Accra–Kumasi road and the western arm of Lake Volta. With an average elevation of around 450m, and a maximum altitude of 762m, this extensive highland boasts a relatively temperate and disease-free climate, one that proved highly attractive to early missionaries, who established many churches and schools in the hills. Though seldom visited by travellers today, the plateau offers some worthwhile opportunities for off-the-beaten-track exploration. The most obvious goals for short forays are Abetifi, which is the highest town on the plateau, and the traverse road via Mpraeso to the ferry terminus at Adowso on the eastern shore of Lake Volta (for more details, see box, pages 348–9). The plateau is well endowed with hotels and easy to get around on public transport, but there is not much in the way of an organised tourist infrastructure, which can be a blessing or a curse, depending on your viewpoint – certainly it is one of the few comparably scenic parts of Ghana that can be explored independently without any pressure to engage guides or embark on formal activities. See inset on map, page 336, for more details.

NKAWKAW Situated about 50km northwest of Bunso Junction and 100km southeast of Kumasi, Nkawkaw is the district capital of Kwahu West and main road springboard to the Kwahu Plateau, which rises in spectacular fashion immediately to the east. A rather scruffy town of 60,000, it is dominated by a long, winding main road that must rank close to being the most hectic and pedestrian-unfriendly in Ghana, though it has calmed down somewhat since the construction of the Accra–Kumasi bypass several years back. Since 2003, the cliffs above the town have been the site of the annual **Ghana Paragliding Festival** (*www.ghanaparagliding.com*), a fun fundraising event that also includes traditional ceremonies and live music, and is held over three days every Easter.

Getting there and away Nkawkaw is a major transport hub, and plenty of transport runs there from Accra, Kumasi and most places in between. Note that if you are driving yourself on to the Kwahu Plateau, you have the choice of two ascent roads from Nkawkaw to Mpraeso. The old 9km direct road, signposted to the northeast at the main intersection in Nkawkaw, was closed for surfacing works in early 2016, but it's as scenic as any road in Ghana, following a dramatic series of switchbacks up a jungle-clad slope. The newer and better-maintained 10km road via Obomeng, which leaves Nkawkaw about 1km further towards Kumasi, was the only way up or down the plateau when we visited.

⌂ **Where to stay and eat** In the unlikely event that you need to overnight there, it is also well endowed with budget and moderate hotels, ranging from the flash **Rojo Hotel** (*34 rooms;* ☏ *03431 22221;* m *0244 250593; US$32/37 self-contained with queen-/king-sized bed*), which has a swimming pool and views of the escarpment from some rooms, to the cheaper **Top Way Hotel** (m *0208 559770/0245 476633;* e *samboah@live.com; rooms in the US$10–25 range*), both on the Mpraeso road. Plenty of street food is available along the main road through the town centre, and there is a reasonable restaurant with indoor and outdoor seating behind the Goil garage.

CROSSING LAKE VOLTA VIA THE AFRAM PLAINS

Stephen Gee, updated by Philip Briggs

The Afram Plains is a sparsely populated and poorly developed part of Eastern Region that has found itself isolated since the creation of Lake Volta, which forms its southern and eastern boundaries. The economy is based on subsistence agriculture. The soil is very fertile and it was once a cocoa-growing region. In recent times, possibly due to the creation of the lake, the climate has changed sufficiently to cause cocoa harvests to fail and leave the population with little or no exportable produce. For these reasons the Afram Plains is considered by the present government to be an underdeveloped region of Ghana.

Owing to the poor condition of the roads to the north, transport to and from the plains entails crossing the lake by ferry only, and electricity is supplied only to those settlements along the route linking the main town of Donkorkrom with the ferry ports of Ekye-Amanfrom (for Adowso) and Agordeke (for Kpandu). However, the westerly ferry between Agordeke and Kpandu broke down in 2011 and was still not operating five years later. This means that, for the time being, the full trip cannot be undertaken in a private car, but it is still possible using public transport, since smaller boats with room for maybe 50 foot passengers still provide an informal link between Agordeke and Kpandu.

The Afram Plains lack any tourist attractions of note, but the boat crossings from Kpandu and Adowso can be enchanting in the morning mist, and the sense of isolation from the urbanity of Accra or Kumasi, or even from the relatively cosmopolitan likes of Ho or Hohoe, will provide a more balanced view of modern Ghana. The views across the lake are also very pretty. More pragmatically, for those travelling between the eastern highlands and Kumasi, the route through the Afram Plains offers an appealing and adventurous alternative to the longer road via Koforidua or Accra, one that can be undertaken without having to sit for too many hours in hot and bumpy trotros. The route is described below from east to west, but it could as easily be travelled in the reverse direction.

The eastern springboard for the trip across the Afram Plains is Kpandu (see pages 321–4). The ferry service from Agordeke used to leave at 06.00 and 11.00 and Kpandu at 08.00 and 13.00 daily, taking about two hours in either direction, but this shows no signs of returning any time soon. For the foreseeable future, there is only an informal boat service for foot passengers. This doesn't run to any fixed schedule, but there are usually one to three departures daily, mainly in the morning.

When you arrive on foot at Agordeke, which has quite a pleasant beach with a small bar selling drinks and snacks, you'll need to board one of the trotros that take about 40 minutes to reach the regional capital, Donkorkrom. In the past,

MPRAESO Nkawkaw's high-altitude twin, Mpraeso is perched at an elevation of 475m atop the sandstone cliffs that lie immediately to the east of Nkawkaw. The district capital of Kwahu South, it is the main junction town on the east side of the hills, where the two ascent roads from Nkawkaw converge with the road running north to Abetifi and Abene and the road running northeast to Kwahu Tafo and Adowso. Mpraeso is surrounded by protected forests, which can be explored with the permission of the helpful Forestry Services Division office, 200m uphill from the roundabout on the Obomeng road. Regular passenger taxis run from Nkawkaw and Mpraeso, and the pick of a few inexpensive lodges is the **Ohene Nana Classic**

heavy rainfall could transform the poor road from Agordeke to Donkorkrom into an impassable one, but this has improved following recent roadworks.

The best place to stay in Donkorkrom is St Michael's Hotel (✆ *03424 22043;* m *0209 019079*), where self-contained rooms with a fan and television cost around US$15, but there is also the cheaper Genesis Guesthouse. St Michael's Hotel also serves food but it is advisable to let staff know in advance if you intend to eat there. There are also a number of street vendors and chop bars where you can try the local grasscutter. Fresh produce is available at Donkorkrom, particularly on the market days of Wednesday and Thursday – enjoyable unless the smell of fish makes you ill – but better markets can be found at Kpandu and Nkawkaw before arriving in the Afram Plains.

In Donkorkrom, a very enthusiastic local entrepreneur has set up a tie-dye and batik business called Stephanmanu Enterprises, where you can buy ready-made fabrics or, if you want a more personal souvenir, create your own unique design in his workshop at very reasonable prices (creating your own design takes up to three hours). The shop can be found in the main market and the workshop is just a 10-minute walk away. There's a Ghana Commercial Bank with ATM in town, and Donkorkrom Hospital can cope with many medical problems. Fuel is available here, as well as in Forefori, Ekye-Amanfrom and Tease.

Donkorkrom is of note as the southern administrative centre for Ghana's second-largest conservation area, Digya National Park, which extends over 3,750km^2 north of the Afram Plains and west of Lake Volta. Proclaimed in 1971, Digya has never formally opened to the public because of difficulty of access, but its potential is enormous, thanks to a remarkable diversity of habitats and a mammal checklist that includes red-flanked duiker, elephant, manatee, hippopotamus, buffalo, lion, leopard, bongo antelope and half a dozen species of monkey. Until recently, the park was practically unknown in ornithological terms, but its rich biodiversity is reflected by an incredible tally of 297 bird species recorded by the Dowsetts over three pioneering expeditions in 2005, 2008 and 2009, and further exploration is almost certain to produce a checklist of well over 300 species. (A detailed report on their expeditions can be found at www.africanbirdclub.org/sites/default/files/MiscRep57%28Digya%29.pdf). It is presumably only a matter of time before this alluring park is developed for tourism; check with the wildlife division in Donkorkrom for the current details. The wildlife division in Atebubu manages the northern sector of the park.

Moving on from Donkorkrom, trotros south to the port of Ekye-Amanfrom (or just Ekye – pronounced 'echay' – to its friends) generally take about 90 minutes. Trotros in both directions work around the ferry timetable between Ekye and Adowso, which lies at the northern base of the Kwahu Plateau – for details of the ferry, see pages 351–2.

15

Hotel (m *0209 690002/0208 175084; map, page 336*), which lies 1km from the main junction in the direction of Abetifi, and charges US$18/26 for a self-contained singlegl/double with air-conditioning. There's a Ghana Commercial Bank with ATM here as well.

OBO   About 560m above sea level, the tranquil small town of Obo is a destination of choice for wealthy Kwahu residents when it comes time to build their vacation homes, and the sheer number of unexpectedly large houses lining the road into town from Obomeng indicate there are more than a few sons and daughters of Kwahu who've gone on to do quite well for themselves in Accra and beyond. The town is also renowned for producing an outsized number of musicians, but none bigger than highlife star Nana Kwame Ampadu, who founded the legendary African Brothers Band in 1963.

Today, though, Obo is home to one of the plateau's most unexpected and welcome tourist developments in the form of a new canopy walkway and Ghana's first ever zip-line course. Privately run, they're part of the Jays Lodge & AirJays complex, which sits about 2.2km from the Nkawkaw road junction in Obomeng. Zip line and canopy activities are booked at AirJays (⊕ *08.00–17.00 daily*), which sits directly adjacent to Jays Lodge and is the starting point for 855 thigh-burning steps up the ridge, which eventually land you at the zip line and canopy walk, 745m above sea level and nearly 200m above the lodge itself. The 150m zip line (*US$5*) and four-span canopy walkway (*US$5*) are built to European safety standards and visitors are provided with Petzl climbing gear. On a clear day, the canopy walkway offers views from the ridgeline all the way to the Afram River and plains beyond. Occasional shared taxis run here from Mpraeso and Obomeng, or an inexpensive 'dropping' taxi can easily be found on the main road.

⌂ **Where to stay and eat**   If your legs have turned into jelly after all those stairs (and flying through the air), the attached **Jays Lodge** ✳ (*25 rooms;* ✆ *03029 75356;* m *0507 979710;* e *info@jayslodge.com; www.jayslodge.com; map, page 336*) offers excellent accommodation in two stylish stone and wood buildings at the bottom of the ridge for US$52/58 standard single/double and US$65/71 executive single/double. The tile or wood-floored en-suite rooms come with flatscreen satellite TV, air conditioning, hot water, private terraces, and the executive rooms also have a fridge. Table tennis, board games and mountain bikes are all provided free for guests, and there's a restaurant attached.

ABETIFI   Recently appointed capital of Kwahu East District, the picturesque small town of Abetifi, situated at an elevation of 650m about 10km north of Mpraeso, is the highest settlement on the Kwahu Plateau, and one of the coolest places anywhere in the country. In 1869, the Presbyterian missionary Fritz Ramseyer and his family were held hostage for several months at Abetifi by the Ashanti army. Ramseyer returned seven years later to establish one of the country's oldest Basel Missions, and the charming mission house that still stands there today. A plaque commemorating Ramseyer stands outside the Dutch-style Presbyterian church, built in 1907, which has the largest bell in Ghana, a ten-ton artefact carried by boat to Adowso in 1910, and then pulled by teams of men along the 50km road ascent to Abetifi. There is also a memorial outside the church certifying Abetifi as the highest inhabited place in Ghana, a claim that might have been true a century ago, but which ceased to be the case when the significantly higher settlement of Amedzofe (formerly part of German

Togoland) was annexed to the Gold Coast Colony in the aftermath of World War I. Abene, perched on the escarpment a few kilometres north of Abetifi, is the stool of the Kwahumanhene, the paramount chief of all Kwahu, a position that has been unfilled since the death of Daasebre Akuamoah Boateng II, who had ruled continuously since his enstoolment in 1971.

In terms of travel practicalities, plenty of trotros run back and forth between Mpraeso and Abetifi throughout the day. We couldn't see any accommodation in town, but a couple of decent options exist close by. Most unexpected is the large and not-quite-so-smart-as-it-thinks-it-is **Modak Royal Hotel** (*75 rooms;* m *0207 377549/0249 817519/0506 760948;* e *modakroyal4u@gmail.com; www. modakroyalhotelghana.com; map, page 336*), which boasts an attractive location in Pepease, 2km east of Abetifi, good facilities including a (half-full but usable) swimming pool, gym, restaurant and pleasant self-contained rooms with Wi-Fi, satellite TV, AC, and kitchenette in the chalets for US$40/53 double/chalet, yet somehow exudes a slightly unfinished and deserted aura. Far less pretentious, situated 2km along the Mpraeso road, amid green slopes lined with trees and the unfinished mansions characteristic of Kwahu, the **Top Hotel** (*31 rooms;* m *0548 333183/0274 263663; map, page 336*) has a decent restaurant/bar attached and charges US$12/16 for a self-contained single/double with fan, and US$24 for a room with TV, queen-size bed, and air conditioning.

TAFO Often referred to as Kwahu Tafo to avoid confusion with its namesake near Bunso, the busy farming service town of Tafo is arguably best known as the birth and burial place of the actor Gyearbuor Asante, who played the Gambian student Matthew in the British television series *Desmond's*. His bust sits proudly outside Tafo's community library, one of several local projects part-funded by Friends of Tafo (*www.friendsoftafo.org*), a UK-based charity run by the producer of *Desmond's*, Humphrey Barclay, who was awarded a British Empire Medal for his services to Tafo in the 2013 Queen's Birthday Honours List. Friends of Tafo have recently launched the Kwahu Tourism Initiative (m *0249 202869/0264 349058*) here, and they can help with local information down to the region's tiniest villages. Just outside town, on the Kotoso road, is a small waterfall scenically set in a very shaded spot near a quarry.

Visible to the left about 5km out of town along the Adowso road, Buruku Rock Pillar Shrine, an immense and rather phallic rock sitting on a small hill, is the paramount shrine in the Tafo area. Believed to be home to a powerful god, the rock shrine is shrouded in superstitions and is said to watch over and protect all the villages in the surrounding area like a giant eye. The round walk to Buruku from Tafo will take about five hours and, with a good guide, it's a great opportunity to find out more about local folklore and wildlife.

Tafo lies 23km east of Mpraeso and is connected by regular trotros. The chief's own **Blessed Arrival Guest House** (m *0244 213075*) offers basic en-suite double rooms for US$10–15, or it's equally easy to visit as a day trip.

ADOWSO Situated at the northeast base of the Kwahu Plateau 20km east of Tafo, and reached via a wild descent road passing through relatively dry rocky savannah overlooked by the prominent Buruku Rock Pillar, Adowso is the most important port on this part of the Lake Volta shore, linked to Ekye-Amanfrom on the Afram Plains by a motor ferry several times daily. As a result, Adowso is a busy port town, with a constant stream of traffic travelling to and from the ferry jetty along the Kwahu Tafo road, mainly lorries or trotros carrying produce or people to and from markets on the Afram Plains. If you want to get out on the lake, canoe trips can be arranged (ask down by the ferry terminal), or you could just cross to Ekye and back by ferry. For hikers, the escarpment above Adowso can be climbed following a steep track, from where footpaths can be taken to Asikiman then along the Asuboni River to Kwahu Tafo. Alternatively, the road can be followed to the last borehole before Tafo at Nkyenenkyene (pronounced 'enchinni-enchinni') and on to Kwahu Tafo itself.

Plenty of shared taxis connect Adowso to Mpraeso and Nkawkaw. The ferry to Ekye (m *0203 773889*) usually runs about five times daily in either direction, starting at around 07.30, taking 20 minutes to cross, then leaving back and forth when it is full. The charge is around US$5 per vehicle and less than US$1 per foot passenger. There are also plenty of local pirogues that can be hired to punt you across, should you not want to wait for the ferry. The only accommodation in Adowso, situated behind the Crown filling station, 500m from the ferry terminal, is the **Crown Motel**, which charges a very reasonable US$9 for a self-contained double with air conditioning and fan. There is also a bar-restaurant at the filling station, and plenty of street food near the ferry terminal.

Part Five

CENTRAL GHANA

The next three chapters cover the central Ghanaian interior west of Lake Volta, and south of Tamale and Mole National Park. Culturally and geographically, the area is dominated by Ashanti Region, home to the kingdom of the same name, as well as to its ancient capital Kumasi, which is the main route focus and road funnel between the coast and the north. The other administrative region to fall in this section is Brong-Ahafo, which was split off from Ashanti in 1958, shortly after independence, and named after the dominant Brong and Ahafo ethnic groups. Centred on the regional capital Sunyani, the boundaries of modern Brong-Ahafo more or less conform to those of the defunct Bono State, an important medieval gold-trading empire to which most of the modern Akan peoples of Ghana – including the Ashanti and Fante – trace their ancestry.

The first chapter in this section deals with Kumasi, which is the second-largest city in Ghana, yet altogether more cohesive than Accra, and studded with sites of cultural interest. The second covers the Greater Ashanti region, an area that warrants several days' exploration thanks to the many Ashanti cultural shrines, forest reserves and other beauty spots that lie within day-tripping or overnight distance of Kumasi. The last chapter covers the main through route between Kumasi and Tamale, a route that passes through the heart of Brong-Ahafo, including Sunyani, and offers access to the region's two main attractions, Kintampo Falls and the Boabeng-Fiema Monkey Sanctuary.

BEST OF CENTRAL GHANA

KUMASI CITY CENTRE Combining chaotic modernity with cultural and architectural landmarks such as the 19th-century fort, Prempeh II Jubilee Museum and historic Okomfo Anokye Sword, central Kumasi is easily explored on foot and studded with a few great eateries. Pages 356–76.

KEJETIA MARKET At the north end of central Kumasi, Ghana's largest and most labyrinthine market is crammed with around 10,000 traders selling everything from traditional crafts to vegetables and car spares, though scheduled redevelopment works spell big changes for the market. Pages 373–4.

AKWASIDAE FESTIVAL Held every sixth Sunday at Kumasi's Manhyia Palace, this colourful highlight of the Ashanti calendar is when the Asantehene (king) holds court before his subjects and various lesser chiefs to a dramatic aural backdrop of traditional drumming and blaring horns. Page 375.

ADANWOMASE An important centre of kente-weaving for more than 300 years, this peaceful little village has a visitor centre offering fascinating guided tours. It's also a good place to buy the cloth, which is practically synonymous with Ashanti. Pages 379–82.

LAKE BOSOMTWE This beautiful lake, nestled within a circular meteorite crater south of Kumasi, is the largest natural freshwater body in Ghana, and its shores are dotted with affordable resorts, as well as offering superb horseriding opportunities. Pages 384–8.

BONKRO PICATHARTES SITE A forest-enclosed cave within walking distance of the remote village of Bonkro is renowned among bird enthusiasts as the most reliable place globally to look for the bizarre white-necked picathartes. Pages 389–91.

ASHANTI TRADITIONAL SHRINES The only UNESCO World Heritage Site in the Ghanaian interior comprises ten ancient fetish shrines, several of which are still in active use and/or beautifully decorated, the most accessible being the cluster around Ejisu on the Accra road east of Kumasi. Pages 390–1.

BOBIRI BUTTERFLY SANCTUARY Supporting a wealth of colourful butterflies and localised forest birds, as well as four species of monkey, this well-organised reserve east of Kumasi also houses a forest resthouse ideal for those seeking an affordable rustic retreat. Pages 395–6.

BOABENG-FIEMA MONKEY SANCTUARY Also serviced by an affordable and winningly unpretentious resthouse, this tiny forest reserve is the best place in Ghana for close-up encounters with Lowe's mona and black-and-white colobus monkey, both held sacred by the local villagers. Pages 413–15.

KINTAMPO FALLS Situated on the outskirts of the town of the same name, this accessible forest-fringed waterfall, which plunges around 70m in three separate stages, is most impressive during the rains. Page 417.

16

Kumasi

The modern capital of Ashanti Region, Kumasi has also served as the royal capital of the Ashanti Kingdom for longer than three centuries. Yet, contrary to the sort of expectations conjured up by the epithet 'ancient Ashanti capital', one's first impression upon arriving in Kumasi, particularly if you disembark near Kejetia Circle, is less likely to be rustic traditionalism than daunting developing-world urbanity. This is the largest settlement in the Ghanaian interior, with a population of slightly more than two million according to the 2012 census, and one of the most hectic cities we've encountered anywhere in Africa. Surging throngs of humanity and constant traffic jams emanate in every direction from the market and lorry station, creating an emphatically modern mood that can be positively overwhelming to newcomers, particularly those arriving from the relatively provincial north. For all that, Ghana's second city ranks as a 'must-see' in most people's book. True, historical Kumasi amounts to little more than the late 19th-century fort and a cluster of colonial-era buildings in the old city centre (known as Adum). But the city boasts several worthwhile sites of interest, ranging from the Prempeh II Jubilee Museum to the fantastically sprawling and soon to be redeveloped Kejetia Market, and is also a useful base for any number of day or overnight trips into rural Ashanti, as detailed in the chapter *Greater Ashanti* (pages 378–400).

HISTORY

The foundation of Kumasi is shrouded in legend. Some oral traditions suggest that it became capital of the Oyoko Abohyen dynasty (to which all the kings of Ashanti have belonged) in around 1640, when Otumfuo Nana Oti Akenten relocated his capital there from Kwaaman. Others state that the relocation from Kwaaman to Kumasi occurred between 1695 and 1701 under Otumfuo Nana Osei Tutu Opemsoo, the first proper Asantehene (see also box, pages 360–1). According to legend, it was here in Kumasi, in what are now the hospital grounds, that Okomfo Anokye, the priestly chief advisor to Otumfuo Nana Osei, summoned the Golden Stool of Ashanti from the sky, and followed this up by thrusting an irremovable sword into the ground as a symbol of the Ashanti unity.

As capital of Ashanti, Kumasi rapidly acquired the status of the largest and most important city in the Ghanaian interior, and was the inland terminus of most of the major 18th-century slave-trading routes to the coast. Accounts by early 19th-century visitors suggest Kumasi was then a spacious, attractive city of whitewashed buildings with steep thatched roofs. In the latter part of the century, however, Kumasi became the focus of hostilities between aspirant British colonists and the Ashanti. The old city was burnt to the ground by Sir Garnet Wolseley in 1873, resulting in the Anglo–Ashanti Peace Treaty of March 1874 and a period of prolonged infighting within the Ashanti state. Following the Yaa Asantewaa War of 1900–01, Kumasi (or Kumase as it was then spelt) was annexed to the British Gold Coast Colony on 1 January 1902.

GETTING THERE AND AWAY

BY AIR Starbow (m *0245 000000;* e *info@flystarbow.com; www.flystarbow. com; online booking at www.ghanaticketservice.com*) and **Africa World Airlines** (m *0242 438888; www.flyawa.com.gh*) both fly a few times daily in either direction between Accra and Kumasi. Fares start at around US$80 one-way, including taxes and surcharges. Africa World also flies between Kumasi and Tamale four times a week. All flights land and depart at Kumasi Airport [359 G1], which lies just off the Eastern bypass about 6km northeast of the city. The airport was upgraded to international standard in 2015, though it was only serving domestic routes as of 2016. Taxis are available at the airport.

BY RAIL The rail service between Takoradi and Kumasi, once quite popular with travellers, was suspended in 2006, ostensibly because of high fuel costs. The government reputedly secured a substantial loan from China to rehabilitate the line in 2011 and works were under way in Takoradi in 2016, but a functioning passenger rail service between the two cities likely remains some years off.

BY ROAD Kumasi lies about 270km northwest of Accra along a fair surfaced road, a drive that usually takes 4 hours, depending on traffic volumes on the outskirts of the two cities, as well as on the extent of roadworks, which usually hold things up somewhere. The route through Mamfe and Koforidua was for years a better prospect than the slightly more direct road via Nsawam and Kibi, though roadworks on the latter will hopefully be complete by the time you read this, making the two routes more or less interchangeable. The two roads meet at Bunso Junction, which is now more widely known as 'Linda Dor' after the popular restaurant at the rest stop there, and then continue north to Kumasi

KUMASI *Orientation*
For listings, see pages 365–71

🛏 **Where to stay**

1	Ahema Guesthouse	C3
2	Ashanti Gold	C2
3	Ceeta Kel Guesthouse	F6
4	Golden Bean	D6
5	Golden Tulip Kumasi City	D5
6	Hotel Georgia	E7
7	Hotel Rexmar	A7
8	Justice	G4
9	Kumasi Catering Resthouse	C4
10	Noks	F6
11	Sleepers Lodge	E5

Off map

Four Villages Inn	E7
Help Our Village Bed & Breakfast	E7
Pink Panther	C7
Royal Basin Resort	H5
Royal Park	E7
Samaritan Villa Guesthouse	A7
Sir Max	E7
Wadoma Royale	A2

✖ **Where to eat and drink**

12	Chopsticks	D7
13	Cultural Jazz Club	C3
14	Doris Door	C3
15	Friend's Garden	B4
	Golden Tulip Kumasi City	(see 5)
	Hotel Georgia	(see 6)
	Hotel Rexmar	(see 7)
16	L'Italy Ice Cream	A7
17	Jofel Catering Services	G1

	Kentish Kitchen (see National Cultural Centre)	C3
18	Ki-Vis Night Club	D6
19	KFC	F7
	Kumasi Catering Resthouse	(see 9)
20	Moti Mahal	F7
21	Nik's Pizza	E6
22	Sports Hotel	F6
23	Vienna City Pub	D6

Off map

Bonne Arrivée	E7
Cheers Bar	E7
Gina's Kitchen	E7
Gisgo Cottage	A2
Relax	E7
Royal Park (see Royal Park)	E7
Sir Max	E7
The View Bar & Grill	E7

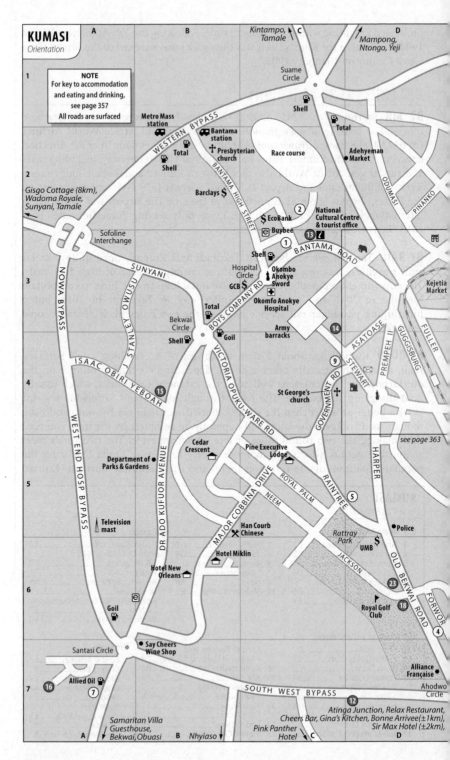

KUMASI
Orientation

NOTE
For key to accommodation and eating and drinking, see page 357
All roads are surfaced

Kintampo, Tamale

Mampong, Ntongo, Yeji

Suame Circle

Shell

Total

Metro Mass station

WESTERN BYPASS

Bantama station

Presbyterian church

Total

Shell

Race course

Adehyeman Market

ODUMASI

PINANKO

Gisgo Cottage (8km), Wadoma Royale, Sunyani, Tamale

Barclays $

BANTAMA HIGH STREET

Sofoline Interchange

EcoBank $

Buybee

National Cultural Centre & tourist office

BANTAMA ROAD

Kejetia Market

SUNYANI

Shell

Hospital Circle

Okombo Anokye Sword

GCB $

Okomfo Anokye Hospital

ASATOASE

PREMPEH II

GUGGISBURG

FULLER

NOWA BYPASS

J STANLEY OWUSU

BOYS COMPANY RD

Total

Bekwai Circle

Goil

Army barracks

14

9

Shell

ISAAC OBIRI YEBOAH

15

VICTORIA OPUKU-WARE RD

GOVERNMENT RD

St George's church

STEWART

see page 363

WEST END HOSP BYPASS

DR ADO KUFUOR AVENUE

Cedar Crescent

Pine Executive Lodge

ROYAL PALM

RAINTREE

HARPER

Department of Parks & Gardens

MAJOR COBBINA DRIVE

NEEM

5

Television mast

Han Courb Chinese

Rattray Park

Police

Hotel Miklin

UMB $

JACKSON

OLD BEKWAI ROAD

Goil

Hotel New Orleans

23

18

FORWOR

Royal Golf Club

4

Santasi Circle

Say Cheers Wine Shop

Alliance Française

16

Allied Oil

7

SOUTH WEST BYPASS

12

Ahodwo Circle

Samaritan Villa Guesthouse, Bekwai, Obuasi

Nhyiaso

Pink Panther Hotel

Atinga Junction, Relax Restaurant, Cheers Bar, Gina's Kitchen, Bonne Arrivee(±1km), Sir Max Hotel (±2km),

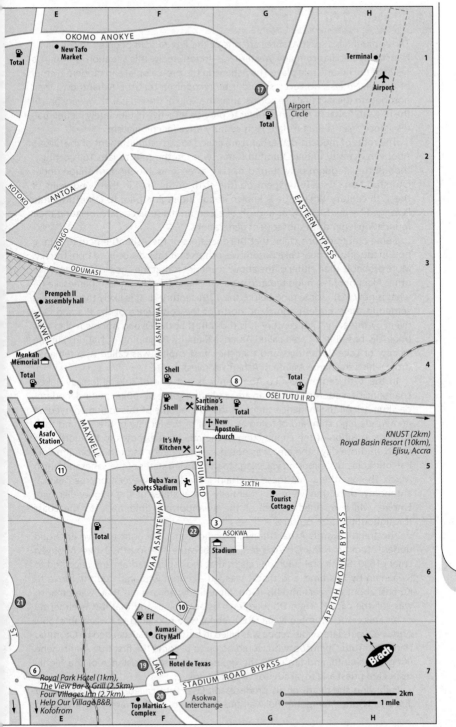

OKOMO ANOKYE

Total

New Tafo
Market

Terminal

Airport

17

Airport
Circle

Total

KOTOKO

ANTOA

ZONGO

ODUMASI

EASTERN BYPASS

Prempeh II
assembly hall

MAXWELL

VAA ASANTEWAA

Menkah
Memorial

Total

Shell

8

Total

OSEI TUTU II RD

Shell

Santino's
Kitchen

Total

KNUST (2km)
Royal Basin Resort (10km),
Ejisu, Accra

Asafo
Station

MAXWELL

New
Apostolic
church

It's My
Kitchen

11

Baba Yara
Sports Stadium

SIXTH

Tourist
Cottage

STADIUM RD

Total

VAA ASANTEWAA

22

3

ASOKWA

Stadium

APPIAH MONKA BYPASS

21

Elf

10

Kumasi
City Mall

N

Bradt

6

19

LAKE

Hotel de Texas

STADIUM ROAD BYPASS

Royal Park Hotel (1km),
The View Bar & Grill (2.5km),
Four Villages Inn (2.7km),
Help Our Village B&B,
Kofofrom

20

Top Martin's
Complex

Asokwa
Interchange

0   2km
0   1 mile

E   F   G   H

The Ashanti (also spelt 'Asante') are one of the few African peoples whose name is instantly familiar to many Westerners. Undoubtedly, this situation is in part a result of the unique role played by Ashanti in the pre-colonial and modern history of Ghana. No less, however, should it be recognised that the Ashanti owe their notoriety to the fact that like, for instance, the Zulu or the Maasai, they were one of the few sub-Saharan African peoples to provide effective (if ultimately ineffectual) resistance against Britain's late 19th-century drive for colonialism.

The roots of modern-day Ashanti are linked to the establishment of the Oyoko Abohyen dynasty under Otumfuo Nana Twum in the mid to late 16th century, though the kingdom only started to take a recognisable modern shape under Otumfuo Nana Osei Tutu Opemsoo (the sixth in the line) in the dying years of the 17th century. What little is known about the region prior to Osei Tutu's rule is fogged by myth, partly as a result of a ban on his subject states relating their foundation legends to subsequent generations.

Some oral traditions claim that the ancestors of the Ashanti emerged from a hole in the ground near Lake Bosomtwe, others that they descended from the sky. More probable than either of the above scenarios is that the ancestral Ashanti, like other Akan peoples, migrated into modern Ghana from its ancient namesake (in what is now Mali) some time before the 13th century AD. It is likely that they had settled in their modern homeland north of the confluence of the Pra and Oda rivers by the early 17th century. It is thought that the Oyoko Abohyen clan was originally based in an area called Amanse (literally 'Beginning of Nations') in the vicinity of Lake Bosomtwe, and that their first capital was called Asantemanso (from which the name Asante or Ashanti derives).

In the 17th century, Oyoko Abohyen was just one of several loosely linked chieftaincies scattered through an area radiating some 30–50km around modern-day Kumasi. All the evidence suggests that the people of this region enjoyed an immensely high standard of living as a result of the fertility of the soil and their strategic position at the conjunction of the main trade routes to the north and south. In those days, the area was noted particularly for its production of mildly narcotic kola nuts, exported via Salaga to the Muslim states of the Sahel and North Africa. The one thing that these chieftaincies lacked, however, was true political autonomy, since they were all essentially vassal states of the mighty Denkyira Empire, which retained control of the all-important gold trade to the coast throughout the 17th century.

The trend towards Ashanti military unification is thought to have emerged under Otumfuo Nana Oti Akenten, who became the fourth Oyoko Abohyen chief c1630. Some oral traditions claim that the capital had already relocated to Kwaaman by this time, and that it was Oti Akenten who initiated the move to Kumasi about 20 years into his reign. More likely, however, is that Asantemanso was still the capital when Oti Akenten was enstooled, and that it was either he or his successor, Otumfuo Nana Obiri Yeboa, who relocated to Kwaaman c1660. About 20 years later, Obiri Yeboa was killed in battle, to be succeeded by Otumfuo Nana Osei Tutu Opemsoo, who would go on to become the first true Asantehene (King of Ashanti), and arguably the greatest, with the assistance of the highly respected priest and royal advisor Okomfo Anokye.

Following the death of his predecessor, Osei Tutu called upon the states of Juaben, Nsuta, Mampong, Bekwai and Kokofu to confederate with Kwaaman against the more powerful state of Denkyira. The chiefs of the six states assembled at present-day Kumasi, whereupon the priest Okomfo Anokye summoned a Golden Stool from the sky to land in the lap of Osei Tutu, signifying that he should assume the role of paramount king of the new confederation. It is also claimed that the priest planted three palm (kum) trees in various parts of the union, and the first one to start growing was nominated as the site of the Ashanti capital, Kumasi (which means 'Under the Kum Tree').

When the Denkyirahene (King of Denkyira) heard about the Ashanti Confederation, he increased his tax demands on the six member states. When they refused to comply, he insisted that the Asantehene hand over the Golden Stool, thereby dissolving the union, and that each of the member states' chiefs should chop off a finger to send him. Instead, the newly formed confederation decided to go to war with Denkyira, though after Okomfo Anokye warned that the chief who led Ashanti to victory would not live for more than seven days after the battle, it was decided that Osei Tutu should remain in Kumasi. The Mamponhene (King of Mampong) volunteered to lead the army in Osei Tutu's place, provided that his stool was made second to that of the Asantehene (the Silver Stool of Mampong is to this day regarded to be second in importance only to the Golden Stool of Kumasi). In 1701, the Denkyirahene was captured and beheaded at Feyiase, and his kingdom became Ashanti's first subject by conquest.

Using revolutionary military tactics, and fuelled by its growing importance in the emergent slave trade, Ashanti grew from strength to strength in the 18th century. In 1717, Osei Tutu was killed by snipers while crossing the Pra River, but after a brief period of internal instability, his successor, Otumfuo Nana Opuku Ware Katakyie (1720–50), pursued a policy of military expansion that resulted in most of the Akan states of southern Ghana being subject to Ashanti by 1740. In 1744, Accra was briefly captured by the Ashanti army, and later in the same decade much of what is now northern Ghana fell under Ashanti rule. Indeed, during the reign of Otumfuo Nana Osei Tutu Kwame Asiba Bonsu (1804–24), the kingdom covered an area larger than that of modern Ghana, spilling over into parts of what are now Ivory Coast, Togo and Burkina Faso.

The 19th-century decline of Ashanti is linked to the parallel decline in the transatlantic slave trade, which lay at the heart of the kingdom's economy. It was more or less sealed in 1896 when Britain occupied Kumasi and deported Asantehene Otumfuo Nana Prempeh I to the Seychelles, along with several other important dignitaries. In 1900, led by the aged queen mother, Yaa Asantewaa, the Ashanti made one last brave but ill-fated attempt to remove Britain from Kumasi Fort, with the net result that even more of its traditional leaders were deported and Ashanti was formally annexed to Britain's Gold Coast Colony. However, while this may have resulted in the core states of the Ashanti confederation losing their autonomy, they have never lost their identity. Indeed, Britain was practically forced to release Prempeh I from exile in 1924 and restore him as Asantehene two years later, and his successors – Otumfuo Nana Osei Tutu Agyeman Prempeh II (1931–70), Otumfuo Opoku Ware II (1970–99) and Otumfuo Nana Osei Tutu II (1999–present) – have, at any given point in time, been regarded as the most important traditional leader in Ghana.

continued overleaf

16

It is one thing to sum up the history of the Ashanti, altogether another trying to come to grips with their cultural institutions. Every Ashanti is a member of one of seven matrilineal 'families' as well as his or her clan, and of a patrilineal spiritual group known as a *nton*. Like many African cultures, great emphasis is placed on communality and the subservience of the individual to the nation (as an example, until recent times all land was communal, the nominal property of the Asantehene), yet, paradoxically, the highest of all Ashanti goals is personal power (one classic Ashanti proverb translates thus: 'If power is up for sale, then sell your mother to obtain it – once you have the power there are several ways of getting her back').

If you are interested in finding out more, seek out one of the books written by Ghanaians and available for next to nothing in bookshops in Accra or Kumasi. Although many of them are based in part on dubious history, they still give insight into the facts and vicarious truths of Ashanti legend. The latest, and we suspect among the more credible, is Nana Otamakuro Adubofour's self-published *Asante: The Making of a Nation*, sold at the Palace Museum in Kumasi.

via Nkawkaw. The other main surfaced routes to Kumasi from the coast are the 220km road from Cape Coast, taking 3–4 hours, and 230km road from Takoradi via Tarkwa and Obuasi, which is in rough shape and will take considerably longer.

Most transport for these and other destinations south of Kumasi leaves from and arrives at **Asafo Station** [359 E5], sometimes referred to locally as Cape Coast for the influx of workers from that city who come to live there. The station sprawls for about 500m along Fuller Road, just south of the bridge across the old railway line, only 10 minutes' walk from the city centre. Most of the major long-haul coach operators, including VIP/VVIP, Diplomatic and Executive, have their main Kumasi terminal at Asafo. The pick of the coach operators is VIP/VVIP, which runs about two dozen air-conditioned buses daily between Accra and Kumasi (leaving Accra from the terminus near Nkrumah Circle) on a fill-up-and-go basis, and charges US$9–13 depending on whether it's a VIP or VVIP coach. Asafo is also the place to pick up air-conditioned Stanbic and Ford minibus services to Accra, Cape Coast and Takoradi, as well as trotros to the likes of Obuasi, Lake Bosomtwe and Nkawkaw.

The most central long-haul terminal is the **STC station** [363 C6] off Adum Road, but services here have collapsed almost entirely and, as of early 2016, there was one daily bus to Tamale at 07.00 (*US$11*) and no other destinations were served.

Another important station is the outlying **Metro Mass terminus** [358 B2] on the Western bypass near the junction with Bantama High Street. Metro Mass operates coaches to almost every corner of Ghana, including a steady stream of transport to Accra, Cape Coast, Takoradi, Sunyani, Tamale and Wa, with several coaches daily leaving for all these destination on a fill-up-and-go basis.

KUMASI *City Centre*
For listings, see pages 365–71

🛏 **Where to stay**

1 Basel Mission Guesthouse.....B5
2 Daddy's Lodge............................C6
3 Hotel de Kingsway..................B5
4 Sanbra......................................B3

✖ **Where to eat and drink**

5 Eclipse Bar.................................C4
6 Kenny Joe's................................B3
  Old Timer's Bar...................(see 3)
7 Queen's Gate............................B4
8 Saarnak Vegetarian
  Food & Health Shop..............A4
  Sanbra...................................(see 4)
9 Vic Baboo's Café.......................D5

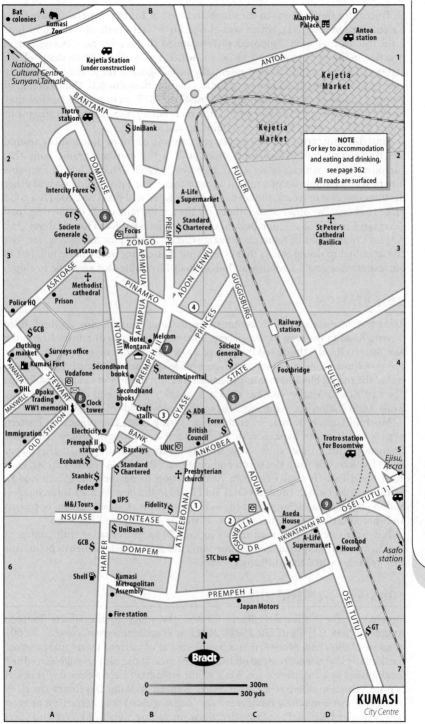

KUMASI
City Centre

Trotros for destinations to the north and west of Kumasi generally leave from **Kejetia Station** [363 A1], which was closed for a total overhaul starting in June 2015. All trotros were supposed to relocate to the nearby racecourse, but in practice many drivers refused to do so, which means that the contents of the station (traders included) have essentially just disgorged on to the surrounding streets, making for an even more chaotic situation than normal. Construction of the new station is slated to last until at least late 2017, so until then (unless they finally manage to get everyone over to the racecourse) it seems that locating your trotro here will involve a fair bit of pointing and asking.

Thus, for short trips out of Kumasi, you can waste a lot of time milling around Kejetia finding your trotro (and more still in the constant traffic jams that surround it), for which reason it is often easier to catch a shared taxi to a suitable junction and gamble on picking up a trotro there. For Ejisu, Effiduase and other destinations east of Accra, the corner of Fuller Road and the Accra road is a good place to stand. For other destinations, try the appropriate circle on the ring road – **Santasi Circle** [358 A7] for Bekwai or Obuasi, **Sunyani Road Roundabout** [358 A3] for Owabi Wildlife Sanctuary, **Suame Circle** [358 C1] for Mampong, etc. The risk attached to doing this is that everything that comes past will be full, but in our experience you'll seldom wait longer than 15 minutes for a vehicle to stop.

ORIENTATION

The city centre consists of an asymmetrical maze of roads sloping downhill from Stewart Road in the west to Guggisberg Road and the (disused) railway line in the east. Stewart Road is the closest thing there is to a main road, flanked by several banks and government offices, as well as the post office and the fort, though the northern end of the road is blocked to non-pedestrian traffic by a gate and military roadblock. The vast Kejetia Market and bus station lie at the northern end of the city centre, while Asafo Station lies to the southeast on the opposite side of the railway line.

Much of Greater Kumasi is enclosed by a 'ring road', comprising an Eastern bypass and Western bypass, with a total diameter of roughly 10km. The most important trunk routes connecting the city centre to the Ring Road are Harper Road (which runs from the south end of Stewart Road to Ahodwo Circle), Osei Tutu Road (which runs east from Asafo Station to become the Accra Road), Stadium Road (which connects Osei Tutu Road to the new Asokwa Interchange), and the Bantama and Sunyani roads in the northwest. A steady stream of trotros and shared taxis plies all these routes, as well as circling the Ring Road.

It is worth noting that road names in Kumasi seem to change with confusing regularity, with many roads being named after influential businessmen or politicians then renamed when their influence wanes.

TOURIST INFORMATION

Situated in the National Cultural Centre, the office of the **Ghana Tourism Authority** [358 C3] (✆ 03220 35848/26243; e gtaashanti@gmail.com; ⊕ 08.00–noon & 13.00–17.00 Mon–Fri) is a useful source of current travel information, particularly if you want to head off the beaten track. It can also arrange accredited local guides at a negotiable fee. Most of the upmarket hotels offer day tours in private vehicles, albeit at a higher price. **Kumasi Walking Day Tours** (m 0249 885370; e kwesiannan7@gmail.com) also offers guided tours (starting at your hotel) to all of Kumasi's major attractions, including Kejetia Market and local communities for US$17/24 half-/full-day tour. Guided 'pub crawls' to dance clubs and drinking dens are available at the weekend.

SAFETY

Kumasi is a reasonably safe city, and we've had very few reports of armed crime against tourists. A few years back, the hassle factor from aspirant guides and other chancers was quite high, particularly around the post office and in the National Cultural Centre. This sort of annoyance seems to have abated in recent years, though you might still be approached by the occasional artist or craftsman, often claiming to be from a neighbouring country, who will try to befriend you, then offer you jewellery or other craftwork at a wildly inflated price in the hope that you'll not negotiate too hard.

WHERE TO STAY

There must be more than 100 hotels and guesthouses scattered around Kumasi and its suburbs, most of them rather bland and indifferent set-ups aimed at business travellers. The following listings are highly selective and represent a few of the most reliable bets in each category.

LUXURY

Golden Tulip Kumasi City Hotel
[359 D5] (160 rooms) \03220 83777;
e reservations@goldentulipkumasicity.com;
www.goldentulipkumasicity.com. Tarted up comprehensively after being acquired by the Golden Tulip chain a few years back, Kumasi's first 4-star hotel, with its sleek air-conditioned interiors & shiny new fittings, has no real competition at the very top end of the price & comfort scale. Set in spacious forest-fringed grounds just opposite the new Rattray Park less than 2km south of the city centre, this multi-storey hotel has excellent facilities, including a complimentary hotel shuttle, a forex bureau (with good rates), ATM, pool, excellent restaurant, Wi-Fi, coffee shop & casino. All rooms come with AC, satellite TV, 24hr room service, minibar, coffee & tea facilities & safe. *US$180/211 B&B standard sgl/dbl; exec rooms & suites from US$519/551 sgl/dbl.* **$$$$$**

UPMARKET

✱ **Four Villages Inn** [359 E7]
(4 rooms) \03220 22682; m 0207 667559;
e fourvillagesinn@gmail.com; www.
fourvillages.com. This award-winning small inn, situated on the Old Bekwai (now Melcolm) road 2.8km past Ahodwo Circle, is the most individualistic upmarket option in Kumasi, &

it has received the highest praise from many readers of previous editions who have stayed there. Owned & managed by a very helpful & committed Ghanaian–Canadian family, it has a cosy common lounge & dining room furnished with books & photographs that give it the feel of a family home, while a shady patio overlooks the compact green gardens. The spacious rooms all come with AC, minibar, TV & DVD, while other facilities include Wi-Fi, a great selection of free DVDs, golf-club hire, complimentary tea & coffee. Delicious home-cooked meals are available by request (expect to pay US$25 for a full 4-course meal), or you can grab a cheap local meal & beer at Gina's Kitchen opposite. Highly recommended. *USUS$90/100/110 B&B self-contained sgl/dbl/trpl, plus 17.5% VAT.* **$$$$–$$$**

Royal Park Hotel [359 E7] (24 rooms) \03220 33388; m 0244 182790;
e info@royalparkhotelksi.com; www. royalparkhotelksi.com. Located in the suburb of Adiebra, about 500m south of Ahodwo Circle, this smart hotel has comfortable rooms with Wi-Fi, AC & flatscreen satellite TV. The attached Chinese restaurant (⊕ 11.30–23.00 daily) serves authentic dishes at reasonable prices & has a choice of excellent set menus. *US$86/104/125 B&B self-contained sgl/dbl/suite.* **$$$$–$$$**

Sir Max Hotel [359 E7] (21 rooms) \03220 25278; m 0270 635909; e sirmaxhotel@gmail. com; www.sirmaxhotel.com. This comfortable 3-star hotel, located just off the Old Bekwai (now Melcolm) road in Ahodwo, is regularly recommended by readers for its spacious well-priced rooms, excellent service & good facilities. There's plenty to entertain, with a very pleasant swimming pool, terrace bar, gift shop & pool table as well as an attractive Lebanese restaurant & coffee shop. *US$73/88 B&B self-contained sgl/dbl with AC; from US$91 suite.* **$$$**

Golden Bean Hotel [358 D6] (51 rooms) \03220 86000; e info@goldenbeanhotel.com; www.goldenbeanhotel.com. Though it's not quite on the level of the Golden Tulip, the facilities at this new business-class hotel are still excellent & they're clearly aiming for the top end of Kumasi's market. Set in spacious green grounds near the Alliance Française, rooms here are clean & modern, with flatscreen TV, desk, fridge, kettle & Wi-Fi. There are 3 bars on the property, a buffet restaurant, gym, swimming pool, on-site travel agent & 24hr room service. *US$122/142 standard sgl/dbl; US$143/163 exec sgl/dbl; suites from US$235.* **$$$$**

Hotel Georgia [359 E7] (30 rooms) \03220 23915/24154; e info@hotelgeorgia. net; www.hotelgeorgia.net. Situated off Ahodwo Roundabout, this 3-star multi-storey concrete monolith is especially suitable for package groups, but also a fair bet for individual travellers following some relatively recent renovations. Though somewhat characterless, it has reasonable facilities including a large swimming pool, restaurant, bar, Wi-Fi, conference hall & Royal Bank ATM. The neat, spacious rooms come with king-size bed, writing desk, tiled floor, hardwood furniture, satellite TV & fridge. *US$65/78/91 B&B self-contained sgl/dbl/ suite.* **$$$**

MODERATE

Ashanti Gold Hotel [358 C2] (30 rooms) \03220 25875; m 0541 481488; e ashgoldhotel@yahoo.com. In a rather hotchpotch compound behind the National Cultural Centre, this 'homely and discipline' hotel (as described on one of their signs) has won several local tourism awards & gets regular praise from our readers, though we've also had some complaints about the speed of the restaurant. Its

self-contained rooms with AC & fridge are very reasonably priced & there's a rather cramped swimming pool. *US$18/21/31/37 sgl/dbl/twin/ suite.* **$$**

Wadoma Royale Hotel [358 A2] (40 rooms) \03222 96089; m 0249 404047; e info@wadomaroyalehotel.com; www. wadomaroyalehotel.com. Situated about 1km from Abuakwa Junction, this smart service-orientated hotel is rather inconvenient for those with business in central Kumasi, but it makes for a useful overnight stop for self-drivers or tour groups bound for Sunyani or points further north. The comfortable rooms come with free Wi-Fi, AC, satellite TV, minibar & hot shower, while facilities include a well-priced restaurant & swimming pool area. Good value. *US$40/45/50/65 B&B self-contained sgl/dbl/twin/suite.* **$$$**

Kumasi Catering Resthouse [358 C4] (20 rooms) \03220 26506; m 0204 307627; e grandregency@jso-group.com. This conveniently located former government hotel lies in an attractive green compound off Stewart Rd, immediately south of the city centre. The large, tiled chalet-like rooms all have AC, fan, satellite TV, Wi-Fi, fridge & hot shower, plus an inexpensive restaurant is attached. It's justifiably popular with local businessmen, & quite often full, so it's worth ringing in advance. *US$42/52/78 self-contained sgl/dbl/suite.* **$$$**

Royal Basin Resort [359 H2] (21 rooms) \03220 60144; m 0244 627999; e info@ royalbasinresort.com; www.royalbasinresort.com. This deservedly popular & very reasonably priced 3-star hotel is situated next to the regional Peace Corps office, 10km out of town off the main Accra road. The comfortable rooms have AC, satellite TV & Wi-Fi. Other facilities include a swimming pool, gym & gift shop. Recommended. *US$40/44/47 self-contained sgl/dbl/twin; US$60 suite.* **$$$**

Hotel Rexmar [358 A7] (62 rooms) \03220 29111; m 0240 869834; e info@hotelrexmar. com; fb.me/RexmarHotel. Among the better of Kumasi's numerous business-type hotels, the Rexmar is situated in large grounds centred on a swimming pool a few hundred metres south of Santasi Circle. The rooms are based around a green courtyard & come with king-sized bed, satellite TV, AC & private balcony. A good restaurant specialises in charcoal-grilled meat. *US$52/65/91 B&B self-contained sgl/dbl/suite.* **$$$**

Pink Panther Hotel [358 C7] (15 rooms) 03220 38340/1; e reservations@ pinkpantherhotel.com; www.pinkpantherhotel. com. Set in landscaped grounds a block or 2 east of Atinga Junction in Adiebra, outside the circle road, this quirky little hotel is decorated with pictures of prominent African leaders & 'great authors'. Facilities include an international restaurant, free internet & business centre. The rooms are small but neat & come with satellite TV, mini-hifi, fan, AC, & hot tub/shower. *US$35/45 B&B dbl/suite.* **$$$–$$**

Ceeta Kel Guesthouse [359 F6] (25 rooms) 03220 27652. This small guesthouse is perhaps the best value among a cluster of mostly quite overpriced hotels close to the stadium. The staff are friendly, the adequately clean rooms come with satellite TV & Wi-Fi, & there's a free laundry service (exc tip). *US$27 self-contained sgl with fan; US$31/39 sgl/dbl with AC; suites from US$65.* **$$$–$$**

BUDGET

Basel Mission Guesthouse [363 B5] (30 rooms) 03220 26966; m 0203 080900; e pcgap@hotmail.com; www.asantepresbytery. org. Also known as the Presbyterian Guesthouse, this ramshackle colonial-era building, with wide wooden balcony overlooking the leafy grounds of the Basel Mission, now sits attached to a glossy new wing, where the very tidy new rooms come with fridge & TV. It's long been one of the most important backpacker crossroads in the Ghanaian interior & is recommended for the central location & recently upgraded rooms, though the staff remain somewhat grumpy & unobliging. *US$13 dbl with fan & shared shower; US$20 self-contained dbl; US$36 executive room (new wing); US$8pp camping.* **$$–$**

Help Our Village Bed & Breakfast [359 E7] m 0241 798791/0244 797158; e helpourvillage@gmail.com; www. helpourvillage.org; f fb.me/ HelpOurVillageFoundation. In a private home down the old Bekwai (now Melcom) road past Four Villages Inn (call for directions), this unpretentious family-run B&B is affiliated to the ecotourism programme at Adaklu Mountain near Ho, & used mainly by volunteers working with that organisation. There are basic but reasonably comfortable rooms with fan using shared bath,

as well as a couple of self-contained rooms, & facilities include free use of onsite internet café, a basketball court, & a Kumasi highlights tour upon request. Local & Western dishes are served in the US$3–5 range. *US$11pp B&B.* **$$–$**

Noks Hotel [359 F6] (18 rooms) 03220 24438. Set in large, flowering gardens in a quiet suburb off Stadium Road, this friendly 2-star hotel is one of the best deals in its range. The neat & clean rooms all come with fan, AC & DSTV, & the adequate restaurant has garden seating & a varied menu of Chinese & Western dishes in the US$6–8 range. *US$22/25/31/39 self-contained sgl/twin/ dbl/suite.* **$$**

Sanbra Hotel [363 B3] (22 rooms) 03220 31257/8; m 0230 406219; e info@ sanbrahotelgh.com; www.sanbrahotelgh. com. Several readers have recommended this affordable hotel, which is centrally located just off Prempeh II St, not far from Kejetia Market, but we have also had one isolated report of theft from a room. The popular restaurant serves affordable Ghanaian & international cuisines & an excellent hair salon is attached. Good value. *US$24/32/63 B&B self-contained dbl/twin/suite with AC.* **$$$–$$**

Sleepers Lodge [359 E5] (13 rooms) 03220 47680; m 0243 802769. Conveniently located near to Asafo Bus Station, this 2nd-floor hotel is also pretty good value. The neat tiled rooms all have dbl bed, fan, AC & satellite TV, but the noise from the street below could be quite intrusive, so try to get a room facing in the other direction. *US$19 self-contained dbl.* **$$**

Hotel de Kingsway [363 B5] (16 rooms) 03220 26228. The most central option in this range, the venerable Hotel de Kingsway lies in the heart of Adum. It's an adequate fallback but none too clean & a bit overpriced. *US$11 dbl with shared bath & fan; US$18–22 self-contained dbl.* **$$–$**

SHOESTRING

Samaritan Villa Guesthouse [358 A7] (26 rooms) 03220 23559; m 0208 159961/0245 008899; www.kumasicatholic.org. Assuming that you don't mind staying out of town, this clean little guesthouse in the tranquil, leafy grounds of the rustic St Hubert's Seminary is easily the best-value accommodation in the city. Private taxis will drop you at the hotel, or you can get a shared taxi 1km south of Santasi Circle down the Obuasi road &

ask to be dropped at the junction (from where it is another 1km walk through the grounds to the guesthouse). A canteen serves unpretentious meals at around US$4 per plate, along with soft drinks & beer. *US$8 immaculate self-contained sgl with fan; US$11/13 self-contained sgl/dbl with fan; US$17 dbl with AC, TV & lounge; all rates B&B.* **$$-$**

🏠 **Daddy's Lodge** [363 C6] (18 rooms) 📞03220 22128; m 0240 869 255/0233 333598; e info@daddyslodge.com; www.daddyslodge. com. Formerly known as Guestline Lodge but under new management since the end of 2015, this is still the closest thing in Kumasi to a backpacker hostel, & centrally located in a breezy old trpl-storey house next to the STC station. The high-ceilinged rooms are all newly renovated & looking trim with en-suite facilities, ceiling fan, fridge, desk, TV, AC & hot water, & there are also a couple of budget sgl rooms using fan only & shared ablutions. The 6–8-bed dorms are very clean, & it's possible they'll also get AC at

some point in the future. Beer & cold drinks are available, & there are Ghanaian meals at request. Paid Wi-Fi. Recommended. *US$12 sgl with shared bath & fan; US$14.50 en-suite sgl with fan; US$21/24 dbl/exec with AC; US$29 family room sleeping 4; US$6.50 dorm bed with fan.* **$$-$**

🏠 **Ahema Guesthouse** [358 C3] (8 rooms) m 0277 355023/0240 705887. Situated off bustling Bantama Rd, close to the National Cultural Centre, this has decent dbl rooms with a writing desk. Certainly scruffy, but as good as you could hope for at the price. *US$10 dbl with shared bath; US$12 self-contained dbl.* **$**

🏠 **Justice Hotel** [359 G4] 📞03220 22525. The long-serving Justice Hotel lies east of the city centre on Osei Tutu II Rd, but it's close to a rank where you can pick up shared taxis & trotros into the city centre or out towards Ejisu. The self-contained rooms are rather basic & none too clean, but they do come with TV & are about as cheap as it gets in Kumasi. *US$10 dbl with fan; US$15 dbl with AC.* **$**

✖ WHERE TO EAT AND DRINK

There are surprisingly few places to eat out in central Kumasi, and most of what is on offer is geared to local rather than international palates and budgets, the main exception – at least where variety is concerned – being the superb (and newly relocated) Vic Baboo's Café. Most bespoke restaurants in Adum close on Sundays, but you can still eat at hotel restaurants, of which the **Sanbra** and **Kumasi Catering Resthouse** are the pick of the more central options.

Kumasi's pricier eateries lie outside the city centre, and include the restaurants of several of the hotels listed in the upmarket and moderate ranges. Notables not mentioned below include the **Hotel Georgia** and **Royal Park Hotel** (both Chinese), and the **Rexmar**. Also worth a special mention is the superb but pricey coffee and pastry shop in the foyer of the **Golden Tulip Kumasi City Hotel**. Suburban restaurants are generally open for lunch and dinner only, but unlike the restaurants in the city centre, they mostly open on Sundays.

CITY CENTRE
Moderate

✳✖ **Vic Baboo's Café** [363 D5] m 0506 161574/0203 737816/0547 614324; ⏲ 10.00–22.00 Mon–Sat, 13.00–21.00 Sun. After a short closure in 2015, this reasonably priced & perennially popular Indian-owned restaurant is happily back in action at a new location, serving from the same menu that would take weeks to work through, with plenty of vegetarian choices. We've always ordered from the Indian selections & have yet to be disappointed, so we suspect

that mixed reader feedback is down to a drop in quality when you stray into other areas of the menu (it also serves burgers, pizzas, grills & Chinese). The blasting AC is welcome after a few hours wandering around town, & it serves cocktails & filling fruit lassis, as well as the usual range of chilled soft drinks, beer & cocktails. All main courses are in the US$5–8 range. **$$**

✖ **Queen's Gate Restaurant** [363 B4] m 0208 137083/0245 920340; ⏲ 08.30–19.00 Mon–Sat. Accessed up an inauspicious staircase, this (very) poorly signposted restaurant feels surprisingly upmarket in a retro kind of way, with bizarre décor that includes a massive bronze of the Last Supper & a sizeable aquarium. The restaurant serves Ghanaian standards for around US$4, or delicious Chinese & fish upwards of US$5 – which can be eaten inside below whining but effective fans, or outside on a breezy balcony that runs the length of the restaurant & makes for a great spot for people-watching with a cocktail or a cool beer. $$–$

Budget

✷ ✕ **Saarnak Vegetarian Food & Health Shop** [363 A4] m 0261 839233; ⏲ 09.00–17.00 Mon–Fri. Centrally located next to the post office, this welcome addition to Kumasi's eateries consists of a shop at the front selling wholewheat loaves & specialised health food & vegetarian ingredients, as well as a canteen at the back serving a nutritious vegetarian stew of the day, together with brown rice, rice balls & the usual local staples. Great value at US$1.50 per plate. $

✕ **Kumasi Club** [363 A4] m 0242 208073; ⏲ 10.00–22.00 daily. This long-serving institution behind Kumasi Fort serves decent local lunches in the US$3–5 range Mon–Fri, & it's a relaxed & retro spot for a drink at other times. $$–$

SUBURBS
Expensive

✕ **Moti Mahal Restaurant** [359 F7] ☎03220 29698; www.motimahalgh.com; ⏲ noon–15.00 & 19.00–23.00 daily. Now located in the Top Martin's Complex on the southwest side of Asokwa flyover, this superb Indian restaurant comes as a refreshing – though by no means inexpensive – treat after the ubiquitous Chinese & Western dishes served in most parts of Ghana. Many readers cite it as the best Indian food they've eaten in Ghana, if not the Western world. Mains around US$10–15. $$$

✕ **Nik's Pizza** [359 E6] m 0243 222006; ⏲ 13.00–22.00 daily. This popular restaurant on Jackson Road has been recommended by a number of readers for excellent wood-oven pizzas, which are available to eat alfresco at the leafy restaurant or to take away. Expect to pay around US$8 for a large pizza. $$$–$$

✕ **The View Bar & Grill** [359 E7] m 0244 668880; ◼ fb.me/theviewbarandgrill; ⏲ 10.00– midnight Tue–Thu & Sun, 10.00–late Fri–Sat. On the 3rd floor of an unmissable building on the

Melcolm Rd some 2.5km south of Ahodwo circle, this soigné new place has swiftly raised the bar for style in Kumasi. The menu covers salads, burgers, grills & bar snacks, but steaks are what people come here for. The chic wood-floored interior opens on to huge windows & 2 terraces overlooking Kumasi, & the whole place turns into a dance party after dinner at w/ends. Mains US$10–25. $$$

Moderate

✕ **Bonne Arrivée** [359 E7] ☎03220 22783; m 0208 114846/0249 874347; ⏲ 10.00–21.30 daily. Located in Ahodwo just off Melcolm (Old Bekwai) Rd at Atinga junction, this owner-managed Ivorian restaurant serves up tasty Senegalese & Ivorian dishes (the grills are particularly good) along with a bunch of Chinese options. Mains are priced around US$5–10. $$

✕ **Friend's Garden** [358 B4] m 0208 179906; ⏲ noon–21.00 daily. With several awards under its belt, this convivial restaurant with its nice shady courtyard is justifiably a popular choice for local & international cuisine. It serves an excellent range of Ghanaian dishes including palm-nut soup & omo tuo, as well as a good sprinkling of continental choices such as pizzas & steaks. Most mains are in the US$5–10 bracket. $$

✕ **Relax Indian & Chinese Restaurant** [359 E7] ☎03220 99671; m 0243 978462; ⏲ 15.00– 23.00 Tue–Sun. Superb Indian & adequate Chinese fare is served at this reasonably priced eatery at Atinga Junction. It also has a bar & the choice of indoor & outdoor seating. Mains US$7–10. $$

✕ **Sir Max Restaurant** [359 E7] ☎03220 25278; www.sirmaxhotel.com; ⏲ 07.00–23.00 daily. Attached to its namesake hotel in Ahodwo (page 366), this place is a surprise winner for reasonably priced Lebanese mezze for lunch or dinner & a good coffee shop stocked with plenty of pastries for earlier in the day. Meals are taken on the poolside terrace, & there are flavoured shisha pipes to puff on afterwards. Mains US$4–10. $$

✕ **L'Italy Ice Cream & Restaurant** [358 A7] m 0506 629219; ⏲ 10.30–22.30 daily. Hidden away in a leafy plot on a side road just south of Santasi Circle, this tranquil new place puts the ice cream first in their name so you can get an idea as to where their focus lies, but their pizzas, grills & pastas hold their own just fine. On Sat & Sun they set up a bouncy castle, face painting & other fun stuff for the kids, while later on Sat evenings it's BBQ & shisha night. Mains US$7–14. $$$–$$

✗ **Gisgo Cottage** [358 A2] m 0271 944077/0265 410680/0501 363292; e gisgocottage@yahoo.com; ⏰ 09.00–21.00 Mon–Sat, noon–21.00 Sun. It would be a stretch to apply the adjective 'idyllic' to this unusual stilted restaurant, which overlooks a small artificial lake on a tilapia farm surrounded by forest patches hosting plenty of birds. But it is a reasonably attractive spot for a drink or meal, with the speciality being delicious grilled tilapia served with banku, which starts at around US$5 per plate. You can also take a boat out on to the lake or enjoy a therapeutic massage at the attached spa, & if you don't feel like going anywhere afterwards, they've got a few rooms for rent as well. It lies on a backroad in Atwima Boko, 8km west of the city centre near the Amen Scientific Hospital. $$

✗ **Kentish Kitchen** [358 C3] m 0244 570476; ⏰ 08.00–18.00 daily. Situated in the National Cultural Centre near Kejetia Circle, this restaurant serves a selection of uncomplicated Western & Ghanaian dishes at reasonable prices, but service is slow & quality variable, though this may be compensated for by the fairly attractive garden setting. Mains US$5–6. $$–$

✗ **Chopsticks Restaurant** [359 D7] m 0243 374247/0505 128152; ⏰ 11.00–late daily. Recently moved to a new location on the Southwest Bypass opposite +2 Pub, Chopsticks has long been rated as the best Chinese restaurant in Kumasi, though reader feedback has been somewhat less than overwhelming. Main courses start at around US$6. $$

✗ **KFC** [359 F7] ☎ 03022 29962; ⏰ 10.00–23.00 daily. There's not much that needs to be said about this American fast-food stalwart, but local finger-lickers were quite excited when Kumasi's first outlet opened here in 2015, at the Shell garage near Asokwa Interchange. Mains US$2–5.

Budget

✗ **Doris Door** [358 C3] ⏰ 08.00–17.00 Mon–Sat. Situated to the right about 50m past the military gate & checkpoint on Stewart Road, this popular local lunch venue serves a good selection of cheap local dishes for around US$2. $

✗ **Gina's Kitchen** [359 E7] ⏰ lunch & dinner daily. This agreeable open-air bar opposite Four Villages Inn serves good local-style chicken/fish with chips or rice in the US$3–5 range. $

BARS AND NIGHTLIFE

CITY CENTRE

♀ **Eclipse Bar** [363 C4] ⏰ 09.30–midnight daily. Situated on Adum Rd, a couple of blocks south of Queen's Gate, this is primarily a drinking hole, & a very pleasant one, too, with indoor & pavement seating. They don't serve food themselves, but there's plenty of fried rice & other goodies to soak up the beer within shouting distance. It's a mainly local clientele, with a fair bit of dancing at night.

♀ **Kenny Joe's** [363 B3] Situated near the corner of Asatoase St & Dominase Rd, this pleasant pavement bar serves decent meals for around US$3 per plate.

♀ **Old Timer's Bar** [363 B5] Part of the Hotel de Kingsway, this is one of the most pleasant drinking holes in the city centre – admittedly rather dead on w/days, but sometimes thriving on Sat.

SUBURBS

♀ **Cheers Bar** [359 E7] m 0509 123333; ⏰ 18.00–late Tue–Sun. Situated opposite the Relax Restaurant & under the same ownership, this

is a pretty typical sports bar with a good variety of drinks, large-screen TV, a couple of pool tables & a welcoming atmosphere.

♀ **Cultural Jazz Club** [358 C3] m 0244 329000/654800; 📷 @culturaljazzclubkumasi; ⏰ 13.00–late daily. There's live music here every Fri night, & the rest of the time it serves as a drinking hole with a nice open-air setting at the National Cultural Centre, & a difficult-to-ignore sound system that was being abused by execrably tasteful elevator funk when we last dropped by.

♀ **Jofel Catering Services** [358 G1] ☎ 03223 90865/6; m 0208 995478; www. jofelcateringservices.com; ⏰ 10.00–midnight Mon–Fri, 11.00–04.00 Sat–Sun. Situated northeast of the city centre near Airport Circle, this award-winning bar & restaurant is the place to head for live music on Sat, usually starting at around 19.00.

☆ **Ki-Vis Night Club** [358 D6] ☎ 03220 27815; m 0544 141824; ⏰ 22.00–05.00 Fri & Sat. The hippest nightclub in Kumasi offers free entrance to ladies but men pay a cover of US$5. It's on the Old Bekwai (now Melcolm) Rd a short distance south of Vienna City Pub, & there are snooker tables if you want to give your dance moves a rest.

♀ **Sports Hotel** [359 F6] ☎ 03220 29066. The terrace bar at this difficult-to-miss bright-blue hotel on Stadium Rd has live bands at w/ends & doesn't ask for a cover charge. Expect homegrown highlife & hip-life (Ghanaian hip hop) on Fri & Sat starting at 19.00, & plenty of wailing at the Almighty during Sun's 'Gospel Light Splash'.

♀ **Vienna City Pub** [358 D6] ☎ 03220 23500; www.viennacity.com.gh; ⊕ 24hrs. This gaudy restaurant/bar/casino has about as much to do with Vienna as with Ghana. It's a reliable escape if you fancy some acceptable international food in an AC environment, plus the opportunity to play some pool & watch sports on the wide-screen TV. At night, the atmosphere can get rather seedy, when it's largely populated by prostitutes.

SHOPPING

BOOKS Reading material is pretty hard to come by in Kumasi. There are central secondhand bookstalls on Stewart Road and Prempeh II, but neither has much that is likely to be of interest to travellers. The only place that seems to sell a (limited) range of new novels is the gift shop in the Golden Tulip Kumasi City Hotel [358 D5].

CRAFTS The numerous craft villages around Kumasi are covered in detail in the *Greater Ashanti* chapter, but their products – including kente cloth – can easily be bought at **Kejetia Market** [363 C/D1–2] (assuming it's not under renovation), and at the craft shop in the **National Cultural Centre** [358 C3], where you can also see them being made. Several of the smarter hotels also have craft shops attached, and numerous stalls are dotted around the city centre. For kente cloth, adinkra and other dyed clothing, try the row of cloth and clothing stalls on Ananta Lane behind the Kumasi Fort [363 A4].

SUPERMARKETS Quite a number of reasonable supermarkets are to be found in the vicinity of Prempeh II Street. By far the most varied selection of groceries in Kumasi is available at the excellent **A-Life Supermarket** [363 D6] (between the STC and railway stations), which also serves ice-cream cones and other snacks on the veranda café. A second branch of the same supermarket lies on Prempeh II Street next to the Standard Chartered Bank [363 B2]. More centrally, **Opoku Trading** [363 A4] is also well stocked, and probably has the largest wine selection in town. On a (much) larger scale, **Kumasi City Mall** [359 F7] is scheduled to open just north of Asokwa Interchange in 2017, and will have a Shoprite, Game, Edgars, and eventually 61 other shops and restaurants, along with a five-screen cinema.

OTHER PRACTICALITIES

CAR RENTAL Kitticilly Tours (m *0244 258404/985254/846724*; e *info@kitticilly. com*; 🔲 *fb.me/KitticillyTours*), in the foyers of the Golden Tulip Kumasi City Hotel [358 D5], and Golden Bean Hotel [358 D6], rents sedan cars and 4x4s with driver for US$100–150 per day.

FOREIGN EXCHANGE All of Ghana's major banks are represented with multiple branches in Kumasi. In the city centre, Stanbic, Standard Chartered, EcoBank and Barclays Bank all have Visa ATMs within metres of Prempeh II Circle [363 B5], while nearby, Ghana Commercial Bank, GT Bank and UniBank have ATMs accepting MasterCard as well. Most of these banks also have foreign exchange counters, but you'll generally get a better rate and quicker service at any of the numerous private forex bureaux that are dotted around the city centre. Intercity Forex Bureau [363 C5] usually has very good rates. The Aries Forex Bureau on Asokwa Road has a reputation for swindling travellers. Less centrally, there are also several banks with Visa and MasterCard ATMs clustered in the commercial area ('Tech Junction') of the KNUST campus (pages 375–6).

IMMIGRATION The visa extension service here is far quicker than in Accra: two or three days as opposed to two weeks, and you may even be able to get it done overnight if you can persuade the immigration officers that it's urgent.

INTERNET Several internet cafés are dotted around central Kumasi, with the more reliable ones marked on the map. The best is the **Vodafone Internet Café** [363 A4] (\ *03220 20094/49110; ⊕ 07.00–23.00 daily*), which has a branch on Stewart Road next to the post office and another, open 24 hours daily, in the School of Engineering at the KNUST Campus. Also recommended is the air-conditioned **UNIC Internet** [363 B5], next to the British Council, which has about two dozen fast machines and opens seven days a week.

SPORT It can be fun to watch a game of football at **Baba Yara Sports Stadium** [359 F5] (also known as Kumasi Stadium) on Stadium Road – tickets for league matches cost around US$1 and those for more important matches might cost up to US$5. There's a great atmosphere, and armed guards to escort the referee off the pitch, but do watch out for pickpockets, especially on the way in and out.

You can get in a round of golf at the 18-hole **Royal Golf Club** [358 D6/7] (\ *03220 23930;* m *0224 429264/0227 679292*). Green fees are US$20 per person, club rental is US$8, and caddies are available at US$2/4 for nine/18 holes. There's also a driving range. It's not quite up to Western standards but it's a great way to kill a Sunday morning. A strict dress code applies, though they might bend the rules for a visitor with the right attitude.

SWIMMING There is no public swimming pool, but the ones at the Hotel Georgia [359 E7], Hotel Rexmar [358 A7] and Golden Bean [358 D6] are open to non-residents for a fee of around US$3–6. The Golden Tulip Hotel [358 D5] has the nicest pool in town, but it's pricier at US$10 day entry.

WHAT TO SEE AND DO

In addition to the sights detailed below, Kumasi is the obvious base for numerous day trips and overnight excursions, most of which are described in the next chapter, *Greater Ashanti*.

ARMED FORCES MUSEUM [363 A4] (\ *03220 23103; ⊕ 08.00–17.00 Tue–Sat; entrance US$4/3 non-Ghanaian adults/students*) The most central of Kumasi's prescribed tourist attractions is the Armed Forces Museum, which lies in the Kumasi Fort, on Stewart Road, near Prempeh II Circle. This is probably the oldest building in the city, though not as old as many of the traditional shrines in rural Ashanti. Some sources suggest – wholly inaccurately – that the foundation of the fort and some of the walls date to 1820, when Otumfuo Osei Tutu Kwame decided to build a replica of the fort at Cape Coast. The fort as it stands today was completed in 1897 by the British using granite blocks transported to Kumasi from the coast. The fortress was surrounded in March 1900, during the so-called Ashanti Rebellion, and 29 Britons were trapped within its walls for several weeks before they were able to escape. The Queen Mother of Ejisu, Ohemaa Yaa Asantewaa, the prime initiator of the Ashanti Rebellion, was imprisoned here for a week before being exiled to Cape Coast and later the Seychelles, where she died. A well-maintained British Military Cemetery about 200m northwest of the fort contains the graves of British casualties of the Yaa Asantewaa War.

The highly informative guided tour of the museum is well worth the expenditure. True, it starts unpromisingly with a collection of weapons and the spoils from various campaigns in which the Gold Coast Regiment has been involved (we were surprised to see how heavily the Gold Coast Regiment had featured in booting the Italians out of Ethiopia during World War II). More interesting, in our opinion, are the many portraits of Ashanti notables (notably Yaa Asantewaa), the first African soldiers to be promoted to various ranks during colonial rule, and two of the World War II veterans who were killed when an anti-colonial protest outside Osu Castle in Accra was fired upon by colonial police. The tour gradually takes on several unexpected dimensions: a potted history of 20th-century conflict, as seen through the collected memorabilia of a relatively obscure African regiment, and, more tellingly, an exposure of the minutiae of cruel colonial arrogance, which for many years forbade African soldiers in their regiments to wear shoes.

KEJETIA MARKET [363 C/D1–2] Sprawling over 12ha immediately southeast of Kejetia Circle, this is reputedly the largest open market in West Africa, hosting around 10,000 traders within its confines (a figure that excludes the innumerable stalls that spill out along the surrounding streets). It has been restored to its gloriously hectic former self after it was partially destroyed by fire in 1995 and sadly again in 2009, and excellent overviews can be obtained from the tall building on its western edge. Once inside, the market takes on a labyrinthine aspect, confusing at first, but in fact quite orderly, with clothing, textile and food stalls clustered in the west, pottery and metal in the northeast, and tailors in the southwest. Aside from the decidedly smelly part of the market where fish and meat are sold, this is a fascinating place, well worth dedicating an afternoon or morning to, and a great place to buy curios and crafts in an environment where tourists form a fraction of the clientele. Getting lost is part of the fun – the market isn't so large that you are likely to lose your bearings for long – and there is little cause for concern about hassle or theft, though many travellers do prefer to explore the market with a local guide. For collectors, the market is a great place to buy old trade beads, but you're advised to enter at Roman Hill to avoid a tiresome slog through the main household goods and food sections. There seem to be very few drinking spots in the market, so carry a big bottle of water with you. Guided tours arranged through Kumasi Walking Day Tours (pages 364–5) or Four Villages Inn (page 365) have been recommended by several readers.

Kejetia Market won't exist in its current, irascible form for much longer, however. The Kumasi Metropolitan Assembly recently commissioned a massive, US$298m redevelopment of Kejetia Market and lorry station, which is being undertaken in partnership with the Brazilian engineering firm Contracta (*www.contracta.com.br*) and is scheduled to take a total of five years divided into three phases to complete. Phase one, the redevelopment of the lorry station, began in June 2015 and is slated to last until late 2017 or early 2018, when phases two and three, involving the closure and total redevelopment of Kejetia Market proper, will begin. When complete, the market complex will contain more than 45,000 market stalls available for traders, and will reputedly be the second-largest such facility on the African continent.

Practically speaking, it's hard to predict what sort of contingency plans will go into effect once the market shuts down. If it's anything like the closure of the trotro

16

park, the streets surrounding the market will somehow become even more densely choked with traffic and traders, though many of the merchants will probably be relocated to Race Course, Adyeheman, Sofoline, Abinkyi, and other smaller markets around the city. For a visitor, it will probably become considerably more difficult to track down a particular item (ie beads), but visits to the overflow markets ought to be compelling nonetheless. Either of the previously mentioned tour providers should be able to give you a better picture of what sort of market visits around Kumasi might be possible once Kejetia's redevelopment begins.

KUMASI ZOO [363 A1] (⏱ *09.00–17.00 daily; entrance US$5 with a 50% discount to students*) Situated on the north side of Kejetia Circle, this zoo consists of a few depressingly cramped cages harbouring various primates (many are in solitary confinement, a fate as cruel to a chimp or a monkey as to a person), as well as a rather more aesthetically pleasing duiker-breeding scheme and a few more recent additions in the form of lions, an elephant and other refugees from the zoo in Accra. Altogether more phenomenal than the inmates of the zoo are the thousands upon thousands of fruit bats that rest in the trees of their own volition. This is a quite incredible sight (not to say sound – they chatter away like demented mice), and worth the nominal entrance fee if you've never before seen a large bat colony. Even more spectacular is the sight of the hungry fruit bats as they flock through the sky towards dusk. For those not content merely to see the bats, a couple of enterprising vendors serve them freshly grilled on the pavement next to the zoo (though do be warned that the initial transmission to humans of several diseases, including the SARS and Ebola virus, have been linked to eating bats, which can also carry rabies).

NATIONAL CULTURAL CENTRE [358 C3] Situated on Bantama Road, about 5 minutes' walk north of Kejetia Circle, this is as good a place as any to start your explorations of Ashanti. The regional tourist office can be found here, and the staff are likely to be clued up about any new tourist developments in the region. An excellent craft market makes goods onsite, and has been recommended by several readers as far friendlier and cheaper than its counterpart in Accra.

A highlight of the cultural centre, offering a good overview of Ashanti history, the **Prempeh II Jubilee Museum** (⏱ *09.00–17.00 Mon–Fri, 10.00–16.00 Sat/Sun; entrance US$2.50 covers an informative guided tour; photography forbidden*) is named after Otumfuo Nana Osei Agyeman Prempeh II, a very popular Asantehene who ascended to the Golden Stool in May 1931 and reigned until his death almost 40 years later, in 1970. Most of the artefacts in the museum relate to his reign, a largely peaceful period during which the Ashanti Empire, shattered in several respects by the British colonists, re-established much of its former cultural cohesion. Several black-and-white photos are on display, most strikingly a vibrant portrait of the young Asantehene taken at his coronation. A number of royal stools include the fake Golden Stool handed to Lord Baden-Powell in an attempt to fool the British authorities in 1900, and there's a photo of the real Golden Stool, which last appeared in public at the enstoolment of the present Asantehene in 1999. Perhaps the most historically significant artefact in the museum is the royal cask, which dates back 300 years to the rule of Nana Osei Tutu; its contents are unknown, since tradition holds that opening it would bring about the fall of Ashanti.

Recently added to the centre, the generously air-conditioned Kejetia Central Market Exhibition Centre (**m** *0248 752296*; ⏱ *10.00–17.00 Tue–Sun*) is an unexpectedly interesting little exhibit sponsored by the Brazilian firm that's renovating Kejetia Market and station. The small exhibit is home to evocative photos and profiles of market sellers from Kejetia, along with an intriguing video history of the market's more than century-long history and an enormous scale model of what the new market-station complex will eventually look like.

OKOMFO ANOKYE SWORD [358 C3] (☺ *09.00–17.00 Mon–Sat, 09.00–14.00 Sun*) Close to Bantama Road, about 500m past the National Cultural Centre, the Okomfo Anokye Sword is situated behind Block C of the Okomfo Anokye Hospital. According to tradition, the sword was planted in the ground by the priest and royal advisor Okomfo Anokye, at the very spot where the Golden Stool descended from the sky into the lap of Nana Osei Tutu. An important symbol of Ashanti unity, the sword has been stuck in the ground in the same position for 300 years, and legend has it that the state would collapse should it ever be removed. It is now housed in a small circular building, and an entrance fee of US$2 is charged to see it.

RATTRAY PARK [358 C/D 5–6] (m *0245 090093*; ☺ *09.00–23.00 daily*; *www. rattrayparkkumasi.com; entry US$2.50/1.25 adults/kids*) It might seem difficult to believe at times, but Kumasi's nickname has long been 'the garden city', and while the moniker can often seem hopelessly obsolete today, this new park, rather unexpectedly named after Scottish colonial official and early student of the Ashanti, Robert Sutherland Rattray, makes a valiant effort at keeping the garden city nickname relevant. Opened in 2015 on 4ha of immaculately tended, grassy grounds criss-crossed by cobblestone paths and centred around several busts of Ashanti royalty and a large, dancing fountain, the peace and quiet here (save the piped-in smooth jazz) is worth the price of admission alone. There's a children's playground and some outdoor fitness equipment, along with reasonably clean toilets and two restaurants that had yet to open when we dropped in. If you need a breather from Kumasi's oft-frantic pace, you could do worse than an afternoon here with a picnic basket. There's also Wi-Fi.

MANHYIA PALACE [363 D1] Situated on Antoa Road, about 1km from the National Cultural Centre, this surprisingly low-key palace was built in 1926 following the return from exile of Prempeh II's predecessor and uncle, Asantehene Nana Prempeh I. It remains in use today, and houses a small but interesting **history museum** (☺ *09.00–17.00 daily; entrance US$3.50*), where photography is predictably, but for no apparent reason, forbidden. The best time to visit the palace is Akwasidae Sunday or Awukudae Wednesday, both held every six weeks in accordance with the 40- to 42-day Adae cycle, a set of nine month-like divisions recognised within each calendar year.

The **Akwasidae Festival** days, which are usually peaking in activity between 11.30 and 13.00, is when the Asantehene receives homage from his subjects, as well as from subservient chiefs – a truly spectacular occasion, with a variety of traditional dress on show, great drumming displays, traditional horns blaring and all the rest. The Awukudae, starting at around 10.00, is less dramatic but still worth checking out if you happen to be in town at the time. You're allowed to take photos of the drummers and of the audience (including chiefs with their company), but not the Asantehene, whose bodyguards can be quite rude if you point a camera in his general direction. The dates of upcoming festivals are posted at the tourist office at the National Cultural Centre, and are also posted online at www.manhyiaonline.org.

KWAME NKRUMAH UNIVERSITY OF SCIENCE AND TECHNOLOGY (KNUST) [359 H5] (☏ *03220 60021*; e *uro@knust.edu.gh; www.knust.edu.gh*) Founded by Kwame Nkrumah in 1952, KNUST is one of the most prominent universities in Ghana, situated about 6km east of the city centre, off the Accra road. It is worth visiting for the botanical garden alone, a peaceful and often deserted oasis of tropical vegetation on the city outskirts, with fine displays of bamboo and flowering trees, many labelled specimens, and beautiful butterflies. There is also a museum, archaeological site and swimming pool on campus.

KOFOFROM Those with an interest in traditional sculpture might want to head out to is small village, which lies on the Old Bekwai (now Melcolm) Road roughly 6km south of Ahodwo Circle. The village is famous for its **brass-moulding co-operative** (m 0244 518093), the main product of which is cremation urns, though statues and other figurines are also made and sell from around US$3 upwards, and it is also perhaps the main centre of brass bead production in Ghana. The craftsmen use recycled brass, melting down old taps and pipes, etc, and will gladly show interested visitors how they create the mould, using a combination of beeswax, clay and coconut hairs. You can visit independently or arrange a tour through Four Villages Inn (page 365).

BIA NATIONAL PARK AND RESOURCE RESERVE

Situated along the Ivorian border west of Kumasi, the 280km² Bia Resource Reserve and 78km² Bia National Park (*entrance US$5 non-Ghanaian adult, with a 50% discount for students; US$2.50pp/hr for a guide*) protect a remote and seldom visited tract of forest that was effectively closed to tourists until a guesthouse opened there in 2008. Bia protects an important area of virgin rainforest, noted for its enormous biodiversity. In addition to trees reaching a height of 60m, the reserve harbours many mammal species, including bongo, forest elephant, and all eight of the forest-associated higher primates that occur in Ghana, but tourists should not expect to see mammals in rainforest conditions. The bird list now stands at 203, while 668 species of butterfly have been recorded.

Various walking trails have been cut through the national park, and it is possible to drive into the reserve from the eastern side. A 3km loop walk from the guesthouse at Kunkumso takes you to the Apaso Rock, which offers spectacular views of the forest in an area teeming with birdlife. The rock and its pools form a shrine for the local people, who believe it to be the home of spirits that exercise a great deal of power, assisting people to have good fortune and helping barren women procreate. There is an annual Yam Festival in honour of these spirits. Visitors are welcome, but are asked to respect the rules and conditions of visiting the rock.

GETTING THERE AND AWAY Administratively, this isolated reserve falls into Western Region, but since it is most easily visited as a round trip from Kumasi, we have chosen to include it in this chapter. This can be done using public transport, but it is a long and, for the last part, bumpy ride, so worth doing only if you intend to spend at least three nights in the reserve. It is best visited during the dry season as the unsealed roads can be hazardous during the rains.

The main entrance to Bia lies at New Debiso (aka Kunkumso), about 240km west of Kumasi along a road that is surfaced for all but the last 94km. A couple of trotros run between Kumasi and Debiso daily, taking about seven hours, and passing through Bibiani (Ashanti Goldfields' opencast mine), Sefwi Bekwai and Sefwi Wiawso. The road from Sefwi Wiawso to the Ivorian border is now being rebuilt to a very high standard.

From here the road is gravel and can be very bumpy in the wet season. About 2km past the market town of Asawinso, turn right at the police barrier and take the road to Debiso through the Krokosua Hills and the village of Asempanye. The Bia National Park headquarters (**m** *0205 386665/0201 703083*) is signposted on the left but the park entrance is at **Kunkumso**, 23km further on. Kunkumso is situated at the north end of the national park on a road junction. The northern road (straight ahead) goes to Debiso (5km) and the western road goes to the border. Both have customs barriers at New Debiso. The entrance gate to the national park is about 20m past the left-hand barrier on the left of the road to the border. (If you miss New Debiso, a taxi back there from Debiso takes about 15 minutes.)

WHERE TO STAY AND EAT About 100m from the entrance gate lies **Kunkumso Guesthouse**, a one-storey cabin consisting of two double rooms with bedding provided, en-suite toilet and shower, electricity, and a shared kitchen and dining room with gas stove, pots, plates and cutlery. Visitors should bring all their own food. **Camping** is permitted next to the guesthouse. Rooms are US$13 per person; camping costs US$5.50 per person.

SEND US YOUR SNAPS!

We'd love to follow your adventures using our *Ghana* guide – why not send us your photos and stories via Twitter (🐦 @BradtGuides) and Instagram (📷 @bradtguides) using the hashtag #ghana. Alternatively, you can upload your photos directly to the gallery on the Ghana destination page via our website (*www.bradtguides.com*).

17

Greater Ashanti

The lush countryside within a 50km radius of Kumasi is the core region of Ashanti, comprising as it does the six states that combined forces in the late 17th century under the Golden Stool. It is also a region that offers some great opportunities for unstructured travel, with its mix of cultural and natural attractions ranging from 19th-century fetish houses and several kente-weaving and other craft villages to pedestrian-friendly forest reserves and the lovely Lake Bosomtwe.

Travellers generally explore the region using Kumasi as a base (of the places listed in this chapter, only Lake Bosomtwe is more often visited as an overnight excursion than a day trip), and the regional capital is certainly far better equipped than anywhere else in Ashanti when it comes to hotels and restaurants. For those who prefer to get away from tourist hubs, however, small towns such as Mampong or Ejisu could also serve as a base for exploring Ashanti, as could the likeable Moon and Star Guesthouse in Banko, and it would also be possible to travel around whimsically, staying overnight at wherever you happened to end up. One obvious advantage of steering clear of Kumasi is that it would eliminate the need to navigate the city's legendary traffic jams whenever you want to get out.

Given that tastes and interests differ, it would be restrictive to describe the places covered in this chapter in the form of a prescribed circuit. Instead, we've chosen to follow them in roughly anticlockwise sequence, starting immediately northeast of Kumasi with the textile-production villages of Ntonso, Bonwire, Wonoo and Adanwomase, then continuing westwards to Owabi Wildlife Sanctuary, southwards to Lake Bosomtwe, east to Ejisu and Bobiri Butterfly Sanctuary, and finally spiralling outwards to the more remote northeastern towns of Effiduase, Kumawu and Mampong. With the exception of Owabi and to a lesser extent Bosomtwe, you can travel between virtually any of the places listed in this chapter without returning to Kumasi, making use of the small trotros and shared taxis that connect just about any two villages in the area. Alternatively, if you have time restrictions or can't be bothered with using public transport, you can arrange a taxi for the day out of Kumasi – expect to pay around US$30 for about six hours of driving around.

CRAFT VILLAGES NORTHEAST OF KUMASI

Ashanti lies at the heart of Ghana's traditional cloth industry (see box, pages 382–3), and four of the region's most renowned centres of textile production form an arc about 20km northeast of Kumasi. Running from east to west, the four villages are Bonwire (the country's best-known centre of kente cloth production), then Adanwomase and Wonoo (formerly known for kente cloth) and Ntonso (a major adinkra production centre on the Mampong road). Any of these villages can be visited as an easy day trip out of Kumasi, with Adanwomase having superseded Bonwire as the most popular option in recent years due to its well-organised community tourism programme. It should be noted that while these artisanal villages are good places to see traditional kente weavers and adinkra dyers at work, they are not necessarily the best places to buy the product, as overcharging is rife.

NTONSO Straddling the main Mampong road about 20km northeast of Kumasi, Ntonso is Ghana's major centre for the design and manufacture of adinkra – the red-and-black dyed cloth that you often see older Ghanaians wearing draped around them as a toga on Saturdays, since it is the customary attire for funerals. It is not the cloth itself – either plain kente or imported cotton – that is made in Ntonso, but rather the dye stamps, which can be bought here as well as the stamped product. Once rather a chaotic experience, tourism to Ntonso has now been formalised (and to some extent sanitised) by the opening of a **visitor centre** (m *0249 547110/596759;* ☺ *08.00–18.00 Mon–Sat*) on the right side of the road as you enter the village coming from Kumasi. The centrepiece of the visitor centre is a shop selling adinkra cloth dyed onsite (expect to pay around US$30 for a 2m² strip or US$125 for 15m²), and there is also a kiosk selling cold drinks. They will also demonstrate the dyeing process from start to finish, which takes around 45 minutes and costs US$1.50. So far as we can ascertain, the village tours once offered by the visitor centre have been discontinued.

In theory, Ntonso is a straightforward 20- to 30-minute drive northeast of Kumasi along the Mampong road, though it may take a lot longer in practice, due to heavy traffic. Any trotro heading between Kumasi and Mampong can drop you at Ntonso; these can be picked up at Kejetia Station or by waiting at Suame Traffic Circle. If you want to overnight in Ntonso, the **Dapaah Siakwan Executive Lodge** (*4 rooms;* m *0205 232084; map, pages 380–1*), about 1km along the Adanwomase road, is a very agreeable and reasonably priced set-up charging US$8/14 for a clean, self-contained room with fan or air conditioning.

Between Kumasi and Ntonso, the villages of Ahwiaa and Pankrona are known respectively for their woodcarvings and pottery. In both cases, however, you've little chance of seeing the craftsmen at work. At one point, the level of aggro meant these places were worth visiting only if you planned to buy, but recent reports suggest that this is no longer the case at Ahwiaa.

ADANWOMASE Also known as Adangomase, this peaceful little village is one of the five original kente stools founded by Denkyira exiles, who settled around Kumasi shortly after their homeland was conquered by King Osei Tutu in 1701. It is still a good place to see kente being made today, and more accessible than in previous years following the set up of a community-based tourism venture that stands out for its friendly and informative attitude. Two one-hour tours are available, both of them fascinating in their own right. Tours must be arranged through the **visitor centre** (m *0209 162925/0548 067989/0249 098609/0240 884409;* ☺ *06.00–18.00 daily*), which lies 100m to the right of the main road coming from Ntonso or Kumasi. The charge is US$4 per person for each of the tours for non-Ghanaians, or US$5.50 for both, with discounts for volunteers and students.

The kente tour follows the production of this famous cloth from the spun thread through to the finished strip, weaving around the village where locals work in a new communal workshop or alone under the trees, and comes with explanations of the various types of cloth and the symbolism of their patterns. The village tour takes in the chief's palaces (both old and new), a traditional healer's shrine, local cocoa farms, and the *danwoma* tree for which the village was named: rather chilling local tradition has it that Adanwomase was founded when the seed was planted in the ground along with a human being who was buried alive.

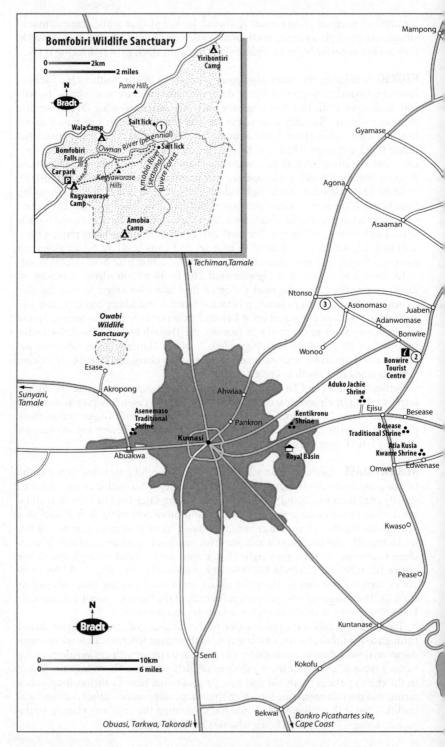

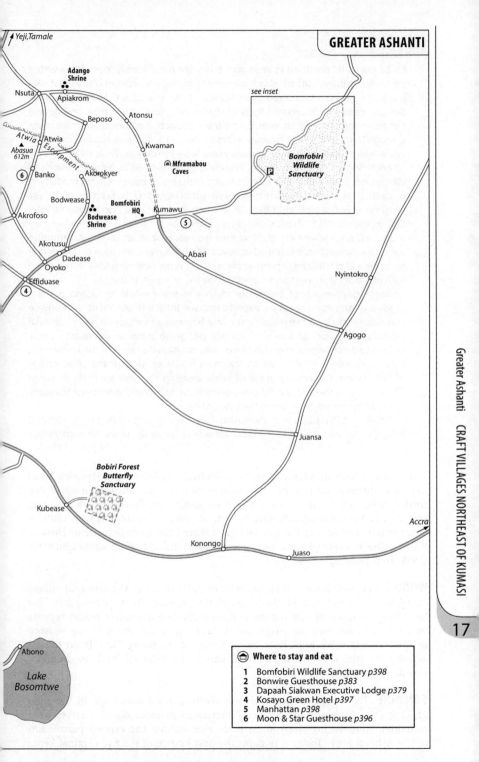

↑ Yeji, Tamale

Nsuta

Adango Shrine

Apiakrom

Beposo

Atonsu

Atwia Escarpment

Atwia

Abasua 612m

6 Banko

Akorokyer

Kwaman

Mframabou Caves

Bodwease

Akrofoso

Bodwease Shrine

Bomfobiri HQ

Kumawu

5

Akotusu

Dadease

Abasi

Oyoko

Effiduase

4

Nyintokro

Agogo

Juansa

Bobiri Forest Butterfly Sanctuary

Kubease

Accra

Konongo

Juaso

Abono

Lake Bosomtwe

see inset

Bomfobiri Wildlife Sanctuary

P

Where to stay and eat

1 Bomfobiri Wildlife Sanctuary *p398*
2 Bonwire Guesthouse *p383*
3 Dapaah Siakwan Executive Lodge *p379*
4 Kosayo Green Hotel *p397*
5 Manhattan *p398*
6 Moon & Star Guesthouse *p396*

Of all the crafts practised in West Africa, few are more readily identifiable with a particular country than kente cloth with Ghana. Strongly associated with the Ashanti, modern kente is characterised by intricately woven and richly colourful geometric designs, generally dominated by bold shades of yellow, green, blue, orange and red. However, in its earliest form, before the introduction of exotic fabrics and dyes through trade with the European castles of the coast, kente cloth was somewhat less kaleidoscopic, since white and navy blue were the only available dyes.

According to Ashanti tradition, kente design originated at Bonwire, the small village close to Kumasi that still serves as one of the main centres of kente production in south-central Ghana. Five kente stools were proclaimed by the first king of Kumasi, of which only Bonwire and Adanwomase remain active. The Ewe people of Volta Region, the country's other important centre of kente production, maintain that they were the first kente weavers, and that their techniques were adopted in Ashanti after some Ewe weavers were captured as slaves. While the Ewe claim has a certain ring of truth, the reality is that most people now associate kente cloth with Ashanti, where the skills of the finest weavers are reserved for the use of royalty to this day.

These days, much of the kente cloth you see on sale in Ghana is mass produced, and considered by experts to have little intrinsic merit. At Bonwire and Adanwomase, however, almost every homestead includes a few traditional weavers, who work at looms of ancient design to produce top-quality cloth. Visitors to Volta Region may also like to visit traditional centres of the kente craft, such as Kpetoe, a small town on the main Ho–Aflao road, or the small village of Tafi Abuipe. The best example of kente weaving that you are likely to see in Ghana today is the century-old piece of cloth on display in the National Museum, formerly the property of one of the kings of Ashanti.

Adinkra cloth is popular in many Akan societies, but is most strongly associated with the Ashanti. Like kente cloth, adinkra is generally worn by men in the

The easiest route to Adanwomase from Kumasi is to follow the Mampong Road to Ntonso, then (about 1km past that village's visitors centre) turn right into a side road signposted for Bonwire and follow it for about 5km. Trotros to Adanwomase run directly from Kumasi's Kejetia station, or you can combine it with visits to other artisanal villages in the area and get a shared taxi from Bonwire or Ntonso. It is possible to overnight at a basic **guesthouse** affiliated to the visitors centre for US$8–16 depending on the room.

WONOO Less well known than Bonwire or Adanwomase, the artisanal village of Wonoo was not one of the original five Ashanti kente stools, but also has a long tradition of weaving the famous cloth. Unfortunately, reader reports in 2015 and our own investigations in 2016 revealed the seeming closure of the weaving workshops here, so as things stand today there is no tourist activity in Wonoo and visitors will simply be referred back to Bonwire or Adanwomase.

BONWIRE The village of Bonwire first received royal patronage in the time of King Osei Tutu, and for centuries afterwards its most skilful weavers were forbidden from selling cloth to anybody else without the express permission of the Ashanti king. Today it remains the best known of the five original kente

form of a toga, but its use is reserved for funerals and other relatively sombre occasions rather than for celebrations, and adinkra symbolism takes the form of monochrome graphics as opposed to the colourful geometric abstractions of kente. Most contemporary adinkra cloth is made using a plain white calico textile that is then decorated with various ancient designs using calabash stamps and a dye obtained by boiling the bark of the badie tree (*Bridelia micranta*).

More than 60 different adinkra symbols are in use, each of them signifying a specific tradition or proverb. The most popular of these is the rather Chinese-looking *Gye Nyame*, which symbolises the omnipotence of God, and can be seen all over the country on everything from signboards to plastic chairs, jewellery, and concrete blocks. Another popular symbol is *sankofa*, heart-shaped with two whirls inside, which has taken on a particular resonance in the post-independence era since it signifies the value of building on one's cultural roots. The *kuntinkantan* design of five interlocking circles depicts the value of pride in one's state or society over pride in oneself, while the *pempansie* (like two opposing figures of '3' linked by a concave bar) symbolises a chain and stresses the importance of each member of a society as part of the whole. These and other traditional designs remain at the core of most adinkra designs, but many modern craftsmen will experiment with variations reflecting the changing nature of Ghanaian society.

The origin of the adinkra dyeing technique is uncertain. It is thought to have been adopted by the Ashanti in around 1818, when King Osei Bonsu defeated the Gyaman, whose chief at the time was called Adinkra. Oral traditions differ as to whether the craft originated in the neighbouring territory of Denkyira or in the Jaman Kingdom in what is now Ivory Coast, both of which were vassal states of Ashanti during its early 19th-century peak. Today, the main centre of adinkra production is the village of Ntonso on the main Kumasi–Mampong road.

stools, but perhaps this is why it is also the one where visitors are most likely to be swindled or hassled. All the same, it's a good souvenir pit stop and still a good place to see weavers at work. Several guides are bound to approach you on arrival (they won't ask a fee but will expect a fair tip) but it is easy enough to find your own way to the main **weaving centre** (m *0547 878287;* ☉ *06.00–18.00 daily*), a hassle-free set-up where you can take a short tour (free, but again a tip would be expected) and buy all the cloth you like, though starting prices are somewhat higher than at Adanwomase.

A direct 20km road connects Bonwire to Kumasi, from where it can easily be visited as a self-standing day trip. Trotros to Bonwire leave Kumasi from Manhyia Station, close to the synonymous palace, and take about 30 minutes in either direction, traffic permitting. If you are planning on visiting several craft villages, Bonwire only lies about 2km southeast of Adanwomase (and thus about 7km from Ntonso) along a road that carries a fair volume of traffic. Bonwire can also be reached by shared taxi from Ejisu, following a signposted 3km dirt road that branches west from the Effiduase road a few kilometres south of Juaben. If you want to spend the night, the municipal assembly-run **Bonwire Guesthouse** (m *0243 835163; map, pages 380–1*) is next door to the weaving centre and has clean en-suite rooms with hot water and ceiling fans for US$9 for a double.

17

OWABI WILDLIFE SANCTUARY

One of Ghana's smallest conservation areas, covering a mere 13km², Owabi Wildlife Sanctuary (*entrance US$5pp, 50% discount to students; guide US$2.50/hr*) nevertheless protects a good selection of forested and aquatic habitats, making it an excellent day retreat for wildlife lovers seeking respite from the chaos of Kumasi. The sanctuary was gazetted in 1971 to protect the chunk of pristine forest and reed beds surrounding the Owabi Reservoir, which was constructed by the British on the eponymous rocky river in 1928, and served for many years as Kumasi's sole source of drinking water. Crossed by several footpaths, the sanctuary harbours a great many varieties of butterfly, and more than 100 bird species have been identified – the raucous pied hornbill is among the most conspicuous of the forest birds, while the likes of African finfoot and African jacana might be seen on the reservoir, and kingfishers, barbets, greenbuls and herons are generally well represented. A fair number of large mammals are present: casual visitors stand a reasonable chance of glimpsing Campbell's mona monkey, the population of which is estimated at 500, as well as the semi-habituated Cusimanse mongoose, but are unlikely to see more secretive terrestrial species such as bushpig, bushbuck, Maxwell's duiker or royal antelope.

Easily visited in conjunction with Owabi, **Asenemaso Traditional Shrine** is one of the most unusual of the old fetish houses in Ashanti, since it consists of one large enclosed building rather than four semi-open rooms around a courtyard. Nevertheless, the murals here are excellent, and it is unique in having retained its original ceiling.

GETTING THERE AND AWAY Owabi lies roughly 16km from Kumasi and 3km from the main Sunyani road. The turn-off to the sanctuary is at Akropong, which can be reached by a regular trotro service from Kumasi's Kejetia Station. Most trotros going from Kumasi to Akropong continue along the Owabi turn-off as far as Esase, from where it's a 10-minute walk to the reserve entrance, where you'll have to pay the entrance fee, as well as an additional charge for a mandatory guide.

The village of Asenemaso lies on the Sunyani–Owabi road, 8km from Kumasi, and perhaps 200m past Abuakwa on the junction of the Bibiani road. The shrine itself lies along the road to Akropong and is difficult to find unless you ask around for directions.

LAKE BOSOMTWE

Cupped within a near-circular meteorite crater about 35km south of Kumasi, Lake Bosomtwe (also sometimes spelt Bosumtwi) is Ghana's most expansive natural freshwater body, with an average diameter of 8km and a total surface area of more than 50km². It was declared a UNESCO biosphere reserve in 2016 and is an undoubtedly beautiful spot, with the muddy lake waters being encircled by thickly vegetated and raggedly mountainous crater walls that reach an altitude of greater than 600m. The springboard for visits is the pretty village of Abono, which lies on the northwest shore at the terminus of a surfaced road from Kumasi via Kuntanase. Bosomtwe is now serviced by half a dozen or so lakeshore lodges, most of which lie within a few kilometres of Abono, and it offers plenty of opportunities for outdoor activities such as walking, birding, swimming and horseriding.

BACKGROUND AND HISTORY The origin of the crater that houses Bosomtwe was once hotly debated, but a recent geological study confirmed that it is not volcanic; it

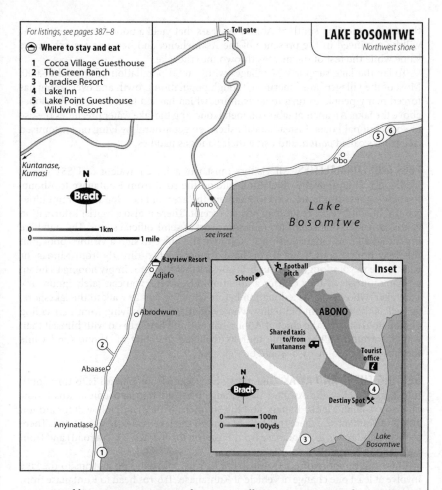

For listings, see pages 387–8

⊜ **Where to stay and eat**
1 Cocoa Village Guesthouse
2 The Green Ranch
3 Paradise Resort
4 Lake Inn
5 Lake Point Guesthouse
6 Wildwin Resort

Kuntanase,
Kumasi

Toll gate

Obo

*L a k e
B o s o m t w e*

see inset

Bayview Resort
Adjafo

Abrodwum

Abaase

Anyinatiase

Inset

School

Football
pitch

ABONO

Shared taxis
to/from
Kuntananse

Tourist
office

Destiny Spot

*Lake
Bosomtwe*

0 — 100m
0 — 100yds

0 — 1km
0 — 1 mile

was created by a meteorite impact about one million years ago. In prehistoric times, the lake level has risen and fallen quite dramatically, influenced both by climatic change and by the availability of water outlets. During periods of heavy rainfall, the lakeshore reached close to the crater rim, leaving sediments rich in fish fossils near the top of what are now tall hills. By contrast, as recently as 300 years ago, the lake itself was little more than a small pond enclosed by rainforest. Today it has a maximum depth of 90m, and the water level is steadily rising, a phenomenon that has resulted in the submersion of several lakeshore villages within living memory.

According to legend, the name Bosomtwe, meaning 'God's antelope', dates to the mid 17th century. The story goes that an Ashanti hunter called Akora Bompe was led to the lake by an injured antelope and settled there when he found it to be a rich source of fish. Lake Bosomtwe is still held sacred by Ashanti traditionalists, who claim that it is the abode of a deity called Twi, and is also visited by the souls of the departed on their passage to eternity. It is also the sacred water body of the Bosomtwe (one of five divisions in the patrilineal *nton* system that the Ashanti and other Akan peoples believe passes a father's attributes to his children), on account of it being as round as the sun, the model for members of the Bosomtwe *nton*. The most important spiritual shrine is the Abrodwum Stone, in the lakeshore village of

the same name 2km south of Abono. In years that yield a poor fish harvest, a cow will be sacrificed in the presence of the Asantehene, and her guts are left on the stone while the rest of the meat is thrown into the lake.
Today the lake supports 27 villages with a total population of around 25,000.
Most of the villagers are fishermen, though population growth and overfishing has forced many people to turn to agriculture, which has led to erosion on the slopes above the lake. An ancient taboo on metal touching the lake water precludes the use of conventional boats. Instead, local fishermen get around by lying on customised tree trunks called *padua*, and using their hands as paddles.

FEES AND FORMALITIES All visitors must pay a fee equivalent to US$1 (up to US$5 on holidays) at the official toll gate on the road from Kuntanase to Abono. In theory, these funds are used to maintain the area and develop the communities around Bosomtwe, so request an official receipt. There is also a tourist information centre in Abono that seems to enjoy some sort of semi-official status. The staff here insist that all non-Ghanaians must stop in at the office to sign a visitors' book, but this may not be convenient if you have arranged a taxi directly from Kumasi or Kuntanase to your lodge, and our best guess is that they are simply hoping to hit up as many tourists as they can for a donation. Elsewhere, you can safely ignore any 'caretaker' who demands a donation before allowing you to walk to the lakeshore, as well as the persistent old fellow who evidently makes a living from persuading gullible tourists that the chief of Abono has nothing better to do with himself than wander around telling gullible tourists that he's the chief of Abono (and while they're about it, some cash would be welcome ...!).

GETTING THERE AND AWAY The most direct route from Kumasi is to turn south into Lake Road at the Asokwa Interchange (the junction of Stadium Road, now officially Appiah Menka Bypass, and the Southern bypass) and follow it for around 30km to Kuntanase, where the descent road to the lake is clearly signposted. There are also good roads to Kuntanase from Ejisu (on the Kumasi–Accra road) and from Bekwai (via Kokofu).
There are no more direct trotros from Kumasi to Abono, so all trips to the lake involve at least one change of vehicle at Kuntanase. Trotros head to Kuntanase from both Kejetia and Asafo stations (trotros from Asafo may require another change at Atonsu-Agogo), as well as from 'Tech Junction' (KNUST) east of the city centre. There are also trotros from Bekwai and Ejisu to Kuntanase, though coming from Ejisu you may need to change vehicles at Piase and Kwaso. Once in Kuntanase, you can pick up a shared taxi to Abono without much trouble.
Note that, with the exception of Lake Inn and Lake Bosomtwe Paradise Resort, most of the accommodation listed below lies at least 2km from Abono along rough roads that aren't serviced by any public transport. If you don't fancy walking, it might be easiest to charter a private taxi in Kuntanase, which should cost around US$10 to any of the lakeshore resorts. It should be about US$5 for a private taxi from Abono, but drivers frequently demand double that, so if you're planning to hire a taxi anyway, you may be better off just doing so directly in Kuntanase.
A considerably more enticing and cost-effective alternative would be to hire a boatman in Abono to ferry you to your hotel. Samuel (m 0505 955384/0541 647828) has a motorboat and can usually be found at Destiny Spot (see map, pages 380–1) in Abono, and a one-way transfer to most of the lakeshore hotels should be about US$5. He can also be hired for longer tours around the lake at US$37/hour for up to 12 passengers.

WHERE TO STAY AND EAT *Map, page 385*

Moderate

Paradise Resort (20 rooms) 03220 95803; m 0205 275724/0203 338805; e info@paradiseresortlakebosomtwe.com; www.paradiseresortlakebosomtwe.com. Ostensibly the most upmarket resort on Bosomtwe, & certainly the most convenient, this place lies in attractive lakeshore grounds immediately south of Abono (accessed along a dirt track to the right of the main road just after the school). The landscaped gardens, dominated by non-indigenous trees, slope down to a secluded beach, & there's a good 1st-floor restaurant with a view over the water. Accommodation is in very spacious & reasonably clean chalets with AC, satellite TV, fridge & en-suite hot shower. The service gets mixed reviews & overall it feels like the place has gone downhill slightly over the last couple of years. *US$49/59 B&B self-contained sgl/dbl.* **$$$**

Budget

✶ **The Green Ranch** (3 rooms) m 0202 917058/0203 534870; e sistaelo@hotmail.com; www.greenranchlakebosomtwe.com. Owned & managed by a delightful Ghanaian–French couple, this much-praised ranch near Abaase, 3km southwest of Abono, started life a few years back as the 1st (& only) horse stable on Lake Bosomtwe, but it has since branched out to offer accommodation in 2 neat en-suite stone rooms & a wooden cabin dorm, all on a cliff offering a great view over the lake below. In addition to horseback excursions, it offers free canoeing on the lake, & a setting well suited to birdwatchers. For overnight guests, fabulous home-cooked vegetarian fare (including a 3-course dinner) is offered, using fresh local produce, organic where possible, plus homemade yoghurts, ice cream, & cottage cheese. Meals are also available to horseriders & other outside visitors by advance arrangement. *US$13/24/35 sgl/dbl/trp; 4-bed dorm US$8pp.* **$$–$**

✶ **Lake Point Guesthouse** (9 rooms) m 0243 452922; e lakepointguest5@gmail.com; www.lakepointguesthouse.com. Set in landscaped gardens with its own private beach near the village of Obo, 2km east of Abono, this attractive Ghanaian–Austrian-owned lodge fits the backpacker budget but could just as easily please mid-range travellers. Neat but rustic en-suite huts with king-sized beds & individualistic,

immaculately finished interiors are dotted around a flourishing garden planted with palm & mango trees, & there is also a 10-bed dorm. The food is widely regarded to be the best on the lake (the menu changes daily according to availability, but most mains are in the US$7–12 range) & it also has filter coffee. *Great value at US$17/22 self-contained dbl/trpl; US$5.50pp dorm bed.* **$$–$**

Cocoa Village Guesthouse (4 rooms) m 0208 612675; e info@cocoa-village.com; www.cocoa-village.com. This bright & creative resort opened here in 2012 and lies in a neat grassy plot on the lakeshore 5km southwest of Abono, near the village of Anyinatiase. There is a pleasant stilted wooden bar & restaurant serving pizzas, pastas & home-baked bread, & accommodation is in airy hand-painted bungalows with fan & lake-facing balcony, & there is also a 6-bed dorm. Bicycles, canoes, traditional paduas & stand-up paddleboards are available for hire, & there's an on-site art studio where guests can take lessons in painting, batik, screenprinting, weaving & more. *US$35 self-contained dbl; US$40 4-bed bungalow; US$9pp dorm bed; US$6pp camping.* **$$–$**

Wildwin Resort (8 rooms) 03220 93265; m 0206 728613/0540 988613; e info@wildwinresort.com; www.wildwinresort.com. Situated 2.5km east of Abono, just past Lake Point Guesthouse, this newish resort has attractive large grounds running down to a good beach, a friendly hands-on owner-manager, & a great little thatched restaurant serving a varied selection of meals for around US$8. The large, tiled en-suite rooms with fan, though decent enough at the price, are set in a rather characterless block set back a few hundred metres from the lake. *US$28–36 self-contained dbl, depending on room size; US$8 dorm bed.* **$$**

Lake Inn (12 rooms) 03222 99399; m 0206 034289; e rawilsonii@gmail.com; www.lakeinnghana.com. Set in a 2-storey block along the lakeshore in Abono, rooms at this new American-owned hotel don't take much advantage of the lakefront location, but they're spacious & comfortable nonetheless, & the friendly owner-manager is happy to arrange boats, bikes, & hikes around the lake. The restaurant serves good-value grills & Ghanaian dishes, & there's a weekly bonfire & cultural performance on Sat nights. The budget rooms weren't ready when we checked in, but should be by the time you read this. *US$11 budget* *dbl with fan; US$18 self-contained twin with fan; US$21/26 self-contained dbl/king with AC.* **$$–$**

WHAT TO SEE AND DO Plenty of people swim in the lake (there is reputedly no bilharzia, though this sort of assertion is difficult to confirm) and traditional padua canoes can be arranged through the various lakeshore lodgings. Informal trips around the lake can be arranged with local boat owners (page 386), and a small passenger boat normally circumnavigates the lake every Sunday ferrying locals between the different villages.

The lake is also circumnavigated by roads and tracks with a total length of around 32km, offering ample opportunities for walking and birding. Among the more interesting sites close to Abono are the Abrodwum Stone in the eponymous village 2km to the southwest, and the butterfly-rich Obo river valley 2km to the east. Further afield, the village of Banso, on the southern lakeshore 10km from Abono, is the site of an old Catholic church as well as the mouth of the clear Aberewa River, which is worshipped as the 'Mother of the Lake', while nearby Hantase hosts a large breeding colony of weaver birds. On the west side of the lake, an old overflow channel running downhill from Konkoma supports a belt of lush riparian woodland frequented by plentiful birds and small numbers of monkeys. It's also possible to rent a bicycle from several of the lodges, allowing you to explore more remote parts of the lakeshore.

The most recent additions to Bosomtwe's portfolio of tourist activities are the horseback excursions operated from the Green Ranch. These have been universally praised by readers since they started up in 2011, and range from short excursions, charged at US$15/hour, to a full 9–10-hour trip around the lake, which costs around US$105 for the first person and US$91 for each additional rider. By advance arrangement, they can also prepare excellent vegetarian meals for after the ride.

OBUASI

Situated some 85km south of Kumasi, Obuasi is Ghana's most important gold-mining centre and the home of the AngloGold Ashanti mining company, which stopped offering guided tours of its workings several years ago. Despite an attractive setting in a valley ringed by verdant hills, this town of 400,000 inhabitants couldn't have much less going for it aesthetically, though it is a good place to buy locally produced gold jewellery, or to buy the gold dust and design it yourself. There's also an attractive **golf course** (✆ *0582 40494*; m *0244 419565*) behind the Catholic church. In Patakro, on the Kumasi road about 10km north of Obuasi, lies the most southerly of the extant 19th-century *obosomfies* (Ashanti shrine houses) and, in front of it, four statues of similar vintage.

GETTING THERE AND AWAY Obuasi is connected to Kumasi by regular minibus-taxis as well as an hourly Metro Mass bus. There's also public transport to the south, but self-drivers should note that the road to Takoradi via Tarkwa is in notoriously bad shape.

⌂ **WHERE TO STAY AND EAT** The best hotel by far is the two-star **Coconut Grove Miners Lodge** (*24 rooms;* ✆*03225 40550/1;* e *minerslodge@coconutgrovehotelsghana. com; www.coconutgrovehotelsghana.com*), where adequately comfortable rooms with air conditioning, satellite television and hot water cost around US$60 for a double. Recently opened, both **Cofkans Hotel** (✆ *03225 41200;* m *0208 000092;* e *info@cofkans.com; www.cofkanshotel.com/new*) and **Golden Icon Hotel** (✆ *03223*

94386; e info@goldeniconhotel.com; www.goldeniconhotel.com) boast swimming pools and similar standard business-orientated accommodation. The reader-recommended **Anyinam Lodge** (m 03225 40473; e anyinamlodgeanglogodashanti@ yahoo.com) also has a pool, while budget options include the **Silence Hotel** (m 0271 863869/0244 450024), which lies no more than 5 minutes' walk from the lorry station via the market, and cheaper **New Paradise Lodge** (m 03225 82283) next to the lorry station. Ghana Commercial Bank and Standard Chartered are represented here with ATMs, and **Goldfinger Restaurant** (m 0276 329966), near the central roundabout and post office, has been recommended as the best restaurant/bar in town.

BONKRO PICATHARTES SITE

Based primarily on a 2012 trip report by Noëlle and Hervé Jacob
The village of Bonkro, 14km east of New Edubiase (administrative capital of the forested district of Adansi South), is probably the most reliable place globally to look for the white-necked picathartes, a peculiar and highly localised bird that ranks as Ghana's top ornithological attraction (see box, pages 406–7). The picathartes breeds in a cave that lies about 45 minutes' walk from Bonkro, along a footpath through lush rainforest, and whose walls are covered with up to 30 of the distinctive cupped mud nests constructed by this unusual bird. The odds of a sighting are very good throughout the year, provided you head out in the late afternoon, and are prepared to wait until the birds return to their nests for the night, usually some time after 17.00. A community fee equivalent to US$15 per person is charged, and the mandatory guide(s) will expect a tip – around US$5 per head seems fair.

Although it is unusual to miss out on the picathartes, assuming you are at the cave at the right hour, dedicated birders might want to allow time for a second visit, just in case they are out of luck first time. Either way, these birds are IUCN listed as Vulnerable, the guides at Bonkro are poorly trained (though the Wildlife Division hopes to secure funding to improve training) and too much human disturbance could ultimately result in the abandonment of their nests and nesting sites. To avoid this, it is best to wait for the birds away from the nest site as much as possible (at least 7m from the cliff) and not against the cliff, as is often done. Once the birds arrive, refrain from creating any unnecessary noise or other disturbance, and discourage the guides from taking you too close to the nests (particularly for better photographs), or staying on once you have had a good sighting. For large groups, individuals should take turns to view the birds from a vantage point away from the rock outcrop. Avoid using the camera flash too many times.

GETTING THERE AND AWAY The springboard for visits to Bonkro is the small town of New Edubiase, situated about 75km south of Kumasi on the main road to Assin Fosu and Cape Coast. Coming from the north, after arriving in New Edubiase you need to turn left at the Ghana Commercial Bank intersection, and keep going straight, past a filling station, taking the only fork to the left, until you arrive at the village of Breku after about 13km. It is another 500m or so from here to Bonkro, and everybody will know why you have visited, so you'll have no problem finding a guide to take you to the nesting site. Using public transport, it is straightforward enough to get to New Edubiase from Kumasi and most other nearby towns, but it is unclear whether any public transport heads out to Bonkro. Even if it does, given that you're only likely to return from the cave after nightfall, you are probably safer chartering a taxi from New Edubiase and having it wait for you in Bonkro.

Greater Ashanti   BONKRO PICATHARTES SITE

17

Designated as Ghana's second UNESCO World Heritage Site in 1980 (and still one of only two such sites in the country), the Ashanti Traditional Buildings Site comprises a scattered collection of ten ancient fetish shrines or *abosomfie* (singular *obosomfie*), most of which lie to the east or northeast of Kumasi. Originally constructed in the 18th or 19th century, these vulnerable mud, wood and straw buildings have been described by UNESCO as 'the last material remains of the great Ashanti civilisation'. For the most part, they remain active shrines, and their existence provides curious travellers with a strong incentive to explore a mystical aspect of Ashanti tradition easily overlooked in the urban bustle of modern Kumasi.

The most accessible of the shrines, and the only one formally geared up for tourism, is the restored Besease Traditional Shrine near Ejisu, some 20km east of Kumasi. It is a fine example of an obosomfie, a building traditionally regarded to be the spiritual abode of a particular Obosom, the name given to one of the lesser deities who mediate between mortals and the supreme god Nyame. The Obosom maintains a permanent presence in its shrine, but manifests itself only on set occasions through the medium of a fetish priest or Okomfo, who becomes possessed by the spirit and acts as its mouthpiece. Traditionally, the Okomfo is regarded to be the most important member of a community, and he or she works closely with the chief, who will call on the Obosom for advice before any important decision is made.

Over the last century, the importance of the fetish houses has diminished greatly. Speak to many Christians in Ashanti, and they will dismiss the traditional beliefs embodied by these shrines as pure superstition. And yet it is also the case, particularly in rural areas, that many Ashanti people adhere concurrently to Christianity and their traditional systems of faith. The ambiguities can be difficult for outsiders to come to grips with. At Bodwease, for instance, the last fetish priest has been dead for more than two decades, yet the shrine is still maintained by the local community in the belief that the resident Obosom is still there, and just waiting to settle on a human medium to act as their fetish priest.

Many of the extant shrine houses are still inhabited by a fetish priest, who sits in session on specific days (typically Sunday and/or Friday) and is consulted by a stream of locals requiring spiritual advice. A fetish priest can be male or female, and although the role is occasionally hereditary, it can fall on anybody who is called to service by the resident Obosom. There are also many fetish priests in Ashanti who operate outside of a traditional shrine house.

When the ten extant abosomfie of Ashanti joined the coastal forts and castles on the UNESCO World Heritage Sites list, it was not solely for their spiritual significance, but also because they form the only surviving examples of traditional Ashanti architecture. Not easy to imagine today, but Kumasi, prior to being razed by the British in 1874, was by all accounts an unusually beautiful city, the wide streets lined by airy houses of a unique architectural style. The typical house of the period consisted of several rooms centred on a quadrangular courtyard and shaded by steep thatched roofs, often rising at an angle greater than 60 degrees. The lower walls were polished orange, while the upper walls were whitewashed. Another characteristic feature of

⌂ **WHERE TO STAY AND EAT** There is no accommodation in Bonkro, but you can stay overnight in New Edubiase – a good idea because the best time to look for the picathartes is after 17.00. The **Hotel Boa Temaa Lodge** (m *0272 203483/0243 468327*) has adequate double rooms for around US$12, while

19th-century Ashanti homesteads was carved murals of symbols similar to those found on adinkra cloth. Much of what is known of pre-colonial Kumasi comes from the verbal accounts of European travellers such as Bowdich (1819) and Winniett (1884), but the handful of black-and-white photographs that survive do provide a visual record of what Kumasi must have looked like in its heyday.

The ten extant abosomfie, some of which are said to be more than 200 years old, are of typical pre-colonial Ashanti construction in general appearance, while also boasting certain features unique to fetish houses. With a couple of exceptions, the abosomfie all conform to a ground plan of four rooms facing into a large courtyard. Three of these rooms – the drumming, singing and cooking rooms – are open on the courtyard side, while the fourth, which houses the actual shrine, is screened off and may be entered only by the priest and his assistants. In the courtyard of all the shrines stands a *Nyame Dua* – the altar to the supreme god, which generally consists of a pot wedged on a forked branch. Many of the shrines are littered with a variety of fetishes, most unexpectedly the tortoises that mill around the base of the *Nyame Dua* ('when they die, they don't need coffins, because they have their own …').

Tourists are generally welcome to any priest or shrine. For the casual visitor, the most interesting of these is at Besease, about 1km from Ejisu. This is the only ancient building in Ashanti where the roof has been fully restored, and it also contains a number of informative displays. Curious travellers who prefer to visit a shrine under less formal circumstances might want to seek out two further examples in the immediate vicinity of Besease, at Edwenase and Aduko Jachie. There are also superb examples at Bodwease (see *Effiduase*, page 397), Apiakrom (see *Mampong*, page 400), Patakro (see *Obuasi*, page 388) and Asenemaso (see *Owabi Wildlife Sanctuary*, page 384).

With the exception of Besease, which to all intents and purposes functions as a museum, none of the fetish houses is formally established as a tourist site. In most cases, the shrines are held sacred by the surrounding community, and many are still occupied by a priest. Some charge an official entrance fee, while others don't, but under no circumstances should you enter a shrine without offering a libation in advance and/or making a donation afterwards. The mood differed at every shrine house that we visited, and it might well differ from one day to the next at any given shrine, which makes it difficult to offer hard and fast advice. In hindsight, our feeling is that the best approach is to follow the local custom when visiting a chief or fetish priest, which is to offer a bottle of schnapps as a libation (one bottle would be fine for two people visiting together). If you prefer to offer a donation, then a reasonable guideline would be the price of a bottle of schnapps (check this in Kumasi) or the entrance fee to Besease shrine (about US$2 per person at the time of writing).

A lavish booklet entitled *Asante Traditional Buildings*, published by the Ghana Museums and Monuments Board in 1999, and available at most museums in the country as well as at Besease Traditional Shrine, is highly recommended to those with an interest in the local architecture.

Nina's Guesthouse is better quality but slightly pricier. Better but more remote accommodation is available in Assin Fosu, where the one-star **Babeven Hotel** (m *0242 670628/0245 539606*) is a popular base for ornithological tours to the region.

EJISU AND SURROUNDS

The busy little junction town of Ejisu, situated 20km east of Kumasi at the intersection of the main road to Accra and branch roads leading north to Effiduase and south to Kuntanase, lies within striking distance of three of the region's most accessible abosomfie shrines, all described fully in the box on pages 390–1. Ejisu is best known historically as the birthplace and home of Yaa Asantewaa, the queen mother who instigated the Ashanti siege of Kumasi Fort in 1900. Sadly, the out-of-town Yaa Asantewaa Museum burnt down in 2004, consuming many items that once belonged to the queen mother, and there are no indications it will ever be rebuilt. However, a statue of Ejisu's most famous daughter now stands prominently on the main traffic circle, while 100m further south, on the left side of the Kuntanase road, the original Yaa Asantewaa House is still lived in by her descendants, who will show visitors around and recount her history for a small fee. On Sundays, the stretch of road in front of the Yaa Asantewaa House transforms into a pedestrian mall hosting one of the region's most spectacular markets.

GETTING THERE AND AWAY Ejisu straddles the main road to Accra about 30 minutes' drive from Kumasi (longer when traffic is heavy) and a steady stream of minibuses runs throughout the day in both directions. Coming from central Kumasi, rather than head to the trotro station, the best place to pick up transport to Ejisu is at the interchange west of the railway bridge at the intersection of Fuller and Osei Tutu II roads (you're unlikely to wait more than five minutes for something to come past).

There are also regular trotros connecting Ejisu to Effiduase and Kuntanase (the latter more usually via a series of short hops) – just wait at the traffic circle [393 D3]. The taxi station close to the main traffic circle and Yaa Asantewaa House [393 D3] is the place to pick up shared taxis to local destinations.

WHERE TO STAY AND EAT Although Ejisu can easily be visited as a day trip out of Kumasi, it boasts a couple of decent hotels, and could serve as a useful base for exploring the Kumasi area.

Upmarket

⌂ **Anita Hotel** [393 E1] (86 rooms) ✆03220 35550; m 0248 631124; e info@anita-hotelgh. com; www.anita-hotelgh.com. Situated on the Accra road about 1km past the main traffic circle in Ejisu, this smart new business-class hotel might feel rather overstated for its surrounds, but it is the equal of anything in Kumasi when it comes to value for money in a similar price range. Large tiled rooms look very clean & comfortable & come with free Wi-Fi, satellite TV, AC, fridge & hairdryer. Facilities include a good restaurant, a large swimming pool & a gym. *US$47/57/77 sgl/ dbl/suite.* **$$$**

Budget

⌂ **Gina Pee Guesthouse** [393 E2] (14 rooms) ✆03221 95444; m 0240 751066/0244 535417.

Situated about 1.5km out of town along the Kuntanase road, this pleasantly rustic guesthouse has clean, sensibly priced rooms & a friendly feel, with the only drawback being that there is a bar but no restaurant, so you would need to walk or drive to town to eat. *US$7 self-contained dbl with fan; US$8.50/14.50 self-contained dbl with fan/ AC & TV.* **$**

⌂ **Ejisu Hotel** [393 C3] (15 rooms) m 0244 036726/0245 070830. This friendly budget hotel, situated in the town centre only 50m from the main Accra road, is one of the best deals in the region, though we have had a nocturnal mugging reported along the alley between it & the main road. Rooms are large & clean, & while no meals are available, plenty of street food & bars can be found in town. *US$6.50 dbl with fan & shared bath; US$8–11 self-contained dbl depending on size.* **$**

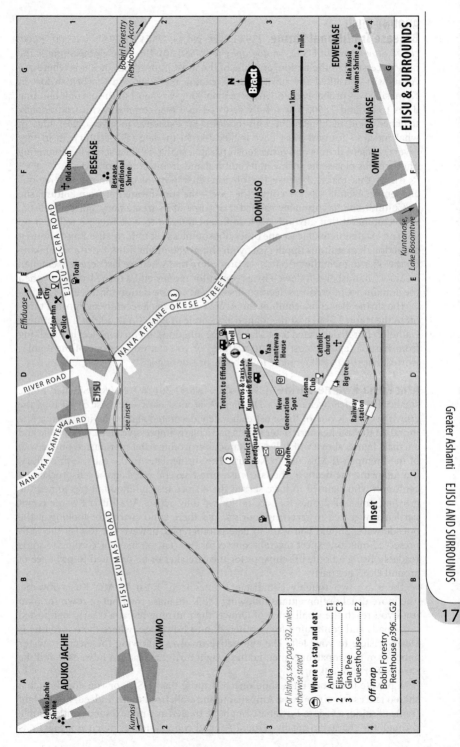

EJISU & SURROUNDS

Off map
Bobiri Forestry
Resthouse p396.....G2

For listings, see page 392, unless
otherwise stated
Where to stay and eat
1 Anita...............E1
2 Ejisu...............C3
3 Gina Pee
   Guesthouse.......E2

AROUND EJISU

Besease Traditional Shrine [393 F1] (✪ *N6 43.425 W1 26.984;* ⏰ *08.00–17.00, closed Sun; entrance US$2, photography fee US$0.50*) This lovely obosomfie is the most accessible in the region, and one of the most important, since it is where Yaa Asantewaa consulted the spirits before leading the attack on the British fort in Kumasi. It was probably founded more than 300 years ago, but the current building dates to around 1850. It was fully restored in 1998, complete with traditionally thatched roof, making it the only building in existence to give a clear idea of what much of Kumasi must have looked like in the late 19th century. Inside are several ancient drums and other fetish paraphernalia, while a series of fascinating photographs places the shrine in its cultural and architectural context.

All of this makes Besease the obvious first port of call among the region's abosomfie, even if – as is so often the case – the transformation from cultural site to Cultural Site has arguably robbed it of some of its immediacy. For this reason, we recommend that anybody with sufficient interest to visit Besease follow it up with an excursion to at least one other obosomfie as yet unformalised into a tourist attraction. If gratuitous tipping isn't your thing, you might think twice about taking up the offer to meet the priestess – a procedure that when we last acceded, entailed a cursory handshake, followed by a request for money and a turned-up nose when the amount we offered was deemed insufficient compensation for her efforts.

The shrine lies 200m south of the Accra road, along a recently signposted turn-off to the right, 2.5km past the main traffic circle in Ejisu (look out for a prominent Catholic church dedicated to St Mary on the junction). If you don't feel like walking from Ejisu, a taxi will cost next to nothing, or you can wait for one of the regular trotros that run past it *en route* to Kubease or Konongo.

Atia Kusia Kwame Shrine [393 G4] (✪ *N6 41.301 W1 26.083*) Situated in the small village of Edwenase (aka Dwenease), around 6km southeast of Ejisu as the crow flies, this is one of the most elaborately decorated abosomfie in Ashanti. The mural on the southeastern outer wall is particularly impressive, depicting a male and a female figure, above which lies the famous crocodile relief reproduced on the wall of the Prempeh II Museum in Kumasi. The shrine dates to the early 19th century, but following the death of the last fetish priest several years ago, a self-proclaimed centurion who claimed to have served there since his childhood, it has joined the growing ranks of shrines that are no longer fully active. Atia Kusia Kwame is not particularly geared to receiving tourists, and there is no charge for looking at the outside walls. Should you want to take photographs, however, or to visit the well-preserved interior, expect several requests for tips (far too many, according to some readers). Bring a bottle of schnapps for the caretaker or be prepared to pay a fee of around US$5 per party.

There are two roughly equidistant routes from Ejisu to Atia Kusia Kwame. The more usual option entails following the Kuntanase road out of town for 6km until you reach the small town of Omwe, then turning left at a clearly signposted crossroads and continuing for another 2km to Edwenase, where the obosomfie is clearly visible to your left. The alternative involves following the Accra road for about 6km to Ampabame, then taking a right turn that leads to Edwenase and the shrine after about 3km.

A private taxi from Ejisu shouldn't cost more than US$5, or you could catch a shared taxi as far as Omwe or Ampabame and walk from there. Indeed, in the right frame of mind, a visit to Edwenase might be treated as a pretext for a gentle ramble through the characteristically verdant Ashanti countryside, as much as a goal in its own right. The route from Ejisu is pretty flat, and it shouldn't take longer than 90 minutes to cover in either direction.

Aduko Jachie Shrine [393 A1] (✪ *N6 43.422 W1 30.678*) Despite being situated no more than 10 minutes' walk from the main Kumasi–Accra road, this striking obosomfie is visited by few tourists. It used to be kept by a flamboyantly dreadlocked fetish priest, who has since upped and gone – depending on who you talk to, he left to become a musician, was fired after an altercation with the queen mother, was destooled after fitting the shrine with electric lights, or opted to relocate to a less ancient shrine after being called by a different spirit. The outer wall is decorated with a few rather primitive and unpromising paintings, but the well-maintained interior – decorated with beautiful murals, and housing numerous fetishes and artefacts dating to the last priest's time there – is well worth a look.

Aduko Jachie Shrine lies a short distance north of the main road between Kumasi and Ejisu. Coming from Kumasi, the (unsignposted) junction is to your left about 4km before Ejisu. Follow this dirt road for slightly more than 1km until you reach Jachie village, and turn left when you see a building with statues of lions on the outside. The shrine is enclosed within the next compound. The friendly female caretaker lives close by and will charge around US$5 per person to let you inside, though the price is negotiable for larger groups.

BOBIRI BUTTERFLY SANCTUARY

Situated within walking distance of the main Accra road about 30km east of Kumasi as the crow flies, Bobiri is one of the most worthwhile day or overnight destinations in the Ashanti Region, particularly for those seeking a peaceful and affordable forest retreat rattling with animal life. Set aside as a forest reserve in 1939, the sanctuary comprises 55km² of near-pristine semi-deciduous forest, and though some parts are logged selectively on a 40-year cycle, significant sections of high canopy forest preserve some fine examples of giant African teak (*Milicia excelsa*) and mahogany-like *Entandrophragma* trees. Six plots are used as research sites by the Forestry Research Institute of Ghana, including some that have been studied for longer than 50 years. Bobiri supports a very rich fauna, most prolifically butterflies, of which more than 400 different species have been identified, including several endemics. March–May and September–November represent the best times for butterfly spotting, but Bobiri is also probably the best site in the region for forest birds, with some of the more iconic species recorded being long-tailed hawk, black dwarf hornbill, red-billed dwarf hornbill, African grey parrot and blue-throated roller. It is also a good site for African piculet (the continent's smallest woodpecker) as well as the diminutive tit-hylia (the smallest African bird of any type). Nocturnals likely to be heard and possibly seen near the resthouse include red-chested owlet, African wood-owls, Fraser's eagle-owl and brown nightjar. Mammals are more scarce and secretive, but mona, white-nosed, green and black-and-white colobus monkeys are present in small numbers. The entrance fee is US$1.50 per person, and an additional guide fee of US$1.50 person is levied for a 1–2-hour guided walk.

GETTING THERE AND AWAY The turn-off to the sanctuary lies at Kubease along the road to Accra, about 35km east of Kumasi and 14km past Ejisu. Coming from the direction of Ejisu, the junction is signposted immediately after the toll gate at the western end of the Kubease. From there it's about 3km to the forest station and resthouse, following a fair dirt road. The only place where you could go wrong *en* *route* is at a signposted fork slightly more than 1km out of Kubease, where you ought to head to the right.

To reach Kubease from Kumasi or Ejisu by public transport, ask any Konongo-bound minibus to drop you there, ideally at the toll gate. Shared taxis from Ejisu to Kubease can also easily drop you here. There is no public transport from here to the forest, but taxis are available and charge about US$4 one-way. Alternatively, it's a lovely 30–40-minute walk out. The first half of the road passes through lush, marshy vegetation, dotted with palms, and absolutely heaving with birds in the early morning (serious twitchers could spend a happy two hours along this stretch sorting out the myriad weavers, waxbills and bulbuls). After around 2km, a signpost, and abrupt change in vegetation and drop in temperature, signal your entry to the forest proper, after which it's a straightforward 10–15-minute walk to the resthouse.

🏠 WHERE TO STAY AND EAT

✳ 🏠 **Bobiri Forestry Resthouse** [393 G2] (8 rooms) m 0208 382704/0262 905620/0270 106290. Set in a small clearing in the heart of the forest, this delightfully unpretentious old guesthouse offers the choice of smallish rooms with 1 dbl using shared baths, or self-contained twins with 2 dbl beds, plenty of cupboard space & a writing desk. Simple inexpensive meals can be prepared from scratch with a few hours' notice, using ingredients bought fresh in Kubease, & beers & soft drinks are normally available. There is also a comfortable lounge & screened outdoor seating. *Brilliant value at US$8 dbl with shared bath; US$11 self-contained twin.* **$$–$**

EFFIDUASE AND SURROUNDS

Situated about 50km from Kumasi along a good surfaced road branching north from the Accra highway at Ejisu, the relaxed market town of Effiduase (sometimes spelt Effiduasi) forms a pleasant retreat into small-town Ashanti, away from the major tourist circuits. Local attractions include the fascinating Bodwease Shrine and scenic Atwia Escarpment, both of which lie to the north of Effiduase towards Nsuta. Effiduase is also conveniently situated for exploring most other places listed in this chapter: the manic trotro station has good public transport links in every imaginable direction, while a couple of adequate budget hotels in town are supplemented by the backpacker-friendly Moon and Star Guesthouse at Banko.

GETTING THERE AND AWAY Regular trotros run directly between Kumasi to Effiduase, but it's just as easy to pick up something going along the Accra road as far as Ejisu and to change vehicles there. From the trotro station in Effiduase, you'll find shared taxis or minibuses heading to most local destinations, including Bodwease, Kumawu, Mampong, Nsuta, Banko and Bonwire.

🏠 WHERE TO STAY AND EAT

✳ 🏠 **Moon & Star Guesthouse** [map, pages 380–1] (5 rooms) ✪ N6 55.976 W1 23.451; m 0543 709331; e moonandstarguesthouse@ hotmail.com; www.moonandstarguesthouse. com. Situated on the outskirts of Banko, a village of 5,000 at the base of the Atwia Escarpment about 10km north of Effiduase, this cosy Dutch owner-managed guesthouse is a great place to chill out for a few days in a relaxed communal environment. It is conveniently based for visiting Abasua Mountain & Bodwease Shrine, but also offers a bunch of more low-key activities ranging from traditional cooking lessons to village tours, or just playing with the dogs. Tasty home-cooked meals on a rotating fixed menu (vegetarian meals at request) are eaten communally & other facilities include a terrace bar facing a small patch of gallery forest, a lounge with satellite TV, board games, book swap, & plenty of hammocks. A swimming pool is planned. To get there from Effiduase, follow the Kumawu road north for about 4km as far as Oyoko, then turn left on to a newly surfaced road, passing through the small villages of Bomeng & Akrofoso, before you see the guesthouse to your left after about 8km. Shared taxis from Effiduase to Banko can drop you right outside the gate. *US$8/11/13 self-contained sgl/dbl/twin with fan; US$18 family room sleeping 4.* **$$-$**

🏠 **Kosayo Green Hotel** [map, pages 380–1] (28 rooms) m 0264 529292/0244 749024; e kosayo.greenhotel@yahoo.com. This quiet & decent little hotel lies alongside the Kumasi road

a few kilometres south of town. The light & airy rooms come with satellite TV & fridge, & there's now a restaurant. *US$13–16 self-contained sgl with fan; US$17/26 dbl/suite with AC.* **$$-$**

🏠 **Zanamat Hotel** (12 rooms) ☎ 03220 20243; m 0205 778666/0242 333733. Situated about 500m from the trotro station & towards Efface Secondary School, this clean, friendly place has rather clueless management, but the bar & restaurant & self-contained rooms with fan, flatscreen TV & fridge are fine at the price. *US$11/16 dbl/twin.* **$**

AROUND EFFIDUASE

Bodwease Shrine (✪ *N6 55.091 W1 20.272*) This ancient shrine, set in the village of Bodwease, is as architecturally impressive as any obosomfie in the region. It effectively forms an extension of the neighbouring chief's palace, a handsome but semi-abandoned 12-room building where six chiefs are buried, the first of them back in 1750, indicating that the complex might be around 260 years old. The last fetish priest at Bodwease died in 1985, leaving a vacuum that remains unfilled more than 30 years later, but the spirit is still regarded to inhabit the shrine, and locals say that it will eventually select another priest to act as its medium. Within the shrine, a marvellous collection of fetishes and other artefacts (bead necklaces, clay fertility dolls, ancient drums and animal bones) is looking considerably more dusty and neglected than it did a few years back, and the pair of tortoises that once dawdled around the building are now evidently slumbering in the coffins they carry on their back.

Despite this decline, the caretaker still welcomes visitors. Indeed, one senses that the only thing that might keep this lovely shrine from total decay is the trickle of tourist income it generates. The entrance fee is a rather steep US$5 per person, plus the customary bottle of schnapps (or equivalent cash) per party. For this, you also get to poke around the old palace, and might possibly meet the chief if he happens to be around. To reach the shrine from Effiduase, follow the main Kumawu road for 8km to Akotusu, where a surfaced road to your left brings you to Bodwease Shrine after another 5–6km. Regular shared taxis connect Effiduase to Bodwease.

Abasua Prayer Mountain One of the most sacred Christian sites in Ghana, Abasua (sometimes spelt Abesua) Mountain is situated 5km north of Banko, on the west side of the jungle-flanked road that winds northwards along the base of the Atwia Escarpment towards Nsuta and Mampong. The mountain often attracts hundreds of pilgrims daily, particularly over weekends and holidays, when it offers a fascinating insight into the more extrovert side of Christianity in Ghana. One of the highest outcrops along the Atwia Escarpment, with an altitude of 612m and prominence of 300m, its peak offers magnificent views over the forested footslopes and the plains below.

To get there from Banko, follow the Nsuta road north for about 4km to the village of Atwia (✪ *N6 57.844 W1 23.500*), where a left turn leads to the base village of Abasua after another 1.5km or so. From here, the hike to the top takes about one hour, following a clear and well-used footpath that incorporates several hundred stone steps. You are unlikely to get lost, but guides are available at the base. It can easily be visited as a self-guided or guided day trip from the Moon and Star Guesthouse in Banko, or as a day trip from most other towns in Ashanti. An entrance fee equivalent to US$1 is charged.

17

Gazetted in 1975, this 53km² wildlife sanctuary, situated about 10km north of the medium-sized town of Kumawu, is centred on the seasonally impressive Bomfobiri waterfall, which lies on the perennial Ownan River. Home to a small population of Nile crocodile, the sanctuary also harbours a wide variety of forest and savannah mammals, including Campbell's mona monkey, buffalo, bushbuck, red river hog and two species of duiker, though the only species likely to be seen by day visitors are green monkey and olive baboon. The widely reported presence of the very rare bare-headed rock fowl in Bomfobiri has no apparent foundation, but the bird checklist of 140 species is still of great interest for the likes of great blue turaco, yellow-casqued hornbill, black-and-white casqued hornbill, red-fronted parrot and Johanna's sunbird.

Several trails run through the sanctuary, the most popular being the hilly 2km hike to the Bomfobiri Falls, which takes around 45 minutes in either direction. Areas of interest that require more legwork to reach include the riparian woodland along the seasonal Amobia River, a good location for forest birds; and two salt licks, one situated about 500m southwest of the confluence of the Amobia and Ownan, and another about 1km north of it.

FEES The sanctuary charges a one-off entrance fee of US$5 per person for non-Ghanaian adults, plus a guide fee of US$2.50 per person per hour *or* a birding fee of US$13 per person per two hours, including the services of a guide. No visits are permitted on Thursday due to a local taboo, and call ahead on Sundays as the office may not be staffed.

GETTING THERE AND AWAY The main entrance to Bomfobiri Wildlife Sanctuary, and the car park for the footpath to Bomfobiri Falls, lies around 10km east of Kumawu (✪ N6 56.362 W1 12.333). Before heading out there, however, you are obliged to visit the sanctuary headquarters (✆ 03029 35478; m 0208 223667/0267 038031/0502 779477; e bomfobiriwswd.fc@gmail.com) in Kumawu to make all arrangements and payments, and collect your mandatory guide. This office is on the left side of the road just before you enter town coming from the direction of Effiduase (✪ N6 54.601 W1 17.346).

Self-drivers approaching Bomfobiri from the direction of Effiduase must go straight across the main traffic circle in Kumawu, then after 2.3km (just past the Manhattan Hotel) take the fork to the left, and then after another 700m the clearly signposted dirt road to the left. The car park is poorly signposted to the right about 6km along this road.

Using public transport, you'll have no problem reaching Kumawu, which is only 30 minutes from Effiduase along a good surfaced road traversed by regular trotros. Getting from Kumawu to the reserve entrance could be problematic. Unless you're prepared to walk, the only viable option at present is to charter a taxi, which will cost around US$5 per hour, and is best arranged through the sanctuary headquarters. For more details, see map inset, page 380.

🏠 **WHERE TO STAY** *Map, pages 380–1*

🏠 **Manhattan Hotel** (19 rooms) m 0246 623423. Situated about 2km past central Kumawu on the right side of the road towards Bomfobiri, this adequate local hotel has spacious, clean rooms with satellite TV, as well as a bar & meals at request. *US$11 self-contained dbl with fan; US$19 self-contained sgl/dbl with AC.* **$$–$**

🏠 **Bomfobiri Wildlife Sanctuary** There are long-standing plans to build overnight hides at the salt licks, as well as a simple mobile tented camp. For now, however, self-sufficient campers can overnight anywhere in the park, ideally at one of the salt licks, where buffalo, red river hog & bushbuck are regularly seen at night. Note, however, that while the camping fee is only US$5pp, a guide is mandatory & as things stand this means paying an hourly guide fee of US$2.50pp, which would, for instance, add up to a daunting US$80 for 2 people spending a total of 16 hours in the park! We pointed out this anomaly to the head warden but it doesn't seem to have been addressed, so you may have to do a bit of negotiating for an overnight rate.

MAMPONG AND SURROUNDS

Situated about 45km northeast of Kumasi, Mampong is one of the oldest and largest towns in Ashanti, with a population of around 45,000. The paramount chief is the Mamponhene (sometimes spelt Mamponghene), who has a silver stool befitting his designation as Ashanti's second most important traditional ruler, one whose roles include serving as regent during the period between the death of an Asantehene and the election of his successor. Less sprawling than most Ghanaian towns of comparable size, Mampong is centred on a compact, bustling core, dotted with fading colonial-era buildings in the town centre. Though little visited by tourists and lacking for any formal attractions, Mampong is the site of an important market, which is busiest on Wednesdays, and it could be used as a base for visiting the nearby Adango Shrine and Mframabuo Caves.

GETTING THERE AND AWAY Mampong is connected to Kumasi by a good surfaced road and regular minibus trotros, which take about an hour and cost US$1.50 for a seat. It also has good transport links to Nsuta and Effiduase.

🏠 WHERE TO STAY

🏠 **Antiedu Lodge** (10 rooms) m 0503 623705/0244 168838/0208 421828/0200 480011. By far the most appealing lodging in Mampong, this new hotel on the fringes of a small pond & just around the corner from Video City has a surprisingly scenic location given that it is right in the city centre. The spacious AC rooms are well equipped with flatscreen TVs, ceiling fan, fridge & hot water, while fan rooms are smaller but similarly equipped. There's a restaurant/bar & block of new 1st-floor rooms under construction that will boast views over the water once completed. *US$16/21 dbl with fan/AC.* **$$**

🏠 **Mampong Guesthouse & Restaurant** (11 rooms) m 0248 629766. This small out-of-town guesthouse has gone from a solid pick to solidly underwhelming in the past few years. Located 100m down a dirt road on the north side of the police barrier about 500m along the road to Kumasi, it has a pleasantly quiet location, but there's no longer a restaurant, making it rather inconvenient for those on foot. Still, the self-contained rooms are all large & clean, & shared taxis regularly connect the police barrier & the town centre. *US$6.50/8 sgl/dbl with fan; US$9 dbl with AC.* **$**

🏠 **Video City Hotel** (23 rooms) m 0243 845705. About 200m west of the trotro station, this conspicuous purple hotel next to the eponymous cinema was obviously conceived as an upmarket set-up, but it is looking rather run-down these days, & notable only for the friendly management & a courtyard centred on an empty pond & disco-lit bar. Also, the hand-painted movie posters decorating the cinema next door are absolutely worth a look. *US$10 self-contained dbl with fan.* **$**

✗ WHERE TO EAT AND DRINK
The **Simple Stores Restaurant** on the main road south of the trotro station is very popular with locals for ice-cold drinks and hearty meals (around US$3 a plate), which can be eaten inside or in the courtyard bar. The **Obama Chop House** near the Video City Hotel serves adequate rice and chicken.

AROUND MAMPONG

Adango Shrine (✦ *N7 01.105 W1 22.013*) This small obosomfie in the village of Apiakrom is less architecturally interesting than others of its ilk, since the modern building is clearly a 20th-century construction, but it is studded with some impressive statues, notably a singular figure of a person lying on his back on the floor ('this is how you will lie when God punishes you'). It can be visited at almost any time, for a fee of US$2.50 per person, the exception being if the fetish priest is at a funeral (most likely on a Saturday) or every sixth Sunday, when a secret ceremony is held there. Photography will cost extra. The fetish priest has a history of the shrine, written by his predecessor, in which it is claimed it was founded in 1799 by one Nana Akwesi Acheampong.

To get to the shrine, you first need to head to Nsuta, a substantial town that lies about 8km southeast of Mampong along the road to Banko and Effiduase. From Nsuta, you need to head along the main road to Kwaaman for 2km to Apiakrom, where the shrine is in a plain white building on the left side of the road just before a prominent Presbyterian kindergarten. Regular shared taxis connect Nsuta to Mampong, and there is also less frequent public transport from Effiduase via Banko. From Nsuta, any shared taxi heading to Kwaaman will drop you at Apiakrom, but the walk only takes about 20 minutes.

Mframabuo Caves These little-known caves can be reached from Mampong by catching a shared taxi to Kwaaman (possibly changing vehicles at Nsuta), where the chief can organise a guide. The caves lie two hours from Kwaaman on foot, with the last stretch being rather tough – with luck you'll be offered lunch and liquid at a cocoa farm near the caves. There is nowhere to stay in Kwaaman, though vague plans to build a resthouse may be abetted by an increase in tourism. Note that Kwaaman lies within sight of Kumawu, but the gorge that separates the towns is passable only on foot, a 5–10km hike depending on whom you believe.

18

From Kumasi to Tamale

Most travellers heading northwards from Kumasi travel along the main north–south highway to Tamale, passing through Techiman and Kintampo. This 400km trip takes about 6 hours by coach, which is the best way to go if you're doing it in one stretch. Alternatively, it can be broken up using a mixture of shared taxis and trotros. The most alluring diversion is the excellent and readily accessible **Boabeng-Fiema Monkey Sanctuary**, which many visitors have rated as the highlight of their time in Ghana, though the more adventurous might be tempted to divert through Sunyani and Wenchi to the little-visited **Bui National Park** on the River Volta northwest of Wenchi. Other more low-key attractions include the **Tano Sacred Grove** and **Buoyem Caves** near Techiman, and the **Kintampo Falls** near the town of the same name.

It's worth noting that Mole National Park does in fact lie along a side road departing from the Kumasi–Tamale road at Fufulsu, on which basis it might reasonably be considered to belong in the present chapter, but the park has its own dedicated chapter starting on page 439.

SUNYANI

A district capital since 1924, and capital of Brong-Ahafo Region since it was created in 1958, Sunyani lies at the heart of one of Ghana's main areas of cocoa and kola-nut production. The town's name is reputedly a corruption of *ason ndwae*, an Akan phrase meaning 'place where elephants are skinned', which dates to a distant time when the surrounding forest provided hunters with a rich source of income in the form of ivory. These days, there's not a great deal of virgin vegetation around Sunyani, and the elephants are long gone, but the remote southwest of Brong-Ahafo still supports extensive tracts of rainforest known in ornithological circles as the place to search for the mega-rare white-necked rockfowl. Otherwise, this town of around 90,000 residents holds little of specific interest and is visited by very few travellers, but it's still a pleasant enough place to spend a couple of days, with a friendly atmosphere and no hustlers. The impressive Nana Bosoma Market on the east side of the town centre is busiest on Wednesdays.

GETTING THERE AND AWAY Sunyani lies about 130km northwest of Kumasi along a good surfaced road through Bekyem. The drive should take around 2 hours, depending greatly on traffic on the outskirts of central Kumasi, which can be horrendous leaving town in this direction. Regular trotros between Kumasi and Sunyani charge around US$2, as do something like 30 Metro Mass buses daily, starting from 05.00, and leaving when full. There is also a daily Metro Mass coach from Sunyani to Tamale, leaving at 05.00 and charging US$5, and another to Bolgatanga, leaving at 05.30 and charging US$8. Metro Mass buses and trotros

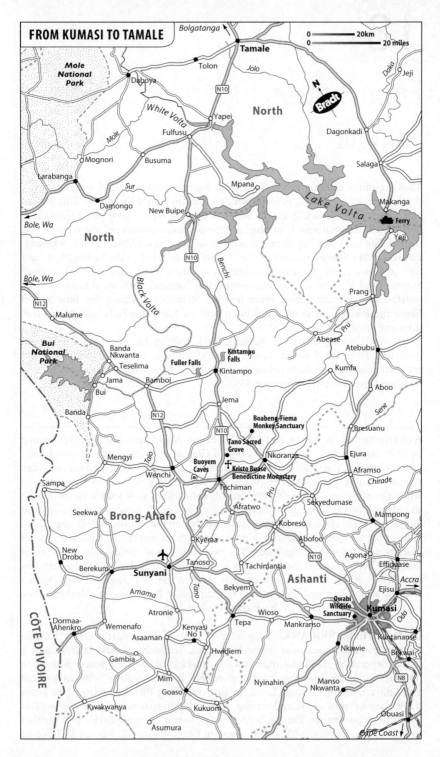

to other long-haul destinations leave from **Nana Bosoma Station** [404 D4] on the east side of the town centre next to the eponymous market. For shared taxis and trotros to Techiman (*US$1.50*), Wenchi (*US$1.50*) or Kintampo (*US$2*), head to the **smaller station** [404 B3] about 200m north of the Ecobank on Bosoma High Street. More comfortably, OA Tours (m *0269 042901; www.oatravels.com*) run one bus daily to Accra at 20.30 (*US$11*) and one bus daily to Tamale and Bolgatanga at 07.00 (*US$11*) from their station diagonally opposite Cocoa House in the centre of town [404 A5]. VIP (m *0560 027198*) also runs to Accra daily from their station near Bosoma Market [404 D5].

Sunyani is potentially a good stopover for the Ivorian border. There are quicker road connections to Yamoussoukro via the Ivorian town of Abengourou (if you have your own vehicle) than anywhere else in Ghana. A good tarmac road, much of it quite newly surfaced, runs west from Sunyani directly to the Ivorian border at Sampa, taking around two hours and passing through Berekum.

By air, **Starbow** (m *0245 000000;* e *info@flystarbow.com; www.flystarbow.com; online booking at www.ghanaticketservice.com*) flies to Sunyani from Accra four times weekly for US$100 one-way, and tickets can be booked at the Eusbett Hotel.

TOURIST INFORMATION The **Ghana Tourism Authority** office for Brong-Ahafo Region [404 A1] (✆ *03520 27108;* e *brongahafo@ghana.travel.com;* ⊕ *08.00–12.30 & 13.30–17.00 Mon–Fri*) is on the first floor of the Brong-Ahafo Regional Co-ordinating Council Office.

🏠 WHERE TO STAY

Upmarket

🏠 **Eusbett Hotel** [404 A4] (109 rooms) ✆03520 24393/4; m 0547 099002; e reservations@eusbetthotel.com; www. eusbetthotel.com. The title of 'best hotel in Brong-Ahafo' is not exactly hotly contested, but this well-established & plush multi-storey block, though rather short on character, is clearly it. About 1km west of the town centre, it has modern facilities including a good restaurant/bar, swimming pool (*US$2.50/day for non-guests*), cinema, 1st-class gym, internet café, well-stocked supermarket & Wi-Fi. The smart self-contained rooms all come with AC, satellite TV, fridge & hot water. *US$37 budget dbl; US$45 junior dbl; US$68 std dbl; US$82/91 exec dbl/twin; US$181 suite.* **$$$$–$$**

Moderate

🏠 **Glamossay Hotel** [404 D7] (36 rooms) ✆03520 23642/23629; m 0208 337600; e info@ glamossayhotelgh.com; www.glamossayhotelgh. com. Situated at Abesim, about 6km from central Sunyani along the main road to Kumasi, this well-organised 3-storey hotel has a good restaurant, friendly staff, gym, swimming pool, & large, spotless rooms with fridge, hot water, writing desk, fan, AC & satellite TV. *US$35 B&B self-*

contained dbl; US$50 with king-sized bed; US$82 suite.* **$$$–$$**

Budget

🏠 **Oti Yeboah Hotel** [404 A1] (8 rooms) m 0261 701892/0265 956746/0246 515180. Housed in large green grounds about 500m from the town centre along the airport road, this venerable resthouse offers very reasonably priced accommodation in self-contained cottages with hot water, AC & TV. The attached Lifetime Restaurant & Bar serves a few local staples & chilled drinks in a setting that feels very suburban despite its proximity to the town centre. It hosts occasional reggae & highlife dance parties, mainly catering for the crowd from the local polytechnic, at w/ends. *US$16 suite.* **$$**

🏠 **Bob Pierce Memorial Centre** [404 C7] (18 rooms) ✆03520 27152; m 0244 131790/0201 188927. This strange establishment, tucked away on a backroad at the southeast end of town, was funded by World Vision (& named after its founder), & turned over to the local community to run. The upshot is a bleak but friendly operation with compact, clean & well-maintained self-contained rooms but no restaurant or bar. *US$12/14 dbl/twin with TV & fan; US$18 twin with AC.* **$$–$**

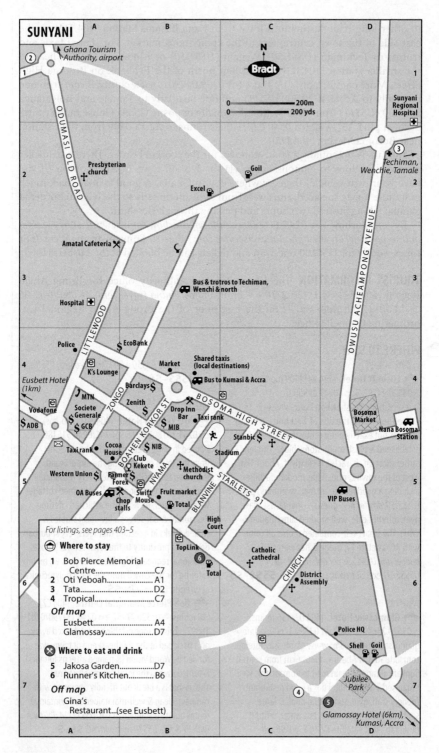

SUNYANI

N

Bradt

| | 0 | 200m |
| | 0 | 200 yds |

Ghana Tourism Authority, airport

Sunyani Regional Hospital

Techiman, Wenchie, Tamale

Presbyterian church

Goil

Excel

Amatal Cafeteria

Hospital

Bus & trotros to Techiman, Wenchi & north

Police

EcoBank

Eusbett Hotel (1km)

K's Lounge

Market

Shared taxis (local destinations)

Bus to Kumasi & Accra

Barclays

Vodafone

MTN

Societe Generale

Zenith

Drop Inn Bar

Taxi rank

Bosoma Market

Nana Bosoma Station

ADB

GCB

MIB

BOSOMA HIGH STREET

Taxi rank

Cocoa House

NIB

Stanbic

Western Union

Club Kekete

Stadium

Methodist church

VIP Buses

OA Buses

Farmer Forex

Swift Mouse

Fruit market

Chop stalls

Total

BLANVINE

STARLETS 91

High Court

TopLink

Total

Catholic cathedral

District Assembly

CHURCH

Police HQ

Shell   Goil

Jubilee Park

For listings, see pages 403–5

Where to stay
1 Bob Pierce Memorial Centre...........................C7
2 Oti Yeboah.........................A1
3 Tata...............................D2
4 Tropical...........................C7

Off map
Eusbett...............................A4
Glamossay..........................D7

Where to eat and drink
5 Jakosa Garden.................D7
6 Runner's Kitchen............B6

Off map
Gina's Restaurant...(see Eusbett)

Glamossay Hotel (6km), Kumasi, Accra

404

⌂ Tropical Hotel [404 C7] (40 rooms)
☎ 03520 27179/24398. Situated a few doors away from the Bob Pierce Memorial Centre, this substantial but rather time-worn hotel offers adequate self-contained accommodation, & local & continental dishes by request. *US$11 sgl with ¾ bed & fan; US$12/16 dbl with cold/hot water, AC & satellite TV; US$18.50 suite.* **$$-$**

Shoestring

⌂ Tata Hotel [404 D2] (22 rooms) m 0241 673446. Situated about 1km from the town centre on the Techiman road, this unpretentious hotel offers the cheapest (& dingiest) rooms in town, all using common showers. It's probably best to get rooms away from the road, to avoid traffic noise in the early morning. The bar has a good atmosphere, with highlife music played in the evening at the w/end. *US$7-10 dbl.* **$**

✗ WHERE TO EAT AND DRINK Sunyani's finest eatery is **Gina's Restaurant**, on the ground floor of the Eusbett Hotel [404 A4], which serves a good selection of continental, Chinese and Ghanaian mains, as well as tasty pizzas, for around US$8. For cheaper eats, the **Jakosa Garden Restaurant** [404 D7] (m *0244 732473*), next to the Tropical Hotel, serves traditional Ghanaian dishes for around US$2-3 a plate. **Runner's Kitchen** [404 B6], near the TopLink Internet Café, has also been recommended.

OTHER PRACTICALITIES

Foreign exchange Forex bureaux are unexpectedly prolific (far more so than in larger and more touristed centres such as Tamale or Bolgatanga), but rates are quite variable so shop around. Most of Ghana's major banks are represented in the city centre with ATMs accepting Visa, and Ghana Commercial Bank [404 A4] also accepts MasterCard.

Internet Although several internet cafés are marked on the map, connections can be slow and unreliable. At the time of research, the two best were **Swift Mouse** [404 B5] and **TopLink** [404 B6], both on the main road.

ASUMURA CONSERVATION INITIATIVE

Situated about 120km west of Kumasi and 80km southwest of Sunyani as the crow flies, the remote village of Asumura (sometimes spelt Asubura) lies on the western border of the Subim Forest Reserve, which together with the contiguous Ayum and Bonsam Bepo forest reserves extends over an area of 488km² within the Asunafo North and South districts of Brong-Ahafo. The three reserves protect a cover dominated by moist semi-deciduous forest, parts of which have been compromised by intensive logging, as well as a rich forest fauna that includes forest buffalo, bongo antelope, bushbuck, yellow-backed duiker, Maxwell's duiker, common chimpanzee, Lowe's mona monkey, spot-nosed monkey, olive colobus and black-and-white colobus. Subim also protects a truly impressive variety of forest birds, most notably the rare white-necked rockfowl, which was rediscovered here in 2003 after having gone unrecorded in Ghana for 40 years (see box, pages 406-7).

In 2011, a formal ecotourism project called the Asumura Conservation Initiative (☎ *03220 47066/8;* ⊕ *07.00-18.00 daily*) was established in the village, which lies within moderately easy walking distance of a rockfowl breeding site almost as reliable as its counterpart at Bonkro (see pages 389-91). The status of this project was uncertain in 2016, but even if it is not formally running, there is at least one private lodging (Eco Home) in the village, and visits to the rockfowl site can be arranged with a local guide called Akbeku, who can be contacted through the aforementioned lodge. The round trip to the rockfowl breeding site takes around two hours, and involves a bit of clambering. It is best undertaken in the early morning or late afternoon, when the birds are most likely to be at their nest, though there is less chance of a sighting in the main dry season (December to March).

The rockfowl aside, Asumura is a great base for general forest birding, since a road runs straight out of the village into the heart of the forest, and there are also many old logging roads. Among the more interesting species likely to be seen here are Cassin's hawk-eagle, red-fronted parrot, white-headed woodhoopoe, yellow-billed barbet, red-billed helmetshrike, brown illadopsis and West African batis. Mammals are much less likely to be seen, though there is a slight possibility of black-and-white colobus and other monkeys.

GETTING THERE AND AWAY The springboard for visiting Asumura is Goaso (sometimes spelt Gwaso), the low-key district capital of Asunafo North. Goaso lies 135km from Kumasi along a decent surfaced road through Mankranso, Wioso, Tepa and Hwidiem, a drive that takes up to 2 hours in a private vehicle once you've cleared the city outskirts. There are a few different routes from Sunyani, but the best option is to head directly south to Hwidiem, where you need to turn right for Goaso (you could also go via Mim, turning right from Hwidiem at an unmarked junction about 5km south of Atronie, but this entails about 40km of dirt roads).

WHITE-NECKED PICATHARTES

Among the most peculiar of African birds, the white-necked picathartes (*Picathartes gymnocephalus*) is often ranked among the top five most eagerly sought birds in Africa, and it certainly tops the wish list of most dedicated birdwatchers visiting Ghana. Also known as the yellow-headed rockfowl, or by its local Ghanaian name *anamea*, it is endemic to the section of the Upper Guinean Forest Belt running between Ghana and Sierra Leone, and is IUCN listed as Vulnerable, with a probable global population of around 2,500–5,000. The distribution of this enigmatic bird is extremely fragmented due to the very specific habitat requirements associated with its nesting habits. Although it inhabits medium-altitude evergreen forests, the picathartes builds an elaborate thick-walled cupped nest of mud and plant fibres inside a cave about 3m above the ground on a cliff face or large boulder.

The peculiar breeding habits and innate scarcity of the white-necked picathartes account for part of its allure to birdwatchers. But it is also an exceptionally strange-looking bird, intermediate in size between a cuckoo and a turaco, with a long tail, black and white body, long legs, and a bare bright orange-yellow head with contrasting black eyes and cap, and a heavy dark bill it uses to snap up prey as large as frogs. It can fly, but spends most of its time hopping around on the forest floor, seldom straying far from its nesting site (indeed, an individual's home range is limited to a radius of about 300m from its nest), and is almost never seen outside the forest. Contrary to appearances, it is classified as a passerine, one of two species in the genus *Picathartes*, the other being the grey-necked picathartes *P. oreas*, which has a more southerly distribution in the rainforest running from southeast Nigeria to Gabon.

The bird's broader taxonomic affiliations have long mystified biologists. The white-necked picathartes was first described in 1825 by the Dutch bird

From Goaso, turn left (south) at the T-junction as you exit town. After about 5km (⊕ *N6 45.816 W2 30.370*) you need to turn right towards Akrodie (⊕ *N6 41.652 W2 33.265*), which you'll reach after another 15km. The asphalt ends at Akrodie, but you just need to keep going straight for another 27km before you finally emerge at Asumura. This road passes right though the Bonsam Bepo, Ayum and Subim forest reserves, and it is flanked by genuine forest for the last 18km before Asumura, offering some great opportunities to stop and look for birds. Once you reach Asumura, turn right at the main junction (⊕ *N6 42.117 W2 45.661*) and you'll reach the conservation project and guesthouse after about 600m.

Despite its remoteness, Asumura is quite easy to reach on public transport. Regular trotros to Goaso depart from Kejetia Station in Kumasi, taking at least three hours and costing around US$3. Trotros between Sunyani and Goaso are just as regular, take about two hours, and cost US$2. Once at Goaso, about half a dozen trotros leave daily for Asumura, costing around US$3 and usually taking at least two hours. If you want to spend the night in Goaso, or arrive there too late to pick up transport to Asumura, the 28-room King Khana Hotel has adequate rooms starting at US$14 self-contained double with television and fan, and there is a restaurant almost directly opposite. Though it's 25km further away in Hwidiem, Hotel Sanbra (m *0244 429529*; e *info@hotelsanbra.com*; *www.hotelsanbra.com*) has rooms from US$9–26 and is another good option, particularly if you've got your own transport.

taxonomist Coenraad Temminck, who placed it in the crow family and named it *Corvus gymnocephalus* (literally naked-headed crow). Three years later, the French ornithologist René Primevère Lesson reassigned it to a new genus, *Picathartes*, combining the Latin genera *Pica* (Eurasian and related magpies) and *Cathartes* (a type of New World vulture). Since then, the genus *Picathartes* has been shuffled between the crow, starling, flycatcher, babbler and warbler families without much conviction, before finally being placed in its own mono-generic family Picathartidae in 1952. Today, some ornithologists believe that two *Picathartes* species are relicts of an ancient and otherwise extinct bird order. However, recent DNA analysis suggests the rockfowls are most closely related to the rockjumpers, an endemic southern African family that is very different in appearance from the rockfowls, but that is also associated with rocky habitats, and that the two lines split more than 40 million years ago.

The white-necked rockfowl, though most common in Sierra Leone and southern Guinea, is not easily located in either country, largely due to the poor infrastructure associated with years of political instability. Ghana, by contrast, is now regarded to be the easiest place to see this rare species, even though it was long thought to be extinct there, due to a lack of confirmed sightings since the late 1960s. However, since 2003, when an individual was trapped in a net in Subim Forest Reserve, more than ten active nests have been discovered across the Subim, Ayum and Bonsam Bepo forest reserves, along with half a dozen other nesting sites in suitable habitats elsewhere in Ghana, including Bonkro in southern Ashanti (see pages 389–91). And because rockfowl tend to breed colonially in nesting sites they reuse twice a year, and to return to their nest every evening when breeding, sightings are almost certain if you visit an active site in season with a guide who knows the location.

WHERE TO STAY AND EAT

Eco Home Lodge (4 rooms) ☎03520 99116; m 0246 138368. About 400m & signposted to the left of the main road as you enter the village, this no-frills family-run set-up has simple rooms using a shared bath. Food can be prepared with a bit of notice. *US$5 sgl with ¾bed.* $

Asumura Conservation Initiative Guesthouse (5 rooms) ☎03220 47066/8. Though it opened as recently as 2011, the official guesthouse 600m out of town was unstaffed & looking rather neglected when we popped past. Assuming it is still operational, it has a superb birding location right on the forest boundary, & it should be possible to arrange meals. *US$10 dbl.* $

BUI NATIONAL PARK

This seldom-visited national park (*entry US$5/2.50 foreigners/students*) near the Ivorian border is the third largest in Ghana, extending over 1,821km² on either side of the Black Volta River as it runs along the border between Brong-Ahafo and Northern regions. Since a controversial dam on the Black Volta came online here in 2013, nearly 444km² — almost 25% of the park — has been submerged under what's now known as the Bui Reservoir. Prior to the flooding, Bui supported the country's largest population of hippos, roughly 200 individuals, along with small numbers of terrestrial mammals such as roan antelope, hartebeest, waterbuck, kob, bushbuck, warthog, green and patas monkeys, spotted hyena and leopard, however there have been no surveys undertaken since the dam's inauguration to see how the park's animals have been faring since. Three crocodile species inhabit the river and reservoir, including the localised dwarf and long-snouted crocodiles, but they are seldom observed by casual visitors. More than 220 bird species have been recorded, including several interesting forest species associated with the lush riparian woodland along the river, though many of the best-preserved tracts of this forest are unfortunately now underwater.

The national park is named after the Bui Gorge, which hems in the Black Volta at its southern end and is now the site of the aforementioned 400MW hydro-electric dam (*www.buipower.com*), which controversially came online at the end of 2013. The idea for this dam was conceived as long ago as 1925 by the British-Australian geologist Sir Albert Kitson, who was also the first person to recognise the potential of building the dam at Akosombo that created Lake Volta. Finally, after an initial Australian-backed venture was abandoned in 1978 as a result of a spate of coups, construction of the 90m-high, 490m-long dam began in 2009, a collaboration between the government and a Chinese construction company called Sino Hydro. Bui is now home to the third-largest lake in Ghana, and the dam has gone some way towards easing the energy crisis that has been responsible for regular blackouts in most Ghanaian cities in recent years.

Unfortunately, the dam's completion has also had numerous implications for the ecology of the park. All land below the 180m contour has been flooded, resulting in the loss of much riparian forest and numerous forested islands in the Volta River, and the likely death or evacuation of most of the park's monkeys, duikers and forest-associated birds. The permanent submergence of the fertile seasonal floodplains flanking the Volta is likely to have knocked the hippo population, which depended on these plains for grazing. And although there is some ongoing talk of extending the park's boundaries in compensation, much of this surrounding land is in poor ecological condition, and it lacks the biodiversity of the riparian woodland and grasslands lost in the flood. On a human level, eight local communities totalling more than 1,200 people in the path of the flooding also had to be resettled, and most of these evacuees now live in the newly constructed Bui resettlement village (known locally as Bui Camp) or the town of Jama, some 10km away.

Today, Bui National Park sees very few visitors (it had been three months since the last signature in the guestbook when we stopped by), and one gets the sense that while the park is still operational, little has been done to formulate any sort of tourism plan based on the park's drastically altered and newly aquatic circumstances. The **Park Headquarters** (✆ *8.24641 -2.2539*; m *0202 578867*) has been relocated to the resettlement village at Bui Camp, and all activities must be arranged here – although your options are more or less limited to boat cruises on the reservoir and theoretical hikes. The boats take a maximum of 15 passengers each, setting out in the morning for US$42 for the first hour and US$13 for every additional hour. Traditionally, the boat trips were a good way to look for hippos (most readily seen during the dry season of December to May), as well as monkeys, monitor lizards and a variety of bird species associated with water and riparian forest, but the drastic changes to the ecosystem here mean it's unclear what you can expect to see today, and recent reports indicate that most of the hippos have moved to shallower waters far upstream that are well beyond the range of a short boat cruise.

As for hiking, there are no designated trails in the park, but the staff assured us that it was possible to go out with a ranger (*US$2.50/hr*) and explore nonetheless, should you feel like bushwhacking. There are also no campsites, but we were again told bush camping is possible for self-sufficient travellers, though the rather nonsensical US$31 guide fee per overnight (in addition to the US$5pp camping fee) might act as a deterrent to finding out. More reasonably, you could spend the day in the park and sleep in one of the basic en-suite rooms available at park HQ for a considerably more reasonable US$7 per double.

GETTING THERE AND AWAY The new park HQ at the relocated Bui Camp sits 17km from the Wenchi–Bole road, via surfaced access roads branching west at either Banda Nkwanta (which is also home to an 18th-century mosque – see page 449) or Teselima villages. Any vehicle headed between Wenchi and Bole can drop you at either junction, and there are periodic trotros from Banda Nkwanta to Bui Camp throughout the day for US$2. If you're self-driving, keep left at the unmarked junction after Jama village, as the road to the dam itself is closed to the public. **Wenchi** is 85km from the park HQ and linked by regular trotros to Bole, Sunyani and Techiman, and (should you need to spend the night) is serviced by a couple of adequate budget lodges, namely the **Baah Hotel** (*28 rooms;* ✆ *03524 22690*) and **Pony Hotel** (*22 rooms;* ✆ *03524 22343*).

TECHIMAN AND SURROUNDS

The second-largest settlement in Brong-Ahafo, with a population approaching 80,000, the ancient market town of Techiman (sometimes spelt Tekyiman) lies about 60km northeast of Sunyani and 120km north of Kumasi, at the junction of the main roads running northeast to Tamale and northwest to Wa. Equipped with plenty of hotels, Techiman is most often visited by travellers as the springboard for the popular Boabeng-Fiema Monkey Sanctuary, which lies about 50km to the northeast by road. The town is most notable today for its sprawling food market, which is reputedly the largest of its kind in the country. It is also bisected by the River Tono, whose sacred fishes and crocodiles are sometimes seen in town. Other local attractions include the Tano Sacred Grove, the Buoyem Caves, the Kristo Buase Monastery, and Nkoranza *en route* to Boabeng-Fiema.

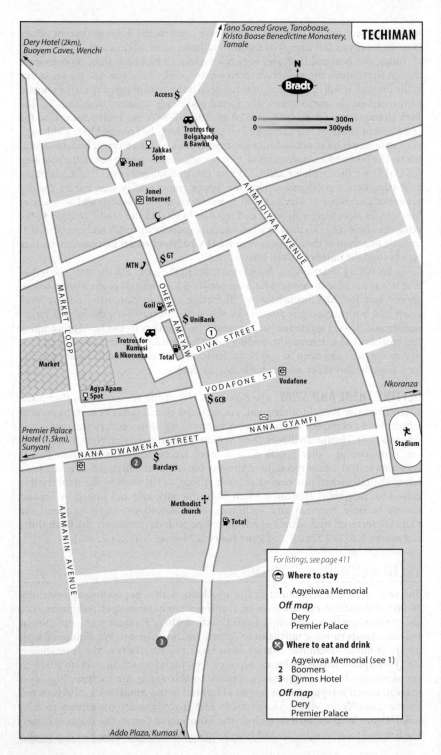

Dery Hotel (2km),
Buoyem Caves, Wenchi

Tano Sacred Grove, Tanoboase,
Kristo Boase Benedictine Monastery,
Tamale

TECHIMAN

N

Bradt

Access $

Trotros for
Bolgatanga
& Bawku

0 — 300m
0 — 300yds

Jakkas
Spot

Shell

Jonel
Internet

AHMADIYAA AVENUE

$ GT

MTN

MARKET LOOP

Goil

Ohene Ameyaw

$ UniBank

Trotros for
Kumasi
& Nkoranza

Total

① DIVA STREET

Nkoranza

Market

VODAFONE ST

Vodafone

Agya Apam
Spot

$ GCB

Premier Palace
Hotel (1.5km),
Sunyani

NANA DWAMENA STREET

NANA GYAMFI

Stadium

②

$
Barclays

Methodist
church

Total

AMMANIN AVENUE

③

For listings, see page 411

🛏 Where to stay

1 Agyeiwaa Memorial

Off map
Dery
Premier Palace

🍴 Where to eat and drink

Agyeiwaa Memorial (see 1)
2 Boomers
3 Dymns Hotel

Off map
Dery
Premier Palace

Addo Plaza, Kumasi ↓

HISTORY One of the country's oldest market towns, Techiman is situated at the ancient crossroads of two important medieval trade routes (precursors to the modern roads north to Tamale and Wa) that linked the goldfields of what is now southern Ghana to the Sahel. According to oral tradition, Techiman lay at the heart of the first centralised Akan state, and is from where the Fante migrated southwards in the 13th century to found the Mankessim Kingdom. Since 1740, the town has been the capital of Techiman-Bono, which was founded in 1740, originally as a vassal state of Ashanti, by refugees from the once powerful Bono Kingdom following its defeat by the Asantehene's army in 1723. The rule of the incumbent paramount chief Oseadeeyo Akumfi Ameyaw IV, who was enstooled in 2007 as the 16th Techimanhene in a line stretching back to 1782, has been marked by ongoing disputes with the Asantehene over the allegiance of several stools in the Techiman Traditional Area, among them Buoyem and Tuobodom.

GETTING THERE AND AWAY Techiman is arguably the most important route crossroads north of Kumasi, and you'll have absolutely no problem finding a trotro or shared taxi there from Sunyani, Kintampo or Tamale. Almost all buses and trotros leave and depart from the main bus station, which has a very central location opposite the Agyeiwaa Memorial Hotel. Coming from Kumasi, your best bests are the express trotros that leave from Kejetia Station, cost US$2.50 and take up to three hours (but do note that there is another village called Techiman in the area, so check you're heading to the right one). In addition, Metro Mass, which is based in the central station, offers direct daily services from Techiman to Kintampo, Sunyani and Wenchi. Heading directly to/from Accra, two air-conditioned OA coaches (m 0246 953444/0206 728703) leave daily between 19.00 and 21.00 in either direction, taking up to seven hours, and costing US$8–12 depending on which service you choose.

WHERE TO STAY *Map, opposite*

Budget

Agyeiwaa Memorial Hotel (29 rooms) 03525 684856; m 0271 416787/0203 684856; e agyeiwaahotel@hotmail.com. This 2-storey block, centred on a shady garden bar, is conveniently located about 100m from the main lorry station, & the friendly staff & good-value accommodation are routinely praised by readers – though mosquitoes can be a problem. The restaurant serves a good selection of reasonably priced Chinese, continental & local meals. *US$17/23/26 self-contained dbl/queen/twin with AC.* **$$**

Dery Hotel (30 rooms) 03520 91211; m 0249 926053. Situated next to a filling station about 2.5km out of town along the Wenchi road,

this large hotel stands out for its pleasant outdoor bar/restaurant & swimming pool. It also has a varied menu & clean spacious rooms that seem a little spartan in terms of furnishings, but are fine at the price. *US$13 B&B self-contained dbl with fan; US$21/26 dbl/exec with AC.* **$$**

Premier Palace Hotel (32 rooms) 03520 91299; m 0208 119670. Situated some 1.5km out of town along the Sunyani road, this relatively smart hotel is notable for its bright modern décor & attractive grounds, but it is a little pricier than most of the competition, & standards of service & cleanliness have come in for quite a bit of reader criticism. Facilities include a decent restaurant/bar, clothing boutique, & internet café. *US$12–16 AC dbl; US$23 AC twin; US$26 exec dbl..* **$$–$**

WHERE TO EAT AND DRINK *Map, opposite*

The restaurants at the **Premier Palace**, **Agyeiwaa Memorial**, **Dery** and **Dymns** hotels are all good. The best stand-alone restaurant is **Boomers** on the Sunyani road, which serves local and continental meals for around US$3, though we've recently had complaints about the quality of food and service. If it is street food you are after, there is no shortage of choice around the bus station and market area.

AROUND TECHIMAN

Tano Sacred Grove The more accessible of two ecotourist sites operating around Techiman, the Tano Sacred Grove is situated close to the village of Tanoboase on the main Tamale road north of town. It consists of an attractive cluster of sandstone rock formations, now formally protected within a community-run sanctuary, which lie at the source of the Tano River. The stretch of river protected within the sanctuary is believed to house Taakora, the greatest of the earthly Akan gods, and it is the site of an annual cleansing festival called the Apoo, in April or May. In addition to its spiritual significance, the sanctuary protects a variety of mammals and birds. Patas monkey and baboon had become very rare here in recent years, but seem to have multiplied in number since the sanctuary was created and a ranger station established. A trip to the grove can incorporate a cultural visit to the village of Baafi, and – assuming you're reasonably fit and fearless – a hike up steep rock surfaces to the top of the escarpment and a stunning lookout point used during the 18th-century Ashanti–Bono wars. Other attractions include the fruit bat colony in the trees of the sacred grove, and a tour of historical sites related to the 18th-century Ashanti–Bono wars.

Tanoboase lies 13km north of Techiman, and the two are connected by regular shared taxis. The **ecotourism project information centre** (m *0241 844668*) lies 700m along a dirt road running to the right from the main junction in the village. The return hike to the sacred grove costs US$3.50 per person (with discounts for volunteers), and takes around one to two hours. It is easy to visit as a day trip from Techiman, but if you fancy overnighting at the site, a four-bedroom guesthouse attached to the information centre opened in May 2013, and charges US$8 per person per night.

A more alluring overnight option in the area is the **Kristo Buase Benedictine Monastery** (m *0200 862699/0269 498449/0240 289243*; e *kristobuasemonastery@gmail.com*; *www.kristobuasemonastery.org*), which was founded in 1987 in collaboration with three abbeys in the UK. As its name (literally 'Christ in the Rocks') suggests, this beautiful abbey is built into a spectacular rockscape, set in huge peaceful grounds within walking distance of Tanoboase. It has seven guest rooms for male or female visitors, who can eat with the monks, too (though note that meals are taken on a fixed schedule: 07.15 breakfast, 12.45 lunch, and 18.30 dinner), in exchange for a recommended donation equivalent to US$11 per person per day. The on-site shop sells a variety of homemade preserves and fruit wines, but there's no bar or restaurant as such. The expansive grounds are ripe for exploring, and easy strolls can be had through the shady cashew plantation out front, and a scramble up the towering sandstone rocks reveals commanding views over the surrounding countryside. The abbey is clearly signposted on the east side of the Techiman road, 1.7km south of Tanoboase, about 250m south of the toll booth. They lock the gate at 18.30 daily, so be sure to call and warn them if you think you'll arrive after this.

Buoyem Caves The centrepiece of this semi-functional ecotourism site near the village of Buoyem, 12km from Techiman, is a large sandstone bat cave where the Bono people retreated after their defeat by the Ashanti in the early 18th century. Unfortunately, the cave, which lies about an hour's walk from the village, has been closed since at least 2013 due to an infestation of bees, and plans to move the hive have remained just that for several years now. Other worthwhile (and functional) attractions here include the 3-hour hike through the Mprisi rainforest via the impressive Africa Rock and Bibiri Waterfall, which is good for a swim. The fee is US$1.50 per person to visit the caves and US$2.50 per person for the hike to Africa Rock and Bibiri Waterfall; it's also customary to tip your guide.

The junction for Buoyem lies along the Wenchi road, 3km past the main traffic circle in Techiman. Take a right turning on to a dirt road, bear right after 1.4km, and you'll see the Buoyem Information Centre and Guesthouse to your right after another 7.5km or so. Shared taxis cost US$1, take about 30 minutes, and leave Techiman from the main bus station on market days (Wednesday, Thursday and Friday) or from the Wenchi Station on other days. The community-run **guesthouse** (which may or may not be taken over as temporary accommodation for soldiers) charges US$5 for a basic room with a double bed using a shared toilet and showers. No food is served, but a few chop shops can be found in the village.

Nkoranza The small town of Nkoranza, set in green wooded hills some 28km east of Techiman, was once of interest to travellers solely as the place to change vehicles *en route* to Boabeng-Fiema. But this has all changed with the setting up of a budget guesthouse at **Operation Hand in Hand** (m *0242 731095/0244 533343;* e *handinhandcommunity@ gmail.com; www.operationhandinhand.nl*), a community-based project for mentally handicapped children run by a Dutch doctor. The project provides shelter to 80 mentally handicapped children who might otherwise be homeless and lies in a compound on the outskirts of town behind the St Theresa hospital.

The guesthouse consists of 14 stone-built huts with running water that sleep two to four people, set in a beautiful location a short distance further out towards the hills. Accommodation includes budget single rooms for US$5–8, double huts with private outdoor shower for US$11–17, and houses sleeping up to four for US$20–25. Booking is recommended, especially over weekends and during the months of July, August and December.

Other attractions and facilities include a simple restaurant, a swimming pool, an internet café (located in town), and an onsite craft shop that sells jewellery, attractive postcards and other items made by the children. Visitors are encouraged to interact with the children, who all seem very happy and stimulated, and you can ask about local cultural points of interest such as the traditional religion and the chief. The guesthouse can also be used as a base to explore Boabeng-Fiema (half an hour away in a private vehicle) and Kintampo Falls (one hour away).

Plenty of trotro traffic runs between Techiman and Nkoranza. Direct public transport from Kumasi's Racecourse or Kejetia stations takes about two hours, and OA Travel (m *0242 754874*) runs coaches to Accra from here. The Hand in Hand Guesthouse is situated directly behind St Theresa Hospital, and the road there passes through the hospital compound. Arriving on public transport, you can walk there in about 10 minutes. To get to the PCC (as the community is known locally), ask for directions to the hospital, which lies about 500m from the lorry park, then go through the hospital gate, keeping to the right, and after about 100m cross a bridge over a gutter directly opposite the main hospital building, from where it's another 300m or so to the project.

BOABENG-FIEMA MONKEY SANCTUARY

This small but rather wonderful 2km² sanctuary (⊕ *07.00–17.00 daily*) was created in 1974 to protect the monkey population supported within a small patch of semi-deciduous forest centred on the villages of Boabeng and Fiema, which lie 1km apart in Nkoranza District. Two monkey species occur in significant numbers: Lowe's mona and black-and-white colobus. The mona population is thought to stand at around 400 individuals, living in troops of 15–50 animals, several of which now have a territory in the forest fringe and adjacent woodland. The black-and-white

18

colobus, with a population of 200 animals divided into 13 troops, are rarely seen outside the true forest. Recent reports of green, patas, spot-nosed and Diana monkeys remain unsubstantiated, but the forest does support a good variety of birds and butterflies.

Guided walks can be arranged at the visitor centre located beside the resthouse at the forest entrance. The village is the best place to see monkeys at close range. The unruly monas that scavenge here are particularly tame and spend a great deal of time on the ground; it is highly rewarding to be able to watch these normally shy forest monkeys interact at such close quarters. The colobus monkeys are more timid and tend to stick to the trees, but you should easily get a clear view of them, and it's wonderful to see them leap between the trees with their feathery white tails in tow. A longer guided walk along some of the 10km of footpaths that emanate from the village provides an opportunity to see some of the many birds and butterflies, as well as a giant mahogany tree thought to be more than 150 years old. Small plastic bottles of the excellent local honey are on sale at the entrance.

BACKGROUND AND HISTORY The reason why significant monkey populations have survived at Boabeng and Fiema, but not in most other parts of Ghana, is that the inhabitants of both villages have a taboo on killing monkeys. There are several stories about how this taboo arose. One is that Boabeng was founded by a Brong warrior who, seeing two mona and two black-and-white colobus monkeys guarding a piece of white calico, consulted his patron god, Daworoh, and was told that the monkeys would bring him good fortune. A variation on this states that Daworoh married Abodwo, the patron saint of Ashanti-founded Fiema, and that the monkeys are their offspring. Another tradition is that a former chief who had the ability to turn people into monkeys and back at will, something that was useful in battle, died before he was able to transform some 'monkeys' back into human form. According to this version of events, the colobuses are men and the mona monkeys are women, and the two interbreed freely!

Oral tradition dates the taboo to 1831, when the villages were founded. And it is taken so seriously that whenever a monkey dies, the villagers conduct a formal burial and funeral service. In addition, a special festival is held for the monkeys every November. However, like most traditions, the taboo has been undermined in recent years by the rising influence of Christianity, for which reason it is now illegal to hunt monkeys within a 5km radius of either village.

FEES An entrance fee of US$5 per person is valid for the duration of your stay, and while there was no guide fee when we dropped by in early 2016, we were told that prices were likely to increase slightly in the near term.

GETTING THERE AND AWAY The monkey sanctuary lies about 6km from the back road that connects Nkoranza to Jema, along a clearly signposted turn-off to the east at the junction village of Tankor. The normal springboard for visits is Techiman, from where you will first need to take a shared taxi to Nkoranza, 28km to the east. From Nkoranza, you shouldn't have to wait too long for a shared taxi heading directly northwards to Fiema, another roughly 25km trip. Ask to be dropped at the visitor centre, on the left side of the road about 1km before you enter Fiema. With luck, you can get from Techiman to Fiema in about one hour, and even on a slow day you should be there in 2 hours. If you don't mind more frequent changes, one reader recommends doing the trip in a series of shorter trotro journeys, along the back roads via Tanoboase, then Kranka, Yeffi and Tanko, for less traffic and dust.

Travellers leaving Fiema for points further north should note that, while shared taxis do run along the road connecting Nkoranza to Jema, they are normally full when they pass Tankor. In other words, rather than trying to head directly between Fiema and Jema, you might be better heading back to Techiman and picking up a northbound vehicle there.

🏠 WHERE TO STAY AND EAT

✴ 🏠 **Boabeng-Fiema Resthouse** (8 rooms) m 0247 419530/0246 403478. Just outside the sanctuary entrance, this agreeable little resthouse has an idyllic setting in the forest. Basic twin rooms with light & fan are very good value. Facilities include a shower & toilet block, & a thatched garden hut serving inexpensive basic meals, beers & soft drinks. *US$5 twin; US$2.50pp to camp, with possible price increases to come.* **$**

🏠 **DK Damoah Hotel** (7 rooms) m 0244 171815/0504 843389. Situated about 5km from the sanctuary at the junction village of Tankor, this offers adequate accommodation in green gardens with a restaurant & bar, but lacks the sense of place of the Boabeng-Fiema Resthouse. *US$5–8 self-contained dbl with fan.* **$**

KINTAMPO

Sprawling along the main northern road almost exactly halfway between Kumasi and Tamale, this rather scruffy and amorphous town of around 50,000 is best known as the site of the impressive Kintampo Falls, which lie on the right side of the Tamale road a short distance north of the town centre. Kintampo might also be of interest to trivia lovers for lying at the 'official Centre of Ghana' as it was measured in colonial times – the exact site, decorated by a local artist, lies about 100m left of the main road as you enter town from Kumasi, behind a football field and under a big mango tree.

GETTING THERE AND AWAY Situated as it is on the main north–south road through Ghana, Kintampo is easily reached by bus or trotro from Kumasi, Techiman, Wenchi, Nkoranza or Tamale. The **main bus station**, in the town centre opposite the Total filling station, is where most long-haul coaches (including STC, VVIP and OA) stop, while **trotros** have their own station 400m to the north. Metro Mass operates out of a separate station at the **Falls Rest Stop** right next to Kintampo Falls.

🏠 WHERE TO STAY *Map, page 416*

Moderate

🏠 **Falls Executive Lodge** (5 rooms, more u/c) m 0247 511189/0241 875243. Situated 100m to the west of the main road & 1km south of the trotro station, this comfortable lodge has spacious well-equipped rooms & the attached restaurant & garden bar are popular with local expats. Wi-Fi coming soon, apparently. *US$18/24 dbl with queen-/king-sized bed, fan, AC, satellite TV & writing desk.* **$$**

🏠 **Falls Palace Hotel** (23 rooms) m 0206 794295/0243 081373. Right next to the Falls Rest Stop in a can't-miss-it, 2-storey yellow-&-white building, this newly opened place is obviously well located to visit the falls, & offers what are probably the sharpest rooms in town. The cavernous halls open on to rather cramped standard rooms, but

the executive & official rooms allow a bit more space to swing a cat, & all are equipped with fridge, flatscreen TV, telephone, AC, Wi-Fi, & hot water. There's a restaurant if Falls Rest Stop is closed. *US$21/26/39 dbl/exec/official; US$52 family room sleeping 4.* **$$$–$$**

Budget

🏠 **Prince of Peace Guesthouse** (8 rooms) m 0263 729171/0576 403047/0206 394077. This clean & friendly establishment, situated 1km south of the trotro station opposite the Falls Executive Lodge, is probably the best budget deal. *US$7 dbl with fan & shared bath; US$9 self-contained dbl with fan, AC & TV.* **$**

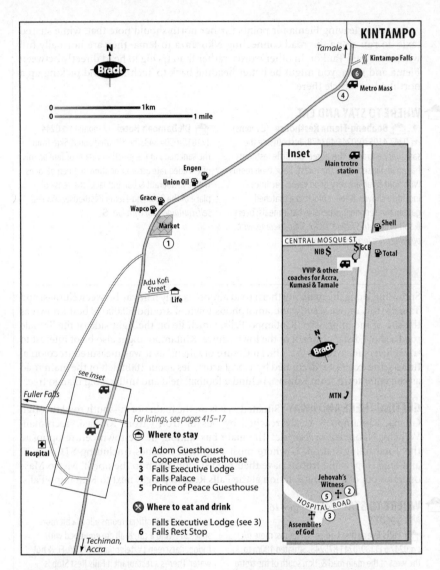

KINTAMPO

Tamale ↑

≈ Kintampo Falls

Metro Mass

N

Bradt

0 — 1km
0 — 1 mile

Engen

Union Oil

Grace
Wapco

Market

①

Adu Kofi
Street

Life

see inset

Fuller Falls

Hospital

/ Techiman,
Accra

Inset

Main trotro
station

Shell

CENTRAL MOSQUE ST.

NIB $ $ GCB Total

VVIP & other
coaches for Accra,
Kumasi & Tamale

N

Bradt

MTN ♪

Jehovah's
Witness

⑤ ✝ ②

HOSPITAL ROAD

③

Assemblies
of God

For listings, see pages 415–17

🏠 **Where to stay**
1 Adom Guesthouse
2 Cooperative Guesthouse
3 Falls Executive Lodge
4 Falls Palace
5 Prince of Peace Guesthouse

✖ **Where to eat and drink**
   Falls Executive Lodge (see 3)
6 Falls Rest Stop

🏠 **Cooperative Guesthouse** (8 rooms)
m 0502 208561. Situated next to the Prince of
Peace, this is probably the least inviting of the
lodges in the cluster south of the trotro station, but
it is still a very pleasant set-up if the other 2 are
full. *US$8/9 self-contained dbl with ¾bed & fan/
AC; US$11/12 self-contained with king-sized bed,
AC & TV.* **$**

🏠 **Adom Guesthouse** (7 rooms) m 0243
656699/0204 447848. This decent cheapie, situated
opposite the market about 1.5km north of the trotro
station, has a variety of dbl rooms, & a good chop
bar is attached. *US$5/6.50 sgl/dbl with fan & TV
using shared bath; US$8 self-contained dbl with fan;
US$16 self-contained with king-sized bed & AC.* **$**

✖ **WHERE TO EAT AND DRINK** *Map, above*
If you are staying at one of the cluster of lodges south of the trotro station, try the
onsite restaurant at the **Falls Executive Lodge**, which also has a pleasant garden

bar. For cheap eats, there's a row of chop stalls and bars in the lorry station and along the road towards the Shell garage. You can also eat well at the well-organised **Falls Rest Stop** (🕐 *07.00–18.30 daily*), where a canteen serves tasty local meals for around US$2.

WHAT TO SEE AND DO

Kintampo Falls (*entrance US$1.50 for non-Ghanaians, plus US$1.50 camera fee, inc an unnecessary but mandatory guide who will expect a tip*) Said to have been discovered by roving hunters in the 18th century (though presumably it would have been known to local residents since time immemorial), this impressive waterfall lies on the Pumpum River, a tributary of the Black Volta. It was called Saunders Falls in the colonial era, after a British medical officer stationed at Kintampo, and briefly renamed Nkrumah Falls in honour of Ghana's first president shortly after independence. Falling around 70m in three separate stages, the waterfall is most impressive during the rains, but still worth visiting in the dry season.

All three stages can be seen on the guided 15-minute round walk from the entrance gate. The walk culminates at a flight of 152 concrete stairs (built in the mid 1960s, when the construction of a State House at the waterfall was aborted following the 1966 coup that ousted Nkrumah) leading down to the lovely pool at the base. There's a large cave a short distance further upstream, while the fringing riparian forest is dominated by mahogany trees up to 40m high and looks promising for birding. According to a local brochure, the waterfall is home to a large but harmless aquatic snake, which is sometimes seen by visitors, as well as a band of human dwarfs whose existence 'has not been proved yet, since none of them has ever been seen'.

Kintampo Falls is prominently signposted on the right side of the Tamale road, exactly 4km north of the central market, immediately after the conspicuous Falls Rest Stop. Any public transport heading along the Tamale road can drop you there, but you'll probably end up paying full fare to wherever it is headed. Better perhaps to charter a taxi from the lorry station in Kintampo, which shouldn't cost more than US$3 one-way, and either ask the driver to wait for you, or else wait on the roadside for a lift when you're finished. Alternatively, you could walk from the town centre in around one hour.

Fuller Falls (*entrance US$2.50*) Situated on the Yoko River near the village of Yabraso about 8km from Kintampo, the seldom-visited Fuller Falls is named after the British surveyor who 'discovered' it in 1911. The 10m-high upper waterfall is very pretty, and the pool below it is safe for swimming, but the most remarkable feature is that the stream below the waterfall disappears underground for some 40m before re-emerging. An entrance fee is now charged to enter the church-run compound around the waterfall. Fuller Falls lies along a rather obscure side road to New Longoro – there's no public transport so you'll have to charter a taxi. If you do find a vehicle to drop you at the turn-off (✪ *8.071547, -1.798906*), it's just over 1km from here to the falls themselves.

18

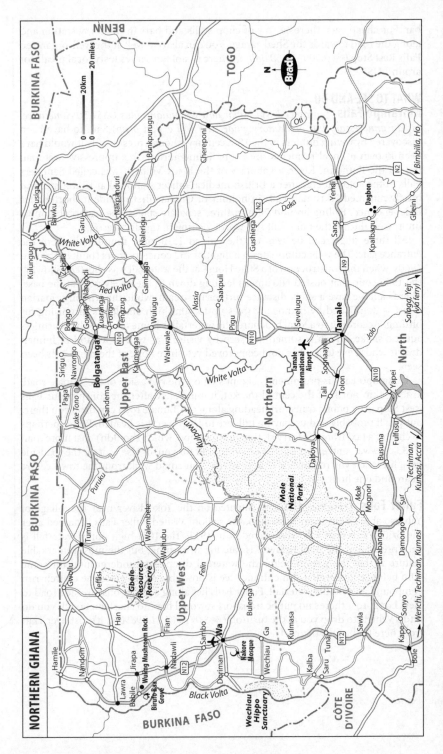

NORTHERN GHANA

Part Six

NORTHERN GHANA

OVERVIEW

The vast and relatively thinly populated savannah country that lies to the north of Lake Volta and the Black Volta River was annexed to the Gold Coast Colony in 1902. Formerly known as the Northern Territory, it is now divided into three administrative regions. The Northern Region is the largest of these, covering an area of 70,384km² (more than one-quarter of the country's surface area), and its regional capital Tamale is now the country's third most populous city. Much smaller than the Northern Region (and, somewhat paradoxically, lying to its north) are the Upper East and Upper West, whose respective capitals, Bolgatanga and Wa, both retain a likeable aura of provinciality.

Northern Ghana is, in many respects, a historically and culturally discrete entity from the southern and central regions. Unlike the various Akan groups who live to the south of the Black Volta, the predominantly Mole-Dagbani groupings of the north generally follow patrilineal lines of inheritance and they share a common oral tradition that suggests they arrived in modern-day Ghana in the 12th or 13th century following a militarised migration from the Lake Chad region. Historically, the Mole-Dagbani have had far stronger trade and cultural links with the Islamic world than with the Christian Europeans who settled along the Gold Coast, as witnessed by the large number of mosques throughout the region, including several centuries-old West Sudanese-style whitewashed mud-and-stick mosques in the northwest.

Situated along the main south–north trunk road between the Atlantic coastline and the Burkina Faso border, the city of Tamale, connected to Accra and Kumasi by daily flights and a plethora of coaches and trotros, is the main travel gateway to the north. And while Tamale has no major tourist attractions, it does boast a good range of amenities, and it's an agreeable place to hang out for a day or two before continuing on to the likes of Bolgatanga or Mole National Park. A second main access road from the south connects Kumasi to Wa via Bole, passing several beautiful old mosques *en route*.

BEST OF NORTHERN GHANA

MOLE NATIONAL PARK Thrilling guided walks in search of elephants, serene canoe trips along the bird-rich Mole River near Mognori, and the scenic setting of the Mole Motel make this Ghana's top safari destination. Pages 439–51.

SIRIGU Home to one of the best organised of the north's numerous community tourism programmes, Sirigu is renowned for the curvaceous adobe architecture and brightly painted exteriors of its houses. Pages 458–9.

PAGA Renowned for its sacred crocodiles, which are so tame they allow visitors to touch them, Paga is also the base for visits to the moving Pikworo Slave Camp and impressive Paga Pia's Palace. Pages 467–70.

LARABANGA MOSQUE Situated close to the entrance of Mole, this is the oldest and best known of the surreal West Sudanese-style mud-and-stick mosques that stud northeast Ghana. Pages 445–8.

BOLE AND NAKORE MOSQUES Though less well publicised than their counterpart at Larabanga, these two fine examples of West Sudanese architecture offer a more satisfying experience in most respects. Pages 449 and 476.

WA NAA'S PALACE Recently reoccupied by the paramount chief of Wa after sitting vacant for 14 years, this well-known landmark has the most impressive exterior of any palace in northern Ghana. Pages 475–6.

WECHIAU COMMUNITY HIPPO SANCTUARY Though not as well managed as it might be, this community reserve on the Burkina Faso border near Wa is a good place to see hippos during the dry season, and one of the region's top birding sites throughout the year. Pages 476–9.

TAMALE CENTRE FOR NATIONAL CULTURE True, there's not much more to this central Tamale landmark than craft stalls, but the variety of items on offer makes it a fine one-stop shop for craft lovers and other shopaholics. Page 433.

CATHEDRAL OF OUR LADY OF THE SEVEN SORROWS, NAVRONGO Built entirely from traditional mud-bricks, this century-old cathedral is decorated with earthy frescoes originally created by the women of Sirigu. Page 466.

WULING MUSHROOM ROCK Admittedly rather low-key, this bizarre rock formation outside Babile is among the most striking natural landmarks in the region. Page 481.

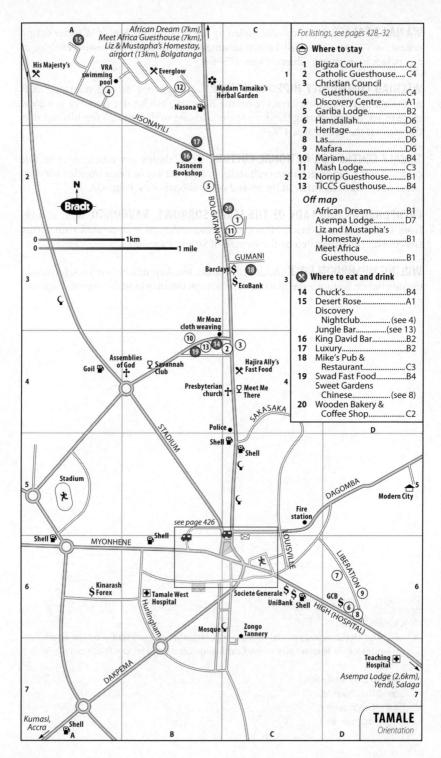

For listings, see pages 428–32

Where to stay
1 Bigiza Court.....................C2
2 Catholic Guesthouse......C4
3 Christian Council
   Guesthouse...................C4
4 Discovery Centre............A1
5 Gariba Lodge..................B2
6 Hamdallah......................D6
7 Heritage..........................D6
8 Las..................................D6
9 Mafara.............................D6
10 Mariam...........................B4
11 Mash Lodge....................C3
12 Norrip Guesthouse........B1
13 TICCS Guesthouse..........B4

Off map
African Dream..................B1
Asempa Lodge................D7
Liz and Mustapha's
   Homestay.....................B1
Meet Africa
   Guesthouse.................B1

Where to eat and drink
14 Chuck's...........................B4
15 Desert Rose....................A1
   Discovery
   Nightclub................(see 4)
   Jungle Bar...............(see 13)
16 King David Bar..............B2
17 Luxury............................B2
18 Mike's Pub &
   Restaurant...................C3
19 Swad Fast Food.............B4
   Sweet Gardens
   Chinese...................(see 8)
20 Wooden Bakery &
   Coffee Shop.................C2

TAMALE
Orientation

19

Tamale and Surrounds

The administrative capital of the Northern Region and third-largest settlement in Ghana, Tamale is a rapidly growing city, with a population of 540,000 in 2012. It also ranks among the country's fastest-changing towns, barely recognisable today as the 'hot, flat and quite incredibly dusty' provincial backwater described in the first edition of this guidebook. Indeed, the distinctive red-dirt suspension that once enveloped Tamale is today sealed beneath a modern grid of freshly surfaced roads, while the US$80 million football stadium constructed for the 2008 Africa Cup of Nations is emblematic of its growing infrastructure and modernity.

Despite this, the cultural divide between northern and southern Ghana soon becomes evident in this predominantly Islamic city, as haunting mosque calls, elements of Sahelian architecture, striped plastic pots (used by local Muslims for ablutions before prayers), and the diverse meats (beef and lamb) associated with more northerly francophone territories start shading into the former British colony. A striking facet of the city centre is the astonishing infestation of bicycles, whose riders' propensity for weaving whimsically between pedestrians can be positively hazardous (a danger only slightly reduced by the presence – in our experience of Africa, unique – of bicycle lanes running parallel to the main thoroughfares).

Tamale is the most important route focus in northern Ghana – it would take quite some effort to travel through the north without passing through it at least once – and the most convenient springboard for visits to the popular Mole National Park. It is also the main focal point for NGO and aid workers in northern Ghana, typically engendering more loyalty among locally based volunteers than any major town in the south thanks to its friendly atmosphere. That said, while the hassle-free atmosphere and good selection of relatively inexpensive travel amenities make Tamale a pleasant place to settle into for a few days, sightseeing opportunities within the city limits are somewhat meagre.

HISTORY

Not much is known about the early history of Tamale. However, the oldest part of town, which incorporates the present-day Grand Mosque and central market, has been settled for hundreds of years, having served as an important crossroads on the caravan route connecting the Sahel to the coast during the slave-trading era, and possibly before that. Originally known as Gulkpegu, it was then ruled by the Gulkpe Naa, one of seven district chieftaincies that comprise the Dagomba Kingdom of Dagbon, whose paramount chief, the Ya Naa, has been based in Yendi since the early 19th century. In 1899, when Dagbon was partitioned by the Anglo–German colonial border, Yendi ended up on the German side, as did the Gulkpe Naa, who happened to be visiting the Ya Naa at the time of the split. In his absence, a popular local fetish priest installed himself as the Chief of Tamale under the title Dakpema Naa.

In 1907, Tamale, then a small adobe settlement supporting a population of around 1,400, embarked on the path to modern prominence under the Dakpema Naa, who persuaded the British to relocate their regional administrative headquarters there from Gambaga. In the aftermath of World War I, however, Dagbon was reunited under British rule, and the Ya Naa insisted that the Dakpema Naa be replaced by the Gulkpe Naa, whom he regarded to be Tamale's legitimate chief. The British agreed to reinstall the Gulkpe Naa but only after the death of the incumbent Dakpema Naa, which transpired in 1930. Since then, both rulers have maintained palaces in Tamale, and while the Gulkpe Naa has always enjoyed official recognition as the representative of the Ya Naa, ongoing rivalry with the Dakpema Naa has led to frequent confusion about their respective roles, as well as political tension that has occasionally welled up into violence.

Tamale grew rapidly under British rule, particularly after the construction of the Great North Road from Kumasi and Accra in the 1920s, which sealed its future significance – over then-larger towns such as Bawku and Navrongo – as the main transport and economic hub in the north. Between 1920 and 1960, the population increased from 3,900 to 48,000, at a rate faster than either Accra or Kumasi, and from the 1930s onwards, several foreign trading companies established themselves there, selling goods imported by lorry from the south to local traders that distributed them to outlying villages by bicycle. Tamale remained the capital of the Northern Region after independence, and since the turn of the millennium it has often been cited as the fastest-growing city in West Africa, in terms of population as well as amenities, though the significant role foreign aid organisations have played in this boom has led to it being dubbed 'the NGO capital of Ghana'. The city is administered by the Tamale Metropolitan Council, under a mayor appointed by the incumbent national president. The Gulkpe Naa and Dakpema Naa still play an important role in local politics, with both frequently being referred to as the Chief of Tamale, though the outspoken Alhassan Dawuni, installed as Dakpema Naa in 2009 following the death of his father two years earlier, is currently the more prominent of the two figures.

GETTING THERE AND AWAY

BY AIR A speedy (and these days relatively affordable) alternative to the long bus trip between Accra and Tamale are the hour-long flights operated by **Starbow** (m *0245 000000*; e *info@flystarbow.com*; *www.flystarbow.com*; *online booking at www.ghanaticketservice.com*) and **Africa World Airlines** (m *0242 438888*; *www.flyawa.com.gh*). Both carriers operate twice daily in either direction, once in the morning and once in the afternoon, and ticket prices start at US$90–100 one-way, including taxes and surcharges. As of April 2016, Africa World also runs a Kumasi–Tamale flight four times weekly for around US$55 one-way. All flights land and depart at **Tamale International Airport** [422 B1], which lies about 20km north of the town centre off the Bolgatanga Road, and taxis are available at the airport. Be aware that flights to Tamale are frequently cancelled during the November–March harmattan season due to poor visibility, so allow time in your schedule in case you need to get down to Accra by road.

BY BUS AND TROTRO Tamale is the pivotal transport hub in northern Ghana, and – unusually for a Ghanaian town of its size – the main trotro and coach stations could scarcely be more central, situated right next to the main market. The main station is easy to navigate, as individual termini for all destinations are clearly signposted, and the STC station is right next door to it. However, several of the more popular coach companies operate from more remote stations. The Metro Mass and OA stations are situated 500m west of the main station, while the VVIP/VIP station is off Gulkpegu Road behind the Grand Mosque.

Coaches to/from Kumasi take 6 hours and tickets cost about US$15, while those to/from Accra take 12 hours and the fare is around US$20. For these long-haul destinations, the most swift and comfortable option is **VVIP/VIP** (m *0243 543337/219121*), which operates two fixed-departure air-conditioned coaches daily in either direction between Accra and Tamale (via Kumasi) at 16.00 and 17.00. Tickets can usually be booked on the day, though advance booking is safer. The once pre-eminent STC now only operates one daily service to/from Accra via Kumasi at 06.30. Comparable in price and standard are the two daily coaches to Accra operated by **OA Tours** (m *0248 691360/0208 083644; www.oatravels.com*), which leave at 15.00 and 16.00 and stop in Kumasi. A few blocks away, **GH Express** (m *0206 317512*) runs a similar service at 16.00 and 17.00. The best of the operators in the main coach terminal is probably Imperial, which runs a morning bus to Accra at 08.00 daily.

Metro Mass operates a vast array of services all around the country. They formerly offered the only transport to Mole National Park, but this service has been discontinued (see pages 440–2 for details on getting to Mole). Though the buses are not air conditioned, Metro Mass still operates what are probably the most reliable daily fixed-departure services to Wa (*US$5; 05.00*), Makongo (*for Yeji; US$4; 05.00*) and Yendi (*US$4; 05.00 & 07.00*), as well as one bus daily to Bolgatanga (*US$3; 09.30*) and four to Kumasi (*US$7; 05.00, 06.00, 08.00, 09.30*).

A great many other **private trotros and/or buses** run between Tamale and most other towns along the surfaced road south to Kumasi and north to Bolgatanga. Just head to the right terminus and ask for the next vehicle heading there. From the main station, vehicles run several times per day to Wa (*US$6*), Yendi (*US$1.50*), and Salaga (*for Yeji/Makongo; US$5*), and there's at least one departure daily to Bimbilla (*US$3*), from where there are occasional vehicles to Kete-Krachi and Nkwanta in the Volta Region. Fares are generally slightly more expensive than Metro Mass for vehicles with air conditioning, and a bit cheaper for those without. If you're a glutton for punishment, you could consider a trotro to Accra, but most people would consider it worth paying extra for air conditioning.

BY BOAT Especially for those coming from Volta Region, a considerable chunk of the trip between southern Ghana and Tamale can be covered on the MV *Yapei Queen*, a passenger boat that does a weekly run on Lake Volta connecting Akosombo to Kete Krachi and Yeji (see box, page 292). For those just seeking an opportunity to spend an hour or so on this vast lake, there is also the *Nana Besemuna*, a motor ferry that typically leaves from Makongo (on the north shore 160km south of Tamale) at about 08.00 and noon, and from Yeji (on the south shore opposite Makongo) at about 10.00 and 14.00, and is supplemented by small motorised boats that take around 45 minutes between the two ports.

Travellers using the *Yapei Queen* to get to Tamale are advised not to disembark at Kete Krachi but to continue to Yeji, a rather unappealing port town that has a few grotty places to crash if you arrive late in the day (try the Volta and Alliance hotels). A fair selection of road transport, including one Metro Mass bus daily, runs from Makongo (opposite Yeji) to Tamale, though you may need to change vehicles at Salaga, 40km along the Tamale road (pages 436–7). There is nowhere to stay in Makongo, so don't cross from Yeji in the afternoon unless you can be sure of reaching Salaga.

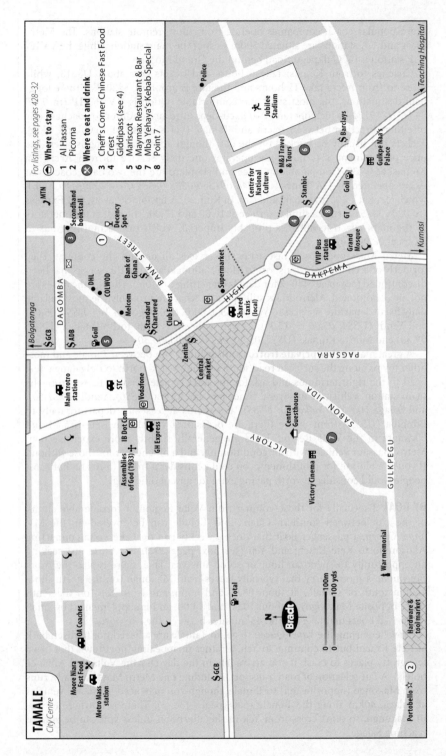

TAMALE
City Centre

For listings, see pages 428–32

Where to stay
1 Al Hassan
2 Picorna

Where to eat and drink
3 Cheff's Corner Chinese Fast Food
4 Crest
Giddipass (see 4)
5 Mariscot
6 Maymax Restaurant & Bar
7 Mba Yehaya's Kebab Special
8 Point 7

It is of course equally possible to do this trip in reverse, and boats headed south towards Akosombo depart from Yeji every Wednesday around 05.00, stopping in Kete-Krachi that evening. For a status report, try ringing the harbourmasters in Yeji (m *0201 656388*) or Kete-Krachi (m *0207 947788*).

GETTING AROUND

BY TAXI As with other large towns in Ghana, inexpensive shared taxis ply along most major roads in Tamale. The most useful to travellers are those that run along the Bolgatanga Road as far north as Jisonayili Junction, starting from a rank just past the traffic lights diagonally opposite the main lorry and coach station. Charter taxis are also widely available.

TOURIST INFORMATION

The **Ghana Tourist Board**'s Northern Regional Office (\ *03720 24834–5;* e *gtanorthern@gmail.com;* ☉ *08.00–12.30 & 13.30–17.00 Mon–Fri*) is in the Regional Co-ordinating Council offices on the outskirts of the town centre. It stocks a few brochures, as well as being able to connect you with reliable guides.

GUIDES AND TOURS

The only established operator with a branch in Tamale is the long-serving and well-respected **M&J Travel and Tours** (\ *03720 28213;* m *0202 533013/0201 568390;* e *info@mandjtravelghana.com; www.mandjtravelghana.com*) near the Centre for National Culture. It can arrange bespoke tours all around Ghana, as well as renting out chauffeur-driven pick-ups and 4x4s.

A newish operator, started by the same person who helped set up Mognori Eco-Village near Mole National Park, **Travel Ghana** (m *0249 507413;* e *savannaghana@ gmail.com; www.savannatourism.com*), on the Kumasi road almost opposite Japan Motors, offers safaris to Mole, hotel reservations and a guiding service to most local attractions. Other new options include **AY Transport** (m *0246 678296/0553 315129;* e *ibrahimmatinu@yahoo.com; www.ibrahimmatinu.wordpress.com*) and **Grassroot Tours** (m *0541 668682/0503 722405;* e *info@grassroottours.com; www. grassroottours.com*), both of which can make all the usual arrangements, including transport to and from Mole.

Otherwise, the best way to get hold of a reliable guide is through the tourist board. You could also contact **Walisu Alhassan** (m *0243 822633/0206 797148/0274 471509;* e *alwalisu@yahoo.co.uk*), who left the tourist office to establish Ti-Kali, and has been recommended by numerous readers.

SAFETY

A handful of swindling teens – known locally as 419s after the Nigerian penal code for fraud – hang around the bus station and Crest Bar, trying to latch on to newly arrived travellers and clocking their every move. They're clearly after one thing – cash – but they're a relatively unsophisticated (and good-humoured) bunch and can be shaken off fairly easily if you make it clear you're not going to give or buy anything.

More seriously, the last couple of years have seen a spate of after-dark muggings by machete-wielding henchmen around Tamale, so it's definitely worth getting a taxi home or walking with a trusted local if you plan to be out in the late evening.

UPMARKET

⌂ **African Dream Hotel** [422 B1] (11 rooms) ✆03720 91127; m 0243 623179/0245 345738; e africandreamhotel@yahoo.com; www.africandreamhotel.com. Set on a 10ha plot alongside the Bolgatanga Rd 7km north of Jisonayili Junction, this comfortable new hotel is quickly garnering an enviable reputation for its helpful & hospitable Swiss–Ghanaian owner-managers, tasty international cuisine, 5 well-equipped AC rooms in the main building, & 6 thatched huts in the garden aimed at budget travellers. The out-of-town location won't suit all, but it is easy enough to pick up transport to/from the city centre. The restaurant has outdoor seating & serves tasty local & international dishes in the US$8–14 range. *US$55/63 B&B self-contained sgl/dbl with queen-sized bed, AC, satellite TV, fan, fridge, smoke alarm, erratic Wi-Fi & hot tub/shower; US$71 larger exec dbl with king-sized bed.* **$$$**

⌂ **Gariba Lodge** [422 B2] (32 rooms) ✆03720 23041–3; m 0236 786634/0244 606342; e garibalodge@yahoo.com; www.garibalodge. com. Set on the Bolgatanga Rd about 3km north of the city centre, just south of Jisonayili Junction, this comfortable 3-star lodge, though notable more for its efficient management than any discernible character, is widely regarded as the best business-style hotel in northern Ghana. The rooms are tastefully decorated & amenities include a good open-air international restaurant. *US$63/72 B&B self-contained sgl/twin with AC, flatscreen satellite TV, fridge & free Wi-Fi; US$90 executive dbl.* **$$$**

⌂ **Mariam Hotel** [422 B4] (45 rooms) ✆03720 23548/25446; e hotelmariamgh@gmail. com. With its puzzlingly purple exterior, Mariam's is certainly not as attractive as the Gariba, & probably 2nd choice to it, but the clean rooms & helpful staff make it a more than adequate alternative. An onsite restaurant serves good Ghanaian & international staples. Overpriced at *US$102/113 B&B self-contained sgl/dbl with AC, flatscreen satellite TV & free Wi-Fi; US$117/137 sgl/dbl for slightly larger exec rooms.* **$$$$**

MODERATE

⌂ **Picorna Hotel** [map, page 426] (22 rooms) ✆03720 22672; m 0208 160548; e picornahotel@ hotmail.com; www.picornahotel.com. Once the smartest option in Tamale, the Picorna might have seen better days, but it remains the only centrally located hotel to bridge the substantial gap in quality between the upmarket & budget ranges, with a convenient location about 10mins' walk from the central bus station. The upstairs restaurant serves acceptable Chinese, continental & local dishes priced around US$5–6, & you can also eat in the garden. The clean, comfortable rooms are a standout deal, since prices haven't changed in something like 5 years. *From US$19/24 self-contained sgl/dbl with AC & satellite TV.* **$$**

⌂ **Bigiza Court Hotel** [422 C2] (30 rooms) ✆03720 23531; e info@bigizacourthotel.com; www.bigizacourthotel.com. Despite the grounds looking rather faded, this reasonably priced but characterless multi-storey hotel was still fully booked when we stopped by in 2016. Just off the Bolgatanga Rd, its main selling point is still the large swimming pool, but the rooms are decent value, too, & a good restaurant is attached. *US$34 self-contained dbl with AC, fan & satellite TV; larger dbls US$40–55.* **$$$–$$**

⌂ **Mash Lodge** [422 C3] (16 rooms) ✆03720 28463; m 0506 437534; e mashlodge@gmail. com; www.mashlodge.com. On the Bolgatanga Rd right next door to the excellent Wooden Bakery & Café, this new hotel is set in a multi-storey block that isn't much to write home about, but the business-like rooms are sparklingly clean, and all come with AC, ceiling fan, fridge, flatscreen TV, Wi-Fi, & bathtub with hot water. There's no restaurant (again – Wooden is right next door), but cold drinks are available. *Good value at US$31 self-contained dbl with AC, fan & satellite TV; larger dbls US$39–52.* **$$$–$$**

⌂ **Heritage Hotel** [422 D6] (10 rooms) ✆03720 91137; m 0244 946730. Situated on Liberation Rd about 1km east of the city centre, this workmanlike hotel may not have the most convenient location, but the rooms are comfortable, agreeably decorated, clean & very good value, as is the attached restaurant. *US$37 self-contained dbl with fan & satellite TV; US$41 exec dbl with balcony, king-sized bed, fridge & writing desk.* **$$**

⌂ **Mafara Hotel** [422 D6] (12 rooms) ✆0372 098818; m 0200 535784; e info@mafarahotel.

com; www.mafarahotel.com. This sensibly priced hotel lies just off Liberation Rd, practically opposite the Heritage Hotel, & is very similar in quality & price. It has a restaurant, internet, & the spacious, pleasantly furnished rooms all come with flatscreen satellite TV, AC, fridge, balcony and hot shower. *US$31/34 B&B dbl with queen-/king-sized bed; US$40 suite.* **$$**

🏠 **Discovery Centre** [422 A1] (40 rooms) m 0262 761976; e info@discoverygroup.com.gh; www.discoverygroup.com.gh. A bit of an oddity, this hotel off Jisonayili Rd, with its large grounds, free-form swimming pool, good restaurant, & children's playground, sounds a lot more appealing on paper than it is in the concrete-dominated flesh. It hosts the city's most popular nightclub on Fri & Sat nights, which might be a mixed blessing for overnight guests. The rooms are spacious, but facilities are impressively shoddy, even by Ghanaian standards. Still, it's undeniably cheap. *US$8/16 self-contained sgl/dbl; US$26 executive room.* **$$–$**

BUDGET

🏠 **Asempa Lodge** [422 D7] (7 rooms) ✪ 9.37884, -0.81604; m 0207 090065; e info@ asempalodge.com; www.asempalodge.com. Tucked away in the backstreets southeast of the town centre, this recently relocated lodge is owned by a Dutch & Belgian team with deep roots in Tamale. Positives include the friendly & articulate staff, good food, peaceful atmosphere, & newly built en-suite accommodation. But the remote location means it can feel quite moribund when no other guests are present, & the sparse grounds would benefit from a bit of care & planting. Services & amenities include Wi-Fi, dance & cooking lessons by arrangement, guided tours around the nearby village of Zozogu, & easily arranged trips throughout the region. If you are coming from Kumasi, go right at the first roundabout entering Tamale & carry on for 4km until the signposted turnoff on the right. *US$11/13 sgl/dbl with fan; US$13/16 sgl/dbl with AC. Discount offered to long-term volunteers.* **$$–$**

🏠 **Meet Africa Guesthouse** [422 B1] (4 rooms) m 0249 243142/0205 911748/0244 248110/0243 618742; e meetafrica.tamale@ yahoo.com; www.ontmoetafrika.nl. Situated in Sognaayilli, a traditional village set in a landscape of open savannah 7km northwest of Tamale (see

pages 434–5), this rustic guesthouse comprises a traditional compound of connected round adobe huts. The twin/dbl rooms all have a private bucket shower, but there is no electricity & the (eco friendly) toilets are outside. Moderately priced meals are available by request. *Accommodation costs US$13pp.* **$**

🏠 **Liz and Mustapha's Homestay** [422 B1] (1 room) m 0262 980167/0244 849604; e lizzygentilcore@yahoo.co.uk; fb.me/ tamalehomestay. This well-travelled British– Ghanaian couple living close to Sognaayilli, 15mins' taxi ride north of Tamale, have a self-contained guest room with fan, sleeping up to 3, located outside their main living area. There is also a fully equipped kitchen, a bicycle for rent & they can arrange drumming & dancing lessons. *US$8pp B&B.* **$**

🏠 **Catholic Guesthouse** [422 C4] (41 rooms) ☎ 03720 22265. Set in rambling green grounds 1.5km north of the town centre alongside the Bolgatanga Rd, this stalwart guesthouse has long been a popular budget retreat, offering quiet, clean accommodation at very reasonable prices. The restaurant serves inexpensive hearty meals (the guineafowl is especially good), & there's also a great outdoor bar (& Chuck's is just around the block). Highly recommended. *US$12/13 self-contained sgl with fan/AC; US$17/18 twin/dbl with fan/AC; US$26 exec dbl.* **$$–$**

🏠 **Tamale Institute of Cross Cultural Studies (TICCS) Guesthouse** [422 B4] (16 rooms) ☎ 03720 22836; m 0205 106773; e ticcs@ africaonline.com.gh; www.ticcs.com. Situated in attractive wooded grounds around the corner from the Catholic Guesthouse, this is another long-serving & popular option, offering clean accommodation in boring-looking blocks. Run by TICCS (which, despite its right-on name, is actually a Christian organisation dedicated to 'fostering a deeper understanding of African culture for the enculturation of the gospel'), it also has an excellent library relating to northern Ghana & elsewhere in West Africa. The breezy Jungle Bar is one of the most pleasant eateries in Tamale. For guests, a separate dining room serves up a substantial b/fast for US$3pp. Paid Wi-Fi is available. Ring first as it's often full. *US$12/18 self-contained sgl/dbl with fridge & fan.* **$$–$**

🏠 **Norrip Guesthouse** [422 B1] (6 rooms) m 0247 263027/0248 114752. Tucked away along the road to the Volta River Authority swimming pool a short walk west of the Bolgatanga Rd, this small institutional guesthouse has a rather isolated & rustic setting, but the clean, spacious rooms are exceptionally good value. No food is served but you could eat at the nearby Everglow Restaurant. *US$14/20 self-contained dbl/queen with AC, TV, fridge & fan.* **$$**

SHOESTRING

⌂ **Las Hotel** [422 D6] (25 rooms) ☏03720 26097. If reader feedback is any indicator, this shabbily comfortable hotel has gone well downhill in recent years, but it's still a just about adequate pick in this range. The rooms are large, & an added attraction is the attached (but unaffiliated) Sweet Gardens Chinese Restaurant, one of the best in town. *US$11/15 self-contained dbl with fan/AC & cold water only.* **$**

⌂ **Hamdallah Hotel** [422 D6] (46 rooms) ☏03720 23228/25448; m 0245 367189. The clean rooms at this multi-storey block have become the preferred shoestring option since the drop in standards at the Las Hotel, & given that there's no alcohol permitted on the premises, late-night

shenanigans are also less likely. *US$11/13 self-contained sgl/dbl with fan; US$16 dbl with AC & TV; US$22–26 exec rooms with hot water.* **$$–$**

⌂ **Al Hassan Hotel** [map, page 426] (38 rooms) ☏03720 23638. Owing much of its enduring popularity with backpackers to its central location, the perennially rundown Al Hassan is especially convenient for catching early-morning buses. The rooms are as variable in standard as price: nothing much wrong with the large self-contained ground-floor dbls or their enthusiastic showers, but the shabby 1st-floor 'hotboxes' are best avoided unless you're really strapped for cash or partial to long, sweaty, sleepless nights. *US$7/9 sgl/dbl with common shower; US$11/13 self-contained dbl with fan/AC.* **$**

⌂ **Christian Council Guesthouse** [422 C4] (12 rooms) ☏03720 23278/22991. The tired-looking rooms at this little guesthouse on the Bolgatanga Rd are a useful fallback if the Catholic Guesthouse opposite is full, but otherwise offer considerably less value for money. *US$8.50 dbl with fan using common showers; US$13.50 self-contained dbl with AC.* **$**

✖ WHERE TO EAT AND DRINK

CITY CENTRE
Moderate

❋ ✖ **Chuck's Bar & Restaurant** [422 B4] m 0553 997379/0554 819346; ▐ fb.me/ ChucksTamale; ⏱ 17.00–late Wed–Sun, 11.00–15.00 Sun. Run by two amiable Swedish friends, this place has almost instantaneously become the go-to hangout in Tamale since it opened here in 2015. The bar & dining area are set out in the open air in a large grassy compound just off Mariam junction, & the menu throws a bar-food life belt to anyone who's had one bowl of fufu too many. The thoroughly satisfying pizzas, burgers, & pasta all check in between US$8–12. Both the playlist & the cocktail list are refreshingly eclectic, & dinner here has a way of turning into a late night out before you've realised it. There's beer on draft (with a microbrew operation, believe it or not), Wi-Fi, & brunch every Sun. **$$$–$$**

✖ **Sweet Gardens Chinese Restaurant** [422 D6] On the roof of the Las Hotel; m 0547 999177; ⏱ 10.30–14.30 & 18.30–22.00 daily. Situated 1km from the town centre along Hospital Rd, the

misleadingly named Sweet Gardens is widely regarded to serve the best Chinese food in town, & it's far more reasonably priced than the more central Crest. Mains US$4–6. **$$–$**

✖ **Mba Yehaya's Kebab Special** [map, page 426] ⏱ lunch & dinner daily. This no-frills kiosk opposite the Victory Cinema Building is renowned for its whole flame-grilled guineafowl, which costs US$10, but it also serves kebabs, all accompanied by salad & spicy garnish. **$$**

✖ **Maymax Restaurant & Bar** [map, page 426] m 0208 309429; ⏱ 08.00–midnight Mon–Sat. Grilled tilapia is the speciality at this semi-outdoor eatery next to the National Cultural Centre, but it serves a selection of other local staples as well as the usual chilled beers to a predominantly local clientele. Mains US$4–6. **$**

✖ **Crest Restaurant** [map, page 426] m 0244 707608; ⏱ lunch & dinner daily. On the 1st floor of the Giddipass Building, this well-established restaurant serves Chinese & Ghanaian dishes that seem very overpriced given it gets such mixed reviews. Mains US$8–12. **$$–$$**

Budget

✳ ✕ **Cheff's Corner Chinese Fast Food** [map, page 426] m 0243 310977; ⏱ 10.30–23.00 Mon–Sat. Our runaway budget pick in Tamale, this cheap & very cheerful take-away, set in an old container around the corner from the Al Hassan Hotel, rustles up tasty fried rice with shredded beef, chicken or vegetables to order, for a bargain US$2–3 per plate. **$**

✕ **Mariscot Restaurant** [map, page 426] Located in the Goil filling station opposite the main coach station, this superior chop shop doesn't have much character, but it is very clean, & the local dishes are good value. Mains US$3. **$**

BOLGATANGA ROAD

✳ ✕ **Swad Fast Food** [422 B4] ☎03720 23588; m 0244 712942; e swadtamale@gmail. com; ⏱ 09.00–22.00 daily. This perennially popular garden restaurant lies about 1.5km from the town centre off the Bolgatanga Rd, a few doors from the Catholic Guesthouse. The extensive menu, dominated by Indian & other Asian dishes, but also including pizzas & various continental & Ghanaian staples, caters to meat-eaters & vegetarians. You can eat indoors or under thatched canopies in the well-kept, shady garden. Mains US$6–8. **$$**

✕ **Wooden Bakery & Coffee Shop** [422 C2] ☎03720 28743; www.wooden-gh.com; ⏱ 07.00–23.00 daily. This unexpected gem on the Bolgatanga Rd serves up a long menu of pizzas, burgers, sandwiches, pasta, & Lebanese specialties for US$4–9, alongside coffee, cupcakes, croissants, & other baked goods you wouldn't expect to see in Tamale. The indoor seating is stiflingly hot, but the large shady terrace & green lawn out front make for an agreeable place to while away the hours with the free Wi-Fi or a glass of wine. **$$**

✕ **Mike's Pub & Restaurant** [422 C3] ☎03720 27799; m 0262 027799; ⏱ 11.00–23.00 daily. Situated just off the Bolgatanga Rd behind Barclays Bank, this Lebanese-owned garden eatery is set below tall, shady trees that host a large fruit bat colony, making it interesting at dusk! A cosmopolitan menu includes Lebanese staples – hummus, falafel, kebabs – plus salads, pizzas, grills & a small selection of desserts. The bar is well stocked, smokers can indulge in a flavoured shisha pipe, & major football matches are shown live on a large outdoor screen. Snacks & salads US$5–6; mains US$10. **$$**

✕ **Luxury Restaurant** [422 B2] m 0507 463655; ⏱ 08.00–22.00 Mon–Sat, noon–22.00 Sun. This stylish but unpretentious & good-value eatery at the junction of the Jisonayili & Bolgatanga roads serves a varied selection of Chinese dishes, including a few vegetarian selections, as well as burgers, pizzas, sub sandwiches, real coffee & Ghanaian staples. The lengthy wine list (with bottles for sale at their shop) & dessert menu are added attractions. Mains US$3–7. **$$–$**

✕ **Jungle Bar** [422 B4] In TICCS Guesthouse; ⏱ 16.00–22.00 daily. Cane furniture & hundreds of tropical pot plants make this breezy & cheerful rooftop bar unusually characterful. A pleasant spot for a beer or 2, it also serves a selection of pizza, burgers, hot dogs & grilled meat. Snacks & mains US$4–8. **$$–$**

✕ **Desert Rose** [422 A1] m 0244 031746; ⏱ 08.00–23.30 daily. Tucked away in the backroads 500m north of Jisonayili Rd, this looks like a pretty ordinary semi-outdoor bar from the outside, but it also doubles as a popular restaurant best known for its tasty burgers & grilled guineafowl (or antelope!). The friendly proprietress is happy to take special orders with notice. Mains US$4–7. **$$–$**

BARS AND NIGHTCLUBS

Of the restaurants listed above, Chuck's stands out as the runaway favourite for a Tamale night out, but Jungle Bar, Mike's Pub and Desert Rose are also pleasant spots for a drink. Also recommended are the following.

♀ **Giddipass** [map, page 426] The rooftop of the distinctive dbl-storey Giddipass Building is quite simply the best spot in central Tamale for an early evening drink, thanks to the welcome breeze, scene-setting dusk views over the city, & opportunities for subsequent stargazing. The 1st-floor bar & dance floor is comparatively mundane & has a reputation for attracting sketchy characters.

♀ **Point 7** [map, page 426] Directly opposite the Giddipass, there's cheaper beer but less breeze at this bar, which is popular with locals & volunteers alike, & where you have the choice of sitting indoors or on the semi-enclosed pavement.

♀ **King David Bar** [422 B2] This sprawling semi-outdoor bar at Jisonayili Junction is very popular with locals & especially lively at weekends.

☆ **Discovery Nightclub** Discovery Centre; ⏱ 23.00–06.00 Fri & Sat. The most popular nightclub in Tamale, situated off Jisonayili Road, plays a lively mix of reggae, hip-hop & hip-life (Ghanaian hip-hop). There's usually a cover charge of between US$2.50 & US$5.

SHOPPING

BOOKS The secondhand bookstall next to Cheff's Corner Chinese has a small selection of pre-read novels selling at around US$5 each. A much larger range of secondhand novels is available for around US$2 apiece at **Tasneem Bookshop** [422 B2] on Jisonayili Road, just before King David Bar.

CURIOS Try the stalls around the Centre for National Culture, which have been recommended as far better than most in the country. One of the best is the award-winning **Ragems** (✆ 03720 27223; m 0244 379769; e ragems66@yahoo.com), run by Mrs Asana Awaah Abugre, which specialises in batik and tie-dye as well as baskets, slippers and other products from the Northern Region.

For traditional Gonja shirts and other woven material, try visiting **Mr Moaz** [422 B4] (m 0244 685434/0209 093817), the traditional weaver who operates in two containers off the Bolgatanga Road, more or less opposite the TICCS Guesthouse. The busy **central market** is also a good place to buy local crafts, cloths and beads.

Tucked away behind the DHL office is **COLWOD** (m 0246 223865; ⏱ 09.00–17.00 Mon–Sat), which stands for Collaboration with Women in Distress. Founded in 1995, this small charity helps abandoned women achieve economic independence through teaching them skills such as tie-dyeing, batik and sewing. The shop offers a good range of handmade products including cards, aprons, tablecloths, shirts and blouses, among many other things.

A more recent reader recommendation is the **GIGDEV (Girls Growth and Development) Centre** situated at Jisonayili (✆ 03720 91033; www.gigdev.org; ⏱ 09.00–15.00 Mon–Fri), an educational facility funded partly by proceeds from an excellent shop selling a beautiful selection of handmade products including aprons, bags, rucksacks, jewellery and clothing.

OTHER PRACTICALITIES

DRUMMING AND DANCING Established in 1985, the **Tamale Youth Home Cultural Group** (m 0244 708222/0203 636908/0242 315820; e lisedrewes@hotmail.com; www. yhcg.net), based at the eponymous organisation's headquarters, offers drumming and dancing courses, including traditional dances such as fume, kpalongo, pacha, bamaaya, tora, taai and fast agbeko. The group usually practises from 16.00 to 18.00 Monday to Friday and visitors are warmly welcomed to observe (or join in!), while private and group lessons are also easily arranged.

Drumming and dancing lessons are also offered by the **Yemgarnayili Cultural Troupe**, which is based at the Centre for National Culture. Performances can be arranged through the centre's artistic director (✆ 03720 22855; m 0249 833652) or by contacting instructor Mohammed Ofei (m 0242 102475). Also based at the centre and warmly recommended by readers, Maigah (m 0543 769675) teaches both traditional and contemporary Ghanaian dance, along with a variety of drums and other instruments. He does fixed lessons on Thursdays at 17.00, but private instruction is easily arranged.

FOREIGN EXCHANGE All of Ghana's major banks are represented with ATMs in central Tamale. Barclays Bank has foreign exchange facilities for cash and travellers' cheques, as well as an ATM where local currency can be drawn against a Visa card. The ATMs at GT Bank, Ghana Commercial Bank and UniBank also accept MasterCard. Oddly, the only private forex bureau in Tamale is Kinarash Forex [422 A6], which lies about 1km west of the city centre near the Tamale West Hospital. Generally, though, travellers carrying cash will get a better deal if they change it in Bolgatanga (coming from the north) or Kumasi (coming from the south). Should you be heading on to Mole, best to make sure you have enough local currency to pay for everything there, as the motel works a low exchange rate (though they do accept Visa and MasterCard).

INTERNET AND EMAIL Vodafone Internet (✎ *03720 26635/23646;* ⏰ *07.00–23.00 daily*), next to the central coach station, is generally regarded to have the most reliable and fastest connection. Several other internet cafés are dotted around town and shown on the map.

MEDICAL CARE The Tamale Teaching Hospital [422 D7] (✎ *03720 22454/22458*), which lies along Hospital Road about 3km east of the city centre, is generally regarded as the best medical facility in Tamale. It has an eye clinic and dental facilities.

SWIMMING POOL The pool at the **Volta River Authority (VRA) Clubhouse** [422 A1] (⏰ *10.00–17.30 Wed–Sun; entrance US$1pp*), 1.5km east of the Bolgatanga Road, is well maintained with shaded tables and showers, along with tennis courts and a tranquil bar. A more central and expensive option is the smaller pool at the **Bigiza Court Hotel** (*US$2.50pp*).

WHAT TO SEE AND DO

CENTRAL TAMALE The large **central market** is interesting to explore, in particular the fetish section, which sells scraps of leopard skin, horses' tails and other weird animal artefacts for use in traditional medicine. It's also a good spot for fabric and beads, and you'll certainly want to pause to watch the Gonja cloth weavers at work. Nearby, the **Grand Mosque** on Gulkpegu Road, though of limited architectural interest, is the city's most impressive landmark, with its domed roof enclosed by four cream-coloured minarets that reach six stories into the sky. Ask nicely outside of prayer times and you may be allowed inside the mosque, though a small tip will be expected.

A couple of minutes' walk east of the mosque, the **Gulkpe Naa's Palace** (also called Chief's Palace) used to provide an interesting taster for northern architectural styles, but the old compound of traditional thatched buildings has evidently been replaced by a few undistinguished modern buildings. In the past, any photography or poking around was met with a certain amount of hostility. Now it has opened to visitors in return for a discretionary donation, but it's questionable whether there's anything worth seeing in the first place. Near to the palace, the **Centre for National Culture** is really little more than a glorified craft market, but the various stalls here do stock a great range of artefacts from all around northern Ghana, and you can get a cold drink at Maymax Restaurant next door when you're all crafted out.

An interesting short excursion for craft enthusiasts entails walking south from the Grand Mosque along Hausa Zongo Road for 10 minutes, then – literally – following your nose to the quite pungent open-air **Zongo Tannery** [422 C6], where hundreds of sheep, goat and cow hides (as well as the odd crocodile skin from the Volta) are pinned down to dry in the sun. The people who work at this extensive tannery will show tourists the leather-making process from start to finish for a small negotiable fee. Nearby stalls sell sandals and other leatherwork to a predominantly local clientele.

Further afield, legend has it that a 'mystery tree' in the grounds of the **Tamale Teaching Hospital** [422 D7] (about 2km from the town centre along Hospital Road) was pulled down several times during the construction of the hospital, but always resurrected itself overnight. Another low-key botanical attraction, on the east side of the Bolgatanga Road a short distance north of Jisonayili Junction, is **Madam Tamaiko's Herbal Garden** [422 B1], where a wide variety of medicinal herbs are cultivated in a patch of baobab woodland for use by traditional healers.

TI-KALI CULTURAL EXCHANGE PROGRAMME Formerly known as Kalpohin, the first of six different local communities it now works with, Walisu Alhassan's respected programme operates short participatory tours into traditional villages that are situated about 20 minutes' moto ride or drive from central Tamale, but feel much further away. The main activities you can see or participate in are the spinning of cotton, which the men make into traditional Dagomba smocks, as well as shea butter production and pottery. The price of a standard 2½-hour tour is around US$10. Arrangements can also be made for groups to enjoy lunch or dinner with entertainment from the local drumming and dancing troupes (the performance fee is around US$80 per party). Visitors who want to engage in other activities for more than one day have the opportunity to try preparing traditional meals on the three-stone hearth in a traditional compound. Ideally, all programmes should be arranged at least two days ahead. Proceeds go towards the upkeep of an early day care centre called Early Academy, as well as a vocational training programme for girls. By advance notice, volunteers are welcome to help teach at the school or to help out in other areas. All queries and bookings can be addressed to Walisu Alhassan (m *0243 822633/0206 797148/0274 471509;* e *alwalisu@yahoo.co.uk*).

SOGNAAYILLI Situated about 7km northwest of central Tamale, the village of Sognaayilli hosts a worthwhile community-based tour programme set up by the Dutch/Ghanaian volunteer organisation Meet Africa. Operating under the name **Meet Africa Rural Village Experience and Lodging (MARVEL)**, it offers visitors the opportunity to experience a rural northern culture through homestays, where you live with a local family and help with everyday duties such as cooking, fetching water, sweeping, washing dishes and gardening/farming. Tours can also take in activities such as shea butter or peanut oil extraction, smock weaving, dawadawa (a néré bean-based condiment used as stock) processing, indigenous bathing of babies, cotton spinning, traditional medicinal processing, pottery, basketry, brewing of pito (beer), tobacco processing, local housing systems, drumming and dancing, traditional cooking, funeral-rite performances, and visits to active shrines. Half-day tours cost around US$10 per person, while full-day tours cost US$17–23 per person depending on group size. You can also stay overnight in Sognaayilli, whether at the Meet Africa Guesthouse or at Liz and Mustapha's Homestay (page 429).

All visits and stays must be arranged through Meet Africa (m *0249 243142/0205 911748/0244 248110/0243 618742;* e *meetafrica.tamale@yahoo.com;* www.

ontmoetafrika.nl), ideally with a little advance notice. To get to the Tamale office of Meet Africa, which lies about 5km out of town along the Bolgatanga Road, catch a shared taxi towards Kamina, and disembark just after the village of Kanvilli. The office is on the right side of the road opposite a Nasona fuel station.

EXCURSIONS FURTHER AFIELD

The most popular excursion from Tamale is undoubtedly to Mole National Park, which is covered in *Chapter 20*. However, several towns of relatively minor interest can be visited out of Tamale.

YENDI Situated about 100km east of Tamale, the small town of Yendi is the seat of the Ya Naa of Dagbon (aka Dagomba), an ancient Mole-Dagbani offshoot of the even older Mamprusi Kingdom founded, according to oral tradition, 1415 by the militaristic Chief Nyagse. The first Dagomba capital, Yendi Dabari, which lay some 30km southwest of present-day Yendi, was the base from where Nyagse expanded his empire to incorporate a great many smaller kingdoms, most strategically the salt-producing village of Daboya on the White Volta. The Dagomba influence appears to have declined following the rise of the Gonja Kingdom, c1620, when Gonja expansionists forced Chief Dariziogo of Dagomba to relocate his capital to modern-day Yendi. From around 1750 to 1874, Dagomba was a vassal state of Ashanti, and from 1902 until after World War I, the state was split between the British Gold Coast and German Togoland, with Yendi falling into the latter territory. Despite the economic ascendancy of Tamale since it was made capital of the Northern Territory in 1907, Yendi remains the traditional centre of Dagomba power.

At the time of writing the position of Ya Naa is unfilled. On 27 March 2002, Ya Naa Yakubu Andani II, who ascended the throne in controversial circumstances in 1974, was decapitated and at least 30 of his guards and elders were murdered during a three-day siege on his Gbewaa Palace. Nobody has ever been convicted for the massacre, and as recently as the 14th anniversary in March 2016, the Andani family once again called upon the government to reopen investigations. The killings also triggered a bitter secession dispute between the Andani and Abudu families that remains unresolved to this day.

The situation cooled somewhat in April 2006, when the late king was finally laid to rest in a state funeral, but Yendi remains home to two feuding pretenders to the throne, the semi-official Andani caretaker Abdoulaye Yakubu III and his Abudu rival Abdulai Mahamadu, known as the Bolin Lana, both of whom live practically next door to the original bullet-scarred Gbewaa Palace, a crime scene enclosed by barbed wire and watched over by the military. Meanwhile, for the best part of two decades, nobody has been able to perform tasks traditionally assigned to the paramount chief, most importantly signing new land leases, and the resulting economic stagnation has discouraged any form of investment, making Yendi one of the poorest districts in the country.

In happier times, Yendi was best visited on Monday or Friday mornings, when the Ya Naa held an open court in the company of his 30-odd shaven wives. But it seems unlikely that the long-simmering dispute will be resolved anytime soon, and inter-family politics could well flare up into violence at any time, so ask around about security before heading out. Assuming that all's well, there are several trotros daily from Tamale to Yendi, taking around 2½ hours in either direction, and a few inexpensive places to stay: **Eyarro's Lodge** (m *0205 651793*), signposted off the road towards Bimbilla, where clean self-contained rooms with television, fridge

19

and running water cost around US$15; the more upmarket **Kamil Legacy Hotel** (m *0265 868887/0203 030135*) 1.5km along the road to Saboba where you'll find neat air-conditioned rooms; and the basic **District Assembly Guesthouse**, which charges around US$5 for a room.

DABOYA Set on the northwest bank of the White Volta, 67km west of Tamale, Daboya is the best place to see high-quality *fugu* being made – the hand-spun white and indigo-dyed cloth worn as a smock by men throughout northern Ghana, also known as 'ash and white' – and it makes a very pleasant day trip from Tamale. The town might also be the most ancient extant settlement in northern Ghana thanks to its location at a good river crossing close to a salt pond, which was of great commercial significance as a source of this precious commodity until very recent times. According to Gonja oral tradition, the present-day settlement at Daboya dates to the mid-17th-century reign of Chief Jakpa Lanta, whose son Denyawuri became Daboya's first Wasipewura (chief), a title still in use today. However, Dagomba traditions, backed up by archaeological investigation, indicate that Daboya was probably settled and mined centuries before the arrival of Jakpa Lanta. Although salt is still mined in Daboya today, it happens on a far smaller scale than it did during the pre-colonial era, when salt was a treasured commodity with which to barter for slaves and other items of trade.

From Tamale, the drive to the eastern riverbank opposite Daboya takes about 60–90 minutes in a private vehicle, while public transport is limited to two daily Metro Mass bus services in either direction, leaving from Tamale at 05.00 and 07.00 and returning when they feel like it. *En route*, it might be worth checking out the Jaagpo Sacred Grove (near Tali, about halfway between the two towns) and its giant baobab tree indented by the hoofprints of the horse of a local chief who rode up the trunk! A dugout canoe ferries passengers across the river to Daboya itself, for a nominal fee. Homestays can be arranged through the local assembly man or chief.

SALAGA Set roughly 120km southeast of Tamale along the Yeji road, the small town of Salaga, though rather nondescript today, was for several centuries the commercial hub of northern Ghana, situated at the crossroads of several key caravan routes that ran north towards Burkina Faso, Mali and Nigeria, and south to Ashanti. Throughout the 19th century, merchants from the north and the south converged on Salaga – which at its peak reputedly boasted seven different marketplaces – to barter salt, kola nuts, cowries, gold, livestock, gunpowder, guns and other imported European goods and local produce. But the small town is most notorious today for its large 19th-century central market, which served as the most important slave-trading emporium in this part of West Africa, the place where villagers captured in present-day northern Ghana, Burkina Faso and Mali would be offered for sale to coastal and Ashanti traders for eventual resale to the European coastal forts and export to the Americas.

Salaga can easily be visited as an excursion from Tamale. The infamous former slave market couldn't be easier to find, since it is now the central trotro station. It holds little for the untrained eye, aside from a white signpost reading Salaga Slave Market, and a young baobab planted in 1989 to replace the original tree to which slaves were once tied. Rusting metal shackles, antique rifles and other slave trade relics are still in the possession of many of the town's more established households.

The old well that stands in the former market, protected by a padlocked concrete bunker, is one of several dozen excavated before or during the 19th century in the vicinity of Salaga. The best known of these, signposted alongside a river crossing

2km along the Tamale road, is known as 'Ouankan Baya' – Bathing Place of Slaves – in the local Hausa dialect. According to local tradition, newly arrived slave traders from the north would bathe their human captives here, then rub them with shea butter to make them shine, and feed them up to make them look strong, before taking them to the market to be sold. Another network of underground cisterns, together with the remains of 17th-century walls associated with Chief Jakpa, the founder of the Gonja state, can be seen at Jakpa Wuto near Grushi Zongo, 5km southeast of Salaga.

Reasonably regular public transport runs between Tamale and Salaga from the main trotro station (*US$5*), taking up to 3 hours in either direction. If you're planning to visit as a day trip, best get an early start with the Metro Mass bus to Makongo that departs from Tamale at 05.00. It would also be possible to stop off in Salaga *en route* between Kumasi and Tamale via the Yeji–Makongo ferry – indeed, northbound travellers might well be forced to change vehicles at Salaga. Should you need accommodation, there are four self-contained double rooms with air conditioning and fan at the **Salaga Community Centre**, 200m from the trotro station. Cheaper rooms using common showers are available at the **Catholic Guesthouse**.

SAAKPULI Situated about halfway between Tamale and Bolgatanga, Saakpuli was one of the region's most important slave-trading centres in the early 19th century. The village was founded c1700 by Asante settlers first stationed in the area during a dispute between the Asantehene and the Dagbon king Naa Gariba, but peaked in importance under a local chief called B'laima during the reign of Naa Yakuba (1824–49). During this period, it doubled as a military base and a slaving market, and is said to have consisted of several hundred 12-pole reception halls, each of which housed a platoon of around 50 young men.

Saakpuli has preserved a great deal of evidence dating from the 19th-century slave trade. A stand of massive baobab trees, to which slaves were chained, still overlooks the former market. A small museum containing a four-page history of Saakpuli and a few slave trade artefacts was built by Americans in the early 1990s, and the remains of a slave warehouse and a cluster of water cisterns lie 1.5km northwest of the old market.

The visitor reception centre at Saakpuli lies 6.5km east of the Tamale–Bolgatanga road along a dirt road signposted at Disiga, 46km north of Savelugu. There are no eateries or lodgings in the village, so you would need to visit as a day trip, which is only really feasible with a private vehicle. There's no formal fee as such, but expect to be expected to dole out around US$10 per visitor in the form of donations and tips to the elders, chiefs and guide.

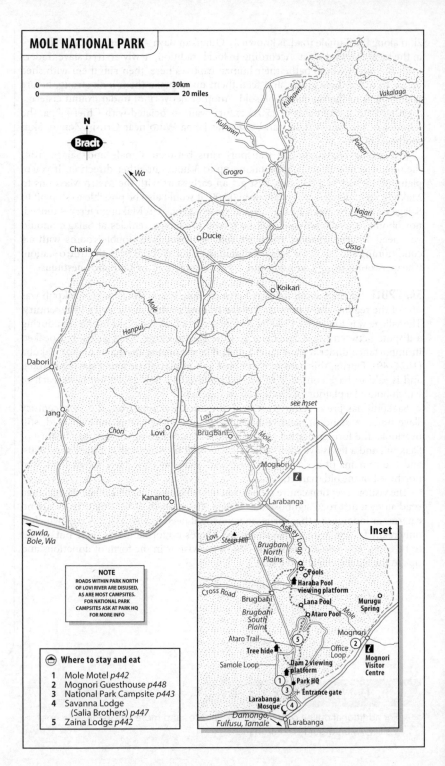

MOLE NATIONAL PARK

0 ——————— 30km
0 ——————— 20 miles

N
Bradt

Wa

Kulpawn

Vakalaga

Grogro

Polzen

Najari

Ducie

Chasia

Koikari

Oisso

Mole

Hanpui

Dabori

Jang

Chori

Lovi

Brugbani

see inset

Lovi

Mole

Moghori

i

Kananto

Larabanga

Sawla,
Bole, Wa

NOTE
ROADS WITHIN PARK NORTH
OF LOVI RIVER ARE DISUSED,
AS ARE MOST CAMPSITES.
FOR NATIONAL PARK
CAMPSITES ASK AT PARK HQ
FOR MORE INFO

Where to stay and eat

1   Mole Motel *p442*
2   Mognori Guesthouse *p448*
3   National Park Campsite *p443*
4   Savanna Lodge
    (Salia Brothers) *p447*
5   Zaina Lodge *p442*

Inset

Lovi   Steep Hill

Asibey Loop

Brugbani
North
Plains

Pools

Haraba Pool
viewing platform

Murugu
Spring

Cross Road   Brugbani

Lana Pool

Mole

Brugbani
South
Plains

Ataro Pool

Ataro Trail

5

Mognori

Tree hide

Office
Loop

2   *i*

Samole Loop

Mognori
Visitor
Centre

Dam 2 viewing
platform

1   Park HQ

3   Entrance gate

Larabanga
Mosque

4

Damongo,
Fulfusu, Tamale   Larabanga

20

Mole National Park

Ghana's largest wildlife sanctuary, Mole (pronounced Mo-*lay*) National Park is one of the best places anywhere in West Africa for general game viewing. Serviced by the rather rundown but relatively affordable Mole Motel and, since 2015, the fabulous new Zaina Lodge, it is also comparatively easy and affordable to visit, whether on public transport or in a private vehicle, and well worth the effort for the opportunity to see a varied range of savannah wildlife at close quarters, most prolifically in the dry season (October–March). Both Zaina Lodge and the motel have memorable settings on a cliff overlooking several waterholes regularly visited by elephant, especially in the dry season, and the adjacent park headquarters offer a range of activities including guided walks, game drives in open 4x4s, and specialist birding excursions.

Although Mole is undoubtedly Ghana's premier wildlife destination, its immense potential as the linchpin of the northern tourist circuit remains largely unrealised, a bizarre oversight that is not only detrimental to travellers and to regional tourism development, but also works to the probable advantage of subsistence poachers. This has improved in recent years, with the surfacing of the road to the park, long-overdue introduction of organised game drives, and the opening of Zaina Lodge, which offers a luxurious tented camp experience that's entirely unique to Ghana and would be right at home in the parks of eastern or southern Africa. Nevertheless, as things stand, the game-viewing circuit is limited to a 40km network of poorly maintained roads to the south of the Lovi River, leaving about 95% of the park inaccessible to visitors, and the infrastructure falls below the standard normally associated with national parks in southern and eastern Africa.

FEES

A one-off entrance fee equivalent to US$10 per person for foreigners or US$5 for Ghanaian nationals covers the duration of your stay. Self-drivers must also pay a one-off entrance fee equivalent to US$2 for locally registered or US$5 for foreign-registered vehicles. These are paid at the entrance gate as you enter the park, unless you're staying at Zaina Lodge, where park fees are included in the accommodation rate.

With regard to activities, game drives in an open 4x4 cost the equivalent of US$21 per party per hour (for a group of up to eight) plus a guide fee of US$2.50 per person per hour. Other charges are US$2.50 per person per hour for guided walks (plus optional tip), or US$13 per person for 2 hours of birdwatching, plus US$2.50 for each additional hour. All activities can be arranged and paid for on the spot at the tourist office in the park headquarters 100m from the Mole Motel.

HISTORY AND WILDLIFE

Set aside as a game reserve in 1958, a year after Ghana attained independence, Mole protects a vast tract of undulating and relatively dry savannah woodland that had always been thinly populated due to an abundance of tsetse flies and lack of perennial water. It was gazetted as a national park in 1971, following the controversial resettlement of the relatively few villagers who lived within its boundaries, and was extended to its present size of 4,840km² in 1991. The park lies at an average altitude of about 150m, but is bisected by the 250m-high Konkori Escarpment, on which the Mole Motel and Zaina Lodge are situated. The two main watercourses are the seasonal Lovi and Mole rivers, tributaries of the White Volta River that seldom flow in the dry season, but feed a scattering of more permanent waterholes.

More than 90 mammal species have been recorded in Mole, though several of the more charismatic larger mammals are locally extinct, or in critical danger of that fate. The last African wild-dog sighting, for instance, was back in 1978, and while anecdotal evidence suggests that lions might still be present in small numbers, a survey undertaken over four months in 2008/09 for the *African Journal of Ecology* obtained 'no unequivocal evidence' of their continued presence. More pleasingly, the same survey concluded that the spotted hyena remains reasonably common, and it also captured several images of leopards on nocturnal photographic traps. A 2011–14 survey for *Animal Biodiversity and Conservation* was similarly frustrated in producing hard evidence of lions' continued presence at Mole, but nonetheless concluded that 'the presence of a few individual lions in Mole National Park should not be ruled out a priori', based on multiple roars heard by researchers and rangers, as well as a buffalo bearing the marks of a lion attack spotted in October 2013, and anecdotal reports of two lions sighted by poachers in August 2014.

Other mammal populations seem reasonably stable despite the presence of more than 30 villages close to the park boundaries and associated problems with subsistence hunting. The elephant population probably stands at between 400 and 600 individuals, and is mostly concentrated in the southern half of the park. There used to be a significant seasonal fluctuation in this population, as many herds followed a pair of well-established migration routes into southern Burkina Faso, but it is unclear to what extent elephants still use these corridors, which have become increasingly heavily settled by humans. The park also supports more than 1,000 buffalo, and significant populations of hippo, warthog and antelope species such as Defassa waterbuck, kob, roan, hartebeest, bushbuck, and various duikers. Five primate species are present, most visibly olive baboon, but also patas and green monkey. A dozen or so small carnivores are also present, but the only ones likely to be seen are various types of mongoose.

Mole National Park has the longest checklist for any site in Ghana, with a total of at least 316 species now recorded. It is the main Ghanaian stronghold for several raptors and other large birds that have become scarce in more settled areas, for instance white-backed vulture, bateleur, martial eagle, Beaudouin's snake eagle, and marabou and saddle-billed stork. It is also an important site for species associated with the Guinean savannah biome, such as Senegal parrot, northern carmine bee-eater, blue-bellied roller, northern red-billed hornbill and bearded barbet.

GETTING THERE AND AWAY

Mole is relatively cheap and easy to get to, certainly by comparison with the more renowned savannah reserves of eastern and southern Africa, most of which can only be visited on costly organised safaris. Described as 'legendarily dusty and bumpy' as recently as the last edition of this guide, the 150km road to Mole between Sawla and Fulfusu saw the completion of surfacing works in late 2015, turning what was once an arduous and inconveniently timed slog into as (relatively) painless a trip as you'd expect to find anywhere in Ghana.

BY BUS Previously, the *only* places where you could pick up public transport to Mole National Park or Larabanga were Tamale, Bole and Wa. This is no longer the case, and there are now several reasonably convenient ways to reach the park depending on which direction you are coming from.

Starting in either Wa or Tamale, **trotros** (Toyota Coasters, usually) make the 5-hour trip back and forth between the two cities several times per day, stopping in Larabanga *en route*. You'll likely have to pay the full fare even if dropping at Larabanga, but at US$6, it's not too much of a burden.

Coming from the south, there was previously no transport to Larabanga from either Fulfusu or Sawla junctions, but the newly surfaced road has changed all that. Assuming you don't mind a couple of vehicle changes, you can start from the junction in Fulfusu and catch a trotro to Damongo for US$2, from where there are shared taxis covering the remaining 15km to Larabanga for less than US$1. Coming from Sawla in the west, trotros connect to Larabanga (and onwards to Damongo) throughout the day for US$2. Once in Larabanga, however, there's no public transport to the park itself, so you've either got to hire a cab or hoof it the last few miles. A charter taxi from Larabanga to the park HQ and Mole Motel will run you about US$8, while hiring a motorbike for the same should come in just under US$5. It is also permitted to walk the 6km to the motel, which takes 60–90 minutes, depending on your pace, and is best undertaken in the cool of the early morning or late afternoon. Alternatively, you can rent a bicycle from Savana Lodge (Salia Brothers) in Larabanga for a few dollars per day.

The daily **Metro Mass bus** that was for many years the most popular way of reaching Mole seemed to have stopped for good when we visited in early 2016, but in the unlikely event that services resume, buses used to depart Tamale at around 14.00–15.00, and would start the return trip from Mole Motel at 04.00 sharp. A few other Metro Mass buses still pass through Larabanga daily. Most useful is the service between Tamale and Wa, which leaves at 05.00 in either direction. If it departs on time, it should reach Larabanga before 08.00, allowing plenty of time to see the mosque, have a bite, and make it to Mole in time for an afternoon activity. Another service runs daily in either direction from Tamale to Bole, leaving in either direction at 06.00. A disadvantage of all these buses is that you need to be at the bus station by 04.30 to be certain of getting a seat, since tickets cannot be booked prior to the day of travel. Also, departure times are somewhat theoretical, and the buses often leave a few hours later than scheduled.

BY CAR For self-drivers, getting to Mole is now straightforward in any vehicle, and the tarmac runs all the way up to Mole Motel's front door. The turn-offs at Fulfusu and Sawla are hard to miss, and the park HQ sits about 85km and 75km from Fulfusu and Sawla, respectively. From the (clearly signposted) turn-off in Larabanga, it is 3.5km to the park entrance gate, and another 2.5km to Mole Motel. If time is an issue, a one-way charter taxi from Tamale will cost around US$80–100, or 4x4s arranged through either AY Transport (m *0246 678296/0553 315129*; e *ibrahimmatinu@yahoo.com*; *www.ibrahimmatinu.wordpress.com*) or the Tamale-based Grassroot Tours (m *0541 668682/0503 722405*; e *info@*

grassroottours.com; www.grassroottours.com) go for around US$120 per day including usage within the park.

BY AIR The airstrip at Mole has been out of service for ages, but the 2015 opening of Zaina Lodge means there's rather serious talk of getting it up and running again in the years to come. As it stands today, Mole is about 2½ hours by car from Tamale Airport, and Zaina Lodge arranges airport transfers for guests at US$150 round-trip.

WHERE TO STAY AND EAT *Map, page 438*

In addition to the accommodation listed below, cheap rooms are available in Larabanga and at Mognori. For those who want to see the park at its best, but keep costs to a minimum, a good compromise might be to spend one night at the motel in the park, then a second night at one of the villages outside.

Mole Motel m 0277 564444/0244 316777; e motel.mole@yahoo.com or info@molemotelgh. com; www.molemotelgh.com. Built in 1961 on a cliff overlooking 2 watering holes, this idyllically situated hotel is an amazing place to wake up – as likely as not to the sound of baboons clattering over the roof – and it often offers great in-house game viewing. The rooms & 6-bed dorms get mixed reviews, & are definitely far from luxurious, but they seem comfortable enough & pretty good value at the price (especially when you consider how dauntingly expensive game lodges have become elsewhere in Africa – or even elsewhere in Mole!). The standard of service & food has also attracted plenty of criticism over the years, but it seems to have improved of late. Water & power cuts are also sporadic problems, though the motel is now connected to the national power grid. A more insurmountable drawback, as implied by the 'motel' moniker, is the almost startling architectural insensitivity of the long, white accommodation blocks, which stand in glaring contrast to the wild surrounds. More happily, the swimming pool at the edge of the escarpment is generally clean & inviting, & a great spot to cool down after a walk in the park. The poolside bar serves fairly priced sodas, beers & mineral water, & though it's officially open from 06.00–22.00 daily, it's been known to close early without warning. The restaurant serves decent meals for around US$8–10, which are best ordered an hour or so in advance. If you eat outdoors during daylight hours, watch out for thieving baboons. Booking is advisable, especially over a w/end. Visa & MasterCard accepted. *US$16pp dorm bed; US$47/57 self-contained sgl/twin with AC, satellite TV & fridge; US$21/37/55 sgl/dbl/trp family room with fan;*

US$26/47/71 sgl/dbl/trp family room with AC; US$78 dbl chalet with AC & private balcony overlooking the waterhole. **$$$–$$**

Zaina Lodge (25 rooms) \ 0303 938736; m 0540 111504/5; e info@zainalodge.com; www. zainalodge.com. Entirely one of its kind in Ghana, & among a tiny handful of lodges anywhere in West Africa to possess a sensibility & aesthetic in line with the best bush lodges in eastern & southern Africa, Zaina Lodge has thoroughly reimagined the possibilities of Mole National Park, & a visit here would rightly rank among the highlights of any trip to Ghana. The luxurious en-suite standing tents are spread out along the edge of the escarpment, decorated in local textiles & carvings, & all are handsomely appointed with flatscreen satellite TVs, AC, ceiling fan, cold-box minibar, reading lamps, writing desk, indoor & outdoor shower, dual sinks, terracotta floors, & a private deck offering views over the savannah and waterholes below. The thatched, open-air restaurant & bar soars to nearly 20m in height, centred around an impressively large mud & stick pillar built by local craftsmen & carved top-to-bottom in traditional motifs by female artisans from Larabanga. The women of Sirigu in the Upper East were brought on to decorate other walls of the restaurant in the geometric patterns they're famous for, & the whole area opens up on to a wide terrace & infinity pool with expansive views over two new waterholes. The food ranges from continental to Indian, pan-Asian, & Ghanaian, & is almost certainly the finest cuisine to be had anywhere in Ghana north of Accra. Special meals & sundowners can be put on at a variety of private sites around the lodge, & while there's no spa, plans are in the works to bring a masseuse on board. All game drives, walks &

other park activities are arranged directly with the lodge & begin right at the front door. There's 1 room accessible to visitors with mobility problems, Wi-Fi, a business centre, soon to be an organic garden, & a percentage of revenue is earmarked to support community development & environmental management. Airport transfers from Tamale are available for US$150/vehicle round trip & day visitors are welcome for US$25/45/75 for pool use/plus lunch/plus a game drive. *US$250/400 sgl/dbl B&B; US$350pp all-inclusive (food, drink, & activities).* **$$$$$**

⚔ National Park Campsite m 0249 890298. The main campsite lies about 10mins' walk from the motel in the direction of the entrance gate, and is made up of 3 camping areas, each able to accommodate 4–5 tents, & parking spaces. There is a long-drop toilet & water onsite. Excitingly, it's now possible to spend the night under the stars on one of the park's strategically positioned tree platforms (though there's a US$15 charge per vehicle if you need a lift to them). There are a limited number of mattresses (*US$3*), mozzie nets (*US$3*) & tents (*US$13*) available for hire, but you should have a backup plan in case they're unavailable. Several other very basic campsites are dotted around the reserve & can theoretically be visited with a ranger, but guides are reluctant to go to them. In all cases, campers will need to be self-sufficient for food & beverages. *US$5pp/night basic campsites; US$8pp/night main campsite & tree platforms.* **$**

WHAT TO SEE AND DO

Whether you're staying at Zaina Lodge or Mole Motel, there are worse ways to pass a day than sitting on the terrace, cold drink in hand, swimming pool a few paces away, and two waterholes clearly visible below. In the dry season even this most passive (and at the motel, inexpensive) approach to safari-going should reward you with sightings of elephant, kob antelope, Defassa waterbuck, bushbuck, warthog, olive baboon, green monkey and numerous birds during the course of any given day. If you're hanging around the motel, do drop in at the small museum in the staff quarters, which contains elephant skins, skulls and embryos, as well as some good sketches (but expect a bit of a wait while somebody locates the keys).

Note that Larabanga and, to a lesser extent, Mognori Eco-Village, both covered separately later in the chapter, are both realistic goals for day trips from either of the park's hotels.

GUIDED GAME WALKS The most popular activity at Mole is the guided game walks that usually run twice daily from the headquarters to the base of the cliff below the motel. (Walks for Zaina guests start directly at the lodge.) You won't necessarily see a greater variety of large mammals than you will from up on the escarpment, but usually you'll get far closer to them. Indeed, the elephants resident in this area are reasonably habituated to human pedestrians and often allow visitors to approach to within 20m. On foot, you can also be reasonably sure of seeing Nile crocodiles in the dam, and of mutually startling a few water monitors – bulky lizards that measure more than 1m long and habitually crash gracelessly to safety when disturbed.

Walking in the park (except along the road between Larabanga and Mole Motel) without an armed ranger is expressly forbidden, and properly so, given the number of elephants around. Guided walks cost the equivalent of US$2.50 per person per hour, regardless of group size, and there are enough rangers for every group to have its own guide. The walks generally depart at 07.00 and 15.30, but can be arranged at other times with notice. It is customary to tip the ranger.

Note that it is mandatory to wear closed shoes (as opposed to sandals or flip-flops) on guided walks; visitors who don't comply with this ruling will be forced to rent bulky (and blister-inducing) rubber boots.

Mole National Park is easily the most important non-forested birding site in Ghana, with some 315 species recorded, including many species whose Ghanaian distribution is limited to the drier northern woodland. What's more, the likes of the oriole warbler, violet turaco and several species of kingfisher, bee-eater, roller, barbet, sunbird and starling create a riot of colour!

The grounds of Mole Motel form a superb starting point for dry-county birds. Seed-eaters abound, including mixed flocks of lavender and orange-cheeked waxbill, red-cheeked cordon-bleu, red-billed and bar-breasted firefinch, pin-tailed and long-tailed paradise-whydah, chestnut-crowned sparrow-weaver, grey-headed sparrow and yellow-fronted canary. The rocky escarpment harbours family groups of stone partridge and double-spurred francolin, along with freckled nightjar, Abyssinian ground-hornbill, rock-loving and Dorst's cisticola, white-fronted black-chat and cinnamon-breasted bunting.

The moist woodland surrounding the swamp below the lodge is home to some special birds, in particular the highly desirable oriole warbler, one of West Africa's most beautiful birds. In fact, colourful birds are here the rule rather than the exception. The noisy but elusive yellow-crowned gonolek is common, as is the red-throated bee-eater (a colony of which nests in the vicinity). Even the most hardened birder will be dazzled by one gem after the next: Bruce's green-pigeon, violet turaco, rose-ringed parakeet, blue-breasted and grey-headed kingfisher, northern carmine bee-eater, Abyssinian and blue-bellied roller, bearded barbet, half a dozen species of sunbird, sulphur-breasted and grey-headed bush-shrike, and purple and long-tailed glossy-starling.

Other target species in these woodlands are white-throated francolin, vinaceous dove, green woodhoopoe, black scimitar-bill, yellow-fronted tinker-bird, greater and lesser honeyguide, fine-spotted, grey and brown-backed woodpecker, Fanti sawwing, white-breasted and red-shouldered cuckoo-shrike, yellow-throated greenbul, African thrush, Senegal eremomela, northern crombec, yellow-bellied hyliota, several species of overwintering Palaearctic warblers, northern black, African blue, European pied and swamp flycatcher, white-crowned robin-chat, brown-throated wattle-eye, Senegal batis, blackcap and brown babbler, white-winged black-tit, spotted creeper, African golden oriole, northern puffback, yellow-billed shrike, brubru, white helmetshrike (this race topped with an enormous, floppy crest), red-headed weaver, black-faced and black-bellied firefinch, and brown-rumped and Cabanis's bunting.

Raptors are particularly prolific in Mole and regularly encountered species include white-backed, white-headed and hooded vulture, short-toed and brown snake-eagle, bateleur, several species of migrant harrier, lizard buzzard, Wahlberg's, martial and long-crested eagle, Ayres' and African hawk-eagle, lanner falcon, and African hobby.

BIRDWATCHING While the variety of large mammals to be seen in Mole is limited, the birdlife is fantastic. Larger birds likely to be seen in the vicinity of the motel and waterholes include martial eagle, woolly-necked and saddle-billed stork, white-backed and palm-nut vulture, and various herons and egrets. Colour, too, is not lacking, as noted by Adam Riley in his box, *Birding Mole* (see above). All in all, you might easily pick up 60-plus species in the course of a 3- to 4-hour walk around the waterholes and motel. Birdwatching is now treated as an official activity at Mole, attracting a special fee equivalent to US$13 per person for 2 hours, plus US$2.50 for each additional hour, inclusive of a guide. Dedicated birders will also usually be allocated a ranger who is especially knowledgeable (the legendary Zechariah Wareh is one of the best birding guides in Ghana, but several other guides are well versed in the local avifauna).

GAME DRIVES A relatively recent, and long overdue, addition to the limited selection of activities on offer at Mole is a guided game drive in an open 4x4. These usually run twice daily from the park headquarters, at the same time as the walks, which is the best time to see wildlife, though there is some flexibility about timing – midday drives can also be arranged. Zaina guests should note that the lodge operates their own closed-top safari vehicles (with AC!) and game drives for guests begin directly at the lodge. As with game walks, you are very likely to see elephants on a game drive, as well as the other wildlife that tends to haunt the waterholes below the escarpment, but the capacity to head out a bit further improves the odds of seeing other large mammal species, such as buffalo, hartebeest, roan antelope and patas monkey. Arguably even more exciting are night drives, which offer the opportunity to look for nocturnal creatures such as spotted hyena, civet, genet and marsh mongoose – not to mention the oddball aardvark, which has been observed a few times on recent night drives.

The cost of a diurnal game drive works out at around US$21 per hour for the vehicle including fuel and driver, plus US$2.50 per person per hour, while night drives are charged at the same vehicle rate, plus US$8 per person per hour. The 4x4s can take up to eight passengers, so it is clearly worth trying to get a group together if you want to keep down costs. That said, if you have special interests, such as wildlife photography or birding, it might be more productive to arrange a private game drive.

Visitors who arrive in their own 4x4 are permitted to conduct their own game drives. No fee is charged except for the vehicles initial entry into the park, but it is mandatory to take a guide/ranger at US$2.50 per person per hour.

AROUND MOLE NATIONAL PARK

Easily visited in conjunction with the park is the striking Larabanga Mosque, the most famous and reputedly oldest of half a dozen West Sudanese-style mud-and-stick buildings dotted around northwestern Ghana, and an interesting community project at Mognori Eco-Village. Also of interest, depending on whether you approach the park from east or west, are the small traditional towns of Damongo and Bole, with the latter in particular offering access to some of the most interesting adobe architecture in the north.

LARABANGA MOSQUE Only 3km southeast of the entrance gate to Mole National Park, at the T-junction with the main road between Damongo and Sawla, stands the best-known and possibly oldest of the few West Sudanese structures that survive in northern Ghana. This is Larabanga Mosque: a broadly rectangular timber-frame structure whose whitewashed mud walls are supported by around a dozen bulbous buttresses spiked with protruding timber struts. The tallest parts of this rather surreal apparition are the mihrab and minaret, which take the form of pyramidal towers rising almost twice as high as the main building. The western wall is shaded by a baobab that some claim matches the building itself for antiquity.

Few visitors to Mole would want to miss out on seeing Larabanga Mosque, which is not only a masterpiece of West Sudanese architecture, but also an important pilgrimage site for local followers of Islam. Furthermore, the mosque is set in a village of 4,000, also known as Larabanga, that forms perhaps the most southerly accessible example of the flat-roofed adobe architecture typical of certain parts of the Sahel, making it of particular interest to travellers who won't be exploring other parts of northern Ghana.

History and background
The mosque at Larabanga may well be the oldest extant building in Ghana. Yet, oddly enough, nobody seems to agree on just how old it is, or even who built it. Some sources date it to the 13th century, which if not impossible is certainly improbable given that Islam had barely infiltrated the region at that time. At the other extreme, some traditions claim the founder of the mosque was one Imam Yidan Braimah, a 17th-century migrant from Medina in Saudi Arabia whose illuminated Koran – supposedly delivered to him by angels – is still preserved in the mosque today.

The most widely accepted tradition locally accredits the mosque's construction to a medieval Islamic trader called Ayuba, who was travelling through the region in AD1421 when he found the so-called Mystic Stone that lies on the outskirts of Larabanga (in the direction of Wa) and decided to sleep there. During the night, Ayuba had a strange dream about a mosque, the foundations of which were mysteriously in place when he awoke. So he completed the construction of the mosque and settled at Larabanga – whose name reputedly derives from the Mole-Dagbani for 'speakers of Arabic'. It is said that after his death Ayuba's remains were buried beneath the large baobab tree that still shades the mosque today.

The accuracy of the year 1421 is anybody's guess. But a construction date in the early 15th century would tie in those given by imams of other similar mosques, as well as the period that is generally agreed to be when Islam expanded into what is now northern Ghana. And if this is the case, then visitors to Larabanga are probably looking at the oldest extant building in Ghana, some 50 years older than the first Portuguese castle at Elmina.

In all probability, the various mud-and-stick mosques of northern Ghana were built in close succession along a well-established Islamic trade route. The special venerated status of Larabanga Mosque is not so much due to its age as the widely held belief that its foundations were divinely built. Nevertheless, Larabanga's claim to be the oldest of Ghana's mud-and-thatch mosques is probably supported by its status as a surrogate Mecca for Ghanaian Muslims. But nobody knows for sure.

What's more, the people of Larabanga tend to deny the existence of similar mosques elsewhere in the country. Say that you've actually seen them yourself, and they'll still turn up their nose at any suggestion that a 'manmade replica' might be of similar antiquity to their divinely created original. And the sense that Larabanga isn't above a bit of conscious myth-making is heightened when you are taken to the Mystic Stone a short distance west of the village. When the Sawla road was originally constructed in the 1950s, this venerated boulder obstructed the intended route, but every time the roadmakers moved it out of the way, it 'mysteriously' reappeared overnight. Eventually, the road was diverted to go around it.

Whenever it was built, Larabanga Mosque, like others of its ilk, is obviously very old, and a truly strange and inspiring sight. But while it has retained much of its architectural integrity over the centuries, the structural fabric was critically undermined when a layer of waterproof cement was applied to the exterior in the 1970s, trapping moisture within the earthen walls, weakening them significantly, and allowing termites to infest the wooden support beams. In 2001, following the collapse of part of the walls, the mosque was placed on the World Monuments

Fund (WMF)'s Watch List of 100 Most Endangered Sites. A year later, a grant from American Express allowed the WMF to train a team of local artisans in the dying craft of mud-plaster maintenance, and to oversee the restoration of the crumbling mosque to its full former glory.

Getting there and away   All visitors to Mole pass through Larabanga *en route*, and many budget travellers stay in the village, using it as an alternative base for exploring the national park.

For those who intend to stay in the park, you'll probably first be dropped off at the junction in Larabanga, from where it's only a minute or two's walk to the mosque, so you may as well visit it before you head out to the national park.

Once in Larabanga, the mosque itself is easy enough to find, situated only 100m northwest of the junction to Mole National Park. In any case, one of the town's plethora of official and unofficial guides will doubtless find you first, and escort you to a small office (m *0504 117381/0275 820970/0263 168105*) where you'll pay the receiptable viewing fee (equivalent to US$2). This fee allows you to spend as long as you like admiring and photographing the mosque's striking exterior, but be aware that non-Islamic visitors are forbidden from entering the mosque or climbing to the roof.

Cons and hassles   For some years, Larabanga was notorious not only for a high level of hassle (travellers disembarking from the bus were routinely mobbed by ten or more self-styled guides), but also for the formidable litany of fees, charges, donations and tips associated with visiting the mosque. Thankfully, however, we've had no reports of mobbings or overt aggression from guides over the past several years, and transport on the new road means that visitors show up unannounced throughout the day, leaving less notice for the crowd of would-be guides to meet you. More importantly, there is now just one reasonable and receiptable official fee. So on the face of things, the situation is much improved compared with when we researched earlier editions of the guide, but we do continue to receive negative feedback from readers regarding their experiences in town.

Perhaps it would be most accurate to say that the hassle at Larabanga has simply become more subtle. The guides who work the mosque are masterful at pressurising even the most experienced and sceptical of travellers into parting with sums of money far more substantial than the official viewing fee. You may be asked to fund the building of a school or hospital, or to help a sick friend or a local football team, the variations are numerous, and they are good at making it difficult to refuse. But refuse you should, because it is basically just a con, and any money you give your guide will essentially be a hefty 'tip' extorted under false pretences. If you're clear from the outset in your intention *only* to pay the official viewing fee, you can expect something of a frosty reception, but should be largely left alone to view the mosque after the guides give up on you.

🏠 **Where to stay and eat**   *Map, page 438*

Should you stay in Larabanga in preference to Mole, we advise against taking up any offer of a private homestay made by so-called guides – we've had more than one report of such an offer resulting in theft from the room.

🏠 **Savanna Lodge (Salia Brothers)**
(5 rooms) m 0275 544453/0275 544071/0509 130367; e bamdese@yahoo.com. After closing

their eponymous guesthouse at the main junction in Larabanga, the Salia Brothers have put their focus into Savanna Lodge, which was always the more rustic & comfortable of their 2 guesthouses anyway. Set in a patch of thornbush about 1km from the town centre along the road to Mole National Park, the traditional round huts here come with thatched roofs, brightly painted (though peeling) exteriors, mozzie nets & fans, &

there's also a high-ceilinged dormitory sleeping 3. All rooms use shared bucket showers & cold drinks & meals are available at around US$3 each. En-suite rooms are planned but seem a long way off. Village tours can be arranged & bicycles rented for visits to Mole. *US$8 dbl; US$4.50 dorm bed.* **$**

MOGNORI ECO-VILLAGE Situated just outside the southern national park boundary 10km northeast of Mole Motel, this wonderfully hassle-free traditional adobe village is the focal point of a worthwhile ecotourism project conceived in 2003 after the local crop was destroyed by elephants. The main attraction here is a canoe safari along the stretch of the Mole River running from the village into the park, which costs around US$8/13 for parties of one to two or three to five for 1 hour. Crocodiles are frequently seen on the river, and there is also a chance of other large mammals, even elephant. The canoe trip is also of particular interest to birdwatchers, both for the presence of the elusive African finfoot, most often seen close to the bank below overhanging vegetation, as well as of gallery forest species such as yellowbill, Narina trogon, blue-breasted kingfisher, shining-blue kingfisher, blue flycatcher, blackcap babbler, square-tailed drongo and bar-breasted firefinch. All revenue from tourist visits is put into a community development fund. Other activities at Mognori include village walks at US$3 per person, and Gonja dancing performances (*US$18/31/44 per party of 1–10/11–20/21+*). For more details contact Moses (m *0249 507413;* e *moleboy2007@hotmail.com*).

Getting there and away To get to Mognori, follow the road from Larabanga towards Mole National Park for about 2km until you reach a T-Junction about 1km before the park entrance gate. Take the right fork (the opposite direction to the entrance gate), and you will reach the village after about 10km. No trotros cover this route, but you can charter a motorbike for around US$10. Alternatively, if you are staying at Mole Motel, the park headquarters at Mole charges around US$35 per group for a return 4x4 road transfer to Mognori. If the visitor reception centre is unmanned when you get there, ask around for one of the guides: Kwame Anawra, Mahama Abukbakari or Saidu Passo.

⌂ **Where to stay and eat** *Map, page 438*
⌂ **Mognori Guesthouse** (5 rooms) m 0249 507413/0241 343392; e moleboy2007@hotmail. com. Operated as part of the ecotourism project, this no-frills guesthouse offers simply furnished but surprisingly comfortable rooms within a

traditional mud compound. During the dry season you can join the locals & sleep on the roof under a blanket of stars. Meals can be provided for around US$2pp. *US$8pp.* **$**

DAMONGO The largest town flanking the road from Tamale to Mole National Park, Damongo, the birthplace of President John Mahama, is the capital of West Gonja, the largest and most thinly populated of the 20 districts comprising Northern Region. Though seldom visited by tourists, it boasts some good examples of traditional northern architecture and, more practically, a GCB bank with ATM, however its utility as a stopover for visitors headed to or from Mole is rather questionable given the transportation improvements associated with the new road. The only real attraction here is the recently established **Bi Konu Tu Drumming and Cultural Group** (m *0275 543076;* e *kimbsharif@yahoo.com*), which organises half-day traditional Gonja dance performances and drumming workshops for under US$5 per person. The group is based out of Jakpa Palace (the residence of the paramount chief or Yagbon Waa) and performances and workshops are best arranged in advance otherwise just ask around at the palace for Mohammed or Aziz. Bi Konu Tu can also arrange for visitors to volunteer in the community school, or to visit a traditional Gonja farm.

Getting there and away Any transport headed between Tamale and Wa will pass through Damongo, and there are regular enough trotros originating here and headed for Fulfusu/Tamale (*US$3*) and Sawla/Wa (*US$4*) as well, with more trips on Saturdays for the weekly market. Shared taxis between Damongo and Larabanga also leave throughout the day, and it's likely you'll have to change vehicles here if you're doing the journey to Mole in stages from Fulfusu.

🏠 Where to stay and eat

🏠 **Home Touch Guesthouse** (24 rooms) m0201 048987/0553 697871/0261 651256. Situated about 1km east of the town centre on the main road through town in the direction of Fulfusu (just behind the Nasona fuel station), this reasonably priced & reader-recommended place is the most comfortable option in town, with simple & clean tiled rooms with minifridge & TV set around a bare courtyard. The major downside is there's no food available, but it's not too terribly far

into town, where you could give the Palace View Canteen or Flemish Bar a try. *US$14/17 sgl/dbl with fan, US$16/18 sgl/dbl with AC.* **$$–$**

🏠 **Kigbonmato Guesthouse** (5 rooms) m 0243 815406/0249 705194. Formerly the Mahama Guesthouse & still usually referred to by that name, this place seems a little chaotic, but the rooms are decent at the price, & the popular restaurant is reputedly the best in town. US$8 self-contained twin with fan. **$**

BOLE AND SURROUNDS The small district capital of Bole, situated on the main Kumasi–Wa road about 40km south of Sawla, is best known for its beautiful mud-and-stick mosque, which is often claimed to be the second-oldest of its type in the country. The ancient **mosque** isn't readily visible from the main road, but it's easy enough to find, situated about 50m behind the modern mosque, a major landmark with its five-storey parapet. Although it may not be as old as its counterpart at Larabanga, Bole Mosque also suffers from far less hype and bureaucracy. The chief imam, whose palace is signposted next door, is more than happy to show visitors around for a small tip (around US$2 feels appropriate). He is also very relaxed about women visitors and photography, and may well offer to take you inside the mosque and up to the roof.

Two other mud-and-stick mosques stand alongside the modern road running north from Techiman to Bole. Both are said to date to the 18th century, and are notable for having minarets that are very tall relative to the rest of the building. Coming from the south, the first mosque you'll encounter stands on the west side of the road at **Banda Nkwanta** (where you'll also find the turn-off for Bui National Park). The second lies on the east side of the road as you pass through the forest-fringed village of **Maluwe**. The presence of these mosques along the modern road suggests that it approximates to a much older Islamic trade route.

The flat-roofed adobe architecture characteristic of this part of Ghana arguably reaches its apex in **Sonyo** (shown on some maps as Senyon), a sprawling village of around 5,000 Choruba-speakers situated about 18km further northeast. The oldest part of Sonyo comprises a few large clusters of connected homesteads whose interiors are most easily accessed via an enclosed courtyard from the roofs, which are used rather like an aerial network of pathways. The community also plays host to the Soonyor Kipo Shrine, which is sworn on as one would the Bible and is believed to have the power instantly to kill anyone who lies. The best time

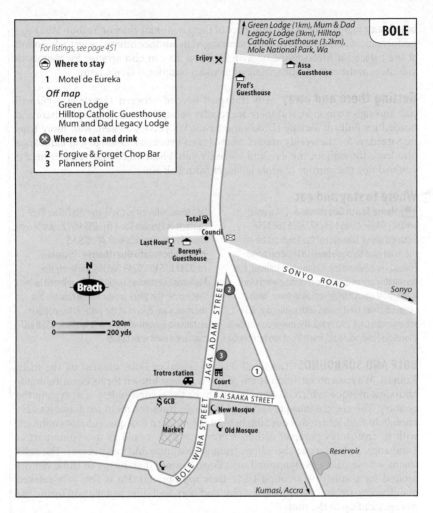

For listings, see page 451

BOLE

Green Lodge (1km), Mum & Dad
Legacy Lodge (3km), Hilltop
Catholic Guesthouse (3.2km),
Mole National Park, Wa

Erijoy

Assa
Guesthouse

Prof's
Guesthouse

Where to stay

1   Motel de Eureka

Off map
Green Lodge
Hilltop Catholic Guesthouse
Mum and Dad Legacy Lodge

Where to eat and drink

2   Forgive & Forget Chop Bar
3   Planners Point

Total

Council

Last Hour

Borenyi
Guesthouse

SONYO ROAD

Sonyo

N

Bradt

0   200m
0   200 yds

JAGA ADAM STREET

Trotro station

Court

GCB

B A SAAKA STREET

New Mosque

Market

Old Mosque

BOLE WURA STREET

Reservoir

Kumasi, Accra

to be there is during the culturally vibrant five-day Deng Festival, usually held in late April or early May, and said (rather improbably) to culminate in an orgy of informal rooftop wife-swapping! But the unique adobe architecture makes it a fascinating place to visit at any time of year. Guided village tours can be arranged through the tourist officer Joseph Kupo (m *0261 149097*), and cost around US$4 per person, with discounts for volunteers and no restrictions on photography.

Getting there and away Bole straddles the main road between Kumasi/ Techiman and Wa, and is serviced by frequent trotros in both directions. There is also a daily Metro Mass bus from Tamale, leaving in either direction at around 06.00 and taking around 3½ hours. The 18km dirt road to Sonyo via Kape leaves from the north end of Bole, more or less opposite the Total filling station, and takes around 30 minutes to cover in a private vehicle. The Bole–Sonyo road is serviced by up to five trotros daily, more on market day (Friday), but if you don't feel like waiting around for something to leave, a one-way moto ride won't cost more than a few dollars.

⌂ Where to stay *Map, opposite*

In addition to the hotels listed below, the tourist officer at Sonyo can arrange private homestays, ideally with a couple of days' advance notice, for a negotiable rate inclusive of meals.

Budget

⌂ **Mum and Dad Legacy Lodge** (18 rooms) m 0505 140993/0206 403555. Flanking the road to Wa about 3km north of the town centre, this agreeable newish hotel has large comfortable rooms, a large courtyard with seating, & a decent restaurant with contemporary wooden furnishing. *US$11 self-contained dbl with fan & hot shower; US$16 dbl with queen-size bed & AC.* [$$–$

⌂ **Green Lodge** (11 rooms) m 0242 070437/0262 346779/0247 937587. Another good-value set-up, this hotel on the Wa road about 1.5km north of the town centre has a good restaurant & bar, & spacious clean rooms with en-suite hot showers. It was closed for renovations in early 2016, but should be back up & running by the time you read this. *US$11 self-contained dbl with fan & satellite TV; US$15 dbl with king-size bed & AC.* $$–$

Shoestring

⌂ **Hilltop Catholic Guesthouse** (6 rooms) m 0241 683333. Situated in large green grounds about 200m from Mum and Dad Legacy Lodge, this offers cheap accommodation to sgl travellers. Rooms are basic but clean, & the setting is pleasant, though feeling more than a bit forlorn upon last inspection. They only serve drinks, so you'll have to drop by Mum & Dad's for a meal. *US$5.50 sgl with fan & shared bathroom; US$7 self-contained sgl.* $

⌂ **Motel de Eureka** (10 rooms) m 0244 896662. The pick of a few less-than-appealing hotels in the town centre, this friendly family-run establishment has adequate rooms with fans or AC. *US$5.50 fan sgl using shared bathroom; US$8–11 en-suite AC dbl.* $

✖ Where to eat and drink *Map, opposite*

✖ **Forgive & Forget Chop Bar** m 0507 216783; ⏱ 06.00–22.00 Mon–Sat. This superior chop shop serves tasty jollof rice & various other local dishes for around US$2 per plate. $

✖ **Planners Point Restaurant** m 0541 590364/0507 808112; ⏱ 07.30–22.30 daily. Situated about 100m north of the main trotro station on Jaga Adam St, this well-regarded & inexpensive eatery is a good place to try local Gonja dishes. $

Mole National Park AROUND MOLE NATIONAL PARK

20

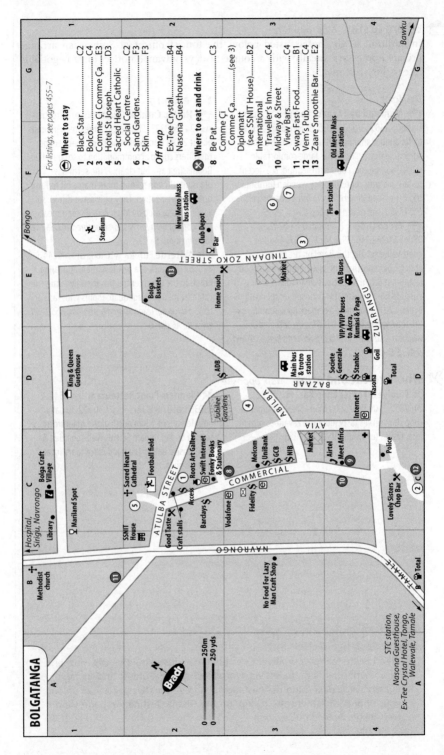

BOLGATANGA

For listings, see pages 455–7

Where to stay

1 Black Star........................C2
2 Bolco..............................C4
3 Comme Çi Comme Ça...E3
4 Hotel St Joseph..............D3
5 Sacred Heart Catholic
   Social Centre................C2
6 Sand Gardens................F3
7 Skin................................F3

Off map

Where to eat and drink

8 Be Pat.............................C3
   Comme Çi
   Comme Ça...........(see 3)
   Diplomatt
   (see SSNIT House)........B2
9 International
   Traveller's Inn.............C4
10 Midway & Street
    View Bars...................C4
11 Swap Fast Food..............B1
12 Vem's Pub.....................C4
13 Zaare Smoothie Bar......E2

452

21

Bolgatanga and the Upper East

Because the Upper East Region is so remote from the coast and capital, the few travellers who pass through are generally backpackers or overlanders crossing into Burkina Faso. Those who do visit the Upper East, however, will find it offers plenty of off-the-beaten-track rewards. The regional capital Bolgatanga is a chaotic but rather captivating town, and a good base for day visits to Sirigu, with its wonderful painted adobe houses, as well as the rhyming villages of Bongo and Tongo. Situated right at the main border crossing into Burkina Faso, Paga is famed for its sacred crocodile pool, while Navrongo is the site of a beautiful church with a unique mud-sculpted interior. Somewhat more remote, the pretty Gambaga Escarpment (which actually lies within Northern Region) is most easily visited as an easterly excursion from Bolgatanga.

BOLGATANGA

The burgeoning capital of Upper East Region, Bolgatanga, though far smaller than Tamale, has a similarly hectic aura, as if it is about to do the urban equivalent of bursting at the seams. Like many towns in the north, Bolga (as you'll soon come to call it) lacks for specific tourist attractions, though the small ethnographic museum behind the **Sacred Heart Catholic Social Centre** [452 C2] is worth an hour or two. No less interesting is the busy **market** [452 E3], which peaks in activity every three days and is best known for the fine and often very affordable leatherwork, basketry, straw hats and striped cloth shirts produced for a predominantly local market by the Frafra people. Hat salesmen, heads layered high with samples of their wares, are a familiar sight around town. Bolga is also a good base for day trips to nearby tourist sites such as Paga, Tongo and Bongo.

HISTORY Bolgatanga was founded in medieval times, probably under a different name, on a southern arm of the trans-Sahara trade, when it served as an important funnel through which gold from the south reached the Niger River to be transported to Timbuktu. According to oral tradition, the town's first Frafra chief, Bolga Naba Apasinyaba, a migrant from Zecco in the Moshi region of present-day Burkina Faso, was installed as a prize after winning a dancing competition. This probably occurred in the early 19th century, given that the present-day chief Bolga Naba Martin Abilba III, enskinned in 1970, is the sixth or seventh in the line. A relatively insignificant town in colonial times, Bolgatanga was selected as the administrative capital of Upper Region when the original Northern Region was split in two in 1960, and as capital of Upper East following a regional reorganisation in 1983. In common with Tamale, the population of Bolgatanga has grown rapidly in recent decades, from fewer than 20,000 people in 1970, to around 131,500, according to the 2010 census.

GETTING THERE AND AWAY

By air Although there are no direct flights to Bolgatanga, it is less than 2 hours' drive from Tamale International Airport, to which it is connected by a daily shuttle service with **Jet 3:16** (m *0244 769254/0202 527577*), leaving from in front of the **STC station** [452 A4] at 04.00 daily. Bolgatanga is actually supposed to get an airport of its own, but works slated to begin in 2015 showed no sign of doing so when we passed through in 2016. When completed, the airport will be some 15km towards Navrongo at Anateem village.

By road Bolgatanga is an important regional route focus and transport hub, situated about 165km north of Tamale and 40km southeast of Paga (on the Burkina Faso border) along a good surfaced road. The **main bus and trotro station** [452 D3], centrally located on Bazaar Street, is where you'll find regular transport to all destinations, including Tamale, Navrongo, Paga, Tumu, Bawku, Bongo, Tongo and Gambaga. Several other important stations are dotted around the town centre. These include the **VIP/VVIP** [452 D4] (m *0243 543337/364429*) and **OA Tours** [452 E3] (m *0208 294602; www. oatravels.com*) stations on Zuarangu Road, the **STC station** [452 B4] a few hundred metres along the Tamale road, and the **Metro Mass station** [452 F4] on the Bawku road next to the junction for the Sand Gardens Hotel, but note that this is scheduled to move to a new location [452 F2] about 500m to the north some time in 2016.

Heading to or coming from Tamale, it is possible to hook up with the air-conditioned VIP/VVIP or OA Tours services that run a few times daily between Accra and Paga. However, it's probably easier to catch one of the several Metro Mass buses that run between Bolgatanga and Tamale daily, or the regular trotros and taxis that leave from the main station and take about 2½ hours in either direction. For southerly travel beyond Tamale, however, the best options are undoubtedly the VIP/VVIP or OA Tours services to Kumasi and Accra. OA Tours runs two buses daily to Accra at 14.00 and 15.00 for US$18/24 depending on type of coach, and VIP/VVIP has one bus daily at 14.00 for a similar price. (VIP and VVIP are the same company but the VVIP buses are even more 'Very'.)

Metro Mass also runs a direct service between Bolgatanga and Wa. In theory, this leaves at 06.00 daily except Sundays in both directions and take about 9 hours, but it's not unusual to arrive after dark owing to delays and unscheduled stops. Tickets cannot be booked before the departure date, which means you ought to be at the station between 04.30 and 05.00 to be certain of a seat. It's also possible (and given the newly improved roads, very likely faster) to travel to or from Wa by trotro, changing vehicles at Tamale. If you'd prefer to go via Tumu, be aware that while it's possible to get through to Wa in a day coming from Bolga, you'll almost certainly need to overnight in Tumu coming from Wa.

TOURIST INFORMATION The Upper East Region's **tourist office** [452 C1] (☏ *03820 23416;* e *gtuer@ghana.com;* ⊕ *08.00–12.30 & 13.30–17.00 Mon–Fri*) lies alongside the Navrongo road a short distance north of Swap Fast Food. The staff seem pretty clued up and helpful, and if nothing else they can give you a selection of pamphlets covering ecotourism sites in and around Bolga.

GUIDES AND TOURS A good source of local information, the well-organised **Tanga Tours** [452 C2] (m *0249 874044;* e *abdulfuseini2@yahoo.com or tangatoursgh@ gmail.com*) is a Belgian/Ghanaian NGO with an office on the ground floor of the Black Star Hotel. It can arrange scooter and bike hire, as well as a variety of guided excursions in the Upper East and further afield.

At the southern end of Commercial Road opposite Twin Bar (Midway/Street View bars), is the regional office for **Meet Africa** [452 C4] (**m** *0249 333184; www. ontmoetafrika.nl*), a Dutch/Ghanaian NGO that offers travellers the opportunity to experience traditional life in the nearby villages of Gowrie and Karimenga. The very helpful staff can also arrange a number of guided tours around the region.

A couple of readers have recently recommended Adombila (aka Joseph) Adugbire (**m** *0209 335955;* **e** *josephadugbire@yahoo.com*) as an excellent laidback guide with no agenda. He owns the Nongre Craft & Culture shop by the Ex-Tee Crystal Hotel [452 B4] and can be contacted through Sand Gardens Hotel [452 F3]. The scooter and bike excursions with **Bolga Boy Tours** (**m** *0241 512377; bolgaboytours@gmail. com*) have also been recently recommended; a full-day tour starts around US$20 and self-guided options are also available.

WHERE TO STAY Accommodation options in Bolgatanga, plentiful though they are, mostly rank as mediocre, or somewhere south of that, and those looking for a more rustic experience might think about basing themselves at the simple but attractive Tongo Oasis near Tongo, SWOPA Guesthouse in Sirigu or Green House in Karimenga.

Upmarket

Ex-Tee Crystal Hotel [452 B4] (52 rooms) 03820 22975; **m** 0264 810969/0244 290412/0549 628446; **e** exteecrystalhotel@ gmail.com or crystalextee@yahoo.com; www. exteecrystalhotel.com. Situated off the Tamale Rd 3km south of the town centre, this is ostensibly the smartest hotel in Bolgatanga, aimed squarely at the business end of the market. The comfortable self-contained rooms match expectations, with modern décor, AC, free Wi-Fi, flatscreen satellite TV & hot water, & the rates are very reasonable, too. Unfortunately, however, in lieu of any outdoor seating or a proper restaurant (the latter remains unfinished some years after the hotel opened), the only functional common area is a sweaty makeshift café, serving a few indifferent local staples in the reception area, which makes it a rather depressing place to stay unless you have means to get to a restaurant in town. They've recently added a swimming pool, but it was disappointingly desiccated when we stopped in. *US$22/31/44/65 self-contained sgl/dbl/twin/suite.* **$$$–$$**

Moderate

Comme Çi Comme Ça Hotel [452 E3] (8 rooms) 03820 22355; **m** 0277 837143/0205 761102; **e** commecihotel@gmail.com. For many years the top eatery in Bolga, this central set-up opposite the market also now offers decent & sensibly priced rooms set in leafy gardens behind the main building. If the service was on a par with the accommodation & food, this would

be a thoroughly commendable establishment, but the indifference implied in the name seems to have rubbed off on the staff, who are notoriously sluggish & inattentive. If you can get past that, the spacious tiled rooms, which come with AC, flatscreen satellite TV & hot shower/tub, seem like exceptional value, especially as you are just a few paces way from the outstanding restaurant. *US$26/33/39 self-contained sgl/dbl/twin.* **$$**

Nasona Guesthouse [452 B4] (7 rooms) 03820 91692; **m** 0541 479482; **e** nasonahouse@gmail.com. This clean, friendly & attractively priced guesthouse has only 1 major drawback (at least for those without transport), that being its rather isolated location, 3km from the town centre, near the Ex-Tee Crystal Hotel. There is no bar, & food is by advance request only, but otherwise the spacious tiled rooms with king-sized bed, fan, satellite TV & hot water seem like great value. *US$11/18 self-contained dbl with fan/ AC.* **$$–$**

Budget

Sand Gardens Hotel [452 F3] (30 rooms) 03820 23464; **m** 0200 965917; **e** sandgardenshotel@yahoo.com. It says much about the overall standard of accommodation in Bolga that this comfortable but flawed hotel keeps emerging as the pick, edition after edition. It has a convenient location, close to the Metro Mass station & about 10mins' walk east of the main bus station, & a selection of neat clean rooms to suit most budget & shoestring travellers (though the cheaper rooms can be a little musty). Reasonable Chinese, Ghanaian & continental meals cost around US$4–5, & can be eaten outdoors or in the AC restaurant, though service can be slow. The hotel's best feature is the immense courtyard garden after which it is named – no longer sandy but gravelled, & shaded by leafy mango trees – which is a thoroughly pleasant spot for a drink, especially as the sound system is played at non-distortive levels until it shuts down at around 22.30, after which the frogs & cicadas take over. It is popular with conferences & travelling professionals, so best book in advance. *US$9 dbl with fan & shared bath; US$13 self-contained dbl with fan & TV; US$16/17 dbl/twin with AC.* **$$–$**

🏠 **Skin Hotel** [452 F3] (6 rooms) m 0205 129609/0209 113023. Despite its unfortunately suggestive name, this newish family-run hotel next to the Sand Gardens is clean, comfortable & good value. There is a living room/TV lounge, but no restaurant. *US$11 dbl with fan & shared bathroom; US$15 self-contained dbl with AC & satellite TV.* **$$–$**

🏠 **Black Star Hotel** [452 C2] (11 rooms) ✆ 038 2022346; m 0246 334042. Once Bolga's most upmarket offering, the Black Star Hotel has certainly seen better days, but the central location is convenient, & the spacious rooms, though somewhat frayed at the seams, are acceptable at the asking price. Be warned that it can be noisy on Sat nights when the ground-floor disco blasts into action. *US$9/13 sgl/dbl with fan, using common showers; US$13/17/20 self-contained sgl/dbl/twin with AC.* **$$–$**

Shoestring

🏠 **Sacred Heart Catholic Social Centre** [452 C2] (15 rooms) ✆ 03820 23216; m 0205 123143/0244 607000; e msgrroger-bolga@yahoo. com; www.nbdiocese.wordpress.com. Some might find the aura of shabby institutionalism a little off-putting, but the central location & cheap canteen go a long way to compensating. Clean dbl rooms at this poorly signposted guesthouse are decent value, using immaculate common showers, whilst the dorms (which must be taken as a unit) are outstanding value for small groups. *US$8 twin with fan & shared bath; US$11/12 self-contained twin with fan/AC; US$21 dorm sleeping up to 6.* **$**

🏠 **Hotel St Joseph** [452 D3] (19 rooms) ✆ 03820 23214. Tucked away behind the disused stadium, this central multi-storey block is a lot better than its rather sleazy exterior might suggest & is well placed for travellers planning to catch an early-morning bus. There's a lively outdoor bar, but the noise doesn't permeate to the rooms to a disturbing degree. *US$8/9 sgl/twin with fan, using common bath; US$13–20 self-contained dbl with AC.* **$$–$**

🏠 **Bolco Hotel** [452 C4] (15 rooms) m 0207 500321. About the most uninspiring of the central hotels, this rundown hotel next to the affiliated Vem's Pub is probably only worth considering if all the other places in this range are full. Renovations were under way in 2016, & not a moment too soon. *US$7 dbl using shared bath; US$8/9 self-contained sgl/dbl with fan; US$13 dbl with AC.* **$$–$**

✖ **WHERE TO EAT AND DRINK** The town centre is scattered with chop stalls, with the greatest concentration situated around the southern end of Commercial Road. You can also get inexpensive fresh bread every morning from the open-air clay oven bakery next to the Black Star Hotel. The following sit-down places stand out.

Favourite spots for a relaxed outdoor drink in reasonably rustic surrounds include the Sand Gardens Hotel and Comme Çi Comme Ça, with the latter hosting live music on the last Saturday of the month. Elsewhere, despite its Islamic feel, central Bolga is certainly not short of low-key local bars.

Moderate

✖ **Comme Çi Comme Ça Restaurant** [452 E3] ⏱ b/fast, lunch & dinner daily. Attached to the eponymous hotel, this ranks among the best restaurants in northern Ghana on a good day, serving a varied international selection of tasty dishes including several northern specials (try the guineafowl in spicy tomato sauce with yam chips). You can eat in the AC dining hall or in one of several fan-cooled thatched shelters. It's a good place to drink, too, especially on the last Sat of the month, when there's usually live music. On a bad day, the lackadaisical service can quickly start to grate, & the variety of dishes available might be a small subset of the written menu. You might want to check the bill, too, as it has a reputation for overcharging. Mains around US$5–7. **$$–$**

✕ **Swap Fast Food** [452 B1] 📞0382 095677; 📱 0200 230991; ⏱ 09.00–22.00 Mon–Sat, noon–22.00 Sun. Though not affiliated to its near namesake in Tamale, this has a similarly varied menu, with Indian cuisine being the speciality, supplemented by some Chinese & Western dishes, including sandwiches, burgers & pizzas. Vegetarians are well catered for, too, with the falafel wrap being recommended. Situated just off the Navrongo Rd opposite SSNIT House, the new gazebos out front should be ready to eat under by the time you read this. Pizzas US$10; other mains & snacks US$3–6. **$$–$**

✕ **Diplomatt Restaurant** [452 B2] 📱 0244 827799; ⏱ 07.00–18.00 Mon–Sat. A popular lunching spot for local businessmen & NGO workers, this well-ventilated establishment in SSNIT House serves a limited selection of local dishes, notably grilled tilapia, in the US$4–7 range. **$$–$**

Budget
🖵 **Zaare Smoothie Bar** [452 E2] 📱 0502 770741; (08.00–20:00 Mon–Sat. A pro-poor tourism project linked to the Youth Harvest Foundation Ghana (YHFG) & the Greenhouse in Karimenga, this alluring new eatery a few hundred metres south of the stadium offers a wide range of freshly made sandwiches, snacks & mixed smoothies, all 100% natural. It also aims to become a multi-cultural meeting place reflecting the mixture of local & Western influences on the menu. Smoothies & sandwiches cost around US$1. **$**

🖵 **International Traveller's Inn** [452 C4] 📞0382 022356; ⏱ 06.00–late Mon–Sat, 08.00–23.00 Sun. Housed in a nondescript storefront at the southern end of Commercial Rd, this place has excellent egg sandwiches & tea for a few cedi. **$**

✕ **Be Pat** [452 C3] 📱 0208 241042; ⏱ 08.00–20.00 Mon–Sat. This superior chop shop serves excellent jollof rice & a good selection of other local staples for around US$2 per plate. **$**

BARS AND NIGHTCLUBS
🍷 **Midway/Street View Bars** [452 C4] Directly opposite the International Traveller's Inn, these 2 legendarily down-to-earth local drinking holes (known together as Twin Bar) serve chilled beer at rock-bottom prices, to the usual accompaniment of blaring distorted music.

☆ **Vem's Pub** [452 C4] ⏱ 20.00–late Wed, Fri, Sat, Sun. This is the only nightclub in Bolga, situated right alongside the Bolco Hotel.

SHOPPING
The **central market** [452 E3], which peaks in activity every third day, is well known as a good place to buy the traditional baskets, hats and smocks associated with this part of Ghana. A varied selection is also sold at the dozen or so stalls comprising the **Bolga Craft Village** [452 C1] near the regional library. Several good crafts stalls are dotted around the town centre, including two at the north end of Commercial Road near Barclays Bank, one close to the International Travellers Inn at the south end of the same road, and the fantastically named **No Food For Lazy Man Craft Shop** [452 B3] on Navrongo Road. Also worth a look if you want to buy baskets in bulk is **Bolga Baskets** [452 E2] near the stadium.

Roots Art Gallery [452 C2] 📱 0244 854478; ⏱ 08.30–19.00 daily. In addition to an interesting selection of paintings, baskets, jewellery & other handicrafts, this gallery serves delicious freshly ground coffee & smoothies, & stocks a decent range of secondhand novels. It is also a good place

to ask about drumming lessons or tours around town.

Fonky Books and Stationery [452 C2] This unassuming shop on the north end of Commercial Road sells a fair range of modern novels at reasonable prices.

OTHER PRACTICALITIES
Foreign exchange Barclays Bank, on Commercial Road opposite the post office, has a foreign exchange service and a Visa-only ATM. Several other banks, including

the Stanbic Bank on Bazaar Road and Ghana Commercial or Access banks on Commercial Road, also have ATMs from where you can draw cash against a Visa or MasterCard.

Internet Several internet cafés are dotted around town. The best at the time of writing is the **Vodafone Internet Café** [452 C3] next to the post office, and, almost directly opposite, **Swift Internet** [452 C2] beside Roots Art Gallery.

Medical Situated along the Navrongo Road north of the town centre, **Bolgatanga Regional Hospital** (✆ 03820 22461/2) doesn't have a great reputation, but it is still the best option in an emergency.

AROUND BOLGATANGA

In addition to the sites listed below, Paga and Navrongo – neither more than an hour's drive away, and covered under their own headings later in the chapter – would make a perfectly feasible goal for a day trip out of Bolgatanga. The Gambaga Escarpment, also covered later in the chapter, would only be worth considering with two or three days to spare.

SIRIGU Nestled close to the Burkina Faso border 20km northwest of Bolgatanga as the crow flies, Sirigu is known throughout Ghana not only for the superb pottery and basketwork produced by its women, but also for the elaborate symbolic wall paintings with which the artists decorate their flat-roofed adobe houses. Also very striking is the elaborate facial scarring – like a spider's web in complexity – practised by the Nakarisi people who live in and around the village. Since 1997, Sirigu has been the site of an excellent community-based tourism project centred on a guesthouse and gallery run by the Sirigu Women's Organisation for Pottery and Art (SWOPA), a local organisation dedicated to the preservation of these traditional crafts, and of using them to promote the social and economic advancement for local women. The SWOPA Visitors' Centre Gallery sells a well-priced selection of local pottery and other craft work.

The main activity here is guided village tours, which must be arranged at the visitor centre. These usually take in two traditionally painted homesteads, as well as other local sites of interest, and cost US$4 per person. Other guided tours run to the local market, and to a nearby orphanage, while three-hour pottery, painting and basketry workshops are available by prior arrangement for US$5 per person.

Getting there and away Sirigu lies 35km from Bolgatanga by road and can be reached by following the Navrongo road for 18km then turning right into a signposted dirt side road at Kandiga Junction. Minibuses to Sirigu leave Bolgatanga throughout the day, departing from the main trotro station, and take about one hour in either direction. They can take a while to fill up, so it might be worth paying for some extra seats to get things rolling. These minibuses now approach Sirigu using a turnoff from the Bongo road, and since SWOPA lies about 1km south of the village towards Kandiga and the Navrongo Road, you'll have to walk or charter a taxi for the last kilometre.

Coming from Navrongo, there is no direct public transport to Sirigu and it is difficult to pick up a lift at Kandiga Junction, so either you must travel via Bolgatanga or charter a taxi. If you are in private transport, it may also be worth knowing that a rough but adequate direct road connects Sirigu to Paga.

⌂ Where to stay and eat

⌂ SWOPA Guesthouse (5 rooms) **m** 0205 880712/0243 012967/0202 436446; **e** siriguart@ yahoo.com; www.swopa.org. Regularly praised by readers, this attractive, traditionally styled guesthouse next to the visitor centre offers accommodation in comfortable thatched huts with nets, fans or AC, running water and earthy décor provided by the local women. There is also a 5-berth dorm, & a restaurant serving simple meals in the US$3–5 range. *US$13/17 self-contained dbl with fan/AC; US$27 5-bed dorm, taken as a unit.* **$$–$**

BONGO About 15km north of Bolgatanga, the small town of Bongo lies at the heart of a truly memorable landscape of smooth rocky outcrops, magnificent baobab trees, and round-hutted compounds covered in stencil-like painted figures. The main attraction here, the aptly named Bongo Rock, emits a convincingly resonant vibrating boom when struck. Also of interest is the elaborately decorated Chief's Palace opposite the trotro station, and the Bongo Women Weavers Association, a few hundred metres back towards Bolgatanga, which sells well-priced traditional baskets.

Getting there and away Regular shared taxis and trotros to Bongo leave Bolgatanga from the main trotro station, costing less than US$1 and taking about 30 minutes. Bongo Rock lies 20–30 minutes' walk from Bongo; to get there follow the main road back from the trotro station to the church, then continue for another 800m to St Anne's Primary School, where a footpath to the left leads to the taller and more distant of two hills. Between Bolgatanga and Bongo, you might want to stop at Yorogo (also known as Nyariga), where the roadside Single Mothers Association Craft Centre (*next to Yorogo Primary School;* ⊕ *Mon–Sat*) sells baskets, hats, leatherwork and other traditional products made onsite.

TONGO AND THE TENGZUG HILLS The small town of Tongo lies about 15km southeast of Bolgatanga at the base of the horseshoe-shaped Tengzug Hills, a granitic range known for its striking balancing-rock formations and the whistling sound made by the harmattan as it passes through cracks in the boulders from December to February. Most of all, this striking rockscape is venerated for its many Talensi ancestral shrines, the most sacred and powerful being Ba'ar Tonna'ab Ya'nee. A popular site of pilgrimage for Ashanti traditionalists (who call it Nana Tongo), this shrine has also been visited by several modern dignitaries, including the former president Jerry Rawlings during his time in power.

Listed as a tentative UNESCO World Heritage Site since 2000, the Tengzug Hills are now the subject of a well-established ecotourism project based out of a visitor centre (**m** *0246 215975/0249 160699*) in the village of Tengzug, a cluster of mud huts set on a baobab-clad rocky plateau about 20 minutes' walk from Ba'ar Tonna'ab Ya'nee. Two-hour guided tours to Ba'ar Tonna'ab Ya'nee cost around US$9 per person, and also incorporate a visit to the labyrinthine chief's compound, which has reputedly sheltered more than 300 people at times, and the Hyena Caves. Traditionally, visitors to Ba'ar Tonna'ab Ya'nee need to disrobe completely in order to enter the shrine. This rule has been relaxed slightly to accommodate the ecotourism project, but it is still required that all visitors, whether male or female, are naked from the waist up. No photography is permitted in or immediately around the shrine.

If you're in the area during late October, ask about the exact dates of the **Boar Dam Harvest Festival**, which is centred on Ba'ar Tonna'ab Ya'nee and other Talensi ancestral shrines. Also worth asking about is March's Golob Festival at Nnon Shrine. Baare, 3km from Tengzug, is the site of a sacred bat tree, but it's debatable whether this is worth the hassle of a special visit, since the bats aren't always there, and numbers pale by comparison with the colonies in parts of Accra and Kumasi.

History The Talensi people of the Tengzug/Tongo Hills are sedentary agriculturists whose rich oral traditions and unusual agricultural practices – which include stone terracing and strong taboos against starting uncontrollable fires and the felling of trees in certain areas – suggest they have occupied the area for many centuries. For much of the 19th century, the Talensi suffered heavily at the hands of slave raiders, partially because Tongo formed something of a no-man's-land between Mossi and Dagbon territory, but they still resisted any significant cultural assimilation into the more powerful neighbouring states. The Talensi also offered staunch resistance to British rule, inspired by the powerful ancestral spirits and oracle housed in Ba'ar Tonna'ab Ya'nee. Even after 1911, when they were finally subjugated by a colonial military expedition and evicted from the hills, the Talensi took little heed of a ban on attending their hilltop shrines, resulting in a second – and essentially ineffective – British military foray into the hills in 1915. The so-called Hiding Caves and Hyena, close to the legendary shrine, are where the chief took shelter and commanded his forces against the British.

Getting there and away Tengzug lies 17km from Bolgatanga by road. To get there, follow the Tamale road south for 5km as far as the signposted junction to the left at Winkogo (✪ *N10 43.108 W0 51.975*). Follow this dirt road for another 7km and you reach Tongo (✪ *N10 42.486 W0 48.413*), where you need to turn right on to a rougher road that climbs into the hills, reaching Tengzug and the signposted visitor centre (✪ *N10 40.409 W0 48.867*) after another 5km. Several trotros and shared taxis connect Bolgatanga and Tongo daily, but there is no transport on to Tengzug except on market days (every third day). On other days, you'll either need to walk the 5km between Tongo and Tengzug, or charter a taxi to do the round trip from Bolgatanga, which should cost around US$20–25.

🏠 Where to stay and eat

✳ 🏠 **Tongo Oasis** (7 rooms) m 0249 116646/0248 527352/0203 079893; www. tongooasis.com. Situated halfway between Winkogo & Tongo, this underpublicised retreat, surrounded by hills & overlooking a small lake, is owned by a friendly Ghanaian couple who received a year's training from locally based PCVs (Peace Corps Volunteers) in preparing US & Mexican food, from salads & smoothies to brownies & burritos. The varied international menu, with prices ranging from US$2–3 for local dishes to US$10 for burritos & fajitas, is undoubtedly the main attraction, & well worth the excursion from Bolgatanga in its own right. Inexpensive accommodation is also available in a creatively designed compound of traditional muds huts with fan, shared kitchen (with fridge) & outdoor shower. There is also a Western-style 1-bedroom house with fan, living room, kitchen, bathroom & roof terrace. *US$5.50pp for the huts; US$22 dbl for the house.* **$$–$**

KARIMENGA AND WULUGU Located about 30km south of Bolgatanga along the Tamale road, Karimenga is an agricultural village of around 500 people founded c1790 by one Naa Satenbla, reputedly the ancestor of the present-day chief Naa Kulayim. In recent years, with the help of a Dutch volunteer organisation, it has been developed as a community-based ecotourism project, centred on a traditionally built guesthouse called the Green House. The project offers visitors the opportunity to experience several facets of local culture and rural life, for instance meeting the local herbalist, drumming lessons, learning fishing, beekeeping and traditional cooking, or renting a bicycle to explore the surrounding backroads.

Straddling the Tamale road 10km south of Karimenga, Wulugu is the site of one of Ghana's most peculiar Islamic monuments. This is Zayaa Mosque, a fort-like multi-storey construction of rich red earth that rises like a gigantic sculpted termite mound in surreal isolation some 50m west of the main road. Contrary to appearances, this elevated warren of tiny rooms and cramped passages is not of any great antiquity, but was constructed c1990 by one Sheik Abdul Karim (also known as Abu Bakar) as a residence as well as a place of prayer. Local sources claim that the building was inspired by a vision the sheik received at his home in Bawku. He then spent years travelling around the Upper East Region looking for a suitable site before he settled on one between the two hand-dug wells that flank the building today, and whose waters are said to be a powerful cure for illness when mixed together. The sheik lived in the building until his death in 1994, since when it has been maintained as a shrine by his many ancestors, who are happy to show visitors around for an unofficial fee equivalent to around US$5.

Getting there and away Direct transport between Bolgatanga and Karimenga or Wulugu is rather thin on the ground. Better to catch one of the shared taxis and trotros to Walewale (15km past Wulugu along the Tamale road) that leave regularly throughout the day from the main trotro station, and ask to be dropped at Karimenga or Wulugu. Coming from Tamale, which lies about 150km to the south, you can either do the trip in short hops, a somewhat tedious exercise, or – more practically – pay the full fare on a bus or trotro heading to Bolgatanga and 'drop'.

Where to stay and eat

Green House (5 rooms, 1 dorm)
m 0503 706117/0208 913117/0249 333184;
e greenhouseghana@gmail.com; www.
greenhouseghana.com. Situated 300m from the main tar road & clearly signposted, this simple but attractive guesthouse, built in the style of a traditional adobe compound, offers spotless & affordable accommodation in cosy, naturally ventilated rooms & a 6-bed dorm, with nets & solar lighting. There's also the option of sleeping local-style on the roof. A small menu of basic meals is available at around US$3 per plate. There's a rain-fed swimming pond in season, & it's best to make advance contact before pitching up. *US$8/10 sgl/twin using shared bathroom, US$9/12 self-contained sgl/dbl, US$6 dorm bed.* **$**

THE GAMBAGA ESCARPMENT

Running in an easterly direction from the main Tamale–Bolgatanga road, the Gambaga Escarpment is the most significant physical feature in northeastern Ghana, around 60km long, and rising several hundred metres above the surrounding plains. Rich in Mamprusi tradition and culture, the area remains practically undeveloped for tourism, but adventurous travellers could explore it along a circular route leading from Walewale (on the main Bolga–Tamale road) via Gambaga and Nalerigu to Nakpanduri at the eastern edge of the escarpment, then returning to Bolga via Bawku and Pusiga. There is a strong element of 'travel for its own sake' attached to this circuit, and the main attraction is arguably the sense of being away from any beaten tourist trail.

Coming from Walewale, the first main town you'll reach, after about 45km, is **Gambaga**, whose main claim to fame, or infamy, is the so-called Witch Camp that lies on its outskirts (for the history, see box page 462). Visitors are welcome, though they should first visit the office of the Presbyterian Church's Outcast Home Project, about 10 minutes' walk from the trotro station, and a donation will be expected.

The notorious Witch Camp at Gambaga dates back to the 19th century, when it was founded by the Gambaga Rana (Chief of Gambaga), who is accredited with the hereditary power to exorcise evil spirits from alleged witches. Today it shelters an estimated 150–200 women, some from as far afield as Burkina Faso and Togo, and many of whom have lived there for decades. Since 1994, it has been managed in collaboration with the Presbyterian Church's Outcast Home Project, which has attempted to reduce poverty by teaching the women income-generating activities such as cotton-spinning and bead-making. It is also perhaps the only village in Ghana where every homestead has its own 'front garden' – cultivated out of necessity, as social convention prevents the 'witches' from inheriting land or buying any nearby.

Traditionally, it doesn't require any effort – just a bit of misfortune – for a woman in northern Ghana to be stigmatised as a witch. It is customary, for instance, for a charge of sorcery to be levelled at an elder female relative of anybody who dies prematurely of measles, epilepsy, malaria, cholera or any other disease, while elder wives are also often accused of casting a spell to make their polygamous husband impotent or his younger wives barren. The accused will be tried according to local custom, which varies from one community to the next, but is generally somewhat arbitrary – for instance, the chief might strangle a chicken, throw it into the air, and decide the case on the basis of how the fowl lands. If the accused is found guilty, she might at worst be beaten to death by angry relatives of the deceased, but just as often she will be forced to flee and placed by relatives, or take refuge herself, in a witches' camp.

The witch camp has attracted a great deal of controversy in recent years. Human-rights activists and feminists argue convincingly that it functions as a prison wherein hundreds of women charged with imaginary crimes are detained on what is effectively a life sentence. The Gambaga Rana and associated church workers reject this charge, preferring to characterise it as a sanctuary, one that has for decades offered refuge to social outcasts with nowhere else to go.

Indeed, in 1998, more than 100 'witches' were formally released in response to outside pressure. They simply refused to leave. Their septuagenarian leader, a camp resident of more than three decades' standing, said, 'We will not go anywhere; we are safe here' – and cited the example of another 'witch' who had recently returned home only to come back to the camp a few days later with one ear cut off by angry locals, who told her that if she returned home again, then the other ear would be cut off, too.

Closing the witches' camp would be akin more to treating the symptom than to curing the disease. So long as the women are stigmatised in this manner, they are probably safest from persecution in Gambaga, whose chief is believed to render witches harmless whilst they are in his presence. In that sense, the inhabitants of the camp are prisoners not so much of the Gambaga Rana, but of the superstitions about witchcraft that still prevail in much of northern Ghana.

For further background, a recommended starting point is Yaba Badoe's award-winning 2010 documentary, *The Witches of Gambaga*, and the associated website (*www.witchesofgambaga.com*).

You can also visit the new meeting place, built by the East Mamprusi District Assembly, where the older women do beadwork and make soap to help generate an income for themselves.

Although most sources refer to Gambaga as the ancient capital of Mamprugu, **Nalerigu**, 8km further to the east, appears to be the older settlement and houses the Nayiri's Palace. The Naa Jaringa Walls, which lie under a grove of trees to the left of the dam wall a short distance from the town centre in the direction of Gambaga, were reputedly built with stones, mud, honey and milk during the 16th-century rule of their namesake. Though the main aim of the wall was to protect the village from raiders, it also ensured that the name of Naa Jaringa – whose only son was not accepted as his successor because he was blind in one eye – would not be forgotten after his death.

Perched at a breezy altitude of 420m on the highest point along the Gambaga Escarpment, some 25km east of Nalerigu, **Nakpanduri** is a striking collection of circular traditional compounds interspersed with massive baobab trees. It affords some great views to the northern plains, and hikers and birdwatchers will enjoy the stretch of the Bawku road that descends through a forest reserve to the base of the escarpment, where a bridge crosses a forest-fringed tributary of the Volta River.

The largest town in the far northeast, **Bawku**, situated 60km north of Nakpanduri, has experienced significant unrest following a chieftaincy dispute that left several buildings pitted with gunshot marks in 2005 and enforced the imposition of a strict curfew in 2009, which has been variously lifted and re-imposed several times in the years since. It was fine to visit when this seventh edition was researched, but you're advised to seek up-to-date advice before visiting. The town is absorbing on market days (every third day), and a good place to buy the attractive fugu shirts characteristic of the far northeast. Some 15km east of Bawku, Pusiga is the site of an important shrine dedicated to Naa Gbewaa, who is often regarded to have been the first paramount chief of Mamprugu.

HISTORY The escarpment is named after the town of Gambaga, which once served as the capital of the Mamprugu Kingdom, and was also the first British administrative centre in the Northern Territory prior to the relocation to Tamale in 1907. The kingdom of the Mamprusi people, Mamprugu is widely regarded to be the oldest of the Mole-Dagbani states, and quite possibly the most ancient extant political entity anywhere in Ghana. All Mole-Dagbani traditions agree that it was founded before AD1200 by the descendants of a light-skinned chief remembered by the name Toha-jie ('The Red Warrior'), who led his people from somewhere further east to Pusiga on what is now the Ghana–Burkina Faso border. Toha-jie's grandson, Naa Gbewaa, is thought to have been the first true paramount Mamprugu chief, and the site of his palace and probable burial place at Pusiga is revered as one of the most important shrines in northern Ghana. It is said to have been Naa Gbewaa who forged the union with the Tengdana priests of Gambaga that led to the incorporation of the area into Mamprugu. Today, Nalerigu, 8km east of Gambaga, houses the Palace of the Nayiri (the paramount chief of Mamprugu), an important regional leader who is traditionally called upon to settle internal disputes in neighbouring Mossi and Dagomba.

GETTING THERE AND AROUND Roads in this part of the country are a mixed bag. Between Walewale and Nakpanduri, you're on good dirt for the first 30km, then it's surfaced as far as Gambaga and on to Nalerigu, then rough dirt to Nakpanduri. The road between Nakpanduri and Bawku is dirt the whole way and mostly quite rough, but you are back on well-maintained tar from Bawku back to Bolgatanga.

A few buses daily run directly between the main station in Bolgatanga and Nakpanduri, stopping at Gambaga and Nalerigu. If you can't find a direct vehicle, pick up a trotro to Walewale from the Tamale Station, and change there for Gambaga or Nalerigu (though do note that eastbound trotros from Walewale leave not from the main station but from the junction). A steady stream of shared taxis covers the 8km asphalt road between Gambaga and Nalerigu, and there is also plenty of transport between Nalerigu and Nakpanduri.

There's something of a hiatus in public transport between Nakpanduri and Bawku, except on market days, which are every third day. On other days, a solitary bus leaves Bawku at 06.00, passes through Nakpanduri at about 09.00 and terminates at Nalerigu an hour later, starting the return trip at around 15.00 to pass through Nakpanduri at about 16.00 and arrive in Bawku after dark. Transport between Bawku and Bolgatanga's main trotro station is plentiful.

WHERE TO STAY AND EAT Accommodation in this part of the country tends to be cheap and quite basic, but there is at least one adequate place to stay in each of the towns mentioned above.

In Gambaga, the best options are the friendly **Norrip Guesthouse** (*7 rooms;* m *0245 850811; US$11/13 self-contained dbl with fan/AC*), which also prepares good meals with advance notice, and the more central and very friendly **Marta Memorial Guesthouse** (*8 rooms;* m *0208 385269; US$8/11 self-contained dbl with fan/AC*). The only hotel proper in Nalerigu is the **Chesterfield Guesthouse** (*5 rooms;* m *0241 318363; US$11/14 self-contained sgl/dbl*).

In Nakpanduri, the **Government Resthouse**, about 1km south of the main junction opposite the signpost for Nakpanduri Weaver, has a truly superb location on the escarpment rim, and adequate rooms with fan and common bucket showers for around US$6, but the caretaker is often difficult to locate. A more reliable option is the privately owned **Sillim Guesthouse** (m *0246 120654; ¾ bed US$5.50/8 with fan/ AC*), which lies in the same direction about 100m past the prominently signposted Skyview Spot and Restaurant, and has adequate rooms.

Set between GN Bank and the Total filling station on the main road in Bawku, the centrally located **Sunrise Guesthouse** (m *0274 520576; US$8/14 for a self-contained dbl/exec with fan/AC*) is the pick of several small hotels in town.

NAVRONGO

Coming from Tamale or Bolgatanga, this quiet, small rustic town, situated close to the main border crossing into Burkina Faso, feels remarkably orderly and shady, despite the presence of a few skeletal concrete relics of an ambitious development plan initiated in the 1970s by the short-lived Acheampong government. According to oral tradition, Navrongo was founded in the early 18th century by three brothers from Zecco, 25km to the northeast in what is now Burkina Faso. The eldest brother Butto named his new home 'Nagavoro', meaning 'Soft on the Foot', in reference to its sandy soil. This was later bastardised to Navrongo.

Navrongo was an important trading post in the 19th century, but its modern-day significance can be traced to 1901, when Chief Kwara, in exchange for protection against the slave raiders who still made regular forays into the region, invited a British expedition to establish a military encampment next to his palace. Five years later, a Catholic mission was founded alongside the British military encampment by a group of pioneering 'White Fathers' led by the Canadian missionary Oscar Morin, who had travelled to the area from Ouagadougou via the then little-known

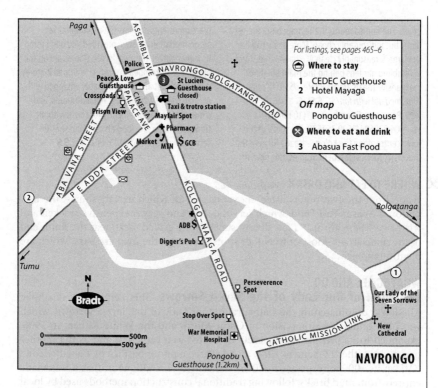

south of Burkina Faso. Widely regarded to be the home of Catholicism in northern Ghana, Navrongo is highly unusual for the area in so far as it is predominantly Christian, with only 5% of its 28,000 inhabitants following Islam. Navrongo's main attraction is the Cathedral of Our Lady of the Seven Sorrows, with its unique mud-decorated interior.

GETTING THERE AND AWAY Navrongo is less than 30km west of Bolgatanga and around 12km south of Paga. Shared taxis run in both directions every few minutes throughout the day. If you are thinking of heading on to Wa, the Metro Mass bus from Bolgatanga is usually full by the time it reaches Navrongo (around 07.00), which means standing at least as far as Tumu. Better to go to Bolgatanga and pick up the bus at the terminus. Road surfacing works to Tumu were well under way in 2016, but as things stand there are still only a couple of trotros per day between the towns; set off early or risk a very long wait.

WHERE TO STAY *Map, above*

Hotel Mayaga (30 rooms) m 0556 868605/0240 591813. This likeable family-run hotel, situated at least 500m from the lorry station along the Wa road, & clearly signposted, is a little rundown from the outside but has good spacious rooms inside. The restaurant is affordable, but the choice is limited & it's worth ordering in advance as food is cooked from scratch. A shady outdoor bar serves chilled beer & cold drinks. *US$9 dbl with fan* & common shower; US$20 self-contained dbl with AC; US$31 family room sleeping 4. **$$–$**

CEDEC Guesthouse (24 rooms) ☎ 03821 22161; m 0242 130404; www.nbdiocese. wordpress.com. Situated alongside the Catholic Mission, this inexpensive guesthouse is part of the church-affiliated Centre for Development Communications (CEDEC), which also houses a printing press & a small shop stocking religious books. The fanned rooms in the main block are very dingy but indisputably cheap. More attractive are the large & reasonably clean AC chalets that stand in rambling gardens behind the main building. Inexpensive meals are available. *US$9/17 self-contained dbl with fan/AC.* **$$–$**

🏠 **Pongobu Guesthouse** (10 rooms) m 0504 820604/0500 357579. Set south of the town centre along the Kologo–Naaga Rd near the University for Development Studies, this newish

place represents perhaps the most upmarket accommodation in town, provided you don't mind its rather out-of-the-way locale. Rooms are on the bland side & arranged in a rather cramped 2-storey compound, but all are comfortably equipped with AC, flatscreen TV, hot water, big bathrooms, and a mini-fridge. Inconveniently for those without transport, there's no food on offer, but they do serve cold drinks. *US$21/26 dbl/exec.* **$$**

✕ WHERE TO EAT AND DRINK Map, page 465

Aside from the two hotels listed above, neither of which exactly shines, the best option is **Abasua Fast Food**, which serves decent and very inexpensive chicken and fried rice. There are also a few decent stalls selling grilled meat near the south end of the main street. Most of the other spots shown on the map are **bars**, which are plentiful indeed.

WHAT TO SEE AND DO

Cathedral of Our Lady of the Seven Sorrows This century-old Catholic

Mission is dominated by the Cathedral of Our Lady of the Seven Sorrows, which was built under the supervision of Oscar Morin and the White Fathers in 1906, expanded to its present size in 1920, dedicated as a cathedral and as the mother parish of northern Ghana in 1934, and declared a minor basilica by Pope Benedict XVI on its 100th anniversary in 2006. The cathedral is unique in that it was made entirely from mud bricks, following traditional construction methods used by local women, and the exterior is sealed and waterproofed with a cement-like mixture of mud, cow dung and dawa-dawa fruit extracts. The colonnaded interior is decorated with dozens of simple but beautiful frescoes – depicting biblical scenes, animals and geometric patterns – created in 1972 using kerite oil and soil-based pigments by seven craftswomen from Sirigu. A small museum housing displays on local history and culture stands adjacent to the church. The mission lies about 1.5km from the town centre, and is particularly worth visiting when a service is on the go, as the singing can be phenomenal. There are several routes to the cathedral, the most straightforward being to follow the Kologo–Naaga Road south past the Ghana Commercial Bank for 10–15 minutes, then turn left on to Catholic Mission Link (opposite the War Memorial Hospital), and continue for another five minutes or so.

Lake Tono Situated some 5km west of Navrongo, Tono is one of the largest

agricultural dams in West Africa, held in by a 2km-long wall and providing irrigation to around 2,500ha of nearby farmland. It is also known as one of the most productive birding sites in northern Ghana. Adam Riley, of Rockjumper Tours, notes that it is: 'home to a healthy population of waterbirds including herons, egrets, waders and one of Africa's most sought-after birds, the seasonally resident Egyptian plover. Other target species include grasshopper buzzard, Beaudouin's snake-eagle, Stanley and white-bellied bustard, black-headed lapwing, Forbes's plover, four-banded sandgrouse, swallow-tailed bee-eater, rufous-rumped and sun lark, rufous cisticola, pygmy sunbird, piacpiac, chestnut-bellied starling, bush petronia, speckled-fronted weaver, red-winged pytilia, African silverbill and white-rumped seedeater. Nocturnal excursions are good for owls and often yield sightings of the incredible standard-winged nightjar, the male of which has a 50cm-long bare feather shaft ending in the so-called 'standard' – a large feather vane off each wing – making for one of the world's most unusual birds, particularly during its display flight.

To get there, follow the Tumu road out of Navrongo for roughly 3km then turn right on to a surfaced turn-off, which leads to the lake after about 4km. Without private transport, you'll probably have to charter a taxi.

PAGA

Situated 12km north of Navrongo along a good surfaced road, Paga is the most popular crossing point between Ghana and Burkina Faso, though you'd scarcely know it from the subdued mood of the rustic town centre – a chaotic northern counterpart to Aflao or Elubo it most definitely isn't! International connections aside, Paga is best known for its sacred crocodiles, which can be seen at unusually close quarters, and form the centrepiece of a perennially popular community tourist project. Other attractions include the Paga Pia's Palace near the taxi park and Pikworo Slave Camp 2km from the town centre.

GETTING THERE AND AWAY Paga is connected to Navrongo and Bolgatanga by regular shared taxis. The one-way trip takes about 20 minutes and 90 minutes respectively. If you're coming for the crocodile pools or other facets of the ecotourism project, ask to be dropped at the visitor centre, a prominent, traditionally painted building opposite the Chief's Pool (as opposed to the parking lot next to the border post 1.5km further north, or the central taxi park 1.5km back towards Navrongo).

The **border with Burkina Faso** lies at the northern end of the town, 1.5km past the Chief's Pool. Shared taxis from Navrongo or Bolgatanga will drop passengers here on request, practically alongside the building where Ghanaian border formalities must be completed. Bush taxis and other transport on to Ouagadougou, the capital of Burkina Faso, line up about 200m into no-man's-land, and – because the Burkina Faso border post lies another kilometre or so away – it's conventional for passengers to wait for the vehicle to fill up and leave and then to complete entrance formalities *en masse*. Most visitors require a visa for Burkina Faso, and while they are available at the border, it's a hefty US$41/162 (24,000/94,000CFA) for a 3-day/3-month visa, so it's much cheaper to arrange this in Accra if you can. It's easy enough to change money on the street at the border – whether you want to exchange hard currency cash or change CFA into cedi or vice versa – but the rates are lousy and there is a risk of being conned, so don't change more than you need to see you through to the capital.

OA Tours (m *0208 294602*; *www.oatravels.com*) runs an executive bus to Kumasi and Accra for US$16/23, departing Paga at 12.30 daily.

WHERE TO STAY AND EAT *Map, page 468*

Kubs Lodge (19 rooms) m 0242 366251/0241 098392. Situated about 500m from the border post, this is a good bet in the unlikely event you need to overnight in Paga. The music tends to be a little loud, but the management is very professional & friendly. There's also a chop bar attached, but it seemed to be out of action on last inspection. *US$8 dbl with shared bath & fan. US$11/13 self-contained dbl with fan/AC.* **$**

We Pe Paga Crocodile Restaurant m 0278 130237; ⏲ 07.00–22.00 Mon–Sat. This superior chop bar next to Chief's Pool & the visitors' centre serves a selection of local dishes for around US$2. **$**

WHAT TO SEE AND DO The attractions listed below can be visited only with an official guide recognised by the town's well-run community-based ecotourism project (**m** *0244 189338/691525*). This is based out of a clearly signposted summer hut next to the Chief's Pool, and you are strongly advised against getting involved with any supposed guide who approaches you elsewhere in town. The project charges a one-off entrance fee equivalent to US$3, and another US$3 per person per individual site for a guided tour. There is an additional camera fee of US$1.50 per person, a video fee of US$1.50, and a sacrificial chicken (for the crocodiles) costs an additional US$3 per party.

Directly across the street from the reception centre, the appealing **Beads of Hope** (**m** *0246 206218;* ⏰ *08.00–19.30 Mon–Sat, 14.00–19.30 Sun;* 🄵 *fb.me/ beadsofhopeghana*) jewellery shop is a locally run enterprise that sells an enticing variety of beaded bracelets, necklaces, earrings, and other accessories handmade by a co-operative of women from Paga and surrounding villages.

Crocodile ponds There are two main sacred crocodile pools in Paga, hosting around 200 individual crocodiles of various ages and sizes, though these may disperse into other seasonal pools and swamps during the rains. The ancient **Chief's Pool**, on the west side of the main road directly opposite the visitor centre, probably harbours the greatest number of crocodiles, but the largest individuals are said to live in **Zenga Pond**, which lies no more than 500m along a signposted footpath running east from the main road between the taxi park and the visitor centre. Live chickens, used to bait the crocs on to terra firma, are arranged by the caretaker who stays at each of the ponds. It's a rare treat to be able to touch and photograph crocodiles at such close quarters, though one can't help but feel for them – revered for centuries as vassals for the ancestral spirits, they now suffer the indignity of being leapt on, prodded about and shooed off with a familiarity that might lead more sceptical observers

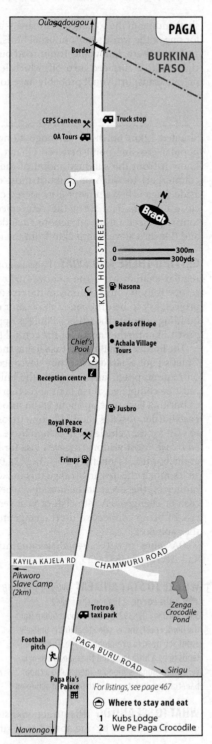

Local tradition has it that Paga was founded in 1670 by Naveh Kampala, the grandson of an important chief whose totem was a crocodile. When the old chief died, Naveh's father Paniogo lost out in the succession dispute and he and his followers were forced to flee from their home on horseback with the new chief and his soldiers in hot pursuit. At a place called Tampala, Paniogo's passage was blocked by a raging river, and in desperation he asked a nearby crocodile to help his party across the river, and pledged that in return he and his followers would never again harm a crocodile. Obligingly, the crocodile dived into the water and beat his tail so hard that the water parted, clearing the way for Paniogo to scurry to the safety of the opposite bank before the water rolled back to block his pursuers' path. After this close escape, the exiles settled in a place called Kampala (in present-day Burkina Faso), which lay close to a grove and crocodile pool that Paniogo declared to be sacred.

Many years later, Paniogo's son Naveh was out hunting when he fell into an aardvark hole whose entrance collapsed. Naveh was trapped in the hole for two full days, and his family assumed him to be dead when his dog returned home alone. But then a crocodile living in the hole saw that Naveh was dying, showed him an escape route, and walked him to a pool to quench his thirst. Naveh reaffirmed his father's pledge to the crocodile, but when he returned to Kampala he realised that his people had broken the taboo by killing and eating crocodiles, and he decided to move away with his family. Then, sometime in 1670, after several months of searching for an appropriate new home, Naveh arrived at the uninhabited margin of the crocodile-infested Chief's Pool and cried out, '*A yi paga ywo!*' – this place pleases my eyes – from which the name Paga derives. Naveh became the first Paga Pia (Chief of Paga) and instated crocodiles as the town's totem – it is said that no person has ever been harmed by one of the crocodiles of Paga, and the town's human residents traditionally view killing a croc to be as sinful as homicide.

At least two other conflicting legends are in circulation to explain how the crocodiles of Paga became sacred, though it's possible that these relate to the circumstance under which they originally became the totem for Naveh Kampala's ancestors. One story is that a hunter trapped between a hungry lion and a river asked a crocodile to carry him across to safety in exchange for which he and his descendants would never eat crocodile meat. The other is that a man who left home after his pet dog had been sacrificed by his parents got lost in a dry area and was nearly dying of thirst when a friendly crocodile led him to a pool and saved his life.

than ourselves to form the conclusion that they are preserved solely for the money they generate. Still, if one were to be reincarnated in Paga, one would rather be a crocodile than a chicken.

Paga Pia's Palace Paga hosts some superb examples of the extended family homesteads that characterise this Burkina Faso border region – fantastic, labyrinthine, fortress-like constructions characterised by their curvaceous earthen walls, flat roofs and cosy courtyards. Many of the complexes are more than a century old, and they may be inhabited by more than ten separate households, each with its own living quarters and courtyards, some marked by rounded mud mounds under which an important family member is buried. The flat roofs are used not only for drying crops, but also as a place to sleep in hot weather, while the mud walls are often covered in symbolic paintings or portraits of animals – a crocodile with a chicken in its mouth being a particular favourite.

It's possible to visit a private compound by arrangement, but the obvious place to start is the Paga Pia's Palace, which lies on the east side of the main road a short distance south of the taxi park. Said to have been founded by Naveh Kampala himself (see box, page 469), this sprawling complex is now home to his descendant Charles Awia Awampaga II, who was enskinned as the 11th Paga Pia in 1971, and more than 300 relatives, including five wives and 15 children. Roughly three-quarters of the buildings in the complex are built in the traditional Sahelian style, several are attractively painted, and some contain centuries-old pottery and other artefacts. The door design of the palace houses, typical of this part of Ghana, is reputedly a relic of the slaving era – the low entrance and high rim immediately inside made it impossible for somebody to enter a house without giving the occupant plenty of time to whack them on the head!

Pikworo Slave Camp Slaving activity around Paga reputedly peaked between 1840 and 1870, when the rocky outcrops of Pikworo – situated some 2km from the town centre – enclosed the most important slave-holding pen in this part of Ghana. At any given time, up to 200 captives from surrounding parts of present-day Ghana and Burkina Faso would be held at Pikworo, eventually to be sold to slave traders from Salaga. Strong local oral traditions relating to the layout of the slave camp suggest that the captives were well looked after – not through any altruism on the part of their captors, but in order that they would fetch a good price – and you can still see their 'eating bowls' carved in neat rows into the rock, as well as the recreational area where they would dance to the accompaniment of a resonant natural rock drum. On the other side of the camp is the cemetery, where dead slaves were buried in mass graves, and the punishment rock on which failed escapees would be seated and bound hand and foot to bake in the heat of the sun. A nearby lookout rock is where the slavers stood guard against attacks – several of which, it is said, were initiated by the Paga Pia, an opponent of slavery who frequently led rescue parties to Pikworo to release captured residents of nearby Paga.

Entrance to Pikworo includes an informative guided tour, and a donation for the drummers who play on the natural rock drum is expected. The site lies about 2km west of Paga, along a dirt road signposted from the main road perhaps 200m south of the Chief's Pool. You can walk there and back, allowing about 30 minutes each way and an hour to explore the camp, but most people either hire a bicycle for around US$1 per hour or charter a taxi for the return trip for around US$7.

Wa and the Upper West

The most remote, unpopulated and little visited of Ghana's administrative regions, the Upper West is something of a dead end in travel terms, and it offers little in the way of formal tourist development. In the right frame of mind, however, these shortcomings might be compensated for by the region's frontier atmosphere and its sense of remoteness from the rest of modern Ghana. The regional capital Wa is a sleepy but rather appealing town, studded with some fine examples of West Sudanese-style mud-and-stick architecture, notably the striking Wa Naa's Palace and lovely Nakore Mosque. Further afield, the Wechiau Hippo Sanctuary protects a herd of 50-odd hippos and abundant birdlife on the Black Volta, while the little-known Gbele Resource Reserve near Tumu road supports several antelope species as well as a rich variety of birds.

WA

The unimposing but amiable capital of the Upper West, Wa is best known to travellers for the palace of the Wa Naa (paramount chief of the Wala people), probably the most impressive construction of its type in the country. The town also forms a useful base for visiting several ancient mosques, and the Wechiau Hippo Sanctuary. Though rather provincial in feel, Wa is one of the oldest towns in the Ghanaian interior, and among the largest, supporting a population of 107,000, according to the 2010 census. A good time to visit is during the Dumba Festival, which started life as a harvest festival, held in late September or early October, but is also an important event on the Wala Islamic calendar. The centrepiece of the festival is a ceremony wherein the Wa Naa has to step over a small recumbent cow. If no part of the chief or his clothing brushes the cow, a good year is predicted, but if any contact is made, then it is believed that he will most likely die before the next year's Dumba.

HISTORY One of the oldest cities in the Ghanaian interior, Wa was founded in the 16th or 17th century as the capital of the emergent Islamic state of Wala, and the seat of the first Wa Naa, who was reputedly called Sorliya and had 99 wives. Back then, Wa was an important market along the trade routes connecting coastal Ghana to the Sahel, and it also had something of a reputation as a centre of Islamic scholarship, as evidenced by the high number of West Sudanese-style mosques dotted around the area. In 1894, the British agent George Ekem Ferguson visited Wa, whose population was then estimated at a substantial 8,000, and noted that the capital of what he called Dagarti 'was not a walled city, but the flat-roofed buildings and date palms present it with an Eastern appearance'. Ferguson signed a 'treaty of friendship' with Wa Naa Saidu Takora, effectively placing Wala under British rule, a claim that was reinforced when a British fort was constructed in the town three years later. Despite this, the traditional

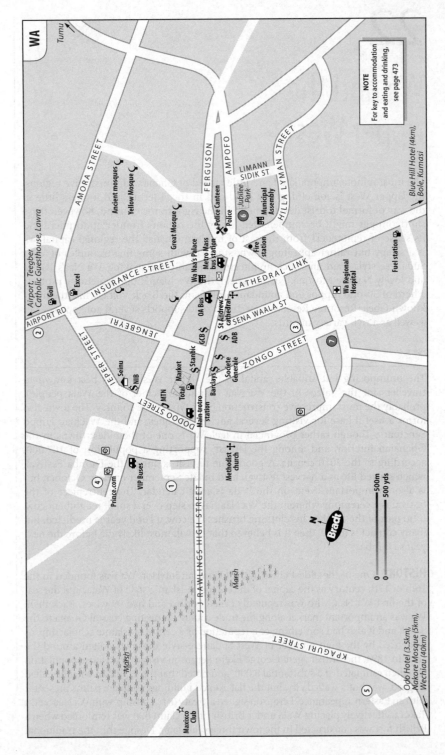

WA

Tumu

AMORA STREET

Ancient mosques
Yellow Mosque

Great Mosque

Excel

Goil

Airport, Teegber
Catholic Guesthouse, Lawra

INSURANCE STREET

Wa Naa's Palace

Metro Mass
bus station

OA Bus

AIRPORT RD

JENGBEYRI

IEPER STREET

Seinu

NIB

MTN

Total

Market

Stanbic

GCB

St Andrew's
cathedral

Barclays

Société
Générale

ADB

SENA WAALA ST

ZONGO STREET

DODOO STREET

Main trotro
station

Prince.com

VIP Buses

Methodist
church

J J RAWLINGS HIGH STREET

Maxixco
Club

Marsh

Marsh

Odo Hotel (3.5km),
Nakore Mosque (5km),
Wechiau (40km)

KPAGURI STREET

FERGUSON

AMPOFO

LIMANN
SIDIK ST

Jubilee
Park

Municipal
Assembly

HILLA LYMAN STREET

Police Canteen

Police

Fire
station

CATHEDRAL LINK

Wa Regional
Hospital

Fuel station

Blue Hill Hotel (4km),
Bole, Kumasi

NOTE
For key to accommodation
and eating and drinking,
see page 473

N

Bradt

0   500m
0   500 yds

1
2
3
4
5
6
7

472

authority of the Wa Naa was recognised throughout the colonial era, though the borders of Wala were frequently disputed and changed. Wa remained an important district capital in the early independence era, and was elevated to regional capital when the Upper West was split from the Upper East in 1983.

Secession disputes, triggered by the January 1998 death of the 28th Wa Naa, the long-serving Momori Bondiri II, have undermined the paramount chief's authority in recent years. Following a protracted and sporadically violent dispute between rival candidates, Naa Yakubu Seidu Soale II was enskinned in 2001, aged 76, but ongoing litigation meant he was never able to occupy the palace prior to his death in 2006. A successor, Naa Fuseini Seidu Pelpuo IV, was enskinned in January 2007, but his status was challenged legally by the leaders of three of the other dynasties that comprise the so-called four royal 'gates' of Wa on the basis that his rather clandestine nomination went against Wala tradition. A court ruling in the Wa Naa's favour in 2010 went under appeal, and tensions between the two factions have remained high ever since, culminating in a June 2012 assassination attempt on the Wa Naa, in which one of his bodyguards was shot dead. Following a favourable ruling by the National House of Chiefs, Fuseini Seidu Pelpuo IV was finally sworn in as Wa Naa at a peaceful ceremony held at the Centre for National Culture in October 2012. He has since reoccupied the palace, and calm once again reigns in the Wa Naa's domain.

GETTING THERE AND AWAY

By air Wa's airport is less than 2km north of the central roundabout and hasn't seen commercial traffic in years, but upgrades seem to be afoot and the official government stance is that it will reopen to passenger traffic in 2016. That may be optimistic, but it's nonetheless quite possible that Starbow or another carrier could begin servicing Wa during the lifespan of this edition.

By road The main terminus for long-haul coaches is in the town centre adjacent to the Wa Naa's Palace. The most reliable service is **OA** (↘ *03022 36917 (Accra);* ↘ *03220 41925 (Kumasi);* m *0209 383060/0544 729597 (Wa); www.oatravels.com*), which runs between Accra and Wa (*US$15–20*) via Kumasi (*US$10*), Sunyani, Techiman and Bole, departing at 16.00 and 17.00 daily. In addition, **VIP Buses** (m *0246 721795*) head to Accra (*US$22*) and Kumasi (*US$12*) from their own station about 1km to the west at 17.00 daily. Either way, the trip typically takes around 14 hours.

Heading towards Tamale and Larabanga (for Mole National Park), **Metro Mass** was previously the best option, but now that the Sawla–Fulfusu road is surfaced, numerous buses and trotros cover this route throughout the day, rendering the Metro Mass and its sadistic early-morning departures largely unnecessary. Still, their bus to/from Bolgatanga via Tumu (departure 05.00 daily) could be of use to eastbound travellers, though it's again worth noting that the upgraded condition of roads to the south means that connecting between Wa and Bolgatanga is almost

Wa and the Upper West WA

22

certainly now more convenient (and faster) via Tamale. There are also Metro Mass buses to Sunyani, Kumasi and Accra.

For more local destinations, such as Wechiau, Lawra, or Hamile (to which road-surfacing works are well under way), the usual motley assortment of trotros and shared taxis can be found at the main station, which lies at the west end of the town centre next to the market. These include sporadic trotros to Tumu, where you'll most likely have to spend the night before heading on to Bolgatanga.

TOURIST INFORMATION The **Ghana Tourist Board**'s Upper West Regional Office (☎ *03920 22431/23431;* e *gtaupperwest@gmail.com;* ⊕ *08.00–12.30 & 13.30–17.00 Mon–Fri*) is on the ground floor of Ministry Block B of the Regional Co-ordinating Council Building.

🏠 WHERE TO STAY *Map, page 472*

Moderate

🏠 **Upland Hotel** (40 rooms) ☎ 03920 22180; m 0209 426520; e upland.hotel@yahoo.com; 🅵 fb.me/uplandhotelgh. A favoured haunt of NGO workers & business travellers, this large, comfortable & well-run hotel is set in compact but leafy grounds along the Nakore road 3km southwest of the town centre. The rooms have good facilities &, though a little rundown, are very comfortable (& renovations are scheduled for later in 2016). It also has the best restaurant in Wa, & a garden bar, though everything closes up by 22.00. *US$30/37 self-contained sgl/dbl with AC, fan, satellite TV & hot water; US$45 larger exec room with queen-sized bed.* **$$$–$$**

🏠 **Blue Hill Hotel** (20 rooms) ☎ 03920 95525; m 0208 816192; e info@bluehillhotel.com; www.bluehillhotel.com. The only rival to the long-serving Upland in this range, the upstart Blue Hill Hotel, situated about 5km south of the town centre along the Kumasi road, lacks the character of its competitor, but the rooms are smarter & feel altogether more modern. The spacious rooms have large bathrooms with hot water, flatscreen satellite TV & AC, & an adequate indoor restaurant serves meals in the US$8–10 range. *US$36/44/52 standard/executive/chalet room with dbl/queen-sized bed.* **$$$–$$**

Budget

🏠 **Teegber Catholic Guesthouse** (40 rooms) ☎ 03920 22375; m 02053 65094. Situated on the east side of the Lawra Rd, past the airstrip & about 2km from the town centre, this well-kept guesthouse is popular with volunteers & the spotless self-contained rooms make it the pick of Wa's cheaper lodgings,

provided you don't mind the rather isolated location. Reasonable meals are available in the US$3–5 range, & there is a friendly garden bar. *US$17/21 sgl/twin or dbl with fan, and satellite TV; US$22–26 dbl with AC.* **$$–$**

Shoestring

🏠 **Kunateh Lodge** (16 rooms) ☎ 03920 22102; m 0206 819267. Probably the best central cheapie, & reasonably convenient for catching early-morning buses, this is a clean & friendly lodge. There are large dbl rooms with fan using common showers, & self-contained dbls, some of which have a balcony. *US$8 dbl with fan & shared bath; US$10/13 self-contained dbl with fan/AC.* **$**

🏠 **Kedge Lodge** (16 rooms) m 0209 518290/0207 600795. This large white multi-storey hotel on the Lawra road is one of Wa's best budget deals. The carpeted rooms, while a little on the pokey side, are adequately clean, & meals are available on request. *US$10 dbl using shared bath; US$11/16 self-contained dbl with fan/AC.* **$$–$**

🏠 **Hotel du Pond** (17 rooms) ☎ 03920 20018. This perennially popular shoestring lodge has a useful central location, but the rooms, set in 2 buildings just across the road from each other, are a bit grubby & musty, though no more so than anywhere else in this range. *US$10 sgl with fan & shared bath; US$13 self-contained dbl with fan; US$15 self-contained dbl with AC.* **$**

🏠 **Odo Hotel** (20 rooms) ☎ 03920 91955; m 0503 660281. Situated along the Nakore Rd another 3km past the Upland Hotel, this rather out-of-the-way spot has a likeable bush location, an adequate restaurant & bar, & clean tiled rooms with TV. *US$11/21 self-contained dbl with fan/AC.* **$$–$**

🏠 **Numbu Hotel** (10 rooms) ☎03920 20460. Set in a maze of unmade roads 500m northwest of the trotro station, this quiet & friendly hotel is

quite grotty but good value at the asking price. *US$6–8 dbl with fan using shared bath; US$9–11 self-contained dbl with fan.* **$$–$**

✗ WHERE TO EAT AND DRINK *Map, page 472*

✗ **Upland Hotel** 🕓 07.30–22.00 daily. This out-of-town hotel has the best restaurant in Wa, serving a varied menu of generously proportioned continental, Chinese & local dishes in the US$5–8 range. You can eat indoors or in the garden bar. **$$**

✗ **Mummy's Kitchen** m 0392 022681; 🕓 08.00–20.00 Mon–Sat. In a smart AC building with large-screen TV, this stalwart on Hospital Ring Road offers an immense selection of international & local dishes (inc guineafowl) in the US$4–5

range, along with what are very likely to be Wa's only pizzas (delivery available). There's an attached supermarket out front, & it's a good b/fast spot, too. **$**

✗ **Jubilee Kitchen** Centrally located next to Jubilee Park & often referred to as 'Ghana @ 50' to commemorate the nation's semi-centennial in 2007, this popular & inexpensive local eatery is well known for its TZ (*tuo zafi*), but it also serves other staples such as rice & banku. **$**

BARS AND NIGHTCLUBS The usual scattering of inexpensive bars can be found in the town centre, but the main cluster of happening places is about 2km along the road towards the university, just after the junction with Kpaguri Street (to Nakore). These include the **Great Top Rock Bar** and **KG Spot**, as well as the ever popular **Maxixco Club** (formerly Wizzy Vill's Nightclub, and still widely known as Wizzy's), which is *the* place for an all-nighter at weekends.

OTHER PRACTICALITIES

Foreign exchange and banks Most of the main bank chains are represented in Wa, including Barclays, Stanbic and Ghana Commercial Banks, all of which have ATMS where local currency can be drawn against a Visa card. There are also foreign exchange facilities at Barclays.

Internet There are plenty of internet cafés dotted around town and shown on the map. **Prince.com**, just around the corner from the Numbu Hotel, is a good option, with about ten PCs and a reliable connection.

Medical The Wa Regional Hospital, on Hospital Ring Road at the south end of the town centre, is the best-equipped medical facility in the Upper West, though not of comparable standard to hospitals elsewhere in the country.

WHAT TO SEE AND DO

Wa Naa's Palace Situated close to the main central traffic circle, the Wa Naa's Palace is a large fortress-like building originally constructed in the flat-roofed style typical of northeast Ghana, but expanded at around the turn of the 20th century in imitation of the West Sudanese mud-brick architectural style more normally associated with the region's ancient mosques. Although much of the palace interior has deteriorated through disuse since the death of Naa Momori Bondiri II in 1998, the buttressed exterior remains in excellent condition, thanks partly to restoration work financed by the World Monuments Fund over 2009/10. Officially reoccupied by Wa Naa Fuseini Seidu Pelpuo IV in 2012, today the palace is once again fully habitable, and the Wa Naa remains in full-time residence. In front of the palace stand the graves of six of the Wa Naa Pelpuo's predecessors, dating back to the early 20th century.

Wa Naa's Palace is not formally managed as a tourist attraction. Indeed, it was boarded up and held under military guard for the duration of the 1998–2012 secession disputes and still remains under police guard today. Attitudes to sightseers during the secession crisis were variable, but today if you approach the police politely they should grant you permission to take photographs of the palace and perhaps even take you up on the rooftop (for no charge!), as they did when we visited in 2016. In addition, the Wa Naa often holds public audiences with his subjects in the afternoons, and these make for a good time to catch a glimpse of his highness. If you ask to speak to his Furko (a kind of traditional liaison officer), you may well be invited in to meet the Wa Naa himself and look around the palace. Should this happen, be warned that the Wa Naa may not be spoken to directly, and that some sort of donation, in the form of kola nuts or money, will be expected.

Old mosques Two semi-ruinous but reasonably well-preserved mud-and-stick mosques in the West Sudanese style are situated alongside each other in the residential backroads about 1km northeast of the central traffic circle. The imam at these mosques is usually very welcoming, and it's unproblematic to take photos, or to go inside, or even to climb on the roof (and since he is a coin collector, you'll be doubly well received if you gift him a foreign coin, no matter how small its value). To get there, follow Insurance Street north from the traffic circle for about 50m, then turn right into Ferguson Street immediately after the Police Canteen. A few hundred metres along this road, you'll see the large white Ahmadiyya/Great Mosque to your left. Follow the dirt road running around the right side of this mosque for about 500m until you reach a smaller yellow mosque. The ancient mosques are immediately behind this.

Nakore Mosque The most impressive West Sudanese construction in the vicinity of Wa is Nakore Mosque, which lies about 1km past the Odo Hotel. The mosque here is taller than its more famous counterpart at Larabanga, and locals claim that it dates to 1516, making it of comparable vintage, though some written sources place its construction in the 18th or 19th century. Either way, the attitude is a lot more relaxed than at Larabanga. The friendly imam (or his helper) charge an entrance fee equivalent to US$3, and will usually show visitors inside, and let them climb to the roof and take photographs.

Nakore Mosque is situated in the village of the same name about 6km from central Wa along the road passing the Upland and Odo hotels. It is an easy, flattish walk, taking perhaps an hour in either direction, or you could cycle there in 20-30 minutes. A taxi charter shouldn't cost more than US$8 for the round trip. Once in Nakore, the mosque is about 200m north of the main road (✪ N10 01.261 W2 32.840).

AROUND WA

WECHIAU COMMUNITY HIPPO SANCTUARY Protecting a 40km stretch of the Black Volta as it flows along the Burkina Faso border southwest of Wa, this remote and little-visited sanctuary, 20km west of the village of Wechiau, represents an admirable attempt to combine community-based tourist and wildlife conservation. The main attraction is the reserve's population of around 50 hippopotami. Generally, the hippos are quite easily located by canoe during the dry season, though do be warned that they seldom stray on to land in daylight, so a sighting may amount to little more than a few ears and snouts twitching above the water, accompanied by some characteristic grunting and harrumphing. The hippos are more elusive during the rainy season, when they disperse widely into seasonal pools, and weeks might pass without a sighting.

Even if there are no hippos in sight, the sanctuary is very beautiful. The riverine savannah and forest are offset by some striking rock formations, and the area supports an impressive tally of 250 bird species, notably exclamatory paradise whydah, malachite kingfisher, Senegal parrot, Abyssinian roller and breeding colonies of red-throated bee-eater. In addition, Wechiau, the nearest village to the sanctuary and springboard for visits, is of some cultural interest. The local Lobi and Biri people live a very traditional lifestyle and are still occasionally seen wearing traditional lip plugs, especially on market days (every six days). Also well worth a look, the Wechiau Naa's Palace, reminiscent of its counterpart in Wa, has a well-maintained façade constructed in West Sudanese style, and the incumbent paramount chief Naa Imoru Nadong Gomah II, a supporter of the community project, is very welcoming to visitors.

The community sanctuary at Wechiau draws mixed feedback from readers. Some have rated it a highlight of their trip to Ghana, while others complain that it is badly organised and the wildlife is a disappointment. A lot will depend on how lucky you are with your guide, whether you spend the night (which greatly improves the odds of seeing hippos), and how prepared you are for the rudimentary accommodation and occasional lapses into organisational chaos. Be aware, too, that the quality of wildlife sightings is highly seasonal, with November to April being the best time to see hippos. It's not realistic to visit Wechiau as a day trip out of Wa on public transport, so plan on spending at least one night, better still two, to be reasonably certain of seeing hippos (in the dry season).

All visits and activities should be arranged at **Wechiau Visitor Centre** (m *0242 805908/0265 773117;* e *info@ghanahippos.com; www.ghanahippos.com or* f *fb.me/ WechiauCommunityHippoSanctuary*), which lies in the village of Wechiau about 100m from the palace, and can also arrange transport along the 20km road to the sanctuary. Entry to the sanctuary costs US$4 per person, with a small discount offered to volunteers and students. Canoe trips on the river cost US$3 per person, and are best undertaken in the early morning or later afternoon, when hippos are most active. Other activities, all charged at the same price as canoe trips, include birdwatching walks, botanical walks and cultural visits to surrounding Lobi communities.

Getting there and away
The village of Wechiau lies about 30km southwest of Wa as the crow flies, and 40km by road. The most direct route entails following the Nakore road out of Wa, past the Upland Hotel and Nakore Mosque, until after about 30km you reach the Vieri T-junction. Turn left here, and continue for another 10km to Wechiau. The drive takes about 45 minutes in a private vehicle (sections of the road are seriously corrugated), and about twice as long with one of the trotros that leave Wa from the main trotro station and cost around US$1 per person. These trotros run rather sporadically, with the most reliable time to pick one up being 07.30–08.00. Leaving Wechiau, you won't find a trotro much after 15.00.

Coming from the south, a good 25km dirt road connects Ga (on the main road between Wa and Bole) to Wechiau, an easy 30–40-minute drive in a private vehicle, but not covered by any public transport. (Should you find yourself at the south end of the reserve, there's another dirt road that connects to the main road at Tuna (via Kalba), but we've got no reports as to its condition.)

From Wechiau, it is still another 20km along a sandy track to the sanctuary and lodge. If you are in private transport, this takes around 30–40 minutes to drive. Otherwise, the best way to get to the lodge is by bicycle, which can be hired at the visitor centre for US$3/5 per day/overnight – the ride takes up to two hours

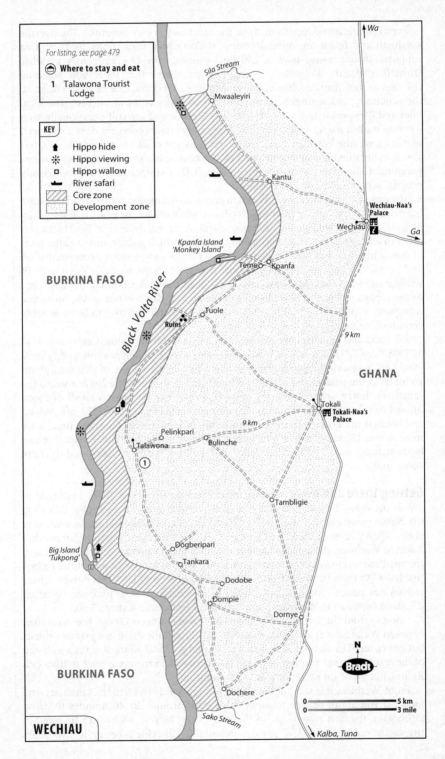

For listing, see page 479

KEY

⬤	Where to stay and eat
1	Talawona Tourist Lodge

KEY

♠	Hippo hide
✳	Hippo viewing
▫	Hippo wallow
⊢	River safari
▨	Core zone
▦	Development zone

↑ *Wa*

Sila Stream

Mwaaleyiri

Kantu

Wechiau-Naa's Palace

Wechiau → *Ga*

Kpanfa Island 'Monkey Island'

Teme ○ Kpanfa

BURKINA FASO

Black Volta River

Tuole

Ruins

9 km

GHANA

Tokali
Tokali-Naa's Palace

Pelinkpari

9 km

Talawona
① Bulinche

Tambligie

Big Island 'Tukpong'

Dogberipari

Tankara

Dodobe

Dompie

Dornye

BURKINA FASO

N

Bradt

Dochere

0		5 km
0		3 mile

Sako Stream

WECHIAU

↓ *Kalba, Tuna*

and can be quite tiring. Alternatively, hiring a motorcycle and driver costs around US$5/10 one-way/overnight, and a hired taxi will run you closer to US$8/16. If you are cycling, you can stash your backpack overnight in the reception centre.

⌂ Where to stay and eat   *Map, opposite*

In addition to the formal accommodation below, the visitor centre in Wechiau can arrange homestays in Wechiau or in a Lobi Compound for around US$4 per person.

⌂**Talawona Tourist Lodge** (4 rooms, 8 under construction) m 0242 805908/0265 773117; e info@ghanahippos.com; www.ghanahippos. com. Also known as Mark Donahue Lodge, this rustic lodge is situated 19km from Wechiau in the tiny village of Talawona, & set back about 1km from the river, close to the departure point for canoe safaris. Simple dbl rooms with mattresses & nets are available, or you can sleep on the roof or (if you have one) in a tent. Until recently, you could stay on 1 of 2 nearby 'hippo hide' tree platforms. These were broken when we checked in, but renovations are promised. There's a self-catering kitchen, but you will need to bring all ingredients from Wa or Wechiau. Pure/bottled water is normally, but not always, available. *US$5pp; US$3 camping.* **$**

KULMASA Straddling the Bole road about 40km south of Wa, this village of traditional mud compounds was once an important southern frontier town on the trade route through Wala. Today, it is best known as the site of two sacred crocodile pools, which – like their counterparts in Paga – form the centrepiece of a low-key community tourism project. Oral tradition has it that these toothsome creatures have been held sacred ever since the founder of Kulmasa stepped on what he thought was a log in a river whilst fleeing his enemies, and found himself being transported to the opposite bank on the back of a friendly crocodile. Ever since, it has been forbidden to harm crocodiles in any way in Kulmasa, or to eat their meat, and dead crocodiles are buried with some ceremony. It is also said that when somebody in Kulmasa is fatally ill, one of the crocodiles will come to their room and sit with them companionably until they die.

All visits to the crocodile pools must be arranged through the tourist reception centre, which is signposted on the east side of the main road. It costs US$4 per person, with a discount offered to volunteers and students. The caretaker – a grandson of the village's original crocodile whisperer – will then try to call the crocs out of the water with a loud, '*Walla Walla*'. It is quite impressive to see some of the larger crocs respond by swimming right across the lake like obedient dogs, but reader feedback indicates that they seldom actually leave the water – quite possibly because tourist visits are still enough of a novelty that the shore tends to fill up with an intimidating horde of noisy children.

SAMBO Situated along the Lawra road about 15km north of Wa, this otherwise unremarkable village is renowned for hosting a sacred colony of the hammer-headed bat (*Hypsignathus monstrosus*), a localised equatorial African species more normally associated with forest interior than human settlements. As its Latin binomial suggests, this dedicated frugivore is a genuinely monstrous creature – the male, with a wingspan of almost 1m, is the largest bat known from the African mainland, and its distinctive lopsided 'hammer' head and a resonant chest cavity allow it to emit a booming but eerie call that can carry for kilometres on a still night. The Sambo colony of several hundred lives in a tall, isolated cashew tree on the right side of the road coming from Wa. Anyone can point it out to you, but you may need binoculars to see the bats' unusual-shaped heads clearly.

LAWRA

Situated 100km north of Wa along the road to the Hamile border post with Burkina Faso, Lawra (pronounced like 'Laura') is something of a backwater today, but it was an important administrative centre in the colonial era. Set within walking distance of the Black Volta, this small town is also home to one of Ghana's most famous craftsmen, the gyil xylophone-maker Newin Baaru. Also of minor interest along the road coming from Wa is the remarkable Wuling Mushroom Rock near Babile. Lawra is especially worth a diversion during the post-harvest Kobine Festival (generally in the first week of October, sometimes later), when it springs into colourful life with music and dancing competitions. At other times of year, market day, which always falls the day after the market in Wa, is the best time to visit.

GETTING THERE AND AWAY Trotros between Wa and the border town of Hamile typically run at least thrice daily in either direction, leaving during the morning and 'dropping' passengers in Lawra town centre. The volume of traffic increases significantly on Lawra's market day and during the Kobine Festival. If you are driving yourself, Wuling Mushroom Rock is 4.5km and signposted from Babile along the Jirapa road. Roadworks were well under way in 2016, so there could be tarmac all the way from Wa to Hamile by the time you read this.

WHERE TO STAY AND EAT

Kontol Lodge (6 rooms) m 0201 641687/0241 212030/0502 385512. Situated at the main junction in Lawra, 50m before the Ghana Commercial Bank coming from Wa, this no-frills guesthouse has a variety of adequate fan rooms. Food is available. *US$8 sgl with shared bath, US$9–10 self-contained dbl.* **$**

District Assembly Guesthouse (17 rooms) m 0209 211705. Situated just past the hospital on the east side of the road, this long-serving dbl-storey lodge has dbls with fan only. You need to call the caretaker at the above number to arrange a room. *US$8 dbl.* **$**

WHAT TO SEE AND DO The Lobi and Dagati people of Lawra and surrounds are known countrywide for their traditional music, which is based around drumming and unique type of 14-key xylophone called a *gyil* (see box, opposite). The region's best-known xylophone-maker Newin Baaru generally welcomes visitors, and will show them some of his instruments, which are made with hardwood keys that reverberate into different-sized calabash gourds, and include a 1.5m-long giant version made by his father. He also gives xylophone lessons by request, ideally over a few days. Mr Baaru has no contact details, but if you stop at the 'Lawra' signpost as you enter town from the Wa side, and ask for him by name, his workshop is only 100m to the left of the main road. Best to knock before you enter his workshop, since it doubles as the family residence.

The **Lawra Naa's Palace**, an elaborate rambling maze of mud buildings, is also worth checking out, and the paramount chief himself can be met by appointment. Another interesting building, situated directly behind the District Assembly Guesthouse, is the colonial **regional administrator's mansion**, which is quite possibly – and somewhat incongruously, given its obscure setting – the grandest colonial-era building anywhere in Ghana. Pitifully derelict and overgrown today, the residence must have been constructed more than 100 years ago and it consists of 15–20 rooms, large grounds, servants' quarters, a separate kitchen complex, and an elaborate swimming pool added in the 1950s.

Though Lawra's Newin Baaru may be the region's most celebrated craftsman of the *gyil* (a unique type of 14-key xylophone), the instrument's undisputed doyen hails from Saru, a pinprick of a village more than 100km to the south, set near the Black Volta between Wechiau and Sawla. Gyil master Kakraba Lobi was the first gyil player to perform and record internationally, and he spent more than 20 years teaching at the University of Ghana's International Centre for African Music and Dance in Accra-Legon. In Lobi society, the gyil's repertoire includes songs to commemorate all aspects of life, from weddings and funerals to a simple weekend's hanging out. Kakraba Lobi's (quite aptly named) 1978 LP *Xylophone Player From Ghana* is a masterful and most important record of Lobi gyil performance, and a thoroughly compelling listen to boot.

Lobi passed away in 2007, but not before spending many years in Saru and Accra training his nephew, S K Kakraba, who also taught alongside his uncle at Legon. Today, Kakraba has taken on his uncle's mantle and remains the gyil's most active performer and ambassador. Based in Los Angeles, he can regularly be found touring in Europe and North America, where his virtuosic solo shows draw on age-old Lobi melodies to hypnotise an altogether new audience. His two 2015 releases, *Yonye* and *Songs of Paapieye* (*paapieye* being the Lobi term for the spider's egg-sac silk used to produce the gyil's distinctive buzz), are genuinely exciting documents of a centuries-old tradition that continues to impress in the modern era.

The **Black Volta** can be reached by following the dirt track west out of the town for 4.5km. If you can locate a boatman, boats can be chartered for a modest fee to sail along the river, which forms the border with Burkina Faso. Birdlife is prolific along the river, and locals claim that hippos and crocs are still around, though the odds of seeing them are infinitesimal.

AROUND LAWRA
Babile About 15km south of Lawra along the Wa road, the small junction town of Babile offers access to two little-known tourist sites. The more interesting of these, some 4.5km out of town on the right side of the Jirapa road, is the **Wuling Mushroom Rock**, a truly remarkable 4m-high formation whose eroded base and bulbous head genuinely resemble a giant mushroom. A larger collection of boulders behind the main formation might reward exploration, as it seems to contain several balancing-rock piles and nascent mushroom formations. Rather less compelling, 4km west of Babile, almost on the Burkina Faso border, is the Birufo Baa Grove, which comprises a small patch of swamp forest fed by natural springs at the base of slope scattered with volcanic rocks.

The only place to stay in Babile is the **Peace and Love Guesthouse** (*15 rooms;* m *0247 576862/0541 258964; US$8 dbl with fan & shared bath or US$11 self-contained dbl*), which feels like significantly better value than either of the lodges in Lawra itself, and also provides meals by request.

Nandom North of Lawra, the small town of **Nandom**, which lies along the Hamile road perhaps 15km south of the border, has a guesthouse based on similar lines to the District Assembly Guesthouse in Lawra. Nandom has little else to recommend it except during the last week in November or first in December, when the Kakube Thanksgiving Festival is marked by vibrant xylophone music and dancing.

Hamile Solely of interest as a relaxed border crossing to Burkina Faso, Ghana's northwestern-most official crossing is mostly of use if you're headed to or from Burkina's second city of Bobo-Dioulasso. It sits just opposite its Burkinabe counterpart of the same name, and serves as the junction for a well-graded (in 2016 anyway) laterite route that tiptoes 95km along Ghana's northern border to Gwollu and Tumu. There are at least a few trotros from Hamile to Wa throughout the day, but your odds of finding something heading towards Tumu from here are slim outside of market days (every six days). There's a once-daily **VIP bus** (m *0248 576608*) from here to Madina Station in Accra, which departs at 22.00 and charges US$24. If you get stuck, try the unpronounceable **Kpebbesaan Hotel** (m *0392 096506/0244 801188/0553 392701*) at the south end of town near the police barrier. There's no ATM in town.

TUMU

The most remote town of its size in Ghana, and arguably the least engaging, Tumu lies a few kilometres south of the Burkina Faso border almost exactly halfway along the bumpy strip of red dust that passes for the main road between Wa and Bolgatanga. The main town of the Sissala people, it is a friendly enough place, but has no specific draws, though this may change if plans to establish a hippo sanctuary in the pretty lake at the northern edge of town ever come to fruition. Otherwise, Tumu is of greatest interest during the two main annual festivals, the Naaba Gbiele (held over the cusp of January and February) and Paari Gbiele (literally 'Farmer's Play', held in mid March), which are usually marked by festive cultural performances attended by the Tumu Kuoro (Paramount Chief of Tumu). Otherwise, the main reason to stop in Tumu is to break up the long road trip between Wa and Bolgatanga, or as a springboard to visit the Gbele Resource Reserve or the Slave Defence Walls at Gwollu.

GETTING THERE AND AWAY Tumu lies about 135km northeast of Wa and 140km west of Bolgatanga along some of the dustiest roads to be found anywhere in Ghana. Either of these drives takes around three hours in a private vehicle and up to five hours on public transport, though encouragingly, surfacing works on the Bolgatanga road were well under way when we passed through in 2016. (The route from Wa, not so much.) From Wa, the best option is the direct Metro Mass bus that departs to Tumu from the Total filling station at 13.00 daily. Alternatively, the Metro Mass bus connecting Wa to Bolgatanga, leaving in either direction at around 06.00 daily, passes through Tumu in the mid to late morning. Wa and Tumu are also connected by a few clapped-out trotros, most of which usually leave at around 05.00–06.00, though there are also sometimes a few later in the day, depending on demand. Trotros between Tumu and Bolgatanga follow a more rigid pattern, leaving Tumu at around 05.30–06.00, and starting the return trip from Bolga at around midday. Northbound, the Burkina Faso border is only 18km away (and the Burkinabe town of Léo 12km further), but transport in this direction is sparse. Avoid travelling after dark, as there have been reports of occasional armed robberies along these roads.

🏠 **WHERE TO STAY** *Map, opposite*
🏠 **Sildep Guesthouse** (19 rooms) m 0541
636810/0208 977865/050 394 1540; e sil.dep4@ | gmail.com or margrit_frempong@sil.org; www.
sildep.org. Affiliated to a well-established NGO

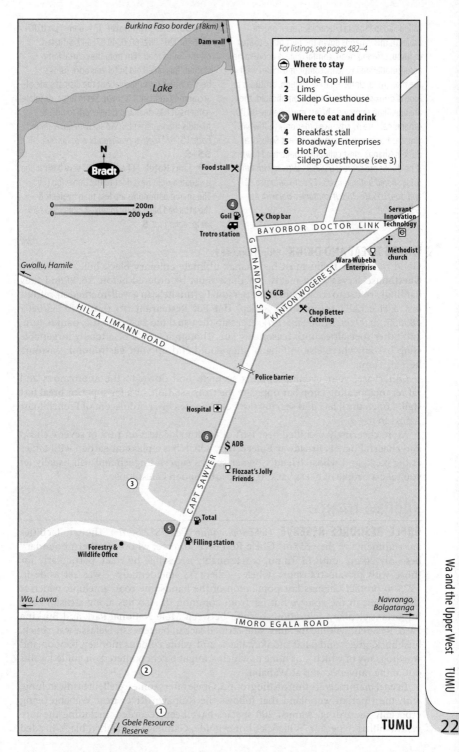

For listings, see pages 482–4

Where to stay
1 Dubie Top Hill
2 Lims
3 Sildep Guesthouse

Where to eat and drink
4 Breakfast stall
5 Broadway Enterprises
6 Hot Pot
   Sildep Guesthouse (see 3)

Burkina Faso border (18km)

Dam wall

Lake

Bradt

N

0 — 200m
0 — 200 yds

Food stall

Goil
Trotro station

Chop bar

Servant Innovation Technology

BAYORBOR DOCTOR LINK

Methodist church

Wara Wubeba Enterprise

Gwollu, Hamile

HILLA LIMANN ROAD

G D NANDZO ST

KANTON WOGERE ST

GCB

Chop Better Catering

Police barrier

Hospital

ADB

Flozaat's Jolly Friends

CAPT SAWYER

Total

Filling station

Forestry & Wildlife Office

Wa, Lawra

IMORO EGALA ROAD

Navrongo, Bolgatanga

Gbele Resource Reserve

TUMU

called Sildep (Sissala Literacy & Development Project), this is hands down the best place to stay in Tumu, offering clean, comfortable & good-value accommodation in a leafy compound 150m west of the main road. Unfortunately, though, attitudes to food & drink seem to be unduly complicated: they are unwilling to provide b/fast much before 08.00, other meals are by advance order only (not what you want to hear when you arrive hot & dusty at dusk in Ghana's most culinarily-challenged town) & no drinks are served. *US$7/8 sgl/twin with fan using shared bathroom; US$11 self-contained dbl with fan; US$16–18 self-contained dbl with AC.* **$$–$**

🛏 **Dubie Top Hill Hotel** (31 rooms) m 0207 074516/0204 082560/0240 078449. Situated off the Bolga road 1km from the central lorry station, this faded old hotel was once Tumu's best – which says much about the dismal state of accommodation in this town. Set in large, desolate gardens, it has clean but time-worn rooms, & friendly management. *US$6 sgl with fan & shared bath; US$8/13 self-contained dbl with fan/AC.* **$$–$**

🛏 **Lims Hotel** (14 rooms) This very basic lodge is situated right next door to the Dubie Top Hill. The shared bathrooms are less than hygienic & the attached bar is quite rowdy at night. *US$3.50 unappealing sgl.* **$**

✕ WHERE TO EAT AND DRINK *Map, page 483*

Good question! Tumu must be Ghana's ultimate culinary black hole. The **Sildep Guesthouse** serves good meals, but these must be ordered before 16.00 and they bafflingly refuse to cook for just one person. Fortunately, in a well-marked storefront just a rice ball's throw from Sildep, **Hot Pot Restaurant** (m *0246 413535/0207 480055;* ⊕ *09.00–21.00 Sun–Fri)* serves up the usual tuo zafi, omo tuo, banku, fufu, and other specialties until reasonably late. Though it would be a totally forgettable chop bar anywhere else in Ghana, they could end up your gastronomic saviours here in Tumu.

Otherwise, your evening options seem to boil down to the anonymous and rather unappealing chop bar opposite the trotro station, or a far superior **breakfast stall** – open until late and serving tasty egg sandwiches reminiscent of French toast – next to it.

More cheeringly, a chilled beer isn't difficult to locate. Our pick of several cheap and cheerful bars is **Broadway Enterprises**, which has a pleasant garden with tables at the back, and whose friendly owner speaks superb English and will usually let you take a couple of beers back to the nearby Sildep Guesthouse.

AROUND TUMU

GBELE RESOURCE RESERVE (*US$5pp, guide fee US$2.50/hr*) Though facilities are rudimentary, the 565km² Gbele Resource Reserve, whose northern boundary lies only 20km south of Tumu, is reasonably accessible by road, particularly for those with private transport. Gbele – silent 'G', incidentally – was set aside in 1975 to protect Ghana's last population of the handsome roan antelope, which is still present in the reserve but far from common. It also lies along a historically important elephant migration corridor between Mole National Park and Burkina Faso. Resident wildlife includes side-striped jackal, hartebeest, Defassa waterbuck, bushbuck, green and patas monkey, black-and-white colobus monkey, baboon and warthog, any of which – or none of which – might be encountered on guided walks out of the rangers' camp at Wahabu.

Even if mammals are thin on the ground, Gbele offers some excellent birdwatching, with the riparian woodland that follows the Kulpawn River near Wahabu being especially rewarding. Almost 200 species have been recorded, including the rare yellow-billed oxpecker, Willcock's honeyguide, Gambaga flycatcher, black-headed weaver, spotted thick-knee, long-tailed parakeet, Senegal parrot, carmine bee-eater, blue-breasted kingfisher, bearded barbet, Vieillot's barbet and yellow-crowned gonolek. The magnificent Egyptian plover is also reputedly quite regular along sandy stretches of riverbank.

Getting there and away Gbele is seldom visited by travellers, and any excursion there should be treated as an expedition. The closest thing to a formal entrance gate is Wahabu Ranger Camp, which lies on the bank of the Kulpawn River close to the southern boundary some 60km south of Tumu along the route to Wa via Walembele. In a private vehicle, the drive from either Tumu or Wa takes up to 2 hours, and may require high clearance and 4x4 during the rains. You could check first at the Wildlife Office in Tumu (\ *03920 22758;* e *gelerr@hotmail.com*). Wahabu can be reached using public transport between Tumu and Wa, but check which of three interchangeable routes the trotro will follow (you need to go via Wahabu rather than via Jeffisi or Gwollu), and you may have a problem finding transport out of the reserve. Alternatively, you can sometimes arrange a lift from Tumu with the Wildlife Office. Inexpensive and very rudimentary accommodation is available in three semi-permanent 'tourist tents'.

GWOLLU Situated on the Burkina Faso border 33km northwest of Tumu, Gwollu is best known as the site of a pair of concentric defensive walls built under the 19th-century paramount chief Gwollu Kuoro Tanjia Limann as protection against the notorious slave raider Babatu Zato. The inner wall enclosed the village homesteads, while a larger outer wall, with a perimeter of 3km, was later constructed to protect the surrounding farmland and water sources. Much of the walls have subsequently collapsed, while other sections have been incorporated into other structures, but parts are still free-standing, notably an 8m-long, 4m-high stretch adjacent to the palace of the present-day Gwollu Kuoro.

A few years back, the defensive wall in Gwollu was earmarked as the centrepiece of a community tourism project that doesn't quite seem to have gelled. The **visitor centre and museum** (m *0274 506148/532553*), clearly signposted next to the Gwollu Kuoro's Palace, was locked up when we dropped past in the course of researching this seventh edition, and nobody seemed too sure where the man with the key might be. A few metres away, the best-preserved nearby stretch of the old wall is fenced off and hung with a few signs reading 'Do not take pictures without permission'. Around the corner, the unadorned tomb of the late President Hilla Limann, a brother of the incumbent Gwollu Kuoro Buktie Limann, can only be viewed if you obtain permission from the elders and offer them a donation.

Whether any of this adds up to a compelling reason to divert to Gwollu might generously be described as debatable. But if you decide to give it a go, it's a bit livelier during the weekly market held every six days, and a fair number of trotros run there from Tumu daily, taking around 45–60 minutes. It would also be worth making advance contact with **Bwana Bukali** (m *0206 398283*), a knowledgeable guide who used to work with the community project. If nothing else, decent and sensibly priced accommodation can be found at the friendly **Tanjia Guesthouse** (*10 rooms;* m *0203 196892; US$9–11 for self-contained doubles with fan*), which lies about 1km along the Wa road.

Appendix 1

LANGUAGE

English is the official language of Ghana, widely spoken in those parts of the country likely to be visited by travellers, to a standard that is matched in few other anglophone African countries. This means that there is little need for short-stay travellers to try to familiarise themselves with any local tongues, though knowing a few words or greetings in a local language will often help open doors and break through barriers, particularly in rural areas.

Numerous different languages and dialects are spoken in Ghana, but you'll find that most people belonging to one or other of the Akan groups – and that means more than half of the population and practically everybody in southern and central Ghana – will speak Twi (pronounced rather like 'Chwee') as a first or second language. Twi is the Ghanaian language taught to most Peace Corps and other volunteers spending a lengthy period of time in the country, and it may help travellers to know a few basic words and phrases. Those who speak Twi will also be able to understand Fante, another widely spoken Akan language.

Note that pronunciation of the words listed below, as of most place names in Ghana, is phonetic (eg: 'ache' is pronounced as 'ah-chee' rather than the English word ache), and that spellings have been simplified to make sense to English-speakers (eg: 'ch' is often spelt 'ky' in Ghana, while 'dz' is pronounced 'j'). Note, too, that vowel sounds are closer to the soft French vowels than hard English ones.

Those who want to learn more could try getting hold of a copy of *Learning Ghanaian Languages*, available from the University Book Shop at the University of Ghana in Accra (e *Unibks@ug.gn.apc.org*).

TWI
Pronunciation
Vowels

a	similar to the 'a' in 'father'
e	as the 'e' in 'wet'
i	as the 'ee' in 'free', but less drawn out
o	somewhere between the 'o' in 'no' and the word 'awe'
u	similar to the 'oo' in 'food'

Basic words and phrases

Do you speak English?	*Wote Borofo ana?*	Good evening	*Mma ajo* (response *yemu*)
equal to	*ya anua*	Good morning	*Mma ache* (response *yemu*)
friend	*madanfo*		
Good afternoon	*Mma aha* (response *yemu*)	Goodbye	*Nanti ye*

How are you?	*Wo ho te sen?* (response *me ho ye*)	Welcome	*Akwaaba* (response: *Ya eja* (to older man); *Ya ema* (to older woman)
How much?	*Sain Me?*		
I'd like ...	*Me pe ...*		
man	*oberima*	What's your name?	*Ye frewo sen?*
No	*Dabe*	My name is ...	*Ye fre me ...*
Please	*Me pawocheo*	What is the cost?	*Eyesen?*
Thank you	*Meda ase*	Where is ...?	*Wo hin ...?*
today	*enne*	woman	*obaa*
tomorrow	*echina*	Yes	*Nyew* (Fante) or *aane* (Ashanti)
water	*nsuo*		
we	*ye*	yesterday	*enra*

Numbers

1	*baako*	21	*aduono baako*
2	*mienu*	30	*aduasa*
3	*miensa*	40	*aduanang*
4	*enang*	50	*aduonum*
5	*enoum*	60	*aduosia*
6	*nsia*	70	*aduosong*
7	*nsong*	80	*aduowotwe*
8	*nwotwe*	90	*aduokrong*
9	*nkrong*	100	*oha*
10	*edu*	1,000	*apem*
11, 12, etc	*dubaako, dumienu,* etc	10,000	*pemdu*
		100,000	*mpemba*
20	*aduono*	1,000,000	*opepe*

Days of the week

Monday	*Uzoada*	Friday	*Fiada*
Tuesday	*Blada*	Saturday	*Memleda*
Wednesday	*Akuada*	Sunday	*Kuasiada*
Thursday	*Yawada*		

EWE The key language to the east of the River Volta is Ewe (pronounced somewhere between 'eh-way' and 'eh-vay'). The main pronunciation points here are that a 'k' before a 'p' is always silent, and makes the 'p' more plosive, and that 'dz' sounds like a soft 'g'.

Useful phrases include:

Good morning	*Ndi* (add -*nami* to end if addressing more than one person)	yes	*eh*
		no	*ow*
		How much?	*Nene?*
Good afternoon	*Ndo* (*nami*)	money	*ga*
Good evening (after 17.00)	*Fieyi* (*nami*)	white person	*yavoo* (literally 'trickish dog' – but with no pejorative meaning)
welcome	*woeso*		
Goodbye	*Miadogo*		
How are you?	*Eh Foa?* (response: *Eh*)	black person	*ameyebo*
		where ...	*fika ...*
Thank you (very much)	*Akpe (ka ka)*		

DAGBANI The main language around Tamale is Dagbani. A 'g' before a 'b' is silent and makes the 'b' plosive – as in Gbele Resource Reserve. Useful phrases include:

Good morning	*Dasiba naa*	Good evening	*Aniwula naa*
	(response *Naa!*)	Welcome	*Maraaba*
Good afternoon	*Autine naa*	How are you?	*A gbihira?*

Note that where words are properly spelt with local characters, we have given an approximation in English characters. Readers are welcome to submit vocabulary lists for other Ghanaian languages (for updates and feedback information, see box, page viii).

GHAN-ENGLISH Travellers whose first language is not English may also appreciate a few 'Ghan-English' phrases – which won't make a lot of sense in English-speaking countries in the Western world, but are useful if you want to make yourself understood in Ghana.

I'll come back later	*I'll go and come/ go come*	How are things?	*How's back?*
see you later	*we shall meet*	mate	*chalay*
tip/bribe	*dash*	flip-flop/thong	*chalay wote*
How are you?	*How?* Or *How is it?* ('*How are you?*' is also used)	small child	*pekin*

Appendix 2

GLOSSARY

Here follows a glossary of terms and names used in this book and/or in Ghana itself.

abekwan	palm-nut soup
abosomfie	Asante traditional shrines – literally home of a 'bosom' or deity (singular: *obosomfie*)
AC	air conditioning
acacia woodland	any woodland dominated by thorn trees of the acacia family
Acheampong, Gen Ignatius	military president of Ghana 1972–78, publicly executed 1979
Adae	Cycle of nine 40- to 42-day month-like divisions recognised by the Ashanti
adinkra	cloth with dyed symbols made in Ashanti, often worn to funerals
adobe	mud building
Afrifa, Brigadier Akwasi	military president of Ghana 1968–69, publicly executed in 1979
Agbamevor	Durable type of kente cloth woven by the Ewe
Akan	most populous of Ghana's linguistic groupings, includes the Asante and coastal Fante
akpeteshie	local gin, distilled from palm wine
akple	local staple, almost indistinguishable from *banku*
Akuffo, Lt Gen	military president of Ghana 1978–79, publicly executed 1979
Akwaaba	Welcome
Ancient Ghana	medieval empire centred on present-day Mali after which Ghana was named
Ankrh, Lt Gen Joseph	military president of Ghana 1966–68
Anokye, Okomfo	spiritual advisor to Asantehene Osei Tutu
Asante	indigenous kingdom centred on Kumasi
Asantehene	King of Asante
Ashanti	see *Asante*
atumpan	talking drum
balance	change (for a payment)
banda	any detached accommodation, such as a hut or chalet
banku	smooth, pasty local staple made by boiling fermented corn/cassava dough in water
bofrot	deep-fried sweet dough-ball, not unlike doughnuts in taste and texture
boma	colonial administrative office

bosom	god or deity
bubra	draught beer
Busia, Dr Kofi	Prime Minister of Ghana 1969–72
chop bar/shop	simple local restaurant ('chop' being a local synonym for 'eat' or 'food')
cedi	local unit of currency
cowry	small white shell used as currency in pre-colonial times
Denkyira	dominant empire in central Ghana prior to the emergence of Asante
doka	old and strong palm wine
dropping taxi	charter taxi, as in Europe (but not metered)
DSTV	South African multi-channel satellite television service
durbar	reception or celebration at the court of a traditional ruler or chief
endemic	unique to a specific area
enskinment	equivalent of the coronation of a chief or king
enstoolment	equivalent of the coronation of a chief or king
exotic	not indigenous, eg: pine plantations
Fante	people of the coast (roughly between Accra and Takoradi)
Ferguson, George Ekem	Ghanaian explorer and colonial political agent; born Ekow Atta, 1864; killed Wa, 1897
forest	wooded area with closed canopy
forex bureau	bureau de change
fufu	popular gooey doughy staple made from pounded cassava, plantain and/or yam
fugu	cloth smock worn in northern Ghana
German Togoland	pre-World War I German territory comprising present-day Togo and Ghana's Volta Region
Ghartey IV, King	King of Winneba 1872–97; founder of Fante Confederation; also referred to as Robert Johnson Ghartey
Golden Stool	ultimate symbol of Asantehene
grasscutter	also known as the cane rat (*Thryonomys* spp), this rodent, weighing up to 8kg, is popularly eaten as bushmeat in Ghana
guesthouse	cheap local hotel
harmattan	dry dusty wind blowing across West Africa from the Sahara in the dry season
Hayford, Joseph Casely	Ghanaian barrister who formed NCBWA to resist British rule after World War I
highlife	homegrown style of music fusing traditional and imported rhythms
ice water	chilled tap water sold in packets
indigenous	occurring in a place naturally
jollof rice	tangy, sometimes very spicy, rice, red in colour, cooked with a tomato base, vegetables and/or meat
kalawole	soft, deep-fried, spicily seasoned plantain cubes
kenkey	maize-based starch ball, wrapped in plantain leaves/corn husks and usually eaten with tomato relish
kente	national cloth woven by the Asante and Ewe people
kola nuts	bitter and mildly narcotic nuts chewed throughout West Africa
krom	town
Kufour, John	elected president of Ghana 2000–2008

Limann, Dr Hilla	civilian president of Ghana 1979–81
lorry	term used locally for any large passenger vehicle (any bus or trotro)
MacLean, Gordon	Governor of the Gold Coast 1830–47, buried in Cape Coast Castle
Mahama, John Dramani	elected president of Ghana 2012–present
Mills, John Atta	elected president of Ghana 2008–12, when he died in office
na	chief (mainly in north)
NCBWA	National Congress of British West Africa
netting	mosquito net
Nkrumah, Kwame	first African prime minister of Gold Coast/Ghana 1952–66; died in exile 1972
nton	patrilineal clan-like division recognised in most Akan societies
ntunkum	mildest form of palm wine
obosomfie	see *abosomfie*
obruni	white person
Okomfo	Asante fetish priest
omo tua	rice balls
palava sauce	spicy tomato-based sauce
panga	local equivalent of a machete
passenger taxi	public transport taxi that carries a full quota of passengers between two fixed places
pito	millet-based beer
posuban	large shrine associated with relatively urbanised Fante settlements
Prempeh I, Asantehene	king exiled by the British to Sierra Leone in 1896; returned to stool, 1926; died 1931
Prempeh II, Asantehene	popular king of Asante 1931–70
pure water	chilled and sealed filtered water sold cheaply in plastic packets
Quarshie, Tetteh	local blacksmith who introduced cocoa to Ghana from Fernando Po in 1876
Rawlings, Flt Lt Jerry	military president of Ghana 1979, 1981–92, elected civilian president 1992–2000
red-red	stew of black-eyed peas served with fried plantains, especially popular in the north
riparian/riverine woodland	strip of forest or lush woodland following a watercourse, often rich in fig trees
Sahel	dry savannah belt dividing the forested coast of West Africa from the Sahara
savannah	grassland with some trees
self-contained	en suite (ie: room with private toilet and shower attached)
spot	unpretentious local bar
shared taxi	*see* passenger taxi
station	bus, trotro or taxi terminal
STC	State Transport Company; operates a depleted network of intercity coaches
stool	symbol of chieftaincy
surfaced (road)	road sealed with asphalt or similar
titale	similar to *kalawole*, but mashed with flour and deep fried as fritters

track	motorable minor road or path
trotro/tro-tro	passenger vehicle larger than a taxi but smaller than a bus
tuo zafi	stiff millet- or maize-based porridge eaten as staple in parts of the north
Tutu Osei, Asantehene	first true Asantehene, and some say also the greatest, enstooled 1697
TZ	see *tuo zafi*
West Sudanese	architectural style using mud and wood typical of mosques of the Sahel
woodland	wooded area lacking closed canopy
Yaa Asantewaa	Queen Mother who led resistance to British colonisation in 1900

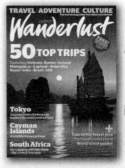

Appendix 3

FURTHER INFORMATION
BOOKS
History and background We consulted quite a number of books while researching the general and local history sections included in this guide, all of which we were able to buy in Ghana, though we can't guarantee you'll be able to do the same. We've listed them all below, but it would be pushing it to class most of them as recommended further reading.

The most readable and up-to-date starting point is Gocking's *History of Ghana*, but unless you can pick it up secondhand, it seems quite insubstantial for the asking price of around £30. Buah's *History of Ghana* is another obvious starting point for those seeking deeper insight into the country's historical background: readable, informative and of manageable length, without really propelling you to turn to the next page. More compelling, oddly enough, is Agbodeka's *Economic History*, while Gadzekpo's otherwise rather flimsy *History of Ghana* is especially strong on prehistory. Also worthwhile is *A Thousand Years of West African History*, a collection of essays covering most aspects of the region's history, probably a bit dated by now, but of great value for the lively, questioning style throughout.

Of the more focused titles, van Dantzig's *Forts and Castles* offers a good introduction to coastal history, brought to life by the final chapter on living conditions in and around the forts, and it's readily available in Accra and Cape Coast. Anquandah's *Castles and Forts of Ghana*, sold at the Accra Museum, and at Cape Coast and Elmina castles, covers similar ground with less substantial, but more readable, text and some wonderful photographs. Debrah's *Asante Traditional Buildings*, also sold at most museums, is a lightweight, but beautiful production well worth buying for further detail on the shrines at Besease and elsewhere in Ashanti.

Superficially somewhat esoteric, Schweizer's *Survivors on the Gold Coast* relates the story of the foundation of the Basel Missionaries, but is of greater interest for its 80-plus pages of monochrome photographs, which date from 1860 onwards and document subjects as diverse as the Asantehene in exile in the Seychelles to Accra street scenes – all in all, a fascinating document.

A highly worthwhile new book about the slave trade out of Ghana is St Clair's *The Grand Slave Emporium*, which is available in an inexpensive paperback edition. By contrast, Meredith's *State of Africa* is a very readable history of 50 years of African independence, which goes a long way to explaining why Africa is as it is, and Guest's *Shackled Continent* is an excellent book looking at development and economic problems in modern Africa.

Agbodeka, F *An Economic History of Ghana* Ghana University Press, 1992
Ajayi, F and Espie, E (eds) *A Thousand Years of West African History* Thomas Nelson, 1965
Amate, C O C *The Making of Ada* Woeli Publishing Services, 1999

Anquandah, K J *Castles and Forts of Ghana* Ghana Museums & Monuments Board, 1999

Arhin, K (ed) *The Cape Coast and Elmina Handbook* University of Ghana, 1995

Buah, F *A History of Ghana* Macmillan, 1980

Buah, F *West Africa Since AD1000* Macmillan, 1974

Davidson, B *A History of West Africa 1000–1800* Longman, 1977

Debrah, I N (ed) *Asante Traditional Buildings* Ghana Museums & Monuments Board, 1999

Gadzekpo, S K *A History of Ghana* Royal Crown Press, 1997

Gocking, Robert *The History of Ghana* Greenwood Press, 2005

Graham, J *Cape Coast in History* Anglican Printing Press, 1994

Guest, Robert *The Shackled Continent* Pan, 2005

Herbstein, M *Ama: A Story of the Atlantic Slave Trade* ereads.com, 2004

Kwadwo, O *An Outline of Asante History* O Kwadwo Enterprises, 1994

Kyeremateng, K *The Akans of Ghana* Sebewie Publishers, 1996

Meredith, Martin *The State of Africa* Free Press, 2005

Moxon, J *Volta: Man's Greatest Lake* André Deutsch, 1969

Nugent, P *Big Men, Small Boys and Politics in Ghana: Power, Ideology and the Burden of History* Pinter Publishing Ltd, 1996

Obeng, E *Ancient Ashanti Chieftaincy* Ghana Publishing Corporation, 1984

Onwubiko, K *History of West Africa 1000–1800* Africana FEP, 1982

Onwubiko, K *History of West Africa 1800–Present Day* Africana FEP, 1985

Packenham, T *The Scramble for Africa* Jonathan Ball, 1991

Sampson, M *Makers of Modern Ghana Volume One* Anowuo Publications, 1969

Sarpong, P *Ghana in Retrospect* Ghana Publishing Corporation, 1974

Schweizer, P A *Survivors on the Gold Coast* Smartline Publishing, 2000

St Clair, William *The Grand Slave Emporium: Cape Coast Castle and the British Slave Trade* Profile Books, 2006

Tufuo, J and Donkor, C *Ashantis of Ghana* Anowuo Publications, 1989

van Dantzig, A *Forts and Castles of Ghana* Sedco, 1980

Ward, W E *A Short History of Ghana* Longman, 1957

Field guides

Borrow, Nik and Demey, Ron *Helm Field Guide to the Birds of Ghana* A&C Black Publishers, 2010. An essential work for anybody with an interest in birds, this current field guide illustrates all 758 confirmed resident, migrant and vagrant species for Ghana across 145 plates, and also has useful short descriptions and distribution maps. The same authors' *Field Guide to the Birds of Western Africa* (Helm Identification Guides, 2004) is more general but worth buying if you intend to visit several countries in the region.

Happold, D C D *Large Mammals of West Africa* Longman, 1973. Once in Ghana, you might be able to get hold of this guide that, despite being rather dated in some respects, is a very handy, lightweight volume with adequate pictures and descriptions.

Kingdon, Jonathon *Field Guide to African Mammals* Academic Press, 1997. This superb and dauntingly comprehensive guide is recommended to serious mammal watchers, especially for its detail on primates, but it's probably too pricey and bulky for most travellers.

Sinclair, Ian, and Ryan, Peter *Birds of Africa South of the Sahara* Struik, 2003. Another useful title, especially for regular visitors to Africa, is this comprehensive and relatively inexpensive guide.

Stuart, Chris and Tilde *Field Guide to the Larger Mammals of Africa* Struik, 1997. A cheaper and more handy volume than Kingdon's guide, but just as useful to those visitors whose interest is confined to large mammals. If you have difficulty locating these, several other inferior guides are more widely available, most visibly those published by Collins.

Travel guides

North American Women's Association's *No More Worries: The Indispensable Insiders' Guide to Accra* (*www.noworriesghana.com*). Highly recommended to those who are spending a while in the capital.

Remy, Mylene *Ghana Today* Jaguar, 1977, 1992. Also worth buying, though more as a souvenir than a guide, is this 30cm-long hardback book packed with good photos, but textually tending towards whimsy and hyperbole.

Time Out Accra for Visitors (2015, *www.timeout.com/accra*). This magazine, which seems to be published every two years or so, is an excellent source of advice and contacts in Accra.

Utley, Ian *Ghana: Culture Smart!* Kuperard, 2009. Providing a detailed look at the attitudes, beliefs and traditions of Ghana.

Other Africa guides For a full list of Bradt's Africa guides, see www.bradtguides.com.

Gibbons, Bob and Pritchard-Jones, Sian *Africa Overland* Bradt Travel Guides, 2014.
Manson, Katrina and Knight, James *Burkina Faso* Bradt Travel Guides, 2011.
Sykes, Tom *Ivory Coast*, Bradt Travel Guides, 2016.

Health

Wilson-Howarth, Dr Jane *Bugs, Bites & Bowels* Cadogan, 2009
Wilson-Howarth, Dr Jane, and Ellis, Dr Matthew *Your Child Abroad: A Travel Health Guide* Bradt Travel Guides, 2014

Fiction and biography

Angelou, Maya *All God's Children Need Travelling Shoes* Virago, 1987. Recounting the story of the American author's return to Ghana to search out her roots.

Casely Hayford, Joseph *Ethiopia Unbound* Frank Cass Publishers, 1969. Ghana has one of the strongest English literary traditions to be found anywhere in Africa, dating back to 1911 and the publication of what is regarded as West Africa's first novel, by a barrister and nationalist politician (see page 23).

Eshun, Ekow *Black Gold of the Sun* Vintage, 2007. Detailing the British-Ghanaian author's search through Ghana to explore his heritage.

Herbstein, Manu *Ama: A Story of the Atlantic Slave Trade* Picador Africa, 2001. Winner of the 2002 Commonwealth Writers' Prize for Best First Book, and was also nominated for the 2003 International IMPAC Dublin Literary Award, for its novelisation of one woman's experience of this bleak period.

Japin, Arthur *The Two Hearts of Kwasi Boachi* Vintage, 2007. Translated from the Dutch, this historical novel is based on the true story of two 19th-century Ashanti princes sent by their father to study in Holland.

Kelman, Stephen *Pigeon English* Houghton Mifflin Harcourt, 2011. A critically lauded murder mystery whose central character is an 11-year-old immigrant from Ghana living on a London housing estate.

Miles, Jo *The Coconut Contract* (Self-published on amazon.co.uk, 2013) The story of how Jo and her husband Tom Miles established the now-defunct Green Turtle Lodge at Akwidaa also doubles as a good-humoured but sharply observed cultural primer of day-to-day life in Ghana.

Noble, Helen *Tears of a Phoenix* Soul Rocks Books, 2012. Highly praised first-person novel about a Ghanaian violent offender serving a life sentence in a UK prison.

Selasi, Taiye *Ghana Must Go* Viking, 2013. This family saga, about a Ghanaian doctor working in the USA, was described by *The Economist* as 'one of the best new novels of the season'.

Selormey, Francis *The Narrow Path* Heinemann African Writers Series, 1992. A vivid and very readable account of a Ghanaian boy's upbringing in the 1920s.

A fair selection of local novels is available in most bookshops around the country, generally at very reasonable prices. A few better-known novels include B Kojo Laing's *Search Sweet Country* (Farrar, Straus & Giroux, 1998); Ayi Kwei Armah's *The Beautyful Ones Are Not Yet Born* Heinemann, 1989) and *Healers* (Heinemann, 1979); Ama Ata Aidoo's *Dilemma of a Ghost* and *Our Sister Killjoy* (both Longman, 1995); and Amma Darko's *Beyond the Horizon* (Heinemann, 1995).

WEBSITES Websites worth checking out before you travel to Ghana include the following:

www.bradtguides.com/ghana Log on for your free Ghana updates.

www.africa-geographic.com Site for the South African publications *Africa Geographic* and *Africa Birds & Birding* – useful news and archives, subscriptions, special offers and tours.

www.fco.gov.uk British Foreign and Commonwealth Office site, whose 'Travel Advice by Country' pages contain up-to-date, generally rather conservative information on trouble spots and places to avoid.

www.ghanahighcommissionuk.com Site of the Ghana High Commission in London, with plenty of background information and details of visa requirements, etc.

www.ghanamuseums.org There's lots of background information on the official site of the Ghana Museums and Monuments Board.

www.ghanaweb.com Probably the best site overall for current affairs and sports news, together with a daunting mass of background information and statistics, as well as comprehensive news archives dating back to 1995.

www.ghct.org.gh Site of the Ghana Heritage Trust, which promotes the preservation and conservation of the country's major historic monuments and sites.

www.graphic.com.gh Online archive of the country's oldest newspaper, plus all the latest news.

www.ncrc-ghana.org Information about ecotourist and community development tourist sites.

www.timeout.com/accra Up-to-date entertainment and other listings for the Ghanaian capital.

www.tougha.com Out-of-date site of the Tour Operators Union of Ghana (TOUGHA) with good information about all aspects of travel in Ghana; especially strong on wildlife.

www.travel.state.gov US Department of State with up-to-date travel information for US citizens.

www.travelafricamag.com Site for the quarterly magazine *Travel Africa* – good news, travel archives and subscriptions.

www.usatoday.com/weather Weather forecasts and archives covering remote parts of Africa; try also www.wunderground.com or www.worldclimate.com.

www.volunteeringinafrica.org/ghana.htm Information for anyone interested in volunteer work in Ghana.

Index

Page numbers in **bold** indicate main entries; those in *italics* indicate maps

INDEX OF ADVERTISERS